INTRODUCTION TO COLLEGE MATHEMATICS

INTRODUCTION TO COLLEGE MATHEMATICS

from

BASIC COLLEGE MATHEMATICS | AN APPLIED APPROACH
INTRODUCTORY ALGEBRA | AN APPLIED APPROACH
INTERMEDIATE ALGEBRA | AN APPLIED APPROACH

Richard N. Aufmann
Palomar College, California

Vernon C. Barker
Palomar College, California

Joanne S. Lockwood
*New Hampshire Community
Technical College, New Hampshire*

and

MATHEMATICAL EXCURSIONS

Richard N. Aufmann
Palomar College, California

Joanne S. Lockwood
*New Hampshire Community
Technical College, New Hampshire*

Richard D. Nation
Palomar College, California

Daniel K. Clegg
Palomar College, California

Houghton Mifflin Company | Boston   New York

BASIC COLLEGE MATHEMATICS, AN APPLIED APPROACH, EIGHTH EDITION
by Richard N. Aufmann, Vernon C. Barker, and Joanne S. Lockwood
Copyright © 2006 by Houghton Mifflin Company. All rights reserved.

Editor-in-Chief: Jack Shira
Senior Sponsoring Editor: Lynn Cox
Associate Editor: Melissa Parkin
Editorial Assistant: Noel Kamm
Senior Project Editor: Carol Merrigan
Editorial Assistant: Eric Moore
Manufacturing Manager: Karen Banks
Senior Marketing Manager: Ben Rivera
Marketing Assistant: Lisa Lawler

Photo Credits appear on page PC1, after the Index.

INTRODUCTORY ALGEBRA: AN APPLIED APPROACH, SEVENTH EDITION
by Richard N. Aufmann, Vernon C. Barker, and Joanne S. Lockwood
Copyright © 2006 by Houghton Mifflin Company. All rights reserved.

Editor-in-Chief: Jack Shira
Senior Sponsoring Editor: Lynn Cox
Associate Editor: Melissa Parkin
Editorial Assistant: Noel Kamm
Editorial Assistant: Julia Keller
Manufacturing Manager: Karen Banks
Senior Marketing Manager: Ben Rivera
Marketing Associate: Lisa Lawler

Photo Credits appear on page PC1, after the Index.

INTERMEDIATE ALGEBRA: AN APPLIED APPROACH, SEVENTH EDITION
by Richard N. Aufmann, Vernon C. Barker, and Joanne S. Lockwood
Copyright © 2006 by Houghton Mifflin Company. All rights reserved.

Editor-in-Chief: Jack Shira
Senior Sponsoring Editor: Lynn Cox
Associate Editor: Melissa Parkin
Editorial Assistant: Noel Kamm
Senior Project Editor: Tamela Ambush
Editorial Assistant: Sage Anderson
Manufacturing Manager: Karen Banks
Senior Marketing Manager: Ben Rivera
Marketing Assistant: Lisa Lawler

Photo Credits appear on page PC1, after the Index.

MATHEMATICAL EXCURSIONS, SECOND EDITION
by Richard N. Aufmann, Joanne S. Lockwood, Richard D. Nation, and Daniel K. Clegg
Copyright © 2007 by Houghton Mifflin Company. All rights reserved.

Publisher: Jack Shira
Senior Sponsoring Editor: Lynn Cox
Development Editor: Lisa Collette
Assistant Editor: Noel Kamm
Senior Project Editor: Kerry Falvey
Manufacturing Manager: Florence Cadran
Senior Marketing Manger: Ben Rivera
Marketing Associate: Lisa Lawler

Photo Credits appear on page PC1, after the Index.

Custom Publishing Editor: Dee Renfrow
Custom Publishing Production Manager: Christina Battista
Project Coordinator: Sara Abbott

Cover Design: Majel Peters
Cover Image: PhotoDisc

This book contains select works from existing Houghton Mifflin Company resources and was produced by Houghton Mifflin Custom Publishing for collegiate use. As such, those adopting and/or contributing to this work are responsible for editorial content, accuracy, continuity and completeness.

Printed in the United States of America.

ISBN-13: 978-0-618-97195-4
ISBN-10: 0-618-97195-5
1023194

1 2 3 4 5 6 7 8 9 – CBP– 09 08 07

 Houghton Mifflin
Custom Publishing

222 Berkeley Street • Boston, MA 02116

Address all correspondence and order information to the above address.

Contents

6 Applications for Business and Consumers   189

Additional Material from Mathematical Excursions

Preface

The initial release of the **Houghton Mifflin Mathematics Custom Courseware (HMMCC 1.0)** program provides mathematically sound and comprehensive coverage of topics considered essential in developmental mathematics. The content available encompasses courses ranging from basic college mathematics through intermediate algebra. The program has been designed not only to meet the needs of traditional college students, but also to serve the needs of returning students whose mathematical proficiency may have declined during years away from formal education.

HMMCC 1.0 draws content from three key author franchises. The bulk of the content comes from Richard N. Aufmann, Vernon C. Barker, and Joanne S. Lockwood's developmental mathematics paperback series. Also included are topical modules written by the Maricopa Project authors – Scott Adamson, Paula Cheslik, Anne Dudley, David Dudley, Teri Glaess, Karen Hay, Alan Jacobs, and Keith Worth – and co-funded by the National Science Foundation®. Both of these author teams have incorporated approaches recommended by AMATYC in their materials. In addition to these materials we also have the content found in the *Math Study Skills Workbook, 2e* by Paul D. Nolting.

The available content from the **Aufmann/Barker/Lockwood** best-selling titles includes:
- *Basic College Mathematics: An Applied Approach, 8e*
- *Introductory Algebra: An Applied Approach, 7e*
- *Intermediate Algebra: An Applied Approach, 7e*

The available content from the **Maricopa Mathematics Modules** includes:
- Beat Ratios and Juggling Proportions
- Data and Graphs
- Exponential Growth and Decay
- Finance
- Functions
- Geometry
- Linear Behavior
- Nonlinear Behavior
- Patterns
- Probability
- Representations of Data
- Right Triangle Trigonometry
- Sampling
- Sets and Logic
- Systems
- Patterns in Numbers and Equations
- Algebraic Patterns
- Visual Patterns

The available content from the Paul D. Nolting, *Math Study Skills Workbook, 2e* is:
- What You Need to Know to Study Math
- How to Discover Your Math-Learning Strengths and Weaknesses
- How to Reduce Math Test Anxiety
- How to Improve Your Listening and Note-Taking Skills
- How to Improve Your Reading, Homework, and Study Techniques
- How to Remember What You Have Learned
- How to improve Your Math Test-Taking Skills

Within **Aufmann/Barker/Lockwood** content, each chapter opens by illustrating a mathematical application reflecting the content of the chapter. At the end of each section exercise set are *Applying the Concepts* exercises that include writing, synthesis, critical thinking, and challenge problems. At the end of most chapters is a *Focus on Problem Solving* that introduces students to various problem-solving strategies, as well as *Projects and Group Activities* that can be used for cooperative learning activities. The **Maricopa Mathematics Modules,** available for customization, feature discovery-based learning by engaging students through activities and enabling them to connect mathematics to the real world. Each module also has students gather and use data to create models and answer questions, taking approximately two to three weeks of class time to complete. The content found in the *Math Study Skills Workbook, 2e* by **Paul D. Nolting,** reinforces skills and minimizes frustration for students in any math class, lab, or study-skills course. It offers a wealth of proven study tips and sound advice on note taking, time management, and reducing math anxiety. The author makes the learning process both manageable and compelling. In addition, numerous opportunities for self-assessment enable students to track their own progress.

FEATURES

Because this courseware is customized to meet specific needs, not all features mentioned below may be found in this text.

Aufmann/Barker/Lockwood Features

AUFMANN INTERACTIVE METHOD (AIM)

An Interactive Method

The Aufmann/Barker/Lockwood pedagogy uses an interactive style that provides a student with an opportunity to try a skill as it is presented. A section is divided into objectives, and every objective contains one or more sets of *Example/You Try It* pairs. The numbered example is worked out; the second example, called *You Try It*, is for the student to work out. By solving this problem, the student actively practices concepts as they are presented in the program.

Every *You Try It* has a completely worked-out solution at the back of the book that students can use to check their work. By comparing their solution to the provided solution, students obtain immediate feedback on and reinforcement of the concept. In addition, the completely worked-out solutions significantly increase the number of examples available for students to refer to during homework or test preparation.

AIM for Success: A Preface for the Student

This preface explains how students can use the program to learn mathematics successfully. *AIM for Success* can be used as a lesson on the first day of class or as a project for students to complete to strengthen their study skills.

CHAPTER OPENING FEATURES

Chapter Opener

Motivating chapter opener photos and captions illustrate an application relevant to the chapter content. The 🌐 at the bottom of the page lets students know of additional online resources at *math.college.hmco.com/students*.

Objective-Specific Approach

Each chapter begins with a list of learning objectives. These objectives provide a framework for a complete learning system. End-of-section exercises are identified by their objective.

Prep Test and Go Figure

Prep Tests occur at the beginning of each chapter and assess a student's mastery of previously covered topics. Knowing these prerequisite skills is necessary for success in the coming chapter. All answers are provided in the answer section at the back of the book. The *Go Figure* problem that follows the *Prep Test* is a playful puzzle problem designed to engage students in problem solving.

PROBLEM SOLVING

Focus on Problem Solving

A *Focus on Problem Solving* feature, which introduces the student to various successful problem-solving strategies, may be found at the end of a chapter. Strategies such as drawing a diagram, applying solutions to other problems, working backwards, inductive reasoning, and trial and error are some of the techniques that are demonstrated.

Problem-Solving Strategies

The program features a carefully developed approach to problem solving that emphasizes the importance of *strategy* when solving problems. Students are encouraged to develop their own strategies—to draw diagrams, to write out the solution steps in words, for example—as part of their solution to a problem. In each case, model strategies are presented as guides for students to follow as they attempt the *You Try It* problem. Having students provide strategies is a natural way to incorporate writing into the math curriculum.

REAL DATA AND APPLICATIONS

Applications

One way to motivate an interest in mathematics is through applications. Several sections present applications that require the student to use problem-solving strategies along with the skills covered in that section. This carefully integrated applied approach generates student awareness of the value of algebra as a real-life problem-solving tool. Applications are taken from many disciplines including agriculture, business, carpentry, chemistry, construction, earth science, education, manufacturing, nutrition, real estate, and sociology.

Real Data

Real data examples and exercises, reflecting current data and trends and often identified by ◕, ask students to analyze and solve problems taken from actual situations. Students are often required to work with tables, graphs, and charts drawn from a variety of disciplines.

STUDENT PEDAGOGY

Annotated Examples

Examples indicated by ➡ use bulleted annotations to explain what is happening in key steps of the complete, worked-out solutions.

Key Terms and Concepts

Key terms, in bold, emphasize important terms. The definitions of key terms also may be repeated in a glossary at the back of the book. Key concepts are presented in boxes to highlight their importance and to provide an easy reference.

Take Note

These margin notes alert students to a point requiring special attention or augment the concept under discussion.

Calculator Note

These margin notes provide suggestions for using a calculator in certain situations.

Point of Interest

These margin notes contain interesting information about mathematics, its history, or its applications.

Icons

The [icon] at objective heads remind students that both a video and a tutorial lesson are available for that objective.

EXERCISES AND PROJECTS

Exercises

Exercise sets emphasize skill building, skill maintenance, and applications. Concept-based writing or developmental exercises have been integrated into the exercise sets.

Icons identify appropriate writing [pencil], data analysis [pie], and calculator [calc] exercises. Included in an exercise set may be an *Applying the Concepts* section that presents extensions of topics, requires analysis, or offers challenge problems. The writing exercises ask students to explain answers, write about a topic in the section, or research and report on a related topic.

Projects and Group Activities

The *Projects and Group Activities* that may be offered at the end of a chapter can be used as extra credit or for cooperative learning activities. The projects cover various aspects of mathematics including the use of calculators, collecting data from the Internet, data analysis, and extended applications.

END OF CHAPTER

Chapter Summary

At the end of a chapter there may be a *Chapter Summary* that includes *Key Words* and *Essential Rules* that were covered in the chapter. Chapter summaries serve as a convenient reference when a student prepares for a test.

Chapter Review

Review exercises may be found at the end of a chapter. These exercises are selected to help the student integrate all of the topics presented in the chapter. All answers are provided in the answer section at the back of the book.

Chapter Test

The *Chapter Test*, which may appear at the end of a chapter, is designed to simulate a possible test of the material in a chapter. All answers are provided in the answer section at the back of the book.

Cumulative Review

Cumulative Review exercises, which may appear at the end of a chapter, help students maintain skills learned in previous chapters. All answers are provided in the answer section at the back of the book.

Maricopa Module Features

Introduction

Each module is divided into lessons. Each lesson introduces the idea or concept to be studied. It lists the objective and the material needed.

Nitty Gritty

If review of a certain skill is appropriate within a lesson, then this feature appears. A short review is provided with examples, along with several skill exercises. Not every lesson or module has a *Nitty Gritty*.

Activity
Each lesson contains several activities. These activities are appropriate for individuals, groups, or classrooms. Data is presented (or student-gathered), models are given (or student-created), and questions are asked to lead students to connect a real-world application to the mathematical concept.

Writing
Writing is integrated in features such as *Activities*, *Wrap-Up*, and *Homework*. Students are asked to write explanations in their own words and to provide real-world models of something written mathematically.

Graph Interpretation Problems
These problems, integrated throughout the modules, are closely related to writing as students see and explain how a real-world model and a mathematical model relate.

Wrap-Up
This summary asks students to write their own lesson summary by encouraging them to be active participants in the learning process.

Glossary
A glossary of key terms is provided with each module.

Selected Answers
Selected answers to *Activities*, *Nitty Gritty*, and *Homework* exercises are provided for the students at the end of each module.

Nolting Features
Each chapter works on building students' confidence by providing study tips, skill-building activities, and advice on time management and note taking.

Chapter 1 What You Need to Know to Study Math
In this chapter students will find out:
- Why learning math is different from learning other subjects
- The differences between high school and college math
- The importance of the first math test

Chapter 2 How to Discover Your Math-Learning Strengths & Weaknesses
In this chapter students will find out:
- How students' knowledge of mathematics affects their grades
- How the quality of math instruction affects students' grades
- How affective math student characteristics affects their math grades
- How to determine their learning style
- How to assess their own strengths and weaknesses
- How to improve their math knowledge

Chapter 3 How to Reduce Math Test Anxiety
In this chapter students will find out:
- How to understand math anxiety
- How to recognize test anxiety
- The causes of test anxiety
- The different types of test anxiety
- How to reduce test anxiety

Chapter 4 How to Improve Your Listening and Note-Taking Skills
In this chapter students will find out:
- How to become an effective listener
- How to become a good note-taker
- When to take notes
- The seven steps to math note-taking
- How to rework their notes

Chapter 5 How to Improve Your Reading, Homework, and Study Techniques
In this chapter students will find out:
- How to read a math textbook
- How to do their homework
- How to solve word problems
- How to work with a study buddy
- The benefits of study breaks

Chapter 6 How to Remember What You Have Learned
In this chapter students will find out:
- How they learn
- How short-term memory affects what students remember
- How working memory affects what students remember
- How long-term memory/reasoning affects what students remember
- How to use memory techniques
- How to develop practice tests
- How to use number sense

Chapter 7 How to Improve Your Math Test-Taking Skills
In this chapter students will find out:
- Why attending class and doing homework may not be enough to pass
- The general pretest rules
- The ten steps to better test-taking
- The six types of test-taking errors
- How to prepare for the final exam

Instructor Print Resources

Instructor's Annotated Editions (IAE)
(Not customizable in this release of HMMCC 1.0)

Aufmann/Barker/Lockwood: For the Aufmann textbooks the IAE material includes a replica of the student text and additional items for just the instructor including *Instructor Notes, Transparency Master Icons, In-Class Examples, Concept Checks, Discuss the Concepts, New Vocabulary/Symbols, Vocabulary/Symbols to Review, Optional Student Activities, Quick Quizzes, Answers to Writing Exercises,* and *Suggested Assignments*. Answers to all exercises are also provided.

Maricopa Modules (IAE): This is a replica of the student text but also features margin annotations with teaching tips along with answers to the exercises.

Instructor's Manual
A customizable print supplement containing completely worked-out solutions to all exercises in the Aufmann textbooks as well as detailed notes on specific modules, test questions, and complete solutions for all exercises in the Maricopa modules.

Printed Test Bank

(Available for Aufmann/Barker/Lockwood content only; not customizable in this release of HMMCC 1.0) The *Printed Test Bank* is a printout of the items in HM Testing. Items that are algorithmic in HM Testing are identified with an asterisk. Instructors can use the test bank to select specific items from the database. Instructors who do not have access to a computer can use the *Printed Test Bank* to create a test being prepared by hand.

Instructor's Resource Manual with Chapter Tests

(Available for Aufmann/Barker/Lockwood content only; not customizable in this release of HMMCC 1.0) The *Instructor's Resource Manual* contains ready-to-use printed Chapter Tests. Eight printed tests (in two formats, free response and multiple choice) are provided for each chapter. Cumulative tests and final exams are also provided. These tests can be downloaded from our website at *math.college.hmco.com/instructors*. The *Instructor's Resource Manual* also includes a lesson plan for the *AIM for Success* student preface.

Instructor Technology Resources

Eduspace Online Learning Environment – Developmental Math Supersite

(Customizable-Eduspace course content includes coverage for all 3 © 2006 Aufmann/Barker/Lockwood Developmental Math Paperbacks.) The Eduspace interactive, online learning environment consists of an integrated set of robust teaching resources and text-specific learning content that enable the instructor to create and manage a mathematics course via an online system. With Eduspace, instructors may assign homework problems in the form of a library of even-numbered problems taken directly from the textbook in use. They also have the option to add or modify questions to the site's existing content.

HM ClassPrep™ with HM Testing

(Standard CD-ROM's available for Aufmann/Barker/Lockwood textbooks only; not customizable in this release of HMMCC 1.0) Each CD-ROM includes HM ClassPrep and HM Testing, which allows an instructor to access both lecture aids and testing software in one place. HM ClassPrep includes resources an instructor can use to develop his or her course, including a transition guide and solutions to all text exercises. HM Testing, the new version of the computerized database, provides instructors with a wide array of algorithmic test items. In addition to producing an unlimited number of tests for each chapter, including cumulative test and final exams, HM Testing also offers online testing and gradebook functions.

Instructor Companion Website

(Standard websites available for Aufmann/Barker/Lockwood textbooks only; not customizable in this release of HMMCC 1.0) Additional instructor resources can be accessed on the text specific site at *math.college.hmco.com/instructors*.

Student Print Resources

Student Manual

A customizable *Student Manual* containing solutions to odd-numbered section exercises from the Aufmann/Barker/Lockwood textbooks and solutions to selected exercises from the Maricopa Modules.

Student Technology Resources

Eduspace Online Learning Environment – Developmental Math Supersite

(Customizable - Eduspace course content includes coverage for all 3 © 2006 Aufmann/Barker/Lockwoood Developmental Math Paperbacks.) The Eduspace interactive, online learning environment combines an algorithmic tutorial program with homework capabilities.

SMARTHINKING™ Online tutoring for students

(Available for the Aufmann/Barker/Lockwood content only; not customizable in this release of HMMCC 1.0) Provides students with live, online, text-specific tutoring when they need it. With SMARTHINKING students can:

- Work one-on-one with an online tutor using a state-of-the-art, mathematically oriented whiteboard.
- Submit a question to receive a response, usually within twenty-four hours.
- Access additional study resources anytime.

HM Mathspace Tutorial CD-Rom

(Available for the Aufmann/Barker/Lockwood content only; not customizable in this release of the HMMCC 1.0) This self-paced tutorial CD-Rom allows students to practice skills and review concepts as many times as necessary by providing algorithmically-generated exercises and step-by-step solutions for practice.

Houghton Mifflin Instructional DVDs by Dana Mosely

(Standard DVDs available for Aufmann/Barker/Lockwood textbooks only; not customizable in this release of HMMCC 1.0) The DVD series provides comprehensive coverage and is available for use in classroom, lab, tutoring center, and/or library settings. The DVDs are available for student purchase.

Student Companion Website

(Standard websites available for Aufmann/Barker/Lockwood textbooks only; not customizable in this release of HMMCC 1.0) Additional student resources for learning can be accessed on the text specific site at *math.college.hmco.com/students*.

AIM for Success

Welcome! As you begin this course, we know two important facts: (1) We want you to succeed. (2) You want to succeed. To do that requires an effort from each of us. For the next few pages, we are going to show you what is required of you to achieve that success and how you can use the features of this text to be successful.

Motivation

One of the most important keys to success is motivation. We can try to motivate you by offering interesting or important ways mathematics can benefit you. But, in the end, the motivation must come from you. On the first day of class, it is easy to be motivated. Eight weeks into the term, it is harder to keep that motivation.

To stay motivated, there must be outcomes from this course that are worth your time, money, and energy.

List some reasons you are taking this course.

_____

_____

_____

> **TAKE NOTE**
>
> Motivation alone will not lead to success. For instance, suppose a person who cannot swim is placed in a boat, taken out to the middle of a lake, and then thrown overboard. That person has a lot of motivation but there is a high likelihood the person will drown without some help. Motivation gives us the desire to learn but is not the same as learning.

Although we hope that one of the reasons you listed was an interest in mathematics, we know that many of you are taking this course because it is required to graduate, it is a prerequisite for a course you must take, or because it is required for your major. Although you may not agree that this course is necessary, it is! If you are motivated to graduate or complete the requirements for your major, then use that motivation to succeed in this course. Do not become distracted from your goal to complete your education!

Commitment

To be successful, you must make a commitment to succeed. This means devoting time to math so that you achieve a better understanding of the subject.

List some activities (sports, hobbies, talents such as dance, art, or music) that you enjoy and at which you would like to become better.

ACTIVITY	TIME SPENT	TIME WISHED SPENT
_____	_____	_____
_____	_____	_____
_____	_____	_____

Thinking about these activities, put the number of hours that you spend each week practicing these activities next to the activity. Next to that number, indicate the number of hours per week you would like to spend on these activities.

Whether you listed surfing or sailing, aerobics or restoring cars, or any other activity you enjoy, note how many hours a week you spend doing it. To succeed in math, you must be willing to commit the same amount of time. Success requires some sacrifice.

The "I Can't Do Math" Syndrome

There may be things you cannot do, such as lift a two-ton boulder. You can, however, do math. It is much easier than lifting the two-ton boulder. When you first learned the activities you listed above, you probably could not do them well. With practice, you got better. With practice, you will be better at math. Stay focused, motivated, and committed to success.

It is difficult for us to emphasize how important it is to overcome the "I Can't Do Math Syndrome." If you listen to interviews of very successful atheletes after a particularly bad performance, you will note that they focus on the positive aspect of what they did, not the negative. Sports psychologists encourage athletes to always be positive—to have a "Can Do" attitude. Develop this attitude toward math.

Strategies for Success

Textbook Reconnaissance Right now, do a 15-minute "textbook reconnaissance" of this book. Here's how:

First, read the table of contents. Do it in three minutes or less. Next, look through the entire book, page by page. Move quickly. Scan titles, look at pictures, notice diagrams.

A textbook reconnaissance shows you where a course is going. It gives you the big picture. That's useful because brains work best when going from the general to the specific. Getting the big picture before you start makes details easier to recall and understand later on.

Your textbook reconnaissance will work even better if, as you scan, you look for ideas or topics that are interesting to you. List three facts, topics, or problems that you found interesting during your textbook reconnaissance.

_____

_____

_____

The idea behind this technique is simple: It's easier to work at learning material if you know it's going to be useful to you.

Not all the topics in this book will be "interesting" to you. But that is true of any subject. Surfers find that on some days the waves are better than others, musicians find some music more appealing than other music, computer gamers find some computer games more interesting than others, car enthusiasts find some cars more exciting than others. Some car enthusiasts would rather have a completely restored 1957 Chevrolet than a new Ferrari.

Know the Course Requirements To do your best in this course, you must know exactly what your instructor requires. Course requirements may be stated in a *syllabus*, which is a printed outline of the main topics of the course, or they may be presented orally. When they are listed in a syllabus or on other printed pages, keep them in a safe place. When they are presented orally, make sure to take complete notes. In either case, it is important that you understand them completely and follow them exactly. Be sure you know the answer to each of the following questions.

1. What is your instructor's name?
2. Where is your instructor's office?
3. At what times does your instructor hold office hours?
4. Besides the textbook, what other materials does your instructor require?
5. What is your instructor's attendance policy?
6. If you must be absent from a class meeting, what should you do before returning to class? What should you do when you return to class?

7. What is the instructor's policy regarding collection or grading of homework assignments?

8. What options are available if you are having difficulty with an assignment? Is there a math tutoring center?

9. If there is a math lab at your school, where is it located? What hours is it open?

10. What is the instructor's policy if you miss a quiz?

11. What is the instructor's policy if you miss an exam?

12. Where can you get help when studying for an exam?

Remember: Your instructor wants to see you succeed. If you need help, ask! Do not fall behind. If you are running a race and fall behind by 100 yards, you may be able to catch up but it will require more effort than had you not fallen behind.

TAKE NOTE

Besides time management, there must be realistic ideas of how much time is available. There are very few people who can *successfully* work full-time and go to school full-time. If you work 40 hours a week, take 15 units, spend the recommended study time given at the right, and sleep 8 hours a day, you will use over 80% of the available hours in a week. That leaves less than 20% of the hours in a week for family, friends, eating, recreation, and other activities.

Time Management   We know that there are demands on your time. Family, work, friends, and entertainment all compete for your time. We do not want to see you receive poor job evaluations because you are studying math. However, it is also true that we do not want to see you receive poor math test scores because you devoted too much time to work. When several competing and important tasks require your time and energy, the only way to manage the stress of being successful at both is to manage your time efficiently.

Instructors often advise students to spend twice the amount of time outside of class studying as they spend in the classroom. Time management is important if you are to accomplish this goal and succeed in school. The following activity is intended to help you structure your time more efficiently.

List the name of each course you are taking this term, the number of class hours each course meets, and the number of hours you should spend studying each subject outside of class. Then fill in a weekly schedule like the one printed below. Begin by writing in the hours spent in your classes, the hours spent at work (if you have a job), and any other commitments that are not flexible with respect to the time that you do them. Then begin to write down commitments that are more flexible, including hours spent studying. Remember to reserve time for activities such as meals and exercise. You should also schedule free time.

	Monday	Tuesday	Wednesday	Thursday	Friday	Saturday	Sunday
7–8 a.m.							
8–9 a.m.							
9–10 a.m.							
10–11 a.m.							
11–12 p.m.							
12–1 p.m.							
1–2 p.m.							
2–3 p.m.							
3–4 p.m.							
4–5 p.m.							
5–6 p.m.							
6–7 p.m.							
7–8 p.m.							
8–9 p.m.							
9–10 p.m.							
10–11 p.m.							
11–12 a.m.							

We know that many of you must work. If that is the case, realize that working 10 hours a week at a part-time job is equivalent to taking a three-unit class. If you must work, consider letting your education progress at a slower rate to allow you to be successful at both work and school. There is no rule that says you must finish school in a certain time frame.

Schedule Study Time As we encouraged you to do by filling out the time management form above, schedule a certain time to study. You should think of this time the way you would the time for work or class—that is, reasons for missing study time should be as compelling as reasons for missing work or class. "I just didn't feel like it" is not a good reason to miss your scheduled study time.

Although this may seem like an obvious exercise, list a few reasons you might want to study.

_____

_____

_____

Of course we have no way of knowing the reasons you listed, but from our experience one reason given quite frequently is "To pass the course." There is nothing wrong with that reason. If that is the most important reason for you to study, then use it to stay focused.

One method of keeping to a study schedule is to form a ***study group***. Look for people who are committed to learning, who pay attention in class, and who are punctual. Ask them to join your group. Choose people with similar educational goals but different methods of learning. You can gain insight from seeing the material from a new perspective. Limit groups to four or five people; larger groups are unwieldy.

There are many ways to conduct a study group. Begin with the following suggestions and see what works best for your group.

1. Test each other by asking questions. Each group member might bring two or three sample test questions to each meeting.
2. Practice teaching each other. Many of us who are teachers learned a lot about our subject when we had to explain it to someone else.
3. Compare class notes. You might ask other students about material in your notes that is difficult for you to understand.
4. Brainstorm test questions.
5. Set an agenda for each meeting. Set approximate time limits for each agenda item and determine a quitting time.

And finally, probably the most important aspect of studying is that it should be done in relatively small chunks. If you can only study three hours a week for this course (probably not enough for most people), do it in blocks of one hour on three separate days, preferably after class. Three hours of studying on a Sunday is not as productive as three hours of paced study.

Text Features That Promote Success

Each chapter is divided into sections, and each section is subdivided into learning objectives.

Preparing for a Chapter   Before you begin a new chapter, you should take some time to review previously learned skills.

One way of preparing for a new chapter is to complete the ***Prep Test***. This test focuses on the particular skills that will be required for the new chapter. The answers for the Prep Test are the first set of answers in the answer section for a chapter. Note that an objective reference is given for each answer. If you answer a question incorrectly, restudy the objective from which the question was taken.

Before the class meeting in which your professor begins a new section, you should read each objective statement for that section. Next, browse through the objective material, being sure to note each word in bold type. These words indicate important concepts that you must know in order to learn the material. Do not worry about trying to understand all the material. Your professor is there to assist you with that endeavor. The purpose of browsing through the material is so that your brain will be prepared to accept and organize the new information when it is presented to you.

Write down the title of the first objective in this book. Under the title of the objective, write down the words in the objective that are in bold print. It is not necessary for you to understand the meaning of these words. You are in this class to learn their meaning.

_____   _____   _____   _____

_____   _____   _____   _____

_____   _____   _____   _____

_____   _____   _____   _____

_____   _____   _____   _____

Math is Not a Spectator Sport   To learn mathematics you must be an active participant. Listening and watching your professor do mathematics is not enough. Mathematics requires that you interact with the lesson you are studying. If you filled in the blanks above, you were being interactive. There are other ways this textbook has been designed to help you be an active learner.

Annotated Examples   An orange arrow indicates an example with explanatory remarks to the right of the work. Using paper and pencil, you should work along as you go through the example.

When you complete the example, get a clean sheet of paper. Write down the problem and then try to complete the solution without referring to your notes or the book. When you can do that, move on to the next part of the objective.

Leaf through the book now and write down the page numbers of two other occurrences of an arrowed example.

You Try Its   One of the key instructional features of this text is the paired examples. Notice that in each example box, the example on the left is completely worked out and the "You Try It" example on the right is not. Study the worked-out example carefully by working through each step. Then work the You Try It. If you get stuck, refer to the page number at the end of the example, which directs you to the place where the You Try It is solved—a complete worked-out solution is provided. Try to use the given solution to get a hint for the step you are stuck on. Then try to complete your solution.

When you have completed your solution, check your work against the solution we provided. Be aware that frequently there is more than one way to solve a problem. Your answer, however, should be the same as the given answer. If you have any question as to whether your method will "always work," check with your instructor or with someone in the math center.

Browse through the textbook and write down the page numbers where two other paired example features occur.

Remember: Be an active participant in your learning process. When you are sitting in class watching and listening to an explanation, you may think that you understand. However, until you actually try to do it, you will have no confirmation of the new knowledge or skill. Most of us have had the experience of sitting in class thinking we knew how to do something only to get home and realize that we didn't.

Word Problems   Word problems are difficult because we must read the problem, determine the quantity we must find, think of a method to do that, and then actually solve the problem. In short, we must formulate a *strategy* to solve the problem and then devise a *solution*.

Note in the paired example below that part of every word problem is a strategy and part is a solution. The strategy is a written description of how we will solve the problem. In the corresponding You Try It, you are asked to formulate a strategy. Do not skip this step, and be sure to write it out.

Rule Boxes   Pay special attention to rules placed in boxes. These rules give you the reasons certain types of problems are solved the way they are. When you see a rule, try to rewrite the rule in your own words.

Chapter Exercises   When you have completed studying an objective, do the exercises in the exercise set that correspond with that objective. The exercises are labeled with the same letter as the objective. Math is a subject that needs to be learned in small sections and practiced continually in order to be mastered. Doing all of the exercises in each exercise set will help you master the problem-solving techniques necessary for success. As you work through the exercises for an objective, check your answers to the odd-numbered exercises with those in the back of the book.

Preparing for a Test   There are features that may be included in this text that can be used to prepare for a test.

- Chapter Summary
- Chapter Review
- Chapter Test

After completing a chapter, read the Chapter Summary. This summary highlights the important topics covered in the chapter.

TAKE NOTE

There is a strong connection between reading and being a successful student in math or any other subject. If you have difficulty reading, consider taking a reading course. Reading is much like other skills. There are certain things you can learn that will make you a better reader.

TAKE NOTE

If a rule has more than one part, be sure to make a notation to that effect.

Following the Chapter Summary are a Chapter Review and a Chapter Test. Doing the review exercises is an important way of testing your understanding of the chapter. The answer to each review exercise is given at the back of the book. After checking your answers, restudy any objective from which a question you missed was taken. It may be helpful to retry some of the exercises for that objective to reinforce your problem-solving techniques.

The Chapter Test should be used to prepare for an exam. We suggest that you try the Chapter Test a few days before your actual exam. Take the test in a quiet place and try to complete the test in the same amount of time you will be allowed for your exam. When taking the Chapter Test, practice the strategies of successful test takers: (1) scan the entire test to get a feel for the questions; (2) read the directions carefully; (3) work the problems that are easiest for you first; and perhaps most importantly, (4) try to stay calm.

When you have completed the Chapter Test, check your answers. If you missed a question, review the material in that objective and rework some of the exercises from that objective. This will strengthen your ability to perform the skills in that objective.

Is it difficult to be successful? YES! Successful music groups, artists, professional athletes, chefs, and Write your major here have to work very hard to achieve their goals. They focus on their goals and ignore distractions. The things we ask you to do to achieve success take time and commitment. We are confident that if you follow our suggestions, you will succeed.

chapter

1 Rational Numbers

These tourists took an excursion boat in order to get a closer look at the icebergs at the end of the glaciers in Antarctica's Paradise Bay. Temperatures in places such as this fall below zero. When this happens, the temperatures are described in negative numbers. Negative numbers are used to express any value below zero, such as debt, altitude below sea level, decreases in stock prices, and golf scores under par.

Need help? For online student resources, such as section quizzes, visit this textbook's website at **math.college.hmco.com/students**.

1. Place the correct symbol, $<$ or $>$, between the two numbers.

54   45

2. What is the distance from 4 to 8 on the number line?

For Exercises 3 to 14, add, subtract, multiply, or divide.

3. $7654 + 8193$

4. $6097 - 2318$

5. 472×56

6. $\dfrac{144}{24}$

7. $\dfrac{2}{3} + \dfrac{3}{5}$

8. $\dfrac{3}{4} - \dfrac{5}{16}$

9. $0.75 + 3.9 + 6.408$

10. $5.4 - 1.619$

11. $\dfrac{3}{4} \times \dfrac{8}{15}$

12. $\dfrac{5}{12} \div \dfrac{3}{4}$

13. 23.5×0.4

14. $0.96 \div 2.4$

15. Simplify: $(8 - 6)^2 + 12 \div 4 \cdot 3^2$

GO FIGURE ••••

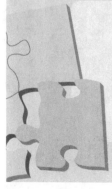

Super Yeast causes bread to double in volume each minute. If it takes one loaf of bread made with Super Yeast 30 minutes to fill the oven, how long does it take two loaves of bread made with Super Yeast to fill one-half the oven?

1.1 Introduction to Integers

Objective A   **To identify the order relation between two integers**

Thus far in the text, we have encountered only zero and the numbers greater than zero. The numbers greater than zero are called **positive numbers.** However, the phrases "12 degrees below zero," "$25 in debt," and "15 feet below sea level" refer to numbers less than zero. These numbers are called **negative numbers.**

The **integers** are . . . , −4, −3, −2, −1, 0, 1, 2, 3, 4, ...

Each integer can be shown on a number line. The integers to the left of zero on the number line are called **negative integers** and are represented by a negative sign (−) placed in front of the number. The integers to the right of zero are called **positive integers.** The positive integers are also called **natural numbers.** Zero is neither a positive nor a negative integer.

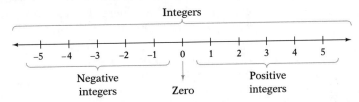

A number line can be used to visualize the order relation between two integers. A number that appears to the left of a given number is less than (<) the given number. A number that appears to the right of a given number is greater than (>) the given number.

2 is greater than negative 4.

$2 > -4$

Negative 5 is less than negative 3.

$-5 < -3$

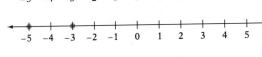

Example 1

The temperature at the North Pole was recorded as 87° below zero. Represent this temperature as an integer.

Solution   −87°

You Try It 1

The surface of the Salton Sea is 232 ft below sea level. Represent this depth as an integer.

Your solution

Example 2

Graph −2 on the number line.

Solution   ⟨—+—+—●—+—+—+—+—+—⟩
           −4 −3 −2 −1 0 1 2 3 4

You Try It 2

Graph −4 on the number line.

Your solution   ⟨—+—+—+—+—+—+—+—+—⟩
              −4 −3 −2 −1 0 1 2 3 4

Example 3

Place the correct symbol, < or >, between the numbers −5 and −7.

Solution $-5 > -7$ • −5 is to the right of −7 on the number line.

You Try It 3

Place the correct symbol, < or >, between the numbers −12 and −8.

Your solution

Objective B   **To evaluate expressions that contain the absolute value symbol**

Two numbers that are the same distance from zero on the number line but on opposite sides of zero are called **opposites.**

−4 is the opposite of 4

and

4 is the opposite of −4.

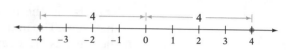

Note that a negative sign can be read as "the opposite of."

−(4) = −4   The opposite of positive 4 is negative 4.

−(−4) = 4   The opposite of negative 4 is positive 4.

The **absolute value of a number** is the distance between zero and the number on the number line. Therefore, the absolute value of a number is a positive number or zero. The symbol for absolute value is | |.

The distance from 0 to 4 is 4.
Thus |4| = 4 (the absolute value of 4 is 4).

The distance from 0 to −4 is 4.
Thus |−4| = 4 (the absolute value of −4 is 4).

The absolute value of a positive number is the number itself. The absolute value of a negative number is the opposite of the negative number. The absolute value of zero is zero.

Example 4   Find the absolute value of 2 and −3.

Solution |2| = 2

|−3| = 3

You Try It 4   Find the absolute value of −7 and 21.

Your solution

Example 5   Evaluate |−34| and |0|.

Solution |−34| = 34

|0| = 0

You Try It 5   Evaluate |2| and |−9|.

Your solution

Example 6   Evaluate −|−4|.

Solution   −|−4| = −4
The minus sign *in front of* the absolute value sign is not affected by the absolute value sign.

You Try It 6   Evaluate −|−12|.

Your solution

1.1 Exercises

Objective A **To identify the order relation between two integers**

For Exercises 1 to 4, represent the quantity as an integer.

1. A lake 120 ft below sea level

2. A temperature that is 15° below zero

3. A share of stock up 2 dollars

4. A loss of 324 dollars

For Exercises 5 to 8, graph the numbers on the number line.

5. 3 and −3

    −6 −5 −4 −3 −2 −1 0 1 2 3 4 5 6

6. −2 and 0

    −6 −5 −4 −3 −2 −1 0 1 2 3 4 5 6

7. −4 and 1

    −6 −5 −4 −3 −2 −1 0 1 2 3 4 5 6

8. 4 and −1

    −6 −5 −4 −3 −2 −1 0 1 2 3 4 5 6

For Exercises 9 to 14, state which number on the number line is in the location given.

9. 3 units to the right of −2

10. 5 units to the right of −3

11. 4 units to the left of 3

12. 2 units to the left of −1

13. 6 units to the right of −3

14. 4 units to the right of −4

For Exercises 15 to 18, use the following number line.

    A *B* *C* *D* *E* *F* *G* *H* *I*

15. **a.** If *F* is 1 and *G* is 2, what number is *A*?

    b. If *F* is 1 and *G* is 2, what number is *C*?

16. **a.** If *G* is 1 and *H* is 2, what number is *B*?

    b. If *G* is 1 and *H* is 2, what number is *D*?

17. **a.** If *H* is 0 and *I* is 1, what number is *A*?

    b. If *H* is 0 and *I* is 1, what number is *D*?

18. **a.** If *G* is 2 and *I* is 4, what number is *B*?

    b. If *G* is 2 and *I* is 4, what number is *E*?

For Exercises 19 to 42, place the correct symbol, $<$ or $>$, between the two numbers.

19. -2 -5

20. -6 -1

21. -16 1

22. -2 13

23. 3 -7

24. 5 -6

25. -11 -8

26. -4 -10

27. 35 28

28. 42 19

29. -42 27

30. -36 49

31. 21 -34

32. 53 -46

33. -27 -39

34. -51 -20

35. -87 63

36. -75 92

37. 86 -79

38. 95 -71

39. -62 -84

40. -91 -70

41. -131 101

42. 127 -150

For Exercises 43 to 51, write the given numbers in order from smallest to largest.

43. $3, -7, 0, -2$

44. $-4, 8, 6, -1$

45. $-3, 1, -5, 4$

46. $-6, 2, -8, 7$

47. $9, -4, 5, 0$

48. $6, -9, -12, 8$

49. $-10, 4, 12, -5, -7$

50. $11, -8, -1, 7, -6$

51. $10, -11, -2, 5, -7$

Objective B   **To evaluate expressions that contain the absolute value symbol**

For Exercises 52 to 61, find the opposite number.

52. 4

53. 16

54. -2

55. -3

56. 22

57. 45

58. -31

59. -59

60. 70

61. -88

For Exercises 62 to 69, find the absolute value of the number.

62. 4   **63.** −4   **64.** −7   **65.** 9

66. −1   **67.** −11   **68.** 10   **69.** −12

For Exercises 70 to 99, evaluate.

70. |2| **71.** |−2| **72.** |−6| **73.** |6| **74.** |8|

75. |5| **76.** |−9| **77.** |−1| **78.** −|−1| **79.** −|−5|

80. −|0| **81.** |16| **82.** |19| **83.** |−12| **84.** |−22|

85. −|29| **86.** −|20| **87.** −|−14| **88.** −|−18| **89.** |−15|

90. |−23| **91.** −|33| **92.** −|27| **93.** |32| **94.** |25|

95. −|−42| **96.** |−74| **97.** |−61| **98.** −|88| **99.** −|52|

For Exercises 100 to 107, place the correct symbol, <, =, or >, between the two numbers.

100. |7| |−9| **101.** |−12| |8| **102.** |−5| |−2| **103.** |6| |13|

104. |−8| |3| **105.** |−1| |−17| **106.** |−14| |14| **107.** |17| |−17|

For Exercises 108 to 113, write the given numbers in order from smallest to largest.

108. |−8|, −3, |2|, −|−5| **109.** −|6|, −4, |−7|, −9   **110.** −1, |−6|, |0|, −|3|

111. −|−7|, −9, 5, |4| **112.** −|2|, −8, 6, |1| **113.** −3, −|−8|, |5|, −|10|

APPLYING THE CONCEPTS

114. 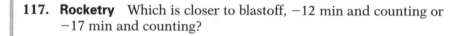 **Meteorology** The graph at the right shows the lowest recorded temperatures, in degrees Fahrenheit, for selected states in the United States. Which state has the lowest recorded temperature?

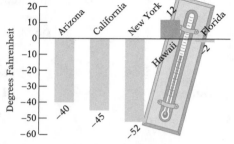

Lowest Recorded Temperatures

Sources: National Climatic Data Center; NESDIS; NOAA; U.S. Dept. of Commerce

115. **a.** Name two numbers that are 5 units from 3 on the number line.
   b. Name two numbers that are 3 units from −1 on the number line.

116. **a.** Find a number that is halfway between −7 and −5.
   b. Find a number that is halfway between −10 and −6.
   c. Find a number that is one-third of the way between −12 and −3.

117. **Rocketry** Which is closer to blastoff, −12 min and counting or −17 min and counting?

118. **Investments** In the stock market, the net change in the price of a share of stock is recorded as a positive or a negative number. If the price rises, the net change is positive. If the price falls, the net change is negative. If the net change for a share of Stock A is −2 and the net change for a share of Stock B is −1, which stock showed the least net change?

119. **Business** Some businesses show a profit as a positive number and a loss as a negative number. During the first quarter of this year, the loss experienced by a company was recorded as −12,575. During the second quarter of this year, the loss experienced by the company was −11,350. During which quarter was the loss greater?

120. Find the values of a for which $|a| = 7$.

121. Find the values of y for which $|y| = 11$.

122. 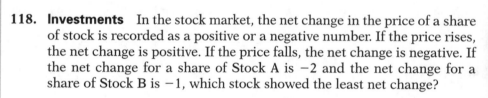 **a.** Describe the *opposite of a number* in your own words.
   b. Describe the *absolute value of a number* in your own words.

1.2 Addition and Subtraction of Integers

Objective A   **To add integers**

An integer can be graphed as a dot on a number line, as shown in the last section. An integer also can be represented anywhere along a number line by an arrow. A positive number is represented by an arrow pointing to the right. A negative number is represented by an arrow pointing to the left. The absolute value of the number is represented by the length of the arrow. The integers 5 and −4 are shown on the number lines below.

The sum of two integers can be shown on a number line. To add two integers, use arrows to represent the addends, with the first arrow starting at zero. The sum is the number directly below the tip of the arrow that represents the second addend.

$4 + 2 = 6$ 

$-4 + (-2) = -6$ 

$-4 + 2 = -2$ 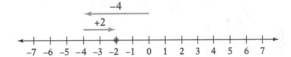

$4 + (-2) = 2$ 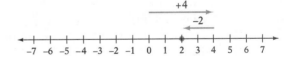

The sums of the integers shown above can be categorized by the signs of the addends.

Here the addends have the same sign:

  $4 + 2$ *positive* 4 plus *positive* 2
$-4 + (-2)$ *negative* 4 plus *negative* 2

Here the addends have different signs:

$-4 + 2$ *negative* 4 plus *positive* 2
 $4 + (-2)$ *positive* 4 plus *negative* 2

The rule for adding two integers depends on whether the signs of the addends are the same or different.

> **Rule for Adding Two Numbers**
>
> To add numbers with the same sign, add the absolute values of the numbers. Then attach the sign of the addends.
>
> To add numbers with different signs, find the difference between the absolute values of the numbers. Then attach the sign of the addend with the greater absolute value.

Point of Interest

Although mathematical symbols are fairly standard in every country, that has not always been true. Italian mathematicians in the 15th century used a "p" to indicate plus. The "p" was from the Italian word *piu*.

HOW TO Add: $(-4) + (-9)$

$|-4| = 4, |-9| = 9$
$4 + 9 = 13$

$(-4) + (-9) = -13$

- Because the signs of the addends are the same, add the absolute values of the numbers.
- Then attach the sign of the addends.

HOW TO Add: $6 + (-13)$

$|6| = 6, |-13| = 13$
$13 - 6 = 7$

$6 + (-13) = -7$

- Because the signs of the addends are different, subtract the smaller absolute value from the larger absolute value.
- Then attach the sign of the number with the larger absolute value. Because $|-13| > |6|$, attach the negative sign.

HOW TO Add: $162 + (-247)$

$162 + (-247) = -85$

- Because the signs are different, find the difference between the absolute values of the numbers and attach the sign of the number with the greater absolute value.

Integrating Technology

To add $-14 + (-47)$ on your calculator, enter the following:

14 +/- + 47 +/- =

HOW TO Find the sum of -14 and -47.

$-14 + (-47) = -61$

- Because the signs are the same, add the absolute values of the numbers and attach the sign of the addends.

When adding more than two integers, start from the left and add the first two numbers. Then add the sum to the third number. Continue this process until all the numbers have been added.

HOW TO Add: $(-4) + (-6) + (-8) + 9$

$(-4) + (-6) + (-8) + 9 = (-10) + (-8) + 9$
$= (-18) + 9$

$= -9$

- Add the first two numbers.
- Add the sum to the next number.
- Continue adding until all numbers have been added.

Example 1 What is -162 added to 98?

Solution $98 + (-162) = -64$ • The signs of the addends are different.

You Try It 1 Add: $-154 + (-37)$

Your solution

Example 2

Add: $-2 + (-7) + 4 + (-6)$

Solution

$$
\begin{aligned}
-2 + (-7) + 4 + (-6) &= -9 + 4 + (-6) \\
&= -5 + (-6) \\
&= -11
\end{aligned}
$$

You Try It 2

Add: $-5 + (-2) + 9 + (-3)$

Your solution

Objective B

To subtract integers

Before the rules for subtracting two integers are explained, look at the translation into words of an expression that is the difference of two integers:

$9 - 3$	positive 9 minus positive 3
$(-9) - 3$	negative 9 minus positive 3
$9 - (-3)$	positive 9 minus negative 3
$(-9) - (-3)$	negative 9 minus negative 3

Note that the sign $-$ is used in two different ways. One way is as a negative sign, as in (-9), *negative* 9. The second way is to indicate the operation of subtraction, as in $9 - 3$, 9 *minus* 3.

Look at the next four subtraction expressions and decide whether the second number in each expression is a positive number or a negative number.

1. $(-10) - 8$ **2.** $(-10) - (-8)$ **3.** $10 - (-8)$ **4.** $10 - 8$

In expressions 1 and 4, the second number is a positive 8. In expressions 2 and 3, the second number is a negative 8.

> **Rule for Subtracting Two Numbers**
>
> To subtract two numbers, add the opposite of the second number to the first number.

This rule states that to subtract two integers, we rewrite the subtraction expression as the sum of the first number and the opposite of the second number.

Here are some examples:

First number	$-$	second number	$=$	first number	$+$	the opposite of the second number	
8	$-$	15	$=$	8	$+$	(-15)	$= -7$
8	$-$	(-15)	$=$	8	$+$	15	$= -23$
(-8)	$-$	15	$=$	(-8)	$+$	(-15)	$= -23$
(-8)	$-$	(-15)	$=$	(-8)	$+$	15	$= -7$

Integrating Technology

The $+/-$ key on your calculator is used to find the opposite of a number. The $-$ is used to perform the operation of subtraction.

HOW TO   Subtract: $(-15) - 75$

$$
\begin{aligned}
(-15) - 75 &= (-15) + (-75) \\
&= -90
\end{aligned}
$$

• To subtract, add the opposite of the second number to the first number.

> **HOW TO**   Subtract: $27 - (-32)$
>
> $27 - (-32) = 27 + 32$ • To subtract, add the opposite of the second
> $\qquad\qquad\quad = 59$ number to the first number.

When subtraction occurs several times in an expression, rewrite each subtraction as addition of the opposite and then add.

> **HOW TO**   Subtract: $-13 - 5 - (-8)$
>
> $-13 - 5 - (-8) = -13 + (-5) + 8$ • Rewrite each subtraction as the
> $\qquad\qquad\qquad\ = -18 + 8$ addition of the opposite and
> $\qquad\qquad\qquad\ = -10$ then add.

Example 3

Find 8 less than -12.

Solution

$-12 - 8 = -12 + (-8)$ • Rewrite "$-$" as "$+$"; the
$\qquad\quad\ = -20$ opposite of 8 is -8.

You Try It 3

Find -8 less 14.

Your solution

Example 4

Subtract: $6 - (-20)$

Solution

$6 - (-20) = 6 + 20$ • Rewrite "$-$" as "$+$"; the
$\qquad\quad\ = 26$ opposite of -20 is 20.

You Try It 4

Subtract: $3 - (-15)$

Your solution

Example 5

Subtract: $-8 - 30 - (-12) - 7$

Solution

$-8 - 30 - (-12) - 7$
$= -8 + (-30) + 12 + (-7)$
$= -38 + 12 + (-7)$
$= -26 + (-7)$
$= -33$

You Try It 5

Subtract: $4 - (-3) - 12 - (-7) - 20$

Your solution

Objective C   **To solve application problems**

Example 6

Find the temperature after an increase of 9°C from -6°C.

Strategy

To find the temperature, add the increase (9°C) to the previous temperature (-6°C).

Solution

$-6 + 9 = 3$

The temperature is 3°C.

You Try It 6

Find the temperature after an increase of 12°C from -10°C.

Your strategy

Your solution

1.2 Exercises

Objective A **To add integers**

For Exercises 1 and 2, name the negative integers in the list of numbers.

1. $-14, 28, 0, -\dfrac{5}{7}, -364, -9.5$

2. $-37, 90, -\dfrac{7}{10}, -88.8, 42, -561$

For Exercises 3 to 30, add.

3. $3 + (-5)$

4. $-4 + 2$

5. $8 + 12$

6. $16 + 23$

7. $-3 + (-8)$

8. $-12 + (-1)$

9. $-4 + (-5)$

10. $-12 + (-12)$

11. $6 + (-9)$

12. $4 + (-9)$

13. $-6 + 7$

14. $-12 + 6$

15. $2 + (-3) + (-4)$

16. $7 + (-2) + (-8)$

17. $-3 + (-12) + (-15)$

18. $9 + (-6) + (-16)$

19. $-17 + (-3) + 29$

20. $13 + 62 + (-38)$

21. $-3 + (-8) + 12$

22. $-27 + (-42) + (-18)$

23. $13 + (-22) + 4 + (-5)$

24. $-14 + (-3) + 7 + (-6)$

25. $-22 + 10 + 2 + (-18)$

26. $-6 + (-8) + 13 + (-4)$

27. $-16 + (-17) + (-18) + 10$

28. $-25 + (-31) + 24 + 19$

29. $-126 + (-247) + (-358) + 339$

30. $-651 + (-239) + 524 + 487$

31. What is -8 more than -12?

32. What is -5 more than 3?

33. What is -7 added to -16?

34. What is 7 added to -25?

35. What is −4 plus 2?

36. What is −22 plus −17?

37. Find the sum of −2, 8, and −12.

38. Find the sum of 4, −4, and −6.

39. What is the total of 2, −3, 8, and −13?

40. What is the total of −6, −8, 13, and −2?

Objective B   To subtract integers

For Exercises 41 to 44, translate the expression into words. Represent each number as positive or negative.

41. −6 − 4

42. −6 − (−4)

43. 6 − (−4)

44. 6 − 4

For Exercises 45 to 48, rewrite the subtraction as the sum of the first number and the opposite of the second number.

45. 9 − (−5)

46. −3 − 7

47. 1 − 8

48. −2 − (−10)

For Exercises 49 to 76, subtract.

49. 16 − 8

50. 12 − 3

51. 7 − 14

52. 6 − 9

53. −7 − 2

54. −9 − 4

55. 7 − (−29)

56. 3 − (−4)

57. −6 − (−3)

58. −4 − (−2)

59. 6 − (−12)

60. −12 − 16

61. −4 − 3 − 2

62. 4 − 5 − 12

63. 12 − (−7) − 8

64. −12 − (−3) − (−15)

65. 4 − 12 − (−8)

66. 13 − 7 − 15

67. −6 − (−8) − (−9)

68. 7 − 8 − (−1)

69. −30 − (−65) − 29 − 4

70. 42 − (−82) − 65 − 7

71. −16 − 47 − 63 − 12

72. 42 − (−30) − 65 − (−11)

73. 47 − (−67) − 13 − 15

74. −18 − 49 − (−84) − 27

75. $167 - 432 - (-287) - 359$

76. $-521 - (-350) - 164 - (-299)$

77. Subtract -8 from -4.

78. Subtract -12 from 3.

79. What is the difference between -8 and 4?

80. What is the difference between 8 and -3?

81. What is -4 decreased by 8?

82. What is -13 decreased by 9?

83. Find -2 less than 1.

84. Find -3 less than -5.

> **Objective C**   **To solve application problems**

85. Temperature   Find the temperature after a rise of 7°C from -8°C.

86. Temperature   Find the temperature after a rise of 5°C from -19°C.

87. Games   During a card game of Hearts, Nick had a score of 11 points before his opponent "shot the moon," subtracting a score of 26 from Nick's total. What was Nick's score after his opponent shot the moon?

88. Games   In a card game of Hearts, Monique had a score of -19 before she "shot the moon," entitling her to add 26 points to her score. What was Monique's score after she shot the moon?

89. Investments   The price of Byplex Corporation's stock fell each trading day of the first week of June. Use the figure at the right to find the change in the price of Byplex stock over the week's time.

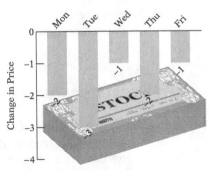

Change in Price of Byplex
Corporation Stock (in dollars)

90. Astronomy   The daytime temperature on the moon can reach 266°F, and the nighttime temperature can go as low as -292°F. Find the difference between these extremes.

91. Earth Science   The average temperature throughout Earth's stratosphere is -70°F. The average temperature on Earth's surface is 45°F. Find the difference between these average temperatures.

Geography The elevation, or height, of places on Earth is measured in relation to sea level, or the average level of the ocean's surface. The table below shows height above sea level as a positive number and depth below sea level as a negative number. Use the table for Exercises 92 to 94.

Continent	Highest Elevation (in meters)		Lowest Elevation (in meters)	
Africa	Mt. Kilimanjaro	5895	Lake Assal	−156
Asia	Mt. Everest	8850	Dead Sea	−411
North America	Mt. McKinley	5642	Death Valley	−28
South America	Mt. Aconcagua	6960	Valdes Peninsula	−86

Mt. Everest

92. What is the difference in elevation between Mt. Kilimanjaro and Lake Assal?

93. What is the difference in elevation between Mt. Aconcagua and the Valdes Peninsula?

94. For which continent shown is the difference between the highest and lowest elevations greatest?

Meteorology The figure at the right shows the highest and lowest temperatures ever recorded for selected regions of the world. Use this graph for Exercises 95 to 97.

95. What is the difference between the highest and lowest temperatures recorded in Africa?

96. What is the difference between the highest and lowest temperatures recorded in South America?

97. What is the difference between the lowest temperature recorded in Europe and the lowest temperature recorded in Asia?

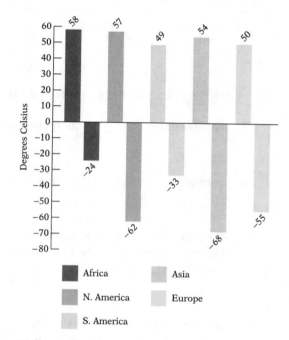

Highest and Lowest Temperatures Recorded (in degrees Celsius)

Source: National Climatic Data Center

APPLYING THE CONCEPTS

98. **Number Problems** Consider the numbers 4, −7, −5, 13, and −9. What is the largest difference that can be obtained by subtracting one number in the list from another number in the list? Find the smallest positive difference.

99. **Number Problems** Fill in the blank squares at the right with integers so that the sum of the integers along any row, column, or diagonal is zero.

−3		1
		3

100. **Number Problems** The sum of two negative integers is −8. Find the integers.

101. ✏️ Explain the difference between the words *negative* and *minus*.

1.3 Multiplication and Division of Integers

Objective A   **To multiply integers**

Multiplication is the repeated addition of the same number.

Several different symbols are used to indicate multiplication:

$$3 \times 2 = 6 \qquad\qquad 3 \cdot 2 = 6 \qquad\qquad (3)(2) = 6$$

When 5 is multiplied by a sequence of decreasing integers, the products decrease by 5.

$$5 \times 3 = 15$$
$$5 \times 2 = 10$$
$$5 \times 1 = 5$$
$$5 \times 0 = 0$$

The pattern developed can be continued so that 5 is multiplied by a sequence of negative numbers. The resulting products must be negative in order to maintain the pattern of decreasing by 5.

$$5 \times (-1) = -5$$
$$5 \times (-2) = -10$$
$$5 \times (-3) = -15$$
$$5 \times (-4) = -20$$

This example illustrates that the product of a positive number and a negative number is negative.

When -5 is multiplied by a sequence of decreasing integers, the products increase by 5.

$$-5 \times 3 = -15$$
$$-5 \times 2 = -10$$
$$-5 \times 1 = -5$$
$$-5 \times 0 = 0$$

The pattern developed can be continued so that -5 is multiplied by a sequence of negative numbers. The resulting products must be positive in order to maintain the pattern of increasing by 5.

$$-5 \times (-1) = 5$$
$$-5 \times (-2) = 10$$
$$-5 \times (-3) = 15$$
$$-5 \times (-4) = 20$$

This example illustrates that the product of two negative numbers is positive.

The pattern for multiplication shown above is summarized in the following rules for multiplying integers.

Integrating Technology
To multiply $(-4)(-8)$ on your calculator, enter the following:
4 +/– × 8 +/– =

> **Rule for Multiplying Two Numbers**
>
> To multiply numbers with the same sign, multiply the absolute values of the factors. The product is positive.
>
> To multiply numbers with different signs, multiply the absolute values of the factors. The product is negative.

$$4 \cdot 8 = 32$$
$$(-4)(-8) = 32$$
$$-4 \cdot 8 = -32$$
$$(4)(-8) = -32$$

HOW TO Multiply: $2(-3)(-5)(-7)$

$2(-3)(-5)(-7) = -6(-5)(-7)$

- To multiply more than two numbers, multiply the first two numbers.

$= 30(-7)$

- Then multiply the product by the third number.

$= -210$

- Continue until all the numbers have been multiplied.

Example 1

Multiply: $(-2)(6)$

Solution
$(-2)(6) = -12$
- The signs are different. The product is negative.

You Try It 1

Multiply: $(-3)(-5)$

Your solution

Example 2

Find the product of -42 and 62.

Solution
$-42 \cdot 62 = -2604$
- The signs are different. The product is negative.

You Try It 2

Find -38 multiplied by 51.

Your solution

Example 3

Multiply: $-5(-4)(6)(-3)$

Solution
$-5(-4)(6)(-3) = 20(6)(-3)$
$= 120(-3)$
$= -360$

You Try It 3

Multiply: $-7(-8)(9)(-2)$

Your solution

Objective B To divide integers

For every division problem, there is a related multiplication problem.

Division: $\dfrac{8}{2} = 4$ Related multiplication: $4 \cdot 2 = 8$

This fact can be used to illustrate the rules for dividing signed numbers.

Rule for Dividing Two Numbers

To divide numbers with the same sign, divide the absolute values of the numbers. The quotient is positive.

To divide numbers with different signs, divide the absolute values of the numbers. The quotient is negative.

$\dfrac{8}{2} = 4$ because $4 \cdot 2 = 8.$

$\dfrac{-8}{-2} = 4$ because $4(-2) = -8.$

$\dfrac{8}{-2} = -4$ because $-4(-2) = 8.$

$\dfrac{-8}{2} = -4$ because $-4(2) = -8.$

Note that $\frac{8}{-2}$, $\frac{-8}{2}$, and $-\frac{8}{2}$ are all equal to -4.

If a and b are two integers, then $\frac{a}{-b} = \frac{-a}{b} = -\frac{a}{b}$.

Properties of Zero and One in Division

Zero divided by any number other than zero is zero.

Any number other than zero divided by itself is 1.

Any number divided by 1 is the number.

Division by zero is not defined.

$\frac{0}{a} = 0$ because $0 \cdot a = 0$

$\frac{a}{a} = 1$ because $1 \cdot a = a$

$\frac{a}{1} = a$ because $a \cdot 1 = a$

$\frac{4}{0} = ?$ $? \cdot 0 = 4$

There is no number whose product with zero is 4.

The examples below illustrate these properties of division.

$$\frac{0}{-8} = 0 \qquad \frac{-7}{-7} = 1 \qquad \frac{-9}{1} = -9 \qquad \frac{-3}{0} \text{ is undefined.}$$

Example 4

Divide: $(-120) \div (-8)$

Solution

$(-120) \div (-8) = 15$ • The signs are the same. The quotient is positive.

You Try It 4

Divide: $(-135) \div (-9)$

Your solution

Example 5

Divide: $95 \div (-5)$

Solution

$95 \div (-5) = -19$ • The signs are different. The quotient is negative.

You Try It 5

Divide: $84 \div (-6)$

Your solution

Example 6

Find the quotient of -81 and 3.

Solution

$-81 \div 3 = -27$

You Try It 6

What is -72 divided by 4?

Your solution

Example 7

Divide: $0 \div (-24)$

Solution

$0 \div (-24) = 0$ • Zero divided by a nonzero number is zero.

You Try It 7

Divide: $-39 \div 0$

Your solution

Objective C   **To solve application problems**

Example 8

The combined scores of the top five golfers in a tournament equaled −10 (10 under par). What was the average score of the five golfers?

Strategy
To find the average score, divide the combined scores (−10) by the number of golfers (5).

Solution
−10 ÷ 5 = −2

The average score was −2.

You Try It 8

The melting point of mercury is −38°C. The melting point of argon is five times the melting point of mercury. Find the melting point of argon.

Your strategy

Your solution

Example 9

The daily high temperatures during one week were recorded as follows: −9°F, 3°F, 0°F, −8°F, 2°F, 1°F, 4°F. Find the average daily high temperature for the week.

Strategy
To find the average daily high temperature:
• Add the seven temperature readings.
• Divide by 7.

Solution
−9 + 3 + 0 + (−8) + 2 + 1 + 4 = −7

−7 ÷ 7 = −1

The average daily high temperature was −1°F.

You Try It 9

The daily low temperatures during one week were recorded as follows: −6°F, −7°F, 1°F, 0°F, −5°F, −10°F, −1°F. Find the average daily low temperature for the week.

Your strategy

Your solution

1.3 Exercises

Objective A   **To multiply integers**

For Exercises 1 to 4, state whether the operation in the expression is addition, subtraction, or multiplication.

1. $5 - (-6)$

2. $4(-9)$

3. $-8(-5)$

4. $-3 + (-7)$

For Exercises 5 to 46, multiply.

5. 14×3

6. 62×9

7. $-4 \cdot 6$

8. $-7 \cdot 3$

9. $-2 \cdot (-3)$

10. $-5 \cdot (-1)$

11. $(9)(2)$

12. $(3)(8)$

13. $5(-4)$

14. $4(-7)$

15. $-8(2)$

16. $-9(3)$

17. $(-5)(-5)$

18. $(-3)(-6)$

19. $(-7)(0)$

20. -32×4

21. -24×3

22. $19 \cdot (-7)$

23. $6(-17)$

24. $-8(-26)$

25. $-4(-35)$

26. $-5 \cdot (23)$

27. $-6 \cdot (38)$

28. $9(-27)$

29. $8(-40)$

30. $-7(-34)$

31. $-4(39)$

32. $4 \cdot (-8) \cdot 3$

33. $5 \times 7 \times (-2)$

34. $8 \cdot (-6) \cdot (-1)$

35. $(-9)(-9)(2)$

36. $-8(-7)(-4)$

37. $-5(8)(-3)$

38. $(-6)(5)(7)$

39. $-1(4)(-9)$

40. $6(-3)(-2)$

41. $4(-4) \cdot 6(-2)$

42. $-5 \cdot 9(-7) \cdot 3$

43. $-9(4) \cdot 3(1)$

44. $8(8)(-5)(-4)$

45. $(-6) \cdot 7 \cdot (-10)(-5)$

46. $-9(-6)(11)(-2)$

47. What is -5 multiplied by -4?

48. What is 6 multiplied by -5?

49. What is -8 times 6?

50. What is -8 times -7?

51. Find the product of -4, 7, and -5.

52. Find the product of -2, -4, and -7.

Objective B   **To divide integers**

For Exercises 53 to 56, write the related multiplication problem.

53. $\dfrac{-36}{-12} = 3$

54. $\dfrac{28}{-7} = -4$

55. $\dfrac{-55}{11} = -5$

56. $\dfrac{-20}{-10} = 2$

For Exercises 57 to 107, divide.

57. $12 \div (-6)$

58. $18 \div (-3)$

59. $(-72) \div (-9)$

60. $(-64) \div (-8)$

61. $0 \div (-6)$

62. $-49 \div 7$

63. $45 \div (-5)$

64. $-24 \div 4$

65. $-36 \div 4$

66. $-56 \div 7$

67. $-81 \div (-9)$

68. $-40 \div (-5)$

69. $72 \div (-3)$

70. $44 \div (-4)$

71. $-60 \div 5$

72. $-66 \div 6$

73. $-93 \div (-3)$

74. $-98 \div (-7)$

75. $(-85) \div (-5)$

76. $(-60) \div (-4)$

77. $120 \div 8$

78. $144 \div 9$

79. $78 \div (-6)$

80. $84 \div (-7)$

81. $-72 \div 4$

82. $-80 \div 5$

83. $-114 \div (-6)$

84. $-91 \div (-7)$

85. $-104 \div (-8)$

86. $-126 \div (-9)$

87. $57 \div (-3)$

88. $162 \div (-9)$

89. $-136 \div (-8)$

90. $-128 \div 4$

91. $-130 \div (-5)$

92. $(-280) \div 8$

93. $(-92) \div (-4)$

94. $-196 \div (-7)$

95. $-150 \div (-6)$

96. $(-261) \div 9$

97. $204 \div (-6)$

98. $165 \div (-5)$

99. $-132 \div (-12)$

100. $-156 \div (-13)$

101. $-182 \div 14$

102. $-144 \div 12$

103. $143 \div 11$

104. $168 \div 14$

105. $-180 \div (-15)$

106. $-169 \div (-13)$

107. $154 \div (-11)$

108. Find the quotient of -132 and -11.

109. Find the quotient of 182 and -13.

110. What is -60 divided by -15?

111. What is 144 divided by -24?

112. Find the quotient of -135 and 15.

113. Find the quotient of -88 and 22.

Objective C   **To solve application problems**

114. Meteorology The daily low temperatures during one week were recorded as follows: 4°F, −5°F, 8°F, −1°F, −12°F, −14°F, −8°F. Find the average daily low temperature for the week.

115. Meteorology The daily high temperatures during one week were recorded as follows: −6°F, −11°F, 1°F, 5°F, −3°F, −9°F, −5°F. Find the average daily high temperature for the week.

116.   Chemistry The graph at the right shows the boiling points of three chemical elements. The boiling point of neon is seven times the highest boiling point shown in the table.
   a. Without actually calculating the boiling point, determine whether the boiling point of neon is above 0°C or below 0°C.
   b. What is the boiling point of neon?

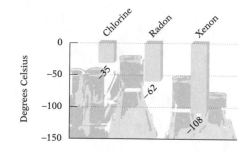

117. Sports The combined scores of the top ten golfers in a tournament equaled −20 (20 under par). What was the average score of the ten golfers?

118. Sports The combined scores of the top four golfers in a tournament equaled −12 (12 under par). What was the average score of the four golfers?

119.   Meteorology The wind chill factor when the temperature is −20°F and the wind is blowing at 15 mph is five times the wind chill factor when the temperature is 10°F and the wind is blowing at 20 mph. If the wind chill factor at 10°F with a 20-mph wind is −9°F, what is the wind chill factor at −20°F with a 15-mph wind?

120. Education To discourage guessing on a multiple-choice exam, an instructor graded the test by giving 5 points for a correct answer, −2 points for an answer left blank, and −5 points for an incorrect answer. How many points did a student score who answered 20 questions correctly, answered 5 questions incorrectly, and left 2 questions blank?

APPLYING THE CONCEPTS

121. a. Number Problems Find the greatest possible product of two negative integers whose sum is −10.
   b. Number Problems Find the least possible sum of two negative integers whose product is 16.

122. Use repeated addition to show that the product of two integers with different signs is a negative number.

123. Determine whether the statement is true or false.
   a. The product of a nonzero number and its opposite is negative.
   b. The square of a negative number is a positive number.

**124.   ** In your own words, describe the rules for multiplying and dividing integers.

1.4 Operations with Rational Numbers

Objective A   **To add or subtract rational numbers**

In this section, operations with rational numbers are discussed. A **rational number** is the quotient of two integers.

> **Rational Numbers**
>
> A rational number is a number that can be written in the form $\frac{a}{b}$, where a and b are integers and $b \neq 0$.

Each of the three numbers shown at the right is a rational number.

$$\frac{3}{4} \qquad \frac{-2}{9} \qquad \frac{13}{-5}$$

An integer can be written as the quotient of the integer and 1. Therefore, **every integer is a rational number.**

$$6 = \frac{6}{1} \qquad -8 = \frac{-8}{1}$$

A mixed number can be written as the quotient of two integers. Therefore, **every mixed number is a rational number.**

$$1\frac{4}{7} = \frac{11}{7} \qquad 3\frac{2}{5} = \frac{17}{5}$$

Recall that every fraction can be written as a decimal by dividing the numerator of the fraction by the denominator. The result is either a terminating decimal or a repeating decimal.

We can write the fraction $\frac{3}{4}$ as the terminating decimal 0.75.

TAKE NOTE

The fraction bar can be read "divided by."

$$\frac{3}{4} = 3 \div 4$$

```
        0.75  ←——— This is a terminating decimal.
   4)−3.00
     −2.80
        20
       −20
         0  ←——— The remainder is zero.
```

We can write the fraction $\frac{2}{3}$ as the repeating decimal $0.\overline{6}$.

TAKE NOTE

A **terminating decimal** is a decimal that has a finite number of digits after the decimal point, which means that it comes to an end and does not go on forever. A **repeating decimal** is a decimal that does not end; it has a repeating pattern of digits after the decimal point.

```
       0.666 = 0.6  ←——— This is a repeating decimal.
   3)−2.000              The bar over the digit 6 in 0.6 is used
     −1.800              to show that this digit repeats.
        200
       −180
         20
        −18
          2  ←——————— The remainder is never zero.
```

All terminating and repeating decimals are rational numbers.

To add or subtract rational numbers in fractional form, first find the least common multiple (LCM) of the denominators.

HOW TO Add: $-\dfrac{7}{8} + \dfrac{5}{6}$

$8 = 2 \cdot 2 \cdot 2$
$6 = 2 \cdot 3$
$\text{LCM} = 2 \cdot 2 \cdot 2 \cdot 3 = 24$

- Find the LCM of the denominators.

$-\dfrac{7}{8} + \dfrac{5}{6} = -\dfrac{21}{24} + \dfrac{20}{24}$

- Rewrite each fraction using the LCM of the denominators as the common denominator.

$= \dfrac{-21 + 20}{24}$

- Add the numerators.

$= \dfrac{-1}{24} = -\dfrac{1}{24}$

TAKE NOTE

In this text, answers that are negative fractions are written with the negative sign in front of the fraction.

HOW TO Subtract: $-\dfrac{7}{9} - \dfrac{5}{12}$

$9 = 3 \cdot 3$
$12 = 2 \cdot 2 \cdot 3$
$\text{LCM} = 2 \cdot 2 \cdot 3 \cdot 3 = 36$

- Find the LCM of the denominators.

$-\dfrac{7}{9} - \dfrac{5}{12} = -\dfrac{28}{36} - \dfrac{15}{36}$

- Rewrite each fraction using the LCM of the denominators as the common denominator.

$= \dfrac{-28}{36} + \dfrac{-15}{36}$

- Rewrite subtraction as addition of the opposite. Rewrite negative fractions with the negative sign in the numerator.

$= \dfrac{-28 + (-15)}{36}$

- Add the numerators.

$= \dfrac{-43}{36} = -\dfrac{43}{36} = -1\dfrac{7}{36}$

To add or subtract rational numbers in decimal form, use the sign rules for adding integers.

HOW TO Add: $47.034 + (-56.91)$

$\begin{array}{r} 56.910 \\ -\,47.034 \\ \hline 9.876 \end{array}$

- The signs are different. Find the difference between the absolute values of the numbers.

$47.034 + (-56.91)$
$= -9.876$

- Attach the sign of the number with the greater absolute value.

HOW TO Subtract: $-39.09 - 102.98$

$$-39.09 - 102.98$$
$$= -39.09 + (-102.98)$$

- Rewrite subtraction as addition of the opposite number.

$$\begin{array}{r} 39.09 \\ + \ 102.98 \\ \hline 142.07 \end{array}$$

- The signs of the addends are the same. Find the sum of the absolute values of the numbers.

$$-39.09 - 102.98 = -142.07$$

- Attach the sign of the addends.

Example 1

Subtract: $\dfrac{5}{16} - \dfrac{7}{40}$

Solution

$$\dfrac{5}{16} - \dfrac{7}{40} = \dfrac{25}{80} - \dfrac{14}{80}$$

- The LCM of 16 and 40 is 80.

$$= \dfrac{25}{80} + \dfrac{-14}{80}$$

- Rewrite as addition of the opposite.

$$= \dfrac{25 + (-14)}{80} = \dfrac{11}{80}$$

You Try It 1

Subtract: $\dfrac{5}{9} - \dfrac{11}{12}$

Your solution

Example 2

Simplify: $-\dfrac{3}{4} + \dfrac{1}{6} - \dfrac{5}{8}$

Solution

$$-\dfrac{3}{4} + \dfrac{1}{6} - \dfrac{5}{8} = -\dfrac{18}{24} + \dfrac{4}{24} - \dfrac{15}{24}$$

- The LCM of 4, 6, and 8 is 24.

$$= \dfrac{-18}{24} + \dfrac{4}{24} + \dfrac{-15}{24}$$

$$= \dfrac{-18 + 4 + (-15)}{24}$$

$$= \dfrac{-29}{24} = -\dfrac{29}{24} = -1\dfrac{5}{24}$$

You Try It 2

Simplify: $-\dfrac{7}{8} - \dfrac{5}{6} + \dfrac{2}{3}$

Your solution

Example 3

Subtract: $42.987 - 98.61$

Solution

$$42.987 - 98.61 = 42.987 + (-98.61)$$

$$\begin{array}{r} 98.610 \\ - \ 42.987 \\ \hline 55.623 \end{array}$$

$$42.987 - 98.61 = -55.623$$

You Try It 3

Subtract: $16.127 - 67.91$

Your solution

Example 4

Simplify: $1.02 + (-3.6) + 9.24$

Solution

$1.02 + (-3.6) + 9.24 = -2.58 + 9.24$
$= 6.66$

You Try It 4

Simplify: $2.7 + (-9.44) + 6.2$

Your solution

Objective B   **To multiply or divide rational numbers**

The product of two rational numbers written as fractions is the product of the numerators over the product of the denominators. Use the sign rules for multiplying integers.

HOW TO   Simplify: $-\dfrac{3}{8} \times \dfrac{12}{17}$

$$-\dfrac{3}{8} \times \dfrac{12}{17} = -\left(\dfrac{3 \cdot 12}{8 \cdot 17}\right) = -\dfrac{9}{34}$$

- **The signs are different.**
  The product is negative.

To divide rational numbers written as fractions, invert the divisor and then multiply. Use the sign rules for dividing integers.

HOW TO   Simplify: $-\dfrac{3}{10} \div \left(-\dfrac{18}{25}\right)$

$$-\dfrac{3}{10} \div \left(-\dfrac{18}{25}\right) = \dfrac{3}{10} \times \dfrac{25}{18} = \dfrac{3 \cdot 25}{10 \cdot 18} = \dfrac{5}{12}$$

- **The signs are the same.**
  The quotient is positive.

To multiply or divide rational numbers written in decimal form, use the sign rules for integers.

HOW TO   Simplify: $(-6.89) \times (-0.00035)$

$$
\begin{array}{r}
6.89 \\
\times\,000.00035 \\
\hline
3445 \\
20675 \\
\hline
0.0024115
\end{array}
$$

2 decimal places
5 decimal places

7 decimal places

- **The signs are the same. Multiply the absolute values.**

$(-6.89) \times (-0.00035) = 0.0024115$

- **The product is positive.**

HOW TO   Divide $1.32 \div (-0.27)$. Round to the nearest tenth.

$$
\begin{array}{r}
4.88 \approx 4.9 \\
0.27.\overline{)1.32.00} \\
-1.08.00 \\
\hline
24.00 \\
-21.60 \\
\hline
2.40 \\
-2.16 \\
\hline
24
\end{array}
$$

- Divide the absolute values. Move the decimal point two places in the divisor and then in the dividend. Place the decimal point in the quotient.

$$1.32 \div (-0.27) \approx -4.9$$

- The signs are different. The quotient is negative.

Example 5

Multiply: $-\dfrac{7}{12} \times \dfrac{9}{14}$

Solution   The product is negative.

$$-\frac{7}{12} \times \frac{9}{14} = -\left(\frac{7 \cdot 9}{12 \cdot 14}\right)$$
$$= -\frac{3}{8}$$

You Try It 5

Multiply: $\left(-\dfrac{2}{3}\right)\left(-\dfrac{9}{10}\right)$

Your solution

Example 6

Divide: $-\dfrac{3}{8} \div \left(-\dfrac{5}{12}\right)$

Solution   The quotient is positive.

$$-\frac{3}{8} \div \left(-\frac{5}{12}\right) = \frac{3}{8} \times \frac{12}{5}$$
$$= \frac{3 \cdot 12}{8 \cdot 5}$$
$$= \frac{9}{10}$$

You Try It 6

Divide: $-\dfrac{5}{8} \div \dfrac{5}{40}$

Your solution

Example 7   Multiply: -4.29×8.2

Solution   The product is negative.

$$
\begin{array}{r}
4.29 \\
\times 48.2 \\
\hline
858 \\
34322 \\
\hline
35.178
\end{array}
$$

$$-4.29 \times 8.2 = -35.178$$

You Try It 7   Multiply: -5.44×3.8

Your solution

Example 8   Multiply: $-3.2 \times (-0.4) \times 6.9$

Solution
$$-3.2 \times (-0.4) \times 6.9$$
$$= 1.28 \times 6.9$$
$$= 8.832$$

You Try It 8   Multiply: $3.44 \times (-1.7) \times 0.6$

Your solution

Example 9   Divide: $-0.0792 \div (-0.42)$
Round to the nearest hundredth.

Solution

$$
\begin{array}{r}
0.188 \approx 0.19 \\
0.42\,)\overline{0.07.920} \\
-4.2 \\
\hline
3.72 \\
-3.36 \\
\hline
360 \\
-336 \\
\hline
24
\end{array}
$$

$-0.0792 \div (-0.42) \approx 0.19$

You Try It 9   Divide: $-0.394 \div 1.7$
Round to the nearest hundredth.

Your solution

Objective C   **To solve application problems**

Example 10

🥧 In Fairbanks, Alaska, the average temperature during the month of July is 61.5°F. During the month of January, the average temperature in Fairbanks is −12.7°F. What is the difference between the average temperature in Fairbanks during July and the average temperature during January?

Strategy
To find the difference, subtract the average temperature in January (−12.7°F) from the average temperature in July (61.5°F).

Solution
$61.5 - (-12.7) = 61.5 + 12.7 = 74.2$

The difference between the average temperature during July and the average temperature during January in Fairbanks is 74.2°F.

You Try It 10

🥧 On January 10, 1911, in Rapid City, South Dakota, the temperature fell from 12.78°C at 7:00 A.M. to −13.33°C at 7:15 A.M. How many degrees did the temperature fall during the 15-min period?

Your strategy

Your solution

1.4 Exercises

Objective A   **To add or subtract rational numbers**

For Exercises 1 to 43, simplify.

1. $\dfrac{5}{8} - \dfrac{5}{6}$

2. $\dfrac{1}{9} - \dfrac{5}{27}$

3. $-\dfrac{5}{12} - \dfrac{3}{8}$

4. $-\dfrac{5}{6} - \dfrac{5}{9}$

5. $-\dfrac{6}{13} + \dfrac{17}{26}$

6. $-\dfrac{7}{12} + \dfrac{5}{8}$

7. $-\dfrac{5}{8} - \left(-\dfrac{11}{12}\right)$

8. $-\dfrac{7}{12} - \left(-\dfrac{7}{8}\right)$

9. $\dfrac{5}{12} - \dfrac{11}{15}$

10. $\dfrac{2}{5} - \dfrac{14}{15}$

11. $-\dfrac{3}{4} - \dfrac{5}{8}$

12. $-\dfrac{2}{3} - \dfrac{5}{8}$

13. $-\dfrac{5}{2} - \left(-\dfrac{13}{4}\right)$

14. $-\dfrac{7}{3} - \left(-\dfrac{3}{2}\right)$

15. $-\dfrac{3}{8} - \dfrac{5}{12} - \dfrac{3}{16}$

16. $-\dfrac{5}{16} + \dfrac{3}{4} - \dfrac{7}{8}$

17. $\dfrac{1}{2} - \dfrac{3}{8} - \left(-\dfrac{1}{4}\right)$

18. $\dfrac{3}{4} - \left(-\dfrac{7}{12}\right) - \dfrac{7}{8}$

19. $\dfrac{1}{3} - \dfrac{1}{4} - \dfrac{1}{5}$

20. $\dfrac{5}{16} + \dfrac{1}{8} - \dfrac{1}{2}$

21. $\dfrac{1}{2} + \left(-\dfrac{3}{8}\right) + \dfrac{5}{12}$

22. $-\dfrac{3}{8} + \dfrac{3}{4} - \left(-\dfrac{3}{16}\right)$

23. $3.4 + (-6.8)$

24. $-4.9 + 3.27$

25. $-8.32 + (-0.57)$

26. $-3.5 + 7$

27. $-4.8 + (-3.2)$

28. $6.2 + (-4.29)$

29. $-4.6 + 3.92$

30. $7.2 + (-8.42)$

31. $-45.71 + (-135.8)$

32. $-35.274 + 12.47$

33. $4.2 + (-6.8) + 5.3$

34. $6.7 + 3.2 + (-10.5)$

35. $-4.5 + 3.2 + (-19.4)$

36. $2.09 - 6.72 - 5.4$

37. $-18.39 + 4.9 - 23.7$

38. $19 - (-3.72) - 82.75$

39. $-3.09 - 4.6 - 27.3$

40. ▦ $-3.89 + (-2.9) + 4.723 + 0.2$

41. ▦ $-4.02 + 6.809 - (-3.57) - (-0.419)$

42. ▦ $0.0153 + (-1.0294) + (-1.0726)$

43. ▦ $0.27 + (-3.5) - (-0.27) + (-5.44)$

Objective B   **To multiply or divide rational numbers**

For Exercises 44 to 79, simplify.

44. $\dfrac{1}{2} \times \left(-\dfrac{3}{4}\right)$

45. $-\dfrac{2}{9} \times \left(-\dfrac{3}{14}\right)$

46. $\left(-\dfrac{3}{8}\right)\left(-\dfrac{4}{15}\right)$

47. $\left(-\dfrac{3}{4}\right)\left(-\dfrac{8}{27}\right)$

48. $-\dfrac{1}{2} \times \dfrac{8}{9}$

49. $\dfrac{5}{12} \times \left(-\dfrac{8}{15}\right)$

50. $\left(-\dfrac{5}{12}\right)\left(\dfrac{42}{65}\right)$

51. $\left(\dfrac{3}{8}\right)\left(-\dfrac{15}{41}\right)$

52. $\left(-\dfrac{15}{8}\right)\left(-\dfrac{16}{3}\right)$

53. $\left(-\dfrac{5}{7}\right)\left(-\dfrac{14}{15}\right)$

54. $\dfrac{5}{8} \times \left(-\dfrac{7}{12}\right) \times \dfrac{16}{25}$

55. $\left(\dfrac{1}{2}\right)\left(-\dfrac{3}{4}\right)\left(-\dfrac{5}{8}\right)$

56. $\dfrac{1}{3} \div \left(-\dfrac{1}{2}\right)$

57. $-\dfrac{3}{8} \div \dfrac{7}{8}$

58. $\left(-\dfrac{3}{4}\right) \div \left(-\dfrac{7}{40}\right)$

59. $\dfrac{5}{6} \div \left(-\dfrac{3}{4}\right)$

60. $-\dfrac{5}{12} \div \dfrac{15}{32}$

61. $-\dfrac{5}{16} \div \left(-\dfrac{3}{8}\right)$

62. $\left(-\dfrac{3}{8}\right) \div \left(-\dfrac{5}{12}\right)$

63. $\left(-\dfrac{8}{19}\right) \div \dfrac{7}{38}$

64. $\left(-\dfrac{2}{3}\right) \div 4$

65. $-6 \div \dfrac{4}{9}$

66. $-6.7 \times (-4.2)$

67. $-8.9 \times (-3.5)$

68. -1.6×4.9

69. -14.3×7.9

70. $(-0.78)(-0.15)$

71. $(-1.21)(-0.03)$

72. $(-8.919) \div (-0.9)$

73. $-77.6 \div (-0.8)$

74. $59.01 \div (-0.7)$

75. $(-7.04) \div (-3.2)$

76. $(-84.66) \div 1.7$

77. $-3.312 \div (0.8)$

78. $1.003 \div (-0.59)$

79. $26.22 \div (-6.9)$

 For Exercises 80 to 85, divide.

80. $(-19.08) \div 0.45$

81. $21.792 \div (-0.96)$

82. $(-38.665) \div (-9.5)$

83. $(-3.171) \div (-45.3)$

84. $27.738 \div (-60.3)$

85. $(-13.97) \div (-25.4)$

Objective C   **To solve application problems**

86.   **Meteorology**   On January 23, 1916, the temperature in Browing, Montana, was 6.67°C. On January 24, 1916, the temperature in Browing was −48.9°C. Find the difference between the temperatures in Browing on these two days.

87.   **Meteorology**   On January 22, 1943, in Spearfish, South Dakota, the temperature fell from 12.22°C at 9 A.M. to −20°C at 9:27 A.M. How many degrees did the temperature fall during the 27-min period?

88.   **Chemistry**   The boiling point of nitrogen is −195.8°C and the melting point is −209.86°C. Find the difference between the boiling point and the melting point of nitrogen.

89.   **Chemistry**   The boiling point of oxygen is −182.962°C. Oxygen's melting point is −218.4°C. What is the difference between the boiling point and the melting point of oxygen?

Investments   The chart at the right shows the closing price of a share of stock on September 15, 2003, for each of five companies. Also shown is the change in the price from the previous day. To find the closing price on the previous day, subtract the change in price from the closing price on September 15. Use this chart for Exercises 90 and 91.

Company	Closing Price	Change in Price
Del Monte Foods Co.	8.77	−0.06
General Mills, Inc.	47.10	−0.11
Hershey Foods, Inc.	72.57	+0.11
Hormel Food Corp.	22.42	−0.08
Sara Lee Corp.	19.18	−0.21

90.   **a.** Find the closing price on the previous day for General Mills.
       b. Find the closing price on the previous day for Hormel Foods.

91.   **a.** Find the closing price on the previous day for Sara Lee.
       b. Find the closing price on the previous day for Hershey Foods.

APPLYING THE CONCEPTS

92.   Determine whether the statement is true or false.
       a. Every integer is a rational number.
       b. Every whole number is an integer.
       c. Every integer is a positive number.
       d. Every rational number is an integer.

93.   **Number Problems**   Find a rational number between $-\frac{3}{4}$ and $-\frac{2}{3}$.

94.   **Number Problems**
       a. Find a rational number between 0.1 and 0.2.
       b. Find a rational number between 1 and 1.1.
       c. Find a rational number between 0 and 0.005.

95.   Given any two different rational numbers, is it always possible to find a rational number between them? If so, explain how. If not, give an example of two different rational numbers for which there is no rational number between them.

1.5

Scientific Notation and the Order of Operations Agreement

Objective A   **To write a number in scientific notation**

Point of Interest

The first woman mathematician for whom documented evidence exists is Hypatia (370–415). She lived in Alexandria, Egypt, and lectured at the Museum, the forerunner of our modern university. She made important contributions in mathematics, astronomy, and philosophy.

Scientific notation uses negative exponents. Therefore, we will discuss that topic before presenting scientific notation.

Look at the powers of 10 shown at the right. Note the pattern: The exponents are decreasing by 1, and each successive number on the right is one-tenth of the number above it. ($100,000 \div 10 = 10,000$; $10,000 \div 10 = 1000$; etc.)

$$10^5 = 100,000$$
$$10^4 = 10,000$$
$$10^3 = 1000$$
$$10^2 = 100$$
$$10^1 = 10$$

If we continue this pattern, the next exponent on 10 is $1 - 1 = 0$, and the number on the right side is $10 \div 10 = 1$.

$$10^0 = 1$$

The next exponent on 10 is $0 - 1 = -1$, and 10^{-1} is equal to $1 \div 10 = 0.1$.

$$10^{-1} = 0.1$$

The pattern is continued on the right. Note that a negative exponent does not indicate a negative number. Rather, each power of 10 with a negative exponent is equal to a number between 0 and 1. Also note that as the exponent on 10 decreases, so does the number it is equal to.

$$10^{-2} = 0.01$$
$$10^{-3} = 0.001$$
$$10^{-4} = 0.0001$$
$$10^{-5} = 0.00001$$
$$10^{-6} = 0.000001$$

Very large and very small numbers are encountered in the natural sciences. For example, the mass of an electron is 0.0000000000000000000000000000000911 kg. Numbers such as this are difficult to read, so a more convenient system called **scientific notation** is used. In scientific notation, a number is expressed as the product of two factors, one a number between 1 and 10, and the other a power of 10.

To express a number in scientific notation, write it in the form $a \times 10^n$, where a is a number between 1 and 10 and n is an integer.

For numbers greater than 10, move the decimal point to the right of the first digit. The exponent n is positive and equal to the number of places the decimal point has been moved.

$$240,000 = 2.4 \times 10^5$$

$$93,000,000 = 9.3 \times 10^7$$

Copyright © Houghton Mifflin Company. All rights reserved.

TAKE NOTE

There are two steps in writing a number in scientific notation: (1) determine the number between 1 and 10, and (2) determine the exponent on 10

For numbers less than 1, move the decimal point to the right of the first nonzero digit. The exponent n is negative. The absolute value of the exponent is equal to the number of places the decimal point has been moved.

$$0.0003 = 3 \times 10^{-4}$$

$$0.0000832 = 8.32 \times 10^{-5}$$

Changing a number written in scientific notation to decimal notation also requires moving the decimal point.

When the exponent on 10 is positive, move the decimal point to the right the same number of places as the exponent.

$$3.45 \times 10^9 = 3,450,000,000$$

$$2.3 \times 10^8 = 230,000,000$$

When the exponent on 10 is negative, move the decimal point to the left the same number of places as the absolute value of the exponent.

$$8.1 \times 10^{-3} = 0.0081$$

$$6.34 \times 10^{-6} = 0.00000634$$

Example 1   Write 824,300,000,000 in scientific notation.

Solution   The number is greater than 10. Move the decimal point 11 places to the left. The exponent on 10 is 11.

$$824,300,000,000 = 8.243 \times 10^{11}$$

You Try It 1   Write 0.000000961 in scientific notation.

Your solution

Example 2   Write 6.8×10^{-10} in decimal notation.

Solution   The exponent on 10 is negative. Move the decimal point 10 places to the left.

$$6.8 \times 10^{-10} = 0.00000000068$$

You Try It 2   Write 7.329×10^6 in decimal notation.

Your solution

Objective B   **To use the Order of Operations Agreement to simplify expressions**

The Order of Operations Agreement has been used throughout this book. In simplifying expressions with rational numbers, the same Order of Operations Agreement is used. This agreement is restated here.

The Order of Operations Agreement

Step 1   Do all operations inside parentheses.

Step 2   Simplify any number expressions containing exponents.

Step 3   Do multiplication and division as they occur from left to right.

Step 4   Rewrite subtraction as addition of the opposite. Then do additions as they occur from left to right.

Exponents may be confusing in expressions with signed numbers.

$$(-3)^2 = (-3) \times (-3) = 9$$
$$-3^2 = -(3)^2 = -(3 \times 3) = -9$$

Note that -3 is squared only when the negative sign is *inside* the parentheses.

HOW TO   Simplify: $(-3)^2 - 2 \times (8 - 3) + (-5)$

$(-3)^2 - 2 \times (8 - 3) + (-5)$

$(-3)^2 - 2 \times 5 + (-5)$

$9 - 2 \times 5 + (-5)$

$9 - 10 + (-5)$

$9 + (-10) + (-5)$

$(-1) + (-5)$

-6

1. Perform operations inside parentheses.

2. Simplify expressions with exponents.

3. Do multiplications and divisions as they occur from left to right.

4. Rewrite subtraction as the addition of the opposite. Then add from left to right.

HOW TO   Simplify: $\left(\dfrac{1}{4} - \dfrac{1}{2}\right)^2 \div \dfrac{3}{8}$

$\left(\dfrac{1}{4} - \dfrac{1}{2}\right)^2 \div \dfrac{3}{8}$

$\left(-\dfrac{1}{4}\right)^2 \div \dfrac{3}{8}$

$\dfrac{1}{16} \div \dfrac{3}{8}$

$\dfrac{1}{16} \times \dfrac{8}{3}$

$\dfrac{1}{6}$

1. Perform operations inside parentheses.

2. Simplify expressions with exponents.

3. Do multiplication and division as they occur from left to right.

Example 3 Simplify: $8 - 4 \div (-2)$	**You Try It 3** Simplify: $9 - 9 \div (-3)$
Solution	**Your solution**

Solution

$8 - 4 \div (-2)$

$= 8 - (-2)$ • Do the division.

$= 8 + 2$ • Rewrite as

$= 10$ addition. Add.

Example 4   Simplify: $12 \div (-2)^2 + 5$

Solution $12 \div (-2)^2 + 5$
$= 12 \div 4 + 5$ • **Exponents**
$= 3 + 5$ • **Division**
$= 8$ • **Addition**

You Try It 4   Simplify: $8 \div 4 \cdot 4 - (-2)^2$

Your solution

Example 5   Simplify: $12 - (-10) \div (8 - 3)$

Solution $12 - (-10) \div (8 - 3)$
$= 12 - (-10) \div 5$
$= 12 - (-2)$
$= 12 + 2$
$= 14$

You Try It 5   Simplify: $8 - (-15) \div (2 - 7)$

Your solution

Example 6   Simplify:
$(-3)^2 \times (5 - 7)^2 - (-9) \div 3$

Solution $(-3)^2 \times (5 - 7)^2 - (-9) \div 3$
$= (-3)^2 \times (-2)^2 - (-9) \div 3$
$= 9 \times 4 - (-9) \div 3$
$= 36 - (-9) \div 3$
$= 36 - (-3)$
$= 36 + 3$
$= 39$

You Try It 6   Simplify:
$(-2)^2 \times (3 - 7)^2 - (-16) \div (-4)$

Your solution

Example 7   Simplify: $3 \div \left(\frac{1}{2} - \frac{1}{4}\right) - 3$

Solution $3 \div \left(\frac{1}{2} - \frac{1}{4}\right) - 3$
$= 3 \div \frac{1}{4} - 3$
$= 3 \times \frac{4}{1} - 3$
$= 12 - 3$
$= 12 + (-3)$
$= 9$

You Try It 7   Simplify: $7 \div \left(\frac{1}{7} - \frac{3}{14}\right) - 9$

Your solution

1.5 Exercises

Objective A   **To write a number in scientific notation**

For Exercises 1 to 12, write the number in scientific notation.

1. 2,370,000

2. 75,000

3. 0.00045

4. 0.000076

5. 309,000

6. 819,000,000

7. 0.000000601

8. 0.00000000096

9. 57,000,000,000

10. 934,800,000,000

11. 0.000000017

12. 0.0000009217

For Exercises 13 to 24, write the number in decimal notation.

13. 7.1×10^5

14. 2.3×10^7

15. 4.3×10^{-5}

16. 9.21×10^{-7}

17. 6.71×10^8

18. 5.75×10^9

19. 7.13×10^{-6}

20. 3.54×10^{-8}

21. 5×10^{12}

22. 1.0987×10^{11}

23. 8.01×10^{-3}

24. 4.0162×10^{-9}

25.   **Physics**   Light travels 16,000,000,000 mi in 1 day. Write this number in scientific notation.

26.   **Earth Science**   Write the mass of Earth, which is approximately 5,980,000,000,000,000,000,000,000 kg, in scientific notation.

27.   **Wars**   The graph at the right shows the monetary cost of four wars. Write the monetary cost of World War II in scientific notation.

28.   **Chemistry**   The electric charge on an electron is 0.00000000000000000016 coulomb. Write this number in scientific notation.

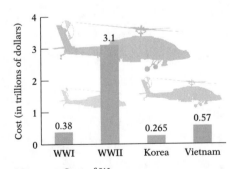

Monetary Cost of Wars

Source: Congressional Research Service, using numbers from the *Statistical Abstract of the United States*

29. **Physics** The length of an infrared light wave is approximately 0.0000037 m. Write this number in scientific notation.

30. **Computers** One unit used to measure the speed of a computer is the picosecond. One picosecond is 0.000000000001 of a second. Write this number in scientific notation.

Objective B **To use the Order of Operations Agreement to simplify expressions**

For Exercises 31 to 92, simplify.

31. $8 \div 4 + 2$

32. $3 - 12 \div 2$

33. $4 + (-7) + 3$

34. $-16 \div 2 + 8$

35. $4^2 - 4$

36. $6 - 2^2$

37. $2 \times (3 - 5) - 2$

38. $2 - (8 - 10) \div 2$

39. $4 - (-3)^2$

40. $(-2)^2 - 6$

41. $4 - (-3) - 5$

42. $6 + (-8) - (-3)$

43. $4 - (-2)^2 + (-3)$

44. $-3 + (-6)^2 - 1$

45. $3^2 - 4 \times 2$

46. $9 \div 3 - (-3)^2$

47. $3 \times (6 - 2) \div 6$

48. $4 \times (2 - 7) \div 5$

49. $2^2 - (-3)^2 + 2$

50. $3 \times (8 - 5) + 4$

51. $6 - 2 \times (1 - 5)$

52. $4 \times 2 \times (3 - 6)$

53. $(-2)^2 - (-3)^2 + 1$

54. $4^2 - 3^2 - 4$

55. $6 - (-3) \times (-3)^2$

56. $4 - (-5) \times (-2)^2$

57. $4 \times 2 - 3 \times 7$

58. $16 \div 2 - 9 \div 3$

59. $(-2)^2 - 5 \times 3 - 1$

60. $4 - 2 \times 7 - 3^2$

61. $7 \times 6 - 5 \times 6 + 3 \times 2 - 2 + 1$

62. $3 \times 2^2 + 5 \times (3 + 2) - 17$

63. $-4 \times 3 \times (-2) + 12 \times (3 - 4) + (-12)$

64. $3 \times 4^2 - 16 - 4 + 3 - (1 - 2)^2$

65. $-12 \times (6 - 8) + 1^2 \times 3^2 \times 2 - 6 \times 2$

66. $-3 \times (-2)^2 \times 4 \div 8 - (-12)$

67. $10 \times 9 - (8 + 7) \div 5 + 6 - 7 + 8$

68. $-27 - (-3)^2 - 2 - 7 + 6 \times 3$

69. $3^2 \times (4 - 7) \div 9 + 6 - 3 - 4 \times 2$

70. $16 - 4 \times 8 + 4^2 - (-18) \div (-9)$

71. $(-3)^2 \times (5 - 7)^2 - (-9) \div 3$

72. $-2 \times 4^2 - 3 \times (2 - 8) - 3$

73. $4 - 6(2 - 5)^3 \div (17 - 8)$

74. $5 + 7(3 - 8)^2 \div (-14 + 9)$

75. $(1.2)^2 - 4.1 \times 0.3$

76. $2.4 \times (-3) - 2.5$

77. $1.6 - (-1.6)^2$

78. $4.1 \times 8 \div (-4.1)$

79. $(4.1 - 3.9) - 0.7^2$

80. $1.8 \times (-2.3) - 2$

81. $(-0.4)^2 \times 1.5 - 2$

82. $(6.2 - 1.3) \times (-3)$

83. $4.2 - (-3.9) - 6$

84. $-\dfrac{1}{2} + \dfrac{3}{8} \div \left(-\dfrac{3}{4}\right)$

85. $\left(\dfrac{3}{4}\right)^2 - \dfrac{3}{8}$

86. $\left(\dfrac{1}{2}\right)^2 - \left(-\dfrac{1}{2}\right)^2$

87. $\dfrac{5}{16} - \dfrac{3}{8} + \dfrac{1}{2}$

88. $\dfrac{2}{7} \div \dfrac{5}{7} - \dfrac{3}{14}$

89. $\dfrac{1}{2} \times \dfrac{1}{4} \times \dfrac{1}{2} - \dfrac{3}{8}$

90. $\dfrac{2}{3} \times \dfrac{5}{8} \div \dfrac{2}{7}$

91. $\dfrac{1}{2} - \left(\dfrac{3}{4} - \dfrac{3}{8}\right) \div \dfrac{1}{3}$

92. $\dfrac{3}{8} \div \left(-\dfrac{1}{2}\right)^2 + 2$

APPLYING THE CONCEPTS

93. Place the correct symbol, $<$ or $>$, between the two numbers.
   a. 3.45×10^{-14} 3.45×10^{-15}
   b. 5.23×10^{18} 5.23×10^{17}
   c. 3.12×10^{12} 3.12×10^{11}

94.   **Astronomy**   Light travels 3×10^8 m in 1 s. How far does light travel in 1 year? (Astronomers refer to this distance as 1 light year.)

95.   **a.** Evaluate $1^3 + 2^3 + 3^3 + 4^3$.
   b. Evaluate $(-1)^3 + (-2)^3 + (-3)^3 + (-4)^3$.
   c. Evaluate $1^3 + 2^3 + 3^3 + 4^3 + 5^3$.
   d. On the basis of your answers to parts a, b, and c, evaluate $(-1)^3 + (-2)^3 + (-3)^3 + (-4)^3 + (-5)^3$.

96. Evaluate $2^{(3^2)}$ and $(2^3)^2$. Are the answers the same? If not, which is larger?

97.   Abdul, Becky, Carl, and Diana were being questioned by their teacher. One of the students had left an apple on the teacher's desk, but the teacher did not know which one. Abdul said it was either Becky or Diana. Diana said it was neither Becky nor Carl. If both those statements are false, who left the apple on the teacher's desk? Explain how you arrived at your solution.

98.   In your own words, explain how you know that a number is written in scientific notation.

99.   **a.** Express the mass of the sun in kilograms using scientific notation.
   b. Express the mass of a neutron in kilograms using scientific notation.

Focus on Problem Solving

Drawing Diagrams   How do you best remember something? Do you remember best what you hear? The word *aural* means "pertaining to the ear"; people with a strong aural memory remember best those things that they hear. The word *visual* means "pertaining to the sense of sight"; people with a strong visual memory remember best that which they see written down. Some people claim that their memory is in their writing hand—they remember something only if they write it down! The method by which you best remember something is probably also the method by which you can best learn something new.

In problem-solving situations, try to capitalize on your strengths. If you tend to understand the material better when you hear it spoken, read application problems aloud or have someone else read them to you. If writing helps you to organize ideas, rewrite application problems in your own words.

No matter what your main strength, visualizing a problem can be a valuable aid in problem solving. A drawing, sketch, diagram, or chart can be a useful tool in problem solving, just as calculators and computers are tools. A diagram can be helpful in gaining an understanding of the relationships inherent in a problem-solving situation. A sketch will help you to organize the given information and can lead to your being able to focus on the method by which the solution can be determined.

HOW TO   A tour bus drives 5 mi south, then 4 mi west, then 3 mi north, then 4 mi east. How far is the tour bus from the starting point?

Draw a diagram of the given information.

From the diagram, we can see that the solution can be determined by subtracting 3 from 5: $5 - 3 = 2$.

The bus is 2 mi from the starting point.

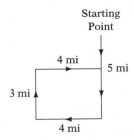

HOW TO   If you roll two ordinary six-sided dice and multiply the two numbers that appear on top, how many different possible products are there?

Make a chart of the possible products. In the chart below, repeated products are marked with an asterisk.

$1 \cdot 1 = 1$	$2 \cdot 1 = 2$ (*)	$3 \cdot 1 = 3$ (*)	$4 \cdot 1 = 4$ (*)	$5 \cdot 1 = 5$ (*)	$6 \cdot 1 = 6$ (*)
$1 \cdot 2 = 2$	$2 \cdot 2 = 4$ (*)	$3 \cdot 2 = 6$ (*)	$4 \cdot 2 = 8$ (*)	$5 \cdot 2 = 10$ (*)	$6 \cdot 2 = 12$ (*)
$1 \cdot 3 = 3$	$2 \cdot 3 = 6$ (*)	$3 \cdot 3 = 9$	$4 \cdot 3 = 12$ (*)	$5 \cdot 3 = 15$ (*)	$6 \cdot 3 = 18$ (*)
$1 \cdot 4 = 4$	$2 \cdot 4 = 8$	$3 \cdot 4 = 12$ (*)	$4 \cdot 4 = 16$	$5 \cdot 4 = 20$ (*)	$6 \cdot 4 = 24$ (*)
$1 \cdot 5 = 5$	$2 \cdot 5 = 10$	$3 \cdot 5 = 15$	$4 \cdot 5 = 20$	$5 \cdot 5 = 25$	$6 \cdot 5 = 30$ (*)
$1 \cdot 6 = 6$	$2 \cdot 6 = 12$	$3 \cdot 6 = 18$	$4 \cdot 6 = 24$	$5 \cdot 6 = 30$	$6 \cdot 6 = 36$

By counting the products that are not repeats, we can see that there are 18 different possible products.

Look at Sections 10.1 and 10.2. You will notice that number lines are used to help you visualize the integers, as an aid in ordering integers, to help you understand the concepts of opposite and absolute value, and to illustrate addition of integers. As you begin your work with integers, you may find that sketching a number line proves helpful in coming to understand a problem or in working through a calculation that involves integers.

Projects and Group Activities

Deductive Reasoning

Suppose that during the last week of your math class, your instructor tells you that if you receive an A on the final exam, you will earn an A in the course. When the final exam grades are posted, you learn that you received an A on the final exam. You can then assume that you will earn an A in the course.

The process used to determine your grade in the math course is deductive reasoning. **Deductive reasoning** involves drawing a conclusion that is based on given facts. The problems below require deductive reasoning.

1. Given that $\Delta\Delta\Delta = \Diamond\Diamond\Diamond\Diamond$ and $\Diamond\Diamond\Diamond\Diamond = ÓÓ$, then $\Delta\Delta\Delta\Delta\Delta\Delta =$ how many Ós?

2. Given that ‡‡ = ••• and ••• = Λ, then ‡‡‡‡ = how many Λs?

3. Given that ÓÓÓ = $\Omega\Omega$ and ¤ = $\Omega\Omega$, then ¤¤ = how many Ós?

4. Given that $\int\int\int\int\int = \partial\partial$ and $\partial\partial\partial\partial = ¥¥¥$, then ¥¥¥¥¥¥ = how many $\int$s?

5. Given that ÔÔÔÔÔ = □□□ and □□□□□□ = §§§§, then §§§§§§ = how many Ôs?

6. Chris, Dana, Leslie, and Pat are neighbors. Each drives a different type of vehicle: a compact car, a sedan, a sports car, or a station wagon. From the following statements, determine which type of vehicle each of the neighbors drives. It may be helpful to use the chart provided below.
   a. Although the vehicle owned by Chris has more mileage on it than does either the sedan or the sports car, it does not have the highest mileage of all four cars.
   b. Pat and the owner of the sports car live on one side of the street, and Leslie and the owner of the compact car live on the other side of the street.
   c. Leslie owns the vehicle with the most mileage on it.

TAKE NOTE
To use the chart to solve this problem, write an X in a box to indicate that a possibility has been eliminated. Write a √ to show that a match has been found. When a row or column has 3 X's, a √ is written in the remaining open box in that row or column of the chart.

	Compact	*Sedan*	*Sports Car*	*Wagon*
Chris				
Dana				
Leslie				
Pat				

7. Four neighbors, Anna, Kay, Michelle, and Nicole, each plant a different vegetable (beans, cucumbers, squash, or tomatoes) in their garden. From the following statements, determine which vegetable each neighbor plants.
   a. Nicole's garden is bigger than the one that has tomatoes but smaller than the one that has cucumbers.
   b. Anna, who planted the largest garden, didn't plant the beans.
   c. The person who planted the beans has a garden the same size as Nicole's.
   d. Kay and the person who planted the tomatoes also have flower gardens.

8. The Ontkeans, Kedrovas, McIvers, and Levinsons are neighbors. Each of the four families specializes in a different national cuisine (Chinese, French, Italian, or Mexican). From the following statements, determine which cuisine each family specializes in.
   a. The Ontkeans invited the family that specializes in Chinese cuisine and the family that specializes in Mexican cuisine for dinner last night.
   b. The McIvers live between the family that specializes in Italian cuisine and the Ontkeans. The Levinsons live between the Kedrovas and the family that specializes in Chinese cuisine.
   c. The Kedrovas and the family that specializes in Italian cuisine both subscribe to the same culinary magazine.

Chapter Summary

Key Words	**Examples**
Positive numbers are numbers greater than zero. *Negative numbers* are numbers less than zero. The *integers* are . . . −4, −3, −2, −1, 0, 1, 2, 3, 4, ... *Positive integers* are to the right of zero on the number line. *Negative integers* are to the left of zero on the number line.	9, 87, and 603 are positive numbers. They are also positive integers. −5, −41, and −729 are negative numbers. They are also negative integers.
Opposite numbers are two numbers that are the same distance from zero on the number line but on opposite sides of zero.	8 is the opposite of −8. −2 is the opposite of 2.
The *absolute value of a number* is its distance from zero on a number line. The absolute value of a number is a positive number or zero. The symbol for absolute value is $\mid\ \mid$.	$\mid 9 \mid = 9$ $\mid -9 \mid = 9$ $-\mid 9 \mid = -9$
A *rational number* is a number that can be written in the form $\frac{a}{b}$, where a and b are integers and $b \neq 0$.	$\frac{3}{7}, -\frac{5}{8}, 9, -2, 4\frac{1}{2}, 0.6$, and $0.\overline{3}$ are rational numbers.

Essential Rules and Procedures	**Examples**
Order Relations A number that appears to the left of a given number on the number line is less than (<) the given number. A number that appears to the right of a given number on the number line is greater than (>) the given number.	$-6 > -12$ $-8 < 4$

To add numbers with the same sign, add the absolute values of the numbers. Then attach the sign of the addends.

$6 + 4 = 10$
$-6 + (-4) = -10$

To add numbers with different signs, find the difference between the absolute values of the numbers. Then attach the sign of the addend with the greater absolute value.

$-6 + 4 = -2$
$6 + (-4) = 2$

To subtract two numbers, add the opposite of the second number to the first number.

$6 - 4 = 6 + (-4) = 2$
$6 - (-4) = 6 + 4 = 10$
$-6 - 4 = -6 + (-4) = -10$
$-6 - (-4) = -6 + 4 = -2$

To multiply numbers with the same sign, multiply the absolute values of the factors. The product is positive.

$3 \cdot 5 = 15$
$-3(-5) = 15$

To multiply numbers with different signs, multiply the absolute values of the factors. The product is negative.

$-3(5) = -15$
$3(-5) = -15$

To divide two numbers with the same sign, divide the absolute values of the numbers. The quotient is positive.

$15 \div 3 = 5$
$(-15) \div (-3) = 5$

To divide two numbers with different signs, divide the absolute values of the numbers. The quotient is negative.

$-15 \div 3 = -5$
$15 \div (-3) = -5$

Properties of Zero and One in Division

Zero divided by any number other than zero is zero.
Any number other than zero divided by itself is 1.
Any number divided by 1 is the number.
Division by zero is not defined.

$0 \div (-5) = 0$
$-5 \div (-5) = 1$
$-5 \div 1 = -5$
$-5 \div 0$ is undefined.

Scientific Notation

To express a number in scientific notation, write it in the form $a \times 10^n$, where a is a number between 1 and 10 and n is an integer.
If the number is greater than 10, the exponent on 10 will be positive.
If the number is less than 1, the exponent on 10 will be negative.

$367{,}000{,}000 = 3.67 \times 10^8$
$0.0000059 = 5.9 \times 10^{-6}$

To change a number written in scientific notation to decimal notation, move the decimal point to the right if the exponent on 10 is positive and to the left if the exponent is negative. Move the decimal point the same number of places as the absolute value of the exponent on 10.

$2.418 \times 10^7 = 24{,}180{,}000$
$9.06 \times 10^{-5} = 0.0000906$

The Order of Operations Agreement

Step 1 Do all operations inside parentheses.

Step 2 Simplify any numerical expressions containing exponents.

Step 3 Do multiplication and division as they occur from left to right.

Step 4 Rewrite subtraction as addition of the opposite. Then do additions as they occur from left to right.

$$\begin{aligned}
(-4)^2 - 3(1 - 5) &= (-4)^2 - 3(-4) \\
&= 16 - 3(-4) \\
&= 16 - (-12) \\
&= 16 + 12 \\
&= 28
\end{aligned}$$

Chapter Review Exercises

1. Find the opposite of 22.

2. Subtract: $-8 - (-2) - (-10) - 3$

3. Subtract: $\frac{5}{8} - \frac{5}{6}$

4. Simplify: $-0.33 + 1.98 - 1.44$

5. Multiply: $\left(-\frac{2}{3}\right)\left(\frac{6}{11}\right)\left(-\frac{22}{25}\right)$

6. Multiply: -0.08×16

7. Simplify: $12 - 6 \div 3$

8. Simplify: $\left(\frac{2}{3}\right)^2 - \frac{5}{6}$

9. Find the opposite of -4.

10. Place the correct symbol, $<$ or $>$, between the two numbers.
$0 \quad -3$

11. Evaluate $-|-6|$.

12. Divide: $-18 \div (-3)$

13. Add: $-\frac{3}{8} + \frac{5}{12} + \frac{2}{3}$

14. Multiply: $\frac{1}{3} \times \left(-\frac{3}{4}\right)$

15. Divide: $-\frac{7}{12} \div \left(-\frac{14}{39}\right)$

16. Simplify: $16 \div 4(8 - 2)$

17. Add: $-22 + 14 + (-18)$

18. Simplify: $3^2 - 9 + 2$

Chapter Review

19. Write 0.0000397 in scientific notation.

20. Divide: $-1.464 \div 18.3$

21. Simplify: $-\dfrac{5}{12} + \dfrac{7}{9} - \dfrac{1}{3}$

22. Multiply: $\dfrac{6}{34} \times \dfrac{17}{40}$

23. Multiply: $1.2 \times (-0.035)$

24. Simplify: $-\dfrac{1}{2} + \dfrac{3}{8} \div \dfrac{9}{20}$

25. Evaluate $|-5|$.

26. Place the correct symbol, $<$ or $>$, between the two numbers.
$-2 \quad -40$

27. Find 2 times -13.

28. Simplify: $-0.4 \times 5 - (-3.33)$

29. Add: $\dfrac{5}{12} + \left(-\dfrac{2}{3}\right)$

30. Simplify: $-33.4 + 9.8 - (-16.2)$

31. Divide: $\left(-\dfrac{3}{8}\right) \div \left(-\dfrac{4}{5}\right)$

32. Write 2.4×10^5 in decimal notation.

33. **Temperatures**   Find the temperature after a rise of $18°$ from $-22°$.

34. **Education**   To discourage guessing on a multiple-choice exam, an instructor graded the test by giving 3 points for a correct answer, -1 point for an answer left blank, and -2 points for an incorrect answer. How many points did a student score who answered 38 questions correctly, answered 4 questions incorrectly, and left 8 questions blank?

35.   **Chemistry**   The boiling point of mercury is $356.58°C$. The melting point of mercury is $-38.87°C$. Find the difference between the boiling point and the melting point of mercury.

Chapter Test

1. Subtract: $-5 - (-8)$

2. Evaluate $-|-2|$.

3. Add: $-\frac{2}{5} + \frac{7}{15}$

4. Find the product of 0.032 and -1.9.

5. Place the correct symbol, $<$ or $>$, between the two numbers.
   $-8 \quad -10$

6. Add: $1.22 + (-3.1)$

7. Simplify: $4 \times (4 - 7) \div (-2) - 4 \times 8$

8. Multiply: $-5 \times (-6) \times 3$

9. What is -1.004 decreased by 3.01?

10. Divide: $-72 \div 8$

11. Find the sum of -2, 3, and -8.

12. Add: $-\frac{3}{8} + \frac{2}{3}$

13. Write 87,600,000,000 in scientific notation.

14. Find the product of -4 and 12.

15. Divide: $\dfrac{0}{-17}$

16. Subtract: $16 - 4 - (-5) - 7$

17. Find the quotient of $-\frac{2}{3}$ and $\frac{5}{6}$.

18. Place the correct symbol, $<$ or $>$, between the two numbers.

0   −4

19. Add: $16 + (-10) + (-20)$

20. Simplify: $(-2)^2 - (-3)^2 \div (1 - 4)^2 \times 2 - 6$

21. Subtract: $-\frac{2}{5} - \left(-\frac{7}{10}\right)$

22. Write 9.601×10^{-8} in decimal notation.

23. Divide: $-15.64 \div (-4.6)$

24. Find the sum of $-\frac{1}{2}, \frac{1}{3},$ and $\frac{1}{4}$.

25. Multiply: $\frac{3}{8} \times \left(-\frac{5}{6}\right) \times \left(-\frac{4}{15}\right)$

26. Subtract: $2.113 - (-1.1)$

27. Temperatures Find the temperature after a rise of 11°C from −4°C.

28. **Chemistry** The melting point of radon is −71°C. The melting point of oxygen is three times the melting point of radon. Find the melting point of oxygen.

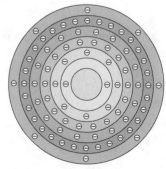

Radon

29. **Meteorology** On December 24, 1924, in Fairfield, Montana, the temperature fell from 17.22°C at noon to −29.4°C at midnight. How many degrees did the temperature fall in the 12-h period?

30. Meteorology The daily low temperature readings for a 3-day period were as follows: −7°F, 9°F, −8°F. Find the average low temperature for the 3-day period.

2 Introduction to Algebra

This family is getting ready to head off on their vacation. They plan to drive 500 miles to their destination, and their car averages 25 miles per gallon of gasoline on the highway. How many gallons of gasoline will the car consume in driving the family there and back? We can use the formula $D = M \cdot G$, where D is the distance traveled, M is the miles per gallon, and G is the number of gallons consumed. Using this formula, we find that the car will need 40 gallons to make the trip.

OBJECTIVES

Section 2.1
A To evaluate variable expressions
B To simplify variable expressions containing no parentheses
C To simplify variable expressions containing parentheses

Section 2.2
A To determine whether a given number is a solution of an equation
B To solve an equation of the form $x + a = b$
C To solve an equation of the form $ax = b$
D To solve application problems using formulas

Section 2.3
A To solve an equation of the form $ax + b = c$
B To solve application problems using formulas

Section 2.4
A To solve an equation of the form $ax + b = cx + d$
B To solve an equation containing parentheses

Section 2.5
A To translate a verbal expression into a mathematical expression given the variable
B To translate a verbal expression into a mathematical expression by assigning the variable

Section 2.6
A To translate a sentence into an equation and solve
B To solve application problems

Need help? For online student resources, such as section quizzes, visit this textbook's website at **math.college.hmco.com/students.**

For Exercises 1 to 9, simplify.

1. $2 - 9$

2. $-5(4)$

3. $-16 + 16$

4. $\dfrac{-7}{-7}$

5. $-\dfrac{3}{8}\left(-\dfrac{8}{3}\right)$

6. $\left(\dfrac{3}{5}\right)^3 \cdot \left(\dfrac{5}{9}\right)^2$

7. $\dfrac{2}{3} + \left(\dfrac{3}{4}\right)^2 \cdot \dfrac{2}{9}$

8. $-8 \div (-2)^2 + 6$

9. $4 + 5(2 - 7)^2 \div (-8 + 3)$

GO FIGURE ● ● ●

In the addition at the right, each letter stands for a different digit. If N = 1, I = 5, U = 7, F = 2, and T = 3, what is the value of S?

$$\begin{array}{r} \text{FUN} \\ \text{IN} \\ +\text{THE} \\ \hline \text{SUN} \end{array}$$

2.1

Variable Expressions

Objective A   **To evaluate variable expressions**

Often we discuss a quantity without knowing its exact value—for example, next year's inflation rate, the price of gasoline next summer, or the interest rate on a new-car loan next fall. In mathematics, a letter of the alphabet is used to stand for a quantity that is unknown or that can change, or *vary*. The letter is called a **variable.** An expression that contains one or more variables is called a **variable expression.**

A company's business manager has determined that the company will make a $10 profit on each radio it sells. The manager wants to describe the company's total profit from the sale of radios. Because the number of radios that the company will sell is unknown, the manager lets the variable n stand for that number. Then the variable expression $10 \cdot n$, or simply $10n$, describes the company's profit from selling n radios.

The company's profit from selling n radios is $\$10 \cdot n = \$10n$.

If the company sells 12 radios, its profit is $\$10 \cdot 12 = \$120$.

If the company sells 75 radios, its profit is $\$10 \cdot 75 = \$750$.

Replacing the variable or variables in a variable expression and then simplifying the resulting numerical expression is called **evaluating a variable expression.**

HOW TO   Evaluate $3x^2 + xy - z$ when $x = -2$, $y = 3$, and $z = -4$.

$3x^2 + xy - z$

$3(-2)^2 + (-2)(3) - (-4)$ • **Replace each variable in the expression with the number it stands for.**

$= 3 \cdot 4 + (-2)(3) - (-4)$ • **Use the Order of Operations Agreement to simplify the resulting numerical expression.**

$= 12 + (-6) - (-4)$

$= 12 + (-6) + 4$

$= 6 + 4$

$= 10$

The value of the variable expression $3x^2 + xy - z$ when $x = -2$, $y = 3$, and $z = -4$ is 10.

Example 1

Evaluate $3x - 4y$ when $x = -2$ and $y = 3$.

Solution
$3x - 4y$

$3(-2) - 4(3) = -6 - 12$
$\qquad\qquad\quad = -6 + (-12) = -18$

You Try It 1

Evaluate $6a - 5b$ when $a = -3$ and $b = 4$.

Your solution

Example 2

Evaluate $-x^2 - 6 \div y$ when $x = -3$ and $y = 2$.

Solution
$-x^2 - 6 \div y$

$-(-3)^2 - 6 \div 2 = -9 - 6 \div 2$
$\qquad\qquad\qquad\quad = -9 - 3$
$\qquad\qquad\qquad\quad = -9 + (-3) = -12$

You Try It 2

Evaluate $-3s^2 - 12 \div t$ when $s = -2$ and $t = 4$.

Your solution

Example 3

Evaluate $-\frac{1}{2}y^2 - \frac{3}{4}z$ when $y = 2$ and $z = -4$.

Solution
$-\frac{1}{2}y^2 - \frac{3}{4}z$

$-\frac{1}{2}(2)^2 - \frac{3}{4}(-4) = -\frac{1}{2} \cdot 4 - \frac{3}{4}(-4)$
$\qquad\qquad\qquad\qquad = -2 - (-3)$
$\qquad\qquad\qquad\qquad = -2 + (3) = 1$

You Try It 3

Evaluate $-\frac{2}{3}m + \frac{3}{4}n^3$ when $m = 6$ and $n = 2$.

Your solution

Example 4

Evaluate $-2ab + b^2 + a^2$ when $a = -\frac{3}{5}$ and $b = \frac{2}{5}$.

Solution
$-2ab + b^2 + a^2$

$-2\left(-\frac{3}{5}\right)\left(\frac{2}{5}\right) + \left(\frac{2}{5}\right)^2 + \left(-\frac{3}{5}\right)^2$

$= -2\left(-\frac{3}{5}\right)\left(\frac{2}{5}\right) + \left(\frac{4}{25}\right) + \left(\frac{9}{25}\right)$

$= \frac{12}{25} + \frac{4}{25} + \frac{9}{25} = \frac{25}{25} = 1$

You Try It 4

Evaluate $-3yz - z^2 + y^2$ when $y = -\frac{2}{3}$ and $z = \frac{1}{3}$.

Your solution

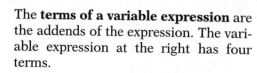

Objective B **To simplify variable expressions containing no parentheses**

The **terms of a variable expression** are the addends of the expression. The variable expression at the right has four terms.

4 terms

$7x^2 \;+\; (-6xy) \;+\; x \;+\; (-8)$

Variable terms   Constant term

Three of the terms are **variable terms:** $7x^2$, $-6xy$, and x.

One of the terms is a **constant term:** -8. A constant term has no variables.

Each variable term is composed of a **numerical coefficient** (the number part of a variable term) and a **variable part** (the variable or variables and their exponents). When the numerical coefficient is 1, the 1 is usually not written. ($1x = x$)

$$\boxed{\text{Numerical coefficient}}$$
$$7x^2 + (-6xy) + 1x + (-8)$$
$$\boxed{\text{Variable part}}$$

Like terms of a variable expression are the terms with the same variable part. (Because $y^2 = y \cdot y$, y^2 and y are not like terms.)

$$\boxed{\text{Like terms}}$$
$$8y^2 + 3y + 9y^2 + 5y$$
$$\boxed{\text{Like terms}}$$

In variable expressions that contain constant terms, the constant terms are like terms.

$$\boxed{\text{Like terms}}$$
$$4x + 9 + 2x + (-7)$$
$$\boxed{\text{Like terms}}$$

The Commutative and Associative Properties of Addition are used to simplify variable expressions. These properties can be stated in general form using variables.

> **Commutative Property of Addition**
>
> If a and b are two numbers, then $a + b = b + a$.

> **Associative Property of Addition**
>
> If a, b, and c are three numbers, then $a + (b + c) = (a + b) + c$.

The phrase **simplifying a variable expression** means *combining* like terms by adding their numerical coefficients. For example, to simplify $2y + 3y$, think

$$2y + 3y = (y + y) + (y + y + y) = 5y$$

HOW TO Simplify: $8z - 5 + 2z$

$$8z - 5 + 2z = 8z + 2z - 5$$
$$= 10z - 5$$

- Use the Commutative and Associative Properties of Addition to group like terms. Combine the like terms $8z + 2z$.

HOW TO   Simplify: $12a - 4b - 8a + 2b$

$$12a - 4b - 8a + 2b = 12a + (-4)b + (-8)a + 2b$$

$$= 12a + (-8)a + (-4)b + 2b$$
$$= 4a + (-2)b$$

$$= 4a - 2b$$

- **Change subtraction to addition of the opposite.**
- **Use the Commutative and Associative Properties of Addition to group like terms. Combine like terms.**
- **Recall that $a + (-b) = a - b$.**

HOW TO   Simplify: $6z^2 + 3 - z^2 - 7$

$$6z^2 + 3 - z^2 - 7 = 6z^2 + 3 + (-1)z^2 + (-7)$$

$$= 6z^2 + (-1)z^2 + 3 + (-7)$$
$$= 5z^2 + (-4)$$
$$= 5z^2 - 4$$

- **Change subtraction to addition of the opposite.**
- **Use the Commutative and Associative Properties of Addition to group like terms. Combine like terms.**

Example 5

Simplify: $6xy - 8x + 5x - 9xy$

Solution
$6xy - 8x + 5x - 9xy$
$= 6xy + (-8)x + 5x + (-9)xy$
$= 6xy + (-9)xy + (-8)x + 5x$
$= (-3)xy + (-3)x$
$= -3xy - 3x$

You Try It 5

Simplify: $5a^2 - 6b^2 + 7a^2 - 9b^2$

Your solution

Example 6

Simplify: $-4z^2 + 8 + 5z^2 - 3$

Solution
$-4z^2 + 8 + 5z^2 - 3$
$= -4z^2 + 8 + 5z^2 + (-3)$
$= -4z^2 + 5z^2 + 8 + (-3)$
$= z^2 + 5$

You Try It 6

Simplify: $-6x + 7 + 9x - 10$

Your solution

Example 7

Simplify: $\frac{1}{4}m^2 - \frac{1}{2}n^2 + \frac{1}{2}m^2$

Solution
$$\frac{1}{4}m^2 - \frac{1}{2}n^2 + \frac{1}{2}m^2 = \frac{1}{4}m^2 + \left(-\frac{1}{2}\right)n^2 + \frac{1}{2}m^2$$

$$= \frac{1}{4}m^2 + \frac{1}{2}m^2 + \left(-\frac{1}{2}\right)n^2$$

$$= \frac{1}{4}m^2 + \frac{2}{4}m^2 + \left(-\frac{1}{2}\right)n^2$$

$$= \frac{3}{4}m^2 + \left(-\frac{1}{2}\right)n^2$$

$$= \frac{3}{4}m^2 - \frac{1}{2}n^2$$

You Try It 7

Simplify: $\frac{3}{8}w + \frac{1}{2} - \frac{1}{4}w - \frac{2}{3}$

Your solution

Objective C   **To simplify variable expressions containing parentheses**

The Commutative and Associative Properties of Multiplication and the Distributive Property are used to simplify variable expressions that contain parentheses. These properties can be stated in general form using variables.

Commutative Property of Multiplication

If a and b are two numbers, then $a \cdot b = b \cdot a$.

Associative Property of Multiplication

If a, b, and c are three numbers, then $a \cdot (b \cdot c) = (a \cdot b) \cdot c$.

The Associative and Commutative Properties of Multiplication are used to simplify variable expressions such as the following.

HOW TO   Simplify: $-5(4x)$

$$-5(4x) = (-5 \cdot 4)x$$ • Use the Associative Property of Multiplication.
$$= -20x$$

HOW TO   Simplify: $(6y) \cdot 5$

$$(6y) \cdot 5 = 5 \cdot (6y)$$ • Use the Commutative Property of Multiplication.
$$= (5 \cdot 6)y = 30y$$ • Use the Associative Property of Multiplication.

The **Distributive Property** is used to remove parentheses from variable expressions that contain both multiplication and addition.

Distributive Property

If a, b, and c are three numbers, then $a(b + c) = ab + ac$.

HOW TO   Simplify: $4(z + 5)$

$$4(z + 5) = 4z + 4(5)$$ • The Distributive Property is used to rewrite the
$$= 4z + 20$$ variable expression without parentheses.

HOW TO   Simplify: $-3(2x + 7)$

$$-3(2x + 7) = -3(2x) + (-3)(7)$$ • Use the Distributive Property.
$$= -6x + (-21)$$
$$= -6x - 21$$ • Recall that $a + (-b) = a - b$.

The Distributive Property can also be stated in terms of subtraction.

$$a(b - c) = ab - ac$$

HOW TO   Simplify: $8(2r - 3s)$

$$8(2r - 3s) = 8(2r) - 8(3s) \qquad \text{• Use the Distributive Property.}$$
$$= 16r - 24s$$

HOW TO   Simplify: $-5(2x - 4y)$

$$-5(2x - 4y) = (-5)(2x) - (-5)(4y) \qquad \text{• Use the Distributive Property.}$$
$$= -10x - (-20y)$$
$$= -10x + 20y \qquad \text{• Recall that } a - (-b) = a + b.$$

HOW TO   Simplify: $12 - 5(m + 2) + 2m$

$$12 - 5(m + 2) + 2m = 12 - 5m + (-5)(2) + 2m \qquad \text{• Use the Distributive}$$
$$= 12 - 5m + (-10) + 2m \qquad \text{Property to simplify}$$
the expression
$-5(m + 2)$.

$$= -5m + 2m + 12 + (-10) \qquad \text{• Use the Commutative and}$$
Associative Properties to
group like terms.

$$= -3m + 2 \qquad \text{• Combine like terms by}$$
adding their numerical
coefficients. Add constant
terms.

The answer $-3m + 2$ can also be written as $2 - 3m$. In this text, we will write answers with variable terms first, followed by the constant term.

Example 8

Simplify: $4(x - 3)$

Solution
$$4(x - 3) = 4x - 4(3)$$
$$= 4x - 12$$

You Try It 8

Simplify: $5(a - 2)$

Your solution

Example 9

Simplify: $5n - 3(2n - 4)$

Solution
$$5n - 3(2n - 4) = 5n - 3(2n) - (-3)(4)$$
$$= 5n - 6n - (-12)$$
$$= 5n - 6n + 12$$
$$= -n + 12$$

You Try It 9

Simplify: $8s - 2(3s - 5)$

Your solution

Example 10

Simplify: $3(c - 2) + 2(c + 6)$

Solution
$$3(c - 2) + 2(c + 6) = 3c - 3(2) + 2c + 2(6)$$
$$= 3c - 6 + 2c + 12$$
$$= 3c + 2c - 6 + 12$$
$$= 5c + 6$$

You Try It 10

Simplify: $4(x - 3) - 2(x + 1)$

Your solution

2.1 Exercises

Objective A   **To evaluate variable expressions**

For Exercises 1 to 34, evaluate the variable expression when $a = -3$, $b = 6$, and $c = -2$.

1. $5a - 3b$ **2.** $4c - 2b$ **3.** $2a + 3c$ **4.** $2c + 4a$

5. $-c^2$ **6.** $-a^2$ **7.** $b - a^2$ **8.** $b - c^2$

9. $ab - c^2$ **10.** $bc - a^2$ **11.** $2ab - c^2$ **12.** $3bc - a^2$

13. $a - (b \div a)$ **14.** $c - (b \div c)$ **15.** $2ac - (b \div a)$ **16.** $4ac \div (b \div a)$

17. $b^2 - c^2$ **18.** $b^2 - a^2$ **19.** $b^2 \div (ac)$ **20.** $3c^2 \div (ab)$

21. $c^2 - (b \div c)$ **22.** $a^2 - (b \div a)$ **23.** $a^2 + b^2 + c^2$ **24.** $a^2 - b^2 - c^2$

25. $ac + bc + ab$ **26.** $ac - bc - ab$ **27.** $a^2 + b^2 - ab$ **28.** $b^2 + c^2 - bc$

29. $2b - (3c + a^2)$ **30.** $\dfrac{2}{3}b + \left(\dfrac{1}{2}c - a\right)$ **31.** $\dfrac{1}{3}a + \left(\dfrac{1}{2}b - \dfrac{2}{3}a\right)$

32. $-\dfrac{2}{3}b - \left(\dfrac{1}{2}c + a\right)$ **33.** $\dfrac{1}{6}b + \dfrac{1}{3}(c + a)$ **34.** $\dfrac{1}{2}c + \left(\dfrac{1}{3}b - a\right)$

For Exercises 35 to 38, evaluate the variable expression when $a = -\dfrac{1}{2}$, $b = \dfrac{3}{4}$, and $c = \dfrac{1}{4}$.

35. $4a + (3b - c)$ **36.** $2b + (c - 3a)$ **37.** $2a - b^2 \div c$ **38.** $b \div (-c) + 2a$

For Exercises 39 to 42, evaluate the variable expression when $a = 3.72$, $b = -2.31$, and $c = -1.74$.

39. $a^2 - b^2$ **40.** $a^2 - b \cdot c$ **41.** $3ac - (c \div a)$ **42.** $2c + (b^2 - c)$

> **Objective B**   To simplify variable expressions containing no parentheses

For Exercises 43 to 46, name the terms of the variable expression. Then underline the constant term.

43. $2x^2 + 3x - 4$ **44.** $-4y^2 + 5$ **45.** $3a^2 - 4a + 8$ **46.** $7 - b$

For Exercises 47 to 50, name the variable terms of the expression. Then underline the coefficients of the variable terms.

47. $3x^2 - 4x + 9$ **48.** $-5a^2 + a - 4$ **49.** $y^2 + 6a - 1$ **50.** $8 - c$

For Exercises 51 to 94, simplify.

51. $7z + 9z$ **52.** $6x + 5x$ **53.** $12m - 3m$

54. $5y - 12y$ **55.** $5at + 7at$ **56.** $12mn + 11mn$

57. $-4yt + 7yt$ **58.** $-12yt + 5yt$ **59.** $-3x - 12y$

60. $-12y - 7y$ **61.** $3t^2 - 5t^2$ **62.** $7t^2 + 8t^2$

63. $6c - 5 + 7c$ **64.** $7x - 5 + 3x$ **65.** $2t + 3t - 7t$

66. $9x^2 - 5 - 3x^2$ **67.** $7y^2 - 2 - 4y^2$ **68.** $3w - 7u + 4w$

69. $6w - 8u + 8w$ **70.** $4 - 6xy - 7xy$ **71.** $10 - 11xy - 12xy$

72. $7t^2 - 5t^2 - 4t^2$ **73.** $3v^2 - 6v^2 - 8v^2$ **74.** $5ab - 7a - 10ab$

75. $-10ab - 3a + 2ab$ **76.** $-4x^2 - x + 2x^2$ **77.** $-3y^2 - y + 7y^2$

78. $4x^2 - 8y - x^2 + y$ **79.** $2a - 3b^2 - 5a + b^2$ **80.** $8y - 4z - y + 2z$

81. $3x^2 - 7x + 4x^2 - x$ **82.** $5y^2 - y + 6y^2 - 5y$ **83.** $6s - t - 9s + 7t$

84. $5w - 2v - 9w + 5v$ **85.** $4m + 8n - 7m + 2n$ **86.** $z + 9y - 4z + 3y$

87. $-5ab + 7ac + 10ab - 3ac$

88. $-2x^2 - 3x - 11x^2 + 14x$

89. $\dfrac{4}{9}a^2 - \dfrac{1}{5}b^2 + \dfrac{2}{9}a^2 + \dfrac{4}{5}b^2$

90. $\dfrac{6}{7}x^2 + \dfrac{2}{5}x - \dfrac{3}{7}x^2 - \dfrac{4}{5}x$

91. $4.235x - 0.297x + 3.056x$

92. $8.092y - 3.0793y + 0.063y$

93. $7.81m + 3.42n - 6.25m - 7.19n$

94. $8.34y^2 - 4.21y - 6.07y^2 - 5.39y$

Objective C   **To simplify variable expressions containing parentheses**

For Exercises 95 to 130, simplify.

95. $5(x + 4)$

96. $3(m + 6)$

97. $(y - 3)4$

98. $(z - 3)7$

99. $-2(a + 4)$

100. $-5(b + 3)$

101. $3(5x + 10)$

102. $2(4m - 7)$

103. $5(3c - 5)$

104. $-4(w - 3)$

105. $-3(y - 6)$

106. $3m + 4(m + z)$

107. $5x + 2(x + 7)$

108. $6z - 3(z + 4)$

109. $8y - 4(y + 2)$

110. $7w - 2(w - 3)$

111. $9x - 4(x - 6)$

112. $-5m + 3(m + 4)$

113. $-2y + 3(y - 2)$

114. $5m + 3(m + 4) - 6$

115. $4n + 2(n + 1) - 5$

116. $8z - 2(z - 3) + 8$

117. $9y - 3(y - 4) + 8$

118. $6 - 4(a + 4) + 6a$

119. $3x + 2(x + 2) + 5x$

120. $7x + 4(x + 1) + 3x$

121. $-7t + 2(t - 3) - t$

122. $-3y + 2(y - 4) - y$ **123.** $z - 2(1 - z) - 2z$ **124.** $2y - 3(2 - y) + 4y$

125. $3(y - 2) - 2(y - 6)$ **126.** $7(x + 2) + 3(x - 4)$ **127.** $2(t - 3) + 7(t + 3)$

128. $3(y - 4) - 2(y - 3)$ **129.** $3t - 6(t - 4) + 8t$ **130.** $5x + 3(x - 7) - 9x$

APPLYING THE CONCEPTS

131. The square and the rectangle at the right can be used to illustrate algebraic expressions. The illustration below represents the expression $2x + 1$.

a. Using similar squares and rectangles, draw a figure that represents the expression $3 + 2x$.
b. Draw a figure that represents the expression $4x + 6$.
c. Draw a figure that represents the expression $3x + 2$.
d. Draw a figure that represents the expression $2x + 4$.
e. The illustration below represents the expression $3(x + 1)$. Rearrange these rectangles so that the x's are together and the 1's are together.
f. Write a mathematical expression for the rearranged figure.

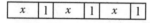

132. **a.** Using squares and rectangles similar to those in Exercise 131, draw a figure that represents the expression $2 + 3x$.
b. Draw a figure that represents the expression $2(2x + 3)$.
c. Draw a figure that represents the expression $4x + 3$.
d. Draw a figure that represents the expression $4x + 6$.
e. Does the figure $2(2x + 3)$ equal the figure $4x + 6$? Explain how this equivalence is related to the Distributive Property.
f. Does the figure $2 + 3x$ equal the figure $5x$? Explain how this equivalence is related to combining like terms.

133. **a.** Simplifying variable expressions requires combining like terms. Give some examples of how this applies to everyday experience.
b. It was stated in this section that the variable terms y^2 and y are not like terms. Use measurements of area and distance to show that these terms would not be combined as measurements.

134. Explain why the simplification of the expression $2 + 3(2x + 4)$ shown at the right is incorrect. What is the correct simplification?

Why is this incorrect?
$$2 + 3(2x + 4) = 5(2x + 4)$$
$$= 10x + 20$$

2.2   Introduction to Equations

Objective A   **To determine whether a given number is a solution of an equation**

Point of Interest

Finding solutions of equations has been a principal aim of mathematics for thousands of years. However, the equals sign did not appear in any text until 1557.

An **equation** expresses the equality of two mathematical expressions. These expressions can be either numerical or variable expressions.

$$\left.\begin{array}{l} 5 + 4 = 9 \\ 3x + 13 = x - 8 \\ y^2 + 4 = 6y + 1 \\ x = -3 \end{array}\right\} \text{Equations}$$

In the equation at the right, if the variable is replaced by 4, the equation is true.

$x + 3 = 7$
$4 + 3 = 7$ A true equation

If the variable is replaced by 6, the equation is false.

$6 + 3 = 7$ A false equation

A **solution of an equation** is a number that, when substituted for the variable, results in a true equation. 4 is a solution of the equation $x + 3 = 7$. 6 is not a solution of the equation $x + 3 = 7$.

> **HOW TO**   Is -2 a solution of the equation $-2x + 1 = 2x + 9$?
>
> $$-2x + 1 = 2x + 9$$
> $$-2(-2) + 1 \overset{?}{=} 2(-2) + 9 \qquad \bullet \textbf{ Replace the variable by the given number.}$$
> $$4 + 1 \overset{?}{=} -4 + 9 \qquad \bullet \textbf{ Evaluate the numerical expressions.}$$
> $$5 = 5 \qquad \bullet \textbf{ Compare the results. If the results are equal, the given number is a solution. If the results are not equal, the given number is not a solution.}$$
>
> Yes, -2 is a solution of the equation $-2x + 1 = 2x + 9$.

Example 1   Is $\frac{1}{2}$ a solution of $2x(x + 2) = 3x + 1$?

Solution

$$2x(x + 2) = 3x + 1$$
$$2\left(\frac{1}{2}\right)\left(\frac{1}{2} + 2\right) \;\middle|\; 3\left(\frac{1}{2}\right) + 1$$
$$2\left(\frac{1}{2}\right)\left(\frac{5}{2}\right) \;\middle|\; \frac{3}{2} + 1$$
$$\frac{5}{2} = \frac{5}{2}$$

Yes, $\frac{1}{2}$ is a solution.

You Try It 1   Is -2 a solution of $x(x + 3) = 4x + 6$?

Your solution

Example 2   Is 5 a solution of
$(x - 2)^2 = x^2 - 4x + 2$?

You Try It 2   Is -3 a solution of
$x^2 - x = 3x + 7$?

Solution

$$\begin{array}{rcl} (x - 2)^2 &=& x^2 - 4x + 2 \\ \hline (5 - 2)^2 &\stackrel{?}{=}& 5^2 - 4(5) + 2 \\ 3^2 &\stackrel{?}{=}& 25 - 4(5) + 2 \\ 9 &\stackrel{?}{=}& 25 - 20 + 2 \\ &\stackrel{?}{=}& 25 + (-20) + 2 \\ 9 &\neq& 7 \quad (\neq \text{ means "is not} \\ && \qquad \text{equal to")} \end{array}$$

No, 5 is not a solution.

Your solution

Objective B   **To solve an equation of the form $x + a = b$**

A solution of an equation is a number that, when substituted for the variable, results in a true equation. The phrase **solving an equation** means finding a solution of the equation.

The simplest equation to solve is an equation of the form *variable = constant*. The constant is the solution of the equation.

If $x = 7$, then 7 is the solution of the equation because $7 = 7$ is a true equation.

In solving an equation of the form $x + a = b$, the goal is to simplify the given equation to one of the form *variable = constant*. The Addition Properties that follow are used to simplify equations to this form.

Addition Property of Zero

The sum of a term and zero is the term.
$$a + 0 = a \qquad 0 + a = a$$

Addition Property of Equations

If a, b, and c are algebraic expressions, then the equations $a = b$ and $a + c = b + c$ have the same solutions.

The Addition Property of Equations states that the same quantity can be added to each side of an equation without changing the solution of the equation.

The Addition Property of Equations is used to rewrite an equation in the form *variable = constant*. Remove a term from one side of the equation by adding the opposite of that term to each side of the equation.

HOW TO   Solve: $x - 7 = -2$

$$x - 7 = -2$$

- The goal is to simplify the equation to one of the form *variable = constant.*

$$x - 7 + 7 = -2 + 7$$
$$x + 0 = 5$$
$$x = 5$$

- Add the opposite of the constant term -7 to each side of the equation. After we simplify and use the Addition Property of Zero, the equation will be in the form *variable = constant.*

The solution is 5.

Because subtraction is defined in terms of addition, the Addition Property of Equations allows the same number to be subtracted from each side of an equation.

HOW TO   Solve: $x + 8 = 5$

$$x + 8 = 5$$

- The goal is to simplify the equation to one of the form *variable = constant.*

$$x + 8 - 8 = 5 - 8$$
$$x + 0 = -3$$
$$x = -3$$

- Add the opposite of the constant term 8 to each side of the equation. This procedure is equivalent to subtracting 8 from each side of the equation.

The solution is -3. You should check this solution.

Example 3   Solve: $4 + m = -2$

Solution
$$4 + m = -2$$
$$4 - 4 + m = -2 - 4 \quad \bullet \text{ Subtract 4 from}$$
$$0 + m = -6 \quad\quad\quad\quad \text{each side.}$$
$$m = -6$$

The solution is -6.

You Try It 3   Solve: $-2 + y = -5$

Your solution

Example 4   Solve: $3 = y - 2$

Solution
$$3 = y - 2$$
$$3 + 2 = y - 2 + 2 \quad \bullet \text{ Add 2 to each}$$
$$5 = y + 0 \quad\quad\quad\quad \text{side.}$$
$$5 = y$$

The solution is 5.

You Try It 4   Solve: $7 = y + 8$

Your solution

Example 5   Solve: $\dfrac{2}{7} = \dfrac{5}{7} + t$

Solution
$$\frac{2}{7} = \frac{5}{7} + t$$
$$\frac{2}{7} - \frac{5}{7} = \frac{5}{7} - \frac{5}{7} + t \quad \bullet \text{ Subtract } \tfrac{5}{7} \text{ from}$$
$$\phantom{\frac{2}{7} - \frac{5}{7} =} \text{each side.}$$
$$-\frac{3}{7} = 0 + t$$
$$-\frac{3}{7} = t$$

The solution is $-\dfrac{3}{7}$.

You Try It 5   Solve: $\dfrac{1}{5} = z + \dfrac{4}{5}$

Your solution

Objective C   **To solve an equation of the form *ax* = *b***

In solving an equation of the form $ax = b$, the goal is to simplify the given equation to one of the form *variable* = *constant*. The Multiplication Properties that follow are used to simplify equations to this form.

Multiplication Property of Reciprocals

The product of a nonzero term and its reciprocal equals 1.

Because $a = \frac{a}{1}$, the reciprocal of a is $\frac{1}{a}$.

$$a\left(\frac{1}{a}\right) = 1 \qquad \frac{1}{a}(a) = 1$$

The reciprocal of $\frac{a}{b}$ is $\frac{b}{a}$.

$$\left(\frac{a}{b}\right)\left(\frac{b}{a}\right) = 1 \qquad \left(\frac{b}{a}\right)\left(\frac{a}{b}\right) = 1$$

Multiplication Property of One

The product of a term and 1 is the term.

$$a \cdot 1 = a \qquad 1 \cdot a = a$$

Multiplication Property of Equations

If *a*, *b*, and *c* are algebraic expressions and $c \neq 0$, then the equation $a = b$ has the same solutions as the equation $ac = bc$.

The Multiplication Property of Equations states that each side of an equation can be multiplied by the same nonzero number without changing the solutions of the equation.

Recall that the goal of solving an equation is to rewrite the equation in the form *variable* = *constant*. The Multiplication Property of Equations is used to rewrite an equation in this form by multiplying each side of the equation by the reciprocal of the coefficient.

HOW TO   Solve: $\frac{2}{3}x = 8$

$$\frac{2}{3}x = 8$$

$$\left(\frac{3}{2}\right)\left(\frac{2}{3}\right)x = \left(\frac{3}{2}\right)8$$

$$1 \cdot x = 12$$

$$x = 12$$

• Multiply each side of the equation by $\frac{3}{2}$, the reciprocal of $\frac{2}{3}$. After simplifying, the equation will be in the form *variable* = *constant*.

Check: $\quad \frac{2}{3}x = 8$

$$\frac{2}{3}(12) \overset{?}{=} 8$$

$$8 = 8$$

The solution is 12.

Because division is defined in terms of multiplication, the Multiplication Property of Equations allows each side of an equation to be divided by the same nonzero quantity.

Study Tip

When we suggest that you check a solution, substitute the solution into the original equation. For instance,

$$-4x = 24$$
$$-4(-6) \mid 24$$
$$24 = 24$$

The solution checks.

HOW TO Solve: $-4x = 24$

$-4x = 24$

- The goal is to rewrite the equation in the form *variable = constant*.

$$\frac{-4x}{-4} = \frac{24}{-4}$$
$$1x = -6$$
$$x = -6$$

- Multiply each side of the equation by the reciprocal of -4. This is equivalent to dividing each side of the equation by -4. Then simplify.

The solution is -6. You should check this solution.

In using the Multiplication Property of Equations, it is usually easier to multiply each side of the equation by the reciprocal of the coefficient when the coefficient is a fraction. Divide each side of the equation by the coefficient when the coefficient is an integer or a decimal.

Example 6   Solve: $-2x = 6$

Solution
$$-2x = 6$$
$$\frac{-2x}{-2} = \frac{6}{-2} \quad \text{• Divide each side by } -2.$$
$$1x = -3$$
$$x = -3$$

The solution is -3.

You Try It 6   Solve: $4z = -20$

Your solution

Example 7   Solve: $-9 = \frac{3}{4}y$

Solution
$$-9 = \frac{3}{4}y$$
$$\left(\frac{4}{3}\right)(-9) = \left(\frac{4}{3}\right)\left(\frac{3}{4}y\right) \quad \text{• Multiply each side by } \frac{4}{3}.$$
$$-12 = 1y$$
$$-12 = y$$

The solution is -12.

You Try It 7   Solve: $8 = \frac{2}{5}n$

Your solution

Example 8   Solve: $6z - 8z = -5$

Solution
$$6z - 8z = -5$$
$$-2z = -5 \quad \text{• Combine like terms.}$$
$$\frac{-2z}{-2} = \frac{-5}{-2} \quad \text{• Divide each side by } -2.$$
$$1z = \frac{5}{2}$$
$$z = \frac{5}{2} = 2\frac{1}{2}$$

The solution is $2\frac{1}{2}$.

You Try It 8   Solve: $\frac{2}{3}t - \frac{1}{3}t = -2$

Your solution

> **Objective D**   **To solve application problems using formulas**

A **formula** is an equation that expresses a relationship among variables. Formulas are used in the examples below.

Example 9	**You Try It 9**
An accountant for a greeting card store found that the weekly profit for the store was $1700 and that the total amount spent during the week was $2400. Use the formula $P = R - C$, where P is the profit, R is the revenue, and C is the amount spent, to find the revenue for the week.	A clothing store's sale price for a pair of slacks is $44. This is a discount of $16 off the regular price. Use the formula $S = R - D$, where S is the sale price, R is the regular price, and D is the discount, to find the regular price.
Strategy	**Your strategy**
To find the revenue for the week, replace the variables P and C in the formula by the given values, and solve for R.	
Solution	**Your solution**

$$P = R - C$$
$$1700 = R - 2400$$
$$1700 + 2400 = R - 2400 + 2400$$
$$4100 = R + 0$$
$$4100 = R$$

The revenue for the week was $4100.

Example 10	**You Try It 10**
A store manager uses the formula $S = R - d \cdot R$, where S is the sale price, R is the regular price, and d is the discount rate. During a clearance sale, all items are discounted 20%. Find the regular price of a jacket that is on sale for $120.	Find the monthly payment when the total amount paid on a loan is $6840 and the loan is paid off in 24 months. Use the formula $A = MN$, where A is the total amount paid on a loan, M is the monthly payment, and N is the number of monthly payments.
Strategy	**Your strategy**
To find the regular price of the jacket, replace the variables S and d in the formula by the given values, and solve for R.	
Solution	**Your solution**

$$S = R - d \cdot R$$
$$120 = R - 0.20R$$
$$120 = 0.80R \qquad \bullet\ R - 0.20R = 1R - 0.20R$$
$$\frac{120}{0.80} = \frac{0.80R}{0.80}$$
$$150 = R$$

The regular price of the jacket is $150.

2.2 Exercises

Objective A   **To determine whether a given number is a solution of an equation**

1. Is -3 a solution of $2x + 9 = 3$?

2. Is -2 a solution of $5x + 7 = 12$?

3. Is 2 a solution of $4 - 2x = 8$?

4. Is 4 a solution of $5 - 2x = 4x$?

5. Is 3 a solution of $3x - 2 = x + 4$?

6. Is 2 a solution of $4x + 8 = 4 - 2x$?

7. Is 3 a solution of $x^2 - 5x + 1 = 10 - 5x$?

8. Is -5 a solution of $x^2 - 3x - 1 = 9 - 6x$?

9. Is -1 a solution of $2x(x - 1) = 3 - x$?

10. Is 2 a solution of $3x(x - 3) = x - 8$?

11. Is 2 a solution of $x(x - 2) = x^2 - 4$?

12. Is -4 a solution of $x(x + 4) = x^2 + 16$?

13. Is $-\frac{2}{3}$ a solution of $3x + 6 = 4$?

14. Is $\frac{1}{2}$ a solution of $2x - 7 = -3$?

15. Is $\frac{1}{4}$ a solution of $2x - 3 = 1 - 14x$?

16. Is $-\frac{1}{3}$ a solution of $5x - 2 = 1 - 2x$?

17. Is $\frac{3}{4}$ a solution of $3x(x - 2) = x - 4$?

18. Is $\frac{2}{5}$ a solution of $5x(x + 1) = x + 3$?

19. 🖩 Is 1.32 a solution of $x^2 - 3x = -0.8776 - x$?

20. 🖩 Is -1.9 a solution of $x^2 - 3x = x + 3.8$?

21. 🖩 Is 1.05 a solution of $x^2 + 3x = x(x + 3)$?

Objective B   **To solve an equation of the form $x + a = b$**

For Exercises 22 to 57, solve.

22. $x + 3 = 9$

23. $x + 7 = 5$

24. $y - 6 = 16$

25. $z - 4 = 10$

26. $3 + n = 4$

27. $6 + x = 8$

28. $z + 7 = 2$

29. $w + 9 = 5$

30. $x - 3 = -7$

31. $m - 4 = -9$

32. $y + 6 = 6$

33. $t - 3 = -3$

34. $v - 7 = -4$

35. $x - 3 = -1$

36. $1 + x = 0$

37. $3 + y = 0$

38. $x - 10 = 5$

39. $y - 7 = 3$

40. $x + 4 = -7$

41. $t - 3 = -8$

42. $w + 5 = -5$

43. $z + 6 = -6$

44. $x + 7 = -8$

45. $x + 2 = -5$

46. $x + \dfrac{1}{2} = -\dfrac{1}{2}$

47. $x - \dfrac{5}{6} = -\dfrac{1}{6}$

48. $y + \dfrac{7}{11} = -\dfrac{3}{11}$

49. $\dfrac{2}{5} + x = -\dfrac{3}{5}$

50. $\dfrac{7}{8} + y = -\dfrac{1}{8}$

51. $\dfrac{1}{3} + x = \dfrac{2}{3}$

52. $x + \dfrac{1}{2} = -\dfrac{1}{3}$

53. $y + \dfrac{3}{8} = \dfrac{1}{4}$

54. $y + \dfrac{2}{3} = -\dfrac{3}{8}$

55. $t + \dfrac{1}{4} = -\dfrac{1}{2}$

56. $x + \dfrac{1}{3} = \dfrac{5}{12}$

57. $y + \dfrac{2}{3} = -\dfrac{5}{12}$

Objective C   **To solve an equation of the form $ax = b$**

For Exercises 58 to 93, solve.

58. $3y = 12$

59. $5x = 30$

60. $5z = -20$

61. $3z = -27$

62. $-2x = 6$

63. $-4t = 20$

64. $-5x = -40$

65. $-2y = -28$

66. $40 = 8x$

67. $24 = 3y$

68. $-24 = 4x$

69. $-21 = 7y$

70. $\dfrac{x}{3} = 5$

71. $\dfrac{y}{2} = 10$

72. $\dfrac{n}{4} = -2$

73. $\dfrac{y}{7} = -3$

74. $-\dfrac{x}{4} = 1$ **75.** $-\dfrac{y}{3} = 5$ **76.** $\dfrac{2}{3}w = 4$ **77.** $\dfrac{5}{8}x = 10$

78. $\dfrac{3}{4}v = -3$ **79.** $\dfrac{2}{7}x = -12$ **80.** $-\dfrac{1}{3}x = -2$ **81.** $-\dfrac{1}{5}y = -3$

82. $\dfrac{3}{8}x = -24$ **83.** $\dfrac{5}{12}y = -16$ **84.** $-4 = -\dfrac{2}{3}z$ **85.** $-8 = -\dfrac{5}{6}x$

86. $-12 = -\dfrac{3}{8}y$ **87.** $-9 = \dfrac{5}{6}t$ **88.** $\dfrac{2}{3}x = -\dfrac{2}{7}$ **89.** $\dfrac{3}{7}y = \dfrac{5}{6}$

90. $4x - 2x = 7$ **91.** $3a - 6a = 8$ **92.** $\dfrac{4}{5}m - \dfrac{1}{5}m = 9$ **93.** $\dfrac{1}{3}b - \dfrac{2}{3}b = -1$

Objective D   To solve application problems using formulas

Investments   In Exercises 94 to 97, use the formula $A = P + I$, where A is the value of the investment after 1 year, P is the original investment, and I is the increase in value of the investment.

94. The value of an investment in a high-tech company after 1 year was $17,700. The increase in value during the year was $2700. Find the amount of the original investment.

95. The value of an investment in a software company after 1 year was $26,440. The increase in value during the year was $2830. Find the amount of the original investment.

96. The original investment in a mutual fund was $8000. The value of the mutual fund after 1 year was $11,420. Find the increase in value of the investment.

97. The original investment in a money market fund was $7500. The value of the mutual fund after 1 year was $8690. Find the increase in value of the investment.

Fuel Efficiency   In Exercises 98 to 101, use the formula $D = M \cdot G$, where D is the distance, M is the miles per gallon, and G is the number of gallons. Round to the nearest tenth.

98. Julio, a sales executive, averages 28 mi/gal on a 621-mile trip. Find the number of gallons of gasoline used on the trip.

99. Over a 3-day weekend, you take a 592-mile trip. If you average 32 mi/gal on the trip, how many gallons of gasoline did you use?

100. The manufacturer of a subcompact car estimates that the car can travel 560 mi on a 15-gallon tank of gas. Find the miles per gallon.

101. You estimate that your car can travel 410 mi on 12 gal of gasoline. Find the miles per gallon.

Markup In Exercises 102 and 103, use the formula $S = C + M$, where S is the selling price, C is the cost, and M is the markup.

102. A computer store sells a computer for $2240. The computer has a markup of $420. Find the cost of the computer.

103. A toy store buys stuffed animals for $23.50 and sells them for $39.80. Find the markup on each stuffed animal.

Markup In Exercises 104 and 105, use the formula $S = C + R \cdot C$, where S is the selling price, C is cost, and R is the markup rate.

104. A store manager uses a markup rate of 24% on all appliances. Find the cost of a blender that sells for $77.50.

105. A music store uses a markup rate of 30%. Find the cost of a compact disc that sells for $18.85.

APPLYING THE CONCEPTS

106. Write out the steps for solving the equation $x - 3 = -5$. Identify each property of real numbers and each property of equations as you use it.

107. Write out the steps for solving the equation $\frac{3}{4}x = 6$. Identify each property of real numbers and each property of equations as you use it.

108. Is 2 a solution of $x = x + 4$? Try -2, 0, 3, 6, and 10. Do you think there is a solution of this equation? Why or why not?

109. Write an equation of the form $x + a = b$ that has -4 as its solution.

110. Write an equation of the form $a - x = b$ that has -2 as its solution.

111. a. In your own words, state the Addition Property of Equations.
b. In your own words, state the Multiplication Property of Equations.

2.3 General Equations: Part I

Objective A   To solve an equation of the form $ax + b = c$

Point of Interest

Evariste Galois, despite being killed in a duel at the age of 21, made significant contributions to solving equations. In fact, there is a branch of mathematics called Galois theory, showing what kinds of equations can be solved and what kinds cannot.

To solve an equation of the form $ax + b = c$, it is necessary to use both the Addition and the Multiplication Properties to simplify the equation to one of the form *variable = constant*.

HOW TO   Solve: $\frac{x}{4} - 1 = 3$

$\frac{x}{4} - 1 = 3$
• The goal is to simplify the equation to one of the form *variable = constant*.

$\frac{x}{4} - 1 + 1 = 3 + 1$
• Add the opposite of the constant term -1 to each side of the equation. Then simplify (Addition Properties).

$\frac{x}{4} + 0 = 4$

$\frac{x}{4} = 4$

$4 \cdot \frac{x}{4} = 4 \cdot 4$
• Multiply each side of the equation by the reciprocal of the numerical coefficient of the variable term. Then simplify (Multiplication Properties).

$1x = 16$

$x = 16$

The solution is 16.
• Write the solution.

TAKE NOTE

$\frac{x}{4} = \frac{1}{4}x$

The reciprocal of $\frac{1}{4}$ is 4.

Example 1   Solve: $3x + 7 = 2$

Solution

$3x + 7 = 2$
$3x + 7 - 7 = 2 - 7$ • Subtract 7 from each side.
$3x = -5$
$\frac{3x}{3} = \frac{-5}{3}$ • Divide each side by 3.
$x = -\frac{5}{3} = -1\frac{2}{3}$

The solution is $-1\frac{2}{3}$.

You Try It 1   Solve: $5x + 8 = 6$

Your solution

Example 2   Solve: $5 - x = 6$

Solution

$5 - x = 6$
$5 - 5 - x = 6 - 5$ • Subtract 5 from each side.
$-x = 1$
$(-1)(-x) = (-1) \cdot 1$ • Multiply each side by -1.
$x = -1$

The solution is -1.

You Try It 2   Solve: $7 - x = 3$

Your solution

Objective B   **To solve application problems using formulas**

Anders Celsius

The Fahrenheit temperature scale was devised by Daniel Gabriel Fahrenheit (1686–1736), a German physicist and maker of scientific instruments. He invented the mercury thermometer in 1714. On the Fahrenheit scale, the temperature at which water freezes is 32°F, and the temperature at which water boils is 212°F. *Note:* The small raised circle is the symbol for degrees, and the capital F is for Fahrenheit. The Fahrenheit scale is used only in the United States.

In the metric system, temperature is measured on the Celsius scale. The Celsius temperature scale was devised by Anders Celsius (1701–1744), a Swedish astronomer. On the Celsius scale, the temperature at which water freezes is 0°C, and the temperature at which water boils is 100°C. *Note:* The small raised circle is the symbol for degrees, and the capital C is for Celsius.

On both the Celsius scale and the Fahrenheit scale, temperatures below 0° are negative numbers.

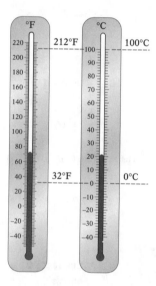

The relationship between Celsius temperatures and Fahrenheit temperatures is given by the formula

$$F = 1.8C + 32$$

where *F* represents degrees Fahrenheit and *C* represents degrees Celsius.

Integrating Technology

You can check the solution to this equation using a calculator. Evaluate the right side of the equation after substituting 37 for *C*. Enter

1.8 $\times$ 37 $+$ 32 $=$

The display reads 98.6, the given Fahrenheit temperature. The solution checks.

HOW TO   Normal body temperature is 98.6°F. Convert this temperature to degrees Celsius.

$$F = 1.8C + 32$$
$$98.6 = 1.8C + 32$$
$$98.6 - 32 = 1.8C + 32 - 32$$
$$66.6 = 1.8C$$
$$\frac{66.6}{1.8} = \frac{1.8C}{1.8}$$
$$37 = C$$

• Substitute 98.6 for *F*.
• Subtract 32 from each side.
• Combine like terms on each side.

• Divide each side by 1.8.

Normal body temperature is 37°C.

Example 3

Find the Celsius temperature when the Fahrenheit temperature is 212°. Use the formula $F = 1.8C + 32$, where F is the Fahrenheit temperature and C is the Celsius temperature.

Strategy

To find the Celsius temperature, replace the variable F in the formula by the given value and solve for C.

Solution

$$F = 1.8C + 32$$
$$212 = 1.8C + 32$$
$$212 - 32 = 1.8C + 32 - 32$$

$$180 = 1.8C$$
$$\frac{180}{1.8C} = \frac{1.8C}{1.8}$$
$$100 = C$$

- **Substitute 212 for F.**
- **Subtract 32 from each side.**
- **Combine like terms.**
- **Divide each side by 1.8.**

The Celsius temperature is 100°.

You Try It 3

Find the Celsius temperature when the Fahrenheit temperature is -22°. Use the formula $F = 1.8C + 32$, where F is the Fahrenheit temperature and C is the Celsius temperature.

Your strategy

Your solution

Example 4

To find the total cost of production, an economist uses the formula $T = U \cdot N + F$, where T is the total cost, U is the cost per unit, N is the number of units made, and F is the fixed cost. Find the number of units made during a week when the total cost was $8000, the cost per unit was $16, and the fixed costs were $2000.

Strategy

To find the number of units made, replace the variables T, U, and F in the formula by the given values and solve for N.

Solution

$$T = U \cdot N + F$$
$$8000 = 16 \cdot N + 2000$$
$$8000 - 2000 = 16 \cdot N + 2000 - 2000$$
$$6000 = 16 \cdot N$$
$$\frac{6000}{16} = \frac{16 \cdot N}{16}$$
$$375 = N$$

The number of units made was 375.

You Try It 4

Find the cost per unit during a week when the total cost was $4500, the number of units produced was 250, and the fixed costs were $1500. Use the formula $T = U \cdot N + F$, where T is the total cost, U is the cost per unit, N is the number of units made, and F is the fixed cost.

Your strategy

Your solution

2.3 Exercises

Objective A To solve an equation of the form $ax + b = c$

For Exercises 1 to 90, solve.

1. $3x + 5 = 14$

2. $5z + 6 = 31$

3. $2n - 3 = 7$

4. $4y - 4 = 20$

5. $5w + 8 = 3$

6. $3x + 10 = 1$

7. $3z - 4 = -16$

8. $6x - 1 = -13$

9. $5 + 2x = 7$

10. $12 + 7x = 33$

11. $6 - x = 3$

12. $4 - x = -2$

13. $3 - 4x = 11$

14. $2 - 3x = 11$

15. $5 - 4x = 17$

16. $8 - 6x = 14$

17. $3x + 6 = 0$

18. $5x - 20 = 0$

19. $-3x - 4 = -1$

20. $-7x - 22 = -1$

21. $12y - 30 = 6$

22. $9b - 7 = 2$

23. $3c + 7 = 4$

24. $8t + 13 = 5$

25. $-2x + 11 = -3$

26. $-4x + 15 = -1$

27. $14 - 5x = 4$

28. $7 - 3x = 4$

29. $-8x + 7 = -9$

30. $-7x + 13 = -8$

31. $9x + 13 = 13$

32. $-2x + 7 = 7$

33. $7d - 14 = 0$

34. $5z + 10 = 0$

35. $4n - 4 = -4$

36. $-13m - 1 = -1$

37. $3x + 5 = 7$

38. $4x + 6 = 9$

39. $6x - 1 = 16$

40. $12x - 3 = 7$

41. $2x - 3 = -8$

42. $5x - 3 = -12$

43. $-6x + 2 = -7$

44. $-3x + 9 = -1$

45. $-2x - 3 = -7$

46. $-5x - 7 = -4$

47. $3x + 8 = 2$

48. $2x - 9 = 8$

49. $3w - 7 = 0$

50. $7b - 2 = 0$

51. $-2d + 9 = 12$

52. $-7c + 3 = 1$

53. $\frac{1}{2}x - 2 = 3$

54. $\frac{1}{3}x + 1 = 4$

55. $\frac{3}{5}w - 1 = 2$

56. $\frac{2}{5}w + 5 = 6$

57. $\frac{2}{9}t - 3 = 5$

58. $\frac{5}{9}t - 3 = 2$

59. $\frac{y}{3} - 6 = -8$

60. $\frac{y}{2} - 2 = 3$

61. $\frac{x}{3} - 2 = -5$

62. $\frac{x}{4} - 3 = 5$

63. $\frac{5}{8}v + 6 = 3$

64. $\frac{2}{3}v - 4 = 3$

65. $\frac{4}{7}z + 10 = 5$

66. $\frac{3}{8}v - 3 = 4$

67. $\frac{2}{9}x - 3 = 5$

68. $\frac{1}{2}x + 3 = -8$

69. $\frac{3}{4}x - 5 = -4$

70. $\frac{2}{3}x - 5 = -8$

71. $1.5x - 0.5 = 2.5$

72. $2.5w - 1.3 = 3.7$

73. $0.8t + 1.1 = 4.3$

74. $0.3v + 2.4 = 1.5$

75. $0.4x - 2.3 = 1.3$

76. $1.2t + 6.5 = 2.9$

77. $3.5y - 3.5 = 10.5$

78. $1.9x - 1.9 = -1.9$

79. $0.32x + 4.2 = 3.2$

80. $5x - 3x + 2 = 8$

81. $6m + 2m - 3 = 5$ **82.** $4a - 7a - 8 = 4$ **83.** $3y - 8y - 9 = 6$

84. $x - 4x + 5 = 11$ **85.** $-2y + y - 3 = 6$ **86.** $-4y - y - 8 = 12$

87. $0.032x - 0.0194 = 0.139$ **88.** $-3.256x + 42.38 = -16.9$

89. $6.09x + 17.33 = 16.805$ **90.** $1.925x + 32.87 = -16.994$

> **Objective B**   **To solve application problems using formulas**

Temperature Conversion In Exercises 91 and 92, use the relationship between Fahrenheit temperature and Celsius temperature, which is given by the formula $F = 1.8C + 32$, where F is the Fahrenheit temperature and C is the Celsius temperature.

91. Find the Celsius temperature when the Fahrenheit temperature is $-40°$.

92. Find the Celsius temperature when the Fahrenheit temperature is $72°$. Round to the nearest tenth of a degree.

Physics In Exercises 93 and 94, use the formula $V = V_0 + 32t$, where V is the final velocity of a falling object, V_0 is the starting velocity of a falling object, and t is the time for the object to fall.

93. Find the time required for an object to increase in velocity from 8 ft/s to 472 ft/s.

94. Find the time required for an object to increase in velocity from 16 ft/s to 128 ft/s.

Manufacturing In Exercises 95 and 96, use the formula $T = U \cdot N + F$, where T is the total cost, U is the cost per unit, N is the number of units made, and F is the fixed cost.

95. Find the number of units made during a week when the total cost was $25,000, the cost per unit was $8, and the fixed costs were $5000.

96. Find the cost per unit during a week when the total cost was $80,000, the total number of units produced was 500, and the fixed costs were $15,000.

Taxes   In Exercises 97 and 98, use the formula $T = I \cdot R + B$, where T is the monthly tax, I is the monthly income, R is the income tax rate, and B is the base monthly tax.

97. The monthly tax that a clerk pays is $476. The clerk's monthly tax rate is 22%, and the base monthly tax is $80. Find the clerk's monthly income.

98. The monthly tax that Marcy, a teacher, pays is $770. Her monthly income is $3100, and the base monthly tax is $150. Find Marcy's income tax rate.

Compensation   In Exercises 99 to 102, use the formula $M = S \cdot R + B$, where M is the monthly earnings, S is the total sales, R is the commission rate, and B is the base monthly salary.

99. A book representative earns a base monthly salary of $600 plus a 9% commission on total sales. Find the total sales during a month in which the representative earned $3480.

100. A sales executive earns a base monthly salary of $1000 plus a 5% commission on total sales. Find the total sales during a month in which the executive earned $2800.

101. Miguel earns a base monthly salary of $750. Find his commission rate during a month in which total sales were $42,000 and he earned $2640.

102. Tina earns a base monthly salary of $500. Find her commission rate during a month when total sales were $42,500 and her earnings were $3560.

APPLYING THE CONCEPTS

103. Explain in your own words the steps you would take to solve the equation $\frac{2}{3}x - 4 = 10$. State the property of real numbers or the property of equations that is used at each step.

104. Make up an equation of the form $ax + b = c$ that has -3 as its solution.

105. Does the sentence "Solve $3x + 4(x - 3)$" make sense? Why or why not?

2.4

General Equations: Part II

Objective A   **To solve an equation of the form** $ax + b = cx + d$

When a variable occurs on each side of an equation, the Addition Properties are used to rewrite the equation so that variable terms are on one side of the equation and constant terms are on the other side of the equation. Then the Multiplication Properties are used to simplify the equation to one of the form *variable = constant.*

HOW TO   Solve: $4x - 6 = 8 - 3x$

$$4x - 6 = 8 - 3x$$

- **The goal is to write the equation in the form** *variable = constant.*

$$4x + 3x - 6 = 8 - 3x + 3x$$
$$7x - 6 = 8 + 0$$
$$7x - 6 = 8$$

- **Add 3x to each side of the equation. Then simplify (Addition Properties). Now only one variable term occurs in the equation.**

$$7x - 6 + 6 = 8 + 6$$
$$7x + 0 = 14$$
$$7x = 14$$

- **Add 6 to each side of the equation. Then simplify (Addition Properties). Now only one constant term occurs in the equation.**

$$\frac{7x}{7} = \frac{14}{7}$$
$$1x = 2$$
$$x = 2$$

- **Divide each side of the equation by the numerical coefficient of the variable term. Then simplify (Multiplication Properties).**

The solution is 2.

- **Write the solution.**

Study Tip

Always check the solution of an equation. For the equation at the right:

$$\frac{4x - 6 = 8 - 3x}{\begin{array}{c|c} 4(2) - 6 & 8 - 3(2) \\ 8 - 6 & 8 - 6 \\ 2 = 2 \end{array}}$$

The solution checks.

Example 1

Solve: $\frac{2}{9}x - 3 = \frac{7}{9}x + 2$

Solution

$$\frac{2}{9}x - 3 = \frac{7}{9}x + 2$$

$$\frac{2}{9}x - \frac{7}{9}x - 3 = \frac{7}{9}x - \frac{7}{9}x + 2$$

- Subtract $\frac{7}{9}x$ from each side.

$$-\frac{5}{9}x - 3 = 2$$

$$-\frac{5}{9}x - 3 + 3 = 2 + 3$$

- Add 3 to each side.

$$-\frac{5}{9}x = 5$$

$$\left(-\frac{9}{5}\right)\left(-\frac{5}{9}\right)x = \left(-\frac{9}{5}\right)5$$

- Multiply each side by $-\frac{9}{5}$.

$$x = -9$$

The solution is -9.

You Try It 1

Solve: $\frac{1}{5}x - 2 = \frac{2}{5}x + 4$

Your solution

Objective B   **To solve an equation containing parentheses**

When an equation contains parentheses, one of the steps in solving the equation requires use of the Distributive Property.

$$a(b + c) = ab + ac$$

The Distributive Property is used to rewrite a variable expression without parentheses.

HOW TO   Solve: $4(3 + x) - 2 = 2(x - 4)$

$4(3 + x) - 2 = 2(x - 4)$

- The goal is to write the equation in the form *variable = constant*.

$12 + 4x - 2 = 2x - 8$

- Use the Distributive Property to rewrite the equation without parentheses.

$10 + 4x = 2x - 8$
$10 + 4x - 2x = 2x - 2x - 8$
$10 + 2x = -8$

- Combine like terms.
- Use the Addition Property of Equations. Subtract 2x from each side of the equation.

$10 - 10 + 2x = -8 - 10$
$2x = -18$

- Use the Addition Property of Equations. Subtract 10 from each side of the equation.

$$\frac{2x}{2} = \frac{-18}{2}$$
$$x = -9$$

- Use the Multiplication Property of Equations. Divide each side of the equation by the numerical coefficient of the variable term.

Check:

$$
\begin{array}{c|c}
4(3 + x) - 2 & = 2(x - 4) \\
\hline
4[3 + (-9)] - 2 & 2(-9 - 4) \\
4(-6) - 2 & 2(-13) \\
-24 - 2 & -26 \\
-26 & = -26
\end{array}
$$

- Check the solution.

A true equation

The solution is -9.

- Write the solution.

The solution to this last equation illustrates the steps involved in solving first-degree equations.

Steps in Solving General First-Degree Equations

1. Use the Distributive Property to remove parentheses.
2. Combine like terms on each side of the equation.
3. Use the Addition Property of Equations to rewrite the equation with only one variable term.
4. Use the Addition Property of Equations to rewrite the equation with only one constant term.
5. Use the Multiplication Property of Equations to rewrite the equation so that the coefficient of the variable is 1.

Example 2

Solve: $3(x + 2) - x = 11$

Solution

$$3(x + 2) - x = 11$$
$$3x + 6 - x = 11$$
$$2x + 6 = 11$$

$$2x + 6 - 6 = 11 - 6$$

$$2x = 5$$

$$\frac{2x}{2} = \frac{5}{2}$$

$$x = 2\frac{1}{2}$$

- Use the Distributive Property.
- Combine like terms on the left side.
- Use the Addition Property of Equations. Subtract 6 from each side.
- Combine like terms on each side.
- Use the Multiplication Property. Divide both sides by 2.
- The solution checks.

The solution is $2\frac{1}{2}$.

You Try It 2

Solve: $4(x - 1) - x = 5$

Your solution

Example 3

Solve: $5x - 2(x - 3) = 6(x - 2)$

Solution

$$5x - 2(x - 3) = 6(x - 2)$$
$$5x - 2x + 6 = 6x - 12$$
$$3x + 6 = 6x - 12$$
$$3x - 6x + 6 = 6x - 6x - 12$$

$$-3x + 6 = -12$$
$$-3x + 6 - 6 = -12 - 6$$

$$-3x = -18$$
$$\frac{-3x}{-3} = \frac{-18}{-3}$$
$$x = 6$$

- Distributive Property
- Combine like terms.
- Subtract 6x from each side.
- Combine like terms.
- Subtract 6 from each side.
- Combine like terms.
- Divide both sides by −3.
- The solution checks.

The solution is 6.

You Try It 3

Solve: $2x - 7(3x + 1) = 5(5 - 3x)$

Your solution

2.4 Exercises

Objective A   To solve an equation of the form $ax + b = cx + d$

For Exercises 1 to 54, solve.

1. $6x + 3 = 2x + 5$

2. $7x + 1 = x + 19$

3. $3x + 3 = 2x + 2$

4. $6x + 3 = 3x + 6$

5. $5x + 4 = x - 12$

6. $3x - 12 = x - 8$

7. $7b - 2 = 3b - 6$

8. $2d - 9 = d - 8$

9. $9n - 4 = 5n - 20$

10. $8x - 7 = 5x + 8$

11. $2x + 1 = 16 - 3x$

12. $3x + 2 = -23 - 2x$

13. $5x - 2 = -10 - 3x$

14. $4x - 3 = 7 - x$

15. $2x + 7 = 4x + 3$

16. $7m - 6 = 10m - 15$

17. $c + 4 = 6c - 11$

18. $t - 6 = 4t - 21$

19. $3x - 7 = x - 7$

20. $2x + 6 = 7x + 6$

21. $3 - 4x = 5 - 3x$

22. $6 - 2x = 9 - x$

23. $7 + 3x = 9 + 5x$

24. $12 + 5x = 9 - 3x$

25. $5 + 2y = 7 + 5y$

26. $9 + z = 2 + 3z$

27. $8 - 5w = 4 - 6w$

28. $9 - 4x = 11 - 5x$

29. $6x + 1 = 3x + 2$

30. $7x + 5 = 4x + 7$

31. $5x + 8 = x + 5$

32. $9x + 1 = 3x - 4$

33. $2x - 3 = 6x - 4$

34. $4 - 3x = 4 - 5x$

35. $6 - 3x = 6 - 5x$

36. $2x + 7 = 4x - 3$

37. $6x - 2 = 2x - 9$
$4x = -7$

38. $4x - 7 = -3x + 2$

39. $6x - 3 = -5x + 8$

40. $7y - 5 = 3y + 9$

41. $-6t - 2 = -8t - 4$

42. $-7w + 2 = 3w - 8$

43. $-3 - 4x = 7 - 2x$

44. $-8 + 5x = 8 + 6x$

45. $3 - 7x = -2 + 5x$

46. $3x - 2 = 7 - 5x$

47. $5x + 8 = 4 - 2x$

48. $4 - 3x = 6x - 8$

49. $12z - 9 = 3z + 12$

50. $4c + 13 = -6c + 9$

51. $\dfrac{5}{7}m - 3 = \dfrac{2}{7}m + 6$

52. $\dfrac{4}{5}x - 1 = \dfrac{1}{5}x + 5$

53. $\dfrac{3}{7}x + 5 = \dfrac{5}{7}x - 1$

54. $\dfrac{3}{4}x + 2 = \dfrac{1}{4}x - 9$

Objective B   To solve an equation containing parentheses

For Exercises 55 to 102, solve.

55. $6x + 2(x - 1) = 14$

56. $3x + 2(x + 4) = 13$

57. $-3 + 4(x + 3) = 5$

58. $8b - 3(b - 5) = 30$

59. $6 - 2(d + 4) = 6$

60. $5 - 3(n + 2) = 8$

61. $5 + 7(x + 3) = 20$

62. $6 - 3(x - 4) = 12$

63. $2x + 3(x - 5) = 10$

64. $3x - 4(x + 3) = 9$

65. $3(x - 4) + 2x = 3$

66. $4 + 3(x - 9) = -12$

67. $2x - 3(x - 4) = 12$

68. $4x - 2(x - 5) = 10$

69. $2x + 3(x + 4) = 7$

70. $3(x + 2) + 7 = 12$

71. $3(x - 2) + 5 = 5$

72. $4(x - 5) + 7 = 7$

73. $3y + 7(y - 2) = 5$

74. $-3z - 3(z - 3) = 3$

75. $4b - 2(b + 9) = 8$

76. $3x - 6(x - 3) = 9$

77. $3x + 5(x - 2) = 10$

78. $3x - 5(x - 1) = -5$

79. $3x + 4(x + 2) = 2(x + 9)$

80. $5x + 3(x + 4) = 4(x + 2)$

81. $2d - 3(d - 4) = 2(d + 6)$

82. $3t - 4(t - 1) = 3(t - 2)$

83. $7 - 2(x - 3) = 3(x - 1)$

84. $4 - 3(x + 2) = 2(x - 4)$

85. $6x - 2(x - 3) = 11(x - 2)$

86. $9x - 5(x - 3) = 5(x + 4)$

87. $6c - 3(c + 1) = 5(c + 2)$

88. $2w - 7(w - 2) = 3(w - 4)$

89. $7 - (x + 1) = 3(x + 3)$

90. $12 + 2(x - 9) = 3(x - 12)$

91. $2x - 3(x + 4) = 2(x - 5)$

92. $3x + 2(x - 7) = 7(x - 1)$

93. $x + 5(x - 4) = 3(x - 8) - 5$

94. $2x - 2(x - 1) = 3(x - 2) + 7$

95. $9b - 3(b - 4) = 13 + 2(b - 3)$

96. $3y - 4(y - 2) = 15 - 3(y - 2)$

97. $3(x - 4) + 3x = 7 - 2(x - 1)$

98. $2(x - 6) + 7x = 5 - 3(x - 2)$

99. $3.67x - 5.3(x - 1.932) = 6.99$

100. $4.06x + 4.7(x + 3.22) = 1.774$

101. $8.45(z - 10) = 3(z - 3.854)$

102. $4(d - 1.99) - 3.92 = 3(d - 1.77)$

APPLYING THE CONCEPTS

103. If $2x - 2 = 4x + 6$, what is the value of $3x^2$?

104. If $3 + 2(4a - 3) = 4$ and $4 - 3(2 - 3b) = 11$, which is larger, a or b?

105. Explain what is wrong with the demonstration at the right, which suggests that $5 = 4$.

$5x + 7 = 4x + 7$

$5x + 7 - 7 = 4x + 7 - 7$ • Subtract 7 from each side of the equation.

$5x = 4x$

$\dfrac{5x}{x} = \dfrac{4x}{x}$ • Divide each side of the equation by x.

$5 = 4$

106. The equation $x = x + 1$ has no solution, whereas the solution of the equation $2x + 3 = 3$ is zero. Is there a difference between no solution and a solution of zero? Explain.

2.5

Translating Verbal Expressions into Mathematical Expressions

Objective A   **To translate a verbal expression into a mathematical expression given the variable**

One of the major skills required in applied mathematics is to translate a verbal expression into a mathematical expression. Doing so requires recognizing the verbal phrases that translate into mathematical operations. Following is a partial list of the verbal phrases used to indicate the different mathematical operations.

Addition	more than	5 more than x	$x + 5$
	the sum of	the sum of w and 3	$w + 3$
	the total of	the total of 6 and z	$6 + z$
	increased by	x increased by 7	$x + 7$
Subtraction	less than	5 less than y	$y - 5$
	the difference between	the difference between w and 3	$w - 3$
	decreased by	8 decreased by a	$8 - a$
Multiplication	times	3 times c	$3c$
	the product of	the product of 4 and t	$4t$
	of	two-thirds of v	$\dfrac{2}{3}v$
	twice	twice d	$2d$
Division	divided by	n divided by 3	$\dfrac{n}{3}$
	the quotient of	the quotient of z and 4	$\dfrac{z}{4}$
	the ratio of	the ratio of s to 6	$\dfrac{s}{6}$

Translating phrases that contain the words *sum, difference, product,* and *quotient* can sometimes cause a problem. In the examples at the right, note where the operation symbol is placed.

the *sum* of x and y $\quad\quad$ $x + y$

the *difference* between x and y $\quad$ $x - y$

the *product* of x and y $\quad\quad$ $x \cdot y$

the *quotient* of x and y $\quad\quad$ $\dfrac{x}{y}$

Note where we place the fraction bar when translating the word *ratio*.

the *ratio* of x to y $\quad\quad$ $\dfrac{x}{y}$

HOW TO   Translate "the quotient of n and the sum of n and 6" into a mathematical expression.

the *quotient* of n and the *sum* of n and 6 $\quad\quad$ $\dfrac{n}{n + 6}$

Example 1 Translate "the sum of 5 and the product of 4 and n" into a mathematical expression.

Solution $5 + 4n$

You Try It 1 Translate "the difference between 8 and twice t" into a mathematical expression.

Your solution

Example 2 Translate "the product of 3 and the difference between z and 4" into a mathematical expression.

Solution $3(z - 4)$

You Try It 2 Translate "the quotient of 5 and the product of 7 and x" into a mathematical expression.

Your solution

Objective B **To translate a verbal expression into a mathematical expression by assigning the variable**

In most applications that involve translating phrases into mathematical expressions, the variable to be used is not given. To translate these phrases, we must assign a variable to the unknown quantity before writing the mathematical expression.

HOW TO Translate "the difference between seven and twice a number" into a mathematical expression.

The difference between seven and twice a number

The unknown number: n

Twice the number: $2n$

$7 - 2n$

- Identify the phrases that indicate the mathematical operations.

- Assign a variable to one of the unknown quantities.

- Use the assigned variable to write an expression for any other unknown quantity.

- Use the identified operations to write the mathematical expression.

Example 3

Translate "the total of a number and the square of the number" into a mathematical expression.

Solution
The *total* of a number and the *square* of the number

The unknown number: x
The square of the number: x^2

$x + x^2$

You Try It 3

Translate "the product of a number and one-half of the number" into a mathematical expression.

Your solution

2.5 Exercises

Objective A   **To translate a verbal expression into a mathematical expression given the variable**

For Exercises 1 to 22, translate into a mathematical expression.

1. 9 less than y

2. w divided by 7

3. z increased by 3

4. the product of -2 and x

5. the sum of two-thirds of n and n

6. the difference between the square of r and r

7. the quotient of m and the difference between m and 3

8. v increased by twice v

9. the product of 9 and 4 more than x

10. the total of a and the quotient of a and 7

11. the difference between n and the product of -5 and n

12. x decreased by the quotient of x and 2

13. the product of c and one-fourth of c

14. the quotient of 3 less than z and z

15. the total of the square of m and twice the square of m

16. the product of y and the sum of y and 4

17. 2 times the sum of t and 6

18. the quotient of r and the difference between 8 and r

19. x divided by the total of 9 and x

20. the sum of z and the product of 6 and z

21. three times the sum of b and 6

22. the ratio of w to the sum of w and 8

Objective B   **To translate a verbal expression into a mathematical expression by assigning the variable**

For Exercises 23 to 44, translate into a mathematical expression.

23. the square of a number

24. five less than some number

25. a number divided by twenty

26. the difference between a number and twelve

27. four times some number

28. the quotient of five and a number

29. three-fourths of a number

30. the sum of a number and seven

31. four increased by some number

32. the ratio of a number to nine

33. the difference between five times a number and the number

34. six less than the total of three and a number

35. the product of a number and two more than the number

36. the quotient of six and the sum of nine and a number

37. seven times the total of a number and eight

38. the difference between ten and the quotient of a number and two

39. the square of a number plus the product of three and the number

40. a number decreased by the product of five and the number

41. the sum of three more than a number and one-half of the number

42. eight more than twice the sum of a number and seven

43. the quotient of three times a number and the number

44. the square of a number divided by the sum of the number and twelve

APPLYING THE CONCEPTS

45. **a.** Translate the expression $2x + 3$ into a phrase.
  b. Translate the expression $2(x + 3)$ into a phrase.

46. **a.** Translate the expression $\frac{2x}{7}$ into a phrase.

  b. Translate the expression $\frac{2 + x}{7}$ into a phrase.

47. ✏ In your own words, explain how variables are used.

48. **Chemistry**   The chemical formula for water is H_2O. This formula means that there are two hydrogen atoms and one oxygen atom in each molecule of water. If x represents the number of atoms of oxygen in a glass of pure water, express the number of hydrogen atoms in the glass of water.

49. **Chemistry**   The chemical formula for one molecule of glucose (sugar) is $C_6H_{12}O_6$, where C is carbon, H is hydrogen, and O is oxygen. If x represents the number of atoms of hydrogen in a sample of pure sugar, express the number of carbon atoms and the number of oxygen atoms in the sample in terms of x.

2.6 Translating Sentences into Equations and Solving

Objective A   To translate a sentence into an equation and solve

Point of Interest

Number puzzle problems similar to the one on this page have appeared in textbooks for hundreds of years. Here is one from a 1st-century Chinese textbook: "When a number is divided by 3, the remainder is 2; when it is divided by 5, the remainder is 3; when it is divided by 7, the remainder is 2. Find the number." There are actually infinitely many solutions to this problem. See whether you can find one of them.

An equation states that two mathematical expressions are equal. Therefore, to translate a sentence into an equation requires recognition of the words or phrases that mean "equals." Some of these phrases are

$$
\left.
\begin{array}{l}
\text{equals} \\
\text{is} \\
\text{is equal to} \\
\text{amounts to} \\
\text{represents}
\end{array}
\right\} \text{translate to } =
$$

Once the sentence is translated into an equation, the equation can be simplified to one of the form *variable = constant* and the solution can be found.

HOW TO   Translate "three more than twice a number is seventeen" into an equation and solve.

The unknown number: n

| Three more than twice a number | is | seventeen |

$$
\begin{aligned}
2n + 3 &= 17 \\
2n + 3 - 3 &= 17 - 3 \\
2n &= 14 \\
\frac{2n}{2} &= \frac{14}{2} \\
n &= 7
\end{aligned}
$$

The number is 7.

- **Assign a variable to the unknown quantity.**

- **Find two verbal expressions for the same value.**

- **Write a mathematical expression for each verbal expression. Write the equals sign. Solve the resulting equation.**

Example 1

Translate "a number decreased by six equals fifteen" into an equation and solve.

Solution

The unknown number: x

| A number decreased by six | equals | fifteen |

$$
\begin{aligned}
x - 6 &= 15 \\
x - 6 + 6 &= 15 + 6 \\
x &= 21
\end{aligned}
$$

The number is 21.

You Try It 1

Translate "a number increased by four equals twelve" into an equation and solve.

Your solution

Example 2

The quotient of a number and six is five. Find the number.

Solution

The unknown number: z

The quotient of a number and six	is	five

$$\frac{z}{6} = 5$$
$$6 \cdot \frac{z}{6} = 6 \cdot 5$$
$$z = 30$$

The number is 30.

You Try It 2

The product of two and a number is ten. Find the number.

Your solution

Example 3

Eight decreased by twice a number is four. Find the number.

Solution

The unknown number: t

Eight decreased by twice a number	is	four

$$8 - 2t = 4$$
$$8 - 8 - 2t = 4 - 8$$
$$-2t = -4$$
$$\frac{-2t}{-2} = \frac{-4}{-2}$$
$$t = 2$$

The number is 2.

You Try It 3

The sum of three times a number and six equals four. Find the number.

Your solution

Example 4

Three less than the ratio of a number to seven is one. Find the number.

Solution

The unknown number: x

Three less than the ratio of a number to seven	is	one

$$\frac{x}{7} - 3 = 1$$
$$\frac{x}{7} - 3 + 3 = 1 + 3$$
$$\frac{x}{7} = 4$$
$$7 \cdot \frac{x}{7} = 7 \cdot 4$$
$$x = 28$$

The number is 28.

You Try It 4

Three more than one-half of a number is nine. Find the number.

Your solution

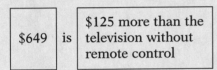 **To solve application problems**

Example 5

The cost of a television with remote control is $649. This amount is $125 more than the cost of the same television without remote control. Find the cost of the television without remote control.

Strategy

To find the cost of the television without remote control, write and solve an equation using C to represent the cost of the television without remote control.

Solution

| $649 | is | $125 more than the television without remote control |

$$649 = C + 125$$
$$649 - 125 = C + 125 - 125$$
$$524 = C$$

The cost of the television without remote control is $524.

You Try It 5

The sale price of a pair of slacks is $38.95. This amount is $11 less than the regular price. Find the regular price.

Your strategy

Your solution

Example 6

By purchasing a fleet of cars, a company receives a discount of $1972 on each car purchased. This amount is 8% of the regular price. Find the regular price.

Strategy

To find the regular price, write and solve an equation using P to represent the regular price of the car.

Solution

| $1972 | is | 8% of the regular price |

$$1972 = 0.08 \cdot P$$
$$\frac{1972}{0.08} = \frac{0.08P}{0.08}$$
$$24{,}650 = P$$

The regular price is $24,650.

You Try It 6

At a certain speed, the engine rpm (revolutions per minute) of a car in fourth gear is 2500. This is two-thirds of the rpm of the engine in third gear. Find the rpm of the engine when it is in third gear.

Your strategy

Your solution

Example 7

Ron Sierra charged $1105 for plumbing repairs in an office building. This charge included $90 for parts and $35 per hour for labor. Find the number of hours he worked in the office building.

Strategy

To find the number of hours worked, write and solve an equation using N to represent the number of hours worked.

Solution

$1105	included	$90 for parts and $35 per hour for labor

$$1105 = 90 + 35N$$
$$1105 - 90 = 90 - 90 + 35N$$
$$1015 = 35N$$
$$\frac{1015}{35} = \frac{35N}{35}$$
$$29 = N$$

Ron worked 29 h.

You Try It 7

The total cost to make a model Z100 television is $300. The cost includes $100 for materials plus $12.50 per hour for labor. How many hours of labor are required to make a model Z100 television?

Your strategy

Your solution

Example 8

The state income tax for Tim Fong last month was $256. This amount is $5 more than 8% of his monthly salary. Find Tim's monthly salary.

Strategy

To find Tim's monthly salary, write and solve an equation using S to represent his monthly salary.

Solution

$256	is	$5 more than 8% of the monthly salary

$$256 = 0.08 \cdot S + 5$$
$$256 - 5 = 0.08S + 5 - 5$$
$$251 = 0.08S$$
$$\frac{251}{0.08} = \frac{0.08S}{0.08}$$
$$3137.50 = S$$

Tim's monthly salary is $3137.50.

You Try It 8

Natalie Adams earned $2500 last month for temporary work. This amount was the sum of a base monthly salary of $800 and an 8% commission on total sales. Find Natalie's total sales for the month.

Your strategy

Your solution

2.6 Exercises

Objective A   **To translate a sentence into an equation and solve**

For Exercises 1 to 26, write an equation and solve.

1. The sum of a number and seven is twelve. Find the number.

2. A number decreased by seven is five. Find the number.

3. The product of three and a number is eighteen. Find the number.

4. The quotient of a number and three is one. Find the number.

5. Five more than a number is three. Find the number.

6. A number divided by four is six. Find the number.

7. Six times a number is fourteen. Find the number.

8. Seven less than a number is three. Find the number.

9. Five-sixths of a number is fifteen. Find the number.

10. The total of twenty and a number is five. Find the number.

11. The sum of three times a number and four is eight. Find the number.

12. The sum of one-third of a number and seven is twelve. Find the number.

13. Seven less than one-fourth of a number is nine. Find the number.

14. The total of a number divided by four and nine is two. Find the number.

15. The ratio of a number to nine is fourteen. Find the number.

16. Five increased by the product of five and a number is equal to 30. Find the number.

17. Six less than the quotient of a number and four is equal to negative two. Find the number.

18. The product of a number plus three and two is eight. Find the number.

19. The difference between seven and twice a number is thirteen. Find the number.

20. Five more than the product of three and a number is eight. Find the number.

21. Nine decreased by the quotient of a number and two is five. Find the number.

22. The total of ten times a number and seven is twenty-seven. Find the number.

23. The sum of three-fifths of a number and eight is two. Find the number.

24. Five less than two-thirds of a number is three. Find the number.

25. [calculator] The difference between a number divided by 4.186 and 7.92 is 12.529. Find the number.

26. [calculator] The total of 5.68 times a number and 132.7 is the number minus 29.265. Find the number.

Objective B   **To solve application problems**

27. Consumerism   Sears has a pair of shoes on sale for $72.50. This amount is $4.25 less than the pair sells for at Target. Find the price at Target.

28. Compensation   As a restaurant manager, Uechi Kim is paid a salary of $832 a week. This is $58 more a week than the salary Uechi received last year. Find the weekly salary paid to Uechi last year.

29. Depreciation   The value of a sport utility vehicle this year is $16,000, which is four-fifths of what its value was last year. Find the value of the vehicle last year.

30. Real Estate   This year the value of a lakefront summer cottage is $175,000. This amount is twice the value of the cottage 6 years ago. What was its value 6 years ago?

31. [icon] **Bridges**   The length of the Akashi Kaikyo Bridge is 1991 m. This is 1505 m greater than the length of the Brooklyn Bridge. Find the length of the Brooklyn Bridge.

32. [icon] **Debt**   According to CardWeb.com, the average household credit card balance ten years ago was $3275, which is $5665 less than the average credit card balance today. Find the average credit card balance today.

Akashi Kaikyo Bridge

33. Finances   Each month the Manzanares family spends $1360 for their house payment and utilities, which amounts to one-fourth of the family's monthly income. Find the family's monthly income.

34. Consumerism   The cost of a graphing calculator is now three-fourths of what the calculator cost 5 years ago. The cost of the graphing calculator is now $72. Find the cost of the calculator 5 years ago.

35. **Business** Assume that the Dell Computer Corp. has increased its output of computers by 400 computers per month. This amount represents an 8% increase over last year's production. Find the monthly output last year.

36. **Sports** The average number of home runs per major league game today is 2.21. This represents 135% of the average number of home runs per game 40 years ago. (*Source:* Elias Sports Bureau) Find the average number of home runs per game 40 years ago. Round to the nearest hundredth.

37. **Nutrition** The nutrition label on a bag of Baked Tostitos tortilla chips lists the sodium content of one serving as 200 mg, which is 8% of the recommended daily allowance of sodium. What is the recommended daily allowance of sodium? Express the answer in grams.

38. **Markup** The price of a pair of skis at the Solitude Ski Shop is $340. This price includes the store's cost for the skis plus a markup at the rate of 25%. Find Solitude's cost for the skis.

39. **Contractors** Budget Plumbing charged $400 for a water softener and installation. The charge included $310 for the water softener and $30 per hour for labor. How many hours of labor were required for the job?

40. **Compensation** Sandy's monthly salary as a sales representative was $2580. This amount included her base monthly salary of $600 plus a 3% commission on total sales. Find her total sales for the month.

41. **Conservation** In Central America and Mexico, 1184 plants and animals are known to be at risk of extinction. This represents approximately 10.7% of all the species known to be at risk of extinction on Earth. (*Source:* World Conservation Union) Approximately how many plants and animals are known to be at risk of extinction in the world?

42. **Taxes** When you use your car for business, you are able to deduct the expense on your income tax return. In 2003 the deduction was 36 cents per mile driven. How many business-related miles did a taxpayer who deducted a total of $1728 drive?

43. **Insecticides** Americans spend approximately $295 million a year on remedies for cockroaches. The table at the right shows the top U.S. cities for sales of roach insecticides. What percent of the total is spent in New York? Round to the nearest tenth of a percent.

City	Roach Insecticide Sales
Los Angeles	$16.8 million
New York	$9.8 million
Houston	$6.7 million

Source: IRI InfoScan for Combat

44. **Consumerism** McPherson Cement sells cement for $75 plus $24 for each yard of cement. How many yards of cement can be purchased for $363?

45. Conservation   A water flow restrictor has reduced the flow of water to 2 gal/min. This amount is 1 gal/min less than three-fifths the original flow rate. Find the original rate.

46. Temperature Conversion   The Celsius temperature equals five-ninths times the difference between the Fahrenheit temperature and 32. Find the Fahrenheit temperature when the Celsius temperature is 40°.

47. Compensation   Assume that a sales executive receives a base monthly salary of $600 plus an 8.25% commission on total sales per month. Find the executive's total sales during a month in which she receives total compensation of $4109.55.

Environment   The graph at the right shows projected world carbon dioxide emissions, in billions of metric tons. Use the graph for Exercises 48 and 49. Round to the nearest hundredth of a billion.

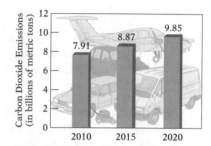

Projected World Carbon Dioxide Emissions

Source: U.S. Energy Information Administration

48. The projected world carbon dioxide emissions in 2020 are equal to 160.4% of the emissions in 1998. Find the world carbon dioxide emissions in 1998.

49. The projected world carbon dioxide emissions in 2015 are equal to 152.1% of the emissions in 1990. Find the world carbon dioxide emissions in 1990.

APPLYING THE CONCEPTS

50. A man's boyhood lasted $\frac{1}{6}$ of his life, he played football for the next $\frac{1}{8}$ of his life, and he married 5 years after quitting football. A daughter was born after he had been married $\frac{1}{12}$ of his life. The daughter lived $\frac{1}{2}$ as many years as her father. The man died 6 years after his daughter. How old was the man when he died? Use a number line to illustrate the time. Then write an equation and solve it.

51. It is always important to check the answer to an application problem to be sure the answer makes sense. Consider the following problem. "A 4-quart mixture of fruit juices is made from apple juice and cranberry juice. There are 6 more quarts of apple juice than of cranberry juice. Write and solve an equation for the number of quarts of each juice used." Does the answer to this question make sense? Explain.

52. A formula is an equation that relates variables in a known way. Find two examples of formulas that are used in your college major. Explain what each of the variables represents.

Focus on Problem Solving

From Concrete to Abstract

As you progress in your study of algebra, you will find that the problems become less concrete and more abstract. Problems that are concrete provide information pertaining to a specific instance. Abstract problems are theoretical; they are stated without reference to a specific instance. Let's look at an example of an abstract problem.

How many cents are in d dollars?

How can you solve this problem? Are you able to solve the same problem if the information given is concrete?

How many cents are in 5 dollars?

You know that there are 100 cents in 1 dollar. To find the number of cents in 5 dollars, multiply 5 by 100.

$100 \cdot 5 = 500$ There are 500 cents in 5 dollars.

Use the same procedure to find the number of cents in d dollars: multiply d by 100.

$100 \cdot d = 100d$ There are $100d$ cents in d dollars.

This problem might be taken a step further:

If one pen costs c cents, how many pens can be purchased with d dollars?

Consider the same problem using numbers in place of the variables.

If one pen costs 25 cents, how many pens can be purchased with 2 dollars?

To solve this problem, you need to calculate the number of cents in 2 dollars (multiply 2 by 100) and divide the result by the cost per pen (25 cents).

$$\frac{100 \cdot 2}{25} = \frac{200}{25} = 8$$ If one pen costs 25 cents,
8 pens can be purchased with 2 dollars.

Use the same procedure to solve the related abstract problem. Calculate the number of cents in d dollars (multiply d by 100) and divide the result by the cost per pen (c cents).

$$\frac{100 \cdot d}{c} = \frac{100d}{c}$$ If one pen costs c cents, $\frac{100d}{c}$ pens
can be purchased with d dollars.

At the heart of the study of algebra is the use of variables. It is the variables in the problems above that make them abstract. But it is variables that enable us to generalize situations and state rules about mathematics.

Try the following problems.

1. How many nickels are in *d* dollars?

2. How long can you talk on a pay phone if you have only *d* dollars and the call costs *c* cents per minute?

3. If you travel *m* miles on one gallon of gasoline, how far can you travel on *g* gallons of gasoline?

4. If you walk a mile in *x* minutes, how far can you walk in *h* hours?

5. If one photocopy costs *n* nickels, how many photocopies can you make for *q* quarters?

Projects and Group Activities

Averages   We often discuss temperature in terms of average high or average low temperature. Temperatures collected over a period of time are analyzed to determine, for example, the average high temperature for a given month in your city or state. The following activity is planned to help you better understand the concept of "average."

1. Choose two cities in the United States. We will refer to them as City X and City Y. Over an 8-day period, record the daily high temperature each day in each city.

2. Determine the average high temperature for City X for the 8-day period. (Add the eight numbers, and then divide the sum by 8.) Do not round your answer.

3. Subtract the average high temperature for City X from each of the eight daily high temperatures for City X. You should have a list of eight numbers; the list should include positive numbers, negative numbers, and possibly zero.

4. Find the sum of the list of eight differences recorded in Step 3.

5. Repeat Steps 2 through 4 for City Y.

6. Compare the two sums found in Steps 4 and 5 for City X and City Y.

7. If you were to conduct this activity again, what would you expect the outcome to be? Use the results to explain what an average high temperature is. In your own words, explain what "average" means.

Chapter Summary

Key Words

Examples

A *variable* is a letter of the alphabet used to stand for a quantity that is unknown or that can change. An expression that contains one or more variables is a *variable expression*. Replacing the variable or variables in a variable expression and then simplifying the resulting numerical expression is called *evaluating the variable expression*.

Evaluate $5x^3 + 2y - 6$ when $x = -1$ and $y = 4$.

$5x^3 + 2y - 6$
$5(-1)^3 + 2(4) - 6 = 5(-1) + 2(4) - 6$
$\qquad\qquad\qquad\quad = -5 + 8 - 6$
$\qquad\qquad\qquad\quad = 3 - 6$
$\qquad\qquad\qquad\quad = 3 + (-6) = -3$

The *terms of a variable expression* are the addends of the expression. A *variable term* consists of a *numerical coefficient* and a *variable part*. A *constant term* has no variable part.

The variable expression $-3x^2 + 2x - 5$ has three terms: $-3x^2$, $2x$, and -5.
$-3x^2$ and $2x$ are variable terms.
-5 is a constant term.
For the term $-3x^2$, the coefficient is -3 and the variable part is x^2.

Like terms of a variable expression have the same variable part. Constant terms are also like terms.

$-6a^3b^2$ and $4a^3b^2$ are like terms.

An *equation* expresses the equality of two mathematical expressions.

$5x + 6 = 7x - 3$
$y = 4x - 10$
$3a^2 - 6a + 4 = 0$

A *solution of an equation* is a number that, when substituted for the variable, results in a true equation.

6 is a solution of $x - 4 = 2$ because $6 - 4 = 2$ is a true equation.

Solving an equation means finding a solution of the equation. The goal is to rewrite the equation in the form *variable = constant*.

$x = 5$ is in the form *variable = constant*. The solution of the equation $x = 5$ is the constant 5 because $5 = 5$ is a true equation.

A *formula* is an equation that expresses a relationship among variables.

The relationship between Celsius temperatures and Fahrenheit temperatures is given by the formula $F = 1.8C + 32$, where F represents degrees Fahrenheit and C represents degrees Celsius.

Some of the words and phrases that translate to *equals* are *is, is equal to, amounts to,* and *represents*.

"Eight plus a number is ten" translates to $8 + x = 10$.

Essential Rules and Procedures

Examples

Commutative Property of Addition
$a + b = b + a$

$-9 + 5 = 5 + (-9)$

Associative Property of Addition
$(a + b) + c = a + (b + c)$

$(-6 + 4) + 2 = -6 + (4 + 2)$

Commutative Property of Multiplication
$a \cdot b = b \cdot a$

$-5(10) = 10(-5)$

Associative Property of Multiplication
$(a \cdot b) \cdot c = a \cdot (b \cdot c)$

$(-3 \cdot 4) \cdot 6 = -3 \cdot (4 \cdot 6)$

Distributive Property
$a(b + c) = ab + ac$
$a(b - c) = ab - ac$

$2(x + 7) = 2(x) + 2(7) = 2x + 14$
$5(4x - 3) = 5(4x) - 5(3) = 20x - 15$

Addition Property of Zero
The sum of a term and zero is the term.
$a + 0 = a$ or $0 + a = a$

$-16 + 0 = -16$

Addition Property of Equations
If a, b, and c are algebraic expressions, then the equations $a = b$ and $a + c = b + c$ have the same solutions.

The same number or variable expression can be added to each side of an equation without changing the solution of the equation.

$$x + 7 = 20$$
$$x + 7 + (-7) = 20 + (-7)$$
$$x = 13$$

Multiplication Property of Reciprocals
The product of a nonzero term and its reciprocal equals 1.

$8 \cdot \dfrac{1}{8} = 1$

Multiplication Property of One
The product of a term and 1 is the term.

$-7(1) = -7$

Multiplication Property of Equations
If a, b, and c are algebraic expressions and $c \neq 0$, then the equation $a = b$ has the same solutions as the equation $ac = bc$.

Each side of an equation can be multiplied by the same nonzero number without changing the solution of the equation.

$$\frac{3}{4}x = 24$$
$$\frac{4}{3} \cdot \frac{3}{4}x = \frac{4}{3} \cdot 24$$
$$x = 32$$

Steps in Solving General First-Degree Equations

1. Use the Distributive Property to remove parentheses.
2. Combine like terms on each side of the equation.
3. Use the Addition Property of Equations to rewrite the equation with only one variable term.
4. Use the Addition Property of Equations to rewrite the equation with only one constant term.
5. Use the Multiplication Property of Equations to rewrite the equation so that the coefficient of the variable is 1.

$$8 - 4(2x + 3) = 2(1 - x)$$
$$8 - 8x - 12 = 2 - 2x$$
$$-8x - 4 = 2 - 2x$$
$$-8x + 2x - 4 = 2 - 2x + 2x$$
$$-6x - 4 = 2$$
$$-6x - 4 + 4 = 2 + 4$$
$$-6x = 6$$
$$\frac{-6x}{-6} = \frac{6}{-6}$$
$$x = -1$$

Chapter Review Exercises

1. Simplify: $-2(a - b)$

2. Is -2 a solution of the equation $3x - 2 = -8$?

3. Solve: $x - 3 = -7$

4. Solve: $-2x + 5 = -9$

5. Evaluate $a^2 - 3b$ when $a = 2$ and $b = -3$.

6. Solve: $-3x = 27$

7. Solve: $\frac{2}{3}x + 3 = -9$

8. Simplify: $3x - 2(3x - 2)$

9. Solve: $6x - 9 = -3x + 36$

10. Solve: $x + 3 = -2$

11. Is 5 a solution of the equation $3x - 5 = -10$?

12. Evaluate $a^2 - (b \div c)$ when $a = -2$, $b = 8$, and $c = -4$.

13. Solve: $3(x - 2) + 2 = 11$

14. Solve: $35 - 3x = 5$

15. Simplify: $6bc - 7bc + 2bc - 5bc$

16. Solve: $7 - 3x = 2 - 5x$

17. Solve: $-\frac{3}{8}x = -\frac{15}{32}$

18. Simplify: $\frac{1}{2}x^2 - \frac{1}{3}x^2 + \frac{1}{5}x^2 + 2x^2$

19. Solve: $5x - 3(1 - 2x) = 4(2x - 1)$

20. Solve: $\frac{5}{6}x - 4 = 5$

21. Fuel Efficiency A tourist drove a rental car 621 mi on 27 gal of gas. Find the number of miles per gallon of gas. Use the formula $D = M \cdot G$, where D is distance, M is miles per gallon, and G is the number of gallons.

22. Temperature Conversion Find the Celsius temperature when the Fahrenheit temperature is 100°. Use the formula $F = 1.8C + 32$, where F is the Fahrenheit temperature and C is the Celsius temperature. Round to the nearest tenth.

23. Translate "the total of n and the quotient of n and five" into a mathematical expression.

24. Translate "the sum of five more than a number and one-third of the number" into a mathematical expression.

25. The difference between nine and twice a number is five. Find the number.

26. The product of five and a number is fifty. Find the number.

27. Discount A compact disc player is now on sale for $228. This is 60% of the regular price. Find the regular price of the CD player.

28. Agriculture A farmer harvested 28,336 bushels of corn. This amount represents a 12% increase over last year's crop. How many bushels of corn did the farmer harvest last year?

Chapter Test

1. Solve: $\frac{x}{5} - 12 = 7$

2. Solve: $x - 12 = 14$

3. Simplify: $3y - 2x - 7y - 9x$

4. Solve: $8 - 3x = 2x - 8$

5. Solve: $3x - 12 = -18$

6. Evaluate $c^2 - (2a + b^2)$ when $a = 3$, $b = -6$, and $c = -2$.

7. Is 3 a solution of the equation $x^2 + 3x - 7 = 3x - 2$?

8. Simplify: $9 - 8ab - 6ab$

9. Solve: $-5x = 14$

10. Simplify: $3y + 5(y - 3) + 8$

11. Solve: $3x - 4(x - 2) = 8$

12. Solve: $5 = 3 - 4x$

13. Evaluate $\frac{x^2}{y} - \frac{y^2}{x}$ for $x = 3$ and $y = -2$.

14. Solve: $\frac{5}{8}x = -10$

15. Solve: $y - 4y + 3 = 12$

16. Solve: $2x + 4(x - 3) = 5x - 1$

17. **Finance**   A loan of $6600 is to be paid in 48 equal monthly installments. Find the monthly payment. Use the formula $L = P \cdot N$, where L is the loan amount, P is the monthly payment, and N is the number of months.

18. **Manufacturing**   A clock manufacturer's fixed costs per month are $5000. The unit cost for each clock is $15. Find the number of clocks made during a month in which the total cost was $65,000. Use the formula $T = U \cdot N + F$, where T is the total cost, U is the cost per unit, N is the number of units made, and F is the fixed costs.

19. **Physics**   Find the time required for a falling object to increase in velocity from 24 ft/s to 392 ft/s. Use the formula $V = V_0 + 32t$, where V is the final velocity of a falling object, V_0 is the starting velocity of a falling object, and t is the time for the object to fall.

20. Translate "the sum of x and one-third of x" into a mathematical expression.

21. Translate "five times the sum of a number and three" into a mathematical expression.

22. Translate "three less than two times a number is seven" into an equation and solve.

23. The total of five and three times a number is the number minus two. Find the number.

24. **Compensation**   Eduardo Santos earned $3600 last month. This salary is the sum of the base monthly salary of $1200 and a 6% commission on total sales. Find his total sales for the month.

25. **Consumerism**   Your mechanic charges you $278 for performing a 30,000-mile checkup on your car. This charge includes $152 for parts and $42 per hour for labor. Find the number of hours the mechanic worked on your car.

chapter

3 Inequalities

You know how to determine the average of four exam scores when each exam has the same weight: add the four scores and divide the sum by 4. But do you know how to determine what score you must receive on a fifth exam to earn a specific average on the five exams? In this chapter you will learn how to use an inequality to determine that fifth and final score.

Need help? For online student resources, such as section quizzes, visit this textbook's website at **math.college.hmco.com/students**.

3.1

The Addition and Multiplication Properties of Inequalities

Objective A   **To solve an inequality using the Addition Property of Inequalities**

Recall that the solution set of an inequality is the set of numbers each element of which, when substituted for the variable, results in a true inequality.

The inequality at the right is true if the variable is replaced by 7, 9.3, or $\frac{15}{2}$.

$$x + 5 > 8$$

$$\left.\begin{array}{l} 7 + 5 > 8 \\ 9.3 + 5 > 8 \\ \dfrac{15}{2} + 5 > 8 \end{array}\right\} \text{True inequalities}$$

The inequality $x + 5 > 8$ is false if the variable is replaced by 2, 1.5, or $-\frac{1}{2}$.

$$\left.\begin{array}{l} 2 + 5 > 8 \\ 1.5 + 5 > 8 \\ -\dfrac{1}{2} + 5 > 8 \end{array}\right\} \text{False inequalities}$$

There are many values of the variable x that will make the inequality $x + 5 > 8$ true. The solution set of $x + 5 > 8$ is any number greater than 3.

At the right is the graph of the solution set of $x + 5 > 8$.

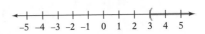

In solving an inequality, the goal is to rewrite the given inequality in the form *variable > constant* or *variable < constant*. The Addition Property of Inequalities is used to rewrite an inequality in this form.

> **Addition Property of Inequalities**
>
> The same term can be added to each side of an inequality without changing the solution set of the inequality.
>
> If $a > b$, then $a + c > b + c$.
>
> If $a < b$, then $a + c < b + c$.

The Addition Property of Inequalities also holds true for an inequality containing the symbol $\geq$ or $\leq$.

The Addition Property of Inequalities is used when, in order to rewrite an inequality in the form *variable > constant* or *variable < constant*, we must remove a term from one side of the inequality. Add the opposite of that term to each side of the inequality.

HOW TO   Solve: $x - 4 < -3$

$$x - 4 < -3$$
$$x - 4 + 4 < -3 + 4 \qquad \bullet \text{ Add 4 to each side of the inequality.}$$
$$x < 1 \qquad\qquad \bullet \text{ Simplify.}$$

At the right is the graph of the solution set of $x - 4 < -3$.

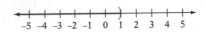

Because subtraction is defined in terms of addition, the Addition Property of Inequalities allows the same term to be subtracted from each side of an inequality.

HOW TO Solve: $5x - 6 \leq 4x - 4$

$$5x - 6 \leq 4x - 4$$

$$5x - 4x - 6 \leq 4x - 4x - 4$$ • Subtract 4*x* from each side of the inequality.

$$x - 6 \leq -4$$ • Simplify.

$$x - 6 + 6 \leq -4 + 6$$ • Add 6 to each side of the inequality.

$$x \leq 2$$ • Simplify.

Example 1

Solve $3 < x + 5$ and graph the solution set.

Solution

$$3 < x + 5$$
$$3 - 5 < x + 5 - 5$$ • Subtract 5.
$$-2 < x$$

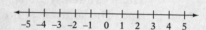

You Try It 1

Solve $x + 2 < -2$ and graph the solution set.

Your solution

Example 2

Solve: $7x - 14 \leq 6x - 16$

Solution

$$7x - 14 \leq 6x - 16$$
$$7x - 6x - 14 \leq 6x - 6x - 16$$ • Subtract 6x.
$$x - 14 \leq -16$$
$$x - 14 + 14 \leq -16 + 14$$ • Add 14.
$$x \leq -2$$

You Try It 2

Solve: $5x + 3 > 4x + 5$

Your solution

Objective B   **To solve an inequality using the Multiplication Property of Inequalities**

In solving an inequality, the goal is to rewrite the given inequality in the form *variable > constant* or *variable < constant*. The Multiplication Property of Inequalities is used when, in order to rewrite an inequality in this form, we must remove a coefficient from one side of the inequality.

Multiplication Property of Inequalities

Each side of an inequality can be multiplied by the same positive number without changing the solution set of the inequality.

$$\text{If } a > b \text{ and } c > 0, \text{ then } ac > bc.$$
$$\text{If } a < b \text{ and } c > 0, \text{ then } ac < bc.$$

If each side of an inequality is multiplied by the same negative number and the inequality symbol is reversed, then the solution set of the inequality is not changed.

$$\text{If } a > b \text{ and } c < 0, \text{ then } ac < bc.$$
$$\text{If } a < b \text{ and } c < 0, \text{ then } ac > bc.$$

TAKE NOTE

Any time an inequality is multiplied or divided by a negative number, the inequality symbol must be reversed. Compare the next two examples.

$2x < -4$ Divide each side by *positive* 2.
$\dfrac{2x}{2} < \dfrac{-4}{2}$

$x < -2$ Inequality *is not* reversed.

$-2x < 4$ Divide each side by *negative* 2.
$\dfrac{-2x}{-2} > \dfrac{4}{-2}$

$x > -2$ Inequality *is reversed*.

$5 > 4$ • **A true inequality**

$5(2) > 4(2)$ • **Multiply by** *positive* **2.**

$10 > 8$ • **Still a true inequality**

$6 < 9$ • **A true inequality**

$6(-3) > 9(-3)$ • **Multiply by** *negative* **3 and** *reverse* **the inequality.**

$-18 > -27$ • **Still a true inequality**

The Multiplication Property of Inequalities also holds true for an inequality containing the symbol $\geq$ or $\leq$.

HOW TO   Solve $-\dfrac{3}{2}x \leq 6$ and graph the solution set.

$$-\dfrac{3}{2}x \leq 6$$

• **Multiply each side of the inequality by** $-\dfrac{2}{3}$ **.**

$$-\dfrac{2}{3}\left(-\dfrac{3}{2}x\right) \geq -\dfrac{2}{3}(6)$$

Because $-\dfrac{2}{3}$ **is a negative number, the inequality symbol must be reversed.**

$$x \geq -4$$

• **Graph** $\{x \mid x \geq -4\}$ **.**

Because division is defined in terms of multiplication, the Multiplication Property of Inequalities allows each side of an inequality to be divided by a nonzero constant.

TAKE NOTE

As shown in the example at the right, the goal in solving an inequality can be *constant* < *variable* or *constant* > *variable*. We could have written the answer to this example as $x > -\dfrac{2}{3}$.

HOW TO   Solve: $-4 < 6x$

$$-4 < 6x$$

$$\dfrac{-4}{6} < \dfrac{6x}{6}$$ • **Divide each side of the inequality by 6.**

$$-\dfrac{2}{3} < x$$ • **Simplify:** $\dfrac{-4}{6} = -\dfrac{2}{3}$ **.**

Example 3 Solve $-7x > 14$ and graph the solution set.

Solution

$$-7x > 14$$

$$\frac{-7x}{-7} < \frac{14}{-7} \quad \bullet \text{ Divide by } -7.$$

$$x < -2$$

You Try It 3 Solve $-3x > -9$ and graph the solution set.

Your solution

Example 4 Solve: $-\dfrac{5}{8}x \le \dfrac{5}{12}$

Solution

$$-\frac{5}{8}x \le \frac{5}{12}$$

$$-\frac{8}{5}\left(-\frac{5}{8}x\right) \ge -\frac{8}{5}\left(\frac{5}{12}\right) \quad \bullet \text{ Multiply by } -\frac{8}{5}.$$

$$x \ge -\frac{2}{3}$$

You Try It 4 Solve: $-\dfrac{3}{4}x \ge 18$

Your solution

Objective C To solve application problems

Example 5

A student must have at least 450 points out of 500 points on five tests to receive an A in a course. One student's results on the first four tests were 94, 87, 77, and 95. What scores on the last test will enable this student to receive an A in the course?

Strategy
To find the scores, write and solve an inequality using N to represent the possible scores on the last test.

Solution

Total number of points on the five tests	is greater than or equal to	450

$$94 + 87 + 77 + 95 + N \ge 450$$

$$353 + N \ge 450 \quad \bullet \text{ Simplify.}$$

$$353 - 353 + N \ge 450 - 353 \quad \bullet \text{ Subtract 353.}$$

$$N \ge 97$$

The student's score on the last test must be greater than or equal to 97.

You Try It 5

An appliance dealer will make a profit on the sale of a television set if the cost of the new set is less than 70% of the selling price. What selling prices will enable the dealer to make a profit on a television set that costs the dealer $314?

Your strategy

Your solution

3.1 Exercises

Objective A   **To solve an inequality using the Addition Property of Inequalities**

For Exercises 1 to 8, solve the inequality and graph the solution set.

1. $x + 1 < 3$

     −5 −4 −3 −2 −1 0 1 2 3 4 5

2. $y + 2 < 2$

     −5 −4 −3 −2 −1 0 1 2 3 4 5

3. $x - 5 > -2$

     −5 −4 −3 −2 −1 0 1 2 3 4 5

4. $x - 3 > -2$

     −5 −4 −3 −2 −1 0 1 2 3 4 5

5. $7 \le n + 4$

     −5 −4 −3 −2 −1 0 1 2 3 4 5

6. $3 \le 5 + x$

     −5 −4 −3 −2 −1 0 1 2 3 4 5

7. $x - 6 \le -10$

     −5 −4 −3 −2 −1 0 1 2 3 4 5

8. $y - 8 \le -11$

     −5 −4 −3 −2 −1 0 1 2 3 4 5

For Exercises 9 to 12, write an inequality that represents the set of numbers shown in the graph.

9.

     −5 −4 −3 −2 −1 0 1 2 3 4 5

10.

     −5 −4 −3 −2 −1 0 1 2 3 4 5

11.

     −5 −4 −3 −2 −1 0 1 2 3 4 5

12.

     −5 −4 −3 −2 −1 0 1 2 3 4 5

For Exercises 13 to 42, solve.

13. $y - 3 \ge -12$

14. $x + 8 \ge -14$

15. $3x - 5 < 2x + 7$

16. $5x + 4 < 4x - 10$

17. $8x - 7 \ge 7x - 2$

18. $3n - 9 \ge 2n - 8$

19. $2x + 4 < x - 7$

20. $9x + 7 < 8x - 7$

21. $4x - 8 \le 2 + 3x$

22. $5b - 9 < 3 + 4b$

23. $6x + 4 \ge 5x - 2$

24. $7x - 3 \ge 6x - 2$

25. $2x - 12 > x - 10$

26. $3x + 9 > 2x + 7$

27. $d + \dfrac{1}{2} < \dfrac{1}{3}$

28. $x - \dfrac{3}{8} < \dfrac{5}{6}$

29. $x + \dfrac{5}{8} \geq -\dfrac{2}{3}$

30. $y + \dfrac{5}{12} \geq -\dfrac{3}{4}$

31. $x - \dfrac{3}{8} < \dfrac{1}{4}$

32. $y + \dfrac{5}{9} \leq \dfrac{5}{6}$

33. $2x - \dfrac{1}{2} < x + \dfrac{3}{4}$

34. $6x - \dfrac{1}{3} \leq 5x - \dfrac{1}{2}$

35. $3x + \dfrac{5}{8} > 2x + \dfrac{5}{6}$

36. $4b - \dfrac{7}{12} \geq 3b - \dfrac{9}{16}$

37. $3.8x < 2.8x - 3.8$

38. $1.2x < 0.2x - 7.3$

39. $x + 5.8 \leq 4.6$

40. $n - 3.82 \leq 3.95$

41. $x - 3.5 < 2.1$

42. $x - 0.23 \leq 0.47$

Objective B | **To solve an inequality using the Multiplication Property of Inequalities**

For Exercises 43 to 52, solve the inequality and graph the solution set.

43. $3x < 12$

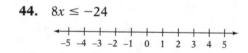

44. $8x \leq -24$

45. $15 \leq 5y$

46. $-48 < 24x$

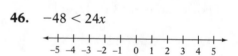

47. $16x \leq 16$

48. $3x > 0$

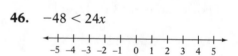

49. $-8x > 8$

50. $-2n \leq -8$

51. $-6b > 24$

52. $-4x < 8$

For Exercises 53 to 79, solve.

53. $-5y \geq 0$

54. $-3z < 0$

55. $7x > 2$

56. $6x \leq -1$

57. $2x \leq -5$

58. $\dfrac{5}{6}n < 15$

59. $\dfrac{3}{4}x < 12$

60. $\dfrac{2}{3}y \geq 4$

61. $10 \leq \dfrac{5}{8}x$

62. $4 \geq \dfrac{2}{3}x$

63. $-\dfrac{3}{7}x \leq 6$

64. $-\dfrac{2}{11}b \geq -6$

65. $-\dfrac{4}{7}x \geq -12$

66. $\dfrac{2}{3}n < \dfrac{1}{2}$

67. $-\dfrac{3}{5}x < 0$

68. $-\dfrac{2}{3}x \geq 0$

69. $-\dfrac{3}{8}x \geq \dfrac{9}{14}$

70. $-\dfrac{3}{5}x < -\dfrac{6}{7}$

71. $-\dfrac{4}{5}x < -\dfrac{8}{15}$

72. $-\dfrac{3}{4}y \geq -\dfrac{5}{8}$

73. $-\dfrac{8}{9}x \geq -\dfrac{16}{27}$

74. $1.5x \leq 6.30$

75. $2.3x \leq 5.29$

76. $-3.5d > 7.35$

77. $-0.24x > 0.768$

78. $4.25m > -34$

79. $-3.9x \geq -19.5$

Objective C   **To solve application problems**

80. Number Sense   Three-fifths of a number is greater than two-thirds. Find the smallest integer that satisfies this inequality.

81. Sports   To be eligible for a basketball tournament, a basketball team must win at least 60% of its remaining games. If the team has 17 games remaining, how many games must the team win to qualify for the tournament?

82. Taxes   To avoid a tax penalty, at least 90% of a self-employed person's total annual income tax liability must be paid in estimated tax payments during the year. What amount of income tax must a person with an annual income tax liability of $3500 pay in estimated tax payments?

83. **Recycling** A service organization will receive a bonus of $200 for collecting more than 1850 lb of aluminum cans during its four collection drives. On the first three drives, the organization collected 505 lb, 493 lb, and 412 lb. How many pounds of cans must the organization collect on the fourth drive to receive the bonus?

84. **Software Development** Computer software engineers are fond of saying that software takes at least twice as long to develop as they think it will. According to that saying, how many hours will it take to develop a software product that an engineer thinks can be finished in 50 h?

85. **Health** A government agency recommends a minimum daily allowance of vitamin C of 60 mg. How many additional milligrams of vitamin C does a person who has already drunk a glass of orange juice with 10 mg of vitamin C need in order to satisfy the recommended daily allowance?

86. **Grading** To pass a course with a B grade, a student must have an average of 80 points on five tests. The student's grades on the first four tests were 75, 83, 86, and 78. What scores can the student receive on the fifth test to earn a B grade?

87. **Grading** A professor scores all tests with a maximum of 100 points. To earn an A grade in this course, a student must have an average of 92 on four tests. One student's grades on the first three tests were 89, 86, and 90. Can this student earn an A grade?

88. **Health** A health official recommends a maximum cholesterol level of 200 units. How many units must a patient with a cholesterol level of 275 units reduce her cholesterol level to satisfy the recommended maximum level?

APPLYING THE CONCEPTS

For Exercises 89 to 94, given that $a > b$ and that a and b are real numbers, determine for which real numbers c the statement is true. Use set-builder notation to write the answer.

89. $ac > bc$

90. $ac < bc$

91. $a + c > b + c$

92. $a + c < b + c$

93. $\dfrac{a}{c} > \dfrac{b}{c}$

94. $\dfrac{a}{c} < \dfrac{b}{c}$

95. ✏ In your own words, state the Addition Property of Inequalities.

96. ✏ In your own words, state the Multiplication Property of Inequalities.

3.2 General Inequalities

Objective A   To solve general inequalities

Solving an inequality frequently requires application of both the Addition and the Multiplication Properties of Inequalities.

HOW TO   Solve: $4y - 3 \geq 6y + 5$

$$4y - 3 \geq 6y + 5$$
$$4y - 6y - 3 \geq 6y - 6y + 5$$ • Subtract **6y** from each side of the inequality.
$$-2y - 3 \geq 5$$ • Simplify.
$$-2y - 3 + 3 \geq 5 + 3$$ • Add 3 to each side of the inequality.
$$-2y \geq 8$$ • Simplify.
$$\frac{-2y}{-2} \leq \frac{8}{-2}$$ • Divide each side of the inequality by −2. Because −2 is a negative number, the inequality symbol must be reversed.
$$y \leq -4$$

When an inequality contains parentheses, one of the steps in solving the inequality requires the use of the Distributive Property.

HOW TO   Solve: $-2(x - 7) > 3 - 4(2x - 3)$

$$-2(x - 7) > 3 - 4(2x - 3)$$
$$-2x + 14 > 3 - 8x + 12$$ • Use the Distributive Property to remove parentheses.
$$-2x + 14 > -8x + 15$$ • Simplify.
$$-2x + 8x + 14 > -8x + 8x + 15$$ • Add **8x** to each side of the inequality.
$$6x + 14 > 15$$ • Simplify.
$$6x + 14 - 14 > 15 - 14$$ • Subtract 14 from each side of the inequality.
$$6x > 1$$ • Simplify.
$$\frac{6x}{6} > \frac{1}{6}$$ • Divide each side of the inequality by 6.
$$x > \frac{1}{6}$$

Example 1   Solve: $7x - 3 \leq 3x + 17$

Solution
$$7x - 3 \leq 3x + 17$$
$$7x - 3x - 3 \leq 3x - 3x + 17$$ • Subtract **3x**.
$$4x - 3 \leq 17$$
$$4x - 3 + 3 \leq 17 + 3$$ • Add 3.
$$4x \leq 20$$
$$\frac{4x}{4} \leq \frac{20}{4}$$ • Divide by 4.
$$x \leq 5$$

You Try It 1   Solve: $5 - 4x > 9 - 8x$

Your solution

Example 2

Solve: $3(3 - 2x) \geq -5x - 2(3 - x)$

Solution

$$3(3 - 2x) \geq -5x - 2(3 - x)$$
$$9 - 6x \geq -5x - 6 + 2x \quad \bullet \text{ Distributive Property}$$
$$9 - 6x \geq -3x - 6$$
$$9 - 6x + 3x \geq -3x + 3x - 6 \quad \bullet \text{ Add } 3x.$$
$$9 - 3x \geq -6$$
$$9 - 9 - 3x \geq -6 - 9 \quad \bullet \text{ Subtract 9.}$$
$$-3x \geq -15$$
$$\frac{-3x}{-3} \leq \frac{-15}{-3} \quad \bullet \text{ Divide by } -3.$$
$$x \leq 5$$

You Try It 2

Solve: $8 - 4(3x + 5) \leq 6(x - 8)$

Your solution

Objective B   **To solve application problems**

Example 3

A rectangle is 10 ft wide and $(2x + 4)$ ft long. Express as an integer the maximum length of the rectangle when the area is less than 200 ft². (The area of a rectangle is equal to its length times its width.)

Strategy

To find the maximum length:

- Replace the variables in the area formula by the given values and solve for x.
- Replace the variable in the expression $2x + 4$ with the value found for x.

Solution

Length times width	is less than	200 ft²

$$10(2x + 4) < 200$$
$$20x + 40 < 200 \quad \bullet \text{ Distributive Property}$$
$$20x + 40 - 40 < 200 - 40 \quad \bullet \text{ Subtract 40.}$$
$$20x < 160$$
$$\frac{20x}{20} < \frac{160}{20} \quad \bullet \text{ Divide by 20.}$$
$$x < 8$$

The length is $(2x + 4)$ ft. Because $x < 8$, $2x + 4 < 2(8) + 4 = 20$. Therefore, the length is less than 20 ft. The maximum length is 19 ft.

You Try It 3

Company A rents cars for $8 a day and $.10 for every mile driven. Company B rents cars for $10 a day and $.08 per mile driven. You want to rent a car for 1 week. What is the maximum number of miles you can drive a Company A car if it is to cost you less than a Company B car?

Your strategy

Your solution

3.2 Exercises

Objective A   To solve general inequalities

For Exercises 1 to 20, solve.

1. $4x - 8 < 2x$

2. $7x - 4 < 3x$

3. $2x - 8 > 4x$

4. $3y + 2 > 7y$

5. $8 - 3x \le 5x$

6. $10 - 3x \le 7x$

7. $3x + 2 > 5x - 8$

8. $2n - 9 \ge 5n + 4$

9. $5x - 2 < 3x - 2$

10. $8x - 9 > 3x - 9$

11. $0.1(180 + x) > x$

12. $x > 0.2(50 + x)$

13. $2(2y - 5) \le 3(5 - 2y)$

14. $2(5x - 8) \le 7(x - 3)$

15. $5(2 - x) > 3(2x - 5)$

16. $4(3d - 1) > 3(2 - 5d)$

17. $4 - 3(3 - n) \le 3(2 - 5n)$

18. $15 - 5(3 - 2x) \le 4(x - 3)$

19. $2x - 3(x - 4) \ge 4 - 2(x - 7)$

20. $4 + 2(3 - 2y) \le 4(3y - 5) - 6y$

Objective B   To solve application problems

21. **Wages**   The sales agent for a jewelry company is offered a flat monthly salary of $3200 or a salary of $1000 plus an 11% commission on the selling price of each item sold by the agent. If the agent chooses the $3200, what dollar amount does the agent expect to sell in 1 month?

22. **Sports**   A baseball player is offered an annual salary of $200,000 or a base salary of $100,000 plus a bonus of $1000 for each hit over 100 hits. How many hits must the baseball player make to earn more than $200,000?

23. **Comparing Services** A computer bulletin board service charges a flat fee of $10 per month or a fee of $4 per month plus $.10 for each minute the service is used. How many minutes must a person use this service to exceed $10?

24. **Comparing Services** A site licensing fee for a computer program is $1500. Paying this fee allows the company to use the program at any computer terminal within the company. Alternatively, the company can choose to pay $200 for each individual computer it has. How many individual computers must a company have for the site license to be more economical for the company?

25. **Health** For a product to be labeled orange juice, a state agency requires that at least 80% of the drink be real orange juice. How many ounces of artificial flavors can be added to 32 oz of real orange juice and have it still be legal to label the drink orange juice?

26. **Health** Grade A hamburger cannot contain more than 20% fat. How much fat can a butcher mix with 300 lb of lean meat to meet the 20% requirement?

27. **Transportation** A shuttle service taking skiers to a ski area charges $8 per person each way. Four skiers are debating whether to take the shuttle bus or rent a car for $45 plus $.25 per mile. Assuming that the skiers will share the cost of the car and that they want the least expensive method of transportation, find how far away the ski area is if they choose the shuttle service.

APPLYING THE CONCEPTS

28. Determine whether the statement is always true, sometimes true, or never true, given that a, b, and c are real numbers.
    a. If $a > b$, then $-a > -b$.
    b. If $a < b$, then $ac < bc$.
    c. If $a > b$, then $a + c > b + c$.

    d. If $a \neq 0$, $b \neq 0$, and $a > b$, then $\frac{1}{a} > \frac{1}{b}$.

For Exercises 29 and 30, use the roster method to list the set of positive integers that are solutions of the inequality.

29. $7 - 2b \leq 15 - 5b$

30. $-6(2 - d) \geq 4d - 9$

For Exercises 31 and 32, use the roster method to list the set of integers that are common to the solution sets of the two inequalities.

31. $5x - 12 \leq x + 8$
    $3x - 4 \geq 2 + x$

32. $3(x + 2) > 9x - 2$
    $4(x + 5) > 3(x + 6)$

33. Determine the solution set of $2 - 3(x + 4) < 5 - 3x$.

34. Determine the solution set of $3x + 2(x - 1) > 5(x + 1)$.

3.3 Graphing Linear Inequalities

Objective A   **To graph an inequality in two variables**

Point of Interest

Linear inequalities play an important role in applied mathematics. They are used in a branch of mathematics called *linear programming*, which was developed during World War II to solve problems in supplying the Air Force with the machine parts necessary to keep planes flying. Today, its applications extend to many other disciplines.

Study Tip

Be sure to do all you need to do in order to be successful at graphing linear inequalities: Read through the introductory material, work through the How To examples, study the paired examples, do the You Try Its, and check your solutions against those in the back of the book. See *AIM for Success.*

The graph of the linear equation $y = x - 2$ separates a plane into three sets:

The set of points on the line
The set of points above the line
The set of points below the line

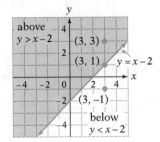

The point $(3, 1)$ is a solution of $y = x - 2$.

$$\frac{y = x - 2}{1 \mid 3 - 2}$$
$$1 = 1$$

The point $(3, 3)$ is a solution of $y > x - 2$.

$$\frac{y > x - 2}{3 \mid 3 - 2}$$
$$3 > 1$$

Any point above the line is a solution of $y > x - 2$.

The point $(3, -1)$ is a solution of $y < x - 2$.

$$\frac{y < x - 2}{-1 \mid 3 - 2}$$
$$-1 < 1$$

Any point below the line is a solution of $y < x - 2$.

The solution set of $y = x - 2$ is all points on the line. The solution set of $y > x - 2$ is all points above the line. The solution set of $y < x - 2$ is all points below the line. The solution set of an inequality in two variables is a **half-plane.**

The following illustrates the procedure for graphing a linear inequality.

HOW TO   Graph the solution set of $2x + 3y \le 6$.

Solve the inequality for y.
$$2x + 3y \le 6$$
$$2x - 2x + 3y \le -2x + 6$$
$$3y \le -2x + 6$$
$$\frac{3y}{3} \le \frac{-2x + 6}{3}$$
$$y \le -\frac{2}{3}x + 2$$

- **Subtract 2x from each side.**
- **Simplify.**

- **Divide each side by 3.**

- **Simplify.**

Change the inequality to an equality and graph $y = -\frac{2}{3}x + 2$. If the inequality is $\ge$ or $\le$, the line is in the solution set and is shown by a solid line. If the inequality is $>$ or $<$, the line is not a part of the solution set and is shown by a dotted line.

If the inequality is $>$ or $\ge$, shade the upper half-plane. If the inequality is $<$ or $\le$, shade the lower half-plane.

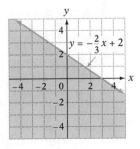

Example 1

Graph the solution set of $3x + y > -2$.

Solution

$$3x + y > -2$$
$$3x - 3x + y > -3x - 2 \quad \bullet \text{ Subtract } 3x.$$
$$y > -3x - 2$$

Graph $y = -3x - 2$ as a dotted line.
Shade the upper half-plane.

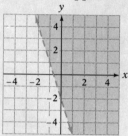

You Try It 1

Graph the solution set of $x - 3y < 2$.

Your solution

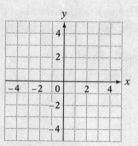

Example 2

Graph the solution set of $2x - y \geq 2$.

Solution

$$2x - y \geq 2$$
$$2x - 2x - y \geq -2x + 2 \quad \bullet \text{ Subtract } 2x.$$
$$-y \geq -2x + 2$$
$$-1(-y) \leq -1(-2x + 2) \quad \bullet \text{ Multiply by } -1.$$
$$y \leq 2x - 2$$

Graph $y = 2x - 2$ as a solid line.
Shade the lower half-plane.

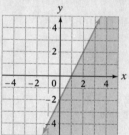

You Try It 2

Graph the solution set of $2x - 4y \leq 8$.

Your solution

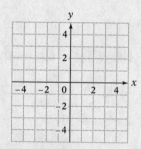

Example 3

Graph the solution set of $y > -1$.

Solution

Graph $y = -1$ as a dotted line.
Shade the upper half-plane.

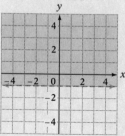

You Try It 3

Graph the solution set of $x < 3$.

Your solution

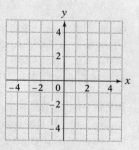

3.3 Exercises

Objective A   **To graph an inequality in two variables**

For Exercises 1 to 18, graph the solution set of the inequality.

1. $x + y > 4$

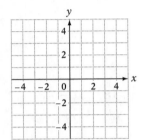

2. $x - y > -3$

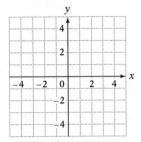

3. $2x - y < -3$

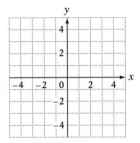

4. $3x - y < 9$

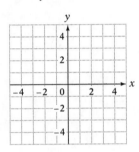

5. $2x + y \geq 4$

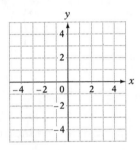

6. $3x + y \geq 6$

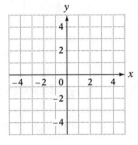

7. $y \leq -2$

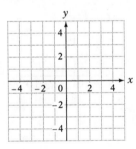

8. $y > 3$

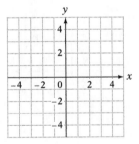

9. $3x - 2y < 8$

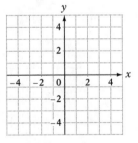

10. $5x + 4y > 4$

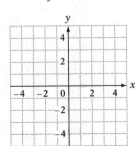

11. $-3x - 4y \geq 4$

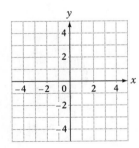

12. $-5x - 2y \geq 8$

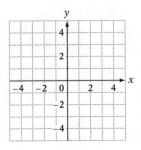

13. $6x + 5y \leq -10$

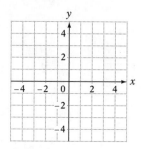

14. $2x + 2y \leq -4$

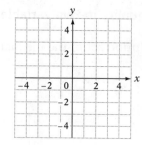

15. $-4x + 3y < -12$

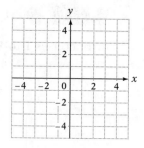

16. $-4x + 5y < 15$

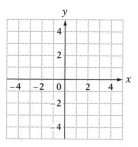

17. $-2x + 3y \leq 6$

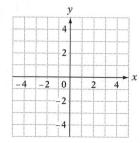

18. $3x - 4y > 12$

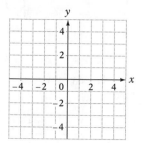

APPLYING THE CONCEPTS

For Exercises 19 to 21, graph the solution set of the inequality.

19. $\dfrac{x}{4} + \dfrac{y}{2} > 1$

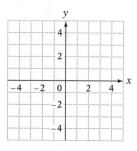

20. $2x - 3(y + 1) > y - (4 - x)$

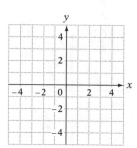

21. $4y - 2(x + 1) \geq 3(y - 1) + 3$

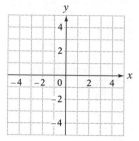

For Exercises 22 to 24, write the inequality given its graph.

22.

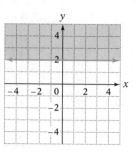

23.

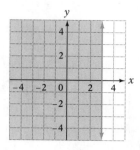

24.

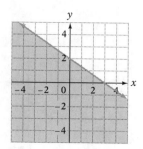

Focus on Problem Solving

Graphing Data

Graphs are very useful in displaying data. By studying a graph, we can reach various conclusions about the data.

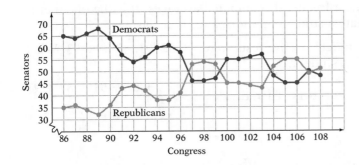

The double-line graph at the left shows the number of Democrats and the number of Republicans in the U.S. Senate for the 86th Congress (1959–1961) through the 108th Congress (2003–2005).

1. How many Democratic and how many Republican senators were in the 90th Congress?

2. In which Congress was the difference between the numbers of Democrats and Republicans the greatest?

3. In which Congress did the majority first change from Democratic to Republican?

4. Between which two Congresses did the number of Republican senators increase but the number of Democratic senators remain the same?

5. In what percent of the Congresses did the number of Democrats exceed the number of Republicans? Round to the nearest tenth.

6. In which Congresses were there a greater number of Republican senators than Democratic senators?

Year	DVD Recorders	DVD Players
2003	1	59
2004	2	62
2005	9	60
2006	18	54
2007	28	44
2008	44	34

The table at the left, based on data from Allied Business Intelligence, Inc., shows the actual and projected number (in millions) of worldwide shipments of DVD players and DVD recorders for the years 2003 through 2008.

7. Make a double-line graph of the data.

8. In which year will the number of DVD recorders shipped first exceed the number of DVD players shipped?

9. Based on this data, for the year 2009, would you expect the difference between the number of DVD recorders shipped and the number of DVD players shipped to be less than or greater than the same number in 2008?

Projects and Group Activities

Mean and Standard Deviation

An automotive engineer tests the miles-per-gallon ratings of 15 cars and records the results as follows:

25 22 21 27 25 35 29 31 25 26 21 39 34 32 28

The **mean** of the data is the sum of the measurements divided by the number of measurements. The symbol for the mean is $\bar{x}$.

$$\text{Mean} = \bar{x} = \frac{\text{sum of all data values}}{\text{number of data values}}$$

Projects and Group Activities

To find the mean for the data on p. 469, add the numbers and then divide by 15.

$$\bar{x} = \frac{25 + 22 + 21 + 27 + 25 + 35 + 29 + 31 + 25 + 26 + 21 + 39 + 34 + 32 + 28}{15}$$

$$= \frac{420}{15} = 28$$

The mean number of miles per gallon for the 15 cars tested was 28 mi/gal.

The mean is one of the most frequently computed averages. It is the one that is commonly used to calculate a student's performance in a class.

The scores for a history student on five tests were 78, 82, 91, 87, and 93. What was the mean score for this student?

To find the mean, add the numbers. Then divide by 5.

$$\bar{x} = \frac{78 + 82 + 91 + 87 + 93}{5}$$

$$= \frac{431}{5} = 86.2$$

The mean score for the history student was 86.2.

Consider two students, each of whom has taken five exams.

Scores for student A

84	86	83	85	87

$$\bar{x} = \frac{84 + 86 + 83 + 85 + 87}{5} = \frac{425}{5} = 85$$

The mean for student A is 85.

Scores for student B

90	75	94	68	98

$$\bar{x} = \frac{90 + 75 + 94 + 68 + 98}{5} = \frac{425}{5} = 85$$

The mean for student B is 85.

For each of these students, the mean (average) for the five exams is 85. However, student A has a more consistent record of scores than student B. One way to measure the consistency, or "clustering" near the mean, of data is to use the **standard deviation.**

To calculate the standard deviation:

Step 1. Sum the squares of the differences between each value of the data and the mean.

Step 2. Divide the result in Step 1 by the number of items in the set of data.

Step 3. Take the square root of the result in Step 2.

The calculation for student A is shown at the right.

Step 1:

x	$x - \bar{x}$	$(x - \bar{x})^2$
84	$84 - 85$	$(-1)^2 = 1$
86	$86 - 85$	$1^2 = 1$
83	$83 - 85$	$(-2)^2 = 4$
85	$85 - 85$	$0^2 = 0$
87	$87 - 85$	$2^2 = 4$
		Total = 10

The symbol for standard deviation is the lowercase Greek letter *sigma*, σ.

Step 2: $\frac{10}{5} = 2$

Step 3: $\sigma = \sqrt{2} \approx 1.414$

The standard deviation for student A's scores is approximately 1.414.

Following a similar procedure for student B shows that the standard deviation for student B's scores is approximately 11.524. Because the standard deviation of student B's scores is greater than that of student A's (11.524 > 1.414), student B's scores are not as consistent as those of student A.

1. The weights in ounces of 6 newborn infants were recorded by a hospital. The weights were 96, 105, 84, 90, 102, and 99. Find the standard deviation of the weights. Round to the nearest hundredth.

2. The numbers of rooms occupied in a hotel on 6 consecutive days were 234, 321, 222, 246, 312, and 396. Find the standard deviation for the number of rooms occupied. Round to the nearest hundredth.

3. Seven coins were tossed 100 times. The numbers of heads recorded for each coin were 56, 63, 49, 50, 48, 53, and 52. Find the standard deviation of the number of heads. Round to the nearest hundredth.

4. The temperatures, in degrees Fahrenheit, for 11 consecutive days at a desert resort were 95°, 98°, 98°, 104°, 97°, 100°, 96°, 97°, 108°, 93°, and 104°. For the same days, temperatures in Antarctica were 27°, 28°, 28°, 30°, 28°, 27°, 30°, 25°, 24°, 26°, and 21°. Which location has the greater standard deviation of temperatures?

5. The scores for 5 college basketball games were 56, 68, 60, 72, and 64. The scores for 5 professional basketball games were 106, 118, 110, 122, and 114. Which scores have the greater standard deviation?

6. The weights in pounds of the 5-man front line of a college football team are 210, 245, 220, 230, and 225. Find the standard deviation of the weights. Round to the nearest hundredth.

7. One student received test scores of 85, 92, 86, and 89. A second student received scores of 90, 97, 91, and 94 (exactly 5 points more on each test). Are the means of the two students the same? If not, what is the relationship between the means of the two students? Are the standard deviations of the scores of the two students the same? If not, what is the relationship between the standard deviations of the scores of the two students?

8. Grade-point average (GPA) is a *weighted* mean. It is called a weighted mean because a grade in a 5-unit course has more influence on your GPA than a grade in a 2-unit course. GPA is calculated by multiplying the numerical equivalent of each grade by the number of units, adding those products, and then dividing by the total number of units. Calculate your GPA for the last quarter or semester.

9. If you average 40 mph for 1 h and then 50 mph for 1 h, is your average speed $\frac{40 + 50}{2} = 45$ mph? Why or why not?

10. A company is negotiating with its employees the terms of a raise in salary. One proposal would add $500 a year to each employee's salary. The second proposal would give each employee a 4% raise. Explain how each of these proposals would affect the current mean and standard deviation of salaries for the company.

Chapter Summary

Key Words

The *empty set* or *null set*, written ∅, is the set that contains no elements.

The *union* of two sets, written $A \cup B$, is the set that contains the elements of A and the elements of B.

The *intersection* of two sets, written $A \cap B$, is the set that contains the elements that are common to both A and B.

Set-builder notation uses a rule to describe the elements of a set.

An *inequality* is an expression that contains the symbol $<$, $>$, $\leq$, or $\geq$. The *solution set of an inequality* is a set of numbers each element of which, when substituted for the variable, results in a true inequality. The solution set of an inequality can be graphed on a number line.

The solution set of a linear inequality in two variables is a *half-plane*.

Examples

The set of cars that can travel faster than 1000 mph is an empty set.

Let $A = \{2, 4, 6, 8\}$ and $B = \{0, 1, 2, 3, 4\}$. Then $A \cup B = \{0, 1, 2, 3, 4, 6, 8\}$.

Let $A = \{2, 4, 6, 8\}$ and $B = \{0, 1, 2, 3, 4\}$. Then $A \cap B = \{2, 4\}$.

Using set-builder notation, the set of real numbers greater than 2 is written $\{x | x > 2, x \in \text{real numbers}\}$.

$3x - 1 < 5$ is an inequality. The solution set of $3x - 1 < 5$ is $\{x | x < 2\}$. The graph of the solution set is ![number line graph from -5 to 5].

The solution set of $3x + 4y \geq 12$ is the half-plane shown at the right.

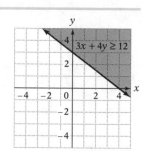

Essential Rules and Procedures

Addition Property of Inequalities
The same term can be added to each side of an inequality without changing the solution set of the inequality.

$\quad$ If $a > b$, then $a + c > b + c$.
$\quad$ If $a < b$, then $a + c < b + c$.

Multiplication Property of Inequalities
Each side of an inequality can be multiplied by the same positive number without changing the solution set of the inequality.

$\quad$ If $a > b$ and $c > 0$, then $ac > bc$.
$\quad$ If $a < b$ and $c > 0$, then $ac < bc$.

If each side of an inequality is multiplied by the same negative number and the inequality symbol is reversed, then the solution set of the inequality is not changed.

$\quad$ If $a > b$ and $c < 0$, then $ac < bc$.
$\quad$ If $a < b$ and $c < 0$, then $ac > bc$.

Examples

$$x - 3 < -7$$
$$x - 3 + 3 < -7 + 3$$
$$x < -4$$

$$4x > -8$$
$$\frac{4x}{4} > \frac{-8}{4}$$
$$x > -2$$

$$-2x < 6$$
$$\frac{-2x}{-2} > \frac{6}{-2}$$
$$x > -3$$

Chapter Review Exercises

1. Solve: $2x - 3 > x + 15$

2. Find $A \cap B$, given $A = \{0, 2, 4, 6, 8\}$ and $B = \{-2, -4\}$.

3. Use set-builder notation to write the set of odd integers greater than -8.

4. Find $A \cup B$, given $A = \{6, 8, 10\}$ and $B = \{2, 4, 6\}$.

5. Use the roster method to write the set of odd positive integers less than 8.

6. Solve: $12 - 4(x - 1) \leq 5(x - 4)$

7. Graph: $\{x \mid x > 3\}$

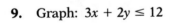

8. Solve: $3x + 4 \geq -8$

9. Graph: $3x + 2y \leq 12$

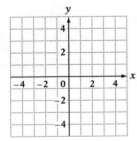

10. Graph: $5x + 2y < 6$

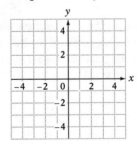

11. Use set-builder notation to write the set of real numbers greater than 3.

12. Solve and graph the solution set of $x - 3 > -1$.

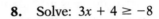

13. Find $A \cap B$, given $A = \{1, 5, 9, 13\}$ and $B = \{1, 3, 5, 7, 9\}$.

14. Graph: $\{x \mid x < 2\} \cup \{x \mid x > 5\}$

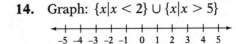

Chapter Review

15. Graph: $\{x | x > -1\} \cap \{x | x \le 2\}$

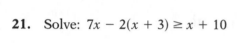

16. Solve: $-15x \le 45$

17. Solve: $6x - 9 < 4x + 3(x + 3)$

18. Solve: $5 - 4(x + 9) > 11(12x - 9)$

19. Solve: $-\dfrac{3}{4}x > \dfrac{2}{3}$

20. Graph: $2x - 3y < 9$

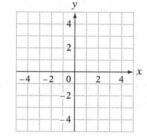

21. Solve: $7x - 2(x + 3) \ge x + 10$

22. **Floral Delivery**   Florist A charges a \$3 delivery fee plus \$21 per bouquet delivered. Florist B charges a \$15 delivery fee plus \$18 per bouquet delivered. A church wants to supply each resident of a small nursing home with a bouquet for Grandparents Day. Find the number of residents of the nursing home if using florist B is more economical than using florist A.

23. **Landscaping**   The width of a rectangular garden is 12 ft. The length of the garden is $(3x + 5)$ ft. Express as an integer the minimum length of the garden when the area is greater than 276 ft². (The area of a rectangle is equal to its length times its width.)

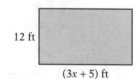

12 ft

$(3x + 5)$ ft

24. **Number Sense**   Six less than a number is greater than twenty-five. Find the smallest integer that will satisfy the inequality.

25. **Grading**   A student's grades on five sociology tests were 68, 82, 90, 73, and 95. What is the lowest score the student can receive on the next test and still be able to attain a minimum of 480 points?

Chapter Test

1. Graph: $\{x \,|\, x < 5\} \cap \{x \,|\, x > 0\}$

   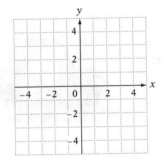

2. Use set-builder notation to write the set of the positive integers less than 50.

3. Use the roster method to write the set of the even positive integers between 3 and 9.

4. Solve: $3(2x - 5) \geq 8x - 9$

5. Solve: $x + \dfrac{1}{2} > \dfrac{5}{8}$

6. Graph: $\{x \,|\, x > -2\}$

7. Solve: $5 - 3x > 8$

8. Use set-builder notation to write the set of the real numbers greater than -23.

9. Graph the solution set of $3x + y > 4$.

   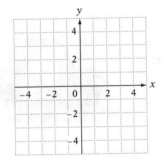

10. Graph the solution set of $4x - 5y \geq 15$.

    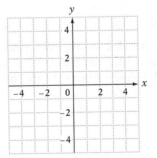

11. Find $A \cap B$, given $A = \{6, 8, 10, 12\}$ and $B = \{12, 14, 16\}$.

12. Solve and graph the solution set of $4 + x < 1$.

    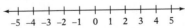

13. Solve: $-\dfrac{3}{8}x \leq 5$

14. Solve: $6x - 3(2 - 3x) < 4(2x - 7)$

15. Solve and graph the solution set of $\frac{2}{3}x \geq 2$.

-5 -4 -3 -2 -1 0 1 2 3 4 5

16. Solve: $2x - 7 \leq 6x + 9$

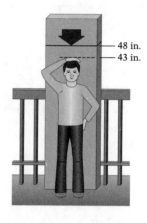

17. Safety To ride a certain roller coaster at an amusement park, a person must be at least 48 in. tall. How many inches must a child who is 43 in. tall grow to be eligible to ride the roller coaster?

18. Geometry A rectangle is 15 ft long and $(2x - 4)$ ft wide. Express as an integer the maximum width of the rectangle if the area is less than 180 ft². (The area of a rectangle is equal to its length times its width.)

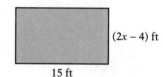

19. Machining A ball bearing for a rotary engine must have a circumference between 0.1220 in. and 0.1240 in. What are the allowable diameters for the bearing? Round to the nearest ten-thousandth. Recall that $C = \pi d$.

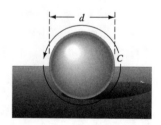

20. Wages A stockbroker receives a monthly salary that is the greater of $2500 or $1000 plus 2% of the total value of all stock transactions the broker processes during the month. What dollar amounts of transactions did the broker process in a month for which the broker's salary was $2500?

chapter

4 Ratio and Proportion

Egypt is known around the world for its enormous pyramids, built thousands of years ago by the pharaohs. This photo shows the pyramids at Giza. The largest pyramid at Giza, called the Great Pyramid, dates to approximately 2600 B.C. and is the oldest of the Seven Ancient Wonders of the World. It is also the only ancient wonder that still survives today. Some historians believe that some of the pyramids of Egypt incorporate a special ratio called the golden ratio. The ratio of the slant height to a side of the base of the pyramid reflects the golden ratio.

Need help? For online student resources, such as section quizzes, visit this textbook's website at **math.college.hmco.com/students.**

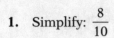

1. Simplify: $\dfrac{8}{10}$

2. Simplify: $\dfrac{450}{650 + 250}$

3. Write as a decimal: $\dfrac{372}{15}$

4. Which is greater, 4×33 or 62×2?

5. Complete: $? \times 5 = 20$

GO FIGURE • • •

Luis, Kim, Reggie, and Dave are standing in line. Dave is not first. Kim is between Luis and Reggie. Luis is between Dave and Kim. Give the order in which the men are standing.

4.1

Ratio

Objective A | **To write the ratio of two quantities in simplest form**

Quantities such as 3 feet, 12 cents, and 9 cars are number quantities written with units.

3 feet
12 cents
9 cars
↑
units

These are some examples of units. Shirts, dollars, trees, miles, and gallons are further examples.

A **ratio** is a comparison of two quantities that have the *same* units. This comparison can be written three different ways:

1. As a fraction
2. As two numbers separated by a colon (:)
3. As two numbers separated by the word *to*

The ratio of the lengths of two boards, one 8 feet long and the other 10 feet long, can be written as

1. $\dfrac{8 \text{ feet}}{10 \text{ feet}} = \dfrac{8}{10} = \dfrac{4}{5}$
2. 8 feet : 10 feet = 8 : 10 = 4 : 5
3. 8 feet to 10 feet = 8 to 10 = 4 to 5

Writing the **simplest form of a ratio** means writing it so that the two numbers have no common factor other than 1.

This ratio means that the smaller board is $\dfrac{4}{5}$ the length of the longer board.

Example 1

Write the comparison $6 to $8 as a ratio in simplest form using a fraction, a colon, and the word *to*.

Solution
$\dfrac{\$6}{\$8} = \dfrac{6}{8} = \dfrac{3}{4}$
$6 : $8 = 6 : 8 = 3 : 4
$6 to $8 = 6 to 8 = 3 to 4

You Try It 1

Write the comparison 20 pounds to 24 pounds as a ratio in simplest form using a fraction, a colon, and the word *to*.

Your solution

Example 2

Write the comparison 18 quarts to 6 quarts as a ratio in simplest form using a fraction, a colon, and the word *to*.

Solution
$\dfrac{18 \text{ quarts}}{6 \text{ quarts}} = \dfrac{18}{6} = \dfrac{3}{1}$
18 quarts : 6 quarts =
18 : 6 = 3 : 1
18 quarts to 6 quarts =
18 to 6 = 3 to 1

You Try It 2

Write the comparison 64 miles to 8 miles as a ratio in simplest form using a fraction, a colon, and the word *to*.

Your solution

Objective B **To solve application problems**

Use the table below for Example 3 and You Try It 3.

Board Feet of Wood at a Lumber Store			
Pine	Ash	Oak	Cedar
20,000	18,000	10,000	12,000

Example 3

Find, as a fraction in simplest form, the ratio of the number of board feet of pine to the number of board feet of oak.

Strategy
To find the ratio, write the ratio of board feet of pine (20,000) to board feet of oak (10,000) in simplest form.

Solution
$$\frac{20{,}000}{10{,}000} = \frac{2}{1}$$

The ratio is $\frac{2}{1}$.

You Try It 3

Find, as a fraction in simplest form, the ratio of the number of board feet of cedar to the number of board feet of ash.

Your strategy

Your solution

Example 4

The cost of building a patio cover was $500 for labor and $700 for materials. What, as a fraction in simplest form, is the ratio of the cost of materials to the total cost for labor and materials?

Strategy
To find the ratio, write the ratio of the cost of materials ($700) to the total cost ($500 + $700) in simplest form.

Solution
$$\frac{\$700}{\$500 + \$700} = \frac{700}{1200} = \frac{7}{12}$$

The ratio is $\frac{7}{12}$.

You Try It 4

A company spends $60,000 a month for television advertising and $45,000 a month for radio advertising. What, as a fraction in simplest form, is the ratio of the cost of radio advertising to the total cost of radio and television advertising?

Your strategy

Your solution

4.1 Exercises

Objective A   To write the ratio of two quantities in simplest form

For Exercises 1 to 24, write the comparison as a ratio in simplest form using a fraction, a colon (:), and the word *to*.

1. 3 pints to 15 pints

2. 6 pounds to 8 pounds

3. $40 to $20

4. 10 feet to 2 feet

5. 3 miles to 8 miles

6. 2 hours to 3 hours

7. 37 hours to 24 hours

8. 29 inches to 12 inches

9. 6 minutes to 6 minutes

10. 8 days to 12 days

11. 35 cents to 50 cents

12. 28 inches to 36 inches

13. 30 minutes to 60 minutes

14. 25 cents to 100 cents

15. 32 ounces to 16 ounces

16. 12 quarts to 4 quarts

17. 3 cups to 4 cups

18. 6 years to 7 years

19. $5 to $3

20. 30 yards to 12 yards

21. 12 quarts to 18 quarts

22. 20 gallons to 28 gallons

23. 14 days to 7 days

24. 9 feet to 3 feet

Objective B   To solve application problems

For Exercises 25 to 28, write ratios in simplest form using a fraction.

Family Budget						
Housing	Food	Transportation	Taxes	Utilities	Miscellaneous	Total
$1600	$800	$600	$700	$300	$800	$4800

25. Budgets   Use the table to find the ratio of housing cost to total expenses.

26. Budgets   Use the table to find the ratio of food cost to total expenses.

27. Budgets   Use the table to find the ratio of utilities cost to food cost.

28. Budgets   Use the table to find the ratio of transportation cost to housing cost.

29. 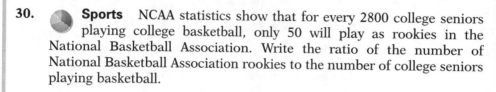 **Sports** National Collegiate Athletic Association (NCAA) statistics show that for every 154,000 high school seniors playing basketball, only 4000 will play college basketball as first-year students. Write the ratio of the number of first-year students playing college basketball to the number of high school seniors playing basketball.

30. 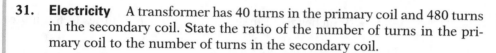 **Sports** NCAA statistics show that for every 2800 college seniors playing college basketball, only 50 will play as rookies in the National Basketball Association. Write the ratio of the number of National Basketball Association rookies to the number of college seniors playing basketball.

31. **Electricity** A transformer has 40 turns in the primary coil and 480 turns in the secondary coil. State the ratio of the number of turns in the primary coil to the number of turns in the secondary coil.

32. **Consumerism** Rita Sterling bought a computer system for $2400. Five years later she sold the computer for $900. Find the ratio of the amount she received for the computer to the cost of the computer.

Primary coil   Secondary coil

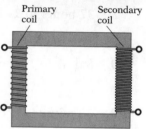

33. **Real Estate** A house with an original value of $90,000 increased in value to $110,000 in 5 years.
a. Find the increase in the value of the house.
b. What is the ratio of the increase in value to the original value of the house?

34. **Energy Prices** The price of gasoline jumped from $1.35 to $1.62 in 1 year.
a. What was the increase in the price per gallon?
b. What is the ratio of the increase in price to the original price?

APPLYING THE CONCEPTS

Banking A bank uses the ratio of a borrower's total monthly debts to the borrower's total monthly income to determine the maximum monthly payment for a potential homeowner. This ratio is called the debt–income ratio. Use the homeowner's debt–income table at the right for Exercises 35 and 36.

Income	Debt
$5500	$1200
$450	$300
$250	$450
	$250

35. Compute the debt–income ratio for the potential homeowner.

36. Central Trust Bank will make a loan to a customer whose debt–income ratio is less than $\frac{1}{3}$. Will the potential homeowner qualify? Explain your answer.

37. **Banking** To make a home loan, First National Bank requires a debt–income ratio that is less than $\frac{2}{5}$. Would the home-owner whose debt–income table is given at the right qualify for a loan using these standards? Explain.

Income		Debt	
Salary	$3400	Mortgage	$1800
Interest	$83	Property tax	$104
Rent	$650	Insurance	$35
Dividends	$34	Liabilities	$120
		Credit card	$234
		Car loan	$197

38. 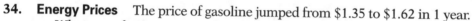 Is the value of a ratio always less than 1? Explain.

4.2   Rates

Objective A   **To write rates**

Point of Interest

Listed below are rates at which some crimes are committed in our nation.

Crime	*Every*
Larceny	4 seconds
Burglary	14 seconds
Robbery	60 seconds
Rape	6 minutes
Murder	31 minutes

A **rate** is a comparison of two quantities that have *different* units. A rate is written as a fraction.

A distance runner ran 26 miles in 4 hours. The distance-to-time rate is written

$$\frac{26 \text{ miles}}{4 \text{ hours}} = \frac{13 \text{ miles}}{2 \text{ hours}}$$

Writing the **simplest form of a rate** means writing it so that the two numbers that form the rate have no common factor other than 1.

Example 1   Write "6 roof supports for every 9 feet" as a rate in simplest form.

Solution $\frac{6 \text{ supports}}{9 \text{ feet}} = \frac{2 \text{ supports}}{3 \text{ feet}}$

You Try It 1   Write "15 pounds of fertilizer for 12 trees" as a rate in simplest form.

Your solution

Objective B   **To write unit rates**

Point of Interest

According to a Gallup Poll, women see doctors more often than men do. On average, men visit the doctor 3.8 times per year, whereas women go to the doctor 5.8 times per year.

A **unit rate** is a rate in which the number in the denominator is 1.

$\frac{\$3.25}{1 \text{ pound}}$ or \$3.25/pound is read "\$3.25 per pound."

To find unit rates, divide the number in the numerator of the rate by the number in the denominator of the rate.

A car traveled 344 miles on 16 gallons of gasoline. To find the miles per gallon (unit rate), divide the numerator of the rate by the denominator of the rate.

$\frac{344 \text{ miles}}{16 \text{ gallons}}$ is the rate.

$16)\overline{344.0}^{\,21.5}$ 21.5 miles/gallon is the unit rate.

Example 2   Write "300 feet in 8 seconds" as a unit rate.

Solution $\frac{300 \text{ feet}}{8 \text{ seconds}}$ $8)\overline{300.0}^{\,37.5}$

37.5 feet/second

You Try It 2   Write "260 miles in 8 hours" as a unit rate.

Your solution

Denver Airport

Objective C   **To solve application problems**

HOW TO The table at the right shows air fares for some routes in the continental United States. Find the cost per mile for the four routes in order to determine the most expensive route and the least expensive route on the basis of mileage flown.

Long Routes	Miles	Fare
New York–Los Angeles	2475	$683
San Francisco–Dallas	1464	$536
Denver–Pittsburgh	1302	$525
Minneapolis–Hartford	1050	$483

Strategy
To find the cost per mile, divide the fare by the miles flown for each route. Compare the costs per mile to determine the most expensive and least expensive routes per mile.

Integrating Technology

To calculate the costs per mile using a calculator, perform four divisions:

683 ÷ 2475 =
536 ÷ 1464 =
525 ÷ 1302 =
483 ÷ 1050 =

In each case, round the number in the display to the nearest hundredth.

Solution

New York–Los Angeles $\dfrac{683}{2475} \approx 0.28$

San Francisco–Dallas $\dfrac{536}{1464} \approx 0.37$

Denver–Pittsburgh $\dfrac{525}{1302} \approx 0.40$

Minneapolis–Hartford $\dfrac{483}{1050} = 0.46$

$0.28 < 0.37 < 0.40 < 0.46$

The Minneapolis–Hartford route is the most expensive per mile, and the New York–Los Angeles route is the least expensive per mile.

Example 3

As an investor, Jung Ho purchased 100 shares of stock for $1500. One year later, Jung sold the 100 shares for $1800. What was his profit per share?

Strategy
To find Jung's profit per share:

• Find the total profit by subtracting the original cost ($1500) from the selling price ($1800).

• Find the profit per share (unit rate) by dividing the total profit by the number of shares of stock (100).

Solution
$1800 - 1500 = 300$

$300 \div 100 = 3$

Jung Ho's profit was $3/share.

You Try It 3

Erik Peltier, a jeweler, purchased 5 ounces of gold for $1625. Later, he sold the 5 ounces for $1720. What was Erik's profit per ounce?

Your strategy

Your solution

4.2 Exercises

Objective A   **To write rates**

For Exercises 1 to 10, write each phrase as a rate in simplest form.

1. 3 pounds of meat for 4 people

2. 30 ounces in 24 glasses

3. $80 for 12 boards

4. 84 cents for 3 bars of soap

5. 300 miles on 15 gallons

6. 88 feet in 8 seconds

7. 20 children in 8 families

8. 48 leaves on 9 plants

9. 16 gallons in 2 hours

10. 25 ounces in 5 minutes

Objective B   **To write unit rates**

For Exercises 11 to 24, write each phrase as a unit rate.

11. 10 feet in 4 seconds

12. 816 miles in 6 days

13. $3900 earned in 4 weeks

14. $51,000 earned in 12 months

15. 1100 trees planted on 10 acres

16. 3750 words on 15 pages

17. $131.88 earned in 7 hours

18. $315.70 earned in 22 hours

19. 628.8 miles in 12 hours

20. 388.8 miles in 8 hours

21. 344.4 miles on 12.3 gallons of gasoline

22. 409.4 miles on 11.5 gallons of gasoline

23. $349.80 for 212 pounds

24. $11.05 for 3.4 pounds

Objective C   **To solve application problems**

25. **Fuel Efficiency**   An automobile was driven 326.6 miles on 11.5 gallons of gas. Find the number of miles driven per gallon of gas.

26. **Travel**   You drive 246.6 miles in 4.5 hours. Find the number of miles you drove per hour.

27.   **Fuel Efficiency**   The Saturn-5 rocket uses 534,000 gallons of fuel in 2.5 minutes. How much fuel does the rocket use per minute?

28. Manufacturing Assume that Regency Computer produced 5000 zip disks for $26,536.32. Of the disks made, 122 did not meet company standards.
   a. How many disks did meet company standards?
   b. What was the cost per disk for those disks that met company standards?

29. Consumerism The Pierre family purchased a 250-pound side of beef for $365.75 and had it packaged. During the packaging, 75 pounds of beef were discarded as waste.
   a. How many pounds of beef were packaged?
   b. What was the cost per pound for the packaged beef?

30. Advertising In 2003, the average price of a 30-second commercial during the sitcom *Friends* was $455,700. (*Source: Time*) Find the price per second.

31. The Film Industry During filming, an IMAX camera uses 65-mm film at a rate of 5.6 feet per second.
   a. At what rate per minute does the camera go through film?
   b. At what rate does it use a 500-foot roll of 65-mm film? Round to the nearest second.

32. Demography The table at the right shows the population and area of three countries. The population density of a country is the number of people per square mile.
   a. Which country has the least population density?
   b. How many more people per square mile are there in India than in the United States? Round to the nearest whole number.

Country	Population	Area (in square miles)
Australia	19,547,000	2,968,000
India	1,045,845,000	1,269,000
United States	291,929,000	3,619,000

Another application of rates is in the area of international trade. Suppose a company in Canada purchases a shipment of sneakers from an American company. The Canadian company must exchange Canadian dollars for U.S. dollars in order to pay for the order. The number of Canadian dollars that are equivalent to 1 U.S. dollar is called the **exchange rate**.

33. Exchange Rates The table at the right shows the exchange rates per U.S. dollar for three foreign countries and for the euro at the time of this writing.
   a. How many euros would be paid for an order of American computer hardware costing $120,000?
   b. Calculate the cost, in Japanese yen, of an American car costing $34,000.

Exchange Rates per U.S. Dollar	
Australian Dollar	1.545
Canadian Dollar	1.386
Japanese Yen	117.000
The Euro	0.9103

APPLYING THE CONCEPTS

34. Compensation You have a choice of receiving a wage of $34,000 per year, $2840 per month, $650 per week, or $18 per hour. Which pay choice would you take? Assume a 40-hour week with 52 weeks per year.

35. The price–earnings ratio of a company's stock is one measure used by stock market analysts to assess the financial well-being of the company. Explain the meaning of the price–earnings ratio.

4.3 Proportions

Objective A   **To determine whether a proportion is true**

A **proportion** is an expression of the equality of two ratios or rates.

$$\frac{50 \text{ miles}}{4 \text{ gallons}} = \frac{25 \text{ miles}}{2 \text{ gallons}}$$

Note that the units of the numerators are the same and the units of the denominators are the same.

$$\frac{3}{6} = \frac{1}{2}$$

This is the equality of two ratios.

A proportion is **true** if the fractions are equal when written in lowest terms.

In any true proportion, the **cross products** are equal.

HOW TO   Is $\frac{2}{3} = \frac{8}{12}$ a true proportion?

$$\frac{2}{3} \diagdown\diagup \frac{8}{12} \begin{array}{l} \rightarrow 93 \times 8 = 24 \\ \rightarrow 2 \times 12 = 24 \end{array}$$

The cross products *are* equal.

$\frac{2}{3} = \frac{8}{12}$ is a true proportion.

A proportion is **not true** if the fractions are not equal when reduced to lowest terms.

If the cross products are not equal, then the proportion is not true.

HOW TO   Is $\frac{4}{5} = \frac{8}{9}$ a true proportion?

$$\frac{4}{5} \diagdown\diagup \frac{8}{9} \begin{array}{l} \rightarrow 5 \times 8 = 40 \\ \rightarrow 4 \times 9 = 36 \end{array}$$

The cross products *are not* equal.

$\frac{4}{5} = \frac{8}{9}$ is not a true proportion.

Example 1   Is $\frac{5}{8} = \frac{10}{16}$ a true proportion?

Solution

$$\frac{5}{8} \diagdown\diagup \frac{10}{16} \begin{array}{l} \rightarrow 8 \times 10 = 80 \\ \rightarrow 5 \times 16 = 80 \end{array}$$

The cross products are equal.
The proportion is true.

You Try It 1   Is $\frac{6}{10} = \frac{9}{15}$ a true proportion?

Your solution

Example 2   Is $\frac{62 \text{ miles}}{4 \text{ gallons}} = \frac{33 \text{ miles}}{2 \text{ gallons}}$ a true proportion?

Solution

$$\frac{62}{4} \diagdown\diagup \frac{33}{2} \begin{array}{l} \rightarrow 4 \times 33 = 132 \\ \rightarrow 62 \times 2 = 124 \end{array}$$

The cross products are not equal.
The proportion is not true.

You Try It 2   Is $\frac{\$32}{6 \text{ hours}} = \frac{\$90}{8 \text{ hours}}$ a true proportion?

Your solution

Objective B   **To solve proportions**

Sometimes one of the numbers in a proportion is unknown. In this case, it is necessary to *solve* the proportion.

To **solve a proportion**, find a number to replace the unknown so that the proportion is true.

HOW TO Solve: $\dfrac{9}{6} = \dfrac{3}{n}$

$$\dfrac{9}{6} = \dfrac{3}{n}$$

$9 \times n = 6 \times 3$ • Find the cross products.

$9 \times n = 18$

$n = 18 \div 9$ • Think of $9 \times n = 18$ as $9\overline{)18}$.

$n = 2$

Check:

$$\dfrac{9}{6} \bowtie \dfrac{3}{2} \quad\begin{array}{l} 6 \times 3 = 18 \\ 9 \times 2 = 18 \end{array}$$

Example 3   Solve $\dfrac{n}{12} = \dfrac{25}{60}$ and check.

Solution

$\begin{aligned} n \times 60 &= 12 \times 25 \\ n \times 60 &= 300 \\ n &= 300 \div 60 \\ n &= 5 \end{aligned}$ • Find the cross products. Then solve for *n.*

Check:

$$\dfrac{5}{12} \bowtie \dfrac{25}{60} \quad\begin{array}{l} 12 \times 25 = 300 \\ 15 \times 60 = 300 \end{array}$$

You Try It 3   Solve $\dfrac{n}{14} = \dfrac{3}{7}$ and check.

Your solution

Example 4   Solve $\dfrac{4}{9} = \dfrac{n}{16}$. Round to the nearest tenth.

Solution

$\begin{aligned} 4 \times 16 &= 9 \times n \\ 64 &= 9 \times n \\ 64 \div 9 &= n \\ 7.1 &\approx n \end{aligned}$ • Find the cross products. Then solve for *n.*

Note: A rounded answer is an approximation. Therefore, the answer to a check will not be exact.

You Try It 4   Solve $\dfrac{5}{7} = \dfrac{n}{20}$. Round to the nearest tenth.

Your solution

Example 5   Solve $\frac{28}{52} = \frac{7}{n}$ and check.

Solution $28 \times n = 52 \times 7$ • **Find the cross**
$28 \times n = 364$ **products. Then**
$\quad\quad n = 364 \div 28$ **solve for n.**
$\quad\quad n = 13$

Check:

$\frac{28}{52} \underset{}{\diagdown\!\!\!\diagup} \frac{7}{13} \quad\begin{matrix}\rightarrow 952 \times 7 = 364 \\ \rightarrow 28 \times 13 = 364\end{matrix}$

You Try It 5   Solve $\frac{15}{20} = \frac{12}{n}$ and check.

Your solution

Example 6   Solve $\frac{15}{n} = \frac{8}{3}$. Round to the nearest hundredth.

Solution $15 \times 3 = n \times 8$
$\quad\quad 45 = n \times 8$
$45 \div 8 = n$
$\quad 5.63 \approx n$

You Try It 6   Solve $\frac{12}{n} = \frac{7}{4}$. Round to the nearest hundredth.

Your solution

Example 7   Solve $\frac{n}{9} = \frac{3}{1}$ and check.

Solution $n \times 1 = 9 \times 3$
$n \times 1 = 27$
$\quad\quad n = 27 \div 1$
$\quad\quad n = 27$

Check:

$\frac{27}{9} \underset{}{\diagdown\!\!\!\diagup} \frac{3}{1} \quad\begin{matrix}\rightarrow 99 \times 3 = 27 \\ \rightarrow 27 \times 1 = 27\end{matrix}$

You Try It 7   Solve $\frac{n}{12} = \frac{4}{1}$ and check.

Your solution

Objective C   **To solve application problems**

The application problems in this objective require you to write and solve a proportion. When setting up a proportion, remember to keep the same units in the numerator and the same units in the denominator.

Example 8

The dosage of a certain medication is 2 ounces for every 50 pounds of body weight. How many ounces of this medication are required for a person who weighs 175 pounds?

Strategy

To find the number of ounces of medication for a person weighing 175 pounds, write and solve a proportion using n to represent the number of ounces of medication for a 175-pound person.

Solution

$$\frac{2 \text{ ounces}}{50 \text{ pounds}} = \frac{n \text{ ounces}}{175 \text{ pounds}}$$

$$2 \times 175 = 50 \times n$$
$$350 = 50 \times n$$
$$350 \div 50 = n$$
$$7 = n$$

• The unit "ounces" is in the numerator. The unit "pounds" is in the denominator.

A 175-pound person requires 7 ounces of medication.

You Try It 8

Three tablespoons of a liquid plant fertilizer are to be added to every 4 gallons of water. How many tablespoons of fertilizer are required for 10 gallons of water?

Your strategy

Your solution

Example 9

A mason determines that 9 cement blocks are required for a retaining wall 2 feet long. At this rate, how many cement blocks are required for a retaining wall that is 24 feet long?

Strategy

To find the number of cement blocks for a retaining wall 24 feet long, write and solve a proportion using n to represent the number of blocks required.

Solution

$$\frac{9 \text{ cement blocks}}{2 \text{ feet}} = \frac{n \text{ cement blocks}}{24 \text{ feet}}$$

$$9 \times 24 = 2 \times n$$
$$216 = 2 \times n$$
$$216 \div 2 = n$$
$$108 = n$$

A 24-foot retaining wall requires 108 cement blocks.

You Try It 9

Twenty-four jars can be packed in 6 identical boxes. At this rate, how many jars can be packed in 15 boxes?

Your strategy

Your solution

4.3 Exercises

Objective A   **To determine whether a proportion is true**

For Exercises 1 to 24, determine whether the proportion is true or not true.

1. $\dfrac{4}{8} = \dfrac{10}{20}$

2. $\dfrac{39}{48} = \dfrac{13}{16}$

3. $\dfrac{7}{8} = \dfrac{11}{12}$

4. $\dfrac{15}{7} = \dfrac{17}{8}$

5. $\dfrac{27}{8} = \dfrac{9}{4}$

6. $\dfrac{3}{18} = \dfrac{4}{19}$

7. $\dfrac{45}{135} = \dfrac{3}{9}$

8. $\dfrac{3}{4} = \dfrac{54}{72}$

9. $\dfrac{16}{3} = \dfrac{48}{9}$

10. $\dfrac{15}{5} = \dfrac{3}{1}$

11. $\dfrac{7}{40} = \dfrac{7}{8}$

12. $\dfrac{9}{7} = \dfrac{6}{5}$

13. $\dfrac{50 \text{ miles}}{2 \text{ gallons}} = \dfrac{25 \text{ miles}}{1 \text{ gallon}}$

14. $\dfrac{16 \text{ feet}}{10 \text{ seconds}} = \dfrac{24 \text{ feet}}{15 \text{ seconds}}$

15. $\dfrac{6 \text{ minutes}}{5 \text{ cents}} = \dfrac{30 \text{ minutes}}{25 \text{ cents}}$

16. $\dfrac{16 \text{ pounds}}{12 \text{ days}} = \dfrac{20 \text{ pounds}}{14 \text{ days}}$

17. $\dfrac{\$15}{4 \text{ pounds}} = \dfrac{\$45}{12 \text{ pounds}}$

18. $\dfrac{270 \text{ trees}}{6 \text{ acres}} = \dfrac{90 \text{ trees}}{2 \text{ acres}}$

19. $\dfrac{300 \text{ feet}}{4 \text{ rolls}} = \dfrac{450 \text{ feet}}{7 \text{ rolls}}$

20. $\dfrac{1 \text{ gallon}}{4 \text{ quarts}} = \dfrac{7 \text{ gallons}}{28 \text{ quarts}}$

21. $\dfrac{\$65}{5 \text{ days}} = \dfrac{\$26}{2 \text{ days}}$

22. $\dfrac{80 \text{ miles}}{2 \text{ hours}} = \dfrac{110 \text{ miles}}{3 \text{ hours}}$

23. $\dfrac{7 \text{ tiles}}{4 \text{ feet}} = \dfrac{42 \text{ tiles}}{20 \text{ feet}}$

24. $\dfrac{15 \text{ feet}}{3 \text{ yards}} = \dfrac{90 \text{ feet}}{18 \text{ yards}}$

Objective B   **To solve proportions**

For Exercises 25 to 52, solve. Round to the nearest hundredth, if necessary.

25. $\dfrac{n}{4} = \dfrac{6}{8}$ 　　　 **26.** $\dfrac{n}{7} = \dfrac{9}{21}$ 　　　 **27.** $\dfrac{12}{18} = \dfrac{n}{9}$ 　　　 **28.** $\dfrac{7}{21} = \dfrac{35}{n}$

29. $\dfrac{6}{n} = \dfrac{24}{36}$ 　　　 **30.** $\dfrac{3}{n} = \dfrac{15}{10}$ 　　　 **31.** $\dfrac{n}{45} = \dfrac{17}{135}$ 　　　 **32.** $\dfrac{9}{4} = \dfrac{18}{n}$

33. $\dfrac{n}{6} = \dfrac{2}{3}$ 　　　 **34.** $\dfrac{5}{12} = \dfrac{n}{144}$ 　　　 **35.** $\dfrac{n}{5} = \dfrac{7}{8}$ 　　　 **36.** $\dfrac{4}{n} = \dfrac{9}{5}$

37. $\dfrac{n}{11} = \dfrac{32}{4}$ 　　　 **38.** $\dfrac{3}{4} = \dfrac{8}{n}$ 　　　 **39.** $\dfrac{5}{12} = \dfrac{n}{8}$ 　　　 **40.** $\dfrac{36}{20} = \dfrac{12}{n}$

41. $\dfrac{n}{15} = \dfrac{21}{12}$ 　　　 **42.** $\dfrac{40}{n} = \dfrac{15}{8}$ 　　　 **43.** $\dfrac{32}{n} = \dfrac{1}{3}$ 　　　 **44.** $\dfrac{5}{8} = \dfrac{42}{n}$

45. $\dfrac{18}{11} = \dfrac{16}{n}$ 　　　 **46.** $\dfrac{25}{4} = \dfrac{n}{12}$ 　　　 **47.** $\dfrac{28}{8} = \dfrac{12}{n}$ 　　　 **48.** $\dfrac{n}{30} = \dfrac{65}{120}$

49. $\dfrac{0.3}{5.6} = \dfrac{n}{25}$ 　　　 **50.** $\dfrac{1.3}{16} = \dfrac{n}{30}$ 　　　 **51.** $\dfrac{0.7}{9.8} = \dfrac{3.6}{n}$ 　　　 **52.** $\dfrac{1.9}{7} = \dfrac{13}{n}$

Objective C   **To solve application problems**

For Exercises 53 to 71, solve. Round to the nearest hundredth.

53. **Nutrition**   A 6-ounce package of Puffed Wheat contains 600 calories. How many calories are in a 0.5-ounce serving of the cereal?

54. **Fuel Efficiency**   A car travels 70.5 miles on 3 gallons of gas. Find the distance that the car can travel on 14 gallons of gas.

55. **Landscaping**   Ron Stokes uses 2 pounds of fertilizer for every 100 square feet of lawn for landscape maintenance. At this rate, how many pounds of fertilizer did he use on a lawn that measures 3500 square feet?

56. **Gardening**   A nursery prepares a liquid plant food by adding 1 gallon of water for each 2 ounces of plant food. At this rate, how many gallons of water are required for 25 ounces of plant food?

57. **Manufacturing**   A manufacturer of baseball equipment makes 4 aluminum bats for every 15 bats made from wood. On a day when 100 aluminum bats are made, how many wooden bats are produced?

58. **Masonry**   A brick wall 20 feet in length contains 1040 bricks. At the same rate, how many bricks would it take to build a wall 48 feet in length?

59. **Cartography**   The scale on the map at the right is "1.25 inches equals 10 miles." Find the distance between Carlsbad and Del Mar, which are 2 inches apart on the map.

60. **Architecture**   The scale on the plans for a new house is "1 inch equals 3 feet." Find the width and the length of a room that measures 5 inches by 8 inches on the drawing.

61. **Medicine**   The dosage for a medication is $\frac{1}{3}$ ounce for every 40 pounds of body weight. At this rate, how many ounces of medication should a physician prescribe for a patient who weighs 150 pounds? Write the answer as a decimal.

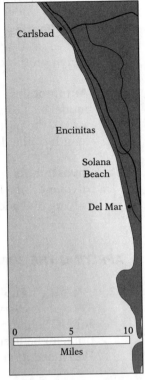

62. **Banking**   A bank requires a monthly payment of $33.45 on a $2500 loan. At the same rate, find the monthly payment on a $10,000 loan.

63. **Elections**   A pre-election survey showed that 2 out of every 3 eligible voters would cast ballots in the county election. At this rate, how many people in a county of 240,000 eligible voters would vote in the election?

64. **Interior Design**   A paint manufacturer suggests using 1 gallon of paint for every 400 square feet of a wall. At this rate, how many gallons of paint would be required for a room that has 1400 square feet of wall?

65. **Insurance**   A 60-year-old male can obtain $10,000 of life insurance for $35.35 per month. At this rate, what is the monthly cost of $50,000 of life insurance?

66. **Manufacturing**   Suppose a computer chip manufacturer knows from experience that in an average production run of 2000 circuit boards, 60 will be defective. How many defective circuit boards can be expected from a run of 25,000 circuit boards?

67. Investments You own 240 shares of stock in a computer company. The company declares a stock split of 5 shares for every 3 owned. How many shares of stock will you own after the stock split?

68. Computers The director of data processing at a college estimates that the ratio of student time to administrative time on a certain computer is 3:2. During a month in which the computer was used 200 hours for administration, how many hours was it used by students?

69. ● **Physics** The ratio of weight on the moon to weight on Earth is 1:6. If a bowling ball weighs 16 pounds on Earth, what would it weigh on the moon?

70. Automobiles When engineers designed a new car, they first built a model of the car. The ratio of the size of a part on the model to the actual size of the part is 2:5. If a door is 1.3 feet long on the model, what is the length of the door on the car?

71. Investments Carlos Capasso owns 50 shares of Texas Utilities that pay dividends of $153. At this rate, what dividend would Carlos receive after buying 300 additional shares of Texas Utilities?

APPLYING THE CONCEPTS

72. ● ◆ **Publishing** In January 2003, *USA Today* reported that for every 100 copies of *Dr. Atkins' New Diet Revolution* sold, John Grisham's *The Summons* sold 7.3 copies. Explain how a proportion can be used to determine the number of copies of *Dr. Atkins' New Diet Revolution* sold given the number of copies of *The Summons* sold.

73. ● ◆ **Social Security** According to the Social Security Administration, the numbers of workers per retiree in the future are expected to be as given in the table below.

Year	2010	2020	2030	2040
Number of workers per retiree	3.1	2.5	2.1	2.0

Why is the shrinking number of workers per retiree of importance to the Social Security Administration?

74. ● ◆ **Compensation** In June 2002, *Time* magazine reported, "In 1980 the average CEO made 40 times the pay of the average factory worker; by 2000 the ratio had climbed to 531 to 1." What information would you need to know in order to determine the average pay of a CEO in 2000? With that information, how would you calculate the average pay of a CEO in 2000?

75. ◆ **Elections** A survey of voters in a city claimed that 2 people of every 5 who voted cast a ballot in favor of city amendment A and that 3 people of every 4 who voted cast a ballot against amendment A. Is this possible? Explain your answer.

76. ◆ Write a word problem that requires solving a proportion to find the answer.

Focus on Problem Solving

Looking for a Pattern

A very useful problem-solving strategy is looking for a pattern.

Problem   A legend says that a peasant invented the game of chess and gave it to a very rich king as a present. The king so enjoyed the game that he gave the peasant the choice of anything in the kingdom. The peasant's request was simple: "Place one grain of wheat on the first square, 2 grains on the second square, 4 grains on the third square, 8 on the fourth square, and continue doubling the number of grains until the last square of the chessboard is reached." How many grains of wheat must the king give the peasant?

Solution   A chessboard consists of 64 squares. To find the total number of grains of wheat on the 64 squares, we begin by looking at the amount of wheat on the first few squares.

Square 1	Square 2	Square 3	Square 4	Square 5	Square 6	Square 7	Square 8
1	2	4	8	16	32	64	128
1	3	7	15	31	63	127	255

The bottom row of numbers represents the sum of the number of grains of wheat up to and including that square. For instance, the number of grains of wheat on the first 7 squares is $1 + 2 + 4 + 8 + 16 + 32 + 64 = 127$.

One pattern to observe is that the number of grains of wheat on a square can be expressed as a power of 2.

The number of grains on square $n = 2^{n-1}$.

For example, the number of grains on square $7 = 2^{7-1} = 2^6 = 64$.

A second pattern of interest is that **the number *below* a square** (the total number of grains up to and including that square) **is 1 less than the number of grains of wheat *on the next* square.** For example, the number *below* square 7 is 1 less than the number *on* square 8 ($128 - 1 = 127$). From this observation, the number of grains of wheat on the first 8 squares is the number on square 8 (128) plus 1 less than the number on square 8 (127): The total number of grains of wheat on the first 8 squares is $128 + 127 = 255$.

From this observation,

$$\begin{array}{c} \text{Number of grains of} \\ \text{wheat on the chessboard} \end{array} = \begin{array}{c} \text{number of grains} \\ \text{on square 64} \end{array} + \begin{array}{c} \text{1 less than the number} \\ \text{of grains on square 64} \end{array}$$

$$= 2^{64-1} + (2^{64-1} - 1)$$

$$= 2^{63} + 2^{63} - 1 \approx 18{,}000{,}000{,}000{,}000{,}000{,}000$$

To give you an idea of the magnitude of this number, this is more wheat than has been produced in the world since chess was invented.

The same king decided to have a banquet in the long banquet room of the palace to celebrate the invention of chess. The king had 50 square tables, and each table could seat only one person on each side. The king pushed the tables together to form one long banquet table. How many people could sit at this table? *Hint:* Try constructing a pattern by using 2 tables, 3 tables, and 4 tables.

Projects and Group Activities

The Golden Ratio   There are certain designs that have been repeated over and over in both art and architecture. One of these involves the **golden rectangle.**

A golden rectangle is drawn at the right. Begin with a square that measures, say, 2 inches on a side. Let *A* be the midpoint of a side (halfway between two corners). Now measure the distance from *A* to *B*. Place this length along the bottom of the square, starting at *A*. The resulting rectangle is a golden rectangle.

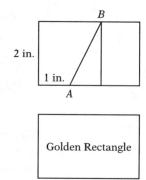

Golden Rectangle

The **golden ratio** is the ratio of the length of the golden rectangle to its width. If you have drawn the rectangle following the procedure above, you will find that the golden ratio is approximately 1.6 to 1.

The golden ratio appears in many different situations. Some historians claim that some of the great pyramids of Egypt are based on the golden ratio. The drawing at the right shows the Pyramid of Giza, which dates from approximately 2600 B.C. The ratio of the height to a side of the base is approximately 1.6 to 1.

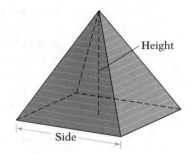

1. There are instances of the golden rectangle in the Mona Lisa painted by Leonardo da Vinci. Do some research on this painting and write a few paragraphs summarizing your findings.

2. What do 3 × 5 and 5 × 8 index cards have to do with the golden rectangle?

3. What does the United Nations Building in New York City have to do with the golden rectangle?

4. When was the Parthenon in Athens, Greece, built? What does the front of that building have to do with the golden rectangle?

Drawing the Floor Plans for a Building

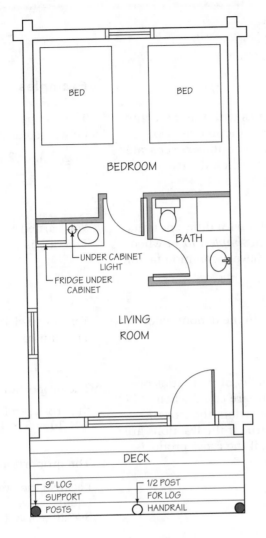

BED

BED

BEDROOM

BATH

UNDER CABINET LIGHT

FRIDGE UNDER CABINET

LIVING ROOM

DECK

9" LOG SUPPORT POSTS

1/2 POST FOR LOG HANDRAIL

The drawing at the left is a sketch of the floor plan for a cabin at a resort in the mountains of Utah. The measurements are missing. Assume that you are the architect and will finish the drawing. You will have to decide the size of the rooms and put in the measurements to scale.

Design a cabin that you would like to own. Select a scale and draw all the rooms to scale.

If you are interested in architecture, visit an architect who is using CAD (computer-aided design) to create a floor plan. Computer technology has revolutionized the field of architectural design.

The U.S. House of Representatives

The framers of the Constitution decided to use a ratio to determine the number of representatives from each state. It was determined that each state would have one representative for every 30,000 citizens, with a minimum of one representative. Congress has changed this ratio over the years, and we now have 435 representatives.

Find the number of representatives from your state. Determine the ratio of citizens to representatives. Also do this for the most populous state and for the least populous state.

 You might consider getting information on the number of representatives for each state and the populations of different states via the Internet.

Chapter Summary

Key Words

Examples

A *ratio* is the comparison of two quantities with the same units. A ratio can be written in three ways: as a fraction, as two numbers separated by a colon (:), or as two numbers separated by the word *to*. A ratio is in *simplest form* when the two numbers do not have a common factor.

The comparison 16 to 24 ounces can be written as a ratio in simplest form as $\frac{2}{3}$, 2:3, or 2 to 3.

A *rate* is the comparison of two quantities with different units. A rate is written as a fraction. A rate is in *simplest form* when the numbers that form the ratio do not have a common factor.

You earned $63 for working 6 hours. The rate is written in simplest form as $\frac{\$21}{2 \text{ hours}}$.

A *unit rate* is a rate in which the number in the denominator is 1.

You traveled 144 miles in 3 hours. The unit rate is 48 miles per hour.

A *proportion* is an expression of the equality of two ratios or rates. A proportion is true if the fractions are equal when written in lowest terms; in any true proportion, the *cross products* are equal. A proportion is not true if the fractions are not equal when written in lowest terms; if the cross products are not equal, the proportion is not true.

The proportion $\frac{3}{5} = \frac{12}{20}$ is true because the cross products are equal: $3 \times 20 = 5 \times 12$.

The proportion $\frac{3}{4} = \frac{12}{20}$ is not true because the cross products are not equal: $3 \times 20 \neq 4 \times 12$.

Essential Rules and Procedures

Examples

To find a unit rate, divide the number in the numerator of the rate by the number in the denominator of the rate.

You earned $41 for working 4 hours.
$$41 \div 4 = 10.25$$
The unit rate is $10.25/hour.

To solve a proportion, find a number to replace the unknown so that the proportion is true.

$$\frac{6}{24} = \frac{9}{n}$$
$6 \times n = 24 \times 9$ • **Find the cross products.**
$6 \times n = 216$
$n = 216 \div 6$
$n = 36$

To set up a proportion, keep the same units in the numerator and the same units in the denominator.

Three machines fill 5 cereal boxes per minute. How many boxes can 8 machines fill per minute?

$$\frac{3 \text{ machines}}{5 \text{ cereal boxes}} = \frac{8 \text{ machines}}{n \text{ cereal boxes}}$$

Chapter Review Exercises

1. Determine whether the proportion is true or not true.
$$\frac{2}{9} = \frac{10}{45}$$

2. Write the comparison 32 dollars to 80 dollars as a ratio in simplest form using a fraction, a colon (:), and the word *to*.

3. Write "250 miles in 4 hours" as a unit rate.

4. Determine whether the proportion is true or not true.
$$\frac{8}{15} = \frac{32}{60}$$

5. Solve the proportion.
$$\frac{16}{n} = \frac{4}{17}$$

6. Write "$300 earned in 40 hours" as a unit rate.

7. Write "$8.75 for 5 pounds" as a unit rate.

8. Write the comparison 8 feet to 28 feet as a ratio in simplest form using a fraction, a colon (:), and the word *to*.

9. Solve the proportion.
$$\frac{n}{8} = \frac{9}{2}$$

10. Solve the proportion. Round to the nearest hundredth.
$$\frac{18}{35} = \frac{10}{n}$$

11. Write the comparison 6 inches to 15 inches as a ratio in simplest form using a fraction, a colon (:), and the word *to*.

12. Determine whether the proportion is true or not true.
$$\frac{3}{8} = \frac{10}{24}$$

13. Write "$15 in 4 hours" as a rate in simplest form.

14. Write "326.4 miles on 12 gallons" as a unit rate.

15. Write the comparison 12 days to 12 days as a ratio in simplest form using a fraction, a colon (:), and the word *to*.

16. Determine whether the proportion is true or not true.
$$\frac{5}{7} = \frac{25}{35}$$

17. Solve the proportion. Round to the nearest hundredth.

$$\frac{24}{11} = \frac{n}{30}$$

18. Write "100 miles in 3 hours" as a rate in simplest form.

19. **Business** In 5 years, the price of a calculator went from $40 to $24. What is the ratio, as a fraction in simplest form, of the decrease in price to the original price?

20. **Taxes** The property tax on a $245,000 home is $4900. At the same rate, what is the property tax on a home valued at $320,000?

21. **Meteorology** The high temperature during a 24-hour period was 84 degrees, and the low temperature was 42 degrees. Write the ratio, as a fraction in simplest form, of the high temperature to the low temperature for the 24-hour period.

22. **Manufacturing** The total cost of manufacturing 1000 cordless phones was $36,600. Of the phones made, 24 did not pass inspection. What is the cost per phone of the phones that *did* pass inspection?

23. **Masonry** A brick wall 40 feet in length contains 448 concrete blocks. At the same rate, how many blocks would it take to build a wall that is 120 feet in length?

24. **Advertising** A retail computer store spends $30,000 a year on radio advertising and $12,000 on newspaper advertising. Find the ratio, as a fraction in simplest form, of radio advertising to newspaper advertising.

25. **Consumerism** A 15-pound turkey costs $13.95. What is the cost per pound?

26. **Travel** Mahesh drove 198.8 miles in 3.5 hours. Find the average number of miles he drove per hour.

27. **Insurance** An insurance policy costs $9.87 for every $1000 of insurance. At this rate, what is the cost of $50,000 of insurance?

28. **Investments** Pascal Hollis purchased 80 shares of stock for $3580. What was the cost per share?

29. **Landscaping** Monique uses 1.5 pounds of fertilizer for every 200 square feet of lawn. How many pounds of fertilizer will she have to use on a lawn that measures 3000 square feet?

30. **Real Estate** A house had an original value of $80,000, but its value increased to $120,000 in 2 years. Find the ratio, as a fraction in simplest form, of the increase to the original value.

Chapter Test

1. Write "$46,036.80 earned in 12 months" as a unit rate.

2. Write the comparison 40 miles to 240 miles as a ratio in simplest form using a fraction, a colon (:), and the word *to*.

3. Write "18 supports for every 8 feet" as a rate in simplest form.

4. Determine whether the proportion is true or not true.
    $$\frac{40}{125} = \frac{5}{25}$$

5. Write the comparison 12 days to 8 days as a ratio in simplest form using a fraction, a colon (:), and the word *to*.

6. Solve the proportion.
    $$\frac{5}{12} = \frac{60}{n}$$

7. Write "256.2 miles on 8.4 gallons of gas" as a unit rate.

8. Write the comparison 27 dollars to 81 dollars as a ratio in simplest form using a fraction, a colon (:), and the word *to*.

9. Determine whether the proportion is true or not true.
    $$\frac{5}{14} = \frac{25}{70}$$

10. Solve the proportion.
    $$\frac{n}{18} = \frac{9}{4}$$

11. Write "$81 for 12 boards" as a rate in simplest form.

12. Write the comparison 18 feet to 30 feet as a ratio in simplest form using a fraction, a colon (:), and the word *to*.

13. **Investments**   Fifty shares of a utility stock pay a dividend of $62.50. At the same rate, what is the dividend paid on 500 shares of the utility stock?

14. **Meteorology**   The average summer temperature in a California desert is 112 degrees. In a city 100 miles away, the average summer temperature is 86 degrees. Write the ratio, as a fraction in simplest form, of the average city temperature to the average desert temperature.

15. **Travel**   A plane travels 2421 miles in 4.5 hours. Find the plane's speed in miles per hour.

16. **Physiology**   A research scientist estimates that the human body contains 88 pounds of water for every 100 pounds of body weight. At this rate, estimate the number of pounds of water in a college student who weighs 150 pounds.

17. **Business**   If 40 feet of lumber costs $69.20, what is the per-foot cost of the lumber?

18. **Medicine**   The dosage of a certain medication is $\frac{1}{4}$ ounce for every 50 pounds of body weight. How many ounces of this medication are required for a person who weighs 175 pounds? Write the answer as a decimal.

19. **Sports**   A basketball team won 20 games and lost 5 games during the season. Write, as a fraction in simplest form, the ratio of the number of games won to the total number of games played.

20. **Manufacturing**   A computer manufacturer discovers through experience that an average of 3 defective hard drives are found in every 100 hard drives manufactured. How many defective hard drives are expected to be found in the production of 1200 hard drives?

chapter

5 Percents

Everyone knows that good health depends on eating right, watching your weight, not smoking, and exercising regularly. In order to get the most out of your workout, the American College of Sports Medicine (ACSM) recommends that you know how to determine your target heart rate. Your target heart rate is the rate at which your heart should beat during any aerobic exercise, such as running, fast walking, or bicycling. Your target heart rate depends on how fit you are, so athletes have higher target heart rates than people who are more sedentary. According to the ACSM, you should reach and then maintain your target heart rate for 20 minutes or more during a workout to achieve cardiovascular fitness.

Need help? For online student resources, such as section quizzes, visit this textbook's website at **math.college.hmco.com/students**.

For Exercises 1 to 6, multiply or divide.

1. $19 \times \dfrac{1}{100}$

2. 23×0.01

3. 0.47×100

4. $0.06 \times 47{,}500$

5. $60 \div 0.015$

6. $8 \div \dfrac{1}{4}$

7. Multiply $\dfrac{5}{8} \times 100$. Write the answer as a decimal.

8. Write $\dfrac{200}{3}$ as a mixed number.

9. Divide $28 \div 16$. Write the answer as a decimal.

GO FIGURE • • •

A whole number that remains unchanged when its digits are written in reverse order is a palindrome. For example, 818 is a palindrome.

a. Find the smallest three-digit multiple of 6 that is a palindrome.

b. Many nonpalindrome numbers can be converted into palindromes: reverse the digits of the number and add the result to the original; continue until a palindrome is achieved. Using this process, what is the palindrome created from 874?

5.1 Introduction to Percents

Objective A | **To write a percent as a fraction or a decimal**

Percent means "parts of 100." In the figure at the right, there are 100 parts. Because 13 of the 100 parts are shaded, 13% of the figure is shaded. The symbol % is the **percent sign**.

In most applied problems involving percents, it is necessary either to rewrite a percent as a fraction or a decimal or to rewrite a fraction or a decimal as a percent.

To write a percent as a fraction, remove the percent sign and multiply by $\frac{1}{100}$.

$$13\% = 13 \times \frac{1}{100} = \frac{13}{100}$$

> **TAKE NOTE**
> Recall that division is defined as multiplication by the reciprocal. Therefore, multiplying by $\frac{1}{100}$ is equivalent to dividing by 100.

To write a percent as a decimal, remove the percent sign and multiply by 0.01.

$$13\% \quad = \quad 13 \times 0.01 \quad = \quad 0.13$$

> Move the decimal point two places to the left. Then remove the percent sign.

Example 1
a. Write 120% as a fraction.
b. Write 120% as a decimal.

Solution
a. $120\% = 120 \times \dfrac{1}{100} = \dfrac{120}{100}$

$\qquad = 1\dfrac{1}{5}$

b. $120\% = 120 \times 0.01 = 1.2$

Note that percents larger than 100 are greater than 1.

You Try It 1
a. Write 125% as a fraction.
b. Write 125% as a decimal.

Your solution

Example 2 Write $16\frac{2}{3}\%$ as a fraction.

Solution
$16\dfrac{2}{3}\% = 16\dfrac{2}{3} \times \dfrac{1}{100}$

$\qquad = \dfrac{50}{3} \times \dfrac{1}{100} = \dfrac{50}{300} = \dfrac{1}{6}$

You Try It 2 Write $33\frac{1}{3}\%$ as a fraction.

Your solution

Example 3 Write 0.5% as a decimal.

Solution $0.5\% = 0.5 \times 0.01 = 0.005$

You Try It 3 Write 0.25% as a decimal.

Your solution

Objective B **To write a fraction or a decimal as a percent**

A fraction or a decimal can be written as a percent by multiplying by 100%.

HOW TO Write $\frac{3}{8}$ as a percent.

$$\frac{3}{8} = \frac{3}{8} \times 100\% = \frac{3}{8} \times \frac{100}{1}\% = \frac{300}{8}\% = 37\frac{1}{2}\% \text{ or } 37.5\%$$

HOW TO Write 0.37 as a percent.

$$0.37 \quad = \quad 0.37 \times 100\% \quad = \quad 37\%$$

Move the decimal point two places to the right. Then write the percent sign.

Example 4 Write 0.015 as a percent.

Solution $0.015 = 0.015 \times 100\%$
$= 1.5\%$

You Try It 4 Write 0.048 as a percent.

Your solution

Example 5 Write 2.15 as a percent.

Solution $2.15 = 2.15 \times 100\% = 215\%$

You Try It 5 Write 3.67 as a percent.

Your solution

Example 6 Write $0.33\frac{1}{3}$ as a percent.

Solution $0.33\frac{1}{3} = 0.33\frac{1}{3} \times 100\%$

$= 33\frac{1}{3}\%$

You Try It 6 Write $0.62\frac{1}{2}$ as a percent.

Your solution

Example 7 Write $\frac{2}{3}$ as a percent.
Write the remainder in fractional form.

Solution $\frac{2}{3} = \frac{2}{3} \times 100\% = \frac{200}{3}\%$

$= 66\frac{2}{3}\%$

You Try It 7 Write $\frac{5}{6}$ as a percent.
Write the remainder in fractional form.

Your solution

Example 8 Write $2\frac{2}{7}$ as a percent.
Round to the nearest tenth.

Solution $2\frac{2}{7} = \frac{16}{7} = \frac{16}{7} \times 100\%$

$= \frac{1600}{7}\% \approx 228.6\%$

You Try It 8 Write $1\frac{4}{9}$ as a percent.
Round to the nearest tenth.

Your solution

5.1 Exercises

Objective A   To write a percent as a fraction or a decimal

For Exercises 1 to 16, write as a fraction and as a decimal.

1. 25%   **2.** 40%   **3.** 130%   **4.** 150%

5. 100%   **6.** 87%   **7.** 73%   **8.** 45%

9. 383%   **10.** 425%   **11.** 70%   **12.** 55%

13. 88%   **14.** 64%   **15.** 32%   **16.** 18%

For Exercises 17 to 28, write as a fraction.

17. $66\frac{2}{3}\%$ **18.** $12\frac{1}{2}\%$ **19.** $83\frac{1}{3}\%$ **20.** $3\frac{1}{8}\%$ **21.** $11\frac{1}{9}\%$ **22.** $\frac{3}{8}\%$

23. $45\frac{5}{11}\%$ **24.** $15\frac{3}{8}\%$ **25.** $4\frac{2}{7}\%$ **26.** $5\frac{3}{4}\%$ **27.** $6\frac{2}{3}\%$ **28.** $8\frac{2}{3}\%$

For Exercises 29 to 43, write as a decimal.

29. 6.5%   **30.** 9.4%   **31.** 12.3%   **32.** 16.7%   **33.** 0.55%

34. 0.45%   **35.** 8.25%   **36.** 6.75%   **37.** 5.05%   **38.** 3.08%

39. 2%   **40.** 7%   **41.** 80.4%   **42.** 36.2%   **43.** 4.9%

Objective B   To write a fraction or a decimal as a percent

For Exercises 44 to 55, write as a percent.

44. 0.16   **45.** 0.73   **46.** 0.05   **47.** 0.01   **48.** 1.07   **49.** 2.94

50. 0.004   **51.** 0.006   **52.** 1.012   **53.** 3.106   **54.** 0.8   **55.** 0.7

For Exercises 56 to 67, write as a percent. Round to the nearest tenth of a percent.

56. $\dfrac{27}{50}$ **57.** $\dfrac{37}{100}$ **58.** $\dfrac{1}{3}$ **59.** $\dfrac{2}{5}$

60. $\dfrac{5}{8}$ **61.** $\dfrac{1}{8}$ **62.** $\dfrac{1}{6}$ **63.** $1\dfrac{1}{2}$

64. $\dfrac{7}{40}$ **65.** $1\dfrac{2}{3}$ **66.** $1\dfrac{7}{9}$ **67.** $\dfrac{7}{8}$

For Exercises 68 to 75, write as a percent. Write the remainder in fractional form.

68. $\dfrac{15}{50}$ **69.** $\dfrac{12}{25}$ **70.** $\dfrac{7}{30}$ **71.** $\dfrac{1}{3}$

72. $2\dfrac{3}{8}$ **73.** $1\dfrac{2}{3}$ **74.** $2\dfrac{1}{6}$ **75.** $\dfrac{7}{8}$

76. Write the part of the square that is shaded as a fraction, as a decimal, and as a percent. Write the part of the square that is not shaded as a fraction, as a decimal, and as a percent.

APPLYING THE CONCEPTS

77. **The Food Industry** In a survey conducted by Opinion Research Corp. for Lloyd's Barbeque Co., people were asked to name their favorite barbeque side dishes. 38% named corn on the cob, 35% named cole slaw, 11% named corn bread, and 10% named fries. What percent of those surveyed named something other than corn on the cob, cole slaw, corn bread, or fries?

78. **Consumerism** A sale on computers advertised $\dfrac{1}{3}$ off the regular price. What percent of the regular price does this represent?

79. **Consumerism** A suit was priced at 50% off the regular price. What fraction of the regular price does this represent?

80. **Elections** If $\dfrac{2}{5}$ of the population voted in an election, what percent of the population did not vote?

81. **a.** Is the statement "Multiplying a number by a percent always decreases the number" true or false?
b. If it is false, given an example to show that the statement is false.

5.2 Percent Equations: Part I

Objective A   **To find the amount when the percent and the base are given**

A real estate broker receives a payment that is 4% of a $285,000 sale. To find the amount the broker receives requires answering the question "4% of $285,000 is what?"

This sentence can be written using mathematical symbols and then solved for the unknown number.

4%   of $285,000 is   what?
↓   ↓   ↓   ↓   ↓

| Percent 4% | × | base 285,000 | = | amount n |

of is written as × (times)
is is written as = (equals)
what is written as n (the unknown number)

$$0.04 \times 285{,}000 = n$$
$$11{,}400 = n$$

Note that the percent is written as a decimal.

The broker receives a payment of $11,400.

The solution was found by solving the **basic percent equation** for amount.

> **The Basic Percent Equation**
>
> | Percent | × | base | = | amount |

In most cases, the percent is written as a decimal before the basic percent equation is solved. However, some percents are more easily written as a fraction than as a decimal. For example,

$$33\frac{1}{3}\% = \frac{1}{3} \qquad 66\frac{2}{3}\% = \frac{2}{3} \qquad 16\frac{2}{3}\% = \frac{1}{6} \qquad 83\frac{1}{3}\% = \frac{5}{6}$$

Example 1   Find 5.7% of 160.

Solution

Percent × base = amount
$$0.057 \times 160 = n$$
$$9.12 = n$$

• The word *Find* is used instead of the words *what is*.

Example 2   What is $33\frac{1}{3}\%$ of 90?

Solution   Percent × base = amount

$$\frac{1}{3} \times 90 = n$$

• $33\frac{1}{3}\% = \frac{1}{3}$

$$30 = n$$

You Try It 1   Find 6.3% of 150.

Your solution

You Try It 2   What is $16\frac{2}{3}\%$ of 66?

Your solution

Objective B   **To solve application problems**

Solving percent problems requires identifying the three elements of the basic percent equation. Recall that these three parts are the *percent,* the *base,* and the *amount.* Usually the base follows the phrase "percent of."

During a recent year, Americans gave $212 billion to charities. The circle graph at the right shows where that money came from. Use these data for Example 3 and You Try It 3.

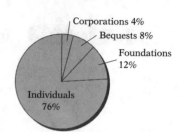

Charitable Giving
Sources: American Association of Fundraising Counsel; AP

Example 3

How much of the amount given to charities came from individuals?

Strategy
To determine the amount that came from individuals, write and solve the basic percent equation using n to represent the amount. The percent is 76%. The base is $212 billion.

Solution   Percent × base = amount
$$76\% \times 212 = n$$
$$0.76 \times 212 = n$$
$$161.12 = n$$

Individuals gave $161.12 billion to charities.

You Try It 3

How much of the amount given to charities was given by corporations?

Your strategy

Your solution

Example 4

A quality control inspector found that 1.2% of 2500 telephones inspected were defective. How many telephones inspected were not defective?

Strategy
To find the number of nondefective phones:

• Find the number of defective phones. Write and solve the basic percent equation using n to represent the number of defective phones (amount). The percent is 1.2% and the base is 2500.
• Subtract the number of defective phones from the number of phones inspected (2500).

Solution $1.2\% \times 2500 = n$
$0.012 \times 2500 = n$
$30 = n$ defective phones

$2500 - 30 = 2470$

2470 telephones were not defective.

You Try It 4

An electrician's hourly wage was $33.50 before an 8% raise. What is the new hourly wage?

Your strategy

Your solution

5.2 Exercises

Objective A   **To find the amount when the percent and the base are given**

1. 8% of 100 is what?

2. 16% of 50 is what?

3. 27% of 40 is what?

4. 52% of 95 is what?

5. 0.05% of 150 is what?

6. 0.075% of 625 is what?

7. 125% of 64 is what?

8. 210% of 12 is what?

9. Find 10.7% of 485.

10. Find 12.8% of 625.

11. What is 0.25% of 3000?

12. What is 0.06% of 250?

13. 80% of 16.25 is what?

14. 26% of 19.5 is what?

15. What is $1\frac{1}{2}$% of 250?

16. What is $5\frac{3}{4}$% of 65?

17. $16\frac{2}{3}$% of 120 is what?

18. $83\frac{1}{3}$% of 246 is what?

19. What is $33\frac{1}{3}$% of 630?

20. What is $66\frac{2}{3}$% of 891?

21. Which is larger: 5% of 95, or 75% of 6?

22. Which is larger: 112% of 5, or 0.45% of 800?

23. Which is smaller: 79% of 16, or 20% of 65?

24. Which is smaller: 15% of 80, or 95% of 15?

25. Which is smaller: 2% of 1500, or 72% of 40?

26. Which is larger: 22% of 120, or 84% of 32?

27. 🖩 Find 31.294% of 82,460.

28. 🖩 Find 123.94% of 275,976.

Objective B   **To solve application problems**

29. 🥧 **Health Insurance**   Approximately 30% of the 44 million people in the United States who do not have health insurance are between the ages of 18 and 24. (*Source:* U.S. Census Bureau) About how many people in the United States aged 18 to 24 do not have health insurance?

30. 🥧 **Aviation**   The Federal Aviation Administration reported that 55,422 new student pilots were flying single-engine planes last year. The number of new student pilots flying single-engine planes this year is 106% of the number flying single-engine planes last year. How many new student pilots are flying single-engine planes this year?

Politics   The results of a survey in which 32,840 full-time college and university faculty members were asked to describe their political views is shown at the right. Use these data for Exercises 31 and 32.

Political View	Percent of Faculty Members Responding
Far Left	5.3%
Liberal	42.3%
Middle of the road	34.3%
Conservative	17.7%
Far right	0.3%

Source: Higher Education Research Institute, UCLA

31. How many more faculty members described their political views as liberal than described their views as far left?

32. How many fewer faculty members described their political views as conservative than described their views as middle of the road?

33. Taxes   A sales tax of 6% of the cost of a car was added to the purchase price of $29,500.
   a. How much was the sales tax?
   b. What is the total cost of the car, including sales tax?

34. Business   During the packaging process for oranges, spoiled oranges are discarded by an inspector. In one day an inspector found that 4.8% of the 20,000 pounds of oranges inspected were spoiled.
   a. How many pounds of oranges were spoiled?
   b. How many pounds of oranges were not spoiled?

35.   **Entertainment**   A USA TODAY.com online poll asked 8878 Internet users, "Would you use software to cut out objectionable parts of movies?" 29.8% of the respondents answered yes. How many respondents did not answer yes to the question? Round to the nearest whole number.

36. Employment   Funtimes Amusement Park has 550 employees and must hire an additional 22% for the vacation season. What is the total number of employees needed for the vacation season?

APPLYING THE CONCEPTS

Sociology   The two circle graphs at the right show how surveyed employees actually spend their time and the way they would prefer to spend their time. Assuming that employees have 112 hours a week of time that is not spent sleeping, answer Exercises 37 to 39. Round to the nearest tenth of an hour.

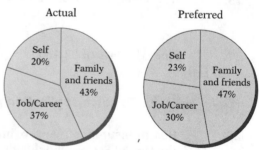

Actual   Preferred

Actual: Self 20%, Family and friends 43%, Job/Career 37%

Preferred: Self 23%, Family and friends 47%, Job/Career 30%

Source: WSJ Supplement, Work & Family, from *Families and Work Institute*

37. What is the actual number of hours per week that employees spend with family and friends?

38. What is the number of hours per week that employees would prefer to spend on job/career?

39. What is the difference between the number of hours an employee preferred to spend on self and the actual amount of time the employee spent on self?

5.3 Percent Equations: Part II

Objective A   **To find the percent when the base and amount are given**

A recent promotional game at a grocery store listed the probability of winning a prize as "1 chance in 2." A percent can be used to describe the chance of winning. This requires answering the question "What percent of 2 is 1?"

The chance of winning can be found by solving the basic percent equation for *percent*.

Integrating Technology

The percent key % on a scientific calculator moves the decimal point to the left two places when pressed after a multiplication or division computation. For the example at the right, enter

1 ÷ 2 % =

The display reads 50.

What percent of   2   is   1?
    ↓   ↓   ↓   ↓   ↓

| Percent n | × | base 2 | = | amount 1 |

$$n \times 2 = 1$$
$$n = 1 \div 2$$
$$n = 0.5$$
$$n = 50\%$$

• **The solution must be written as a percent to answer the question.**

There is a 50% chance of winning a prize.

Example 1   What percent of 40 is 30?

Solution

$$\text{Percent} \times \text{base} = \text{amount}$$
$$n \times 40 = 30$$
$$n = 30 \div 40$$
$$n = 0.75$$
$$n = 75\%$$

You Try It 1   What percent of 32 is 16?

Your solution

Example 2   What percent of 12 is 27?

Solution

$$\text{Percent} \times \text{base} = \text{amount}$$
$$n \times 12 = 27$$
$$n = 27 \div 12$$
$$n = 2.25$$
$$n = 225\%$$

You Try It 2   What percent of 15 is 48?

Your solution

Example 3   25 is what percent of 75?

Solution

$$\text{Percent} \times \text{base} = \text{amount}$$
$$n \times 75 = 25$$
$$n = 25 \div 75$$
$$n = \frac{1}{3} = 33\frac{1}{3}\%$$

You Try It 3   30 is what percent of 45?

Your solution

Objective B   **To solve application problems**

To solve percent problems, remember that it is necessary to identify the percent, base, and amount. Usually the base follows the phrase "percent of."

Example 4

The monthly house payment for the Kaminski family is $787.50. What percent of the Kaminskis' monthly income of $3750 is the house payment?

Strategy

To find what percent of the income the house payment is, write and solve the basic percent equation using n to represent the percent. The base is $3750 and the amount is $787.50.

Solution

$n \times 3750 = 787.50$
$n = 787.50 \div 3750$
$n = 0.21 = 21\%$

The house payment is 21% of the monthly income.

You Try It 4

Tomo Nagata had an income of $33,500 and paid $5025 in income tax. What percent of the income is the income tax?

Your strategy

Your solution

Example 5

On one Monday night, 31.39 million of the approximately 40.76 million households watching television were not watching David Letterman. What percent of these households were watching David Letterman? Round to the nearest percent.

Strategy

To find the percent of households watching David Letterman:

• Subtract to find the number of households that were watching David Letterman (40.76 million − 31.39 million).
• Write and solve the basic percent equation using n to represent the percent. The base is 40.76, and the amount is the number of households watching David Letterman.

Solution

40.76 million − 31.39 million = 9.37 million

9.37 million households were watching David Letterman.

$n \times 40.76 = 9.37$
$n = 9.37 \div 40.76$
$n \approx 0.23$

Approximately 23% of the households were watching David Letterman.

You Try It 5

According to the U.S. Department of Defense, of the 518,921 enlisted personnel in the U.S. Army in 1950, 512,370 people were men. What percent of the enlisted personnel in the U.S. Army in 1950 were women? Round to the nearest tenth of a percent.

Your strategy

Your solution

5.3 Exercises

Objective A   To find the percent when the base and amount are given

1. What percent of 75 is 24?

2. What percent of 80 is 20?

3. 15 is what percent of 90?

4. 24 is what percent of 60?

5. What percent of 12 is 24?

6. What percent of 6 is 9?

7. What percent of 16 is 6?

8. What percent of 24 is 18?

9. 18 is what percent of 100?

10. 54 is what percent of 100?

11. 5 is what percent of 2000?

12. 8 is what percent of 2500?

13. What percent of 6 is 1.2?

14. What percent of 2.4 is 0.6?

15. 16.4 is what percent of 4.1?

16. 5.3 is what percent of 50?

17. 1 is what percent of 40?

18. 0.3 is what percent of 20?

19. What percent of 48 is 18?

20. What percent of 11 is 88?

21. What percent of 2800 is 7?

22. What percent of 400 is 12?

23. 4.2 is what percent of 175?

24. 41.79 is what percent of 99.5?

25. What percent of 86.5 is 8.304?

26. What percent of 1282.5 is 2.565?

Objective B   To solve application problems

27. **Sociology**   Seven in ten couples disagree about financial issues. (*Source:* Yankelovich Partners for Lutheran Brotherhood) What percent of couples disagree about financial matters?

28. **Sociology**   In a survey, 1236 adults nationwide were asked, "What irks you most about the actions of other motorists?" The response "tailgaters" was given by 293 people. (*Source:* Reuters/Zogby) What percent of those surveyed were most irked by tailgaters? Round to the nearest tenth of a percent.

29. **Agriculture**   According to the U.S. Department of Agriculture, of the 63 billion pounds of vegetables produced in the United States in 1 year, 16 billion pounds were wasted. What percent of the vegetables produced were wasted? Round to the nearest tenth of a percent.

30. **Agriculture**   In a recent year, Wisconsin growers produced 281.72 million pounds of the 572 million pounds of cranberries grown in the United States. What percent of the total cranberry crop was produced in Wisconsin? Round to the nearest percent.

31. **Energy**   The typical American household spends $1355 a year on energy utilities. Of this amount, approximately $81.30 is spent on lighting. (*Source:* Department of Energy, Owens Corning) What percent of the total amount spent on energy utilities is spent on lighting?

32. **Education**   To receive a license to sell insurance, an insurance account executive must answer correctly 70% of the 250 questions on a test. Nicholas Mosley answered 177 questions correctly. Did he pass the test?

33. **Agriculture**   According to the U.S. Department of Agriculture, of the 356 billion pounds of food produced in the United States annually, 260 billion pounds are not wasted. What percent of the food produced in the United States is wasted? Round to the nearest percent.

34. **Construction**   In a test of the breaking strength of concrete slabs for freeway construction, 3 of the 200 slabs tested did not meet safety requirements. What percent of the slabs did meet safety requirements?

APPLYING THE CONCEPTS

Pets   The graph at the right shows several categories of average lifetime costs of dog ownership. Use this graph for Exercises 35 to 37. Round answers to the nearest tenth of a percent.

35. What percent of the total amount is spent on food?

36. What percent of the total is spent on veterinary care?

37. What percent of the total is spent on all categories except training?

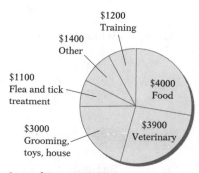

Cost of Owning a Dog

Source: Based on data from the American Kennel Club, *USA Today* research

38. **Sports**   The Fun in the Sun organization claims to have taken a survey of 350 people, asking them to give their favorite outdoor temperature for hiking. The results are given in the table at the right. Explain why these results are not possible.

Favorite Temperature	Percent
Greater than 90	5%
80–89	28%
70–79	35%
60–69	32%
Below 60	13%

5.4   Percent Equations: Part III

Objective A   To find the base when the percent and amount are given

 In 1780, the population of Virginia was 538,000. This was 19% of the total population of the United States at that time. To find the total population at that time, you must answer the question "19% of what number is 538,000?"

19%   of what is 538,000?
 ↓   ↓   ↓

| Percent 19% | base *n* | amount 538,000 |

0.19   ×   *n*   = 538,000
                n   = 538,000 ÷ 0.19
                n   ≈ 2,832,000

- **The population of the United States in 1780 can be found by solving the basic percent equation for the base.**

The population of the United States in 1780 was approximately 2,832,000.

Example 1   18% of what is 900?

Solution

$$\text{Percent} \times \text{base} = \text{amount}$$
$$0.18 \times n = 900$$
$$n = 900 \div 0.18$$
$$n = 5000$$

You Try It 1   86% of what is 215?

Your solution

Example 2   30 is 1.5% of what?

Solution

$$\text{Percent} \times \text{base} = \text{amount}$$
$$0.015 \times n = 30$$
$$n = 30 \div 0.015$$
$$n = 2000$$

You Try It 2   15 is 2.5% of what?

Your solution

Example 3 $33\frac{1}{3}\%$ of what is 7?

Solution

$$\text{Percent} \times \text{base} = \text{amount}$$
$$\frac{1}{3} \times n = 7$$
$$n = 7 \div \frac{1}{3}$$
$$n = 21$$

- **Note that the percent is written as a fraction.**

You Try It 3 $16\frac{2}{3}\%$ of what is 5?

Your solution

Objective B   To solve application problems

To solve percent problems, it is necessary to identify the percent, base, and amount. Usually the base follows the phrase "percent of."

Example 4

A business office bought a used copy machine for $900, which was 75% of the original cost. What was the original cost of the copier?

Strategy

To find the original cost of the copier, write and solve the basic percent equation using n to represent the original cost (base). The percent is 75% and the amount is $900.

Solution

$75\% \times n = 900$
$0.75 \times n = 900$
$n = 900 \div 0.75$
$n = 1200$

The original cost of the copier was $1200.

You Try It 4

A used car has a value of $10,458, which is 42% of the car's original value. What was the car's original value?

Your strategy

Your solution

Example 5

A carpenter's wage this year is $26.40 per hour, which is 110% of last year's wage. What was the increase in the hourly wage over last year?

Strategy

To find the increase in the hourly wage over last year:

• Find last year's wage. Write and solve the basic percent equation using n to represent last year's wage (base). The percent is 110% and the amount is $26.40.
• Subtract last year's wage from this year's wage (26.40).

Solution

$110\% \times n = 26.40$
$1.10 \times n = 26.40$
$n = 26.40 \div 1.10$
$n = 24.00$ • Last year's wage

$26.40 - 24.00 = 2.40$

The increase in the hourly wage was $2.40.

You Try It 5

Chang's Sporting Goods has a tennis racket on sale for $89.60, which is 80% of the original price. What is the difference between the original price and the sale price?

Your strategy

Your solution

5.4 Exercises

Objective A   To find the base when the percent and amount are given

For Exercises 1 to 26, solve. Round to the nearest hundredth.

1.   12% of what is 9?

2.   38% of what is 171?

3.   8 is 16% of what?

4.   54 is 90% of what?

5.   10 is 10% of what?

6.   37 is 37% of what?

7.   30% of what is 25.5?

8.   25% of what is 21.5?

9.   2.5% of what is 30?

10.   10.4% of what is 52?

11.   125% of what is 24?

12.   180% of what is 21.6?

13.   18 is 240% of what?

14.   24 is 320% of what?

15.   4.8 is 15% of what?

16.   87.5 is 50% of what?

17.   25.6 is 12.8% of what?

18.   45.014 is 63.4% of what?

19.   0.7% of what is 0.56?

20.   0.25% of what is 1?

21.   30% of what is 2.7?

22.   78% of what is 3.9?

23.   84 is $16\frac{2}{3}$% of what?

24.   120 is $33\frac{1}{3}$% of what?

25. $66\frac{2}{3}$% of what is 72?

26. $83\frac{1}{3}$% of what is 13.5?

Objective B   To solve application problems

27.    **Travel**   Of the travelers who, during a recent year, allowed their children to miss school to go along on a trip, approximately 1.738 million allowed their children to miss school for more than a week. This represented 11% of the travelers who allowed their children to miss school. (*Source:* Travel Industry Association) About how many travelers allowed their children to miss school to go along on a trip?

28. **Education** In the United States today, 23.1% of the women and 27.5% of the men have earned a bachelor's or graduate degree. (*Source:* Census Bureau) How many women in the United States have earned a bachelor's or graduate degree?

29. **Taxes** A TurboTax online survey asked people how they planned to use their tax refunds. 740 people, or 22% of the respondents, said they would save the money. How many people responded to the survey?

30. **Taxes** The Internal Revenue Service says that the average deduction for medical expenses for taxpayers in the $40,000–$50,000 bracket is $4500. This is 26% of the medical expenses claimed by taxpayers in the over-$200,000 bracket. How much is the average deduction for medical expenses claimed by taxpayers in the over-$200,000 bracket? Round to the nearest thousand.

31. **Manufacturing** During a quality control test, Micronics found that 24 computer boards were defective. This amount was 0.8% of the computer boards tested.
a. How many computer boards were tested?
b. How many computer boards tested were not defective?

32. **Directory Assistance** Of the calls a directory assistance operator received, 441 were requests for telephone numbers listed in the current directory. This accounted for 98% of the calls for assistance that the operator received.
a. How many calls did the operator receive?
b. How many telephone numbers requested were not listed in the current directory?

APPLYING THE CONCEPTS

33. **Demography** At the last census, of the 281,422,000 people in the United States, 28.6% were under the age of 20. (*Source:* U.S. Census 2000) How many people in the United States were age 20 or older in 2000?

Nutrition The table at the right contains nutrition information about a breakfast cereal. Solve Exercises 34 and 35 using information from this table.

34. The amount of thiamin in one serving of cereal with skim milk is 0.45 milligram. Find the recommended daily allowance of thiamin for an adult.

35. The amount of copper in one serving of cereal with skim milk is 0.08 milligram. Find the recommended daily allowance of copper for an adult.

36. Increase a number by 10%. Now decrease the number by 10%. Is the result the original number? Explain.

NUTRITION INFORMATION

SERVING SIZE: 1.4 OZ WHEAT FLAKES WITH
0.4 OZ. RAISINS: 39.4 g. ABOUT 1/2 CUP
SERVINGS PER PACKAGE: 14

	CEREAL & RAISINS	WITH 1/2 CUP VITAMINS A & D SKIM MILK

PERCENTAGE OF U.S. RECOMMENDED DAILY ALLOWANCES (U.S. RDA)

	CEREAL & RAISINS	WITH 1/2 CUP SKIM MILK
PROTEIN	4	15
VITAMIN A	15	20
VITAMIN C	**	2
THIAMIN	25	30
RIBOFLAVIN	25	35
NIACIN	25	35
CALCIUM	**	15
IRON	100	100
VITAMIN D	10	25
VITAMIN B₆	25	25
FOLIC ACID	25	25
VITAMIN B₁₂	25	30
PHOSPHOROUS	10	15
MAGNESIUM	10	20
ZINC	25	30
COPPER	2	4

* 2% MILK SUPPLIES AN ADDITIONAL 20 CALORIES, 2 g FAT, AND 10 mg CHOLESTEROL.
** CONTAINS LESS THAN 2% OF THE U.S. RDA OF THIS NUTRIENT

5.5

Percent Problems: Proportion Method

Objective A   **To solve percent problems using proportions**

Problems that can be solved using the basic percent equation can also be solved using proportions.

The proportion method is based on writing two ratios. One ratio is the percent ratio, written as $\frac{\text{percent}}{100}$. The second ratio is the amount-to-base ratio, written as $\frac{\text{amount}}{\text{base}}$. These two ratios form the proportion

$$\frac{\text{percent}}{100} = \frac{\text{amount}}{\text{base}}$$

To use the proportion method, first identify the percent, the amount, and the base (the base usually follows the phrase "percent of").

Integrating Technology

To use a calculator to solve the proportions at the right for *n*, enter

23 × 45 ÷ 100 =

100 × 4 ÷ 25 =

100 × 12 ÷ 60 =

What is 23% of 45?

$$\frac{23}{100} = \frac{n}{45}$$

$23 \times 45 = 100 \times n$
$1035 = 100 \times n$
$1035 \div 100 = n$
$10.35 = n$

What percent of 25 is 4?

$$\frac{n}{100} = \frac{4}{25}$$

$n \times 25 = 100 \times 4$
$n \times 25 = 400$
$n = 400 \div 25$
$n = 16$
16% of 25 is 4.

12 is 60% of what number?

$$\frac{60}{100} = \frac{12}{n}$$

$60 \times n = 100 \times 12$
$60 \times n = 1200$
$n = 1200 \div 60$
$n = 20$

Example 1   15% of what is 7? Round to the nearest hundredth.

Solution
$$\frac{15}{100} = \frac{7}{n}$$
$15 \times n = 100 \times 7$
$15 \times n = 700$
$n = 700 \div 15$
$n \approx 46.67$

You Try It 1   26% of what is 22? Round to the nearest hundredth.

Your solution

Example 2   30% of 63 is what?

Solution
$$\frac{30}{100} = \frac{n}{63}$$
$30 \times 63 = 100 \times n$
$1890 = 100 \times n$
$1890 \div 100 = n$
$18.90 = n$

You Try It 2   16% of 132 is what?

Your solution

Objective B **To solve application problems**

Example 3

An antiques dealer found that 86% of the 250 items that were sold during one month sold for under $1000. How many items sold for under $1000?

Strategy

To find the number of items that sold for under $1000, write and solve a proportion using n to represent the number of items sold (amount) for less than $1000. The percent is 86% and the base is 250.

Solution

$$\frac{86}{100} = \frac{n}{250}$$
$$86 \times 250 = 100 \times n$$
$$21{,}500 = 100 \times n$$
$$21{,}500 \div 100 = n$$
$$215 = n$$

215 items sold for under $1000.

You Try It 3

Last year it snowed 64% of the 150 days of the ski season at a resort. How many days did it snow?

Your strategy

Your solution

Example 4

In a test of the strength of nylon rope, 5 pieces of the 25 pieces tested did not meet the test standards. What percent of the nylon ropes tested did meet the standards?

Strategy

To find the percent of ropes tested that met the standards:

- Find the number of ropes that met the test standards (25 − 5).
- Write and solve a proportion using n to represent the percent of ropes that met the test standards. The base is 25 and the amount is the number of ropes that met the standards.

Solution

$25 - 5 = 20$ ropes met test standards

$$\frac{n}{100} = \frac{20}{25}$$
$$n \times 25 = 100 \times 20$$
$$n \times 25 = 2000$$
$$n = 2000 \div 25$$
$$n = 80$$

80% of the ropes tested did meet the test standards.

You Try It 4

Five ballpoint pens in a box of 200 were found to be defective. What percent of the pens were not defective?

Your strategy

Your solution

5.5 Exercises

Objective A   To solve percent problems using proportions

1. 26% of 250 is what?

2. What is 18% of 150?

3. 37 is what percent of 148?

4. What percent of 150 is 33?

5. 68% of what is 51?

6. 126 is 84% of what?

7. What percent of 344 is 43?

8. 750 is what percent of 50?

9. 82 is 20.5% of what?

10. 2.4% of what is 21?

11. What is 6.5% of 300?

12. 96% of 75 is what?

13. 7.4 is what percent of 50?

14. What percent of 1500 is 693?

15. 50.5% of 124 is what?

16. What is 87.4% of 255?

17. 120% of what is 6?

18. 14 is 175% of what?

19. What is 250% of 18?

20. 325% of 4.4 is what?

21. 33 is 220% of what?

22. 160% of what is 40?

Objective B   To solve application problems

23. **Charities**   A charitable organization spent $2940 for administrative expenses. This amount is 12% of the money it collected. What is the total amount of money that the organization collected?

24. **Medicine**   A manufacturer of an anti-inflammatory drug claims that the drug will be effective for 6 hours. An independent testing service determined that the drug was effective for only 80% of the length of time claimed by the manufacturer. Find the length of time the drug will be effective as determined by the testing service.

25. **Geography**   The land area of North America is approximately 9,400,000 square miles. This represents approximately 16% of the total land area of the world. What is the approximate total land area of the world?

26. **Fire Departments**   The Rincon Fire Department received 24 false alarms out of a total of 200 alarms received. What percent of the alarms received were false alarms?

27. **Lodging** The graph at the right shows the breakdown of the locations of the 53,500 hotels throughout the United States. How many hotels in the United States are located along highways?

28. **Poultry** In a recent year, North Carolina produced 1,300,000,000 pounds of turkey. This was 18.6% of the U.S. total in that year. Calculate the U.S. total turkey production for that year. Round to the nearest billion.

29. **Mining** During 1 year, approximately 2,240,000 ounces of gold went into the manufacturing of electronic equipment in the United States. This is 16% of all the gold mined in the United States that year. How many ounces of gold were mined in the United States that year?

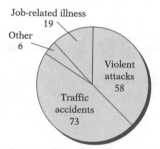

Most Hotels on Highways
Of the 53,500 hotels throughout the USA, most are found along highways. The breakdown:

Highways 42.2%
Suburban 33.6%
Urban 10.2%
Resort 6.3%
Airport 7.7%

Source: American Hotel and Lodging Association

30. **Demography** The table at the right shows the predicted increase in population from 2000 to 2040 for each of four counties in the Central Valley of California.
a. What percent of the 2000 population of Sacramento County is the increase in population?
b. What percent of the 2000 population of Kern County is the increase in population? Round to the nearest tenth of a percent.

County	2000 Population	Projected Increase
Sacramento	1,200,000	900,000
Kern	651,700	948,300
Fresno	794,200	705,800
San Joaquin	562,000	737,400

Source: California Department of Finance

31. **Police Officers** The graph at the right shows the causes of death for all police officers killed in the line of duty during a recent year. What percent of the deaths were due to traffic accidents? Round to the nearest tenth of a percent.

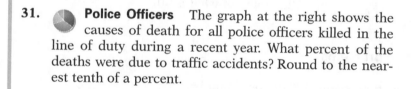

Job-related illness 19
Other 6
Violent attacks 58
Traffic accidents 73

Causes of Death for Police Officers Killed in the Line of Duty

Source: International Union of Police Associations

32. **Demography** According to a 25-city survey of the status of hunger and homelessness by the U.S. Conference of Mayors, 41% of the homeless in the United States are single men, 41% are families with children, 13% are single women, and 5% are unaccompanied minors. How many homeless people in the United States are single men?

APPLYING THE CONCEPTS

33. **The Federal Government** In the 108th Senate, there were 51 Republicans, 48 Democrats, and 1 Independent. In the 108th House of Representatives, there were 229 Republicans, 205 Democrats, and 1 Independent. Which had the larger percent of Republicans, the 108th Senate or the 108th House of Representatives?

Focus on Problem Solving

Using a Calculator as a Problem-Solving Tool

A calculator is an important tool for problem solving. Here are a few problems to solve with a calculator. You may need to research some of the questions to find information you do not know.

1. Choose any single-digit positive number. Multiply the number by 1507 and 7373. What is the answer? Choose another positive single-digit number and again multiply by 1507 and 7373. What is the answer? What pattern do you see? Why does this work?

2. The gross domestic product in 2002 was $10,446,200,000. Is this more or less than the amount of money that would be placed on the last square of a standard checkerboard if 1 cent were placed on the first square, 2 cents were placed on the second square, 4 cents were placed on the third square, 8 cents were placed on the fourth square, and so on, until the 64th square was reached?

3. Which of the reciprocals of the first 16 natural numbers have a terminating-decimal representation and which have a repeating-decimal representation?

4. What is the largest natural number n for which $4^n > 1 \cdot 2 \cdot 3 \cdot 4 \cdot 5 \cdots \cdot n$?

5. If $1000 bills are stacked one on top of another, is the height of $1 billion less than or greater than the height of the Washington Monument?

6. What is the value of $1 + \cfrac{1}{1 + \cfrac{1}{1 + \cfrac{1}{1 + \cfrac{1}{1 + 1}}}}$?

7. Calculate 15^2, 35^2, 65^2, and 85^2. Study the results. Make a conjecture about a relationship between a number ending in 5 and its square. Use your conjecture to find 75^2 and 95^2. Does your conjecture work for 125^2?

8. Find the sum of the first 1000 natural numbers. (*Hint:* You could just start adding $1 + 2 + 3 + \cdots$, but even if you performed one operation every 3 seconds, it would take you an hour to find the sum. Instead, try pairing the numbers and then adding the pairs. Pair 1 and 1000, 2 and 999, 3 and 998, and so on. What is the sum of each pair? How many pairs are there? Use this information to answer the original question.)

9. For a borrower to qualify for a home loan, a bank requires that the monthly mortgage payment be less than 25% of a borrower's monthly take-home income. A laboratory technician has deductions for taxes, insurance, and retirement that amount to 25% of the technician's monthly gross income. What minimum monthly income must this technician earn to receive a bank loan that has a mortgage payment of $1200 per month?

Using Estimation as a Problem-Solving Tool

You can use your knowledge of rounding, your understanding of percent, and your experience with the basic percent equation to quickly estimate the answer to a percent problem. Here is an example.

> **HOW TO** What is 11.2% of 978?
>
> Round the given numbers. $11.2\% \approx 10\%$
> $978 \approx 1000$
>
> Mentally calculate with the rounded numbers. $10\% \text{ of } 1000 = \frac{1}{10} \text{ of } 1000 = 100$
>
> 11.2% of 978 is approximately 100.

TAKE NOTE

The exact answer is $0.112 \times 978 = 109.536$. The exact answer 109.536 is close to the approximation of 100.

For Exercises 1 to 8, state which quantity is greater.

1. 49% of 51, or 201% of 15
2. 99% of 19, or 22% of 55
3. 8% of 31, or 78% of 10
4. 24% of 402, or 76% of 205
5. 10.2% of 51, or 20.9% of 41
6. 51.8% of 804, or 25.3% of 1223
7. 26% of 39.217, or 9% of 85.601
8. 66% of 31.807, or 33% of 58.203

For Exercises 9 to 12, use estimation to provide an approximate number.

9. A company survey found that 24% of its 2096 employees favored a new dental plan. How many employees favored the new dental plan?

10. A local newspaper reported that 52.3% of the 29,875 eligible voters in the town voted in the last election. How many people voted in the last election?

11. 19.8% of the 2135 first-year students at a community college have part-time jobs. How many of the first-year students at the college have part-time jobs?

12. A couple made a down payment of 33% of the $310,000 cost of the home. Find the down payment.

Projects and Group Activities

Health

The American College of Sports Medicine (ACSM) recommends that you know how to determine your target heart rate in order to get the full benefit of exercise. Your **target heart rate** is the rate at which your heart should beat during any aerobic exercise such as running, cycling, fast walking, or participating in an aerobics class. According to the ACSM, you should reach your target rate and then maintain it for 20 minutes or more to achieve cardiovascular fitness. The intensity level varies for different individuals. A sedentary person might begin at the 60% level and gradually work up to 70%, whereas athletes and very fit individuals might work at the 85% level. The ACSM suggests that you calculate both 50% and 85% of your maximum heart rate. This will give you the low and high ends of the range within which your heart rate should stay.

To calculate your target heart rate:

	Example
Subtract your age from 220. This is your maximum heart rate.	$220 - 20 = 200$
Multiply your maximum heart rate by 50%. This is the low end of your range.	$200(0.50) = 100$
Divide the low end by 6. This is your low 10-second heart rate.	$100 \div 6 \approx 17$
Multiply your maximum heart rate by 85%. This is the high end of your range.	$200(0.85) = 170$
Divide the high end by 6. This is your high 10-second heart rate.	$170 \div 6 \approx 28$

1. Why are the low end and high end divided by 6 in order to determine the low and high 10-second heart rates?

2. Calculate your target heart rate, both the low and high end of your range.

Consumer Price Index

The consumer price index (CPI) is a percent that is written without the percent sign. For instance, a CPI of 160.1 means 160.1%. This number means that an item that cost $100 between 1982 and 1984 (the base years) would cost $160.10 today. Determining the cost is an application of the basic percent equation.

$$\text{Percent} \times \text{base} = \text{amount}$$
$$\text{CPI} \times \text{cost in base year} = \text{cost today}$$
$$1.601 \times 100 = 160.1 \qquad \bullet \ 160.1\% = 1.601$$

The table below gives the CPI for various products in July of 2003. If you have Internet access, you can obtain current data for the items below, as well as other items not on this list, by visiting the website of the Bureau of Labor Statistics.

Product	CPI
All items	183.9
Food and beverages	180.3
Housing	185.9
Clothes	116.2
Transportation	156.8
Medical care	297.6
Entertainment	107.7
Education	108.9

1. Of the items listed, are there any items that in 2003 cost more than twice as much as they cost during the base year? If so, which items?

2. Of the items listed, are there any items that in 2003 cost more than one-and-one-half times as much as they cost during the base years but less than twice as much as they cost during the base years? If so, which items?

3. If the cost for textbooks for one semester was $120 in the base years, how much did similar textbooks cost in 2003? Use the "Education" category.

4. If a new car cost $20,000 in 2003, what would a comparable new car have cost during the base years? Use the "Transportation" category.

5. If a movie ticket cost $8 in 2003, what would a comparable movie ticket have cost during the base years? Use the "Entertainment" category.

6. The base year for the CPI was 1967 before the change to 1982–1984. If 1967 were still used as the base year, the CPI for all items in 2003 (not just those listed above) would be 550.9.
  a. Using the base year of 1967, explain the meaning of a CPI of 550.9.
  b. Using the base year of 1967 and a CPI of 550.9, if textbooks cost $75 for one semester in 1967, how much did similar textbooks cost in 2003?
  c. Using the base year of 1967 and a CPI of 550.9, if a family's food budget in 2003 is $800 per month, what would a comparable family budget have been in 1967?

Chapter Summary

Key Words	**Examples**
Percent means "parts of 100."	23% means 23 of 100 equal parts.

Essential Rules and Procedures	**Examples**
To write a percent as a fraction, drop the percent sign and multiply by $\frac{1}{100}$.	$56\% = 56\left(\frac{1}{100}\right) = \frac{56}{100} = \frac{14}{25}$
To write a percent as a decimal, drop the percent sign and multiply by 0.01.	$87\% = 87(0.01) = 0.87$
To write a fraction as a percent, multiply by 100%.	$\frac{7}{20} = \frac{7}{20}(100\%) = \frac{700}{20}\% = 35\%$
To write a decimal as a percent, multiply by 100%.	$0.325 = 0.325(100\%) = 32.5\%$

The Basic Percent Equation
The basic percent equation is

$$\text{Percent} \times \text{base} = \text{amount}$$

Solving percent problems requires identifying the three elements of this equation. Usually the base follows the phrase "percent of."

8% of 250 is what number?
Percent $\times$ base = amount
$$0.08 \times 250 = n$$
$$20 = n$$

Proportion Method of Solving a Percent Problem
The following proportion can be used to solve percent problems.

$$\frac{\text{percent}}{100} = \frac{\text{amount}}{\text{base}}$$

To use the proportion method, first identify the percent, the amount, and the base. The base usually follows the phrase "percent of."

8% of 250 is what number?
$$\frac{\text{percent}}{100} = \frac{\text{amount}}{\text{base}}$$
$$\frac{8}{100} = \frac{n}{250}$$
$$8 \times 250 = 100 \times n$$
$$2000 = 100 \times n$$
$$2000 \div 100 = n$$
$$20 = n$$

Chapter Review Exercises

1. What is 30% of 200?

2. 16 is what percent of 80?

3. Write $1\frac{3}{4}$ as a percent.

4. 20% of what is 15?

5. Write 12% as a fraction.

6. Find 22% of 88.

7. What percent of 20 is 30?

8. $16\frac{2}{3}\%$ of what is 84?

9. Write 42% as a decimal.

10. What is 7.5% of 72?

11. $66\frac{2}{3}\%$ of what is 105?

12. Write 7.6% as a decimal.

13. Find 125% of 62.

14. Write $16\frac{2}{3}\%$ as a fraction.

15. Use the proportion method to find what percent of 25 is 40.

16. 20% of what number is 15? Use the proportion method.

17. Write 0.38 as a percent.

18. 78% of what is 8.5? Round to the nearest tenth.

19. What percent of 30 is 2.2? Round to the nearest tenth of a percent.

20. What percent of 15 is 92? Round to the nearest tenth of a percent.

21. Education Trent missed 9 out of 60 questions on a history exam. What percent of the questions did he answer correctly? Use the proportion method.

22. Advertising A company used 7.5% of its $60,000 advertising budget for newspaper advertising. How much of the advertising budget was spent for newspaper advertising?

23. **Energy** The graph at the right shows the amounts that the average U.S. household spends for energy use. What percent of these costs is for electricity? Round to the nearest tenth of a percent.

24. Consumerism Joshua purchased a video camera for $980 and paid a sales tax of 6.25% of the cost. What was the total cost of the video camera?

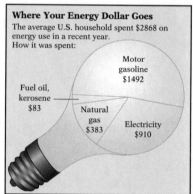

Where Your Energy Dollar Goes
The average U.S. household spent $2868 on energy use in a recent year. How it was spent:

Motor gasoline $1492

Fuel oil, kerosene $83

Natural gas $383

Electricity $910

Source: Energy Information Administration

25. Health In a survey of 350 women and 420 men, 275 of the women and 300 of the men reported that they wore sunscreen often. To the nearest tenth of a percent, what percent of the women wore sunscreen often?

26. **Demography** It is estimated that the world's population will be 9,100,000,000 by the year 2050. This is 149% of the population in 2000. (*Source:* U.S. Census Bureau). What was the world's population in 2000? Round to the nearest hundred million.

27. Computers A computer system can be purchased for $1800. This is 60% of what the computer cost 4 years ago. What was the cost of the computer 4 years ago? Use the proportion method.

28. **Online Transactions** In a recent year, $25.96 billion worth of online transactions were paid for using a Visa card. This represented 50.4% of the online transactions made during the year. (*Source:* The Nilson Report) Find the dollar value of all the online transactions made that year. Round to the nearest billion.

Chapter Test

1. Write 97.3% as a decimal.

2. Write $83\frac{1}{3}\%$ as a fraction.

3. Write 0.3 as a percent.

4. Write 1.63 as a percent.

5. Write $\frac{3}{2}$ as a percent.

6. Write $\frac{2}{3}$ as a percent.

7. What is 77% of 65?

8. 47.2% of 130 is what?

9. Which is larger:
   7% of 120, or 76% of 13?

10. Which is smaller:
    13% of 200, or 212% of 12?

11. **Advertising** A travel agency uses 6% of its $75,000 budget for advertising. What amount of the budget is spent on advertising?

12. **Agriculture** During the packaging process for vegetables, spoiled vegetables are discarded by an inspector. In one day an inspector found that 6.4% of the 1250 pounds of vegetables were spoiled. How many pounds of vegetables were not spoiled?

Nutrition   The table at the right contains nutrition information about a breakfast cereal. Solve Exercises 13 and 14 with information taken from this table.

13. The recommended amount of potassium per day for an adult is 3000 milligrams (mg). What percent, to the nearest tenth of a percent, of the daily recommended amount of potassium is provided by one serving of this cereal with skim milk?

14. The daily recommended number of calories for a 190-pound man is 2200 calories. What percent, to the nearest tenth of a percent, of the daily recommended number of calories is provided by one serving of this cereal with 2% milk?

NUTRITION INFORMATION

SERVING SIZE: 1.4 OZ WHEAT FLAKES WITH
0.4 OZ. RAISINS: 39.4 g. ABOUT 1/2 CUP
SERVINGS PER PACKAGE: 14

	CEREAL & RAISINS	WITH 1/2 CUP VITAMINS A & D SKIM MILK
CALORIES	120	180
PROTEIN, g	3	7
CARBOHYDRATE, g	28	34
FAT, TOTAL, g	1	1*
UNSATURATED, g	1	
SATURATED, g	0	
CHOLESTEROL, mg	0	0*
SODIUM, mg	125	190
POTASSIUM, mg	240	440

* 2% MILK SUPPLIES AN ADDITIONAL 20 CALORIES.
2 g FAT, AND 10 mg CHOLESTEROL.
** CONTAINS LESS THAN 2% OF THE U.S. RDA OF
THIS NUTRIENT

15. **Employment** The Urban Center Department Store has 125 permanent employees and must hire an additional 20 temporary employees for the holiday season. What percent of the permanent employees is the number hired as temporary employees for the holiday season?

16. **Education** Conchita missed 7 out of 80 questions on a math exam. What percent of the questions did she answer correctly? Round to the nearest tenth of a percent.

17. 12 is 15% of what?

18. 42.5 is 150% of what? Round to the nearest tenth.

19. **Manufacturing** A manufacturer of PDAs found 384 defective PDAs during a quality control study. This amount was 1.2% of the PDAs tested. Find the number of PDAs tested.

20. **Real Estate** A new house was bought for $95,000. Five years later the house sold for $152,000. The increase was what percent of the original price?

21. 123 is 86% of what number? Use the proportion method. Round to the nearest tenth.

22. What percent of 12 is 120? Use the proportion method.

23. **Wages** A secretary receives a wage of $16.24 per hour. This amount is 112% of last year's wage. What is the dollar increase in the hourly wage over last year? Use the proportion method.

24. **Demography** A city has a population of 71,500. Ten years ago the population was 32,500. The population now is what percent of what the population was 10 years ago? Use the proportion method.

25. **Fees** The annual license fee on a car is 1.4% of the value of the car. If the license fee during a year is $175.00, what is the value of the car? Use the proportion method.

chapter

6

Applications for Business and Consumers

When you use a credit card to make a purchase, you are actually receiving a loan. This service allows you to defer payment on your purchase until a predetermined date in the future. In exchange for this convenient service, credit card companies will frequently charge you money for using their credit card. This added cost may be in the form of an annual fee, or it may be in the form of interest charges on balances that are not paid off after a certain deadline. These interest charges on unpaid balances are called finance charges and can be calculated using the simple interest formula.

www Need help? For online student resources, such as section quizzes, visit this textbook's website at **math.college.hmco.com/students.**

For Exercises 1 to 6, add, subtract, multiply, or divide.

1. Divide: $3.75 \div 5$

2. Multiply: 3.47×15

3. Subtract: $874.50 - 369.99$

4. Multiply: $0.065 \times 150,000$

5. Multiply: $1500 \times 0.06 \times 0.5$

6. Add: $1372.47 + 36.91 + 5.00 + 2.86$

7. Divide $10 \div 3$. Round to the nearest hundredth.

8. Divide $345 \div 570$. Round to the nearest thousandth.

9. Place the correct symbol, $<$ or $>$, between the two numbers.
    0.379   0.397

GO FIGURE • • •

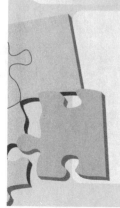

A store manager priced a pair of earrings in dollars and cents such that when 4% sales tax was added, the result was a whole number of dollars and 0 cents. Find the smallest possible number of dollars the items sold for, including the sales tax.

6.1

Applications to Purchasing

Objective A   **To find unit cost**

Frequently, stores promote items for purchase by advertising, say, 2 Red Baron Bake to Rise Pizzas for $10.50 or 5 cans of StarKist tuna for $4.25.

The **unit cost** is the cost of *one* Red Baron Pizza or of *one* can of StarKist tuna. To find the unit cost, divide the total cost by the number of units.

2 pizzas for $10.50	5 cans for $4.25
$10.50 \div 2 = 5.25$	$4.25 \div 5 = 0.85$
$5.25 is the cost of one pizza.	$.85 is the cost of one can.
Unit cost: $5.25 per pizza	Unit cost: $.85 per can

Example 1

Find the unit cost. Round to the nearest tenth of a cent.
a. 3 gallons of mint chip ice cream for $17
b. 4 ounces of Crest toothpaste for $2.29

Strategy
To find the unit cost, divide the total cost by the number of units.

Solution
a. $17 \div 3 \approx 5.667$
    $5.667 per gallon
b. $2.29 \div 4 = 0.5725$
    $.573 per ounce

You Try It 1

Find the unit cost. Round to the nearest tenth of a cent.
a. 8 size-AA Energizer batteries for $7.67
b. 15 ounces of Revlon shampoo for $2.29

Your strategy

Your solution

Objective B   **To find the most economical purchase**

Comparison shoppers often find the most economical buy by comparing unit costs.

One store is selling 6 twelve-ounce cans of ginger ale for $2.99, and a second store is selling 24 twelve-ounce cans of ginger ale for $11.79. To find the better buy, compare the unit costs.

$2.99 \div 6 \approx 0.498$	$11.79 \div 24 \approx 0.491$
Unit cost: $.498 per can	Unit cost: $.491 per can

Because $.491 < $.498, the better buy is 24 cans for $11.79.

Example 2

Find the more economical purchase: 5 pounds of nails for $4.80, or 4 pounds of nails for $3.78.

Strategy
To find the more economical purchase, compare the unit costs.

Solution
4.80 ÷ 5 = 0.96
3.78 ÷ 4 = 0.945
$.945 < $.96

The more economical purchase is 4 pounds for $3.78.

You Try It 2

Find the more economical purchase: 6 cans of fruit for $5.70, or 4 cans of fruit for $3.96.

Your strategy

Your solution

Objective C **To find total cost**

An installer of floor tile found the unit cost of identical floor tiles at three stores.

Store 1	Store 2	Store 3
$1.22 per tile	$1.18 per tile	$1.28 per tile

By comparing the unit costs, the installer determined that store 2 would provide the most economical purchase.

The installer also uses the unit cost to find the total cost of purchasing 300 floor tiles at store 2. The **total cost** is found by multiplying the unit cost by the number of units purchased.

Unit cost	×	number of units	=	total cost
1.18	×	300	=	354

The total cost is $354.

Example 3

Clear redwood lumber costs $5.43 per foot. How much would 25 feet of clear redwood cost?

Strategy
To find the total cost, multiply the unit cost (5.43) by the number of units (25).

Solution

Unit cost	×	number of units	=	total cost
5.43	×	25	=	135.75

The total cost is $135.75.

You Try It 3

Pine saplings cost $9.96 each. How much would 7 pine saplings cost?

Your strategy

Your solution

6.1 Exercises

Objective A   To find unit cost

For Exercises 1 to 12, find the unit cost. Round to the nearest tenth of a cent.

1. Heinz B·B·Q sauce, 18 ounces for $.99

2. Birds-eye maple, 6 feet for $18.75

3. Diamond walnuts, $2.99 for 8 ounces

4. A&W root beer, 6 cans for $2.99

5. Ibuprofen, 50 tablets for $3.99

6. Visine eye drops, 0.5 ounce for $3.89

7. Adjustable wood clamps, 2 for $13.95

8. Corn, 6 ears for $1.85

9. Cheerios cereal, 15 ounces for $2.99

10. Doritos Cool Ranch chips, 14.5 ounces for $2.99

11. Sheet metal screws, 8 for $.95

12. Folgers coffee, 11.5 ounces for $4.79

Objective B   To find the most economical purchase

For Exercises 13 to 24, suppose your local supermarket offers the following products at the given prices. Find the more economical purchase.

13. Sutter Home pasta sauce, 25.5 ounces for $3.29, or Muir Glen Organic pasta sauce, 26 ounces for $3.79

14. Kraft mayonnaise, 40 ounces for $2.98, or Springfield mayonnaise, 32 ounces for $2.39

15. Ortega salsa, 20 ounces for $3.29 or 12 ounces for $1.99

16. L'Oréal shampoo, 13 ounces for $4.69, or Cortexx shampoo, 12 ounces for $3.99

17. Golden Sun vitamin E, 200 tablets for $7.39 or 400 tablets for $12.99

18. Ultra Mr. Clean, 20 ounces for $2.67, or Ultra Spic and Span, 14 ounces for $2.19

19. 16 ounces of Kraft cheddar cheese, $4.37, or 9 ounces of Land O' Lakes cheddar cheese, $2.29

20. Bertolli olive oil, 34 ounces for $9.49, or Pompeian olive oil, 8 ounces for $2.39

21. Maxwell House coffee, 4 ounces for $3.99, or Sanka coffee, 2 ounces for $2.39

22. Wagner's vanilla extract, $3.29 for 1.5 ounces, or Durkee vanilla extract, 1 ounce for $2.74

23. Purina Cat Chow, $4.19 for 56 ounces, or Friskies Chef's Blend, $3.37 for 50.4 ounces

24. Kleenex tissues, $1.73 for 250 tissues, or Puffs tissues, $1.23 for 175 tissues

Objective C **To find total cost**

25. If sliced bacon costs $4.59 per pound, find the total cost of 3 pounds.

26. Used red brick costs $.98 per brick. Find the total cost of 75 bricks.

27. Kiwi fruit cost $.23 each. Find the total cost of 8 kiwi.

28. Boneless chicken filets cost $4.69 per pound. Find the cost of 3.6 pounds. Round to the nearest cent.

29. Herbal tea costs $.98 per ounce. Find the total cost of 6.5 ounces.

30. If Stella Swiss Lorraine cheese costs $5.99 per pound, find the total cost of 0.65 pound. Round to the nearest cent.

31. Red Delicious apples cost $1.29 per pound. Find the total cost of 2.1 pounds. Round to the nearest cent.

32. Choice rib eye steak costs $8.49 per pound. Find the total cost of 2.8 pounds. Round to the nearest cent.

33. If Godiva chocolate costs $7.95 per pound, find the total cost of $\frac{3}{4}$ pound. Round to the nearest cent.

34. Color photocopying costs $.89 per page. Find the total cost for photocopying 120 pages.

APPLYING THE CONCEPTS

35. Explain in your own words the meaning of unit pricing.

36. What is the UPC (Universal Product Code) and how is it used?

ISBN 0-395-75524-7

65)

6.2 Percent Increase and Percent Decrease

Objective A   To find percent increase

Percent increase is used to show how much a quantity has increased over its original value. The statements "Food prices increased by 2.3% last year" and "City council members received a 4% pay increase" are examples of percent increase.

HOW TO 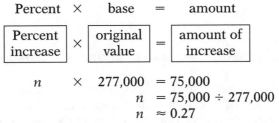 According to the Energy Information Administration, the number of alternative-fuel vehicles increased from approximately 277,000 to 352,000 in four years. Find the percent increase in alternative-fuel vehicles. Round to the nearest percent.

$$\boxed{\begin{array}{c}\text{New}\\\text{value}\end{array}} - \boxed{\begin{array}{c}\text{original}\\\text{value}\end{array}} = \boxed{\begin{array}{c}\text{amount of}\\\text{increase}\end{array}}$$

$$352{,}000 - 277{,}000 = 75{,}000$$

Now solve the basic percent equation for percent.

$$\text{Percent} \times \text{base} = \text{amount}$$

$$\boxed{\begin{array}{c}\text{Percent}\\\text{increase}\end{array}} \times \boxed{\begin{array}{c}\text{original}\\\text{value}\end{array}} = \boxed{\begin{array}{c}\text{amount of}\\\text{increase}\end{array}}$$

$$\begin{aligned} n \times 277{,}000 &= 75{,}000\\ n &= 75{,}000 \div 277{,}000\\ n &\approx 0.27 \end{aligned}$$

Amount of increase (75,000)

Original value (277,000)

New value (352,000)

The number of alternative-fuel vehicles increased by approximately 27%.

Example 1

The average wholesale price of coffee increased from $2 per pound to $3 per pound in one year. What was the percent increase in the price of 1 pound of coffee?

Strategy

To find the percent increase:
- Find the amount of the increase.
- Solve the basic percent equation for *percent*.

Solution

$$\boxed{\begin{array}{c}\text{New}\\\text{value}\end{array}} - \boxed{\begin{array}{c}\text{original}\\\text{value}\end{array}} = \boxed{\begin{array}{c}\text{amount of}\\\text{increase}\end{array}}$$

$$3 - 2 = 1$$

$$\begin{aligned} \text{Percent} \times \text{base} &= \text{amount}\\ n \times 2 &= 1\\ n &= 1 \div 2\\ n &= 0.5 = 50\% \end{aligned}$$

The percent increase was 50%.

You Try It 1

The average price of gasoline rose from $1.46 to $1.83 in 5 months. What was the percent increase in the price of gasoline? Round to the nearest percent.

Your strategy

Your solution

Example 2

Chris Carley was earning $13.50 an hour as a nursing assistant before receiving a 10% increase in pay. What is Chris's new hourly pay?

Strategy

To find the new hourly wage:

• Solve the basic percent equation for *amount*.
• Add the amount of the increase to the original wage.

Solution

Percent × base = amount
  0.10   × 13.50 = *n*
        1.35 = *n*

The amount of the increase was $1.35.

13.50 + 1.35 = 14.85

The new hourly wage is $14.85.

You Try It 2

Yolanda Liyama was making a wage of $12.50 an hour as a baker before receiving a 14% increase in hourly pay. What is Yolanda's new hourly wage?

Your strategy

Your solution

Objective B **To apply percent increase to business—markup**

Some of the expenses involved in operating a business are salaries, rent, equipment, and utilities. To pay these expenses and earn a profit, a business must sell a product at a higher price than it paid for the product.

Cost is the price a business pays for a product, and **selling price** is the price at which a business sells a product to a customer. The difference between selling price and cost is called **markup.**

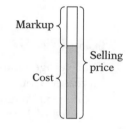

$$\boxed{\text{Selling price}} - \boxed{\text{cost}} = \boxed{\text{markup}}$$
or
$$\boxed{\text{Cost}} + \boxed{\text{markup}} = \boxed{\text{selling price}}$$

Markup is frequently expressed as a percent of a product's cost. This percent is called the **markup rate.**

$$\boxed{\text{Markup rate}} \times \boxed{\text{cost}} = \boxed{\text{markup}}$$

Point of Interest

According to *Managing a Small Business*, from Liraz Publishing Company, goods in a store are often marked up 50% to 100% of the cost. This allows a business to make a profit of 5% to 10%.

HOW TO Suppose Bicycles Galore purchases an AMP Research B-5 bicycle for $2119.20 and sells it for $2649. What markup rate does Bicycles Galore use?

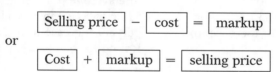

$$\boxed{\text{Selling price}} - \boxed{\text{cost}} = \boxed{\text{markup}}$$

  2649.00 − 2119.20 = 529.80   • **First find the markup.**

  Percent × base = amount   • **Then solve the basic percent equation for *percent*.**

$$\boxed{\text{Markup rate}} \times \boxed{\text{cost}} = \boxed{\text{markup}}$$

   n   × 2119.20 = 529.80
        n = 529.80 ÷ 2119.20 = 0.25

The markup rate is 25%.

Example 3

The manager of a sporting goods store determines that a markup rate of 36% is necessary to make a profit. What is the markup on a pair of skis that costs the store $225?

Strategy

To find the markup, solve the basic percent equation for *amount*.

Solution

Percent × base = amount

$$\boxed{\text{Markup rate}} \times \boxed{\text{cost}} = \boxed{\text{markup}}$$

$$0.36 \quad \times \quad 225 \quad = \quad n$$
$$81 = n$$

The markup is $81.

You Try It 3

A bookstore manager determines that a markup rate of 20% is necessary to make a profit. What is the markup on a book that costs the bookstore $8?

Your strategy

Your solution

Example 4

A plant nursery bought a yellow twig dogwood for $4.50 and used a markup rate of 46%. What is the selling price?

Strategy

To find the selling price:

- Find the markup by solving the basic percent equation for *amount*.
- Add the markup to the cost.

Solution

Percent × base = amount

$$\boxed{\text{Markup rate}} \times \boxed{\text{cost}} = \boxed{\text{markup}}$$

$$0.46 \quad \times \quad 4.50 \quad = \quad n$$
$$2.07 = n$$

$$\boxed{\text{Cost}} + \boxed{\text{markup}} = \boxed{\text{selling price}}$$

$$4.50 \quad + \quad 2.07 \quad = \quad 6.57$$

The selling price is $6.57.

You Try It 4

A clothing store bought a leather suit for $72 and used a markup rate of 55%. What is the selling price?

Your strategy

Your solution

Objective C **To find percent decrease**

Percent decrease is used to show how much a quantity has decreased from its original value. The statements "The number of family farms decreased by 2% last year" and "There has been a 50% decrease in the cost of a Pentium chip" are examples of percent decrease.

HOW TO During a 2-year period, the value of U.S. agricultural products exported decreased from approximately $60.6 billion to $52.0 billion. Find the percent decrease in the value of U.S. agricultural exports. Round to the nearest tenth of a percent.

$$\boxed{\begin{array}{c}\text{Original}\\\text{value}\end{array}} - \boxed{\begin{array}{c}\text{new}\\\text{value}\end{array}} = \boxed{\begin{array}{c}\text{amount of}\\\text{decrease}\end{array}}$$

$$60.6 \quad - \quad 52.0 \quad = \quad 8.6$$

Now solve the basic percent equation for percent.

$$\text{Percent} \times \text{base} = \text{amount}$$

$$\boxed{\begin{array}{c}\text{Percent}\\\text{decrease}\end{array}} \times \boxed{\begin{array}{c}\text{original}\\\text{value}\end{array}} = \boxed{\begin{array}{c}\text{amount of}\\\text{decrease}\end{array}}$$

$$n \quad \times \quad 60.6 \quad = \quad 8.6$$
$$n = 8.6 \div 60.6$$
$$n \approx 0.142$$

The value of agricultural exports decreased approximately 14.2%.

Amount of decrease (8.6) / **New value (52.0)** / **Original value (60.6)**

Study Tip

Note in the example below that solving a word problem includes stating a strategy and using the strategy to find a solution. If you have difficulty with a word problem, write down the known information. Be very specific. Write out a phrase or sentence that states what you are trying to find. See *AIM for Success*.

Example 5

During an 8-year period, the population of Baltimore, Maryland, decreased from approximately 736,000 to 646,000. Find the percent decrease in Baltimore's population. Round to the nearest tenth of a percent.

Strategy

To find the percent decrease:

• Find the amount of the decrease.
• Solve the basic percent equation for *percent*.

Solution

$$\boxed{\begin{array}{c}\text{Original}\\\text{value}\end{array}} - \boxed{\begin{array}{c}\text{new}\\\text{value}\end{array}} = \boxed{\begin{array}{c}\text{amount of}\\\text{decrease}\end{array}}$$

$$736,000 - 646,000 = 90,000$$

$$\text{Percent} \times \text{base} = \text{amount}$$
$$n \times 736,000 = 90,000$$
$$n = 90,000 \div 736,000$$
$$n \approx 0.122$$

Baltimore's population decreased approximately 12.2%.

You Try It 5

During an 8-year period, the population of Norfolk, Virginia, decreased from approximately 261,000 to 215,000. Find the percent decrease in Norfolk's population. Round to the nearest tenth of a percent.

Your strategy

Your solution

Example 6

The total sales for December for a stationery store were $96,000. For January, total sales showed an 8% decrease from December's sales. What were the total sales for January?

Strategy

To find the total sales for January:

- Find the amount of decrease by solving the basic percent equation for *amount*.
- Subtract the amount of decrease from the December sales.

Solution

Percent × base = amount
0.08 × 96,000 = n
7680 = n

The decrease in sales was $7680.

96,000 − 7680 = 88,320

The total sales for January were $88,320.

You Try It 6

Fog decreased the normal 5-mile visibility at an airport by 40%. What was the visibility in the fog?

Your strategy

Your solution

Objective D   **To apply percent decrease to business—discount**

To promote sales, a store may reduce the regular price of some of its products temporarily. The reduced price is called the **sale price.** The difference between the regular price and the sale price is called the **discount.**

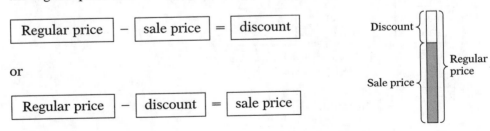

| Regular price | − | sale price | = | discount |

or

| Regular price | − | discount | = | sale price |

Discount is frequently stated as a percent of a product's regular price. This percent is called the **discount rate.**

| Discount rate | × | regular price | = | discount |

Example 7

A GE 25-inch stereo television that regularly sells for $299 is on sale for $250. Find the discount rate. Round to the nearest tenth of a percent.

Strategy

To find the discount rate:

- Find the discount.
- Solve the basic percent equation for *percent*.

Solution

Regular price	–	sale price	=	discount
299	–	250	=	49

Percent	×	base	=	amount
Discount rate	×	regular price	=	discount
n	×	299	=	49

$$n = 49 \div 299$$
$$n \approx 0.164$$

The discount rate is 16.4%.

You Try It 7

A white azalea that regularly sells for $12.50 is on sale for $10.99. Find the discount rate. Round to the nearest tenth of a percent.

Your strategy

Your solution

Example 8

A 20-horsepower lawn mower is on sale for 25% off the regular price of $1125. Find the sale price.

Strategy

To find the sale price:

- Find the discount by solving the basic percent equation for *amount*.
- Subtract to find the sale price.

Solution

Percent	×	base	=	amount
Discount rate	×	regular price	=	discount
0.25	×	1125	=	n
		281.25	=	n

Regular price	–	discount	=	sale price
1125	–	281.25	=	843.75

The sale price is $843.75.

You Try It 8

A hardware store is selling a Newport security door for 15% off the regular price of $110. Find the sale price.

Your strategy

Your solution

6.2 Exercises

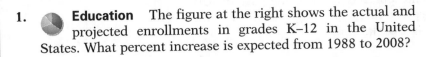 **To find percent increase**

For Exercises 1 to 5, solve. Round percents to the nearest tenth of a percent.

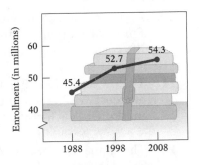

Elementary and Secondary
School Enrollments

Source: National Center for Education

1. **Education**   The figure at the right shows the actual and projected enrollments in grades K–12 in the United States. What percent increase is expected from 1988 to 2008?

2. **Fuel Efficiency**   An automobile manufacturer increased the average mileage on a car from 17.5 miles per gallon to 18.2 miles per gallon. Find the percent increase in mileage.

3. **Business**   In the 1990s, the number of Target stores increased from 420 stores to 914 stores. (*Source:* Target) What was the percent increase in the number of Target stores in the 1990s?

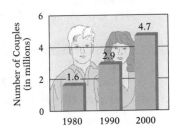

Unmarried U.S. Couples
Living Together

4. **Demography**   The graph at the right shows the number of unmarried American couples living together. (*Source:* U.S. Census Bureau) Find the percent increase in the number of unmarried couples living together from 1980 to 2000. Round to the nearest tenth.

5. **Sports**   In 1924, the number of events in the Winter Olympics was 14. The 2002 Winter Olympics in Salt Lake City included 78 medal events. (*Source:* David Wallenchinsky's *The Complete Book of the Winter Olympics*) Find the percent increase in the number of events in the Winter Olympics from 1924 to 2002.

Year	Number of Households Containing Millionaires
1975	350,000
1997	3,500,000
2005	5,600,000

Source: Affluent Market Institute

6. **Wealth**   The table at the right shows the estimated number of millionaire households in the United States. Find the percent increase in the estimated number of households containing millionaires from 1975 to 2005.

7. **Demography**   The population of Boise City, Idaho, increased 24.3% over an 8-year period. The population initially was approximately 127,000. (*Source:* U.S. Census Bureau) Find the population of Boise City 8 years later.

8. **Television**   During 1 year, the number of people subscribing to direct broadcasting satellite systems increased 87%. If the number of subscribers at the beginning of the year was 2.3 million, how many subscribers were there at the end of the year?

9. **Demography**   From 1970 to 2000, the average age of American mothers giving birth to their first child rose 16.4%. (*Source:* Centers for Disease Control and Prevention) If the average age in 1970 was 21.4 years, what was the average age in 2000? Round to the nearest tenth.

Objective B **To apply percent increase to business—markup**

10. A window air conditioner cost AirRite Air Conditioning Systems $285. Find the markup on the air conditioner if the markup rate is 25% of the cost.

11. The owner of Kerr Electronics purchased 300 Craig portable CD players at a cost of $85 each. If the owner uses a markup rate of 42%, what is the markup on each of the Craig CD players?

12. The manager of Brass Antiques has determined that a markup rate of 38% is necessary for a profit to be made. What is the markup on a brass doorknob that costs $45?

13. Computer Inc. uses a markup of $975 on a computer system that costs $3250. What is the markup rate on this system?

14. Saizon Pen & Office Supply uses a markup of $12 on a calculator that costs $20. What markup rate does this amount represent?

15. Giant Photo Service uses a markup rate of 48% on its Model ZA cameras, which cost the shop $162.
    a. What is the markup?
    b. What is the selling price?

16. The Circle R golf pro shop uses a markup rate of 45% on a set of Tour Pro golf clubs that costs the shop $210.
    a. What is the markup?
    b. What is the selling price?

17. Harvest Time Produce Inc. uses a 55% markup rate and pays $2 for a box of strawberries.
    a. What is the markup?
    b. What is the selling price of a box of strawberries?

18. Resner Builders' Hardware uses a markup rate of 42% for a table saw that costs $160. What is the selling price of the table saw?

19. Brad Burt's Magic Shop uses a markup rate of 48%. What is the selling price of a telescoping sword that costs $50?

Objective C **To find percent decrease**

20. **Travel** A new bridge reduced the normal 45-minute travel time between two cities by 18 minutes. What percent decrease does this represent?

21. **Energy** By installing energy-saving equipment, the Pala Rey Youth Camp reduced its normal $800-per-month utility bill by $320. What percent decrease does this amount represent?

22. **Depreciation** It is estimated that the value of a new car is reduced 30% after 1 year of ownership. Using this estimate, find how much value a $18,200 new car loses after 1 year.

23. **Employment**   A department store employs 1200 people during the holiday. At the end of the holiday season, the store reduces the number of employees by 45%. What is the decrease in the number of employees?

24. **Business**   Because of a decrease in demand for super-8 video cameras, Kit's Cameras reduced the orders for these models from 20 per month to 8 per month.
    a. What is the amount of the decrease?
    b. What percent decrease does this amount represent?

25. **Business**   A new computer system reduced the time for printing the payroll from 52 minutes to 39 minutes.
    a. What is the amount of the decrease?
    b. What percent decrease does this amount represent?

26. **Finance**   Juanita's average monthly expense for gasoline was $76. After joining a car pool, she was able to reduce the expense by 20%.
    a. What was the amount of the decrease?
    b. What is the average monthly gasoline bill now?

27. **Investments**   An oil company paid a dividend of $1.60 per share. After a reorganization, the company reduced the dividend by 37.5%.
    a. What was the amount of the decrease?
    b. What is the new dividend?

28. **Traffic Patterns**   Because of an improved traffic pattern at a sports stadium, the average amount of time a fan waits to park decreased from 3.5 minutes to 2.8 minutes. What percent decrease does this amount represent?

29. **Airplanes**   One configuration of the Boeing 777-300 has a seating capacity of 394. This is 26 more than that of the corresponding 777-200 jet. What is the percent decrease in capacity from the 777-300 to the 777-200 model? Round to nearest tenth of a percent.

30. **The Military**   In 2000, the Pentagon revised its account of the number of Americans killed in the Korean War from 54,246 to 36,940. (*Source: Time*, June 12, 2000) What is the percent decrease in the reported number of military personnel killed in the Korean War? Round to nearest tenth of a percent.

Objective D   **To apply percent decrease to business—discount**

31. The Austin College Bookstore is giving a discount of $8 on calculators that normally sell for $24. What is the discount rate?

32. A discount clothing store is selling a $72 sport jacket for $24 off the regular price. What is the discount rate?

33. A disc player that regularly sells for $340 is selling for 20% off the regular price. What is the discount?

34. Dacor Appliances is selling its $450 washing machine for 15% off the regular price. What is the discount?

35. An electric grill that regularly sells for $140 is selling for $42 off the regular price. What is the discount rate?

36. Quick Service Gas Station has its regularly priced $45 tune-up on sale for 16% off the regular price.
   a. What is the discount?
   b. What is the sale price?

37. Tomatoes that regularly sell for $1.25 per pound are on sale for 20% off the regular price.
   a. What is the discount?
   b. What is the sale price?

38. An outdoor supply store has its regularly priced $160 sleeping bags on sale for $120.
   a. What is the discount?
   b. What is the discount rate?

39. Standard Brands paint that regularly sells for $20 per gallon is on sale for $16 per gallon.
   a. What is the discount?
   b. What is the discount rate?

40. 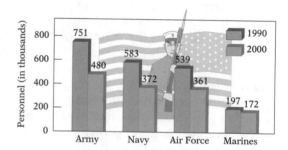 **The Military** The graph at the right shows the number of active-duty U.S. military personnel in 1990 and in 2000.
   a. Which branch of the military had the greatest percent decrease in personnel from 1990 to 2000?
   b. What was the percent decrease for this branch of the service?

Number of Active-Duty U.S. Military Personnel

Source: Fiscal 2000 Annual Report to the President and Congress by the Secretary of Defense

APPLYING THE CONCEPTS

41. Compensation A welder earning $12 per hour is given a 10% raise. To find the new wage, we can multiply $12 by 0.10 and add the product to $12. Can the new wage be found by multiplying $12 by 1.10? Try both methods and compare your answers.

42. Business Grocers, florists, bakers, and other businesses must consider spoilage when deciding the markup of a product. For instance, suppose a florist purchased 200 roses at a cost of $.86 per rose. The florist wants a markup rate of 50% of the total cost of all the roses and expects 7% of the roses to wilt and therefore not be salable. Find the selling price per rose by answering each of the following questions.
   a. What is the florist's total cost for the 200 roses?
   b. Find the total selling price without spoilage.
   c. Find the number of roses the florist expects to sell. *Hint:* The number of roses the florist expects to sell is

   % of salable roses × number of roses purchased

   d. To find the selling price per rose, divide the total selling price without spoilage by the number of roses the florist expects to sell. Round to the nearest cent.

43. **Business** A promotional sale at a department store offers 25% off the sale price. The sale price itself is 25% off the regular price. Is this the same as a sale that offers 50% off the regular price? If not, which sale gives the better price? Explain your answer.

6.3   Interest

Objective A   **To calculate simple interest**

When you deposit money in a bank—for example, in a savings account—you are permitting the bank to use your money. The bank may use the deposited money to lend customers the money to buy cars or make renovations on their homes. The bank pays you for the privilege of using your money. The amount paid to you is called **interest.** If you are the one borrowing money from the bank, the amount you pay for the privilege of using that money is also called interest.

The original amount deposited or borrowed is called the **principal.** The amount of interest paid is usually given as a percent of the principal. The percent used to determine the amount of interest is the **interest rate.**

> **TAKE NOTE**
>
> If you deposit $1000 in a savings account paying 5% interest, the $1000 is the principal and 5% is the interest rate.

Interest paid on the original principal is called **simple interest.** To calculate simple interest, multiply the principal by the interest rate per period by the number of time periods. In this objective, we are working with annual interest rates, so the time periods are years. The simple interest formula for an annual interest rate is given below.

> **Simple Interest Formula for Annual Interest Rates**
>
> Principal × annual interest rate × time (in years) = interest

Interest rates are generally given as percents. Before performing calculations involving an interest rate, write the interest rate as a decimal.

HOW TO   Calculate the simple interest due on a 2-year loan of $1500 that has an annual interest rate of 7.5%.

Principal	×	annual interest rate	×	time (in years)	=	interest
1500	×	0.075	×	2	=	225

The simple interest due is $225.

When we borrow money, the total amount to be repaid to the lender is the sum of the principal and the interest. This amount is called the **maturity value of a loan.**

> **Maturity Value Formula for Simple Interest Loans**
>
> Principal + interest = maturity value

In the example above, the simple interest due on the loan of $1500 was $225. The maturity value of the loan is therefore $1500 + $225 = $1725.

HOW TO Calculate the maturity value of a simple interest, 8-month loan of $8000 if the annual interest rate is 9.75%.

First find the interest due on the loan.

Principal	×	annual interest rate	×	time (in years)	=	interest
8000	×	0.0975	×	$\frac{8}{12}$	=	520

Find the maturity value.

Principal	+	interest	=	maturity value
8000	+	520	=	8520

The maturity value of the loan is $8520.

The monthly payment on a loan can be calculated by dividing the maturity value by the length of the loan in months.

> **Monthly Payment on a Simple Interest Loan**
>
> Maturity value ÷ length of the loan in months = monthly payment

In the example above, the maturity value of the loan is $8520. To find the monthly payment on the 8-month loan, divide 8520 by 8.

Maturity value	÷	length of the loan in months	=	monthly payment
8520	÷	8	=	1065

The monthly payment on the loan is $1065.

Example 1

Kamal borrowed $500 from a savings and loan association for 180 days at an annual interest rate of 7%. What is the simple interest due on the loan?

Strategy

To find the simple interest due, multiply the principal (500) times the annual interest rate (7% = 0.07) times the time, in years (180 days = $\frac{180}{365}$ year).

Solution

Principal	×	annual interest rate	×	time (in years)	=	interest
500	×	0.07	×	$\frac{180}{365}$	≈	17.26

The simple interest due is $17.26.

You Try It 1

A company borrowed $15,000 from a bank for 18 months at an annual interest rate of 8%. What is the simple interest due on the loan?

Your strategy

Your solution

Example 2

Calculate the maturity value of a simple interest, 9-month loan of $4000 if the annual interest rate is 8.75%.

Strategy

To find the maturity value:

- Use the simple interest formula to find the simple interest due.
- Find the maturity value by adding the principal and the interest.

Solution

$$\boxed{\text{Principal}} \times \boxed{\begin{array}{c}\text{annual}\\\text{interest}\\\text{rate}\end{array}} \times \boxed{\begin{array}{c}\text{time}\\\text{(in years)}\end{array}} = \boxed{\text{interest}}$$

$$4000 \quad \times \quad 0.0875 \quad \times \quad \frac{9}{12} \quad = \quad 262.5$$

$$\boxed{\text{Principal}} + \boxed{\text{interest}} = \boxed{\begin{array}{c}\text{maturity}\\\text{value}\end{array}}$$

$$4000 \quad + \quad 262.50 \quad = \quad 4262.50$$

The maturity value is $4262.50.

Example 3

The simple interest due on a 3-month loan of $1400 is $26.25. Find the monthly payment on the loan.

Strategy

To find the monthly payment:

- Find the maturity value by adding the principal and the interest.
- Divide the maturity value by the length of the loan in months (3).

Solution

Principal + interest = maturity value

$$1400 \quad + \quad 26.25 \quad = \quad 1426.25$$

Maturity value ÷ length of the loan = payment

$$1426.25 \quad \div \quad 3 \quad \approx 475.42$$

The monthly payment is $475.42.

You Try It 2

Calculate the maturity value of a simple interest, 90-day loan of $3800. The annual interest rate is 6%.

Your strategy

Your solution

You Try It 3

The simple interest due on a 1-year loan of $1900 is $152. Find the monthly payment on the loan.

Your strategy

Your solution

Objective B   **To calculate finance charges on a credit card bill**

When a customer uses a credit card to make a purchase, the customer is actually receiving a loan. Therefore, there is frequently an added cost to the consumer who purchases on credit. This may be in the form of an annual fee and interest charges on purchases. The interest charges on purchases are called **finance charges.**

The finance charge on a credit card bill is calculated using the simple interest formula. In the last objective, the interest rates were annual interest rates. However, credit card companies generally issue *monthly* bills and express interest rates on credit card purchases as *monthly* interest rates. Therefore, when using the simple interest formula to calculate finance charges on credit card purchases, use a monthly interest rate and express the time in months.

Note: In the simple interest formula, the time must be expressed in the same period as the rate. For an *annual* interest rate, the time must be expressed in years. For a *monthly* interest rate, the time must be in months.

Example 4	You Try It 4
A credit card company charges a customer 1.5% per month on the unpaid balance of charges on the credit card. What is the finance charge in a month when the customer has an unpaid balance of $254?	The credit card that Francesca uses charges her 1.6% per month on her unpaid balance. Find the finance charge when her unpaid balance one month is $1250.
Strategy	**Your strategy**
To find the finance charge, multiply the principal, or unpaid balance (254), times the monthly interest rate (1.5%) times the number of months (1).	
Solution	**Your solution**

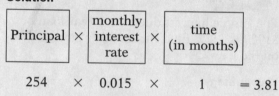

$$254 \times 0.015 \times 1 = 3.81$$

The simple interest due is $3.81.

Objective C   **To calculate compound interest**

Usually, the interest paid on money deposited or borrowed is compound interest. **Compound interest** is computed not only on the original principal but also on interest already earned. Here is an illustration.

Suppose $1000 is invested for 3 years at an annual interest rate of 9% compounded annually. Because this is an *annual* interest rate, we will calculate the interest earned each year.

During the first year, the interest earned is calculated as follows:

Principal	×	annual interest rate	×	time (in years)	=	interest
1000	×	0.09	×	1	=	90

At the end of the first year, the total amount in the account is

$$1000 + 90 = 1090$$

During the second year, the interest earned is calculated on the amount in the account at the end of the first year.

| Principal | × | annual interest rate | × | time (in years) | = | interest |
| 1090 | × | 0.09 | × | 1 | = | 98.10 |

Note that the interest earned during the second year ($98.10) is greater than the interest earned during the first year ($90). This is because the interest earned during the first year was added to the original principal, and the interest for the second year was calculated using this sum. If the account earned simple interest, the interest earned would be the same every year ($90).

At the end of the second year, the total amount in the account is the sum of the amount in the account at the end of the first year and the interest earned during the second year.

$$1090 + 98.10 = 1188.10$$

The interest earned during the third year is calculated using the amount in the account at the end of the second year ($1188.10).

| Principal | × | annual interest rate | × | time (in years) | = | interest |
| 1188.10 | × | 0.09 | × | 1 | ≈ | 106.93 |

TAKE NOTE

The interest earned each year keeps increasing. This is the effect of compound interest.

The amount in the account at the end of the third year is

$$1188.10 + 106.93 = 1295.03$$

To find the interest earned for the three years, subtract the original principal from the new principal.

| New principal | − | original principal | = | interest earned |
| 1295.03 | − | 1000 | = | 295.03 |

Note that the compound interest earned is $295.03. The simple interest earned on the investment would have been only $1000 × 0.09 × 3 = $270.

In this example, the interest was compounded annually. However, compound interest can be compounded

Compounding periods:	annually (once a year)
	semiannually (twice a year)
	quarterly (four times a year)
	monthly (12 times a year)
	daily (365 times a year)

The more frequent the compounding periods, the more interest the account earns. For example, if, in the above example, the interest had been compounded quarterly rather than annually, the interest earned would have been greater.

Calculating compound interest can be very tedious, so there are tables that can be used to simplify these calculations. A portion of a Compound Interest Table is given in the Appendix.

HOW TO What is the value after 5 years of $1000 invested at 7% annual interest compounded quarterly?

To find the interest earned, multiply the original principal (1000) by the factor found in the Compound Interest Table. To find the factor, first find the table headed "Compounded Quarterly" in the Compound Interest Table in the Appendix. Then look at the number where the 7% column and the 5-year row meet.

	Compounded Quarterly						
	4%	*5%*	*6%*	*7%*	*8%*	*9%*	*10%*
1 year	1.04060	1.05094	1.06136	1.07186	1.08243	1.09308	1.10381
5 years	1.22019	1.28204	1.34686	**1.41478**	1.48595	1.56051	1.63862
10 years	1.48886	1.64362	1.81402	2.00160	2.20804	2.43519	2.68506
15 years	1.81670	2.10718	2.44322	2.83182	3.28103	3.80013	4.39979
20 years	2.21672	2.70148	3.29066	4.00639	4.87544	5.93015	7.20957

The factor is 1.41478.

$$1000 \times 1.41478 = 1414.78$$

The value of the investment after 5 years is $1414.78.

Example 5

An investment of $650 pays 8% annual interest compounded semiannually. What is the interest earned in 5 years?

Strategy
To find the interest earned:

- Find the new principal by multiplying the original principal (650) by the factor found in the Compound Interest Table (1.48024).
- Subtract the original principal from the new principal.

Solution
$650 \times 1.48024 \approx 962.16$

The new principal is $962.16.

$962.16 - 650 = 312.16$

The interest earned is $312.16.

You Try It 5

An investment of $1000 pays 6% annual interest compounded quarterly. What is the interest earned in 20 years?

Your strategy

Your solution

6.3 Exercises

Objective A   To calculate simple interest

1. A 2-year student loan of $10,000 is made at an annual simple interest rate of 4.25%. The simple interest on the loan is $850. Identify **a.** the principal, **b.** the interest, **c.** the interest rate, and **d.** the time period of the loan.

2. A contractor obtained a 9-month loan for $80,000 at an annual simple interest rate of 9.75%. The simple interest on the loan is $5850. Identify **a.** the principal, **b.** the interest, **c.** the interest rate, and **d.** the time period of the loan.

3. Find the simple interest Jacob Zucker owes on a 2-year student loan of $8000 at an annual interest rate of 6%.

4. Find the simple interest Kara Tanamachi owes on a $1\frac{1}{2}$-year loan of $1500 at an annual interest rate of 7.5%.

5. To finance the purchase of 15 new cars, the Tropical Car Rental Agency borrowed $100,000 for 9 months at an annual interest rate of 4.5%. What is the simple interest due on the loan?

6. A home builder obtained a preconstruction loan of $50,000 for 8 months at an annual interest rate of 9.5%. What is the simple interest due on the loan?

7. A bank lent Gloria Masters $20,000 at an annual interest rate of 8.8%. The period of the loan was 9 months. Find the simple interest due on the loan.

8. Eugene Madison obtained an 8-month loan of $4500 at an annual interest rate of 6.2%. Find the simple interest Eugene owes on the loan.

9. Shannon O'Hara borrowed $5000 for 90 days at an annual simple interest rate of 7.5%. Find the simple interest due on the loan.

10. Jon McCloud borrowed $8500 for 180 days at an annual simple interest rate of 9.25%. Find the simple interest due on the loan.

11. Jorge Elizondo took out a 75-day loan of $7500 at an annual interest rate of 5.5%. Find the simple interest due on the loan.

12. Kristi Yang borrowed $15,000. The term of the loan was 90 days, and the annual simple interest rate was 7.4%. Find the simple interest due on the loan.

13. The simple interest due on a 4-month loan of $4800 is $320. What is the maturity value of the loan?

14. The simple interest due on a 60-day loan of $6500 is $80.14. Find the maturity value of the loan.

15. An auto parts dealer borrowed $150,000 at a 9.5% annual simple interest rate for 1 year. Find the maturity value of the loan.

16. A corporate executive took out a $25,000 loan at an 8.2% annual simple interest rate for 1 year. Find the maturity value of the loan.

17. William Carey borrowed $12,500 for 8 months at an annual simple interest rate of 4.5%. Find the total amount due on the loan.

18. You arrange for a 9-month bank loan of $9000 at an annual simple interest rate of 8.5%. Find the total amount you must repay to the bank.

19. Capital City Bank approves a home-improvement loan application for $14,000 at an annual simple interest rate of 5.25% for 270 days. What is the maturity value of the loan?

20. A credit union lends a member $5000 for college tuition. The loan is made for 18 months at an annual simple interest rate of 6.9%. What is the maturity value of this loan?

21. Action Machining Company purchased a robot-controlled lathe for $225,000 and financed the full amount at 8% annual simple interest for 4 years. The simple interest on the loan is $72,000. Find the monthly payment.

22. For the purchase of an entertainment center, a $1900 loan is obtained for 2 years at an annual simple interest rate of 9.4%. The simple interest due on the loan is $357.20. What is the monthly payment on the loan?

23. To attract new customers, Heller Ford is offering car loans at an annual simple interest rate of 4.5%.
    a. Find the interest charged to a customer who finances a car loan of $12,000 for 2 years.
    b. Find the monthly payment.

24. Cimarron Homes Inc. purchased a snow plow for $57,000 and financed the full amount for 5 years at an annual simple interest rate of 9%.
    a. Find the interest due on the loan.
    b. Find the monthly payment.

25. Dennis Pappas decided to build onto his present home instead of buying a new, larger house. He borrowed $42,000 for $3\frac{1}{2}$ years at an annual simple interest rate of 9.5%. Find the monthly payment.

26. Rosalinda Johnson took out a 6-month, $12,000 loan. The annual simple interest rate on the loan was 8.5%. Find the monthly payment.

Objective B   **To calculate finance charges on a credit card bill**

27. A credit card company charges a customer 1.25% per month on the unpaid balance of charges on the credit card. What is the finance charge in a month when the customer has an unpaid balance of $118.72?

28. The credit card that Dee Brown uses charges her 1.75% per month on her unpaid balance. Find the finance charge when her unpaid balance one month is $391.64.

29. What is the finance charge on an unpaid balance of $12,368.92 on a credit card that charges 1.5% per month on any unpaid balance?

30. Suppose you have an unpaid balance of $995.04 on a credit card that charges 1.2% per month on any unpaid balance. What finance charge do you owe the company?

31. A credit card customer has an unpaid balance of $1438.20. What is the difference between monthly finance charges of 1.15% per month on the unpaid balance and monthly finance charges of 1.85% per month?

32. One credit card company charges 1.25% per month on any unpaid balance, and a second company charges 1.75%. What is the difference between the finance charges that these two companies assess on an unpaid balance of $687.45?

Objective C   **To calculate compound interest**

33. North Island Federal Credit Union pays 4% annual interest, compounded daily, on time savings deposits. Find the value of $750 deposited in this account after 1 year.

34. Tanya invested $2500 in a tax-sheltered annuity that pays 8% annual interest compounded daily. Find the value of her investment after 20 years.

35. Sal Travato invested $3000 in a corporate retirement account that pays 6% annual interest compounded semiannually. Find the value of his investment after 15 years.

36. To replace equipment, a farmer invested $20,000 in an account that pays 7% annual interest compounded monthly. What is the value of the investment after 5 years?

37. Green River Lodge invests $75,000 in a trust account that pays 8% interest compounded quarterly.
a. What will the value of the investment be in 5 years?
b. How much interest will be earned in the 5 years?

38. To save for retirement, a couple deposited $3000 in an account that pays 7% annual interest compounded daily.
a. What will the value of the investment be in 10 years?
b. How much interest will be earned in the 10 years?

39. To save for a child's education, the Petersens deposited $2500 into an account that pays 6% annual interest compounded daily. Find the amount of interest earned on this account over a 20-year period.

40. How much interest is earned in 2 years on $4000 deposited in an account that pays 6% interest, compounded quarterly?

APPLYING THE CONCEPTS

41. Banking The Mission Valley Credit Union charges its customers an interest rate of 2% per month on money that is transferred into an account that is overdrawn. Find the interest owed to the credit union for 1 month when $800 is transferred into an overdrawn account.

42. Banking Suppose you have a savings account that earns interest at the rate of 6% per year compounded monthly. On January 1, you open this account with a deposit of $100.
a. On February 1, you deposit an additional $100 into the account. What is the value of the account after the deposit?
b. On March 1, you deposit an additional $100 into the account. What is the value of the account after the deposit?
Note: This type of savings plan, wherein equal amounts ($100) are saved at equal time intervals (every month), is called an annuity.

43. Banking At 4 P.M. on July 31, you open a savings account that pays 5% annual interest and you deposit $500 in the account. Your deposit is credited as of August 1. At the beginning of September, you receive a statement from the bank that shows that during the month of August, you received $2.12 in interest. The interest has been added to your account, bringing the total on deposit to $502.12. At the beginning of October, you receive a statement from the bank that shows that during the month of September, you received $2.06 in interest on the $502.12 on deposit. Explain why you received less interest during the second month when there was more money on deposit.

6.4 Wages

To calculate commissions, total hourly wages, and salaries

Commissions, hourly wage, and salary are three ways to receive payment for doing work.

Commissions are usually paid to salespersons and are calculated as a percent of total sales.

HOW TO As a real estate broker, Emma Smith receives a commission of 4.5% of the selling price of a house. Find the commission she earned for selling a home for $175,000.

To find the commission Emma earned, solve the basic percent equation for *amount*.

Percent	×	base	=	amount
Commission rate	×	total sales	=	commission
0.045	×	175,000	=	7875

The commission is $7875.

An employee who receives an **hourly wage** is paid a certain amount for each hour worked.

HOW TO A plumber receives an hourly wage of $18.25. Find the plumber's total wages for working 37 hours.

To find the plumber's total wages, multiply the hourly wage by the number of hours worked.

Hourly wage	×	number of hours worked	=	total wages
18.25	×	37	=	675.25

The plumber's total wages for working 37 hours are $675.25.

An employee who is paid a **salary** receives payment based on a weekly, biweekly (every other week), monthly, or annual time schedule. Unlike the employee who receives an hourly wage, the salaried worker does not receive additional pay for working more than the regularly scheduled workday.

HOW TO Ravi Basar is a computer operator who receives a weekly salary of $695. Find his salary for 1 month (4 weeks).

To find Ravi's salary for 1 month, multiply the salary per pay period by the number of pay periods.

Salary per pay period	×	number of pay periods	=	total salary
695	×	4	=	2780

Ravi's total salary for 1 month is $2780.

Example 1

A pharmacist's hourly wage is $28. On Saturday, the pharmacist earns time and a half (1.5 times the regular hourly wage). How much does the pharmacist earn for working 6 hours on Saturday?

Strategy

To find the pharmacist's earnings:

- Find the hourly wage for working on Saturday by multiplying the hourly wage by 1.5.
- Multiply the hourly wage by the number of hours worked.

Solution

$28 \times 1.5 = 42 \qquad 42 \times 6 = 252$

The pharmacist earns $252.

You Try It 1

A construction worker, whose hourly wage is $18.50, earns double time (2 times the regular hourly wage) for working overtime. Find the worker's wages for working 8 hours of overtime.

Your strategy

Your solution

Example 2

An efficiency expert received a contract for $3000. The expert spent 75 hours on the project. Find the consultant's hourly wage.

Strategy

To find the hourly wage, divide the total earnings by the number of hours worked.

Solution

$3000 \div 75 = 40$

The hourly wage was $40.

You Try It 2

A contractor for a bridge project receives an annual salary of $48,228. What is the contractor's salary per month?

Your strategy

Your solution

Example 3

Dani Greene earns $28,500 per year plus a 5.5% commission on sales over $100,000. During one year, Dani sold $150,000 worth of computers. Find Dani's total earnings for the year.

Strategy

To find the total earnings:

- Find the sales over $100,000.
- Multiply the commission rate by sales over $100,000.
- Add the commission to the annual pay.

Solution

$150,000 - 100,000 = 50,000$
$50,000 \times 0.055 = 2750 \qquad$ • **Commission**
$28,500 + 2750 = 31,250$

Dani earned $31,250.

You Try It 3

An insurance agent earns $27,000 per year plus a 9.5% commission on sales over $50,000. During one year, the agent's sales totaled $175,000. Find the agent's total earnings for the year.

Your strategy

Your solution

6.4 Exercises

Objective A To calculate commissions, total hourly wages, and salaries

1. Lewis works in a clothing store and earns $9.50 per hour. How much does he earn in a 40-hour week?

2. Sasha pays a gardener an hourly wage of $11. How much does she pay the gardener for working 25 hours?

3. A real estate agent receives a 3% commission for selling a house. Find the commission that the agent earned for selling a house for $131,000.

4. Ron Caruso works as an insurance agent and receives a commission of 40% of the first year's premium. Find Ron's commission for selling a life insurance policy with a first-year premium of $1050.

5. A stockbroker receives a commission of 1.5% of the price of stock that is bought or sold. Find the commission on 100 shares of stock that were bought for $5600.

6. The owner of the Carousel Art Gallery receives a commission of 20% on paintings that are sold on consignment. Find the commission on a painting that sold for $22,500.

7. Keisha Brown receives an annual salary of $38,928 as a teacher of Italian. How much does Keisha receive each month?

8. An apprentice plumber receives an annual salary of $27,900. How much does the plumber receive per month?

9. An electrician's hourly wage is $25.80. For working overtime, the electrician earns double time. What is the electrician's hourly wage for working overtime?

10. Carlos receives a commission of 12% of his weekly sales as a sales representative for a medical supply company. Find the commission he earned during a week in which sales were $4500.

11. A golf pro receives a commission of 25% for selling a golf set. Find the commission the pro earned for selling a golf set costing $450.

12. Steven receives $3.75 per square yard to install carpet. How much does he receive for installing 160 square yards of carpet?

13. A typist charges $2.75 per page for typing technical material. How much does the typist earn for typing a 225-page book?

14. A nuclear chemist received $15,000 in consulting fees while working on a nuclear power plant. The chemist worked 120 hours on the project. Find the chemist's hourly wage.

15. Maxine received $3400 for working on a project as a computer consultant for 40 hours. Find her hourly wage.

16. Gil Stratton's hourly wage is $10.78. For working overtime, he receives double time.
   a. What is Gil's hourly wage for working overtime?
   b. How much does he earn for working 16 hours of overtime?

17. Mark is a lathe operator and receives an hourly wage of $15.90. When working on Saturday, he receives time and a half.
   a. What is Mark's hourly wage on Saturday?
   b. How much does he earn for working 8 hours on Saturday?

18. A stock clerk at a supermarket earns $8.20 an hour. For working the night shift, the clerk's wage increases by 15%.
   a. What is the increase in hourly pay for working the night shift?
   b. What is the clerk's hourly wage for working the night shift?

19. A nurse earns $21.50 an hour. For working the night shift, the nurse receives a 10% increase in pay.
   a. What is the increase in hourly pay for working the night shift?
   b. What is the hourly pay for working the night shift?

20. Tony's hourly wage as a service station attendant is $9.40. For working the night shift, his wage is increased 25%. What is Tony's hourly wage for working the night shift?

21. Nicole Tobin, a salesperson, receives a salary of $250 per week plus a commission of 15% on all sales over $1500. Find her earnings during a week in which sales totaled $3000.

APPLYING THE CONCEPTS

Compensation The table at the right shows the average starting salaries for recent college graduates. Use this table for Exercises 22 to 25. Round to the nearest dollar.

22. What was the starting salary in the previous year for an accountant?

23. How much did the starting salary for a chemical engineer increase over that of the previous year?

24. What was the starting salary in the previous year for a computer science major?

25. How much did the starting salary for a political science major decrease from that of the previous year?

Average Starting Salaries		
Bachelor's Degree	Average Starting Salary	Change from Previous Year
Chemical Engineering	$52,169	1.8% increase
Electrical Engineering	$50,566	0.4% increase
Computer Science	$46,536	7.6% decrease
Accounting	$41,360	2.6% increase
Business	$36,515	3.7% increase
Biology	$29,554	1.0% decrease
Political Science	$28,546	12.6% decrease
Psychology	$26,738	10.7% decrease

Source: National Association of Colleges

6.5

Bank Statements

To calculate checkbook balances

A checking account can be opened at most banks and savings and loan associations by depositing an amount of money in the bank. A checkbook contains checks and deposit slips and a checkbook register in which to record checks written and amounts deposited in the checking account. A sample check is shown below.

Payee   Date Check is Written

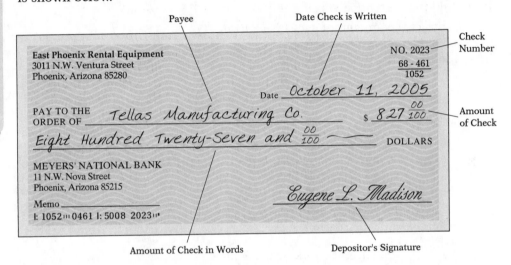

Check Number

East Phoenix Rental Equipment
3011 N.W. Ventura Street
Phoenix, Arizona 85280

NO. 2023

68 - 461
1052

Date *October 11, 2005*

PAY TO THE ORDER OF *Tellas Manufacturing Co.* $ *827 $\frac{00}{100}$*

Eight Hundred Twenty-Seven and $\frac{00}{100}$ ———— DOLLARS

Amount of Check

MEYERS' NATIONAL BANK
11 N.W. Nova Street
Phoenix, Arizona 85215

Memo _____

I: 1052III0461 I: 5008 2023III

Eugene L. Madison

Amount of Check in Words   Depositor's Signature

Each time a check is written, the amount of the check is subtracted from the amount in the account. When a deposit is made, the amount deposited is added to the amount in the account.

A portion of a checkbook register is shown below. The account holder had a balance of $587.93 before writing two checks, one for $286.87 and the other for $202.38, and making one deposit of $345.00.

		RECORD ALL CHARGES OR CREDITS THAT AFFECT YOUR ACCOUNT					BALANCE	
NUMBER	DATE	DESCRIPTION OF TRANSACTION	PAYMENT/DEBIT (–)	√ T	FEE (IF ANY) (–)	DEPOSIT/CREDIT (+)	$ 587	93
108	8/4	Plumber	$286 87		$	$	301	06
109	8/10	Car Payment	202 38				98	68
	8/14	Deposit				345 00	443	68

To find the current checking account balance, subtract the amount of each check from the previous balance. Then add the amount of the deposit.

The current checking account balance is $443.68.

Example 1

A mail carrier had a checking account balance of $485.93 before writing two checks, one for $18.98 and another for $35.72, and making a deposit of $250. Find the current checking account balance.

You Try It 1

A cement mason had a checking account balance of $302.46 before writing a check for $20.59 and making two deposits, one in the amount of $176.86 and another in the amount of $94.73. Find the current checking account balance.

Strategy

To find the current balance:

• Subtract the amount of each check from the old balance.
• Add the amount of the deposit.

Your strategy

Solution

$$
\begin{array}{r}
485.93 \\
-\ 018.98 \quad \text{first check} \\
\hline
466.95 \\
-\ 135.72 \quad \text{second check} \\
\hline
431.23 \\
+\ 250.00 \quad \text{deposit} \\
\hline
681.23
\end{array}
$$

The current checking account balance is $681.23.

Your solution

Objective B **To balance a checkbook**

Each month a bank statement is sent to the account holder. A **bank statement** is a document showing all the transactions in a bank account during the month. It shows the checks that the bank has paid, the deposits received, and the current bank balance.

A bank statement and checkbook register are shown on the next page.

Balancing a checkbook, or determining whether the checking account balance is accurate, requires a number of steps.

1. In the checkbook register, put a check mark (√) by each check paid by the bank and by each deposit recorded by the bank.

RECORD ALL CHARGES OR CREDITS THAT AFFECT YOUR ACCOUNT

NUMBER	DATE	DESCRIPTION OF TRANSACTION	PAYMENT/DEBIT (−)		√ T	FEE (IF ANY) (−)	DEPOSIT/CREDIT (+)		BALANCE $ 840	27
						$	$		$	
263	5/20	Dentist	$ 75	00	√				765	27
264	5/22	Post Office	33	61	√				731	66
265	5/22	Gas Company	67	14					664	52
	5/29	Deposit			√		192	00	856	52
266	5/29	Pharmacy	38	95	√				817	57
267	5/30	Telephone	63	85					753	72
268	6/2	Groceries	73	19	√				680	53
	6/3	Deposit			√		215	00	895	53
269	6/7	Insurance	103	00	√				792	53
	6/10	Deposit					225	00	1017	53
270	6/15	Photo Shop	16	63	√				1000	90
271	6/18	Newspaper	27	00					973	90

CHECKING ACCOUNT Monthly Statement			Account Number: 924-297-8
Date	Transaction	Amount	Balance
5/20	OPENING BALANCE		840.27
5/21	CHECK	75.00	765.27
5/23	CHECK	33.61	731.66
5/29	DEPOSIT	192.00	923.66
6/1	CHECK	38.95	884.71
6/1	INTEREST	4.47	889.18
6/3	CHECK	73.19	815.99
6/3	DEPOSIT	215.00	1030.99
6/9	CHECK	103.00	927.99
6/16	CHECK	16.63	911.36
6/20	SERVICE CHARGE	3.00	908.36
6/20	CLOSING BALANCE		908.36

2. Add to the current checkbook balance all checks that have been written but have not yet been paid by the bank and any interest paid on the account.

Current checkbook balance:	973.90
Checks: 265	67.14
267	63.85
271	27.00
Interest:	+ 4.47
	1136.36

TAKE NOTE

A **service charge** is an amount of money charged by a bank for handling a transaction.

3. Subtract any service charges and any deposits not yet recorded by the bank. This is the checkbook balance.

Service charge:	− 3.00
	1133.36
Deposit:	− 225.00
Checkbook balance:	908.36

4. Compare the balance with the bank balance listed on the bank statement. If the two numbers are equal, the bank statement and the checkbook "balance."

Closing bank balance from bank statement	Checkbook balance
$908.36	= $908.36

The bank statement and checkbook balance.

HOW TO

RECORD ALL CHARGES OR CREDITS THAT AFFECT YOUR ACCOUNT

NUMBER	DATE	DESCRIPTION OF TRANSACTION	PAYMENT/DEBIT (−)		√ T	FEE (IF ANY) (−)	DEPOSIT/CREDIT (+)		BALANCE $ 1620	42
413	3/2	Car Payment	$232	15	√	$	$		1388	27
414	3/2	Utilities	67	14	√				1321	13
415	3/5	Restaurant	78	14					1242	99
	3/8	Deposit			√		1842	66	3085	65
416	3/10	House Payment	672	14	√				2413	51
417	3/14	Insurance	177	10					2236	41

CHECKING ACCOUNT Monthly Statement

Account Number: 924-297-8

Date	Transaction	Amount	Balance
3/1	OPENING BALANCE		1620.42
3/4	CHECK	232.15	1388.27
3/5	CHECK	67.14	1321.13
3/8	DEPOSIT	1842.66	3163.79
3/10	INTEREST	6.77	3170.56
3/12	CHECK	672.14	2498.42
3/25	SERVICE CHARGE	2.00	2496.42
3/30	CLOSING BALANCE		2496.42

Balance the bank statement shown above.

1. In the checkbook register, put a check mark (√) by each check paid by the bank and by each deposit recorded by the bank.

2. Add to the current checkbook balance all checks that have been written but have not yet been paid by the bank and any interest paid on the account.

3. Subtract any service charges and any deposits not yet recorded by the bank. This is the checkbook balance.

4. Compare the balance with the bank balance listed on the bank statement. If the two numbers are equal, the bank statement and the checkbook "balance."

Current checkbook balance:	2236.41
Checks: 415	78.14
417	177.10
Interest:	+ 6.77
	2498.42
Service charge:	− 2.00
Checkbook balance:	2496.42

Closing bank balance from bank statement | Checkbook balance

$2496.42 = $2496.42

The bank statement and checkbook balance.

Example 2 Balance the bank statement shown below.

		RECORD ALL CHARGES OR CREDITS THAT AFFECT YOUR ACCOUNT							BALANCE	
NUMBER	DATE	DESCRIPTION OF TRANSACTION	PAYMENT/DEBIT (−)		√ T	FEE (IF ANY) (−)	DEPOSIT/CREDIT (+)		$ 412	64
345	1/14	Phone Bill	$ 54	75	√	$	$		357	89
346	1/19	News Shop	18	98	√				338	91
347	1/23	Theater Tickets	95	00					243	91
	1/31	Deposit			√		947	00	1190	91
348	2/5	Cash	250	00	√				940	91
349	2/12	Rent	840	00					100	91

CHECKING ACCOUNT Monthly Statement			Account Number: 924-297-8
Date	Transaction	Amount	Balance
1/10	OPENING BALANCE		412.64
1/18	CHECK	54.75	357.89
1/23	CHECK	18.98	338.91
1/31	DEPOSIT	947.00	1285.91
2/1	INTEREST	4.52	1290.43
2/10	CHECK	250.00	1040.43
2/10	CLOSING BALANCE		1040.43

Solution

Current checkbook balance:	100.91
Checks: 347	95.00
349	840.00
Interest:	+ 4.52
	1040.43
Service charge:	− 0.00
	1040.43
Deposit:	− 0.00
Checkbook balance:	1040.43

Closing bank balance from bank statement: $1040.43

Checkbook balance: $1040.43

The bank statement and the checkbook balance.

You Try It 2

Balance the bank statement shown below.

RECORD ALL CHARGES OR CREDITS THAT AFFECT YOUR ACCOUNT

NUMBER	DATE	DESCRIPTION OF TRANSACTION	PAYMENT/DEBIT (–)		√ T	FEE (IF ANY) (–)	DEPOSIT/CREDIT (+)		BALANCE $	
									903	17
	2/15	Deposit	$			$	$ 523	84	1427	01
234	2/20	Mortgage	773	21					653	80
235	2/27	Cash	200	00					453	80
	3/1	Deposit					523	84	977	64
236	3/12	Insurance	275	50					702	14
237	3/12	Telephone	78	73					623	41

CHECKING ACCOUNT Monthly Statement

Account Number: 314-271-4

Date	Transaction	Amount	Balance
2/14	OPENING BALANCE		903.17
2/15	DEPOSIT	523.84	1427.01
2/21	CHECK	773.21	653.80
2/28	CHECK	200.00	453.80
3/1	INTEREST	2.11	455.91
3/14	CHECK	275.50	180.41
3/14	CLOSING BALANCE		180.41

Your solution

6.5 Exercises

Objective A **To calculate checkbook balances**

1. You had a checking account balance of $342.51 before making a deposit of $143.81. What is your new checking account balance?

2. Carmen had a checking account balance of $493.26 before writing a check for $48.39. What is the current checking account balance?

3. A real estate firm had a balance of $2431.76 in its rental-property checking account. What is the balance in this account after a check for $1209.29 has been written?

4. The business checking account for R and R Tires showed a balance of $1536.97. What is the balance in this account after a deposit of $439.21 has been made?

5. A nutritionist had a checking account balance of $1204.63 before writing one check for $119.27 and another check for $260.09. Find the current checkbook balance.

6. Sam had a checking account balance of $3046.93 before writing a check for $1027.33 and making a deposit of $150.00. Find the current checkbook balance.

7. The business checking account for Rachael's Dry Cleaning had a balance of $3476.85 before a deposit of $1048.53 was made. The store manager then wrote two checks, one for $848.37 and another for $676.19. Find the current checkbook balance.

8. Joel had a checking account balance of $427.38 before a deposit of $127.29 was made. Joel then wrote two checks, one for $43.52 and one for $249.78. Find the current checkbook balance.

9. A carpenter had a checkbook balance of $404.96 before making a deposit of $350 and writing a check for $71.29. Is there enough money in the account to purchase a refrigerator for $675?

10. A taxi driver had a checkbook balance of $149.85 before making a deposit of $245 and writing a check for $387.68. Is there enough money in the account for the bank to pay the check?

11. A sporting goods store has the opportunity to buy downhill skis and cross-country skis at a manufacturer's closeout sale. The downhill skis will cost $3500, and the cross-country skis will cost $2050. There is currently $5625.42 in the sporting goods store's checking account. Is there enough money in the account to make both purchases by check?

12. A lathe operator's current checkbook balance is $1143.42. The operator wants to purchase a utility trailer for $525 and a used piano for $650. Is there enough money in the account to make the two purchases?

Objective B **To balance a checkbook**

13. Balance the checkbook.

		RECORD ALL CHARGES OR CREDITS THAT AFFECT YOUR ACCOUNT							
								BALANCE	
NUMBER	DATE	DESCRIPTION OF TRANSACTION	PAYMENT/DEBIT (−)	√ T	FEE (IF ANY) (−)	DEPOSIT/CREDIT (+)		$ 2466	79
223	3/2	Groceries	$ 167 32		$	$		2299	47
	3/5	Deposit				960	70	3260	17
224	3/5	Rent	860 00					2400	17
225	3/7	Gas & Electric	142 35					2257	82
226	3/7	Cash	300 00					1957	82
227	3/7	Insurance	218 44					1739	38
228	3/7	Credit Card	419 32					1320	06
229	3/12	Dentist	92 00					1228	06
230	3/13	Drug Store	47 03					1181	03
	3/19	Deposit				960	70	2141	73
231	3/22	Car Payment	241 35					1900	38
232	3/25	Cash	300 00					1600	38
233	3/25	Oil Company	166 40					1433	98
234	3/28	Plumber	155 73					1278	25
235	3/29	Department Store	288 39					989	86

CHECKING ACCOUNT Monthly Statement		Account Number: 122-345-1	
Date	Transaction	Amount	Balance
3/1	OPENING BALANCE		2466.79
3/5	DEPOSIT	960.70	3427.49
3/7	CHECK	167.32	3260.17
3/8	CHECK	860.00	2400.17
3/8	CHECK	300.00	2100.17
3/9	CHECK	142.35	1957.82
3/12	CHECK	218.44	1739.38
3/14	CHECK	92.00	1647.38
3/18	CHECK	47.03	1600.35
3/19	DEPOSIT	960.70	2561.05
3/25	CHECK	241.35	2319.70
3/27	CHECK	300.00	2019.70
3/29	CHECK	155.73	1863.97
3/30	INTEREST	13.22	1877.19
4/1	CLOSING BALANCE		1877.19

14. Balance the checkbook.

RECORD ALL CHARGES OR CREDITS THAT AFFECT YOUR ACCOUNT

NUMBER	DATE	DESCRIPTION OF TRANSACTION	PAYMENT/DEBIT (−)		√ T	FEE (IF ANY) (−)	DEPOSIT/CREDIT (+)		BALANCE $ 1219	43
	5/1	Deposit	$			$	$ 619	14	1838	57
515	5/2	Electric Bill	42	35					1796	22
516	5/2	Groceries	95	14					1701	08
517	5/4	Insurance	122	17					1578	91
518	5/5	Theatre Tickets	84	50					1494	41
	5/8	Deposit					619	14	2113	55
519	5/10	Telephone	37	39					2076	16
520	5/12	Newspaper	22	50					2053	66
	5/15	Deposit					619	14	2672	80
521	5/20	Computer Store	172	90					2499	90
522	5/21	Credit Card	313	44					2186	46
523	5/22	Eye Exam	82	00					2104	46
524	5/24	Groceries	107	14					1997	32
525	5/24	Deposit					619	14	2616	46
526	5/25	Oil Company	144	16					2472	30
527	5/30	Car Payment	288	62					2183	68
528	5/30	Mortgage Payment	877	42					1306	26

CHECKING ACCOUNT Monthly Statement   Account Number: 122-345-1

Date	Transaction	Amount	Balance
5/1	OPENING BALANCE		1219.43
5/1	DEPOSIT	619.14	1838.57
5/3	CHECK	95.14	1743.43
5/4	CHECK	42.35	1701.08
5/6	CHECK	84.50	1616.58
5/8	CHECK	122.17	1494.41
5/8	DEPOSIT	619.14	2113.55
5/15	INTEREST	7.82	2121.37
5/15	CHECK	37.39	2083.98
5/15	DEPOSIT	619.14	2703.12
5/23	CHECK	82.00	2621.12
5/23	CHECK	172.90	2448.22
5/24	CHECK	107.14	2341.08
5/24	DEPOSIT	619.14	2960.22
5/30	CHECK	288.62	2671.60
6/1	CLOSING BALANCE		2671.60

15. Balance the checkbook.

		RECORD ALL CHARGES OR CREDITS THAT AFFECT YOUR ACCOUNT						BALANCE	
NUMBER	DATE	DESCRIPTION OF TRANSACTION	PAYMENT/DEBIT (–)	√ T	FEE (IF ANY) (–)	DEPOSIT/CREDIT (+)		$ 2035	18
218	7/2	Mortgage	$ 984 60	$		$		1050	58
219	7/4	Telephone	63 36					987	22
220	7/7	Cash	200 00					787	22
	7/12	Deposit				792	60	1579	82
221	7/15	Insurance	292 30					1287	52
222	7/18	Investment	500 00					787	52
223	7/20	Credit Card	414 83					372	69
	7/26	Deposit				792	60	1165	29
224	7/27	Department Store	113 37					1051	92

CHECKING ACCOUNT Monthly Statement			Account Number: 122-345-1	
Date	Transaction		Amount	Balance
7/1	OPENING BALANCE			2035.18
7/1	INTEREST		5.15	2040.33
7/4	CHECK		984.60	1055.73
7/6	CHECK		63.36	992.37
7/12	DEPOSIT		792.60	1784.97
7/20	CHECK		292.30	1492.67
7/24	CHECK		500.00	992.67
7/26	DEPOSIT		792.60	1785.27
7/28	CHECK		200.00	1585.27
7/30	CLOSING BALANCE			1585.27

APPLYING THE CONCEPTS

16. When a check is written, the amount is _____ from the balance.

17. When a deposit is made, the amount is _____ to the balance.

18. In checking the bank statement, _____ to the checkbook balance all checks that have been written but not processed.

19. In checking the bank balance, _____ any service charge and any deposits not yet recorded.

20. Define the words *credit* and *debit* as they apply to checkbooks.

Focus on Problem Solving

Counterexamples

An example that is given to show that a statement is not true is called a **counterexample.** For instance, suppose someone makes the statement "All colors are red." A counterexample to that statement would be to show someone the color blue or some other color.

If a statement is *always* true, there are no counterexamples. The statement "All even numbers are divisible by 2" is always true. It is not possible to give an example of an even number that is not divisible by 2.

In mathematics, statements that are always true are called *theorems,* and mathematicians are always searching for theorems. Sometimes a conjecture by a mathematician appears to be a theorem. That is, the statement appears to be always true, but later on someone finds a counterexample.

One example of this occurred when the French mathematician Pierre de Fermat (1601–1665) conjectured that $2^{(2^n)} + 1$ is always a prime number for any natural number n. For instance, when $n = 3$, we have $2^{(2^3)} + 1 = 2^8 + 1 = 257$, and 257 is a prime number. However, in 1732 Leonhard Euler (1707–1783) showed that when $n = 5$, $2^{(2^5)} + 1 = 4,294,967,297$ and that $4,294,967,297 = 641 \cdot 6,700,417$—without a calculator! Because 4,294,967,297 is the product of two numbers (other than itself and 1), it is not a prime number. This counterexample showed that Fermat's conjecture is not a theorem.

For Exercises 1 and 5, find at least one counterexample.

1. All composite numbers are divisible by 2.

2. All prime numbers are odd numbers.

3. The square of any number is always bigger than the number.

4. The reciprocal of a number is always less than 1.

5. A number ending in 9 is always larger than a number ending in 3.

When a problem is posed, it may not be known whether the problem statement is true or false. For instance, Christian Goldbach (1690–1764) stated that every even number greater than 2 can be written as the sum of two prime numbers. For example,

$$12 = 5 + 7 \qquad 32 = 3 + 29$$

Although this problem is approximately 250 years old, mathematicians have not been able to prove it is a theorem, nor have they been able to find a counterexample.

For Exercises 6 to 9, answer true if the statement is always true. If there is an instance in which the statement is false, give a counterexample.

6. The sum of two positive numbers is always larger than either of the two numbers.

7. The product of two positive numbers is always larger than either of the two numbers.

8. Percents always represent a number less than or equal to 1.

9. It is never possible to divide by zero.

Projects and Group Activities

Buying a Car Suppose a student has an after-school job to earn money to buy and maintain a car. We will make assumptions about the monthly costs in several categories in order to determine how many hours per week the student must work to support the car. Assume the student earns $8.50 per hour.

1. Monthly payment

   Assume that the car cost $8500 with a down payment of $1020. The remainder is financed for 3 years at an annual simple interest rate of 9%.

   Monthly payment = _____

2. Insurance

   Assume that insurance costs $1500 per year.

   Monthly insurance payment = _____

3. Gasoline

   Assume that the student travels 750 miles per month, that the car travels 25 miles per gallon of gasoline, and that gasoline costs $1.50 per gallon.

   Number of gallons of gasoline purchased per month = _____
   Monthly cost for gasoline = _____

4. Miscellaneous

   Assume $.33 per mile for upkeep.

   Monthly expense for upkeep = _____

5. Total monthly expenses for the monthly payment, insurance, gasoline, and miscellaneous = _____

6. To find the number of hours per month that the student must work to finance the car, divide the total monthly expenses by the hourly rate.

   Number of hours per month = _____

7. To find the number of hours per week that the student must work, divide the number of hours per month by 4.

   Number of hours per week = _____

   The student has to work _____ hours per week to pay the monthly car expenses.

If you own a car, make out your own expense record. If you do not own a car, make assumptions about the kind of car that you would like to purchase, and calculate the total monthly expenses that you would have. An insurance company will give you rates on different kinds of insurance. An automobile club can give you approximations of miscellaneous expenses.

Chapter Summary

Key Words	Examples
The *unit cost* is the cost of one item.	Three paperback books cost $36. The unit cost is the cost of one paperback book, $12.
Percent increase is used to show how much a quantity has increased over its original value.	The city's population increased 5%, from 10,000 people to 10,500 people.
Cost is the price a business pays for a product. *Selling price* is the price at which a business sells a product to a customer. *Markup* is the difference between selling price and cost. *Markup rate* is the markup expressed as a percent of a product's cost.	A business pays $90 for a pair of cross trainers; the cost is $90. The business sells the cross trainers for $135; the selling price is $135. The markup is $135 − $90 = $45.
Percent decrease is used to show how much a quantity has decreased from its original value.	Sales decreased 10%, from 10,000 units in the third quarter to 9000 units in the fourth quarter.
Sale price is the price after a reduction from the regular price. *Discount* is the difference between the regular price and the sale price. *Discount rate* is the discount as a percent of a product's regular price.	A movie video that regularly sells for $50 is on sale for $40. The regular price is $50. The sale price is $40. The discount is $50 − $40 = $10.
Interest is the amount paid for the privilege of using someone else's money. *Principal* is the amount of money originally deposited or borrowed. The percent used to determine the amount of interest is the *interest rate*. Interest computed on the original amount is called *simple interest*. The principal plus the interest owed on a loan is called the *maturity value*.	Consider a 1-year loan of $5000 at an annual simple interest rate of 8%. The principal is $5000. The interest rate is 8%. The interest paid on the loan is $5000 × 0.08 = $400. The maturity value is $5000 + $400 = $5400.
The interest charged on purchases made with a credit card are called *finance charges*.	A credit card company charges 1.5% per month on any unpaid balance. The finance charge on an unpaid balance of $1000 is $1000 × 0.015 × 1 = $15.
Compound interest is computed not only on the original principal but also on the interest already earned.	$10,000 is invested at 5% annual interest compounded monthly. The value of the investment after 5 years can be found by multiplying 10,000 by the factor found in the Compound Interest Table in the Appendix. $10,000 × 1.283359 = $12,833.59
A *mortgage* is an amount that is borrowed to buy real estate. The *loan origination fee* is usually a percent of the mortgage and is expressed as *points*.	The loan origination fee of 3 points paid on a mortgage of $200,000 is 0.03 × $200,000 = $6000.
A *commission* is usually paid to a salesperson and is calculated as a percent of sales.	A commission of 5% on sales of $50,000 is 0.05 × $50,000 = $2500.

An employee who receives an *hourly wage* is paid a certain amount for each hour worked.	An employee is paid an hourly wage of $15. The employee's wages for working 10 hours are $15 × 10 = $150.
An employee who is paid a *salary* receives payment based on a weekly, biweekly, monthly, or annual time schedule.	An employee paid an annual salary of $60,000 is paid $60,000 ÷ 12 = $5000 per month.
Balancing a checkbook is determining whether the checkbook balance is accurate.	To balance a checkbook: (1) Put a checkmark in the checkbook register by each check paid by the bank and by each deposit recorded by the bank. (2) Add to the current checkbook balance all checks that have been written but have not yet been paid by the bank and any interest paid on the account. (3) Subtract any charges and any deposits not yet recorded by the bank. This is the checkbook balance. (4) Compare the balance with the bank balance listed on the bank statement. If the two numbers are equal, the bank statement and the checkbook "balance."

Essential Rules and Procedures

Examples

To find unit cost, divide the total cost by the number of units.	Three paperback books cost $36. The unit cost is $36 ÷ 3 = $12 per book.
To find total cost, multiply the unit cost by the number of units purchased.	One melon costs $3. The total cost for 5 melons is $3 × 5 = $15.
Basic Markup Equations Selling price − cost = markup Cost + markup = selling price Markup rate × cost = markup	A pair of cross trainers that cost a business $90 has a 50% markup rate. The markup is 0.50 × $90 = $45. The selling price is $90 + $45 = $135.
Basic Discount Equations Regular price − sale price = discount Regular price − discount = sale price Discount rate × regular price = discount	A movie video is on sale for 20% off the regular price of $50. The discount is 0.20 × $50 = $10. The sale price is $50 − $10 = $40.
Simple Interest Formula for Annual Interest Rates	Principal × annual interest rate × time (in years) = interest The simple interest due on a 2-year
Maturity Value Formula for Simple Interest Loan	Principal + interest = maturity value The interest to be paid on a 2-year loan
Monthly Payment on a Simple Interest Loan Maturity value ÷ length of the loan in months = monthly payment	The maturity value of a simple interest 8-month loan is $8000. The monthly payment is $8000 ÷ 8 = $1000.

Chapter Review Exercises

1. **Consumerism** A 20-ounce box of cereal costs $3.90. Find the unit cost.

2. **Car Expenses** An account executive had car expenses of $1025.58 for insurance, $605.82 for gas, $37.92 for oil, and $188.27 for maintenance during a year in which 11,320 miles were driven. Find the cost per mile for these four items taken as a group. Round to the nearest tenth of a cent.

3. **Investments** An oil stock was bought for $42.375 per share. Six months later, the stock was selling for $55.25 per share. Find the percent increase in the price of the stock for the 6 months. Round to the nearest tenth of a percent.

4. **Markup** A sporting goods store uses a markup rate of 40%. What is the markup on a ski suit that costs the store $180?

5. **Simple Interest** A contractor borrowed $100,000 from a credit union for 9 months at an annual interest rate of 4%. What is the simple interest due on the loan?

6. **Compound Interest** A computer programmer invested $25,000 in a retirement account that pays 6% interest, compounded daily. What is the value of the investment in 10 years? Use the Compound Interest Table in the Appendix. Round to the nearest cent.

7. **Investments** Last year an oil company had earnings of $4.12 per share. This year the earnings are $4.73 per share. What is the percent increase in earnings per share? Round to the nearest percent.

8. **Real Estate** The monthly mortgage payment for a condominium is $523.67. The owner must pay an annual property tax of $658.32. Find the total monthly payment for the mortgage and property tax.

9. **Car Expenses** A used pickup truck is purchased for $24,450. A down payment of 8% is made, and the remaining cost is financed for 4 years at an annual interest rate of 5%. Find the monthly payment. Use the Monthly Payment Table in the Appendix. Round to the nearest cent.

10. **Compound Interest** A fast-food restaurant invested $50,000 in an account that pays 7% annual interest compounded quarterly. What is the value of the investment in 1 year? Use the Compound Interest Table in the Appendix.

11. **Real Estate** Paula Mason purchased a home for $125,000. The lender requires a down payment of 15%. Find the amount of the down payment.

12. **Car Expenses** A plumber bought a truck for $18,500. A state license fee of $315 and a sales tax of 6.25% of the purchase price are required. Find the total cost of the sales tax and the license fee.

13. **Markup**   Techno-Center uses a markup rate of 35% on all computer systems. Find the selling price of a computer system that costs the store $1540.

14. **Car Expenses**   Mien pays a monthly car payment of $122.78. During a month in which $25.45 is principal, how much of the payment is interest?

15. **Compensation**   The manager of the retail store at a ski resort receives a commission of 3% on all sales at the alpine shop. Find the total commission received during a month in which the shop had $108,000 in sales.

16. **Discount**   A suit that regularly costs $235 is on sale for 40% off the regular price. Find the sale price.

17. **Banking**   Luke had a checking account balance of $1568.45 before writing checks for $123.76, $756.45, and $88.77. He then deposited a check for $344.21. Find Luke's current checkbook balance.

18. **Simple Interest**   Pros' Sporting Goods borrowed $30,000 at an annual interest rate of 8% for 6 months. Find the maturity value of the loan.

19. **Real Estate**   A credit union requires a borrower to pay $2\frac{1}{2}$ points for a loan. Find the origination fee for a $75,000 loan.

20. **Consumerism**   Sixteen ounces of mouthwash cost $3.49. A 33-ounce container of the same brand of mouthwash costs $6.99. Which is the better buy?

21. **Real Estate**   The Sweeneys bought a home for $156,000. The family made a 10% down payment and financed the remainder with a 30-year loan at an annual interest rate of 7%. Find the monthly mortgage payment. Use the Monthly Payment Table in the Appendix. Round to the nearest cent.

22. **Compensation**   Richard Valdez receives $12.60 per hour for working 40 hours a week and time and a half for working over 40 hours. Find his total income during a week in which he worked 48 hours.

23. **Banking**   The business checking account of a donut shop showed a balance of $9567.44 before checks of $1023.55, $345.44, and $23.67 were written and checks of $555.89 and $135.91 were deposited. Find the current checkbook balance.

24. **Simple Interest**   The simple interest due on a 4-month loan of $55,000 is $1375. Find the monthly payment on the loan.

25. **Simple Interest**   A credit card company charges a customer 1.25% per month on the unpaid balance of charges on the card. What is the finance charge in a month in which the customer has an unpaid balance of $576?

Chapter Test

1. **Consumerism** Twenty feet of lumber cost $138.40. What is the cost per foot?

2. **Consumerism** Which is the more economical purchase: 3 pounds of tomatoes for $7.49 or 5 pounds of tomatoes for $12.59?

3. **Consumerism** Red snapper costs $4.15 per pound. Find the cost of $3\frac{1}{2}$ pounds. Round to the nearest cent.

4. **Business** An exercise bicycle increased in price from $415 to $498. Find the percent increase in the cost of the exercise bicycle.

5. **Markup** A department store uses a 40% markup rate. Find the selling price of a compact disc player that the store purchased for $215.

6. **Investments** The price of gold dropped from $390 per ounce to $360 per ounce. What percent decrease does this amount represent? Round to the nearest tenth of a percent.

7. **Consumerism** The price of a video camera dropped from $1120 to $896. What percent decrease does this price drop represent?

8. **Discount** A corner hutch with a regular price of $299 is on sale for 30% off the regular price. Find the sale price.

9. **Discount** A box of stationery that regularly sells for $9.50 is on sale for $5.70. Find the discount rate.

10. **Simple Interest** A construction company borrowed $75,000 for 4 months at an annual interest rate of 8%. Find the simple interest due on the loan.

11. **Simple Interest** Craig Allen borrowed $25,000 at an annual interest rate of 9.2% for 9 months. Find the maturity value of the loan.

12. **Simple Interest** A credit card company charges a customer 1.2% per month on the unpaid balance of charges on the card. What is the finance charge in a month in which the customer has an unpaid balance of $374.95?

13. **Compound Interest** Jorge, who is self-employed, placed $30,000 in an account that pays 6% annual interest compounded quarterly. How much interest was earned in 10 years? Use the Compound Interest Table in the Appendix.

14. **Real Estate** A savings and loan institution is offering mortgage loans that have a loan origination fee of $2\frac{1}{2}$ points. Find the loan origination fee when a home is purchased with a loan of $134,000.

15. **Real Estate**   A new housing development offers homes with a mortgage of $222,000 for 25 years at an annual interest rate of 8%. Find the monthly mortgage payment. Use the Monthly Payment Table in the Appendix.

16. **Car Expenses**   A Chevrolet was purchased for $23,750, and a 20% down payment was made. Find the amount financed.

17. **Car Expenses**   A rancher purchased an SUV for $23,714 and made a down payment of 15% of the cost. The balance was financed for 4 years at an annual interest rate of 7%. Find the monthly truck payment. Use the Monthly Payment Table in the Appendix.

18. **Compensation**   Shaney receives an hourly wage of $20.40 an hour as an emergency room nurse. When called in at night, she receives time and a half. How much does Shaney earn in a week when she works 30 hours at normal rates and 15 hours during the night?

19. **Banking**   The business checking account for a pottery store had a balance of $7349.44 before checks for $1349.67 and $344.12 were written. The store manager then made a deposit of $956.60. Find the current checkbook balance.

20. **Banking**   Balance the checkbook shown.

		RECORD ALL CHARGES OR CREDITS THAT AFFECT YOUR ACCOUNT					BALANCE	
NUMBER	DATE	DESCRIPTION OF TRANSACTION	PAYMENT/DEBIT (−)	√ T	FEE (IF ANY) (−)	DEPOSIT/CREDIT (+)	$ 1422	13
843	8/1	House Payment	$ 713 72		$	$	708	41
	8/4	Deposit				852 60	1561	01
844	8/5	Loan Payment	162 40				1398	61
845	8/6	Groceries	166 44				1232	17
846	8/10	Car Payment	322 37				909	80
	8/15	Deposit				852 60	1762	40
847	8/16	Credit Card	413 45				1348	95
848	8/18	Pharmacy	92 14				1256	81
849	8/22	Utilities	72 30				1184	51
850	8/28	Telephone	78 20				1106	31

CHECKING ACCOUNT Monthly Statement		Account Number: 122-345-1	
Date	Transaction	Amount	Balance
8/1	OPENING BALANCE		1422.13
8/3	CHECK	713.72	708.41
8/4	DEPOSIT	852.60	1561.01
8/8	CHECK	166.44	1394.57
8/8	CHECK	162.40	1232.17
8/15	DEPOSIT	852.60	2084.77
8/23	CHECK	72.30	2012.47
8/24	CHECK	92.14	1920.33
9/1	CLOSING BALANCE		1920.33

CHAPTER 6: *Additional Material From:*

MATHEMATICAL EXCURSIONS | SECOND EDITION

Aufmann • Lockwood • Nation • Clegg

SECTION 10.3 | **Credit Cards and Consumer Loans**

Credit Cards

When a customer uses a credit card to make a purchase, the customer is actually receiving a loan. Therefore, there is frequently an added cost to the consumer who purchases on credit. This added cost may be in the form of an annual fee or interest charges on purchases. A **finance charge** is an amount paid in excess of the cash price; it is the cost to the customer for the use of credit.

Most credit card companies issue monthly bills. The due date on the bill is usually 1 month after the billing date (the date the bill is prepared and sent to the customer). If the bill is paid in full by the due date, the customer pays no finance charge. If the bill is not paid in full by the due date, a finance charge is added to the next bill.

Suppose a credit card billing date is the 10th day of each month. If a credit card purchase is made on April 15, then May 10 is the billing date (the 10th day of the month following April). The due date is June 10 (one month from the billing date). If the bill is paid in full before June 10, no finance charge is added. However, if the bill is not paid in full, interest charges on the outstanding balance will start to accrue (be added) on June 10, and any purchase made after June 10 will immediately start accruing interest.

The most common method of determining finance charges is the **average daily balance method.** Interest charges are based on the credit card's average daily balance, which is calculated by dividing the sum of the total amounts owed each day of the month by the number of days in the billing period.

Average Daily Balance

$$\text{Average daily balance} = \frac{\text{sum of the total amounts owed each day of the month}}{\text{number of days in the billing period}}$$

An example of calculating the average daily balance follows.

Suppose an unpaid bill for $315 had a due date of April 10. A purchase of $28 was made on April 12, and $123 was charged on April 24. A payment of $50 was made on April 15. The next billing date is May 10. The interest on the average daily balance is 1.5% per month. Find the finance charge on the May 10 bill.

To find the finance charge, first prepare a table showing the unpaid balance for each purchase, the number of days the balance is owed, and the product of these numbers. A negative sign in the Payments or Purchases column of the table indicates that a payment was made on that date.

Date	Payments or Purchases	Balance Each Day	Number of Days Until Balance Changes	Unpaid Balance Times Number of Days
April 10 – 11		$315	2	$630
April 12 – 14	$28	$343	3	$1029
April 15 – 23	– $50	$293	9	$2637
April 24 – May 9	$123	$416	16	$6656
Total				$10,952

The sum of the total amounts owed each day of the month is $10,952. Find the average daily balance.

$$\text{Average daily balance} = \frac{\text{sum of the total amounts owed each day of the month}}{\text{number of days in the billing period}}$$

$$= \frac{10,952}{30} \approx 365.07$$

Find the finance charge.

$$I = Prt$$
$$I = 365.07(0.015)(1)$$
$$I \approx 5.48$$

The finance charge on the May 10 bill is $5.48.

EXAMPLE 1 ■ Calculate Interest on a Credit Card Bill

An unpaid bill for $620 had a due date of March 10. A purchase of $214 was made on March 15, and $67 was charged on March 30. A payment of $200 was made on March 22. The interest on the average daily balance is 1.5% per month. Find the finance charge on the April 10 bill.

Solution

First calculate the sum of the total amounts owed each day of the month.

Date	Payments or Purchases	Balance Each Day	Number of Days Until Balance Changes	Unpaid Balance times Number of Days
March 10 – 14		$620	5	$3100
March 15 – 21	$214	$834	7	$5838
March 22 – 29	– $200	$634	8	$5072
March 30 – April 9	$67	$701	11	$7711
Total				$21,721

The sum of the total amounts owed each day of the month is $21,721. Find the average daily balance.

$$\text{Average daily balance} = \frac{\text{sum of the total amounts owed each day of the month}}{\text{number of days in the billing period}}$$

$$= \frac{21,721}{31} \approx \$700.68$$

Find the finance charge.

$$I = Prt$$
$$I = 700.68(0.015)(1)$$
$$I \approx 10.51$$

The finance charge on the April 10 bill is $10.51.

CHECK YOUR PROGRESS 1   A bill for $1024 was due on July 1. Purchases of $315 were made on July 7, and $410 was charged on July 22. A payment of $400 was made on July 15. The interest on the average daily balance is 1.2% per month. Find the finance charge on the August 1 bill.

Solution   *See page B-1.*

MathMatters   Credit Card Debt

The graph on the following page shows how long it would take you to pay off a credit card debt of $3000 and the amount of interest you would pay if you made the minimum monthly payment of 3% of the credit card balance each month.

In fact If you have credit card debt and want to determine how long it will take you to pay off the debt, go to **http://www.cardweb.com.** There you will find a calculator that will calculate how long it will take to pay off the debt and the amount of interest you will pay. (*Source:* **CardWeb.com**)

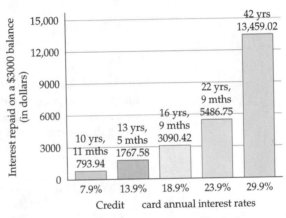

Source: **CardWeb.com,** reprinted by permission of Cardweb.com.

✔ **TAKE NOTE**

Note that both the effective interest rate discussed in Section 10.1 and the annual percentage rate discussed here reflect the cost of a loan on a yearly basis. Both are useful to the consumer interested in comparing loan offers.

Annual Percentage Rate

Federal law, in the form of the Truth in Lending Act, requires that credit customers be made aware of the cost of credit. This law, passed by Congress in 1969, requires that a business issuing credit inform the consumer of all details of a credit transaction, including the true annual interest rate. The **true annual interest rate,** also called the **annual percentage rate (APR)** or **annual percentage yield (APY),** is the effective annual interest rate on which credit payments are based.

The idea behind the APR is that interest is owed only on the *unpaid balance* of the loan. For instance, suppose you decide to borrow $2400 from a bank that advertises a 10% *simple* interest rate. You want a six-month loan and agree to repay the loan in six equal monthly payments. The simple interest due on the loan is

$$I = Prt$$

$$I = \$2400(0.10)\left(\frac{6}{12}\right)$$

$$I = \$120$$

The total amount to be repaid to the bank is

$$A = P + I$$

$$A = \$2400 + \$120$$

$$A = \$2520$$

The amount of each monthly payment is

$$\text{Monthly payment} = \frac{2520}{6} = \$420$$

During the first month you owe $2400. The interest on that amount is

$$I = Prt$$

$$I = \$2400(0.10)\left(\frac{1}{12}\right)$$

$$I = \$20$$

At the end of the first month, of the $420 payment you make, $20 is the interest payment and $400 is applied to reducing the loan. Therefore, during the second month you owe $2400 − $400 = $2000.

During the second month you owe $2000. The interest on that amount is

$$I = Prt$$

$$I = \$2000(0.10)\left(\frac{1}{12}\right) \approx 16.667$$

$$I = \$16.67$$

At the end of the second month, of the $420 payment you make, $16.67 is the interest payment and $403.33 is applied to reducing the loan. Therefore, during the third month you owe $2000 − $403.33 = $1596.67.

The point of these calculations is to demonstrate that each month the amount you owe is decreasing, and not by a constant amount. From our calculations, the loan decreased by $400 the first month and by $403.33 the second month.

The Truth in Lending Act stipulates that the interest rate for a loan be calculated only on the amount owed at a particular time, not on the original amount borrowed. All loans must be stated according to this standard, thereby making it possible for a consumer to compare different loans.

We can use the following formula to estimate the annual percentage rate (APR) on a simple interest rate installment loan.

> **Approximate Annual Percentage Rate (APR) Formula for a Simple Interest Rate Loan**
>
> The annual percentage rate (APR) of a simple interest rate loan can be approximated by
>
> $$\text{APR} \approx \frac{2Nr}{N+1}$$
>
> where N is the number of payments and r is the simple interest rate.

For the loan described above, $N = 6$ and $r = 10\% = 0.10$.

$$\text{APR} \approx \frac{2Nr}{N+1}$$

$$\approx \frac{2(6)(0.10)}{6+1} = \frac{1.2}{7} \approx 0.171$$

The annual percentage rate on the loan is approximately 17.1%. Recall that the simple interest rate was 10%, much less than the actual rate. The Truth in Lending Act provides the consumer with a standard interest rate, APR, so that it is possible to compare loans. The 10% simple interest loan described above is equivalent to an APR loan of about 17%.

EXAMPLE 2 ■ Calculate a Finance Charge and an APR

You purchase a refrigerator for $675. You pay 20% down and agree to repay the balance in 12 equal monthly payments. The finance charge on the balance is 9% simple interest.

a. Find the finance charge.

b. Estimate the annual percentage rate. Round to the nearest tenth of a percent.

Solution

a. To find the finance charge, first calculate the down payment.

Down payment = percent down × purchase price

$$= 0.20 \times 675 = 135$$

Amount financed = purchase price − down payment

$$= 675 - 135 = 540$$

Calculate the interest owed on the loan.

Interest owed = finance rate × amount financed

$$= 0.09 \times 540 = 48.60$$

The finance charge is $48.60.

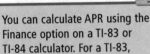

CALCULATOR NOTE

You can calculate APR using the Finance option on a TI-83 or TI-84 calculator. For a TI-83, press [2nd] [FINANCE]; for a TI-83 Plus or TI-84, press [APPS] and then select Finance. Press [ENTER]. Input the values. The screen below is typical. Note that the payment is entered as a negative number. Amounts paid out are normally entered as negative numbers.

```
N=6
I%=0
PV=2400
PMT=-420
FV=0
P/Y=12
C/Y=12
PMT: END BEGIN
```

Move the cursor to I% and then press [ALPHA] [SOLVE]. The actual APR is then displayed next to I%.

```
N=6
■I%=16.94488071
PV=2400
PMT=-420
FV=0
P/Y=12
C/Y=12
PMT: END BEGIN
```

The APR is approximately 16.9%.

b. Use the APR formula to estimate the annual percentage rate.

$$\text{APR} \approx \frac{2Nr}{N + 1}$$

$$\approx \frac{2(12)(0.09)}{12 + 1} = \frac{2.16}{13} \approx 0.166$$

The annual percentage rate is approximately 16.6%.

CHECK YOUR PROGRESS 2   You purchase a washing machine and dryer for $750. You pay 20% down and agree to repay the balance in 12 equal monthly payments. The finance charge on the balance is 8% simple interest.

a. Find the finance charge.

b. Estimate the annual percentage rate. Round to the nearest tenth of a percent.

Solution   *See page B-1.*

Consumer Loans: Calculating Monthly Payments

The stated interest rate for most consumer loans, such as a car loan, is normally the annual percentage rate, APR, as required by the Truth in Lending Act. The payment amount for these loans is given by the following formula.

> **Payment Formula for an APR Loan**
>
> The payment for a loan based on APR is given by
>
> $$PMT = A\left(\frac{i}{1 - (1 + i)^{-n}}\right)$$
>
> where *PMT* is the payment, *A* is the loan amount, *i* is the interest rate per payment period, and *n* is the total number of payments.

It is important to note that in this formula *i* is the interest rate *per payment period*. For instance, if the annual interest rate is 9% and payments are made monthly, then

$$i = \frac{\text{annual interest rate}}{\text{number of payments per year}} = \frac{0.09}{12} = 0.0075$$

QUESTION   *For a four-year loan repaid on a monthly basis, what is the value of n in the formula above?*

ANSWER   *n = (number of years) × (number of payments per year) = 4 × 12 = 48*

The payment formula given above is used to calculate monthly payments on most consumer loans. In Example 3 we calculate the monthly payment for a new television and in Example 4 we calculate the monthly payment for a car loan.

EXAMPLE 3 ■ Calculate a Monthly Payment

 Integrated Visual Technologies is offering anyone who purchases a television an annual interest rate of 9.5% for 4 years. If Andrea Smyer purchases a 50-inch, rear projection television for $5995 from Integrated Visual Technologies, find her monthly payment.

Solution
To calculate the monthly payment, you will need a calculator. The following keystrokes will work on most scientific calculators.

First calculate i and store the result.

$$i = \frac{\text{annual interest rate}}{\text{number of payments per year}} = \frac{0.095}{12}$$

Keystrokes: $0.095 \boxed{\div} 12 \approx 0.00791667 \boxed{\text{STO}}$

Calculate the monthly payment. For a four-year loan, $n = 4(12) = 48$.

$$PMT = A\left(\frac{i}{1 - (1 + i)^{-n}}\right)$$

$$= 5995\left(\frac{0.095/12}{1 - (1 + 0.095/12)^{-48}}\right) \approx 150.61$$

Keystrokes: $5995 \boxed{\times} \boxed{\text{RCL}} \boxed{=} \boxed{\div} \boxed{(} 1 \boxed{-} \boxed{(} 1 \boxed{+} \boxed{\text{RCL}} \boxed{)} \boxed{y^x} 48 \boxed{+/-} \boxed{)} \boxed{=}$

The monthly payment is $150.61.

CHECK YOUR PROGRESS 3   Carlos Menton purchases a new laptop computer from Knox Computer Solutions for $1499. If the sales tax is 4.25% of the purchase price and Carlos finances the total cost, including sales tax, for 3 years at an annual interest rate of 8.4%, find the monthly payment.

Solution   *See page B-2.*

CALCULATOR NOTE

You can calculate the monthly payment using the Finance option on a TI-83 or TI-84 calculator. For a TI-83, press $\boxed{\text{2nd}}$ [FINANCE]; for a TI-83 Plus or TI-84, press $\boxed{\text{APPS}}$ $\boxed{\text{ENTER}}$ $\boxed{\text{ENTER}}$. Input the known values. Typically financial calculations use PV (present value) for the loan amount and FV (future value) for the amount owed at the end of the loan period, usually 0. P/Y = 12 and C/Y = 12 mean that payments and interest are calculated monthly (12 times a year). Now place the cursor at PMT= and press $\boxed{\text{ALPHA}}$ [SOLVE].

```
N=48
I%=9.5
PV=5995
■PMT=-150.6132
FV=0
P/Y=12
C/Y=12
PMT: END BEGIN
```

The monthly payment is $150.61.

EXAMPLE 4 ■ Calculate a Car Payment

A web page designer purchases a car for $18,395.

a. If the sales tax is 6.5% of the purchase price, find the amount of the sales tax.
b. If the car license fee is 1.2% of the purchase price, find the amount of the license fee.
c. If the designer makes a $2500 down payment, find the amount of the loan the designer needs.

d. Assuming the designer gets the loan in part c at an annual interest rate of 7.5% for 4 years, determine the monthly car payment.

Solution

a. Sales tax $= 0.065(18,395) = 1195.675$
The sales tax is $1195.68.

b. License fee $= 0.012(18,395) = 220.74$
The license fee is $220.74.

c. Loan amount = purchase price + sales tax + license fee − down payment
$$= 18,395 + 1195.68 + 220.74 - 2500$$
$$= 17,311.42$$
The loan amount is $17,311.42.

d. To calculate the monthly payment, you will need a calculator. The following keystrokes will work on most scientific calculators.

First calculate i and store the result.

$$i = \frac{APR}{12} = \frac{0.075}{12} = 0.00625$$

Keystrokes: 0.075 $\boxed{\div}$ 12 = 0.00625 $\boxed{STO}$

Calculate the monthly payment.

$$PMT = A\left(\frac{i}{1-(1+i)^{-n}}\right)$$
$$= 17,311.42\left(\frac{0.00625}{1-(1+0.00625)^{-48}}\right) \approx 418.57$$

Keystrokes:

17311.42 $\boxed{\times}$ $\boxed{RCL}$ $\boxed{=}$ $\boxed{\div}$ $\boxed{(}$ 1 $\boxed{-}$ $\boxed{(}$ 1 $\boxed{+}$ $\boxed{RCL}$ $\boxed{)}$ $\boxed{y^x}$ 48 $\boxed{+/-}$ $\boxed{)}$ $\boxed{=}$

The monthly payment is $418.57.

CALCULATOR NOTE

A typical TI-83/84 screen for the calculation in Example 4 is shown below.

```
N=48
I%=7.5
PV=17311.42
■PMT=-418.5711
FV=0
P/Y=12
C/Y=12
PMT: END BEGIN
```

The monthly payment is $418.57.

CHECK YOUR PROGRESS 4   A school superintendent purchases a new sedan for $26,788.

a. If the sales tax is 5.25% of the purchase price, find the amount of the sales tax.

b. The superintendent makes a $2500 down payment and the license fee is $145. Find the amount the superintendent must finance.

c. Assuming the superintendent gets the loan in part b at an annual interest rate of 8.1% for 5 years, determine the superintendent's monthly car payment.

Solution   *See page B-2.*

MathMatters   Payday Loans

An ad reads

Get cash until payday! Loans of \$100 or more available.

These ads refer to *payday* loans, which go by a variety of names, such as cash advance loans, check advance loans, post-dated check loans, or deferred deposit check loans. These types of loans are offered by finance companies and check-cashing companies.

Typically a borrower writes a personal check payable to the lender for the amount borrowed plus a *service fee*. The company gives the borrower the amount of the check minus the fee, which is normally a percent of the amount borrowed. The amount borrowed is usually repaid after payday, normally within a few weeks.

Under the Truth in Lending Act, the cost of a payday loan must be disclosed. Among other information, the borrower must receive, in writing, the APR for such a loan. To understand just how expensive these loans can be, suppose a borrower receives a loan for \$100 for 2 weeks and pays a fee of \$10. The APR for this loan can be calculated using the formula in this section or using a graphing calculator. Screens for a TI-83/84 calculator are shown below.

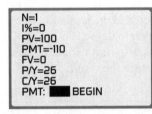

N = 1 (number of payments)
I% is unknown.
PV = 100 (amount borrowed)
PMT = −110 (the payment)
FV = 0 (no money is owed after all the payments)
P/Y = 26 (There are 26 two-week periods in 1 year.)
C/Y = 26

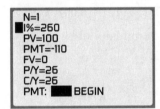

Place the cursor at I%=. Press ALPHA [SOLVE].

The annual interest rate is 260%.

To give you an idea of the enormity of a 260% APR, if the loan on the television set in Example 3, page 680, were based on a 260% interest rate, the monthly payment on the television set would be \$1299.02!

The Federal Trade Commission (FTC) offers suggestions for consumers in need of credit. See **www.ftc.gov/bcp/conline/pubs/alerts/pdayalrt.htm.**

Consumer Loans: Calculating Loan Payoffs

Sometimes a consumer wants to pay off a loan before the end of the loan term. For instance, suppose you have a five-year car loan but would like to purchase a new car after owning your car for 4 years. Because there is still 1 year remaining on the loan, you must pay off the remaining loan before purchasing another car.

This is not as simple as just multiplying the monthly car payment by 12 to arrive at the payoff amount. The reason, as we mentioned earlier, is that each payment includes both interest and principal. By solving the Payment Formula for an APR Loan for A, the amount of the loan, we can calculate the payoff amount, which is just the remaining principal.

APR Loan Payoff Formula

The payoff amount for a loan based on APR is given by

$$A = PMT\left(\frac{1 - (1 + i)^{-n}}{i}\right)$$

where A is the loan payoff, PMT is the payment, i is the interest rate per payment period, and n is the number of *remaining* payments.

EXAMPLE 5 ■ Calculate a Payoff Amount

Allison Werke wants to pay off the loan on her jet ski that she has owned for 18 months. Allison's monthly payment is $284.67 on a two-year loan at an annual percentage rate of 8.7%. Find the payoff amount.

Solution

Because Allison has owned the jet ski for 18 months of a 24-month (two-year) loan, she has six payments remaining. Thus $n = 6$, the number of *remaining* payments. Here are the keystrokes to find the loan payoff.

Calculate i and store the result.

$$i = \frac{\text{annual interest rate}}{\text{number of payments per year}} = \frac{0.087}{12} = 0.00725$$

Keystrokes: 0.087 ÷ 12 = 0.00725 STO

Use the APR Loan Payoff Formula.

$$A = PMT\left(\frac{1 - (1 + i)^{-n}}{i}\right)$$

$$= 284.67\left(\frac{1 - (1 + 0.00725)^{-6}}{0.00725}\right) \approx 1665.50$$

Keystrokes: 284.67 × (1 − (1 + RCL) y^x 6 +/−) ÷ RCL =

The loan payoff is $1665.50.

CHECK YOUR PROGRESS 5   Aaron Jefferson has a five-year car loan based on an annual percentage rate of 8.4%. The monthly payment is $592.57. After 3 years, Aaron decides to purchase a new car and must pay off his car loan. Find the payoff amount.

Solution   *See page B-2.*

Car Leases

Leasing a car may result in lower monthly car payments. The primary reason for this is that at the end of the lease term, you do not own the car. Ownership of the car reverts to the dealer, who can then sell it as a used car and realize the profit from the sale.

The value of the car at the end of the lease term is called the **residual value** of the car. The residual value of a car is frequently based on a percent of the manufacturer's suggested retail price (MSRP) and normally varies between 40% and 60% of the MSRP, depending on the type of lease.

For instance, suppose the MSRP of a car is $18,500 and the residual value is 45% of the MSRP. Then

$$\text{Residual value} = 0.45 \cdot 18,500$$
$$= 8325$$

The residual value is $8325. This is the amount the dealer thinks the car will be worth at the end of the lease period. The person leasing the car, the lessee, usually has the option of purchasing the car at that price at the end of the lease.

In addition to the residual value of the car, the monthly lease payment for a car takes into consideration *net capitalized cost, the money factor, average monthly finance charge,* and *average monthly depreciation.* Each of these terms is defined below.

Net capitalized cost = negotiated price − down payment − trade-in value

$$\textbf{Money factor} = \frac{\text{annual interest rate as a percent}}{2400}$$

Average monthly finance charge
$$= (\text{net capitalized cost} + \text{residual value}) \times \text{money factor}$$

$$\textbf{Average monthly depreciation} = \frac{\text{net capitalized cost} - \text{residual value}}{\text{term of the lease in months}}$$

Using these definitions, we have the following formula for a monthly lease payment.

> **Monthly Lease Payment Formula**
>
> The monthly lease payment formula is given by $P = F + D$, where P is the monthly lease payment, F is the average monthly finance charge, and D is the average monthly depreciation of the car.

EXAMPLE 6 ■ Calculate a Monthly Lease Payment for a Car

The director of human resources for a company decides to lease a car for 30 months. Suppose the annual interest rate is 8.4%, the negotiated price is $29,500, there is no trade-in, and the down payment is $5000. Find the monthly lease payment. Assume that the residual value is 55% of the MSRP of $33,400.

Solution

Net capitalized cost = negotiated price − down payment − trade-in value
$$= 29,500 - 5000 - 0 = 24,500$$

Residual value = 0.55(33,400) = 18,370

$$\text{Money factor} = \frac{\text{Annual interest rate as a percent}}{2400} = \frac{8.4}{2400} = 0.0035$$

TAKE NOTE

The money factor is sometimes written as the product of

$$\frac{\text{net capitalized cost} + \text{residual value}}{2}$$

and $\dfrac{\text{APR}}{12 \times 100}$.

The division by 2 takes the average of the net capitalized cost and the residual value. The division by 12 converts the annual rate to a monthly rate. The division by 100 converts the percent to a decimal. The denominator 2400 in the money factor at the right is the product $2 \times 12 \times 100$.

Various methods are used to calculate monthly lease payments. The method we show here is typically used by car dealerships. In the exercises, we will give another method for calculating a lease payment.

Average monthly finance charge
= (net capitalized cost + residual value) × money factor
= (24,500 + 18,370) × 0.0035
≈ 150.05

$$\text{Average monthly depreciation} = \frac{\text{net capitalized cost} - \text{residual value}}{\text{term of the lease in months}}$$

$$= \frac{24,500 - 18,370}{30}$$

$$\approx 204.33$$

Monthly lease payment
= average monthly finance charge + average monthly depreciation
= 150.05 + 204.33
= 354.38

The monthly lease payment is $354.38.

CHECK YOUR PROGRESS 6   Find the monthly lease payment for a car for which the negotiated price is $31,900, the annual interest rate is 8%, the length of the lease is 5 years, and the residual value is 40% of the MSRP of $33,395. There is no down payment or trade-in.

Solution   *See page B-2.*

Excursion

Leasing versus Buying a Car

In July 2004, the MSRP for a 2005 Dodge Grand Caravan SE Plus was $24,500. We will use this information to analyze the results of leasing versus buying the car. To ensure that we are making valid comparisons, we will assume:

There is no trade-in, the negotiated price is the MSRP, and a down payment of $2500 is made.

The license fee is 1.1% of the negotiated price.

If you purchase a car, then the state sales tax is 5.5% of the negotiated price. If you lease the car, then you make a state tax payment every month. The amount of each of the monthly state tax payments is equal to 5.5% of the monthly lease payment.

The annual interest rate for both a loan and a lease is 6% and the term of the loan or the lease is 60 months.

The residual value when leasing the car is 45% of the MSRP.

1. Determine the loan amount to purchase the car.

2. Determine the monthly car payment to purchase the car.

3. How much will you have paid for the car (excluding maintenance) over the five-year term of the loan?

(continued)

4. At the end of 5 years, you sell the car for 45% of the original MSRP (the residual lease value). Your net car ownership cost is the amount you paid over the 5 years minus the amount you realized from selling the car. What is your net ownership cost?

5. Determine the net capitalized cost for the car.

6. Determine the lease payment. Remember to include the sales tax that must be paid each month.

7. How much will you have paid to lease the car for the five-year term? Because the car reverts to the dealer after 5 years, the net ownership cost is the total of all the lease payments for the 5 years.

8. Which option, buying or leasing, results in the smaller net ownership cost?

9. List some advantages and disadvantages of buying or leasing a car.

Exercise Set 10.3

In Exercises 1–4, calculate the finance charge for a credit card that has the given average daily balance and interest rate.

1. Average daily balance: $118.72; monthly interest rate: 1.25%

2. Average daily balance: $391.64; monthly interest rate: 1.75%

3. Average daily balance: $10,154.87; monthly interest rate: 1.5%

4. Average daily balance: $20,346.91; monthly interest rate: 1.25%

5. **Average Daily Balance** A credit card account had a $244 balance on March 5. A purchase of $152 was made on March 12, and a payment of $100 was made on March 28. Find the average daily balance if the billing date is April 5.

6. **Average Daily Balance** A credit card account has a $768 balance on April 1. A purchase of $316 was made on April 5, and a payment of $200 was made on April 18. Find the average daily balance if the new billing date is May 1.

7. **Finance Charges** A charge account had a balance of $944 on May 5. A purchase of $255 was made on May 17, and a payment of $150 was made on May 20. The interest on the average daily balance is 1.5% per month. Find the finance charge on the June 5 bill.

8. **Finance Charges** A charge account had a balance of $655 on June 1. A purchase of $98 was made on June 17, and a payment of $250 was made on June 15. The interest on the average daily balance is 1.2% per month. Find the finance charge on the July 1 bill.

9. **Finance Charges** On August 10, a credit card account had a balance of $345. A purchase of $56 was made on August 15, and $157 was charged on August 27. A payment of $75 was made on August 15. The interest on the average daily balance is 1.25% per month. Find the finance charge on the September 10 bill.

10. **Finance Charges** On May 1, a credit card account had a balance of $189. Purchases of $213 were made on May 5, and $102 was charged on May 21. A payment of $150 was made on May 25. The interest on the average daily balance is 1.5% per month. Find the finance charge on the June 1 bill.

In Exercises 11 and 12, you may want to use the spreadsheet program available at our web site at **math.college.hmco.com/students.** This spreadsheet automates the finance charge procedure shown in this section.

11. **Finance Charges** The activity date, company, and amount for a credit card bill are shown below. The due date of the bill is September 15. On August 15, there was an unpaid balance of $1236.43. Find the finance charge if the interest rate is 1.5% per month.

Activity Date	Company	Amount
August 15	Unpaid balance	1236.43
August 16	Vetenary clinic	125.00
August 17	Shell	23.56
August 18	Olive's restaurant	53.45
August 20	Seaside market	41.36
August 22	Monterey Hotel	223.65
August 25	Airline tickets	310.00
August 30	Bike 101	23.36
September 1	Trattoria Maria	36.45
September 9	Bookstore	21.39
September 12	Seaside Market	41.25
September 13	Credit card payment	−1345.00

12. **Finance Charges** The activity date, company, and amount for a credit card bill are shown below. The due date of the bill is July 10. On June 10, there was an unpaid balance of $987.81. Find the finance charge if the interest rate is 1.8% per month.

Activity Date	Company	Amount
June 10	Unpaid balance	987.81
June 11	Jan's Surf Shop	156.33
June 12	Albertson's	45.61
June 15	The Down Shoppe	59.84
June 16	NY Times Sales	18.54
June 20	Cardiff Delicatessen	23.09
June 22	The Olde Golf Mart	126.92
June 28	Lee's Hawaiian Restaurant	41.78
June 30	City Food Drive	100.00
July 2	Credit card payment	−1000.00
July 8	Safeway Stores	161.38

 Use a calculator for Exercises 13–42.

In Exercises 13–16, use the Approximate Annual Percentage Rate Formula.

13. **APR** Chuong Ngo borrows $2500 from a bank that advertises a 9% simple interest rate and repays the loan in three equal monthly payments. Estimate the APR. Round to the nearest tenth of a percent.

14. **APR** Charles Ferrara borrows $4000 from a bank that advertises an 8% simple interest rate. If he repays the loan in six equal monthly payments, estimate the APR. Round to the nearest tenth of a percent.

15. **APR** Kelly Ang buys a computer system for $2400 and makes a 15% down payment. If Kelly agrees to repay the balance in 24 equal monthly payments at an annual simple interest rate of 10%, estimate the APR for Kelly's loan.

16. **APR** Jill Richards purchases a stereo system for $1500. She makes a 20% down payment and agrees to repay the balance in 12 equal payments. If the finance charge on the balance is 7% simple interest, estimate the APR. Round to the nearest tenth of a percent.

17. **Monthly Payments** Arrowood's Camera Store advertises a Canon Power Shot 3.34-megapixel camera for $400, including taxes. If you finance the purchase of this camera for 1 year at an annual percentage rate of 6.9%, find the monthly payment.

18. **Monthly Payments** Optics Mart offers a Meade ETX Astro telescope for $1249, including taxes. If you finance the purchase of this telescope for 2 years at an annual percentage rate of 7.2%, what is the monthly payment?

19. **Buying on Credit** Alicia's Surf Shop offers its 9′4″-long Noge Rider surfboard for $649. The sales tax is 7.25% of the purchase price.

    a. What is the total cost, including sales tax?

    b. If you make a down payment of 25% of the total cost, find the down payment.

    c. Assuming you finance the remaining cost at an annual interest rate of 5.7% for six months, find the monthly payment.

20. **Buying on Credit** Waterworld marina offers a motorboat with a mercury engine for $38,250. The sales tax is 6.5% of the purchase price.

    a. What is the total cost, including sales tax?

    b. If you make a down payment of 20% of the total cost, find the down payment.

    c. Assuming you finance the remaining cost at an annual interest rate of 5.7% for three years, find the monthly payment.

21. **Buying on Credit** After becoming a commercial pilot, Lorna Kao decides to purchase a Cessna 182 for $64,995. Assuming the sales tax is 5.5% of the purchase price, find each of the following.

    a. What is the total cost, including sales tax?

    b. If Lorna makes a down payment of 20% of the total cost, find the down payment.

    c. Assuming Lorna finances the remaining cost at an annual interest rate of 7.15% for 10 years, find the monthly payment.

22. **Buying on Credit** Donald Savchenko purchased new living room furniture for $2488. Assuming the sales tax is 7.75% of the purchase price, find each of the following.

    a. What is the total cost, including sales tax?

    b. If Donald makes a down payment of 15% of the total cost, find the down payment.

    c. Assuming Donald finances the remaining cost at an annual interest rate of 8.16% for 2 years, find the monthly payment.

23. **Car Payments** Luis Mahla purchases a Porsche Boxster for $42,600 and finances the entire amount at an annual interest rate of 5.7% for 5 years. Find the monthly payment. Assume the sales tax is 6% of the purchase price and the license fee is 1% of the purchase price.

24. **Car Payments** Suppose you negotiate a selling price of $26,995 for a Ford Explorer. You make a down payment of 10% of the selling price and finance the remaining balance for 3 years at an annual interest rate of 7.5%. The sales tax is 7.5% of the selling price, and the license fee is 0.9% of the selling price. Find the monthly payment.

25. **Car Payments** Margaret Hsi purchases a late model Corvette for $24,500. She makes a down payment of $3000 and finances the remaining amount for 4 years at an annual interest rate of 8.5%. The sales tax is 5.5% of the selling price and the license fee is $331. Find the monthly payment.

26. **Car Payments** Chris Schmaltz purchases a Pontiac GTO for $34,119. Chris makes a down payment of $5000 and finances the remaining amount for 5 years at an annual interest rate of 7.6%. The sales tax is 6.25% of the selling price, and the license fee is $429. Find the monthly payment.

27. **Car Payments** Suppose you purchase a car for a total price of $25,445, including taxes and license fee, and finance that amount for 4 years at an annual interest rate of 8%.

    a. Find the monthly payment.

    b. What is the total amount of interest paid over the term of the loan?

28. **Car Payments** Adele Paolo purchased a Chevrolet Tracker for a total price of $21,425, including taxes and license fee, and financed that amount for 5 years at an annual interest rate of 7.8%.

    a. Find the monthly payment.

    b. What is the total amount of interest paid over the term of the loan?

29. **Loan Payoffs** Angela Montery has a five-year car loan for a Jeep Wrangler at an annual interest rate of 6.3% and a monthly payment of $603.50. After 3 years, Angela decides to purchase a new car. What is the payoff on Angela's loan?

30. **Loan Payoffs** Suppose you have a four-year car loan at an annual interest rate of 7.2% and a monthly payment of $587.21. After $2\frac{1}{2}$ years, you decide to purchase a new car. What is the payoff on your loan?

31. **Loan Payoffs** Suppose you have a four-year car loan at an annual interest rate of 8.9% and a monthly payment of $303.52. After 3 years, you decide to purchase a new car. What is the payoff on your loan?

32. **Loan Payoffs** Ming Li has a three-year car loan for a Mercury Sable at an annual interest rate of 9.3% and a monthly payment of $453.68. After 1 year, Ming decides to purchase a new car. What is the payoff on his loan?

33. **Car Leases** Suppose you decide to obtain a four-year lease for a car and negotiate a selling price of $28,990. The trade-in value of your old car is $3850. If you make a down payment of $2400, the money factor is 0.0027, and the residual value is $15,000, find each of the following.

   a. The net capitalized cost

   b. The average monthly finance charge

   c. The average monthly depreciation

   d. The monthly lease payment

34. **Car Leases** Marcia Scripps obtains a five-year lease for a Ford F-150 pickup and negotiates a selling price of $37,115. The trade-in value of her old car is $2950. Assuming she makes a down payment of $3000, the money factor is 0.0035, and the residual value is $16,500, find each of the following.

   a. The net capitalized cost

   b. The average monthly finance charge

   c. The average monthly depreciation

   d. The monthly lease payment

35. **Car Leases** Jorge Cruz obtains a three-year lease for a Dodge Stratus and negotiates a selling price of $22,100. The annual interest rate is 8.1%, the residual value is $15,000, and Jorge makes a down payment of $1000. Find each of the following.

   a. The net capitalized cost

   b. The money factor

   c. The average monthly finance charge

   d. The average monthly depreciation

   e. The monthly lease payment

36. **Car Leases** Suppose you obtain a five-year lease for a Porsche and negotiate a selling price of $165,000. The annual interest rate is 8.4%, the residual value is $85,000, and you make a down payment of $5000. Find each of the following.

   a. The net capitalized cost

   b. The money factor

   c. The average monthly finance charge

   d. The average monthly depreciation

   e. The monthly lease payment

Extensions

CRITICAL THINKING

37. Explain how the APR Loan Payoff Formula can be used to determine the selling price of a car when the monthly payment, the annual interest rate, and the term of the loan on the car are known. Using your process, determine the selling price of a car that is offered for $235 per month for 4 years if the annual interest rate is 7.2%.

COOPERATIVE LEARNING

38. **Car Trade-Ins** You may have heard advertisements from car dealerships that say something like "Bring in your car, paid for or not, and we'll take it as a trade-in for a new car." The advertisement does not go on to say that you have to pay off the remaining loan balance or that balance gets added to the price of the new car.

   a. Suppose you are making payments of $235.73 per month on a four-year car loan that has an annual interest rate of 8.4%. After making payments for 3 years, you decide to purchase a new car. What is the loan payoff?

   b. You negotiate a price, including taxes, of $18,234 for the new car. What is the actual amount you owe for the new car when the loan payoff is included?

   c. If you finance the amount in part b for 4 years at an annual interest rate of 8.4%, what is the new monthly payment?

39. **Car Leases** The residual value of a car is based on "average" usage. To protect a car dealership from abnormal usage, most car leases stipulate an average number of miles driven annually, that the tires be serviceable when the car is returned, and (in many cases) that all the manufacturer's recommended services be performed over the course of the lease. Basically, the dealership wants a car that can be put on the lot and sold as a used car without much effort.

    Suppose you decide to lease a car for 4 years. The net capitalized cost is $19,788, the residual value is 55% of the MSRP of $28,990, and the interest rate is 5.9%. In addition, you must pay a mileage penalty of $.20 for each mile over 48,000 miles that the car is driven during the 4 years of the lease.

    a. Determine the monthly lease payment using the Monthly Lease Payment Formula given below. This formula is used by some financing agencies to calculate a monthly lease payment.

    Monthly Lease Payment Formula

    The monthly lease payment is given by $P = \dfrac{Ai(1 + i)^n - Vi}{(1 + i)^n - 1}$, where P is the monthly lease payment, A is the net capitalized cost, V is the residual value, i is the interest rate per payment period as a decimal, and n is the number of lease payments.

    ---

    b. If the odometer reads 87 miles when you lease the car and you return the car with 61,432 miles, what mileage penalty will you have to pay?

    c. If your car requires new tires at a cost of $635, what is the total cost, excluding maintenance, of the lease for the 4 years?

EXPLORATIONS

40. **Finance Charges** For most credit cards, no finance charge is added to the bill if the full amount owed is paid by the due date. However, if you do not pay the bill in full, the unpaid amount *and* all current charges are subject to a finance charge. This is a point that is missed by many credit card holders.

    To illustrate, suppose you have a credit card bill of $500 and you make a payment of $499, $1 less than the amount owed. Your credit card activity is as shown in the statement below.

Activity Date	Company	Amount
October 10	Unpaid balance	1.00
October 11	Rick's Tires	455.69
October 12	Costa's Internet Appliances	128.54
October 15	The Belgian Lion Restaurant	64.31
October 16	Verizon Wireless	33.57
October 20	Milton's Cake and Pie Shoppe	22.33
October 22	Fleming's Perfumes	65.00
October 24	Union 76	27.63
October 26	Amber's Books	42.31
November 2	Lakewood Meadows	423.88
November 8	Von's Grocery	55.64

a. Find the finance charge if the interest rate is 1.8% per month. Assume the due date of the bill is November 10. On October 10, the unpaid balance was the $1 you did not pay. You may want to use the spreadsheet program mentioned above Exercise 11.

b. Now assume that instead of paying $499, you paid $200, which is $299 less than the amount paid in part a. Calculate the finance charge.

c. How much more interest did you pay in part b than in part a?

d. If you took the $299 difference in payment and deposited it into an account that earned 1.8% simple interest (the credit card rate) for 1 month, how much interest would you earn?

e. ✎   Explain why the answers to parts c and d are the same.

41. a. Car Leases Use the formula in Exercise 39 to find the monthly lease payment, excluding sales tax, for a car for which the net capitalized cost is $23,488, the residual value is $12,500, the annual interest rate is 7%, and the term of the lease is 4 years.

b. Suppose you negotiate a net capitalized cost of $26,445 for a car and a residual value of $14,000. If the annual interest rate is 6.5% and the term of the lease is 5 years, find the monthly lease payment. The sales tax is 6.25% of the lease payment.

c. Use the formula in Exercise 39 to find the lease payment for Exercise 35. What is the difference between the payment calculated using this method and the payment calculated using the method in Exercise 35?

d. Use the formula in Exercise 39 to find the lease payment for Exercise 36. What is the difference between the payment calculated using this method and the payment calculated using the method in Exercise 36?

42. Credit Card Debt The APR Loan Payoff Formula can be used to determine how many months it will take to pay off a credit card debt if the minimum monthly payment is made each month. For instance, suppose you have a credit card bill of $620.50, the minimum payment is $13, and the interest rate is 18% per year. Using a graphing calculator, we can determine the number of months, n, it will take to pay off the debt. Enter the values shown on the calculator screen at the right. Move the cursor to $N =$ and press ALPHA [SOLVE]. It will take over 84 months (or approximately 7 years) to pay off the credit card debt, assuming you do not make additional purchases.

```
N=84.53746933
■I%=18
 PV=620.5
 PMT=-13
 FV=0
 P/Y=12
 C/Y=12
 PMT: END BEGIN
```

a. Find the number of months it will take to pay off a credit card debt of $1283.34 if the minimum payment is $27 and the annual interest rate is 19.6%. Round to the nearest month.

b. How much interest will be paid on the credit card debt in part a?

c. 🌐   If you have credit card debt, determine how many months it would take to pay off your debt by making the minimum monthly payments. How much interest would you pay? You may want to go to the website at **http://www.cardweb.com,** which was mentioned in the Math Matters on page 676, to determine the answers.

Stocks

Stocks, bonds, and mutual funds are investment vehicles, but they differ in nature.

When owners of a company want to raise money, generally to expand their business, they may decide to sell part of the company to investors. An investor who purchases a part of the company is said to own *stock* in the company. Stock is measured in shares; a **share of stock** in a company is a certificate that indicates partial ownership in the company. The owners of the certificates are called **stockholders** or **shareholders.** As owners, the stockholders share in the profits or losses of the corporation.

A company may distribute profits to its shareholders in the form of **dividends.** A dividend is usually expressed as a per-share amount—for example, $.07 per share.

EXAMPLE 1 ■ Calculate Dividends Paid to a Stockholder

A stock pays an annual dividend of $.84 per share. Calculate the dividends paid to a shareholder who has 200 shares of the company's stock.

Solution

$$(\$.84 \text{ per share}) \times (200 \text{ shares}) = \$168$$

The shareholder receives $168 in dividends.

CHECK YOUR PROGRESS 1   A stock pays an annual dividend of $.72 per share. Calculate the dividends paid to a shareholder who has 550 shares of the company's stock.

Solution   *See page B-2.*

The **dividend yield,** which is used to compare companies' dividends, is the amount of the dividend divided by the stock price and is expressed as a percent. Determining a dividend yield is similar to calculating the simple interest rate earned on an investment. You can think of the dividend as the interest earned, the stock price as the principal, and the yield as the interest rate.

EXAMPLE 2 ■ Calculate a Dividend Yield

A stock pays an annual dividend of $1.75 per share. The stock is trading at $70. Find the dividend yield.

Solution

$$I = Prt$$
$$1.75 = 70r(1)$$ • **Let** I **= annual dividend and** P **= the stock price. The time is 1 year.**

$$1.75 = 70r$$
$$0.025 = r \qquad \bullet \textbf{ Divide each side of the equation by 70.}$$

The dividend yield is 2.5%.

CHECK YOUR PROGRESS 2   A stock pays an annual dividend of $.82 per share. The stock is trading at $51.25. Find the dividend yield.

Solution   *See page B-2.*

The **market value** of a share of stock is the price for which a stockholder is willing to sell a share of the stock and a buyer is willing to purchase it. Shares are always sold to the highest bidder. A **brokerage firm** is a dealer of stocks that acts as your agent when you want to buy or sell shares of stock. The **brokers** in the firm charge commissions for their service. Most trading of stocks happens on a stock exchange. **Stock exchanges** are businesses whose purpose it is to bring together buyers and sellers of stock. The largest stock exchange in the United States is the New York Stock Exchange. Shares of stock are also bought and sold through the National Association of Securities Dealers Automated Quotation System, which is commonly referred to as the NASDAQ. Every working day, each stock exchange provides financial institutions, Internet website hosts, newspapers, and other publications with data on the trading activity of all the stocks traded on that exchange. Table 10.2 is a portion of the stock table printed in the *Wall Street Journal* on August 4, 2004.

Table 10.2

YTD % CHG	52-WEEK HI	52-WEEK LO	STOCK (SYM)	DIV	YLD %	PE	VOL 100s	CLOSE	NET CHG	YTD % CHG	52-WEEK HI	52-WEEK LO	STOCK (SYM)	DIV	YLD %	PE	VOL 100s	CLOSE	NET CHG
8.0	53.54	40.25	♣PanPacProp PNP	2.17	4.2	21	1407	51.45	−0.28	25.1	19.99	6.26	PeriniCp PCR		...	6	649	11.45	−0.12
−40.3	75.44	32.10	PanPharm PRX		...	10	7652	38.88	0.18	0.4	22.59	13.96	PerkinElmer PKI	.28	1.6	29	4475	17.13	−0.27
16.1	12.35	6.08	ParTch PTC		...	22	7	9.28	−0.10	▲ 35.7	11.12	7	PermRltyTr PBT	.83e	7.4	...	820	11.21	0.10
−13.0	30.70	19	ParkElchm PKE	.24	1.0	43	1344	23.05	−0.56	−11.1	14.76	9.67	PerotSys A PER		...	26	5341	11.99	−0.69
36.5	4.49	1.65	ParkerDri PKD		...	dd	8091	3.48	−0.32	−11.1	14.32	7.37	Petrobrs ADS PZE		...	...	306	9.77	−0.08
−3.4	61	43.90	ParkerHan PH	.76	1.3	20	4114	57.45	−0.63	−4.0	53.17	37.56	PetroCnda PCZ	.60g	...	...	641	47.35	0.55
5.4	48.70	36.80	ParkwyProp PKY	2.60	5.9	18	210	43.85	−0.45	−12.0	63.70	29.25	PtroChna ADS PTR	2.16e	4.3	...	2327	50.20	−0.20
−8.9	60.15	46.74	♣PartnerRe PRE	1.36	2.6	6	2982	52.86	0.26	▲ 41.7	32.88	12.80	Ptrokzkhstn A PKZ	.30eg	.9	7	5930	31.90	−0.83
21.0	31.68	14.65	PatinaOil POG s	.20	.7	18	4810	29.65	−0.30	−4.2	35.64	17.76	PetrlBra ADS PBR	1.76e	6.3	5	10196	28.02	0.03
45.4	20	11.46	PaxarCp PXR		...	25	4144	19.48	0.34	−4.3	31.94	16.56	PtrlBras ADS A PBRA	1.76e	6.9	...	4861	25.52	−0.04
−4.3	17.72	11.96	PaylessShoe PSS		...	...	9130	12.82	−0.25	15.1	43.50	27	PfeiffrVac PV	.85e	2.1	...	9	40.32	1.42
33.9	58.34	28.61	Peabdy Egy BTU	.50	.9	31	3750	55.85	−0.22	−8.2	38.89	29.43	Pfizer PFE	.68	2.1	31	169915	32.45	0.25
0.5	12.80	9.17	Pearson ADS PSO	.45e	4.0	...	287	11.27	−0.08	1.3	90.52	41.11	PhelpDodg PD	.25e	.3	16	14948	77.08	−1.29
15.7	71.62	37.50	PediatrixMed PDX		...	18	3743	63.75	0.50	−0.1	25.57	23.20	PhilAuthInd POB	1.64	6.5	...	72	25.08	0.08
▲ 3.2	15.05	14.40	Pengrowth n	.17p		...	5904	15.29	0.31	▲ 32.5	23.41	8.78	PhlpLngDst PHI		...	...	2246	23.09	0.48
−2.0	16.10	11.46	PennAmGp PNG	.24	1.8	10	387	13	−0.02	−18.9	33.38	20.27	PhlpsEl PHG	.44e	1.9	...	14433	23.59	−0.54
1.2	21.58	12.85	PennEngrg PNN	.28	1.5	24	137	19.25	−0.54	3.4	19.95	13.72	PhillipsVanH PVH	.15	.8	dd	976	18.35	−0.38
−1.1	2.67	1.47	PennTreaty PTA		...	dd	609	1.82	0.08	−15.8	14.53	8.67	PhoenixCos PNX	.16e	1.6	14	3784	10.14	−0.32
34.8	40	19.83	♣PennVirginia PVA s	.45	1.2	24	554	37.50	−0.05	−14.9	43.80	28.50	PhoenixCos un	1.81	5.6	...	2	32.11	−0.68
9.6	39	27.25	♣PennVARes PVR	2.16f	5.8	...	603	37.56	0.06	48.9	3.20	0.95	PhosphtRes PLP		...	dd	212	2.83	0.04
51.0	41.50	17.25	PenneyJC JCP	.50	1.3	dd	66959	39.69	−0.51	−4.1	43.95	37.23	PidmntNG PNY	1.72	4.1	...	1308	41.67	0.07
−2.7	37.87	30	♣PA Reit PEI	2.16	6.1	13	1027	35.31	−0.31	−19.9	26.44	16.82	Pier 1 PIR	.40	2.3	14	7163	17.52	−0.32
37.0	34.75	18.38	Pentair PNR s	.44f	1.4	19	7705	31.30	0.21	77.2	32.09	11.25	PilgrmPr PPC	.06	.2	20	3660	28.94	0.59
−6.3	46.03	38.50	PeopEngy PGL	2.16	5.5	16	2262	39.38	0.22	15.7	14.93	5.80	PinnacleEnt PNK		...	dd	1197	10.78	−0.51
−13.8	29.38	14.05	PepBoys PBY	.27	1.4	dd	11159	19.71	−0.68	1.9	41.50	32.87	♣PinaclWCap PNW	1.80	4.4	14	2792	40.80	0.24
−5.8	21.71	16.70	PepcoHldg POM	1.00	5.4	17	3317	18.40	0.07	−23.9	31.25	20.85	PioneerCp PIO	.23e	1.1	...	263	21.44	−0.28
16.0	31.40	20.39	PepsiBttlng PBG	.20f	.7	17	11900	28.04	−0.15	12.1	37.50	22.76	PionrNtrlRes PXD	.10e	.3	11	11662	35.78	0.52
10.1	21.67	13.03	PepsiAm PAS	.08	.4	15	3066	18.85	−0.05	−2.9	59.59	38.70	PiperJaffray PJC n		...	...	1259	40.35	−0.82
9.8	55.71	43.35	PepsiCo PEP	.92	1.8	23	33068	51.20	0.12	4.7	45.21	37.25	PitneyBws PBI	1.22	2.9	19	8263	42.51	−0.13
44.3	25.26	8.34	Perdigao ADS PDA	.55e	2.2	...	32	25.04	0.29	−8.8	19.23	12.23	PlacrDome PDG	.10g	.6	35	15195	16.33	0.20

The headings at the tops of the columns are repeated below, along with the information for Pier 1 (with stock symbol PIR).

YTD %CHG	52-WEEK HI	52-WEEK LO	STOCK (SYM)	DIV	YLD %	PE	VOL 100s	CLOSE	NET CHG
−19.9	26.44	16.82	Pier 1 (PIR)	.40	2.3	14	7163	17.52	−0.32

YTD % CHG The number −19.9 in the first column indicates that the price of a share of Pier 1 stock has decreased 19.9% so far this calendar year.

52-WEEK HI/LO The next two numbers show that in the last 52 weeks, the highest price a share of the stock sold for was $26.44, and the lowest price was $16.82.

DIV The number .40 under the column headed DIV means that the company is currently paying an annual dividend of $.40 per share of stock.

YLD% The current dividend yield on the company's stock is 2.3%. Thus the dividend of $.40 is 2.3% of the current purchase price of a share of the stock.

PE The heading PE refers to the price-to-earnings ratio, the purchase price per share divided by the earnings per share.

VOL 100s 7163 is the number of shares sold that day, in hundreds. $7163 \times 100 = 716{,}300$. 716,300 shares of Pier 1 were sold that day.

CLOSE The next number, 17.52, indicates that the closing price of the stock was $17.52. This means that in the final trade of the day, before the market closed, the price of a share of Pier 1 stock was $17.52 per share.

NET CHG The number −0.32 under the heading NET CHG indicates that the day's closing price was $.32 lower than that of the previous trading day.

EXAMPLE 3 ■ Calculate Profits or Losses and Expenses in Selling Stock

Suppose you owned 500 shares of stock in J.C. Penney (which is listed as PenneyJC in Table 10.2). You purchased the shares at a price of $23.90 per share and sold them at the closing price of the stock given in Table 10.2.

a. Ignoring dividends, what was your profit or loss on the sale of the stock?

b. If your broker charges 2.4% of the total sale price, what was the broker's commission?

Solution

a. From Table 10.2, the selling price per share was $39.69.
The selling price per share is greater than the purchase price per share.
You made a profit on the sale of the stock.

$$\begin{aligned}
\text{Profit} &= \text{selling price} - \text{purchase price} \\
&= 500(\$39.69) - 500(\$23.90) \\
&= \$19{,}845 - \$11{,}950 \\
&= \$7895
\end{aligned}$$

The profit on the sale of the stock was $7895.

b. $$\begin{aligned}
\text{Commission} &= 2.4\%(\text{selling price}) \\
&= 0.024(\$19{,}845) \\
&= \$476.28
\end{aligned}$$

The broker's commission was $476.28.

CHECK YOUR PROGRESS 3   Use Table 10.2. Suppose you bought 300 shares of Pfizer at the 52-week low and sold the shares at the 52-week high.

a. Ignoring dividends, what was your profit or loss on the sale of the stock?

b. If your broker charges 2.1% of the total sale price, what was the broker's commission? Round to the nearest cent.

Solution   *See page B-3.*

Bonds

When a corporation issues stock, it is *selling* part of the company to the stockholders. When it issues a **bond,** the corporation is *borrowing* money from the bondholders; a **bondholder** lends money to a corporation. Corporations, the federal government, government agencies, states, and cities all issue bonds. These entities need money to operate—for example, to fund the federal deficit, repair roads, or build a new factory—so they borrow money from the public by issuing bonds.

Bonds are usually issued in units of $1000. The price paid for the bond is the **face value.** The issuer promises to repay the bondholder on a particular day, called the **maturity date,** at a given rate of interest, called the **coupon.**

Assume that a bond with a $1000 face value has a 5% coupon and a 10-year maturity date. The bondholder collects interest payments of $50 in each of those 10 years. The payments are calculated using the simple interest formula, as shown below.

$$\begin{aligned}
I &= Prt \\
I &= 1000(0.05)(1) \\
I &= 50
\end{aligned}$$

At the end of the 10-year period, the bondholder receives from the issuer the $1000 face value of the bond.

▼ **point of interest**

Municipal bonds are issued by states, cities, counties, and other governments to raise money to build schools, highways, sewer systems, hospitals, and other projects for the public good. The income from many municipal bonds is exempt from federal and/or state taxes.

EXAMPLE 4 ■ Calculate Interest Payments on a Bond

A bond with a $10,000 face value has a 3% coupon and a 5-year maturity date. Calculate the total of the interest payments paid to the bondholder.

Solution

Use the simple interest formula to find the annual interest payments. Substitute the following values into the formula: $P = 10,000$, $r = 3\% = 0.03$, and $t = 1$.

$I = Prt$

$I = 10,000(0.03)(1)$

$I = 300$

Multiply the annual interest payments by the term of the bond.

$300(5) = 1500$

The total of the interest payments paid to the bondholder is $1500.

CHECK YOUR PROGRESS 4   A bond has a $15,000 face value, a 4-year maturity, and a 3.5% coupon. What is the total of the interest payments paid to the bondholder?

Solution   *See page B-3.*

A key difference between stocks and bonds is that stocks make no promises about dividends or returns, whereas the issuer of a bond guarantees that, provided the issuer remains solvent, it will pay back the face value of the bond plus interest.

Mutual Funds

An **investment trust** is a company whose assets are stocks and bonds. The purpose of these companies is not to manufacture a product but to purchase stocks and bonds with the hope that their value will increase. A **mutual fund** is an example of an investment trust.

When investors purchase shares in a mutual fund, they are adding their money to a pool along with many other investors. The investments within a mutual fund are called the fund's portfolio. The investors in a mutual fund share the fund's profits or losses from the investments in the portfolio.

An advantage of owning shares of a mutual fund is that your money is managed by full-time professionals whose job it is to research and evaluate stocks; you own stocks without having to choose which individual stocks to buy or to decide when to sell them. Another advantage is that by owning shares in the fund, you have purchased shares of stock in many different companies. This diversification helps to reduce some of the risks of investing.

Because a mutual fund owns many different stocks, each share of the fund owns a fractional interest in each of the companies. Each day, the value of a share in the fund, called the **net asset value of the fund,** or **NAV,** depends on the performance of the stocks in the fund. It is calculated by the following formula.

Net Asset Value of a Mutual Fund

The net asset value of a mutual fund is given by

$$NAV = \frac{A - L}{N}$$

where A is the total fund assets, L is the total fund liabilities, and N is the number of shares outstanding.

EXAMPLE 5 ■ **Calculate the Net Asset Value of, and the Number of, Shares Purchased in a Mutual Fund**

A mutual fund has $600 million worth of stock, $5 million worth of bonds, and $1 million in cash. The fund's total liabilities amount to $2 million. There are 25 million shares outstanding. You invest $15,000 in this fund.

a. Calculate the NAV.

b. How many shares will you purchase?

Solution

a. $NAV = \dfrac{A - L}{N}$

$= \dfrac{606 \text{ million} - 2 \text{ million}}{25 \text{ million}}$ • **A = 600 million + 5 million + 1 million = 606 million, L = 2 million, N = 25 million**

$= 24.16$

The NAV of the fund is $24.16.

b. $\dfrac{15,000}{24.16} \approx 620$ • **Divide the amount invested by the cost per share of the fund. Round down to the nearest whole number.**

You will purchase 620 shares of the mutual fund.

CHECK YOUR PROGRESS 5 A mutual fund has $750 million worth of stock, $750,000 in cash, and $1,500,000 in other assets. The fund's total liabilities amount to $1,500,000. There are 20 million shares outstanding. You invest $10,000 in this fund.

a. Calculate the NAV.

b. How many shares will you purchase?

Solution *See page B-3.*

Math Matters   Growth of Mutual Funds

Where do Americans invest their money? You might correctly assume that the largest number of Americans invest in real estate, as every homeowner is considered to have an investment in real estate. But more and more Americans are investing their money in the stock market, and many of them are doing so by purchasing shares in mutual funds. The graph below shows the growth of mutual funds from 1985 to 2000. (*Source:* Investment Company Institute)

Year	Number of funds	Total Net Assets (in millions of dollars)	Number of Shareholder Accounts
1985	1528	495,385.1	34,098,401
1990	3079	1,065,190.2	61,947,955
1995	5725	2,811,292.2	131,219,221
2000	8155	6,964,667.0	244,748,546

Excursion

Treasury Bills

✓ TAKE NOTE

You can obtain more information about the various Treasury securities at **http://www.publicdebt. treas.gov.** Using this site, investors can buy securities directly from the government, thereby avoiding the service fee charged by banks and brokerage firms.

The bonds issued by the United States government are called Treasuries. Some investors prefer to invest in Treasury Bills, rather than the stock market, because their investment is backed by the federal government. As such they are considered the safest of all investments. They are grouped into three categories.

U.S. Treasury bills have maturities of under 1 year.

U.S. Treasury notes have maturities ranging from 2 to 10 years.

U.S. Treasury bonds have maturities ranging from 10 to 30 years.

This Excursion will focus on Treasury bills.

The **face value** of a Treasury bill is the amount of money received on the maturity date of the bill. Treasury bills are sold on a **discount basis;** that is, the interest on the bill is computed and subtracted from the face value to determine its cost.

Suppose a company invests in a $50,000 United States Treasury bill at 3.35% interest for 28 days. The bank through which the bill is purchased charges a service fee of $15. What is the cost of the Treasury bill?

To find the cost, first find the interest. Use the simple interest formula.

$$I = Prt$$

$$= 50,000(0.0335)\left(\frac{28}{360}\right)$$

$$\approx 130.28$$

The interest earned is $130.28.

(continued)

Find the cost of the Treasury bill.

Cost = (face value − interest) + service fee

= (50,000 − 130.28) + 15

= 49,869.72 + 15

= 49,884.72

The cost of the Treasury bill is $49,884.72.

Excursion Exercises

1. The face value of a Treasury bill is $30,000. The interest rate is 2.32% and the bill matures in 182 days. The bank through which the bill is purchased charges a service fee of $15. What is the cost of the Treasury bill?

2. The face value of a 91-day Treasury bill is $20,000. The interest rate is 2.96%. The purchaser buys the bill through Treasury Direct and pays no service fee. Calculate the cost of the Treasury bill.

3. A company invests in a 29-day, $60,000 United States Treasury bill at 2.28% interest. The bank charges a service fee of $35. Calculate the cost of the Treasury bill.

4. A $40,000 United States Treasury bill, purchased at 1.96% interest, matures in 92 days. The purchaser is charged a service fee of $20. What is the cost of the Treasury bill?

Exercise Set 10.4

1. Annual Dividends A stock pays an annual dividend of $1.02 per share. Calculate the dividends paid to a shareholder who has 375 shares of the company's stock.

2. Annual Dividends A stock pays an annual dividend of $.58 per share. Calculate the dividends paid to a shareholder who has 1500 shares of the company's stock.

3. Annual Dividends Calculate the dividends paid to a shareholder who has 850 shares of a stock that is paying an annual dividend of $.63 per share.

4. Annual Dividends Calculate the dividends paid to a shareholder who has 400 shares of a stock that is paying an annual dividend of $.91 per share.

5. Dividend Yield Find the dividend yield for a stock that pays an annual dividend of $1.24 per share and has a current price of $49.375. Round to the nearest hundredth of a percent.

6. Dividend Yield The Blackburn Computer Company has declared an annual dividend of $.50 per share. The stock is trading at $40 per share. Find the dividend yield.

7. Dividend Yield A stock that pays an annual dividend of $.58 per share has a current price of $31.75. Find the dividend yield. Round to the nearest hundredth of a percent.

8. Dividend Yield The Moreau Corporation is paying an annual dividend of $.65 per share. If the price of a share of the stock is $81.25, what is the dividend yield on the stock?

Use the portion of the stock table shown below for Exercises 9 to 16. Round dollar amounts to the nearest cent when necessary.

YTD % CHG	52-WEEK HI	LO	STOCK (SYM)	DIV	YLD %	PE	VOL 100s	CLOSE	NET CHG
12.7	51.52	34.45	GallaherGp GLH	2.12e	4.4	...	415	47.95	−0.15
−0.7	19.05	12.52	GameStop A GME		...	14	3149	15.30	−0.38
−5.7	91.38	75.59♣	Gannett GCI	1.00	1.2	18	10658	84.06	−0.07
−4.2	25.72	16.99	Gap Inc GPS	.09	.4	19	37506	22.24	−0.35
15.9	30.30	19.95♣	GardnrDenvr GDI		...	18	530	27.66	0.08
8.5	13.75	8.86	Gartner IT		...	61	7366	12.27	−0.33
12.0	13.06	8.52	Gartner B ITB		...	61	2521	12.19	−0.33
−10.0	6.85	3.64	Gateway GTW		...	dd	12852	4.14	−0.25
−4.0	32.70	17.70	GaylEnt GET		...	dd	1248	28.66	−0.25
9.3	13.53	8.75	GenCorp GY	.12	1.0	dd	1987	11.77	−0.14
1.5	68.25	36.82	Genentech DNA s		...	74	28074	47.50	0.54
15.3	10.23	6.26	GenICbl BGC		...	dd	2002	9.40	−0.26
9.1	101.94	75.59	GenDynam GD	1.44	1.5	18	4787	98.59	−1.44
6.1	34.57	27.18	GenElec GE	.80	2.4	21	157197	32.87	−0.39
12.7	35.30	21.82	GenGrthProp GGP s	1.20	3.8	25	6392	31.27	0.02
63.6	30.42	11.13	GenMaritime GMR		...	8	3176	28.80	−0.20
−0.8	49.17	43.75	GenMills GIS	1.24f	2.8	16	7247	44.92	−0.44
−19.3	55.55	36.11	GenMotor GM	2.00	4.6	6	57115	43.07	−0.23
36.9	25.67	14.30	Genesco GCO		...	15	1688	20.71	−0.71
6.6	26.10	14	♣GeneseWY A GWR s		...	18	1085	22.38	−0.32
13.9	40.20	29.83	GenuinePart GPC	1.20	3.2	18	3739	37.80	−0.38
16.7	23.50	18.75	GnwrthFnl A GNW n	.68p	...	...	8890	22.76	0.04
10.8	29.18	25	GnwrthFnl un n	.33p	...	...	3122	28.15	...
−18.9	24.69	16.40♣	GeoGrp GGI		...	5	328	18.50	−0.25
▲23.9	35.99	20.71	GA Gulf GGC	.32	.9	22	3543	35.79	0.04
9.3	38.60	20.68♣	GA Pac GP	.50	1.5	15	8039	33.53	−0.32

9. **Stock Tables** For Gap, Inc. (GPS):

   a. What is the difference between the highest and lowest prices paid for this stock during the last 52 weeks?

   b. Suppose you own 750 shares of this stock. What dividend do you receive this year?

   c. How many shares of this stock were sold yesterday?

   d. Did the price of a share of this stock increase or decrease during the day shown in the table?

   e. What was the price of a share of this stock at the start of the trading day yesterday?

10. **Stock Tables** For General Motors (GM):

   a. What is the difference between the highest and lowest prices paid for this stock during the last 52 weeks?

   b. Suppose you own 750 shares of this stock. What dividend do you receive this year?

   c. How many shares of this stock were sold yesterday?

   d. Did the price of a share of this stock increase or decrease during the day shown in the table?

   e. What was the price of a share of this stock at the start of the trading day yesterday?

11. **Stock Purchases** At the closing price per share of General Dynamics (GD), how many shares of the stock can you purchase for $5000?

12. **Stock Purchases** At the closing price per share of GenCorp (GY), how many shares of the stock can you purchase for $2500?

13. **Stock Sale** Suppose you owned 1000 shares of stock in Gateway (GTW). You purchased the shares at a price of $3.85 per share and sold them at the closing price of the stock given in the table above.

   a. Ignoring dividends, what was your profit or loss on the sale of the stock?

   b. If your broker charges 1.9% of the total sale price, what was the broker's commission?

14. **Stock Sale** Gary Walters owned 400 shares of stock in General Electric (GE). He purchased the shares at a price of $27.80 per share and sold them at the closing price of the stock given in the table above.

   a. Ignoring dividends, what was Gary's profit or loss on the sale of the stock?

   b. If his broker charges 2.5% of the total sale price, what was the broker's commission?

15. **Stock Sale** Michelle Desjardins bought 800 shares of Genesco (GCO) at the 52-week low and sold the shares at the 52-week high shown in the table above.

   a. Ignoring dividends, what was Michelle's profit or loss on the sale of the stock?

   b. If her broker charges 2.3% of the total sale price, what was the broker's commission?

16. **Stock Sale** Suppose you bought 1200 shares of General Mills (GIS) at the 52-week low and sold the shares at the 52-week high shown in the table above.

   a. Ignoring dividends, what was your profit or loss on the sale of the stock?

   b. If your broker charges 2.25% of the total sale price, what was the broker's commission?

17. **Bonds** A bond with a face value of $6000 and a 4.2% coupon has a 5-year maturity. Find the annual interest paid to the bondholder.

18. **Bonds** The face value on a bond is $15,000. It has a 10-year maturity and a 3.75% coupon. What is the annual interest paid to the bondholder?

19. **Bonds** A bond with an $8000 face value has a 3.5% coupon and a 3-year maturity. What is the total of the interest payments paid to the bondholder?

20. **Bonds** A bond has a $12,000 face value, an 8-year maturity, and a 2.95% coupon. Find the total of the interest payments paid to the bondholder.

21. **Mutual Funds** A mutual fund has total assets of $50,000,000 and total liabilities of $5,000,000. There are 2,000,000 shares outstanding. Find the net asset value of the mutual fund.

22. **Mutual Funds** A mutual fund has total assets of $25,000,000 and total liabilities of $250,000. There are 1,500,000 shares outstanding. Find the net asset value of the mutual fund.

23. **Mutual Funds** A mutual fund has total assets of $15 million and total liabilities of $1 million. There are 2 million shares outstanding. You invest $5000 in this fund. How many shares will you purchase?

24. **Mutual Funds** A mutual fund has total assets of $12 million and total liabilities of $2 million. There are 1 million shares outstanding. You invest $2500 in this fund. How many shares will you purchase?

25. **Mutual Funds** A mutual fund has $500 million worth of stock, $500,000 in cash, and $1 million in other assets. The fund's total liabilities amount to $2 million. There are 10 million shares outstanding. You invest $12,000 in this fund. How many shares will you purchase?

26. **Mutual Funds** A mutual fund has $250 million worth of stock, $10 million worth of bonds, and $1 million in cash. The fund's total liabilities amount to $1 million. There are 13 million shares outstanding. You invest $10,000 in this fund. How many shares will you purchase?

Extensions
CRITICAL THINKING

27. **Load and No-Load Funds** All mutual funds carry fees. One type of fee is called a "load." This is an additional fee that generally is paid at the time you invest your money in the mutual fund. A no-load mutual fund does not charge this up-front fee.

    Suppose you invested $2500 in a 4% load mutual fund two years ago. The 4% fee was paid out of the $2500 invested. The fund has earned 8% during each of the past two years. There was a management fee of 0.015% charged at the end of each year. A friend of yours invested $2500 two years ago in a no-load fund that has earned 6% during each of the past two years. This fund charged a management fee of 0.15% at the end of each year. Find the difference between the values of the two investments now.

COOPERATIVE LEARNING

28. **Investing in the Stock Market** (This activity assumes that the instructor has assigned each student in the class to a group of three or four students.) Imagine that your group has $10,000 to invest in each of ten stocks. Use the stock table in today's paper or use the Internet to determine the price you would pay per share. Determine the number of shares of each stock you will purchase. Check the value of each stock every business day for the next four weeks. Assume that you sell your shares at the end of the fourth week. Calculate the group's profit or loss over the four-week period. Compare your profits or losses with those of the other groups in your class.

EXPLORATIONS

29. Find a mutual fund table in a daily newspaper. You can find one in the same section where the stock tables are printed. Explain the meaning of the heading of each column in the table.

| # Home Ownership

Initial Expenses

When you purchase a home, you generally make a down payment and finance the remainder of the purchase price with a loan obtained through a bank or savings and loan association. The amount of the down payment can vary, but it is normally between 10% and 30% of the selling price. The **mortgage** is the amount that is borrowed to buy the real estate. The amount of the mortgage is the difference between the selling price and the down payment.

Mortgage = selling price − down payment

This formula is used to find the amount of the mortgage. For example, suppose you buy a $240,000 home with a down payment of 25%. First find the down payment by computing 25% of the purchase price.

$$\text{Down payment} = 25\% \text{ of } 240,000 = 0.25(240,000)$$
$$= 60,000$$

Then find the mortgage by subtracting the down payment from the selling price.

$$\text{Mortgage} = \text{selling price} - \text{down payment}$$
$$= 240,000 - 60,000$$
$$= 180,000$$

The mortgage is $180,000.

The down payment is generally the largest initial expense in purchasing a home, but there are other expenses associated with the purchase. These payments are due at the closing, when the sale of the house is finalized, and are called **closing costs.** The bank may charge fees for attorneys, credit reports, loan processing, and title searches. There may also be a **loan origination fee.** This fee is usually expressed in **points.** One point is equal to 1% of the mortgage.

Suppose you purchase a home and obtain a loan for $180,000. The bank charges a fee of 1.5 points. To find the charge for points, multiply the loan amount by 1.5%.

$$\text{Points} = 1.5\% \text{ of } 180,000 = 0.015(180,000)$$
$$= 2700$$

The charge for points is $2700.

EXAMPLE 1 ■ Calculate a Down Payment and the Closing Costs

The purchase price of a home is $392,000. A down payment of 20% is made. The bank charges $450 in fees plus $2\frac{1}{2}$ points. Find the total of the down payment and the closing costs.

Solution
First find the down payment.

$$\text{Down payment} = 20\% \text{ of } 392,000 = 0.20(392,000)$$
$$= 78,400$$

The down payment is $78,400.

Next find the mortgage.

$$\text{Mortgage} = \text{selling price} - \text{down payment}$$
$$= 392{,}000 - 78{,}400$$
$$= 313{,}600$$

The mortgage is $313,600.

Then, calculate the charge for points.

$$\text{Points} = 2\tfrac{1}{2}\% \text{ of } 313{,}600 = 0.025(313{,}600)$$
$$= 7840$$

• $2\tfrac{1}{2}\% = 2.5\% = 0.025$

The charge for points is $7840.

Finally, find the sum of the down payment and the closing costs.

$$78{,}400 + 450 + 7840 = 86{,}690$$

The total of the down payment and the closing costs is $86,690.

CHECK YOUR PROGRESS 1   The purchase price of a home is $410,000. A down payment of 25% is made. The bank charges $375 in fees plus 1.75 points. Find the total of the down payment and the closing costs.

Solution   *See page B-3.*

Mortgages

When a bank agrees to provide you with a mortgage, you agree to pay off that loan in monthly payments. If you fail to make the payments, the bank has the right to **foreclose,** which means that the bank takes possession of the property and has the right to sell it.

There are many types of mortgages available to home buyers today, so the terms of mortgages differ considerably. Some mortgages are **adjustable rate mortgages (ARMs).** The interest rate charged on an ARM is adjusted periodically to more closely reflect current interest rates. The mortgage agreement specifies exactly how often and by how much the interest rate can change.

A **fixed rate mortgage,** or **conventional mortgage,** is one in which the interest rate charged on the loan remains the same throughout the life of the mortgage. For a fixed rate mortgage, the amount of the monthly payment also remains unchanged throughout the term of the loan.

The term of a mortgage can vary. Terms of 15, 20, 25, and 30 years are most common.

The monthly payment on a mortgage is the **mortgage payment.** The amount of the mortgage payment depends on the amount of the mortgage, the interest rate on the loan, and the term of the loan. This payment is calculated by using the Payment Formula for an APR Loan given in Section 10.3. We will restate the formula here.

Mortgage Payment Formula

The mortgage payment for a mortgage is given by

$$PMT = A\left(\frac{i}{1 - (1 + i)^{-n}}\right)$$

where PMT is the monthly mortgage payment, A is the amount of the mortgage, i is the interest rate per payment period, and n is the total number of payments.

EXAMPLE 2 ■ Calculate a Mortgage Payment

Suppose Allison Sommerset purchases a condominium and secures a loan of $134,000 for 30 years at an annual interest rate of 6.5%.

a. Find the monthly mortgage payment.
b. What is the total of the payments over the life of the loan?
c. Find the amount of interest paid on the loan over the 30 years.

Solution

a. First calculate i and store the result.

$$i = \frac{\text{annual interest rate}}{\text{number of payments per year}} = \frac{0.065}{12}$$

Keystrokes: 0.065 ÷ 12 ≈ 0.00541667 STO

Calculate the monthly payment. For a 30-year loan, $n = 30(12) = 360$.

$$PMT = A\left(\frac{i}{1 - (1 + i)^{-n}}\right)$$

$$= 134{,}000\left(\frac{0.065/12}{1 - (1 + 0.065/12)^{-360}}\right) \approx 846.97$$

Keystrokes:

134000 × RCL = ÷ (1 − (1 + RCL) yˣ 360 +/−) =

The monthly mortgage payment is $846.97.

b. To determine the total of the payments, multiply the number of payments (360) by the monthly payment ($846.97).

$$846.97(360) = 304{,}909.20$$

The total of the payments over the life of the loan is $304,909.20.

c. To determine the amount of interest paid, subtract the mortgage from the total of the payments.

$$304{,}909.20 - 134{,}000 = 170{,}909.20$$

The amount of interest paid over the life of the loan is $170,909.20.

CHECK YOUR PROGRESS 2 Suppose Antonio Scarletti purchases a home and secures a loan of $223,000 for 25 years at an annual interest rate of 7%.

a. Find the monthly mortgage payment.
b. What is the total of the payments over the life of the loan?
c. Find the amount of interest paid on the loan over the 25 years.

Solution See page B-3.

A portion of a mortgage payment pays the current interest owed on the loan, and the remaining portion of the mortgage payment is used to reduce the principal owed on the loan. This process of paying off the principal and the interest, which is similar to paying a car loan, is called **amortizing the loan.**

In Example 2, the mortgage payment on a $134,000 mortgage at 6.5% for 30 years was $846.97. The amount of the first payment that is interest and the amount that is applied to the principal can be calculated using the simple interest formula.

$I = Prt$

$= 134{,}000(0.065)\left(\dfrac{1}{12}\right)$ • $P = 134{,}000$, the current loan amount; $r = 0.065$; $t = \dfrac{1}{12}$

≈ 725.83 • **Round to the nearest cent.**

Of the $846.97 mortgage payment, $725.83 is an interest payment. The remainder is applied toward reducing the principal.

Principal reduction = $846.97 − $725.83 = $121.14

After the first month's mortgage payment, the balance on the loan (the amount that remains to be paid) is calculated by subtracting the principal paid on the mortgage from the mortgage.

Loan balance after first month = $134,000 − $121.14 = $133,878.86

The portion of the second mortgage payment that is applied to interest and the portion that is applied to the principal can be calculated in the same manner. In the calculation, the figure used for the principal, P, is the current balance on the loan, $133,878.86.

$I = Prt$

$= 133{,}878.86(0.065)\left(\dfrac{1}{12}\right)$ • $P = 133{,}878.86$, the current loan amount; $r = 0.065$; $t = \dfrac{1}{12}$

≈ 725.18 • **Round to the nearest cent.**

Principal reduction = $846.97 − $725.18 = $121.79

Of the second mortgage payment, $725.18 is an interest payment and $121.79 is a payment toward the principal.

Loan balance after second month = $133,878.86 − $121.79 = $133,757.07

The interest payment, principal payment, and balance on the loan can be calculated in this manner for all of the mortgage payments throughout the life of the loan—all 360 of them! Or a computer can be programmed to make these calculations and print out the information. The printout is called an **amortization schedule.** It lists, for each mortgage payment, the payment number, the interest payment, the amount applied toward the principal, and the resulting balance to be paid.

Each month, the amount of the mortgage payment that is an interest payment decreases and the amount applied toward the principal increases. This is because you are paying interest on a decreasing balance each month. Mortgage payments early in the life of a mortgage are largely interest payments; mortgage payments late in the life of a mortgage are largely payments toward the principal.

The partial amortization schedule below shows the breakdown for the first 12 months of the loan in Example 2.

Amortization Schedule

Loan Amount	$134,000.00
Interest Rate	6.50%
Term of Loan	30
Monthly Payment	$846.97

Month	Amount of Interest	Amount of Principal	New Loan Amount
1	$725.83	$121.14	$133,878.86
2	$725.18	$121.79	$133,757.07
3	$724.52	$122.45	$133,634.61
4	$723.85	$123.12	$133,511.50
5	$723.19	$123.78	$133,387.71
6	$722.52	$124.45	$133,263.26
7	$721.84	$125.13	$133,138.13
8	$721.16	$125.81	$133,012.32
9	$720.48	$126.49	$132,885.84
10	$719.80	$127.17	$132,758.66
11	$719.11	$127.86	$132,630.80
12	$718.42	$128.55	$132,502.25

QUESTION   *Using the amortization schedule above, how much of the loan has been paid off after 1 year?*

EXAMPLE 3 ■ Calculate Principal and Interest for a Mortgage Payment

You purchase a condominium for $98,750 and obtain a 30-year, fixed rate mortgage at 7.25%. After paying a down payment of 20%, how much of the second payment is interest and how much is applied toward the principal?

Solution

First find the down payment by multiplying the percent of the purchase price that is the down payment by the purchase price.

0.20(98,750) = 19,750

The down payment is $19,750.

Find the mortgage by subtracting the down payment from the purchase price.

98,750 − 19,750 = 79,000

The mortgage is $79,000.

ANSWER   *After 1 year (12 months), the loan amount is $132,502.25. The original loan was $134,000. The amount that has been paid off is*
$134,000 − $132,502.25 = $1497.75.

Calculate the mortgage payment.

$$i = \frac{\text{annual interest rate}}{\text{number of payments per year}} = \frac{0.0725}{12}$$

Keystrokes: 0.0725 $\div$ 12 $\approx$ 0.00604167 [STO]

Calculate the monthly payment. For a 30-year loan, $n = 30(12) = 360$.

$$PMT = A\left(\frac{i}{1 - (1 + i)^{-n}}\right)$$

$$= 79{,}000\left(\frac{0.0725/12}{1 - (1 + 0.0725/12)^{-360}}\right) \approx 538.92$$

Keystrokes:

79000 [×] [RCL] [=] [÷] [(] [1] [−] [(] [1] [+] [RCL] [)] [yˣ] 360 [+/−] [)] [=]

The monthly payment is $538.92.

Find the amount of interest paid on the first mortgage payment by using the simple interest formula.

$$I = Prt$$

$$= 79{,}000(0.0725)\left(\frac{1}{12}\right)$$

• **P = 79,000, the current loan amount;**

$$r = 0.0725; t = \frac{1}{12}$$

$$\approx 477.29$$

• **Round to the nearest cent.**

Find the principal paid on the first mortgage payment by subtracting the interest paid from the monthly mortgage payment.

$$538.92 - 477.29 = 61.63$$

Calculate the balance on the loan after the first mortgage payment by subtracting the principal paid from the mortgage.

$$79{,}000 - 61.63 = 78{,}938.37$$

Find the amount of interest paid on the second mortgage payment.

$$I = Prt$$

$$= 78{,}938.37(0.0725)\left(\frac{1}{12}\right)$$

• **P = 78,938.37, the current loan amount;**

$$r = 0.0725; t = \frac{1}{12}$$

$$\approx 476.92$$

• **Round to the nearest cent.**

The interest paid on the second payment was $476.92.

Find the principal paid on the second mortgage payment.

$$538.92 - 476.92 = 62.00$$

The principal paid on the second payment was $62.

CHECK YOUR PROGRESS 3 You purchase a home for $295,000. You obtain a 30-year conventional mortgage at 6.75% after paying a down payment of 25% of the purchase price. Of the first month's payment, how much is interest and how much is applied toward the principal?

Solution *See page B-3.*

When a home is sold before the term of the loan has expired, the homeowner must pay the lender the remaining balance on the loan. To calculate that balance, we can use the APR Loan Payoff Formula from Section 10.3.

APR Loan Payoff Formula

The payoff amount for a mortgage is given by

$$A = PMT\left(\frac{1 - (1 + i)^{-n}}{i}\right)$$

where A is the loan payoff, PMT is the mortgage payment, i is the interest rate per payment period, and n is the number of *remaining* payments.

EXAMPLE 4 ■ Calculate a Mortgage Payoff

A homeowner has a monthly mortgage payment of $645.32 on a 30-year loan at an annual interest rate of 7.2%. After making payments for 5 years, the homeowner decides to sell the house. What is the payoff for the mortgage?

Solution

Use the APR Loan Payoff Formula. The homeowner has been making payments for 5 years, or 60 months. There are 360 months in a 30-year loan, so there are $360 - 60 = 300$ remaining payments.

$$A = PMT\left(\frac{1 - (1 + i)^{-n}}{i}\right)$$

$$= 645.32\left(\frac{1 - (1 + 0.006)^{-300}}{0.006}\right)$$

$$\approx 89,679.01$$

• $PMT = 645.32$; $i = \dfrac{0.072}{12} = 0.006$; $n = 300$, the number of remaining payments

```
N=300
I%=7.2
■PV=89679.0079
PMT=-645.32
FV=0
P/Y=12
C/Y=12
PMT: END BEGIN
```

Here are the keystrokes to compute the payoff on a scientific calculator. The same calculation using a graphing calculator is shown at the left.

Calculate i: 0.072 $\boxed{\div}$ 12 $\boxed{=}$ 0.006 $\boxed{\text{STO}}$

Calculate the payoff: 645.32 $\boxed{\times}$ $\boxed{(}$ $\boxed{1}$ $\boxed{-}$ $\boxed{(}$ $\boxed{1}$ $\boxed{+}$ $\boxed{\text{RCL}}$ $\boxed{)}$ $\boxed{y^x}$ 300 $\boxed{+/-}$ $\boxed{)}$ $\boxed{\div}$ $\boxed{\text{RCL}}$ $\boxed{=}$

The loan payoff is $89,679.01.

CHECK YOUR PROGRESS 4   Ava Rivera has a monthly mortgage payment of $846.82 on her condo. After making payments for 4 years, she decides to sell the condo. If she has a 25-year loan at an annual interest rate of 6.9%, what is the payoff for the mortgage?

Solution   *See page B-4.*

> ## Math Matters   Biweekly and Two-Step Mortgages
>
> A variation of the fixed rate mortgage is the *biweekly mortgage*. Borrowers make payments on a 30-year loan, but they pay half of a monthly payment every 2 weeks, which adds up to 26 half-payments a year, or 13 monthly payments. The extra monthly payment each year can result in the loan being paid off in about $17\frac{1}{2}$ years.
>
> Another type of mortgage is the *two-step mortgage*. Its name is derived from the fact that the life of the loan has two stages. The first step is a low fixed rate for the first 7 years of the loan, and the second step is a different, and probably higher, fixed rate for the remaining 23 years of the loan. This loan is appealing to those homeowners who do not anticipate owning the home beyond the initial low-interest-rate period; they do not need to worry about the increased interest rate during the second step.

Ongoing Expenses

In addition to a monthly mortgage payment, there are other ongoing expenses associated with home ownership. Among these expenses are the costs of insurance, property tax, and utilities such as heat, electricity, and water.

Services such as schools, police and fire protection, road maintenance, and recreational services, which are provided by cities and counties, are financed by the revenue received from taxes levied on real property, or property taxes. Property tax is normally an annual expense that can be paid on a monthly, quarterly, semiannual, or annual basis.

Homeowners who obtain a mortgage must carry fire insurance. This insurance guarantees that the lender will be repaid in the event of a fire.

▼ **point of interest**

The home ownership rate in the United States for the first quarter of 2004 was 68.6%. The following list gives home ownership rates by region during the same quarter.

> Northeast: 65.1%
> Midwest: 73.5%
> South: 70.3%
> West: 63.7%

It is interesting to note that the home ownership rate in the United States in 1950 was 55.0%, significantly lower than it is today. (*Source:* U.S. Bureau of the Census)

EXAMPLE 5 ■ Calculate a Total Monthly Payment

A homeowner has a monthly mortgage payment of $1145.60 and an annual property tax bill of $1074. The annual fire insurance premium is $600. Find the total monthly payment for the mortgage, property tax, and fire insurance.

Solution

Find the monthly property tax bill by dividing the annual property tax bill by 12.

$$1074 \div 12 = 89.50$$

The monthly property tax bill is $89.50.

Find the monthly fire insurance bill by dividing the annual fire insurance bill by 12.

$$600 \div 12 = 50$$

The monthly fire insurance bill is $50.

Find the sum of the mortgage payment, the monthly property tax bill, and the monthly fire insurance bill.

$$1145.60 + 89.50 + 50.00 = 1285.10$$

The monthly payment for the mortgage, property tax, and fire insurance is $1285.10.

CHECK YOUR PROGRESS 5 A homeowner has a monthly mortgage payment of $1492.89, an annual property tax bill of $2332.80, and an annual fire insurance premium of $450. Find the total monthly payment for the mortgage, property tax bill, and fire insurance.

Solution *See page B-4.*

Excursion

Home Ownership Issues

There are a number of issues that a person must think about when purchasing a home. One such issue is the difference between the interest rate on which the loan payment is based and the APR. For instance, a bank may offer a loan at an annual interest rate of 6.5%, but then go on to say that the APR is 7.1%.

The discrepancy is a result of the Truth in Lending Act. This act requires that the APR be based on *all* loan fees. This includes points and other fees associated with the purchase. To calculate the APR, a computer or financial calculator is necessary.

Suppose you decide to purchase a home and you secure a 30-year, $285,000 loan at an annual interest rate of 6.5%.

1. Calculate the monthly payment for the loan.

2. If points are 1.5% of the loan amount, find the fee for points.

3. Add the fee for points to the loan amount. This is the modified mortgage on which the APR is calculated.

4. Using the result from Excursion Exercise 3 as the mortgage and the monthly payment from Excursion Exercise 1, determine the interest rate. (This is where the financial or graphing calculator is necessary. See page 679 for details.) The result is the APR required by the Truth in Lending Act. For this example we have included only points. In most situations, other fees would be included as well.

Another issue to research when purchasing a home is that of points and mortgage interest rates. Usually paying higher points results in a lower mortgage interest rate. The question for the homebuyer is: Should I pay higher points for a lower mortgage interest rate, or pay lower points for a higher mortgage interest rate? The answer to that question depends on many factors, one of which is the amount of time the homeowner plans on staying in the home.

Consider two typical situations for a 30-year, $100,000 mortgage. Option 1 offers an annual mortgage interest rate of 7.25% and a loan origination fee of 1.5 points. Option 2 offers an annual interest rate of 7% and a loan origination fee of 2 points.

5. Calculate the monthly payments for Option 1 and Option 2.

6. Calculate the loan origination fees for Option 1 and Option 2.

7. What is the total amount paid, including points, after 2 years for each option?

8. What is the total amount paid, including points, after 3 years for each option?

9. Which option is more cost effective if you stay in the home for 2 years or less? Which option is more cost effective if you stay in the home for 3 years or more? Explain your answer.

Exercise Set 10.5

1. **Mortgages** You buy a $258,000 home with a down payment of 25%. Find the amount of the down payment and the mortgage amount.

2. **Mortgages** Greg Walz purchases a home for $325,000 with a down payment of 10%. Find the amount of the down payment and the mortgage amount.

3. **Points** Clarrisa Madison purchases a home and secures a loan of $250,000. The bank charges a fee of 2.25 points. Find the charge for points.

4. **Points** Jerome Thurber purchases a home and secures a loan of $170,000. The bank charges a fee of $2\frac{3}{4}$ points. Find the charge for points.

5. **Closing Costs** The purchase price of a home is $309,000. A down payment of 30% is made. The bank charges $350 in fees plus 3 points. Find the total of the down payment and the closing costs.

6. **Closing Costs** The purchase price of a home is $243,000. A down payment of 20% is made. The bank charges $425 in fees plus 4 points. Find the total of the down payment and the closing costs.

7. **Closing Costs** The purchase price of a condominium is $121,500. A down payment of 25% is made. The bank charges $725 in fees plus $3\frac{1}{2}$ points. Find the total of the down payment and the closing costs.

8. **Closing Costs** The purchase price of a manufactured home is $159,000. A down payment of 20% is made. The bank charges $815 in fees plus 1.75 points. Find the total of the down payment and the closing costs.

9. **Mortgage Payments** Find the mortgage payment for a 25-year loan of $129,000 at an annual interest rate of 7.75%.

10. **Mortgage Payments** Find the mortgage payment for a 30-year loan of $245,000 at an annual interest rate of 6.5%.

11. **Mortgage Payments** Find the mortgage payment for a 15-year loan of $223,500 at an annual interest rate of 8.15%.

12. **Mortgage Payments** Find the mortgage payment for a 20-year loan of $149,900 at an annual interest rate of 8.5%.

13. **Mortgage Payments** Leigh King purchased a townhouse and obtained a 30-year loan of $152,000 at an annual interest rate of 7.75%.

    a. What is the mortgage payment?

    b. What is the total of the payments over the life of the loan?

    c. Find the amount of interest paid on the mortgage loan over the 30 years.

14. **Mortgage Payments** Richard Miyashiro purchased a condominium and obtained a 25-year loan of $199,000 at an annual interest rate of 8.25%.

    a. What is the mortgage payment?

    b. What is the total of the payments over the life of the loan?

    c. Find the amount of interest paid on the mortgage loan over the 25 years.

15. **Interest Paid** Ira Patton purchased a home and obtained a 15-year loan of $219,990 at an annual interest rate of 8.7%. Find the amount of interest paid on the loan over the 15 years.

16. **Interest Paid** Leona Jefferson purchased a home and obtained a 30-year loan of $437,750 at an annual interest rate of 7.5%. Find the amount of interest paid on the loan over the 30 years.

17. **Principal and Interest** Marcel Thiessen purchased a home for $208,500 and obtained a 15-year, fixed rate mortgage at 9% after paying a down payment of 10%. Of the first month's mortgage payment, how much is interest and how much is applied to the principal?

18. **Principal and Interest** You purchase a condominium for $173,000. You obtain a 30-year, fixed rate mortgage loan at 12% after paying a down payment of 25%. Of the second month's mortgage payment, how much is interest and how much is applied to the principal?

19. **Principal and Interest** You purchase a cottage for $185,000. You obtain a 20-year, fixed rate mortgage loan at 12.5% after paying a down payment of 30%. Of the second month's mortgage payment, how much is interest and how much is applied to the principal?

20. **Principal and Interest** Fay Nguyen purchased a second home for $183,000 and obtained a 25-year, fixed rate mortgage loan at 9.25% after paying a down payment of 30%. Of the second month's mortgage payment, how much is interest and how much is applied to the principal?

21. **Loan Payoffs** After making payments of $913.10 for 6 years on your 30-year loan at 8.5%, you decide to sell your home. What is the loan payoff?

22. **Loan Payoffs** Christopher Chamberlain has a 25-year mortgage loan at an annual interest rate of 7.75%. After making payments of $1011.56 for $3\frac{1}{2}$ years, Christopher decides to sell his home. What is the loan payoff?

23. **Loan Payoffs** Iris Chung has a 15-year mortgage loan at an annual interest rate of 7.25%. After making payments of $672.39 for 4 years, Iris decides to sell her home. What is the loan payoff?

24. **Loan Payoffs** After making payments of $736.98 for 10 years on your 30-year loan at 6.75%, you decide to sell your home. What is the loan payoff?

25. **Total Monthly Payment** A homeowner has a mortgage payment of $996.60, an annual property tax bill of $594, and an annual fire insurance premium of $300. Find the total monthly payment for the mortgage, property tax, and fire insurance.

26. **Total Monthly Payment** Malcolm Rothschild has a mortgage payment of $1753.46, an annual property tax bill of $1023, and an annual fire insurance premium of $780. Find the total monthly payment for the mortgage, property tax, and fire insurance.

27. **Total Monthly Payment** Baka Onegin obtains a 25-year mortgage loan of $259,500 at an annual interest rate of 7.15%. Her annual property tax bill is $1320 and her annual fire insurance premium is $642. Find the total monthly payment for the mortgage, property tax, and fire insurance.

28. **Total Monthly Payment** Suppose you obtain a 20-year mortgage loan of $198,000 at an annual interest rate of 8.4%. The annual property tax bill is $972 and the annual fire insurance premium is $486. Find the total monthly payment for the mortgage, property tax, and fire insurance.

29. **Mortgage Loans** Consider a mortgage loan of $150,000 at an annual interest rate of 8.125%.

   a. How much greater is the mortgage payment if the term is 15 years rather than 30 years?

   b. How much less is the amount of interest paid over the life of the 15-year loan than over the life of the 30-year loan?

30. **Mortgage Loans** Consider a mortgage loan of $359,960 at an annual interest rate of 7.875%.

   a. How much greater is the mortgage payment if the term is 15 years rather than 30 years?

   b. How much less is the amount of interest paid over the life of the 15-year loan than over the life of the 30-year loan?

31. **Mortgage Loans** The Mendez family is considering a mortgage loan of $349,500 at an annual interest rate of 6.75%.

   a. How much greater is their mortgage payment if the term is 20 years rather than 30 years?

   b. How much less is the amount of interest paid over the life of the 20-year loan than over the life of the 30-year loan?

32. **Mortgage Loans** Herbert Bloom is considering a mortgage loan of $322,495 at an annual interest rate of 7.5%.

   a. How much greater is his mortgage payment if the term is 20 years rather than 30 years?

   b. How much less is the amount of interest paid over the life of the 20-year loan than over the life of the 30-year loan?

33. **Affordability** A couple has saved $25,000 for a down payment on a home. Their bank requires a minimum down payment of 20%. What is the maximum price they can offer for a house in order to have enough money for the down payment?

34. **Affordability** You have saved $18,000 for a down payment on a house. Your bank requires a minimum down payment of 15%. What is the maximum price you can offer for a home in order to have enough money for the down payment?

35. **Affordability** You have saved $39,400 to make a down payment and pay the closing costs on your future home. Your bank informs you that a 15% down payment is required and that the closing costs should be $380 plus 4 points. What is the maximum price you can offer for a home in order to have enough money for the down payment and the closing costs?

Extensions

CRITICAL THINKING

36. **Amortization Schedules** Suppose you have a 30-year mortgage loan for $119,500 at an annual interest rate of 8.25%. For which monthly payment does the amount of principal paid first exceed the amount of interest paid? For this exercise, you will need a spreadsheet program for producing amortization schedules. You can find one at our website at **math.college.hmco.com/students.**

37. **Amortization Schedules** Does changing the amount of the loan in Exercise 36 change the number of the monthly payment for which the amount of principal paid first exceeds the amount of interest paid? For this exercise, you will need a spreadsheet program for producing amortization schedules. You can find one at our website at **math.college.hmco.com/students.**

38. **Amortization Schedules** Does changing the interest rate of the loan in Exercise 36 change the number of the monthly payment for which the amount of principal paid first exceeds the amount of interest paid? For this exercise, you will need a spreadsheet program for producing amortization schedules. You can find one at our website at **math.college .hmco.com/students.**

39. Suppose you are considering a mortgage loan for $250,000 at an annual interest rate of 8%. Explain why the monthly payment for a 15-year mortgage loan is not twice the monthly payment for a 30-year mortgage loan.

COOPERATIVE LEARNING

40. **Buying and Selling a Home** Suppose you buy a house for $208,750, make a down payment that is 30% of the purchase price, and secure a 30-year loan for the balance at an annual interest rate of 7.75%. The points on the loan are 1.5% and there are additional lender fees of $825.

a. How much is due at closing? Note that the down payment is due at closing.

b. After 5 years, you decide to sell your house. What is the loan payoff?

c. Because of inflation, you were able to sell your house for $248,000. Assuming the selling fees are 6% of the selling price, what are the proceeds of the sale after deducting selling fees? Do not include the interest paid on the mortgage. Remember to consider the loan payoff.

d. The percent return on an investment $= \dfrac{\text{proceeds from sale}}{\text{total closing costs}} \times 100$. Find the percent return on your investment. Round to the nearest percent.

41. **Affordability** Assume that you are a computer programmer for a company and that your gross pay is $72,000 per year. You are paid monthly and take home $4479.38 per month. You are considering purchasing a condominium and have looked at one you would like to buy. The purchase price is $134,000. The condominium development company will arrange financing for the purchase. A down payment of 20% of the selling price is required. The interest rate on the 30-year, fixed rate mortgage loan is 9%. The lender charges 2.5 points. The appraisal fee, title fee, and recording fee total $325. The property taxes on the condominium are currently $1152 per year.

The condominium management company charges a monthly maintenance fee for landscaping, trash removal, snow removal, maintenance on the buildings, management costs, and insurance on the property. The monthly fee is currently $120. This fee includes insurance on the buildings and land only, so you will need to purchase separate insurance coverage for your furniture and other personal possessions. You have talked to the insurance agent through whom you buy tenant homeowner's insurance (to cover the personal possessions in your apartment), and you were told that such coverage will cost you approximately $192 per year.

The condominium uses electricity for cooking, heating, and lighting. You have been informed that the unit will use approximately 8750 kilowatt-hours per year. The cost of electricity is currently $.07 per kilowatt-hour.

You have saved $36,000 in anticipation of buying a home, but you do not want your savings account balance to fall below $6000. (You want to have some funds to fall back on in case of an emergency.) You have $900 in your checking account, but you do not want your checking account balance to fall below $600.

a. Calculate the amount to be paid for the down payment and closing costs. Are you willing to take this much out of your accounts?

b. Determine the mortgage payment.

c. Calculate the total of the monthly payments related to ownership of the condominium (mortgage, maintenance fee, property tax, utilities, insurance).

d. Find the difference between your monthly take-home pay and the monthly expenses related to condominium ownership (part c). This figure indicates how much money is available to pay for all other expenses, including food, transportation, clothing, entertainment, dental bills, telephone bills, car bills, etc.

e. What percent of your monthly take-home pay are the condominium-related expenses (part c)?

f. Do you think that, financially, you can handle the purchase of this condominium? Why?

CHAPTER 10   Review Exercises

Use a calculator for Exercises 11–33.

11. **Loans** To help pay your college expenses, you borrow $8000 and agree to repay the loan at the end of 5 years at 7% interest, compounded quarterly.

   a. What is the maturity value of the loan?

   b. How much interest are you paying on the loan?

12. **Present Value** A couple plans to save for their child's college education. What principal must be deposited by the parents when their child is born in order to have $80,000 when the child reaches the age of 18? Assume the money earns 8% interest, compounded quarterly.

13. **Dividend Yield** A stock pays an annual dividend of $.66 per share. The stock is trading at $60. Find the dividend yield.

14. **Bonds** A bond with a $20,000 face value has a 4.5% coupon and a 10-year maturity. Calculate the total of the interest payments paid to the bondholder.

15. **Inflation** In 2001, the price of 1 pound of red delicious apples was $1.29. Use an annual inflation rate of 6% to calculate the price of 1 pound of red delicious apples in 2011. Round to the nearest cent.

16. **Inflation** You purchase a bond that will provide you with $75,000 in 8 years. Assuming an annual inflation rate of 7%, what will be the purchasing power of the $75,000 in 8 years?

17. **Effective Interest Rate** Calculate the effective interest rate of 5.90% compounded monthly. Round to the nearest hundredth of a percent.

18. **Annual Yield** Which has the higher annual yield, 5.2% compounded quarterly or 5.4% compounded semiannually?

19. **Average Daily Balance** A credit card account had a $423.35 balance on March 11. A purchase of $145.50 was made on March 18, and a payment of $250 was made on March 29. Find the average daily balance if the billing date is April 11.

20. **Finance Charges** On September 10, a credit card account had a balance of $450. A purchase of $47 was made on September 20, and $157 was charged on September 25. A payment of $175 was made on September 28. The interest on the average daily balance is 1.25% per month. Find the finance charge on the October 10 bill.

21. **APR** Arlene McDonald borrows $1500 from a bank that advertises a 7.5% simple interest rate and repays the loan in six equal monthly payments.

   a. Find the monthly payment.

   b. Estimate the APR. Round to the nearest tenth of a percent.

22. **APR** Suppose you purchase a DVD player for $449, make a 10% down payment, and agree to repay the balance in 12 equal monthly payments. The finance charge on the balance is 7% simple interest.

   a. Find the monthly payment.

   b. Estimate the APR. Round to the nearest tenth.

23. **Monthly Payments** Photo Experts offers a Nikon camera for $999, including taxes. If you finance the purchase of this camera for 2 years at an annual interest rate of 8.5%, find the monthly payment.

24. **Monthly Payments** Abeni Silver purchases a plasma high-definition television for $9499. The sales tax is 6.25% of the purchase price.

   a. What is the total cost, including sales tax?

   b. If Abeni makes a down payment of 20% of the total cost, find the down payment.

   c. Assuming Abeni finances the remaining cost at an annual interest rate of 8% for 3 years, find the monthly payment.

25. **Car Payments** Suppose you decide to purchase a new car. You go to a credit union to get pre-approval for your loan. The credit union offers you an annual interest rate of 7.2% for 3 years. The purchase price of the car you select is $28,450, including taxes, and you make a 20% down payment. What is your monthly payment?

26. **Loan Payoffs** Dasan Houston obtains a $28,000, five-year car loan for a Windstar at an annual interest rate of 5.9%.

    a. Find the monthly payment.

    b. After 3 years, Dasan decides to purchase a new car. What is the payoff on his loan?

27. **Car Leases** Nami Coffey obtains a five-year lease for a Chrysler 300 and negotiates a selling price of $32,450. Assuming she makes a down payment of $3000, the money factor is 0.004, and the residual value is $16,000, find each of the following.

    a. The net capitalized cost

    b. The average monthly finance charge

    c. The average monthly depreciation

    d. The monthly lease payment using a sales tax rate of 7.5%

28. **Stock Sale** Suppose you purchased 500 shares of stock at a price of $28.75 per share and sold them for $39.40 per share.

    a. Ignoring dividends, what was your profit or loss on the sale of the stock?

    b. If your broker charges 1.3% of the total sale price, what was the broker's commission?

29. **Mutual Funds** A mutual fund has total assets of $34 million and total liabilities of $4 million. There are 2 million shares outstanding. You invest $3000 in this fund. How many shares will you purchase?

30. **Closing Costs** The purchase price of a seaside cottage is $459,000. A down payment of 20% is made. The bank charges $815 in fees plus 1.75 points. Find the total of the down payment and the closing costs.

31. **Mortgage Payments** Suppose you purchase a condominium and obtain a 30-year loan of $255,800 at an annual interest rate of 6.75%.

    a. What is the mortgage payment?

    b. What is the total of the payments over the life of the loan?

    c. Find the amount of interest paid on the mortgage loan over the 30 years.

32. **Mortgage Payments and Loan Payoffs** Garth Santacruz purchased a condominium and obtained a 25-year loan of $189,000 at an annual interest rate of 7.5%.

    a. What is the mortgage payment?

    b. After making payments for 10 years, Garth decides to sell his home. What is the loan payoff?

33. **Total Monthly Payments** Geneva Goldberg obtains a 15-year loan of $278,950 at an annual interest rate of 7%. Her annual property tax bill is $1134 and her annual fire insurance premium is $681. Find the total monthly payment for the mortgage, property tax, and fire insurance.

CHAPTER 10 **Test**

 Use a calculator for Exercises 1–22.

1. **Simple Interest** Calculate the simple interest due on a three-month loan of $5250 if the interest rate is 8.25%.

2. **Simple Interest** Find the simple interest earned in 180 days on a deposit of $6000 if the interest rate is 6.75%.

3. **Maturity Value** Calculate the maturity value of a simple interest, 200-day loan of $8000 if the interest rate is 9.2%.

4. **Simple Interest Rate** The simple interest charged on a two-month loan of $7600 is $114. Find the simple interest rate.

5. **Compound Amount** What is the compound amount when $4200 is deposited in an account earning an interest rate of 7%, compounded monthly, for 8 years?

6. **Compound Interest** Calculate the amount of interest earned in 3 years on $1500 deposited in an account paying 6.3% interest, compounded daily.

7. **Maturity Value** To help pay for a new truck, you borrow $10,500 and agree to repay the loan in 4 years at 9.5% interest, compounded monthly.

    a. What is the maturity value of the loan?

    b. How much interest are you paying on the loan?

8. **Present Value** A young couple wants to save money to buy a house. What principal must be deposited by the couple in order to have $30,000 in 5 years? Assume the money earns 6.25% interest, compounded daily.

9. **Dividend Yield** A stock that has a market value of $40 pays an annual dividend of $.48 per share. Find the dividend yield.

10. **Bonds** Suppose you purchase a $5000 bond that has a 3.8% coupon and a 10-year maturity. Calculate the total of the interest payments you will receive.

11. **Inflation** In 2002 the median value of a single-family house was $158,200. Use an annual inflation rate of 7% to calculate the median value of a single family house in 2022. (*Source:* moneycentral. msn.com)

12. **Effective Interest Rate** Calculate the effective interest rate of 6.25% compounded quarterly. Round to the nearest hundredth of a percent.

13. **Annual Yield** Which has the higher annual yield, 4.4% compounded monthly or 4.6% compounded semiannually?

14. **Finance Charges** On October 15, a credit card account had a balance of $515. A purchase of $75 was made on October 20, and a payment of $250 was made on October 28. The interest on the average daily balance is 1.8% per month. Find the finance charge on the November 15 bill.

15. **APR** Suppose you purchase a Joranda hand-held computer for $629, make a 15% down payment, and agree to repay the balance in 12 equal monthly payments. The finance charge on the balance is 9% simple interest.
    a. Find the monthly payment.
    b. Estimate the APR. Round to the nearest tenth of a percent.

16. **Monthly Payments** Technology Pro offers a new computer for $1899, including taxes. If you finance the purchase of this computer for 3 years at an annual percentage rate of 9.25%, find your monthly payment.

17. **Stock Sale** Suppose you purchased 800 shares of stock at a price of $31.82 per share and sold them for $25.70 per share.
    a. Ignoring dividends, what was your profit or loss on the sale of the stock?
    b. If your broker charges 1.1% of the total sale price, what was the broker's commission?

18. **Mutual Funds** A mutual fund has total assets of $42 million and total liabilities of $6 million. There are 3 million shares outstanding. You invest $2500 in this fund. How many shares will you purchase?

19. **Monthly Payments** Kalani Canfield purchases a high-speed color laser printer for $6575. The sales tax is 6.25% of the purchase price.
    a. What is the total cost, including sales tax?
    b. If Kalani makes a down payment of 20% of the total cost, find the down payment.
    c. Assuming Kalani finances the remaining cost at an annual interest rate of 7.8% for 3 years, find the monthly payment.

20. **Closing Costs** The purchase price of a house is $262,250. A down payment of 20% is made. The bank charges $815 in fees plus 3.25 points. Find the total of the down payment and the closing costs.

21. **Mortgage Payments and Loan Payoffs** Bernard Mason purchased a house and obtained a 30-year loan of $236,000 at an annual interest rate of 6.75%.
    a. What is the mortgage payment?
    b. After making payments for 5 years, Bernard decides to sell his home. What is the loan payoff?

22. **Total Monthly Payment** Zelda MacPherson obtains a 20-year loan of $312,000 at an annual interest rate of 7.25%. Her annual property tax bill is $1044 and her annual fire insurance premium is $516. Find the total monthly payment for the mortgage, property tax, and fire insurance.

chapter

7 Geometry

This is an aerial view of the house of William Paca, who was a Maryland Patriot and a signer of the Declaration of Independence. The house's large, formal garden has been restored to its original splendor. The best way to appreciate the shapes sculpted in the garden is to view it from above, like in this photo. Each geometric shape combines with the others to form the entire garden.

Need help? For online student resources, such as section quizzes, visit this textbook's website at **math.college.hmco.com/students.**

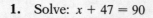

1. Solve: $x + 47 = 90$

2. Solve: $32 + 97 + x = 180$

3. Simplify: $2(18) + 2(10)$

4. Evaluate abc when $a = 2$, $b = 3.14$, and $c = 9$.

5. Evaluate xyz^3 when $x = \frac{4}{3}$, $y = 3.14$, and $z = 3$.

6. Solve: $\frac{5}{12} = \frac{6}{x}$

GO FIGURE • • •

Draw the figure that would come next.

7.1 Angles, Lines, and Geometric Figures

Objective A   **To define and describe lines and angles**

The word *geometry* comes from the Greek words for "earth" (*geo*) and "measure." The original purpose of geometry was to measure land. Today geometry is used in many sciences, such as physics, chemistry, and geology, and in applied fields such as mechanical drawing and astronomy. Geometric form is used in art and design.

Two basic geometric concepts are plane and space.

A **plane** is a flat surface, such as a table-top or a blackboard. Figures that can lie totally in a plane are called **plane figures.**

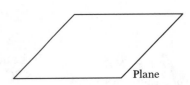

Plane

Space extends in all directions. Objects in space, such as trees, ice cubes, and doors, are called **solids.**

Space

A **line** extends indefinitely in two directions in a plane. A line has no width.

Line

A **line segment** is part of a line and has two endpoints. The line segment *AB* is shown in the figure.

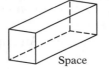

Line segment

The length of a line segment is the distance between the endpoints of the line segment. The length of a line segment may be expressed as the sum of two or more shorter line segments, as shown. For this example, $AB = 5$, $BC = 3$, and $AC = AB + BC = 5 + 3 = 8$.

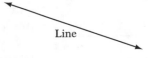

HOW TO   Given that $AB = 22$ and $AC = 31$, find the length of *BC*.

$$AC = AB + BC$$
$$31 = 22 + BC$$
$$31 - 22 = 22 - 22 + BC$$
$$9 = BC$$

• Substitute 22 for *AB* and 31 for *AC*, and solve for *BC*.

Lines in a plane can be parallel or intersecting. **Parallel lines** never meet; the distance between them is always the same. **Intersecting lines** cross at a point in the plane.

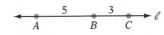

Parallel lines

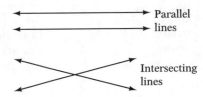

Intersecting lines

The symbol ∥ means "is parallel to." In the accompanying figure, $AB \parallel CD$ and $p \parallel q$. Note that line p contains line segment AB and that line q contains line segment CD. Parallel lines contain parallel line segments.

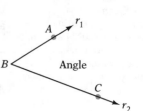

A **ray** starts at a point and extends indefinitely in one direction.

Ray

An **angle** is formed when two rays start from the same point. Rays r_1 and r_2 start from point B. The common endpoint is called the **vertex** of the angle.

Angle

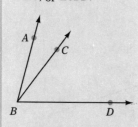
If A and C are points on rays r_1 and r_2 above, respectively, then the angle is called $\angle ABC$, $\angle CBA$, or $\angle B$, where $\angle$ is the symbol for angle. Note that an angle is named by giving three points, with the vertex as the second point listed, or by giving the point at the vertex.

An angle can also be named by writing a variable between the rays close to the vertex. In the figure, $\angle x = \angle QRS = \angle SRQ$ and $\angle y = \angle SRT = \angle TRS$. Note that in this figure, more than two rays meet at the vertex. In this case, the vertex cannot be used to name the angle.

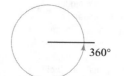

A unit in which angles are measured is the **degree.** The symbol for degree is °. One complete revolution is 360° (360 degrees).

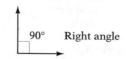

One-quarter of a revolution is 90°. A 90° angle is called a **right angle.** The symbol ∟ represents a right angle.

Perpendicular lines are intersecting lines that form right angles.

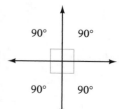

The symbol ⊥ means "is perpendicular to." In the accompanying figure, $AB \perp CD$ and $p \perp q$. Note that line p contains line segment AB and line q contains line segment CD. Perpendicular lines contain perpendicular line segments.

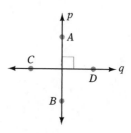

Complementary angles are two angles whose sum is 90°.

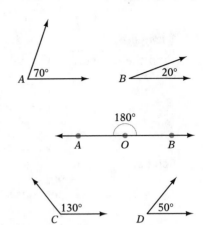

$\angle A + \angle B = 70° + 20° = 90°$
$\angle A$ and $\angle B$ are complementary angles.

One-half of a revolution is 180°. A 180° angle is called a **straight angle**. $\angle AOB$ in the figure is a straight angle.

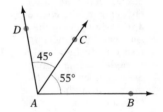

Supplementary angles are two angles whose sum is 180°.

$\angle C + \angle D = 130° + 50° = 180°$
$\angle C$ and $\angle D$ are supplementary angles.

An **acute angle** is an angle whose measure is between 0° and 90°. $\angle D$ in the figure above is an acute angle. An **obtuse angle** is an angle whose measure is between 90° and 180°. $\angle C$ in the figure above is an obtuse angle.

In the accompanying figure, $\angle DAC = 45°$ and $\angle CAB = 55°$.

$\angle DAB = \angle DAC + \angle CAB$
$\qquad = 45° + 55° = 100°$

Example 1

Given that $MN = 15$, $NO = 18$, and $MP = 48$, find the length of OP.

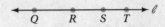

Solution
$MP = MN + NO + OP$
$\quad 48 = 15 + 18 + OP$
$\quad 48 = 33 + OP$
$48 - 33 = 33 - 33 + OP$
$\quad 15 = OP$

You Try It 1

Given that $QR = 24$, $ST = 17$, and $QT = 62$, find the length of RS.

Your solution

Example 2

Find the complement of a 32° angle.

Solution
Let x represent the complement of 32°.

$\quad x + 32° = 90°$ • **The sum of**
$x + 32° - 32° = 90° - 32°$ **complementary**
$\qquad\quad x = 58°$ **angles is 90°.**

58° is the complement of 32°.

You Try It 2

Find the supplement of a 32° angle.

Your solution

Example 3

Find the measure of ∠x.

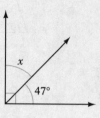

Solution

$$\angle x + 47° = 90°$$
$$\angle x + 47° - 47° = 90° - 47°$$
$$\angle x = 43°$$

You Try It 3

Find the measure of ∠a.

Your solution

Objective B   **To define and describe geometric figures**

A **triangle** is a closed, three-sided plane figure. Figure *ABC* is a triangle. *AB* is called the **base.** The line *CD*, perpendicular to the base, is called the **height.**

> **The Angles in a Triangle**
>
> The sum of the three angles in a triangle is 180°.
>
> $$\angle A + \angle B + \angle C = 180°$$

HOW TO   In triangle *DEF*, ∠D = 32° and ∠E = 88°. Find the measure of ∠F.

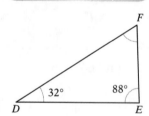

$$\angle D + \angle E + \angle F = 180°$$
$$32° + 88° + \angle F = 180°$$
$$120° + \angle F = 180°$$
$$120° - 120° + \angle F = 180° - 120°$$
$$\angle F = 60°$$

- **The sum of the three angles in a triangle is 180°.**
- **∠D = 32° and ∠E = 88°**
- **Solve for ∠F.**

A **right triangle** contains one right angle. The side opposite the right angle is called the **hypotenuse.** The **legs of a right triangle** are its other two sides. In a right triangle, the two acute angles are complementary.

$$\angle A + \angle B = 90°$$

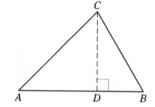

HOW TO   In the right triangle at the left, ∠A = 30°. Find the measure of ∠B.

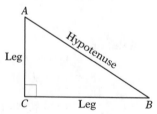

$$\angle A + \angle B = 90°$$
$$30° + \angle B = 90°$$
$$30° - 30° + \angle B = 90° - 30°$$
$$\angle B = 60°$$

- **The two acute angles are complementary.**
- **∠A = 30°**
- **Solve for ∠B.**

A **quadrilateral** is a closed, four-sided plane figure. Three quadrilaterals with special characteristics are described here.

A **parallelogram** has opposite sides parallel and equal. The distance *AE* between the parallel sides is called the **height.**

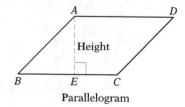

Parallelogram

A **rectangle** is a parallelogram that has four right angles.

A **square** is a rectangle that has four equal sides.

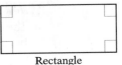
Rectangle

Square

A **circle** is a plane figure in which all points are the same distance from point O, which is called the **center** of the circle.

The **diameter of a circle** (d) is a line segment through the center of the circle with endpoints on the circle. AB is a diameter of the circle shown.

The **radius of a circle** (r) is a line segment from the center to a point on the circle. OC is a radius of the circle.

$$d = 2r \quad \text{or} \quad r = \frac{1}{2}d$$

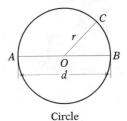
Circle

HOW TO   The line segment AB is a diameter of the circle shown. Find the radius of the circle.

The radius is one-half the diameter. Therefore,

$$r = \frac{1}{2}d$$
$$= \frac{1}{2}(8 \text{ in.}) \quad \bullet \; d = 8 \text{ in.}$$
$$= 4 \text{ in.}$$

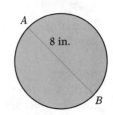

A **geometric solid** is a figure in space, or space figure. Four common space figures are the rectangular solid, cube, sphere, and cylinder.

A **rectangular solid** is a solid in which all six faces are rectangles.

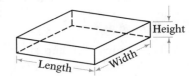
Rectangular solid

A **cube** is a rectangular solid in which all six faces are squares.

Cube

A **sphere** is a solid in which all points on the surface are the same distance from point O, which is called the **center** of the sphere.

The **diameter of a sphere** is a line segment going through the center with endpoints on the sphere. AB is a diameter of the sphere shown.

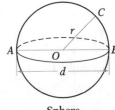
Sphere

The **radius of a sphere** is a line segment from the center to a point on the sphere. OC is a radius of the sphere.

$$d = 2r \quad \text{or} \quad r = \frac{1}{2}d$$

HOW TO The radius of the sphere shown at the right is 5 cm. Find the diameter of the sphere.

$d = 2r$
$\quad = 2(5 \text{ cm})$
$\quad = 10 \text{ cm}$

- The diameter equals twice the radius.
- $r = 5 \text{ cm}$

The diameter is 10 cm.

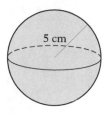

The most common **cylinder** is one in which the bases are circles and are perpendicular to the side.

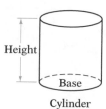

Cylinder

Example 4

One angle in a right triangle is equal to 50°. Find the measure of the other angles.

Solution
In a right triangle, one angle measures 90° and the two acute angles are complementary.

$\angle A + \angle B = 90°$
$\angle A + 50° = 90°$
$\angle A + 50° - 50° = 90° - 50°$
$\angle A = 40°$

The other angles measure 90° and 40°.

You Try It 4

A right triangle has one angle equal to 7°. Find the measure of the other angles.

Your solution

Example 5

Two angles of a triangle measure 42° and 103°. Find the measure of the third angle.

Solution
The sum of the three angles of a triangle is 180°.

$\angle A + \angle B + \angle C = 180°$
$\angle A + 42° + 103° = 180°$
$\angle A + 145° = 180°$
$\angle A + 145° - 145° = 180° - 145°$
$\angle A = 35°$

The measure of the third angle is 35°.

You Try It 5

Two angles of a triangle measure 62° and 45°. Find the measure of the other angle.

Your solution

Example 6

A circle has a radius of 8 cm. Find the diameter.

Solution
$d = 2r$
$\quad = 2 \cdot 8 \text{ cm} = 16 \text{ cm}$

The diameter is 16 cm.

You Try It 6

A circle has a diameter of 8 in. Find the radius.

Your solution

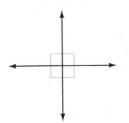

Objective C   **To solve problems involving angles formed by intersecting lines**

Four angles are formed by the intersection of two lines. If the two lines are perpendicular, then each of the four angles is a right angle. If the two lines are not perpendicular, then two of the angles formed are acute angles and two of the angles are obtuse angles. The two acute angles are always opposite each other, and the two obtuse angles are always opposite each other.

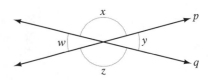

In the figure, $\angle w$ and $\angle y$ are acute angles. $\angle x$ and $\angle z$ are obtuse angles. Two angles that are on opposite sides of the intersection of two lines are called **vertical angles.** Vertical angles have the same measure. $\angle w$ and $\angle y$ are vertical angles. $\angle x$ and $\angle z$ are vertical angles.

$\angle w = \angle y$
$\angle x = \angle z$

Two angles that share a common side are called **adjacent angles.** In the previous figure, $\angle x$ and $\angle y$ are adjacent angles, as are $\angle y$ and $\angle z$, $\angle z$ and $\angle w$, and $\angle w$ and $\angle x$. Adjacent angles of intersecting lines are supplementary angles.

$\angle x + \angle y = 180°$
$\angle y + \angle z = 180°$
$\angle z + \angle w = 180°$
$\angle w + \angle x = 180°$

HOW TO   In the figure at the left, $\angle c = 65°$. Find the measures of angles a, b, and d.

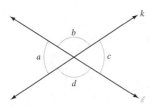

$\angle a = 65°$

- $\angle a = \angle c$ because $\angle c$ and $\angle a$ are vertical angles.

$\angle b + \angle c = 180°$

- $\angle c$ is supplementary to $\angle b$ because $\angle c$ and $\angle b$ are adjacent angles.
- $\angle c = 65°$

$\angle b + 65° = 180°$
$\angle b + 65° - 65° = 180° - 65°$
$\angle b = 115°$

$\angle d = 115°$

- $\angle d = \angle b$ because $\angle b$ and $\angle d$ are vertical angles.

A line intersecting two other lines at two different points is called a **transversal.**

If the lines cut by a transversal are parallel lines and the transversal is perpendicular to the parallel lines, then all eight angles formed are right angles.

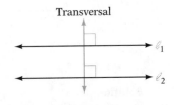

If the lines cut by a transversal are parallel lines and the transversal is not perpendicular to the parallel lines, then all four acute angles have the same measure and all four obtuse angles have the same measure. For the figure at the right,

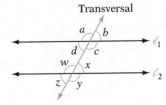

$\angle a = \angle c = \angle w = \angle y$ and $\angle b = \angle d = \angle x = \angle z$

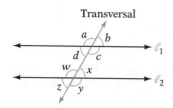

Alternate interior angles are two nonadjacent angles that are on opposite sides of the transversal and between the parallel lines. For the figure at the left, $\angle c$ and $\angle w$ are alternate interior angles. $\angle d$ and $\angle x$ are alternate interior angles. Alternate interior angles have the same measure.

Alternate exterior angles are two nonadjacent angles that are on opposite sides of the transversal and outside the parallel lines. For the figure at the left, $\angle a$ and $\angle y$ are alternate exterior angles. $\angle b$ and $\angle z$ are alternate exterior angles. Alternate exterior angles have the same measure.

Corresponding angles are two angles that are on the same side of the transversal and are both acute angles or are both obtuse angles. For the figure at the top left, the following pairs of angles are corresponding angles: $\angle a$ and $\angle w$, $\angle d$ and $\angle z$, $\angle b$ and $\angle x$, $\angle c$ and $\angle y$. Corresponding angles have the same measure.

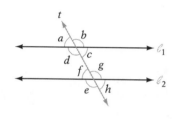

HOW TO   In the figure at the left, $\ell_1 \parallel \ell_2$ and $\angle c = 58°$. Find the measures of $\angle f$, $\angle h$, and $\angle g$.

$\angle f = 58°$

$\angle h = 58°$

$\angle g + \angle h = 180°$
$\angle g + 58° = 180°$
$\angle g = 122°$

- $\angle f = \angle c$ because $\angle f$ and $\angle c$ are alternate interior angles.
- $\angle h = \angle c$ because $\angle c$ and $\angle h$ are corresponding angles.
- $\angle g$ is supplementary to $\angle h$.
- $\angle h = 58°$
- Subtract 58° from each side.

Example 7

In the figure, $\angle a = 75°$. Find $\angle b$.

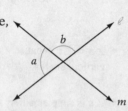

Solution

$\angle a + \angle b = 180°$

$75° + \angle b = 180°$
$\angle b = 105°$

- $\angle a$ and $\angle b$ are supplementary.
- $\angle a = 75°$
- Subtract 75° from each side.

You Try It 7

In the figure, $\angle a = 125°$. Find $\angle b$.

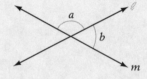

Your solution

Example 8

In the figure, $\ell_1 \parallel \ell_2$ and $\angle a = 70°$. Find $\angle b$.

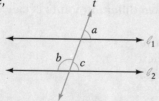

Solution

$\angle c = \angle a = 70°$

$\angle b + \angle c = 180°$
$\angle b + 70° = 180°$
$\angle b = 110°$

- Corresponding angles are equal.
- $\angle b$ and $\angle c$ are supplementary.
- $\angle c = 70°$
- Subtract 70° from each side.

You Try It 8

In the figure, $\ell_1 \parallel \ell_2$ and $\angle a = 120°$. Find $\angle b$.

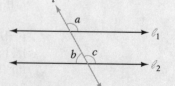

Your solution

7.1 Exercises

To define and describe lines and angles

1. The measure of an acute angle is between ___ and ___.

2. The measure of an obtuse angle is between ___ and ___.

3. How many degrees are in a straight angle?

4. Two lines that intersect at right angles are ___ lines.

5. In the figure, $EF = 20$ and $FG = 10$. Find the length of EG.

6. In the figure, $EF = 18$ and $FG = 6$. Find the length of EG.

7. In the figure, it is given that $QR = 7$ and $QS = 28$. Find the length of RS.

8. In the figure, it is given that $QR = 15$ and $QS = 45$. Find the length of RS.

9. In the figure, it is given that $AB = 12$, $CD = 9$, and $AD = 35$. Find the length of BC.

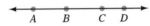

10. In the figure, it is given that $AB = 21$, $BC = 14$, and $AD = 54$. Find the length of CD.

11. Find the complement of a 31° angle.

12. Find the complement of a 62° angle.

13. Find the supplement of a 72° angle.

14. Find the supplement of a 162° angle.

15. Find the complement of a 13° angle.

16. Find the complement of an 88° angle.

17. Find the supplement of a 127° angle.

18. Find the supplement of a 7° angle.

In Exercises 19 and 20, find the measure of angle AOB.

19.

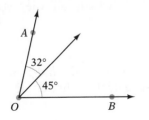

20.

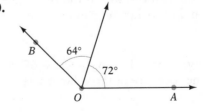

For Exercises 21 to 24, find the measure of angle *a*.

21.

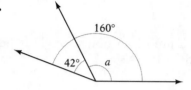

22.

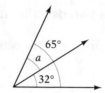

23.

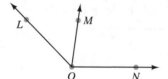

24.

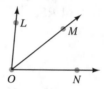

25. In the figure, it is given that ∠LOM = 53° and ∠LON = 139°. Find the measure of ∠MON.

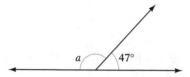

26. In the figure, it is given that ∠MON = 38° and ∠LON = 85°. Find the measure of ∠LOM.

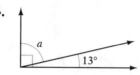

Objective B   **To define and describe geometric figures**

27. What is the sum of the three angles of a triangle?

28. Name the side opposite the right angle in a right triangle.

29. Name a parallelogram with four right angles.

30. Name the rectangle with four equal sides.

31. Name a rectangular solid in which all six faces are squares.

32. Name the solid in which all points are the same distance from the center.

33. Name a quadrilateral in which opposite sides are parallel and equal.

34. Name the plane figure in which all points are the same distance from the center.

35. Name the solid in which the bases are circular and perpendicular to the side.

36. Name a solid in which all the faces are rectangles.

37. A triangle has a 13° angle and a 65° angle. Find the measure of the other angle.

38. A triangle has a 105° angle and a 32° angle. Find the measure of the other angle.

39. A right triangle has a 45° angle. Find the measure of the other two angles.

40. A right triangle has a 62° angle. Find the measure of the other two angles.

41. A triangle has a 62° angle and a 104° angle. Find the measure of the other angle.

42. A triangle has a 30° angle and a 45° angle. Find the measure of the other angle.

43. A right triangle has a 25° angle. Find the measure of the other two angles.

44. Two angles of a triangle are 42° and 105°. Find the measure of the other angle.

45. Find the radius of a circle with a diameter of 16 in.

46. Find the radius of a circle with a diameter of 9 ft.

47. Find the diameter of a circle with a radius of $2\frac{1}{3}$ ft.

48. Find the diameter of a circle with a radius of 24 cm.

49. The radius of a sphere is 3.5 cm. Find the diameter.

50. The radius of a sphere is $1\frac{1}{2}$ ft. Find the diameter.

51. The diameter of a sphere is 4 ft 8 in. Find the radius.

52. The diameter of a sphere is 1.2 m. Find the radius.

| **Objective C** | **To solve problems involving angles formed by intersecting lines** |

For Exercises 53 to 56, find the measures of angles a and b.

53.
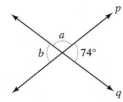

54.
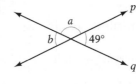

55.
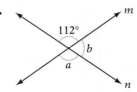

56.
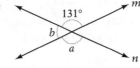

For Exercises 57 to 64, $\ell_1 \parallel \ell_2$. Find the measures of angles a and b.

57.

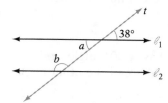

58.

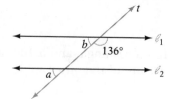

59.

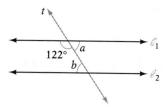

60.

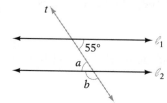

61.

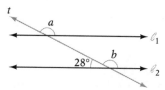

62.

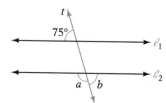

63.

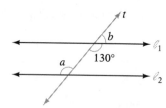

64.

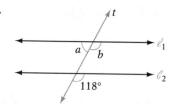

APPLYING THE CONCEPTS

65. **a.** What is the smallest possible whole number of degrees in an angle of a triangle?

b. What is the largest possible whole number of degrees in an angle of a right triangle?

66. Determine whether the statement is always true, sometimes true, or never true.

a. Two lines that are both parallel to a third line are parallel to each other.

b. A triangle contains at least two acute angles.

c. Vertical angles are complementary angles.

67. If AB and CD intersect at point O, and $\angle AOC = \angle BOC$, explain why AB is perpendicular to CD.

7.2 Plane Geometric Figures

Objective A **To find the perimeter of plane geometric figures**

A **polygon** is a closed figure determined by three or more line segments that lie in a plane. The **sides of a polygon** are the line segments that form the polygon. The figures below are examples of polygons.

 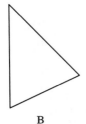 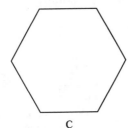 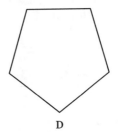 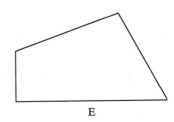

A   B   C   D   E

Point of Interest

Although a polygon is defined in terms of its *sides* (see the definition above), the word actually comes from the Latin word *polygonum*, which means having many *angles*. This is certainly the case for a polygon.

A **regular polygon** is one in which each side has the same length and each angle has the same measure. The polygons in Figures A, C, and D above are regular polygons.

The name of a polygon is based on the number of its sides. The table below lists the names of polygons that have from 3 to 10 sides.

Number of Sides	Name of the Polygon
3	Triangle
4	Quadrilateral
5	Pentagon
6	Hexagon
7	Heptagon
8	Octagon
9	Nonagon
10	Decagon

The Pentagon in Arlington, Virginia

Triangles and quadrilaterals are two of the most common types of polygons. Triangles are distinguished by the number of equal sides and also by the measures of their angles.

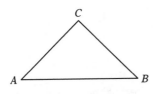 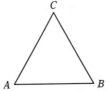 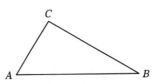

An **isosceles triangle** has two sides of equal length. The angles opposite the equal sides are of equal measure.

$AC \cong BC$

$\angle A = \angle B$

The three sides of an **equilateral triangle** are of equal length. The three angles are of equal measure.

$AB = BC = AC$

$\angle A = \angle B = \angle C$

A **scalene triangle** has no two sides of equal length. No two angles are of equal measure.

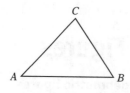

An **acute triangle** has three acute angles.

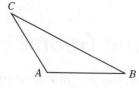

An **obtuse triangle** has one obtuse angle.

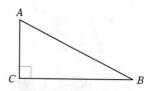

A **right triangle** has a right angle.

Quadrilaterals are also distinguished by their sides and angles, as shown below. Note that a rectangle, a square, and a rhombus are different forms of a parallelogram.

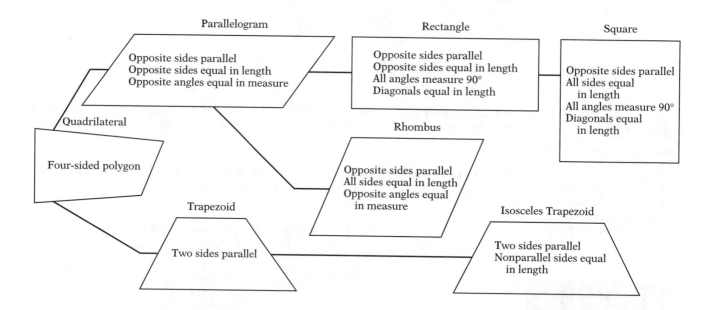

The **perimeter** of a plane geometric figure is a measure of the distance around the figure. Perimeter is used in buying fencing for a lawn or determining how much baseboard is needed for a room.

The perimeter of a triangle is the sum of the lengths of the three sides.

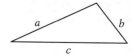

> **Perimeter of a Triangle**
> $P = a + b + c$

HOW TO Find the perimeter of the triangle shown at the right.

$P = a + b + c$
$= 3 \text{ cm} + 5 \text{ cm} + 6 \text{ cm}$
$= 14 \text{ cm}$

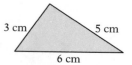

The perimeter of the triangle is 14 cm.

The perimeter of a quadrilateral is the sum of the lengths of the four sides. The perimeter of a square is the sum of the four equal sides.

> **Perimeter of a Square**
> $P = 4s$

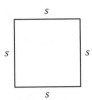

HOW TO Find the perimeter of the square shown at the right.

$P = 4s$
$\quad = 4(3 \text{ ft})$ $\qquad$ • $s = 3$ **ft**
$\quad = 12 \text{ ft}$

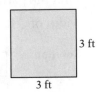

The perimeter of the square is 12 ft.

A rectangle is a quadrilateral with opposite sides of equal length. The length of a rectangle refers to the longer side, and the width refers to the length of the shorter side.

> **Perimeter of a Rectangle**
> $P = 2L + 2W$

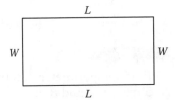

HOW TO Find the perimeter of the rectangle shown at the right.

$P = 2L + 2W$
$\quad = 2(6 \text{ m}) + 2(3 \text{ m})$ $\qquad$ • $L = 6$ **m**, $W = 3$ **m**
$\quad = 12 \text{ m} + 6 \text{ m}$
$\quad = 18 \text{ m}$

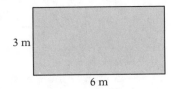

The perimeter of the rectangle is 18 m.

The distance around a circle is called the **circumference.** The circumference of a circle is equal to the product of π (pi) and the diameter.

Point of Interest

Archimedes (c. 287–212 B.C.) was the mathematician who gave us the approximate value of π as $\frac{22}{7} = 3\frac{1}{7}$. He actually showed that π was between $3\frac{10}{71}$ and $3\frac{1}{7}$. The approximation $3\frac{10}{71}$ is closer to the exact value of π, but it is more difficult to use.

> **Circumference of a Circle**
> $C = \pi d$
> $\quad$ or
> $C = 2\pi r$ $\qquad$ • **Because diameter = 2r**

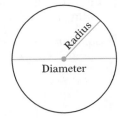

The formula for circumference uses the number π (pi). The value of π can be approximated by a decimal or a fraction.

$$\pi \approx 3.14 \qquad \pi \approx \frac{22}{7}$$

The π key on a calculator gives a closer approximation of π than 3.14.

HOW TO Find the circumference of the circle shown at the right.

$C = 2\pi r$
$\approx 2 \cdot 3.14 \cdot 6$ in.   • $r = 6$ in.
$= 37.68$ in.

The circumference of the circle is approximately 37.68 in.

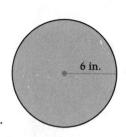
6 in.

Example 1

Find the perimeter of a rectangle with a width of $\frac{2}{3}$ ft and a length of 2 ft.

Solution

$\frac{2}{3}$ ft
2 ft

$P = 2L + 2W$

$P = 2(2 \text{ ft}) + 2\left(\frac{2}{3} \text{ ft}\right)$ • $L = 2$ ft, $W = \frac{2}{3}$ ft

$P = 4 \text{ ft} + \frac{4}{3} \text{ ft}$

$P = 5\frac{1}{3} \text{ ft}$

The perimeter of the rectangle is $5\frac{1}{3}$ ft.

You Try It 1

Find the perimeter of a rectangle with a length of 2 m and a width of 0.85 m.

Your solution

Example 2

Find the perimeter of a triangle with sides 5 in., 7 in., and 8 in.

Solution

5 in.   7 in.
8 in.

$P = a + b + c$
$= 5 \text{ in.} + 7 \text{ in.} + 8 \text{ in.}$
$= 20 \text{ in.}$

The perimeter of the triangle is 20 in.

You Try It 2

Find the perimeter of a triangle with sides 12 cm, 15 cm, and 18 cm.

Your solution

Example 3

Find the circumference of a circle with a radius of 18 cm. Use 3.14 for π.

Solution

18 cm

$C = 2\pi r$
$\approx 2 \cdot 3.14 \cdot 18 \text{ cm}$
$= 113.04 \text{ cm}$

The circumference is approximately 113.04 cm.

You Try It 3

Find the circumference of a circle with a diameter of 6 in. Use 3.14 for π.

Your solution

Objective B   **To find the perimeter of composite geometric figures**

A **composite geometric figure** is a figure made from two or more geometric figures. The following composite is made from part of a rectangle and part of a circle:

$$\text{(figure)} \quad = \quad \text{(rectangle)} \quad + \quad \text{(circle)}$$

Perimeter of the composite figure $= 3$ sides of a rectangle $+ \frac{1}{2}$ the circumference of a circle

Perimeter of the composite figure $= 2L + W + \frac{1}{2}\pi d$

The perimeter of the composite figure below is found by adding the measures of twice the length plus the width plus one-half the circumference of the circle.

(12 m, 4 m figure) $=$ 4 m (12 m rectangle, 12 m) $+$ $\frac{1}{2}\pi \times 4$ m

$$P = 2L + W + \frac{1}{2}\pi d$$

$$P \approx 2(12 \text{ m}) + 4 \text{ m} + \frac{1}{2}(3.14)(4 \text{ m})$$

• $L = 12$ m, $W = 4$ m, $d = 4$ m. *Note:* The diameter of the circle is equal to the width of the rectangle.

$$P = 34.28 \text{ m}$$

The perimeter is approximately 34.28 m.

Example 4

Find the perimeter of the composite figure. Use $\frac{22}{7}$ for π.

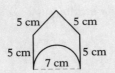

Solution

| Perimeter of composite figure | = | sum of lengths of the 4 sides | + | $\frac{1}{2}$ the circumference of the circle |

$$P = \quad 4s \quad + \quad \frac{1}{2}\pi d$$

$$\approx 4(5 \text{ cm}) + \frac{1}{2}\left(\frac{22}{7}\right)(7 \text{ cm})$$

$$= 20 \text{ cm} + 11 \text{ cm} = 31 \text{ cm}$$

The perimeter is approximately 31 cm.

You Try It 4

Find the perimeter of the composite figure. Use 3.14 for π.

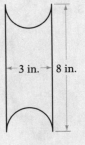

Your solution

Objective C   **To solve application problems**

Example 5

The dimensions of a triangular sail are 18 ft, 11 ft, and 15 ft. What is the perimeter of the sail?

Strategy

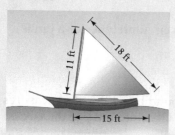

To find the perimeter, use the formula for the perimeter of a triangle.

Solution
$P = a + b + c$
$\quad = 18 \text{ ft} + 11 \text{ ft} + 15 \text{ ft}$
$\quad = 44 \text{ ft}$

The perimeter of the sail is 44 ft.

You Try It 5

What is the perimeter of a standard piece of computer paper that measures $8\frac{1}{2}$ in. by 11 in.?

Your strategy

Your solution

Example 6

If fencing costs $4.75 per foot, how much will it cost to fence a rectangular lot that is 108 ft wide and 240 ft long?

Strategy

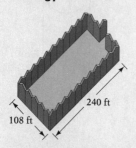

To find the cost of the fence:
- Find the perimeter of the lot.
- Multiply the perimeter by the per-foot cost of fencing.

Solution
$P = 2L + 2W$
$\quad = 2(240 \text{ ft}) + 2(108 \text{ ft})$
$\quad = 480 \text{ ft} + 216 \text{ ft}$
$\quad = 696 \text{ ft}$

Cost $= 696 \times 4.75 = 3306$

The cost is $3306.

You Try It 6

Metal stripping is being installed around a workbench that is 0.74 m wide and 3 m long. At $2.76 per meter, find the cost of the metal stripping. Round to the nearest cent.

Your strategy

Your solution

7.2 Exercises

Objective A   **To find the perimeter of plane geometric figures**

For Exercises 1 to 8, find the perimeter or circumference of the given figures. Use 3.14 for π.

1.

2.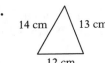

3.

5 ft
5 ft

4.

2 m
2 m

5.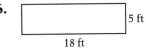

14 cm
32 cm

6.

5 ft
18 ft

7.

15 cm

8.

4 in.

9. Find the perimeter of a triangle with sides 2 ft 4 in., 3 ft, and 4 ft 6 in.

10. Find the perimeter of a rectangle with a length of 2 m and a width of 0.8 m.

11. Find the circumference of a circle with a radius of 8 cm. Use 3.14 for π.

12. Find the circumference of a circle with a diameter of 14 in. Use $\frac{22}{7}$ for π.

13. Find the perimeter of a square in which each side is equal to 60 m.

14. Find the perimeter of a triangle in which each side is $1\frac{2}{3}$ ft.

15. Find the perimeter of a five-sided figure with sides of 22 cm, 47 cm, 29 cm, 42 cm, and 17 cm.

16. Find the perimeter of a rectangular farm that is $\frac{1}{2}$ mi wide and $\frac{3}{4}$ mi long.

Objective B   **To find the perimeter of composite geometric figures**

For Exercises 17 to 24, find the perimeter. Use 3.14 for π.

17.

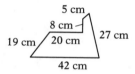

18.

19.

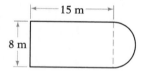

20.

21.

22.

Radius = 6 cm

23.

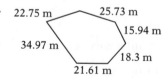

24.

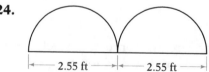

Objective C   **To solve application problems**

25. **Landscaping**   How many feet of fencing should be purchased for a rectangular garden that is 18 ft long and 12 ft wide?

26. **Interior Design**   Wall-to-wall carpeting is installed in a room that is 12 ft long and 10 ft wide. The edges of the carpet are nailed to the floor. Along how many feet must the carpet be nailed down?

27. **Quilting**   How many feet of binding are required to bind the edge of a rectangular quilt that measures 3.5 ft by 8.5 ft?

28. **Carpentry**   Find the length of molding needed to put around a circular table that is 3.8 ft in diameter. Use 3.14 for π.

29. **Landscaping**   The rectangular lot shown in the figure at the right is being fenced. The fencing along the road is to cost $6.20 per foot. The rest of the fencing costs $5.85 per foot. Find the total cost to fence the lot.

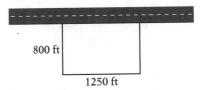

800 ft

1250 ft

30. **Sewing**   Bias binding is to be sewed around the edge of a rectangular tablecloth measuring 72 in. by 45 in. Each package of bias binding costs $3.50 and contains 15 ft of binding. How many packages of bias binding are needed for the tablecloth?

31. **Travel**   A bicycle tire has a diameter of 24 in. How many feet does the bicycle travel when the wheel makes 5 revolutions? Use 3.14 for π.

32. **Travel**   A tricycle tire has a diameter of 12 in. How many feet does the tricycle travel when the wheel makes 8 revolutions? Use 3.14 for π.

33. **Architecture**   The floor plan of a roller rink is shown in the figure at the right.
     a. Use estimation to determine whether the perimeter of the rink is more than 70 m or less than 70 m.
     b. Calculate the perimeter of the roller rink. Use 3.14 for π.

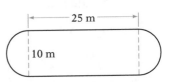

25 m

10 m

34. **Home Improvement**   A rain gutter is being installed on a home that has the dimensions shown in the figure at the right. At a cost of $11.30 per meter, how much will it cost to install the rain gutter?

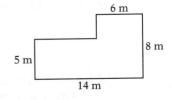

6 m

8 m

5 m

14 m

35. **Home Improvement** Find the length of weather stripping installed around the arched door shown in the figure at the right. Use 3.14 for π.

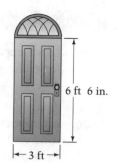

6 ft 6 in.

3 ft

36. 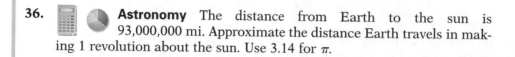 **Astronomy** The distance from Earth to the sun is 93,000,000 mi. Approximate the distance Earth travels in making 1 revolution about the sun. Use 3.14 for π.

37. **Earth Science** The distance from the surface to the center of Earth is 6356 km. Approximate the circumference of Earth. Use 3.14 for π.

APPLYING THE CONCEPTS

38. **a.** If the diameter of a circle is doubled, how many times larger is the resulting circumference?
    b. If the radius of a circle is doubled, how many times larger is the resulting circumference?

39. **Geometry** In the pattern to the right, the length of one side of a square is 1 unit. Find the perimeter of the eighth figure in the pattern.

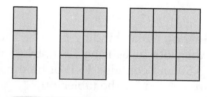

40. **Geometry** Remove six toothpicks from the figure at the right in such a way as to leave two squares.

41. **Geometry** An equilateral triangle is placed inside an equilateral triangle as shown at the right. Now three more equilateral triangles are placed inside the unshaded equilateral triangles. The process is repeated again. Determine the perimeter of all the shaded triangles in Figure C.

2 cm

Figure A   Figure B   Figure C

42. **Metalwork** A wire whose length is given as x inches is bent into a square. Express the length of a side of the square in terms of x.

x

43. A forest ranger must determine the diameter of a redwood tree. Explain how the ranger could do this without cutting down the tree.

7.3 Area

Objective A To find the area of geometric figures

Area is a measure of the amount of surface in a region. Area can be used to describe the size of a rug, a parking lot, a farm, or a national park. Area is measured in square units.

A square that measures 1 in. on each side has an area of 1 square inch, which is written 1 in².

A square that measures 1 cm on each side has an area of 1 square centimeter, which is written 1 cm².

1 in²

1 cm²

Larger areas can be measured in square feet (ft²), square meters (m²), square miles (mi²), acres (43,560 ft²), or any other square unit.

The area of a geometric figure is the number of squares that are necessary to cover the figure. In the figures below, two rectangles have been drawn and covered with squares. In the figure on the left, 12 squares, each of area 1 cm², were used to cover the rectangle. The area of the rectangle is 12 cm². In the figure on the right, 6 squares, each of area 1 in², were used to cover the rectangle. The area of the rectangle is 6 in².

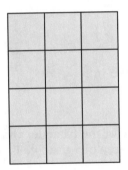

The area of the rectangle is 12 cm².

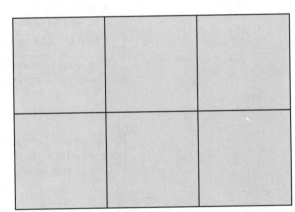

The area of the rectangle is 6 in².

Note from the above figures that the area of a rectangle can be found by multiplying the length of the rectangle by its width.

> **Area of a Rectangle**
> $A = LW$

HOW TO Find the area of the rectangle shown at the right.

$A = LW$
  $= (8 \text{ ft})(5 \text{ ft})$ • $L = 8 \text{ ft}, W = 5 \text{ ft}$
  $= 40 \text{ ft}^2$

The area of the rectangle is 40 ft².

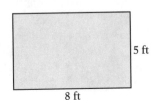

5 ft

8 ft

A square is a rectangle in which all sides are the same length. Therefore, both the length and the width can be represented by a side. Remember that $s \cdot s = s^2$.

> **Area of a Square**
> $A = s^2$

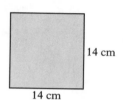

HOW TO Find the area of the square shown at the right.

$A = s^2$
$\quad = (14 \text{ cm})^2 \qquad \bullet \; s = 14 \text{ cm}$
$\quad = 196 \text{ cm}^2$

The area of the square is 196 cm².

The area of a circle is equal to the product of π and the square of the radius.

> **Area of a Circle**
> $A = \pi r^2$

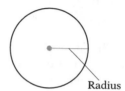

Radius

HOW TO Find the area of the circle shown at the right.

$A = \pi r^2$
$\quad = \pi (8 \text{ in.})^2 = 64\pi \text{ in}^2$
$\quad \approx 64 \cdot 3.14 \text{ in}^2 = 200.96 \text{ in}^2$

The area is exactly 64π in².
The area is approximately 200.96 in².

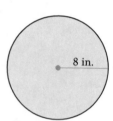

8 in.

In the figure below, AB is the base of the triangle, and CD, which is perpendicular to the base, is the height. The area of a triangle is one-half the product of the base and the height.

> **Area of a Triangle**
> $A = \frac{1}{2}bh$

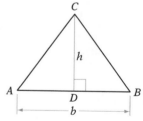

Integrating Technology

To calculate the area of the triangle shown at the right, you can enter

20 × 5 ÷ 2 =

or

.5 × 20 × 5 =

HOW TO Find the area of the triangle shown below.

$A = \frac{1}{2}bh$

$A = \frac{1}{2}(20 \text{ m})(5 \text{ m}) \qquad \bullet \; b = 20 \text{ m}, h = 5 \text{ m}$

$A = 50 \text{ m}^2$

The area of the triangle is 50 m².

5 m

20 m

Example 1 Find the area of a circle with a diameter of 9 cm. Use 3.14 for π.

You Try It 1 Find the area of a triangle with a base of 24 in. and a height of 14 in.

Solution $r = \dfrac{1}{2}d = \dfrac{1}{2}(9 \text{ cm}) = 4.5 \text{ cm}$

$A = \pi r^2$
$\approx 3.14(4.5 \text{ cm})^2 = 63.585 \text{ cm}^2$

The area is approximately 63.585 cm².

Your solution

Objective B   **To find the area of composite geometric figures**

The area of the composite figure shown below is found by calculating the area of the rectangle and then subtracting the area of the triangle.

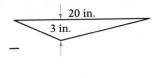

$A = LW - \dfrac{1}{2}bh$

$A = (20 \text{ in.})(8 \text{ in.}) - \dfrac{1}{2}(20 \text{ in.})(3 \text{ in.}) = 160 \text{ in}^2 - 30 \text{ in}^2 = 130 \text{ in}^2$

Example 2

Find the area of the shaded portion of the figure. Use 3.14 for π.

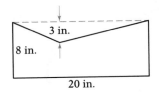

You Try It 2

Find the area of the composite figure.

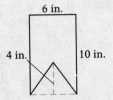

Solution

$$\begin{array}{c}\text{Area of} \\ \text{shaded} \\ \text{portion}\end{array} = \begin{array}{c}\text{area of} \\ \text{square}\end{array} - \begin{array}{c}\text{area of} \\ \text{circle}\end{array}$$

$A = \quad s^2 \quad - \quad \pi r^2$
$= (8 \text{ m})^2 - \pi(4 \text{ m})^2$
$\approx 64 \text{ m}^2 - 3.14(16 \text{ m}^2)$
$= 64 \text{ m}^2 - 50.24 \text{ m}^2 = 13.76 \text{ m}^2$

The area is approximately 13.76 m².

Your solution

Objective C   To solve application problems

Example 3

A walkway 2 m wide is built along the front and along both sides of a building, as shown in the figure. Find the area of the walkway.

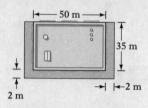

Strategy

To find the area of the walkway, add the area of the front section (54 m · 2 m) and the area of the two side sections (each 35 m · 2 m).

Solution

Area of
walkway = area of front section + 2(area of one side section)

A = (54 m)(2 m) + 2(35 m)(2 m)
  = 108 m² + 140 m²
  = 248 m²

The area of the walkway is 248 m².

You Try It 3

New carpet is installed in a room measuring 9 ft by 12 ft. Find the area of the room in square yards. (9 ft² = 1 yd²)

Your strategy

Your solution

7.3 Exercises

Objective A   **To find the area of geometric figures**

For Exercises 1 to 8, find the area of the given figures. Use 3.14 for π.

1.
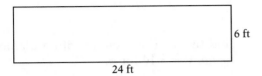
24 ft
6 ft

2.
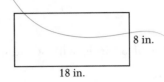
18 in.
8 in.

3.
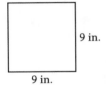
9 in.
9 in.

4.

4 in.
4 in.

5.

4 ft

6.

3 cm

7.
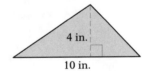
4 in.
10 in.

8.

6 m
7 m

9. Find the area of a right triangle with a base of 3 cm and a height of 1.42 cm.

10. Find the area of a triangle with a base of 3 ft and a height of $\frac{2}{3}$ ft.

11. Find the area of a square with a side of 4 ft.

12. Find the area of a square with a side of 10 cm.

13. Find the area of a rectangle with a length of 43 in. and a width of 19 in.

14. Find the area of a rectangle with a length of 82 cm and a width of 20 cm.

15. Find the area of a circle with a radius of 7 in. Use $\frac{22}{7}$ for π.

16. Find the area of a circle with a diameter of 40 cm. Use 3.14 for π.

Objective B   **To find the area of composite geometric figures**

For Exercises 17 to 24, find the area. Use 3.14 for π.

17.

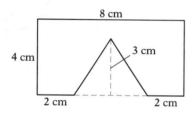

18.

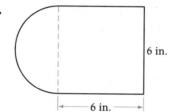

19.

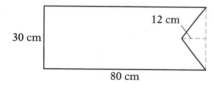

20.

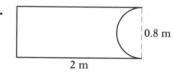

21.

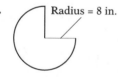

22.

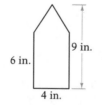

23.

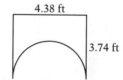

24.

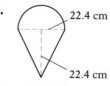

Objective C To solve application problems

25. **Sports** Artificial turf is being used to cover a playing field. If the field is rectangular with a length of 100 yd and a width of 75 yd, how much artificial turf must be purchased to cover the field?

26.  **Telescopes** The telescope lens of the Hale telescope at Mount Palomar, California, has a diameter of 200 in. Find the area of the lens. Leave the answer in terms of π.

27. **Agriculture** An irrigation system waters a circular field that has a 50-foot radius. Find the area watered by the irrigation system. Use 3.14 for π.

28. **Interior Design** A fabric wall hanging is to fill a space that measures 5 m by 3.5 m. Allowing for 0.1 m of the fabric to be folded back along each edge, how much fabric must be purchased for the wall hanging?

29. **Home Improvement** You plan to stain the wooden deck attached to your house. The deck measures 10 ft by 8 ft. A quart of stain will cost $9.95 and will cover 50 ft². How many quarts of stain should you buy?

30. **Interior Design** A carpet is to be installed in one room and a hallway, as shown in the diagram at the right. At a cost of $18.50 per square meter, how much will it cost to carpet the area?

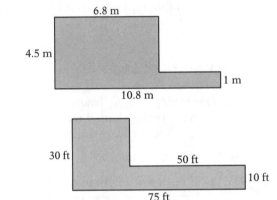

31. **Landscaping** Find the area of a concrete driveway with the measurements shown in the figure.

32. **Interior Design** You want to tile your kitchen floor. The floor measures 12 ft by 9 ft. How many tiles, each a square with side $1\frac{1}{2}$ ft, should you purchase for the job?

33. **Interior Design** You are wallpapering two walls of a child's room. One wall measures 9 ft by 8 ft, and the other measures 11 ft by 8 ft. The wallpaper costs $28.50 per roll, and each roll of the wallpaper will cover 40 ft². What is the cost to wallpaper the two walls?

34. **Construction** Find the area of the 2-meter boundary around the swimming pool shown in the figure.

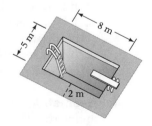

35. Parks An urban renewal project involves reseeding a park that is in the shape of a square, 60 ft on each side. Each bag of grass seed costs $5.75 and will seed 1200 ft². How much money should be budgeted for buying grass seed for the park?

36. Architecture The roller rink shown in the figure at the right is to be covered with hardwood floor.
   a. Without doing the calculations, indicate whether the area of the rink is more than 8000 ft² or less than 8000 ft².
   b. Calculate how much hardwood floor is needed to cover the roller rink. Use 3.14 for π.

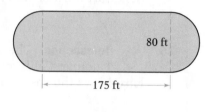

37. Parks Find the total area of the national park with the dimensions shown in the figure. Use 3.14 for π.

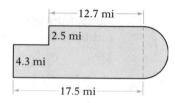

38. Interior Design Find the cost of plastering the walls of a room 22 ft wide, 25 ft 6 in. long, and 8 ft high. Subtract 120 ft² for windows and doors. The cost is $2.50 per square foot.

39. a. A circle has a radius of 8 in. Find the increase in area when the radius is increased by 2 in. Use 3.14 for π.
   b. A circle has a radius of 5 cm. Find the increase in area when the radius is doubled. Use 3.14 for π.

APPLYING THE CONCEPTS

40. Geometry What fractional part of the area of the larger of the two squares is the shaded area? Write your answer as a fraction in simplest form. This problem appeared in *Math Teacher*, vol. 86, No. 3 (September 1993).

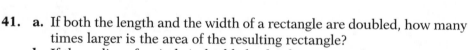

41. a. If both the length and the width of a rectangle are doubled, how many times larger is the area of the resulting rectangle?
   b. If the radius of a circle is doubled, what happens to the area?
   c. If the diameter of a circle is doubled, what happens to the area?

42. The circles at the right are identical. Is the area in the circles to the left of the line equal to, less than, or greater than the area in the circles to the right of the line? Explain your answer.

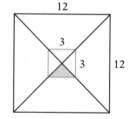

43. Determine whether the statement is always true, sometimes true, or never true.
   a. If two triangles have the same perimeter, then they have the same area.
   b. If two rectangles have the same area, then they have the same perimeter.
   c. If two squares have the same area, then the sides of the squares have the same length.

44. Geometry All of the dots at the right are equally spaced, horizontally and vertically, 1 inch apart. What is the area of the triangle?

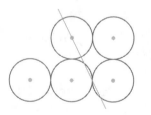

7.4 Volume

Objective A   **To find the volume of geometric solids**

Volume is a measure of the amount of space inside a closed surface, or figure in space. Volume can be used to describe the amount of heating gas used for cooking, the amount of concrete delivered for the foundation of a house, or the amount of water in storage for a city's water supply.

A cube that is 1 ft on each side has a volume of 1 cubic foot, which is written 1 ft³.

A cube that measures 1 cm on each side has a volume of 1 cubic centimeter, which is written 1 cm³.

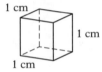

The volume of a solid is the number of cubes that are necessary to fill the solid exactly. The volume of the rectangular solid at the right is 24 cm³ because it will hold exactly 24 cubes, each 1 cm on a side. Note that the volume can be found by multiplying the length times the width times the height.

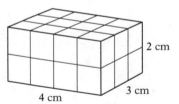

> **Volume of a Rectangular Solid**
>
> $V = LWH$

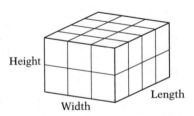

HOW TO   Find the volume of a rectangular solid with a length of 9 in., a width of 3 in., and a height of 4 in.

$V = LWH$
$\quad = (9 \text{ in.})(3 \text{ in.})(4 \text{ in.})$ • $L = 9$ in., $W = 3$ in.,
$\quad = 108 \text{ in}^3$ $H = 4$ in.

The volume of the rectangular solid is 108 in³.

The length, width, and height of a cube have the same measure. The volume of a cube is found by multiplying the side of the cube times itself three times (side cubed).

> **Volume of a Cube**
>
> $V = s^3$

HOW TO Find the volume of the cube shown at the right.

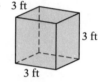

$V = s^3$
$\quad = (3 \text{ ft})^3 \qquad \bullet \ \boldsymbol{s = 3\,ft}$
$\quad = 27 \text{ ft}^3$

The volume of the cube is 27 ft³.

The volume of a sphere is found by multiplying four-thirds times pi (π) times the radius cubed.

> **Volume of a Sphere**
>
> $V = \frac{4}{3}\pi r^3$

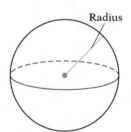

HOW TO Find the volume of the sphere shown below. Use 3.14 for π. Round to the nearest hundredth.

$V = \frac{4}{3}\pi r^3$

$V \approx \frac{4}{3}(3.14)(2 \text{ in.})^3 \qquad \bullet \ \boldsymbol{r = 2\,in}$

$V = \frac{4}{3}(3.14)(8 \text{ in}^3)$

$V \approx 33.49 \text{ in}^3$

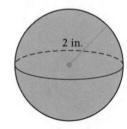

The volume is approximately 33.49 in³.

The volume of a cylinder is found by multiplying the area of the base of the cylinder (a circle) times the height.

> **Volume of a Cylinder**
>
> $V = \pi r^2 h$

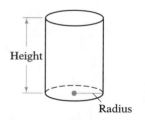

HOW TO Find the volume of the cylinder shown below. Use 3.14 for π.

$V = \pi r^2 h$
$\approx 3.14(3 \text{ cm})^2(8 \text{ cm})$
$= 3.14(9 \text{ cm}^2)(8 \text{ cm})$
$= 226.08 \text{ cm}^3$

• $r = 3 \text{ cm}, h = 8 \text{ cm}$

8 cm

Radius = 3 cm

The volume of the cylinder is approximately 226.08 cm³.

Example 1

Find the volume of a rectangular solid with a length of 3 ft, a width of 1.5 ft, and a height of 2 ft.

Solution
$V = LWH$
$= (3 \text{ ft})(1.5 \text{ ft})(2 \text{ ft})$
$= 9 \text{ ft}^3$

The volume is 9 ft³.

You Try It 1

Find the volume of a rectangular solid with a length of 8 cm, a width of 3.5 cm, and a height of 4 cm.

Your solution

Example 2

Find the volume of a cube that has a side measuring 2.5 in.

Solution
$V = s^3$
$= (2.5 \text{ in.})^3$
$= 15.625 \text{ in}^3$

The volume is 15.625 in³.

You Try It 2

Find the volume of a cube with a side of 5 cm.

Your solution

Example 3

Find the volume of a cylinder with a radius of 12 cm and a height of 65 cm. Use 3.14 for π.

Solution
$V = \pi r^2 h$
$\approx 3.14(12 \text{ cm})^2(65 \text{ cm})$
$= 3.14(144 \text{ cm}^2)(65 \text{ cm})$
$= 29{,}390.4 \text{ cm}^3$

The volume is approximately 29,390.4 cm³.

You Try It 3

Find the volume of a cylinder with a diameter of 14 in. and a height of 15 in. Use $\frac{22}{7}$ for π.

Your solution

Example 4

Find the volume of a sphere with a diameter of 12 in. Use 3.14 for π.

Solution

$r = \dfrac{1}{2}d = \dfrac{1}{2}(12 \text{ in.}) = 6 \text{ in.}$ • Find the radius.

$V = \dfrac{4}{3}\pi r^3$ • Use the formula for the volume of a sphere.

$\approx \dfrac{4}{3}(3.14)(6 \text{ in.})^3$

$= \dfrac{4}{3}(3.14)(216 \text{ in}^3)$

$= 904.32 \text{ in}^3$

The volume is approximately 904.32 in³.

You Try It 4

Find the volume of a sphere with a radius of 3 m. Use 3.14 for π.

Your solution

Objective B **To find the volume of composite geometric solids**

A **composite geometric solid** is a solid made from two or more geometric solids. The solid shown is made from a cylinder and one-half of a sphere.

Volume of the composite solid = volume of the cylinder $+ \dfrac{1}{2}$ the volume of the sphere

HOW TO Find the volume of the composite solid shown above if the radius of the base of the cylinder is 3 in. and the height of the cylinder is 10 in. Use 3.14 for π.

The volume equals the volume of a cylinder plus one-half the volume of a sphere. The radius of the sphere equals the radius of the base of the cylinder.

$V = \pi r^2 h + \dfrac{1}{2}\left(\dfrac{4}{3}\pi r^3\right)$

$\approx 3.14(3 \text{ in.})^2(10 \text{ in.}) + \dfrac{1}{2}\left(\dfrac{4}{3}\right)(3.14)(3 \text{ in.})^3$

$= 3.14(9 \text{ in}^2)(10 \text{ in.}) + \dfrac{1}{2}\left(\dfrac{4}{3}\right)(3.14)(27 \text{ in}^3)$

$= 282.6 \text{ in}^3 + 56.52 \text{ in}^3$

$= 339.12 \text{ in}^3$

The volume is approximately 339.12 in³.

Example 5

Find the volume of the solid in the figure.
Use 3.14 for π.

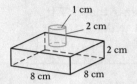

1 cm
2 cm
2 cm
8 cm   8 cm

Solution

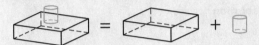

| Volume of the solid | = | volume of rectangu- lar solid | + | volume of cylinder |

$V = LWH + \pi r^2 h$
$\approx (8 \text{ cm})(8 \text{ cm})(2 \text{ cm}) + 3.14(1 \text{ cm})^2(2 \text{ cm})$
$= 128 \text{ cm}^3 + 6.28 \text{ cm}^3$
$= 134.28 \text{ cm}^3$

The volume is approximately 134.28 cm³.

You Try It 5

Find the volume of the solid in the figure.
Use 3.14 for π.

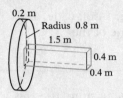

0.2 m
Radius 0.8 m
1.5 m
0.4 m
0.4 m

Your solution

Example 6

Find the volume of the solid in the figure.
Use 3.14 for π.

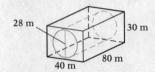

28 m
30 m
40 m   80 m

Solution

| Volume of the solid | = | volume of rectangu- lar solid | − | volume of cylinder |

$V = LWH - \pi r^2 h$
$\approx (80 \text{ m})(40 \text{ m})(30 \text{ m}) - 3.14(14 \text{ m})^2(80 \text{ m})$
$= 96,000 \text{ m}^3 - 49,235.2 \text{ m}^3$
$= 46,764.8 \text{ m}^3$

The volume is approximately 46,764.8 m³.

You Try It 6

Find the volume of the solid in the figure.
Use 3.14 for π.

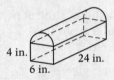

4 in.
24 in.
6 in.

Your solution

Objective C   **To solve application problems**

Example 7

An aquarium is 28 in. long, 14 in. wide, and 16 in. high. Find the volume of the aquarium.

Strategy
To find the volume of the aquarium, use the formula for the volume of a rectangular solid.

Solution
$V = LWH$
$\quad = (28 \text{ in.})(14 \text{ in.})(16 \text{ in.})$
$\quad = 6272 \text{ in}^3$

The volume of the aquarium is 6272 in^3.

Example 8

Find the volume of the bushing shown in the figure below. Use 3.14 for π.

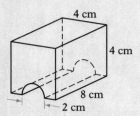

Strategy
To find the volume of the bushing, subtract the volume of the half-cylinder from the volume of the rectangular solid.

Solution

$$\begin{array}{l}\text{Volume} \\ \text{of the} \\ \text{bushing}\end{array} = \begin{array}{l}\text{volume of} \\ \text{rectangu-} \\ \text{lar solid}\end{array} - \begin{array}{l}\frac{1}{2} \text{ the} \\ \text{volume of} \\ \text{cylinder}\end{array}$$

$V = LWH - \dfrac{1}{2}\pi r^2 h$

$V \approx (8 \text{ cm})(4 \text{ cm})(4 \text{ cm}) - \dfrac{1}{2}(3.14)(1 \text{ cm})^2(8 \text{ cm})$

$V = 128 \text{ cm}^3 - 12.56 \text{ cm}^3$
$V = 115.44 \text{ cm}^3$

The volume of the bushing is approximately 115.44 cm^3.

You Try It 7

Find the volume of a freezer that is 7 ft long, 3 ft high, and 2.5 ft wide.

Your strategy

Your solution

You Try It 8

Find the volume of the channel iron shown in the figure below.

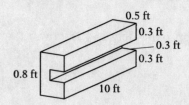

Your strategy

Your solution

7.4 Exercises

Objective A   **To find the volume of geometric solids**

For Exercises 1 to 8, find the volume. Round to the nearest hundredth. Use 3.14 for π.

1.

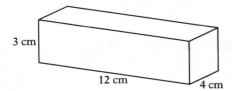

3 cm
12 cm
4 cm

2.

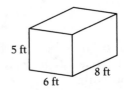

5 ft
6 ft
8 ft

3.

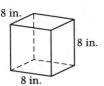

8 in.
8 in.
8 in.

4.

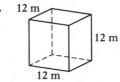

12 m
12 m
12 m

5.

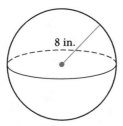

8 in.

6.

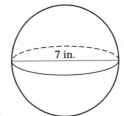

7 in.

7.

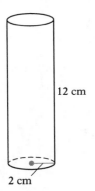

12 cm
2 cm

8.

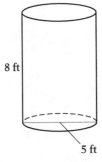

8 ft
5 ft

For Exercises 9 to 16, find the volume.

9. Find the volume, in cubic meters, of a rectangular solid with a length of 2 m, a width of 80 cm, and a height of 4 m.

10. Find the volume of a cylinder with a radius of 7 cm and a height of 14 cm. Use $\frac{22}{7}$ for π.

11. Find the volume of a sphere with an 11-millimeter radius. Use 3.14 for π. Round to the nearest hundredth.

12. Find the volume of a cube with a side of 2.14 m. Round to the nearest tenth.

13. Find the volume of a cylinder with a diameter of 12 ft and a height of 30 ft. Use 3.14 for π.

14. Find the volume of a sphere with a 6-foot diameter. Use 3.14 for π.

15. Find the volume of a cube with a side of $3\frac{1}{2}$ ft.

16. Find the volume, in cubic meters, of a rectangular solid with a length of 1.15 m, a width of 60 cm, and a height of 25 cm.

Objective B **To find the volume of composite geometric solids**

For Exercises 17 to 22, find the volume. Use 3.14 for π.

17.

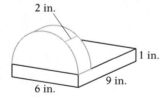

18.

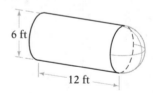

19.

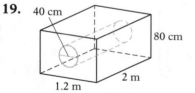

20.

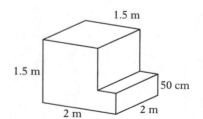

21.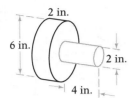

22.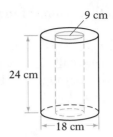

Objective C   **To solve application problems**

For Exercises 23 to 35, solve. Use 3.14 for π.

23.   Fish Hatchery   A rectangular tank at the fish hatchery is 9 m long, 3 m wide, and 1.5 m deep. Find the volume of the water in the tank when the tank is full.

24.   Rocketry   A fuel tank in a booster rocket is a cylinder 10 ft in diameter and 52 ft high. Find the volume of the fuel tank.

25.   Ballooning   A hot air balloon is in the shape of a sphere. Find the volume of a hot air balloon that is 32 ft in diameter. Round to the nearest hundredth.

26.   Petroleum   A storage tank for propane is in the shape of a sphere that has a diameter of 9 m. Find the volume of the tank.

27.   Petroleum   An oil tank, which is in the shape of a cylinder, is 4 m high and has a diameter of 6 m. The oil tank is two-thirds full. Find the number of cubic meters of oil in the tank. Round to the nearest hundredth.

28.   Agriculture   A silo, which is in the shape of a cylinder, is 16 ft in diameter and has a height of 30 ft. The silo is three-fourths full. Find the volume of the portion of the silo that is not being used for storage.

29.   Architecture   An architect is designing the heating system for an auditorium and needs to know the volume of the structure. Find the volume of the auditorium with the measurements shown in the figure.

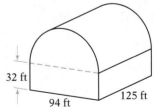

30.   Pools   A swimming pool 50 ft long and 13 ft wide contains water to a depth of 10 ft. Find the total weight of the water in the swimming pool. (1 ft³ weighs 62.4 lb.)

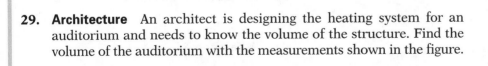

31. Metal Works   Find the volume of the bushing shown at the right.

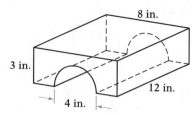

32. Aquariums   How many gallons of water will fill an aquarium that is 12 in. wide, 18 in. long, and 16 in. high? Round to the nearest tenth. (1 gal = 231 in^3)

33. Aquariums   How many gallons of water will fill a fish tank that is 12 in. long, 8 in. wide, and 9 in. high? Round to the nearest tenth. (1 gal = 231 in^3)

34. Petroleum   A truck carrying an oil tank is shown in the figure at the right.
  a. Without doing the calculations, determine whether the volume of the oil tank is more than 240 ft^3 or less than 240 ft^3.
  b. If the tank is half full, how many cubic feet of oil is the truck carrying? Round to the nearest hundredth.

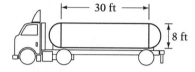

35. Construction   The concrete floor of a building is shown in the figure at the right. At a cost of $5.85 per cubic foot, find the cost of having the floor poured. Round to the nearest cent.

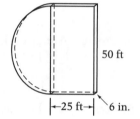

APPLYING THE CONCEPTS

36. Half a sphere is called a hemisphere. Derive a formula for the volume of a hemisphere.

37. a. If both the length and the width of a rectangular solid are doubled, how many times larger is the resulting rectangular solid?
  b. If the length, width, and height of a rectangular solid are all doubled, how many times larger is the resulting rectangular solid?
  c. If the side of a cube is doubled, how many times larger is the resulting cube?

 For Exercises 38 to 41, explain how you could cut through a cube so that the face of the resulting solid is the given geometric figure.

38. A square

39. An equilateral triangle

40. A trapezoid

41. A hexagon

42. Suppose a cylinder is cut into 16 equal pieces, which are then arranged as shown at the right. The figure resembles a rectangular solid. What variable expressions could be used to represent the length, width, and height of the rectangular solid? Explain how the formula for the volume of a cylinder is derived from this approach.

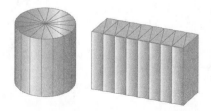

7.5 The Pythagorean Theorem

Objective A To find the square root of a number

The area of a square is 36 in². What is the length of one side?

Area of the square = (side)²
36 = side · side

What number multiplied times itself equals 36?

36 = 6 · 6

The side of the square is 6 in.

The **square root** of a number is one of two identical factors of that number. The square root symbol is $\sqrt{\ }$.

The square root of 36 is 6.

$$\sqrt{36} = 6$$

A **perfect square** is the product of a whole number times itself.

1, 4, 9, 16, 25, and 36 are perfect squares.

The square root of a perfect square is a whole number.

1 · 1 = 1	$\sqrt{1} = 1$
2 · 2 = 4	$\sqrt{4} = 2$
3 · 3 = 9	$\sqrt{9} = 3$
4 · 4 = 16	$\sqrt{16} = 4$
5 · 5 = 25	$\sqrt{25} = 5$
6 · 6 = 36	$\sqrt{36} = 6$

Point of Interest

The square root of a number that is not a perfect square is an irrational number. There is evidence of irrational numbers as early as 500 B.C. These numbers were not very well understood, and they were given the name *numerus surdus*. This phrase comes from the Latin word *surdus*, which means deaf or mute. Thus irrational numbers were "inaudible numbers."

If a number is not a perfect square, its square root can only be approximated. The approximate square roots of numbers can be found using a calculator. For example:

Number	Square Root
33	$\sqrt{33} \approx 5.745$
34	$\sqrt{34} \approx 5.831$
35	$\sqrt{35} \approx 5.916$

Example 1
a. Find the square roots of the perfect squares 49 and 81.
b. Find the square roots of 27 and 108. Round to the nearest thousandth.

You Try It 1
a. Find the square roots of the perfect squares 16 and 169.
b. Find the square roots of 32 and 162. Round to the nearest thousandth.

Solution
a. $\sqrt{49} = 7$ $\sqrt{81} = 9$
b. $\sqrt{27} \approx 5.196$ $\sqrt{108} \approx 10.392$

Your solution

Objective B   **To find the unknown side of a right triangle using the Pythagorean Theorem**

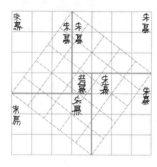

The Greek mathematician Pythagoras is generally credited with the discovery that the square of the hypotenuse of a right triangle is equal to the sum of the squares of the two legs. This is called the **Pythagorean Theorem.** However, the Babylonians used this theorem more than 1000 years before Pythagoras lived.

Square of the hypotenuse	equals	sum of the squares of the two legs
5^2	=	$3^2 + 4^2$
25	=	9 + 16
25	=	25

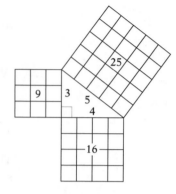

If the length of one side of a right triangle is unknown, one of the following formulas can be used to find it.

If the hypotenuse is unknown, use

$$\text{Hypotenuse} = \sqrt{(\text{leg})^2 + (\text{leg})^2}$$
$$= \sqrt{(3)^2 + (4)^2}$$
$$= \sqrt{9 + 16}$$
$$= \sqrt{25} = 5$$

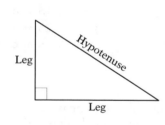

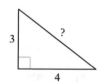

If the length of a leg is unknown, use

$$\text{Leg} = \sqrt{(\text{hypotenuse})^2 - (\text{leg})^2}$$
$$= \sqrt{(5)^2 - (4)^2}$$
$$= \sqrt{25 - 16}$$
$$= \sqrt{9} = 3$$

Example 2

Find the hypotenuse of the triangle in the figure. Round to the nearest thousandth.

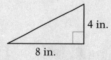

Solution
Hypotenuse $= \sqrt{(\text{leg})^2 + (\text{leg})^2}$
$= \sqrt{8^2 + 4^2}$
$= \sqrt{64 + 16}$
$= \sqrt{80} \approx 8.944$

The hypotenuse is approximately 8.944 in.

You Try It 2

Find the hypotenuse of the triangle in the figure. Round to the nearest thousandth.

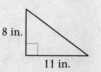

Your solution

Example 3

Find the length of the leg of the triangle in the figure. Round to the nearest thousandth.

12 cm
9 cm

Solution

$\text{Leg} = \sqrt{(\text{hypotenuse})^2 - (\text{leg})^2}$
$= \sqrt{12^2 - 9^2}$
$= \sqrt{144 - 81}$
$= \sqrt{63} \approx 7.937$

The length of the leg is approximately 7.937 cm.

You Try It 3

Find the length of the leg of the triangle in the figure. Round to the nearest thousandth.

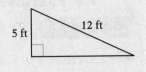
5 ft   12 ft

Your solution

Objective C   **To solve application problems**

Example 4

A 25-foot ladder is placed against a building at a point 21 ft from the ground, as shown in the figure. Find the distance from the base of the building to the base of the ladder. Round to the nearest thousandth.

25 ft
21 ft

Strategy

To find the distance from the base of the building to the base of the ladder, use the Pythagorean Theorem. The hypotenuse is the length of the ladder (25 ft). One leg is the distance along the building from the ground to the top of the ladder (21 ft). The distance from the base of the building to the base of the ladder is the unknown leg.

Solution

$\text{Leg} = \sqrt{(\text{hypotenuse})^2 - (\text{leg})^2}$
$= \sqrt{25^2 - 21^2}$
$= \sqrt{625 - 441}$
$= \sqrt{184} \approx 13.565$

The distance is approximately 13.565 ft.

You Try It 4

Find the distance between the centers of the holes in the metal plate in the figure. Round to the nearest thousandth.

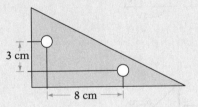
3 cm
8 cm

Your strategy

Your solution

7.5 Exercises

Copyright © Houghton Mifflin Company. All rights reserved.

Objective A   **To find the square root of a number**

For Exercises 1 to 8, find the square root. Round to the nearest thousandth.

1. 7

2. 34

3. 42

4. 64

5. 165

6. 144

7. 189

8. 130

Objective B   **To find the unknown side of a right triangle using the Pythagorean Theorem**

For Exercises 9 to 26, find the unknown side of the triangle. Round to the nearest thousandth.

9.

3 in.
4 in.

10.
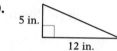
5 in.
12 in.

11.
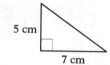
5 cm
7 cm

12.

7 cm
9 cm

13.

15 ft
10 ft

14.
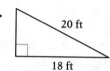
20 ft
18 ft

15.

4 cm
6 cm

16.

9 m
12 m

17.

9 yd
9 yd

18.

20 cm
10 cm

19.

12 ft
6 ft

20.
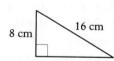
8 cm
16 cm

21.

15 cm
15 cm

22.
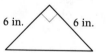
6 in.
6 in.

23.
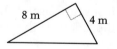
8 m
4 m

24.
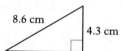
8.6 cm
4.3 cm

25.

11.3 yd
8.1 yd

26.
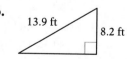
13.9 ft
8.2 ft

Objective C   **To solve application problems**

27. **Ramps**   Find the length of the ramp used to roll barrels up to the loading dock, which is 3.5 ft high. Round to the nearest hundredth.

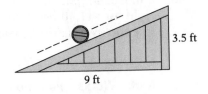
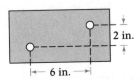

28. **Metal Works**   Find the distance between the centers of the holes in the metal plate in the figure at the right. Round to the nearest hundredth.

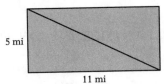

29. **Travel**   If you travel 18 mi east and then 12 mi north, how far are you from your starting point? Round to the nearest tenth.

30. **Travel**   If you travel 12 mi west and 16 mi south, how far are you from your starting point?

31. **Geometry**   The diagonal of a rectangle is a line drawn from one vertex to the opposite vertex. Find the length of the diagonal in the rectangle shown at the right. Round to the nearest tenth.

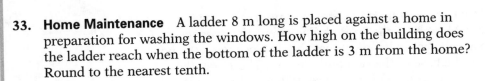

32. **Geometry**   The diagonal of a rectangle is a line drawn from one vertex to the opposite vertex. (See Exercise 31.) Find the length of the diagonal in the rectangle that has a length of 8 m and a width of 3.5 m. Round to the nearest tenth.

33. **Home Maintenance**   A ladder 8 m long is placed against a home in preparation for washing the windows. How high on the building does the ladder reach when the bottom of the ladder is 3 m from the home? Round to the nearest tenth.

34. **Geometry**   Find the perimeter of a right triangle with legs that measure 5 cm and 9 cm. Round to the nearest tenth.

35. **Geometry**   Find the perimeter of a right triangle with legs that measure 6 in. and 10 in.

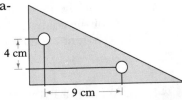

36. **Metal Works**   Find the distance between the centers of the holes in the metal plate shown in the diagram at the right. Round to the nearest tenth.

37. **Parks**   An L-shaped sidewalk from the parking lot to a memorial is shown in the figure at the right. The distance directly across the grass to the memorial is 650 ft. The distance to the corner is 600 ft. Find the distance from the corner to the memorial.

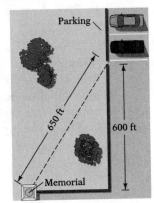

38. Landscaping A fence is built around the plot shown in the figure at the right. At $11.40 per meter, how much did it cost to fence the plot? (*Hint:* Use the Pythagorean Theorem to find the unknown length.)

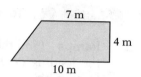
7 m
4 m
10 m

39. Metal Works Four holes are drilled in the circular plate in the figure at the right. The centers of the holes are 3 in. from the center. Find the distance between the centers of adjacent holes. Round to the nearest thousandth.

40. Plumbing Find the offset distance, d, of the length of pipe shown in the diagram at the right. The total length of the pipe is 62 in.

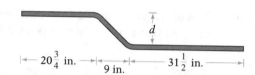
d
$20\frac{3}{4}$ in.
9 in.
$31\frac{1}{2}$ in.

APPLYING THE CONCEPTS

41. Determine whether the statement is always true, sometimes true, or never true.
  a. The sum of the lengths of two sides of a triangle is greater than the length of the third side of the triangle.
  b. The hypotenuse is the longest side of a right triangle.

42. **Home Maintenance** You need to clean the gutters of your home. The gutters are 24 ft above the ground. For safety, the distance a ladder reaches up a wall should be four times the distance from the bottom of the ladder to the base of the side of the house. Therefore, the ladder must be 6 ft from the base of the house. Will a 25-foot ladder be long enough to reach the gutters? Explain how you determined your answer.

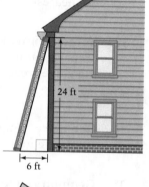
24 ft
6 ft

43. Can the Pythagorean Theorem be used to find the length of side c of the triangle at the right? If so, determine c. If not, explain why the theorem cannot be used.

4
c
6

44. a. What is a Pythagorean triple?
  b. Provide at least three examples of Pythagorean triples.

45. Construction Buildings A and B are situated on opposite sides of a river. A construction company must lay a pipeline between the two buildings. The plan is to connect the buildings as shown. What is the total length of the pipe needed to connect the buildings?

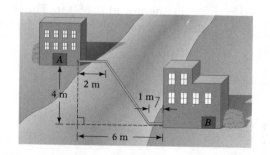
A
2 m
4 m
1 m
B
6 m

Focus on Problem Solving

Trial and Error   Some problems in mathematics are solved by using **trial and error.** The trial-and-error method of arriving at a solution to a problem involves performing repeated tests or experiments until a satisfactory conclusion is reached.

Many of the Applying the Concepts exercises in this text require a trial-and-error method of solution. For example, an exercise in Section 12.4 reads as follows:

Explain how you could cut through a cube so that the face of the resulting solid is **(a)** a square, **(b)** an equilateral triangle, **(c)** a trapezoid, **(d)** a hexagon.

There is no formula to apply to this problem; there is no computation to perform. This problem requires picturing a cube and the results after it is cut through at different places on its surface and at different angles. For part a, cutting perpendicular to the top and bottom of the cube and parallel to two of its sides will result in a square. The other shapes may prove more difficult.

When solving problems of this type, keep an open mind. Sometimes when using the trial-and-error method, we are hampered by our narrowness of vision; we cannot expand our thinking to include other possibilities. Then when we see someone else's solution, it appears so obvious to us! For example, for the Applying the Concepts question above, it is necessary to conceive of cutting through the cube at places other than the top surface; we need to be open to the idea of beginning the cut at one of the corner points of the cube.

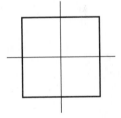

One topic of the Projects and Group Activities in this chapter is symmetry. Here again, the trial-and-error method is used to determine the lines of symmetry inherent in an object. For example, in determining lines of symmetry for a square, begin by drawing a square. The horizontal line of symmetry and the vertical line of symmetry may be immediately obvious to you.

But there are two others. Do you see that a line drawn through opposite corners of the square is also a line of symmetry?

Many of the questions in this text that require an answer of "always true, sometimes true, or never true" are best solved by the trial-and-error method. For example, consider the following statement

If two rectangles have the same area, then they have the same perimeter.

Try some numbers. Each of two rectangles, one measuring 6 units by 2 units and another measuring 4 units by 3 units, has an area of 12 square units, but the perimeter of the first is 16 units and the perimeter of the second is 14 units, so the answer "always true" has been eliminated. We still need to determine whether there is a case when it is true. After experimenting with a lot of numbers, you may come to realize that we are trying to determine whether it is possible for two different pairs of factors of a number to have the same sum. Is it?

Don't be afraid to make many experiments, and remember that *errors*, or tests that "don't work," are a part of the trial-and-*error* process.

Projects and Group Activities

Investigating Perimeter

The perimeter of the square at the right is 4 units.

If two squares are joined along one of the sides, the perimeter is 6 units. Note that it does not matter which sides are joined; the perimeter is still 6 units.

If three squares are joined, the perimeter of the resulting figure is 8 units for each possible placement of the squares.

Four squares can be joined in five different ways as shown. There are two possible perimeters: 10 units for A, B, C, and D, and 8 for E.

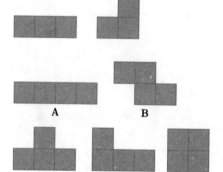

A   B

C   D   E

1. If five squares are joined, what is the maximum perimeter possible?

2. If five squares are joined, what is the minimum perimeter possible?

3. If six squares are joined, what is the maximum perimeter possible?

4. If six squares are joined, what is the minimum perimeter possible?

Symmetry Look at the letter A printed at the left. If the letter were folded along line ℓ, the two sides of the letter would match exactly. This letter has **symmetry** with respect to line ℓ. Line ℓ is called the **axis of symmetry.**

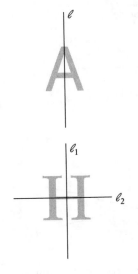

Now consider the letter H printed below at the left. Both lines ℓ₁ and ℓ₂ are axes of symmetry for this letter; the letter could be folded along either line and the two sides would match exactly.

1. Does the letter A have more than one axis of symmetry?

2. Find axes of symmetry for other capital letters of the alphabet.

3. Which lowercase letters have one axis of symmetry?

4. Do any of the lowercase letters have more than one axis of symmetry?

5. Find the number of axes of symmetry for each of the plane geometric figures presented in this chapter.

6. There are other types of symmetry. Look up the meaning of *point symmetry* and *rotational symmetry*. Which plane geometric figures provide examples of these types of symmetry?

7. Find examples of symmetry in nature, art, and architecture.

Chapter Summary

Key Words

Examples

A *line* extends indefinitely in two directions. A *line segment* is part of a line and has two endpoints. The length of a line segment is the distance between the endpoints of the line segment.

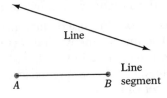

Parallel lines never meet; the distance between them is always the same. The symbol ∥ means "is parallel to." *Intersecting lines* cross at a point in the plane. *Perpendicular lines* are intersecting lines that form right angles. The symbol ⊥ means "is perpendicular to."

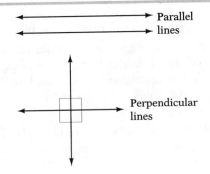

A *ray* starts at a point and extends indefinitely in one direction. An *angle* is formed when two rays start from the same point. The common point is called the *vertex* of the angle. An angle is measured in *degrees*. A 90° angle is a *right angle*. A 180° angle is a *straight angle*. *Complementary angles* are two angles whose measures have the sum 90°. *Supplementary angles* are two angles whose measures have the sum 180°. An *acute angle* is an angle whose measure is between 0° and 90°. An *obtuse angle* is an angle whose measure is between 90° and 180°.

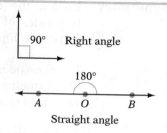

Two angles that are on opposite sides of the intersection of two lines are *vertical angles;* vertical angles have the same measure. Two angles that share a common side are *adjacent angles;* adjacent angles of intersecting lines are supplementary angles.

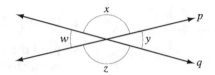

Angles *w* and *y* are vertical angles.
Angles *x* and *y* are adjacent angles.

A line that intersects two other lines at two different points is a *transversal.* If the lines cut by a transversal are parallel lines, equal angles are formed: *alternate interior angles, alternate exterior angles,* and *corresponding angles.*

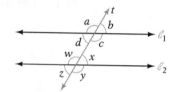

Parallel lines l_1 and l_2 are cut by transversal *t.* All four acute angles have the same measure. All four obtuse angles have the same measure.

A *quadrilateral* is a four-sided polygon. A *parallelogram,* a *rectangle,* and a *square* are quadrilaterals.

A *polygon* is a closed figure determined by three or more line segments. The line segments that form the polygon are its *sides.* A *regular polygon* is one in which each side has the same length and each angle has the same measure. Polygons are classified by the number of sides.

Number of Sides	Name of the Polygon
3	Triangle
4	Quadrilateral
5	Pentagon
6	Hexagon
7	Heptagon
8	Octagon
9	Nonagon
10	Decagon

A *triangle* is a closed, three-sided plane figure.

An *isosceles triangle* has two sides of equal length. The three sides of an *equilateral triangle* are of equal length. A *scalene triangle* has no two sides of equal length. An *acute triangle* has three actue angles. An *obtuse triangle* has one obtuse angle.

A *right triangle* contains a right angle. The side opposite the right angle is called the *hypotenuse.* The other two sides are called *legs.*

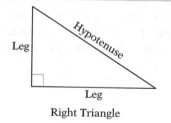

Right Triangle

A *circle* is a plane figure in which all points are the same distance from the center of the circle. A *diameter* of a circle is a line segment across the cricle through the center. A *radius* of a circle is a line segment from the center of the circle to a point on the circle.

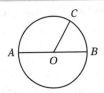

AB is a diameter of the circle.
OC is a radius.

Geometric solids are figures in space. Four common space figures are the rectangular solid, cube, sphere, and cylinder. A *rectangular solid* is a solid in which all six faces are rectangles. A *cube* is a rectangular solid in which all six faces are squares. A *sphere* is a solid in which all points on the sphere are the same distance from the center of the sphere. The most common *cylinder* is one in which the bases are circles and are perpendicular to the side.

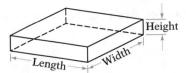

Rectangular Solid

The *square root* of a number is one of two identical factors of that number. The symbol for square root is $\sqrt{\ }$. A *perfect square* is the product of a whole number times itself. The square root of a perfect square is a whole number.

$1^2 = 1, 2^2 = 4, 3^2 = 9, 4^2 = 16,$
$5^2 = 25, \ldots 1, 4, 9, 16, 25, \ldots$ are perfect squares.

$\sqrt{1} = 1, \sqrt{4} = 2, \sqrt{9} = 3, \sqrt{16} = 4, \ldots$

Similar triangles have the same shape but not necessarily the same size. The ratios of corresponding sides are equal. The ratio of corresponding heights is equal to the ratio of corresponding sides. *Congruent triangles* have the same shape and the same size.

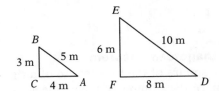

Triangles *ABC* and *DEF* are similar triangles. The ratio of corresponding sides is $\frac{1}{2}$.

Essential Rules and Procedures

Examples

Triangles
Sum of three angles = 180°

Two angles of a triangle measure 32° and 48°. Find the measure of the third angle.

$\angle A + \angle B + \angle C = 180°$
$\angle A + 32° + 48° = 180°$
$\angle A + 80° = 180°$
$\angle A + 80° - 80° = 180° - 80°$
$\angle A = 100°$

The measure of the third angle is 100°.

Formulas for Perimeter (the distance around a figure)

Triangle: $P = a + b + c$
Square: $P = 4s$
Rectangle: $P = 2L + 2W$
Circumference of a circle: $C = \pi d$ or $C = 2\pi r$

The length of a rectangle is 8 m. The width is 5.5 m. Find the perimeter of the rectangle.
$P = 2L + 2W$
$P = 2(8\text{ m}) + 2(5.5\text{ m})$
$P = 16\text{ m} + 11\text{ m}$
$P = 27\text{ m}$
The perimeter is 27 m.

Formulas for Area (the amount of surface in a region)

Triangle: $A = \frac{1}{2}bh$

Square: $A = s^2$
Rectangle: $A = LW$
Circle: $A = \pi r^2$

Find the area of a circle with a radius of 4 cm. Use 3.14 for π.
$A = \pi r^2$
$A \approx 3.14(4\text{ cm})^2$
$A \approx 50.24\text{ cm}^2$
The area is 50.24 cm².

Formulas for Volume (the amount of space inside a figure in space)

Rectangular solid: $V = LWH$
Cube: $V = s^3$

Sphere: $V = \frac{4}{3}\pi r^3$

Cylinder: $V = \pi r^2 h$

Find the volume of a cube that measures 3 in. on a side.
$V = s^3$
$V = 3^3$
$V = 27$
The volume is 27 in³.

Pythagorean Theorem
The square of the hypotenuse of a right triangle is equal to the sum of the squares of the two legs.
If the length of one side of a triangle is unknown, one of the following formulas can be used to find it.
If the hypotenuse is unknown, use

$$\text{Hypotenuse} = \sqrt{(\text{leg})^2 + (\text{leg})^2}$$

If the length of a leg is unknown, use

$$\text{Leg} = \sqrt{(\text{hypotenuse})^2 - (\text{leg})^2}$$

Two legs of a right triangle measure 6 ft and 8 ft. Find the hypotenuse of the right triangle.

$$\begin{aligned}
\text{Hypotenuse} &= \sqrt{(\text{leg})^2 + (\text{leg})^2} \\
&= \sqrt{6^2 + 8^2} \\
&= \sqrt{36 + 64} \\
&= \sqrt{100} \\
&= 10
\end{aligned}$$

The length of the hypotenuse is 10 ft.

Side-Side-Side (SSS) Rule
Two triangles are congruent if three sides of one triangle equal the corresponding sides of the second triangle.

Side-Angle-Side (SAS) Rule
Two triangles are congruent if two sides and the included angle of one triangle equal the corresponding sides and included angle of the second triangle.

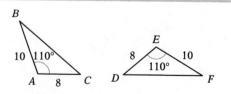

Triangles *ABC* and *DEF* are congruent by the SAS rule.

Chapter Review Exercises

1. The diameter of a sphere is 1.5 m. Find the radius of the sphere.

2. Find the circumference of a circle with a radius of 5 cm. Use 3.14 for π.

3. Find the perimeter of the rectangle in the figure below.

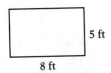

4. Given $AB = 15$, $CD = 6$, and $AD = 24$, find the length of BC.

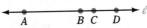

5. Find the volume of the rectangular solid shown below.

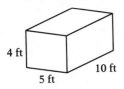

6. Find the unknown side of the triangle in the figure below.

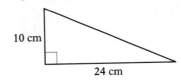

7. Find the supplement of a 105° angle.

8. Find the square root of 15. Round to the nearest thousandth.

9. Triangles ABC and DEF are similar. Find the height of triangle DEF.

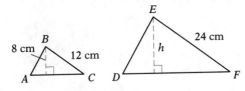

10. Find the area of the circle shown below. Use 3.14 for π.

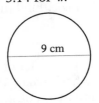

11. Here $\ell_1 \parallel \ell_2$.
 a. Find the measure of angle b.
 b. Find the measure of angle a.

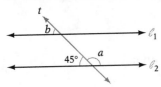

12. Find the area of the rectangle shown below.

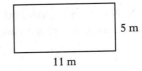

13. Find the volume of the composite figure shown below.

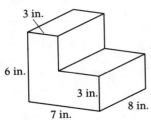

14. Find the area of the composite figure shown below. Use 3.14 for π.

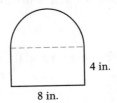

15. Find the volume of a sphere with a diameter of 8 ft. Use 3.14 for π. Round to the nearest tenth.

16. Triangles *ABC* and *DEF* are similar. Find the area of triangle *DEF*.

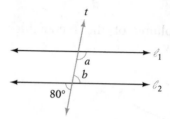

17. Find the perimeter of the composite figure shown below. Use 3.14 for π.

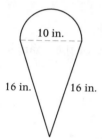

10 in.

16 in.   16 in.

18. Here $\ell_1 \parallel \ell_2$.
   a. Find the measure of angle *b*.
   b. Find the measure of angle *a*.

80°

19. Home Maintenance How high on a building will a 17-foot ladder reach when the bottom of the ladder is 8 ft from the building?

20. A right triangle has a 32° angle. Find the measures of the other two angles.

21. Travel A bicycle tire has a diameter of 28 in. How many feet does the bicycle travel when the wheel makes 10 revolutions? Use 3.14 for π. Round to the nearest tenth of a foot.

28 in.

22. Interior Design New carpet is installed in a room measuring 18 ft by 14 ft. Find the area of the room in square yards. ($9 \text{ ft}^2 = 1 \text{ yd}^2$)

23. Agriculture A silo, which is in the shape of a cylinder, is 9 ft in diameter and has a height of 18 ft. Find the volume of the silo. Use 3.14 for π.

24. Find the area of a right triangle with a base of 8 m and a height of 2.75 m.

25. Travel If you travel 20 mi west and then 21 mi south, how far are you from your starting point?

Chapter Test

1. Find the volume of a cylinder with a height of 6 m and a radius of 3 m. Use 3.14 for π.

2. Find the perimeter of a rectangle that has a length of 2 m and a width of 1.4 m.

3. Find the volume of the composite figure. Use 3.14 for π.

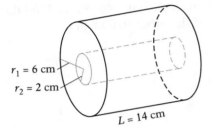

$r_1 = 6$ cm
$r_2 = 2$ cm
$L = 14$ cm

4. Triangles *ABC* and *FED* are congruent right triangles. Find the length of *FE*.

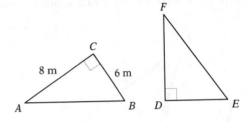

5. Find the complement of a 32° angle.

6. Find the area of a circle that has a diameter of 2 m. Use $\frac{22}{7}$ for π.

7. In the figure below, lines ℓ_1 and ℓ_2 are parallel. Angle *x* measures 30°. Find the measure of angle *y*.

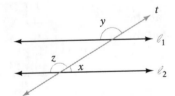

8. Find the perimeter of the composite figure. Use 3.14 for π.

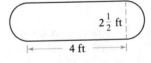

$2\frac{1}{2}$ ft

4 ft

9. Find the square root of 189. Round to the nearest thousandth.

10. Find the unknown side of the triangle shown below. Round to the nearest thousandth.

12 ft

7 ft

11. Find the area of the composite figure.

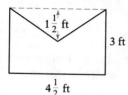

12. In the figure below, lines ℓ_1 and ℓ_2 are parallel. Angle x measures 45°. Find the measures of angles a and b.

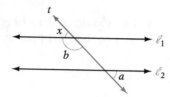

13. Triangles *ABC* and *DEF* are similar. Find side *BC*.

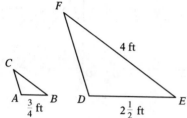

14. A right triangle has a 40° angle. Find the measures of the other two angles.

15. Measurement Use similar triangles to find the width of the canal shown in the figure at the right.

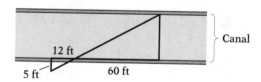

16. Consumerism How much more pizza is contained in a pizza with radius 10 in. than in one with radius 8 in.? Use 3.14 for π.

17. Interior Design A carpet is to be placed as shown in the diagram at the right. At $26.80 per square yard, how much will it cost to carpet the area? Round to the nearest cent. (9 ft² = 1 yd²)

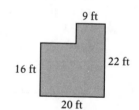

18. Forestry Find the cross-sectional area of a redwood tree that is 11 ft 6 in. in diameter. Use 3.14 for π. Round to the nearest hundredth.

19. Construction Find the length of the rafter needed for the roof shown in the figure.

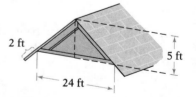

20. Measurement A toolbox is 1 ft 2 in. long, 9 in. wide, and 8 in. high. The sides and bottom of the toolbox are $\frac{1}{2}$ in. thick. Find the volume of the interior of the toolbox in cubic inches.

CHAPTER 7: *Additional Material From:*

MATHEMATICAL EXCURSIONS | SECOND EDITION

Aufmann • Lockwood • Nation • Clegg

Trigonometric Functions of an Acute Angle

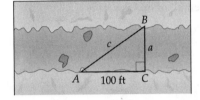

Given the lengths of two sides of a right triangle, it is possible to determine the length of the third side by using the Pythagorean Theorem. In some situations, however, it may not be practical or possible to know the lengths of two of the sides of a right triangle.

Consider, for example, the problem of engineers trying to determine the distance across a ravine so that they can design a bridge that can be built connecting the two sides. Look at the triangle to the left.

It is fairly easy to measure the length of the side of the triangle that is on the land (100 feet), but the lengths of sides *a* and *c* cannot be measured easily because of the ravine.

The study of *trigonometry*, a term that comes from two Greek words meaning "triangle measurement," began about 2000 years ago, partially as a means of solving surveying problems such as the one above. In this section, we will examine *right triangle* trigonometry—that is, trigonometry that applies only to right triangles.

When working with right triangles, it is convenient to refer to the side *opposite* an angle and to the side *adjacent* to (next to) an angle. The hypotenuse of a right triangle is not adjacent to or opposite either of the acute angles in a right triangle.

✔ **TAKE NOTE**

In trigonometry, it is common practice to use Greek letters for angles of a triangle. Here are some frequently used letters: α (alpha), β (beta), and θ (theta). The word *alphabet* is derived from the first two letters of the Greek alphabet, α and β.

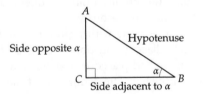

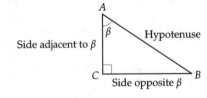

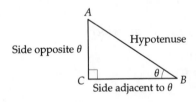

Figure 8.1

Consider the right triangle in Figure 8.1 shown at the left. Six possible ratios can be formed using the lengths of the sides of the triangle.

$$\frac{\text{length of opposite side}}{\text{length of hypotenuse}} \qquad \frac{\text{length of hypotenuse}}{\text{length of opposite side}}$$

$$\frac{\text{length of adjacent side}}{\text{length of hypotenuse}} \qquad \frac{\text{length of hypotenuse}}{\text{length of adjacent side}}$$

$$\frac{\text{length of opposite side}}{\text{length of adjacent side}} \qquad \frac{\text{length of adjacent side}}{\text{length of opposite side}}$$

Each of these ratios defines a value of a trigonometric function of the acute angle θ. The functions are **sine** (sin), **cosine** (cos), **tangent** (tan), **cosecant** (csc), **secant** (sec), and **cotangent** (cot).

The Trigonometric Functions of an Acute Angle of a Right Triangle

If θ is an acute angle of a right triangle ABC, then

$$\sin \theta = \frac{\text{length of opposite side}}{\text{length of hypotenuse}} \qquad \csc \theta = \frac{\text{length of hypotenuse}}{\text{length of opposite side}}$$

$$\cos \theta = \frac{\text{length of adjacent side}}{\text{length of hypotenuse}} \qquad \sec \theta = \frac{\text{length of hypotenuse}}{\text{length of adjacent side}}$$

$$\tan \theta = \frac{\text{length of opposite side}}{\text{length of adjacent side}} \qquad \cot \theta = \frac{\text{length of adjacent side}}{\text{length of opposite side}}$$

As a convenience, we will write opp, adj, and hyp as abbreviations for *the length of the* opposite side, adjacent side, and hypotenuse, respectively. Using this convention, the definitions of the trigonometric functions are written

$$\sin \theta = \frac{\text{opp}}{\text{hyp}} \qquad \csc \theta = \frac{\text{hyp}}{\text{opp}}$$

$$\cos \theta = \frac{\text{adj}}{\text{hyp}} \qquad \sec \theta = \frac{\text{hyp}}{\text{adj}}$$

$$\tan \theta = \frac{\text{opp}}{\text{adj}} \qquad \cot \theta = \frac{\text{adj}}{\text{opp}}$$

All of the trigonometric functions have applications, but the sine, cosine, and tangent functions are used most frequently. For the remainder of this section, we will focus on those functions.

When working with trigonometric functions, be sure to draw a diagram and label the adjacent and opposite sides of an angle. For instance, in the definition above, if we had placed θ at angle A, then the triangle would have been labeled as shown at the left. The definitions of the functions remain the same.

$$\sin \theta = \frac{\text{opp}}{\text{hyp}} \qquad \cos \theta = \frac{\text{adj}}{\text{hyp}} \qquad \tan \theta = \frac{\text{opp}}{\text{adj}}$$

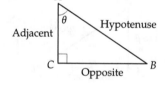

QUESTION   *For the right triangle shown at the left, indicate which side is*

a. adjacent to $\angle A$ *b. opposite θ*
c. adjacent to α   *d. opposite $\angle B$*

EXAMPLE 1 ■ Find the Value of Trigonometric Functions

For the right triangle at the right, find the values of $\sin \theta$, $\cos \theta$, and $\tan \theta$.

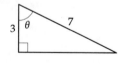

Solution
Use the Pythagorean Theorem to find the length of the side opposite θ.

ANSWER   *a. b b. a c. a d. b*

$$a^2 + b^2 = c^2$$
$$3^2 + b^2 = 7^2 \qquad \bullet \; a = 3, \, c = 7$$
$$9 + b^2 = 49$$
$$b^2 = 40$$
$$b = \sqrt{40} = 2\sqrt{10}$$

Using the definition of the trigonometric functions, we have

$$\sin \theta = \frac{\text{opp}}{\text{hyp}} = \frac{2\sqrt{10}}{7} \qquad \cos \theta = \frac{\text{adj}}{\text{hyp}} = \frac{3}{7} \qquad \tan \theta = \frac{\text{opp}}{\text{adj}} = \frac{2\sqrt{10}}{3}$$

CHECK YOUR PROGRESS 1   For the right triangle at the right, find the values of $\sin \theta$, $\cos \theta$, and $\tan \theta$.

Solution   *See page B-6.*

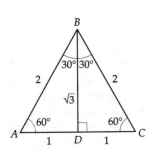

In Example 1, we gave the exact answers. In many cases, approximate values of trigonometric functions are given. The answers to Example 1, rounded to the nearest ten-thousandth, are

$$\sin \theta = \frac{2\sqrt{10}}{7} \approx 0.9035 \quad \cos \theta = \frac{3}{7} \approx 0.4286 \quad \tan \theta = \frac{2\sqrt{10}}{3} \approx 2.1082$$

There are many occasions when we will want to know the value of a trigonometric function for a given angle. Triangle ABC at the left is an equilateral triangle with sides of length 2 units and angle bisector $\overline{BD}$. Because $\overline{BD}$ bisects $\angle ABC$, the measures of $\angle ABD$ and $\angle DBC$ are both 30°. The angle bisector $\overline{BD}$ also bisects $\overline{AC}$. Therefore, $AD = 1$ and $DC = 1$. Using the Pythagorean Theorem, we can find the measure of BD.

$$(DC)^2 + (BD)^2 = (BC)^2$$
$$1^2 + (BD)^2 = 2^2$$
$$1 + (BD)^2 = 4$$
$$(BD)^2 = 3$$
$$BD = \sqrt{3}$$

Using the definitions of the trigonometric functions and triangle BCD, we can find the values of the sine, cosine, and tangent of 30° and 60°.

$$\sin 30° = \frac{\text{opp}}{\text{hyp}} = \frac{1}{2} = 0.5 \qquad\qquad \sin 60° = \frac{\text{opp}}{\text{hyp}} = \frac{\sqrt{3}}{2} \approx 0.8660$$

$$\cos 30° = \frac{\text{adj}}{\text{hyp}} = \frac{\sqrt{3}}{2} \approx 0.8660 \qquad \cos 60° = \frac{\text{adj}}{\text{hyp}} = \frac{1}{2} = 0.5$$

$$\tan 30° = \frac{\text{opp}}{\text{adj}} = \frac{1}{\sqrt{3}} \approx 0.5774 \qquad \tan 60° = \frac{\text{opp}}{\text{adj}} = \sqrt{3} \approx 1.732$$

The properties of an equilateral triangle enabled us to calculate the values of the trigonometric functions for 30° and 60°. Calculating values of the trigonometric functions for most other angles, however, would be quite difficult. Fortunately, many calculators have been programmed to allow us to estimate these values.

CALCULATOR NOTE

Just as distances can be measured in feet, miles, meters, and other units, angles can be measured in various units: degrees, radians, and grads. In this section, we use only degree measurements for angles, so be sure your calculator is in degree mode.

On a TI-83/84, press the MODE key to determine whether the calculator is in degree mode.

```
Normal Sci Eng
Float 0123456789
Radian Degree
Func Par Pol Seq
Connected Dot
Sequential Simul
Real a+bi re^θi
Full Horiz G-T
```

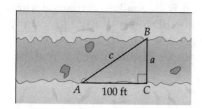

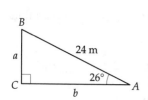

To use a TI-83/84 calculator to find tan 30°, confirm that your calculator is in "degree mode." Press the tan button and key in 30. Then press ENTER.

$$\tan 30° \approx 0.5774$$

Despite the fact that the values of many trigonometric functions are approximate, it is customary to use the equals sign rather than the approximately equals sign when writing these function values. Thus we write $\tan 30° = 0.5774$.

EXAMPLE 2 ■ Use a Calculator to Find the Value of a Trigonometric Function

Use a calculator to find sin 43.8° to the nearest ten-thousandth.

Solution $\sin 43.8° = 0.6921$

CHECK YOUR PROGRESS 2   Use a calculator to find tan 37.1° to the nearest ten-thousandth.

Solution   *See page B-6.*

Using trigonometry, the engineers mentioned at the beginning of this section could determine the distance across the ravine after determining the measure of ∠A. Suppose the engineers measure the angle as 33.8°. Now the engineers would ask, "Which trigonometric function, sine, cosine, or tangent, involves the side opposite an angle and the side adjacent to that angle?" Knowing that the tangent function is the required function, the engineers could write and solve the equation $\tan 33.8° = \dfrac{a}{100}$.

$$\tan 33.8° = \frac{a}{100}$$ • **Multiply each side of the equation by 100.**

$$100(\tan 33.8°) = a$$ • **Use a calculator to find tan 33.8°. Multiply the**
$$66.9 \approx a$$ **result in the display by 100.**

The distance across the ravine is approximately 66.9 feet.

EXAMPLE 3 ■ Find the Length of a Side of a Triangle

For the right triangle shown at the left, find the length of side *a*. Round to the nearest hundredth of a meter.

Solution

We are given the measure of ∠A and the hypotenuse. We want to find the length of side *a*. Side *a* is opposite ∠A. The sine function involves the side opposite an angle and the hypotenuse.

$$\sin A = \frac{\text{opp}}{\text{hyp}}$$
   • **A = 26°, hypotenuse = 24 meters.**
$$\sin 26° = \frac{a}{24}$$
   • **Multiply each side by 24.**
$$24(\sin 26°) = a$$ • **Use a calculator to find sin 26°. Multiply the**
$$10.52 \approx a$$ **result in the display by 24.**

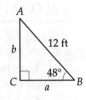

The length of side a is approximately 10.52 meters.

CHECK YOUR PROGRESS 3   For the right triangle shown at the right, find the length of side a. Round to the nearest hundredth of a foot.

Solution   *See page B-6.*

Inverse Trigonometric Functions

Sometimes it is necessary to find one of the acute angles in a right triangle. For instance, suppose it is necessary to find the measure of $\angle A$ in the figure at the left. Because the side adjacent to $\angle A$ is known and the hypotenuse is known, we can write

$$\cos A = \frac{\text{adj}}{\text{hyp}}$$

$$\cos A = \frac{25}{27}$$

The solution of this equation is the angle whose cosine is $\frac{25}{27}$. This angle can be found by using the $\cos^{-1}$ key on a calculator.

$$\cos^{-1}\left(\frac{25}{27}\right) \approx 22.19160657$$

To the nearest tenth, the measure of $\angle A$ is $22.2°$.
The function $\cos^{-1}$ is called the *inverse cosine function*.

> **Definitions of the Inverse Sine, Inverse Cosine, and Inverse Tangent Functions**
>
> For $0° < x < 90°$:
> $y = \sin^{-1}(x)$ can be read "y is the angle whose sine is x."
> $y = \cos^{-1}(x)$ can be read "y is the angle whose cosine is x."
> $y = \tan^{-1}(x)$ can be read "y is the angle whose tangent is x."

Note that $\sin^{-1}(x)$ is used to denote the inverse of the sine function. It is not the reciprocal of $\sin x$ but the notation used for its inverse. The same is true for $\cos^{-1}$ and $\tan^{-1}$.

✔ **TAKE NOTE**

The expression $y = \sin^{-1}(x)$ is sometimes written $y = \arcsin(x)$. The two expressions are equivalent. The expressions $y = \cos^{-1}(x)$ and $y = \arccos(x)$ are equivalent, as are $y = \tan^{-1}(x)$ and $y = \arctan(x)$.

EXAMPLE 4 ■ **Evaluate an Inverse Trigonometric Function**

Use a calculator to find $\sin^{-1}(0.9171)$. Round to the nearest tenth of a degree.

Solution

$\sin^{-1}(0.9171) \approx 66.5°$

• The calculator must be in degree mode. Press the keys for the inverse sine function followed by .9171. Press ENTER .

CALCULATOR NOTE

To find an inverse function on a calculator, usually the INV or 2nd key is pressed prior to pushing the function key. Some calculators have $\sin^{-1}$, $\cos^{-1}$, and $\tan^{-1}$ keys. Consult the instruction manual for your calculator.

✔ **TAKE NOTE**

If

$\sin \theta = 0.7239$,

then

$\theta = \sin^{-1}(0.7239)$.

CHECK YOUR PROGRESS 4   Use a calculator to find $\tan^{-1}(0.3165)$. Round to the nearest tenth of a degree.

Solution   *See page B-6.*

EXAMPLE 5 ■ Find the Measure of an Angle Using the Inverse of a Trigonometric Function

Given $\sin \theta = 0.7239$, find θ. Use a calculator. Round to the nearest tenth of a degree.

Solution

This is equivalent to finding $\sin^{-1}(0.7239)$. The calculator must be in the degree mode.

$$\sin^{-1}(0.7239) \approx 46.4°$$
$$\theta \approx 46.4°$$

CHECK YOUR PROGRESS 5   Given $\tan \theta = 0.5681$, find θ. Use a calculator. Round to the nearest tenth of a degree.

Solution   *See page B-6.*

EXAMPLE 6 ■ Find the Measure of an Angle in a Right Triangle

For the right triangle shown at the left, find the measure of $\angle B$. Round to the nearest tenth of a degree.

Solution

We want to find the measure of $\angle B$, and we are given the lengths of the sides opposite $\angle B$ and adjacent to $\angle B$. The tangent function involves the side opposite an angle and the side adjacent to that angle.

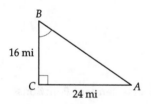

$$\tan B = \frac{\text{opposite}}{\text{adjacent}}$$
$$\tan B = \frac{24}{16}$$
$$B = \tan^{-1}\left(\frac{24}{16}\right)$$
$$B \approx 56.3° \qquad \text{• Use the } \tan^{-1} \text{ key on a calculator.}$$

The measure of $\angle B$ is approximately $56.3°$.

CHECK YOUR PROGRESS 6   For the right triangle shown at the left, find the measure of $\angle A$. Round to the nearest tenth of a degree.

Solution See page B-6.

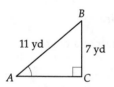

Angles of Elevation and Depression

The use of trigonometry is necessary in a variety of situations. One application, called **line-of-sight problems,** concerns an observer looking at an object.

Angles of elevation and depression are measured with respect to a horizontal line. If the object being sighted is above the observer, the acute angle formed by the line of sight and the horizontal line is an **angle of elevation.** If the object being sighted is below the observer, the acute angle formed by the line of sight and the horizontal line is an **angle of depression.**

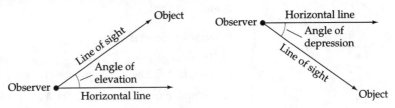

EXAMPLE 7 ■ Solve an Angle of Elevation Problem

The angle of elevation of the top of a flagpole 62 feet away is 34°. Find the height of the flagpole. Round to the nearest tenth of a foot.

Solution
Draw a diagram. To find the height, h, write a trigonometric function that relates the given information and the unknown side of the triangle.

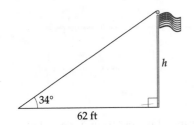

$$\tan 34° = \frac{h}{62}$$
$$62(\tan 34°) = h \qquad \bullet \textbf{ Multiply each side by 62.}$$
$$41.8 \approx h \qquad \bullet \textbf{ Use a calculator to find } \tan 34°. \textbf{ Multiply}$$
$$\textbf{the result in the display by 62.}$$

The height of the flagpole is approximately 41.8 feet.

CHECK YOUR PROGRESS 7   The angle of depression from the top of a lighthouse that is 20 meters high to a boat on the water is 25°. How far is the boat from the base of the lighthouse? Round to the nearest tenth of a meter.

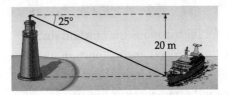

Solution *See page B-6.*

Excursion

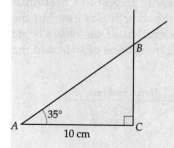

Approximating the Value of Trigonometric Functions

The value of a trigonometric function can be approximated by drawing a triangle with a given angle. To illustrate, we will choose an angle of 35°.

To find the tangent of 35° using the definitions given in this section, we can carefully construct a right triangle containing an angle of 35°. Because any two right triangles containing an angle of 35° are similar, *the value for* tan 35° *is the same no matter what triangle we draw.*

Excursion Exercises

1. Draw a horizontal line segment 10 cm long with left endpoint *A* and right endpoint *C*. See the diagram at the left.

2. Using a protractor, construct at *A* a 35° angle.

3. Draw at *C* a vertical line that intersects the terminal side of angle *A* at *B*. Your drawing should be similar to the one at the left.

4. Measure line segment *BC*.

5. What is the approximate value of tan 35°?

6. Using your value for *BC* and the Pythagorean Theorem, estimate *AB*.

7. Estimate sin 35° and cos 35°.

8. What are the values of sin 35°, cos 35°, and tan 35° as produced by a calculator? Round to the nearest ten-thousandth.

Exercise Set 8.5

1. Use the right triangle at the right and sides *a*, *b*, and *c* to do the following:

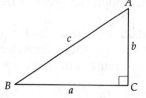

   a. Name the ratio for the trigonometric function sin *A*.
   b. Name the ratio for the trigonometric function sin *B*.
   c. Name the ratio for the trigonometric function cos *A*.
   d. Name the ratio for the trigonometric function cos *B*.
   e. Name the ratio for the trigonometric function tan *A*.
   f. Name the ratio for the trigonometric function tan *B*.

2. Explain the meaning of the notation $y = \sin^{-1}(x)$, $y = \cos^{-1}(x)$, and $y = \tan^{-1}(x)$.

In Exercises 3–10, find the values of sin θ, cos θ, and tan θ for the given right triangle. Give the exact values.

3.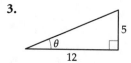

4.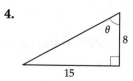

5.

6.

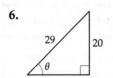

7.

8.

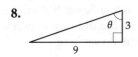

9.

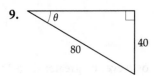

10.

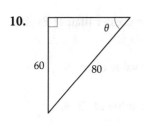

In Exercises 11–26, use a calculator to estimate the value of each of the following. Round to the nearest ten-thousandth.

11. cos 47°	**12.** sin 62°	**13.** tan 55°
14. cos 11°	**15.** sin 85.6°	**16.** cos 21.9°
17. tan 63.4°	**18.** sin 7.8°	**19.** tan 41.6°
20. cos 73°	**21.** sin 57.7°	**22.** tan 39.2°
23. sin 58.3°	**24.** tan 35.1°	**25.** cos 46.9°
26. sin 50°		

In Exercises 27–42, use a calculator. Round to the nearest tenth.

27. Given sin θ = 0.6239, find θ.

28. Given cos β = 0.9516, find β.

29. Find $\cos^{-1}(0.7536)$.

30. Find $\sin^{-1}(0.4478)$.

31. Given tan α = 0.3899, find α.

32. Given sin β = 0.7349, find β.

33. Find $\tan^{-1}(0.7815)$.

34. Find $\cos^{-1}(0.6032)$.

35. Given cos θ = 0.3007, find θ.

36. Given tan α = 1.588, find α.

37. Find $\sin^{-1}(0.0105)$.

38. Find $\tan^{-1}(0.2438)$.

39. Given sin β = 0.9143, find β.

40. Given cos θ = 0.4756, find θ.

41. Find $\cos^{-1}(0.8704)$.

42. Find $\sin^{-1}(0.2198)$.

For Exercises 43–56, draw a picture and label it. Set up an equation and solve it. Show all your work. Round an angle to the nearest tenth of a degree. Round the length of a side to the nearest hundredth of a unit.

43. Ballooning A balloon, tethered by a cable 997 feet long, was blown by a wind so that the cable made an angle of 57.6° with the ground. Find the height of the balloon off the ground.

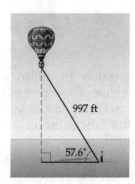

44. Roadways A road is inclined at an angle of 9.8° with the horizontal. Find the distance that one must drive on this road in order to be elevated 14.8 feet above the horizontal.

45. Home Maintenance A ladder 30.8 feet long leans against a building. If the foot of the ladder is 7.25 feet from the base of the building, find the angle the top of the ladder makes with the building.

46. Aviation A plane takes off from a field and rises at an angle of 11.4° with the horizontal. Find the height of the plane after it has traveled a distance of 1250 feet.

47. Guy Wires A guy wire whose grounded end is 16 feet from the telephone pole it supports makes an angle of 56.7° with the ground. How long is the wire?

16 ft

48. Angle of Depression A lighthouse built at sea level is 169 feet tall. From its top, the angle of depression to a boat below measures 25.1°. Find the distance from the boat to the foot of the lighthouse.

49. Angle of Elevation At a point 39.3 feet from the base of a tree, the angle of elevation of its top measures 53.4°. Find the height of the tree.

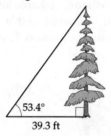

53.4°

39.3 ft

50. Angle of Depression An artillery spotter in a plane that is at an altitude of 978 feet measures the angle of depression of an enemy tank as 28.5°. How far is the enemy tank from the point on the ground directly below the spotter?

51. Home Maintenance A 15-foot ladder leans against a house. The ladder makes an angle of 65° with the ground. How far up the side of the house does the ladder reach?

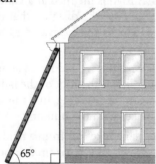

65°

52. Angle of Elevation Find the angle of elevation of the sun when a tree 40.5 feet high casts a shadow 28.3 feet long.

53. Guy Wires A television transmitter tower is 600 feet high. If the angle between the guy wire (attached at the top) and the tower is 55.4°, how long is the guy wire?

54. Ramps A ramp used to load a racing car onto a flatbed carrier is 5.25 meters long, and its upper end is 1.74 meters above the lower end. Find the angle between the ramp and the road.

55. Angle of Elevation The angle of elevation of the sun is 51.3° at a time when a tree casts a shadow 23.7 yards long. Find the height of the tree.

56. Angle of Depression From the top of a building 312 feet tall, the angle of depression to a flower bed on the ground below is 12.0°. What is the distance between the base of the building and the flower bed?

Extensions

CRITICAL THINKING

57. Can the value of sin θ or cos θ ever be greater than 1? Explain your answer.

58. Can the value of tan θ ever be greater than 1? Explain your answer.

59. Let sin $\theta = \dfrac{2}{3}$. Find the exact value of cos θ.

60. Let tan $\theta = \dfrac{5}{4}$. Find the exact value of sin θ.

61. Let cos $\theta = \dfrac{3}{4}$. Find the exact value of tan θ.

62. Let sin $\theta = \dfrac{\sqrt{5}}{4}$. Find the exact value of tan θ.

63. Let sin $\theta = a$, $a > 0$. Find cos θ.

64. Let tan $\theta = a$, $a > 0$. Find sin θ.

EXPLORATIONS

As we noted in this section, angles can also be measured in *radians*. To define a radian, first consider a circle of radius *r* and two radii $\overline{OA}$ and $\overline{OB}$. The angle θ formed by the two radii is a **central angle**. The portion of the circle between *A* and *B* is an **arc** of the circle and is written $\overset{\frown}{AB}$. We say that $\overset{\frown}{AB}$ *subtends* the angle θ. The length of the arc is *s*. (See Figure 1 below.)

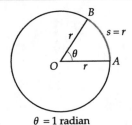

Figure 1

Definition of Radian

One **radian** is the measure of the central angle subtended by an arc of length *r*. The measure of θ in Figure 2 is 1 radian.

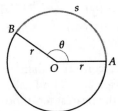

$\theta = 1$ radian

Figure 2

To find the radian measure of an angle subtended by an arc of length *s*, use the following formula.

Radian Measure

Given an arc of length *s* on a circle of radius *r*, the measure of the central angle subtended by the arc is $\theta = \dfrac{s}{r}$ radians.

For example, to find the measure in radians of the central angle subtended by an arc of 9 in. in a circle of radius 12 in., divide the length of the arc (*s* = 9 in.) by the length of the radius (*r* = 12 in.). See Figure 3.

$$\theta = \frac{9 \text{ in.}}{12 \text{ in.}} \text{ radian}$$
$$= \frac{3}{4} \text{ radian}$$

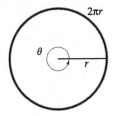

Figure 3

65. Find the measure in radians of the central angle subtended by an arc of 12 cm in a circle of radius 3 cm.

66. Find the measure in radians of the central angle subtended by an arc of 4 cm in a circle of radius 8 cm.

67. Find the measure in radians of the central angle subtended by an arc of 6 in. in a circle of radius 9 in.

68. Find the measure in radians of the central angle subtended by an arc of 12 ft in a circle of radius 10 ft.

Recall that the circumference of a circle is given by $C = 2\pi r$. Therefore, the radian measure of the central angle subtended by the circumference is $\theta = \dfrac{2\pi r}{r} = 2\pi$.

In degree measure, the central angle has a measure of 360°. Thus we have 2π radians = 360°. Dividing each side of the equation by 2 gives π radians = 180°. From the last equation, we can establish the conversion factors $\dfrac{\pi \text{ radians}}{180°}$ and $\dfrac{180°}{\pi \text{ radians}}$. These conversion factors are used to convert between radians and degrees.

Conversion between Radians and Degrees

- To convert from degrees to radians, multiply by $\dfrac{\pi \text{ radians}}{180°}$.
- To convert from radians to degrees, multiply by $\dfrac{180°}{\pi \text{ radians}}$.

For instance, to convert 30° to radians, multiply 30° by $\dfrac{\pi \text{ radians}}{180°}$.

$$30° = 30°\left(\frac{\pi \text{ radians}}{180°}\right) \quad \bullet \text{ Exact answer}$$

$$= \frac{\pi}{6} \text{ radian} \quad \bullet \text{ Approximate answer}$$

$$\approx 0.5236 \text{ radian}$$

To convert 2 radians to degrees, multiply 2 by $\dfrac{180°}{\pi \text{ radians}}$.

$$2 \text{ radians} = 2\left(\frac{180°}{\pi \text{ radians}}\right) \quad \bullet \text{ Exact answer}$$

$$= \left(\frac{360}{\pi}\right)° \quad \bullet \text{ Approximate answer}$$

$$\approx 114.5916°$$

69. What is the measure in degrees of 1 radian?

70. Is the measure of 1 radian larger or smaller than the measure of 1°?

In Exercises 71–76, convert degree measure to radian measure. Find an exact answer and an answer rounded to the nearest ten-thousandth.

71. 45°   **72.** 180°   **73.** 315°

74. 90°   **75.** 210°   **76.** 18°

In Exercises 77–82, convert radian measure to degree measure. For Exercises 80–82, find an exact answer and an answer rounded to the nearest ten-thousandth.

77. $\dfrac{\pi}{3}$ radians   **78.** $\dfrac{11\pi}{6}$ radians

79. $\dfrac{4\pi}{3}$ radians   **80.** 1.2 radians

81. 3 radians   **82.** 2.4 radians

CHAPTER 8   **Review Exercises**

25. Find the unknown side of the triangle. Round to the nearest hundredth of a foot.

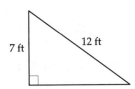

In Exercises 26 and 27, find the values of sin θ, cos θ, and tan θ for the given right triangle.

26.

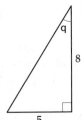

27.

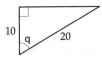

In Exercises 28–31, use a calculator. Round to the nearest tenth of a degree.

28. Find $\cos^{-1}(0.9013)$.

29. Find $\sin^{-1}(0.4871)$.

30. Given $\tan \beta = 1.364$, find β.

31. Given $\sin \theta = 0.0325$, find θ.

32. **Surveying** Find the distance across the marsh in the following figure. Round to the nearest tenth of a foot.

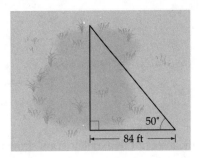

CHAPTER 8   **Test**

1. Find the volume of a cylinder with a height of 6 m and a radius of 3 m. Round to the nearest hundredth of a cubic meter.

2. Find the perimeter of a rectangle that has a length of 2 m and a width of 1.4 m.

3. Find the complement of a 32° angle.

4. Find the area of a circle that has a diameter of 2 m. Round to the nearest hundredth of a square meter.

5. In the figure below, lines ℓ_1 and ℓ_2 are parallel. Angle x measures 30°. Find the measure of angle y.

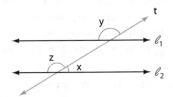

6. In the figure below, lines ℓ_1 and ℓ_2 are parallel. Angle x measures 45°. Find the measures of angles a and b.

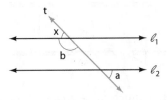

7. Find the area of a square that measures 2.25 ft on each side.

8. Find the volume of the figure. Give the exact value.

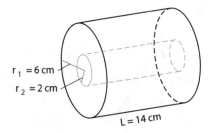

9. Triangles *ABC* and *DEF* are similar. Find side *BC*.

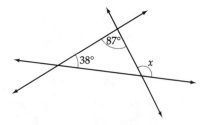

10. A right triangle has a 40° angle. Find the measures of the other two angles.

11. Find the measure of ∠*x*.

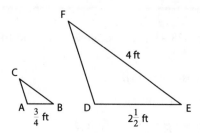

12. Find the area of the parallelogram shown below.

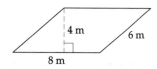

13. Surveying Find the width of the canal shown in the figure below.

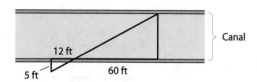

14. Pizza How much more area is in a pizza with radius 10 in. than in a pizza with radius 8 in.? Round to the nearest hundredth of a square inch.

15. Determine whether the two triangles are congruent. If they are congruent, state by what theorem they are congruent.

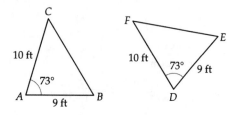

16. For the right triangle shown below, determine the length of side *BC*. Round to the nearest hundredth of a centimeter.

17. Find the values of sin θ, cos θ, and tan θ for the given right triangle.

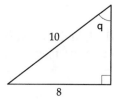

18. Angle of Elevation From a point 27 feet from the base of a Roman aqueduct, the angle of elevation to the top of the aqueduct is 78°. Find the height of the aqueduct. Round to the nearest foot.

19. Trees Find the cross-sectional area of a redwood tree that is 11 ft 6 in. in diameter. Round to the nearest hundredth of a square foot.

20. Toolbox A toolbox is 14 in. long, 9 in. wide, and 8 in. high. The sides and bottom of the toolbox are $\frac{1}{2}$ in. thick. The toolbox is open at the top. Find the volume of the interior of the toolbox in cubic inches.

21. a. State the Euclidean parallel postulate.

   b. State the parallel postulate used in Riemannian geometry.

22. What is the maximum number of right angles a triangle can have in

   a. Lobachevskian geometry?

   b. Riemannian geometry?

23. What is a great circle?

24. Find the area of a spherical triangle with a radius of 12 ft and angles of 90°, 100°, and 90°. Give the exact area and the area rounded to the nearest tenth of a square foot.

25. City Geometry Find the Euclidean distance and the city distance between the points $P(-4, 2)$ and $Q(5, 1)$. Assume that the distances are measured in blocks. Round approximate results to the nearest tenth of a block.

26. City Geometry How many points are on the city circle with center $(0, 0)$ and radius $r = 4$ blocks?

In Exercises 27 and 28, draw stage 2 of the fractal with the given initiator and generator.

27.

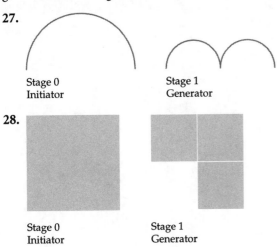

Stage 0
Initiator

Stage 1
Generator

28.

Stage 0
Initiator

Stage 1
Generator

29. Compute the replacement ratio, scale ratio, and similarity dimension of the fractal defined by the initiator and generator in Exercise 27.

30. Compute the replacement ratio, scale ratio, and similarity dimension of the fractal defined by the initiator and generator in Exercise 28.

8 U.S. Customary Units of Measurement

In this chapter, you will be studying the U.S. Customary Units of length, weight, and capacity. As consumers, we are accustomed to these measurements. We purchase fabric by the yard, lumber by the foot, and tomatoes by the pound. We also buy perfume by the ounce, juice by the fluid ounce, and gasoline by the gallon. It is important to know how to convert between units and to perform operations that include different units.

OBJECTIVES

Section 8.1
A To convert measurements of length in the U.S. Customary System
B To perform arithmetic operations with measurements of length
C To solve application problems

Section 8.2
A To convert measurements of weight in the U.S. Customary System
B To perform arithmetic operations with measurements of weight
C To solve application problems

Section 8.3
A To convert measurements of capacity in the U.S. Customary System
B To perform arithmetic operations with measurements of capacity
C To solve application problems

Section 8.4
A To convert units of time

Section 8.5
A To use units of energy in the U.S. Customary System
B To use units of power in the U.S. Customary System

Need help? For online student resources, such as section quizzes, visit this textbook's website at **math.college.hmco.com/students.**

For Exercises 1 to 8, add, subtract, multiply, or divide.

1.   485
    + 217

2.   145
    − 87

3. $36 \times \dfrac{1}{9}$

4. $\dfrac{5}{3} \times 6$

5. $400 \times \dfrac{1}{8} \times \dfrac{1}{2}$

6. $5\dfrac{3}{4} \times 8$

7. $3\overline{)714}$

8. $12\overline{)18}$

GO FIGURE • • •

Mandy walks to work at a constant rate. One-third of the way to work, she passes a bank. Three-fourths of the way to work, she passes a book store. At the bank her watch reads 7:52 A.M., and at the book store it reads 8:02 A.M. At what time is Mandy one-half of the way to work?

8.1 Length

Objective A

To convert measurements of length in the U.S. Customary System

A **measurement** includes a number and a unit.

$$
\begin{array}{cc}
3 & \text{feet} \\
7 & \text{miles} \\
12 & \text{yards} \\
\hline
\text{Number} & \text{Unit}
\end{array}
$$

Standard units of measurement have been established to simplify trade and commerce.

The unit of **length,** or distance, that is called the yard was originally defined as the length of a specified bronze bar located in London.

The standard U.S. Customary System units of length are **inch, foot, yard,** and **mile.**

Equivalences Between Units of Length in the U.S. Customary System

12 inches (in.) = 1 foot (ft)
3 ft = 1 yard (yd)
36 in. = 1 yard (yd)
5280 ft = 1 mile (mi)

These equivalences can be used to form conversion rates; a **conversion rate** is a relationship used to change one unit of measurement to another. For example, because 3 ft = 1 yd, the conversion rates $\frac{3\text{ ft}}{1\text{ yd}}$ and $\frac{1\text{ yd}}{3\text{ ft}}$ are both equivalent to 1.

HOW TO Convert 27 ft to yards.

$$27\text{ ft} = 27\text{ ft} \times \boxed{\dfrac{1\text{ yd}}{3\text{ ft}}}$$

$$= 27\text{ ft} \times \dfrac{1\text{ yd}}{3\text{ ft}}$$

$$= \dfrac{27\text{ yd}}{3}$$

$$= 9\text{ yd}$$

HOW TO Convert 5 yd to feet.

$$5\text{ yd} = 5\text{ yd} \times \boxed{\dfrac{3\text{ ft}}{1\text{ yd}}}$$

$$= 5\text{ yd} \times \dfrac{3\text{ ft}}{1\text{ yd}}$$

$$= \dfrac{15\text{ ft}}{1}$$

$$= 15\text{ ft}$$

Note that in the conversion rate chosen, the unit in the numerator is the same as the unit desired in the answer. The unit in the denominator is the same as the unit in the given measurement.

Example 1 Convert 40 in. to feet.

Solution

$$40 \text{ in.} = 40 \text{ in.} \times \frac{1 \text{ ft}}{12 \text{ in.}}$$

$$= \frac{40 \text{ ft}}{12} = 3\frac{1}{3} \text{ ft}$$

You Try It 1 Convert 14 ft to yards.

Your solution

Example 2 Convert $3\frac{1}{4}$ yd to feet.

Solution

$$3\frac{1}{4} \text{ yd} = \frac{13}{4} \text{ yd} = \frac{13}{4} \text{ yd} \times \frac{3 \text{ ft}}{1 \text{ yd}}$$

$$= \frac{39 \text{ ft}}{4} = 9\frac{3}{4} \text{ ft}$$

You Try It 2 Convert 9240 ft to miles.

Your solution

Objective B **To perform arithmetic operations with measurements of length**

When performing arithmetic operations with measurements of length, write the answer in simplest form. For example, 1 ft 14 in. should be written as 2 ft 2 in.

HOW TO Convert: 50 in. = _____ ft _____ in.

$$\begin{array}{r} 4 \text{ ft } 2 \text{ in.} \\ 12\overline{)-50} \\ \underline{-48} \\ 2 \end{array}$$

• Because 12 in. = 1 ft, divide 50 in. by 12. The whole-number part of the quotient is the number of feet. The remainder is the number of inches.

50 in. = 4 ft 2 in.

Example 3 Convert: 17 in. = _____ ft _____ in.

Solution

$$\begin{array}{r} 1 \text{ ft } 5 \text{ in.} \\ 12\overline{)-17} \\ \underline{-12} \\ 5 \end{array}$$

• 12 in. = 1 ft

17 in. = 1 ft 5 in.

You Try It 3 Convert: 42 in. = _____ ft _____ in.

Your solution

Example 4 Convert: 31 ft = _____ yd _____ ft

Solution

$$\begin{array}{r} 10 \text{ yd } 1 \text{ ft} \\ 3\overline{)-31} \\ \underline{-30} \\ 1 \end{array}$$

• 3 ft = 1 yd

31 ft = 10 yd 1 ft

You Try It 4 Convert: 14 ft = _____ yd _____ ft

Your solution

Example 5   Find the sum of 4 ft 4 in. and 1 ft 11 in.

Solution

$$\begin{array}{r} 4 \text{ ft } 14 \text{ in.} \\ + 1 \text{ ft } 11 \text{ in.} \\ \hline 5 \text{ ft } 15 \text{ in.} \end{array}$$ • **15 in. = 1 ft 3 in.**

5 ft 15 in. = 6 ft 3 in.

You Try It 5   Find the sum of 3 ft 5 in. and 4 ft 9 in.

Your solution

Example 6   Subtract: 9 ft 6 in. − 3 ft 8 in.

Solution

$$\begin{array}{r} {\scriptstyle 8 \text{ ft}} \quad {\scriptstyle 18 \text{ in.}} \\ \cancel{9 \text{ ft } 16 \text{ in.}} \\ - 3 \text{ ft } 18 \text{ in.} \\ \hline 5 \text{ ft } 10 \text{ in.} \end{array}$$ • **Borrow 1 ft (12 in.) from 9 ft and add to 6 in.**

You Try It 6   Subtract: 4 ft 2 in. − 1 ft 8 in.

Your solution

Example 7   Multiply: 3 yd 2 ft × 4

Solution

$$\begin{array}{r} 3 \text{ yd } 2 \text{ ft} \\ \times \qquad 4 \\ \hline 12 \text{ yd } 8 \text{ ft} \end{array}$$ • **8 ft = 2 yd 2 ft**

12 yd 8 ft = 14 yd 2 ft

You Try It 7   Multiply: 4 yd 1 ft × 8

Your solution

Example 8   Find the quotient of 4 ft 3 in. and 3.

Solution

$$\begin{array}{r} 1 \text{ ft} \qquad 5 \text{ in.} \\ 3 \overline{) \, 4 \text{ ft} \qquad 3 \text{ in.}} \\ - \, 3 \text{ ft} \qquad \\ \hline 1 \text{ ft} = 12 \text{ in.} \\ 15 \text{ in.} \\ -15 \text{ in.} \\ \hline 0 \end{array}$$

You Try It 8   Find the quotient of 7 yd 1 ft and 2.

Your solution

Example 9   Multiply: $2\frac{3}{4}$ ft × 3

Solution $2\frac{3}{4}$ ft × 3 = $\frac{11}{4}$ ft × 3

$\qquad\qquad = \frac{33}{4}$ ft

$\qquad\qquad = 8\frac{1}{4}$ ft

You Try It 9   Subtract: $6\frac{1}{4}$ ft − $3\frac{2}{3}$ ft

Your solution

Objective C To solve application problems

Example 10

A concrete block is 9 in. high. How many rows of blocks are required for a retaining wall that is 6′ ft high?

Strategy

To find the number of rows of blocks, convert 9 in. to feet. Then divide the height of the wall (6 ft) by the height of each block.

Solution

$$9 \text{ in.} = \frac{9 \text{ in.}}{1} \cdot \frac{1 \text{ ft}}{12 \text{ in.}} = \frac{9 \text{ ft}}{12} = 0.75 \text{ ft}$$

$$\frac{6 \text{ ft}}{0.75 \text{ ft}} = 8$$

The wall will have 8 rows of blocks.

You Try It 10

The floor of a storage room is being tiled. Eight tiles, each a 9-inch square, fit across the width of the floor. Find the width, in feet, of the storage room.

Your strategy

Your solution

Example 11

A plumber used 3 ft 9 in., 2 ft 6 in., and 11 in. of copper tubing to install a sink. Find the total length of copper tubing used.

Strategy

To find the total length of copper tubing used, add the three lengths of copper tubing (3 ft 9 in., 2 ft 6 in., and 11 in.).

Solution

```
  3 ft 19 in.
  2 ft 16 in.
+ 5 ft 11 in.
  5 ft 26 in.    • 26 in. = 2 ft 2 in.
```

5 ft 26 in. = 7 ft 2 in.

The plumber used 7 ft 2 in. of copper tubing.

You Try It 11

A board 9 ft 8 in. is cut into four pieces of equal length. How long is each piece?

Your strategy

Your solution

8.1 Exercises

Objective A To convert measurements of length in the U.S. Customary System

For Exercises 1 to 15, convert.

1. 6 ft = _____ in.

2. 9 ft = _____ in.

3. 30 in. = _____ ft

4. 64 in. = _____ ft

5. 13 yd = _____ ft

6. $4\frac{1}{2}$ yd = _____ ft

7. 16 ft = _____ yd

8. $4\frac{1}{2}$ ft = _____ yd

9. $2\frac{1}{3}$ yd = _____ in.

10. 5 yd = _____ in.

11. 120 in. = _____ yd

12. 66 in. = _____ yd

13. 2 mi = _____ ft

14. $1\frac{1}{2}$ mi = _____ ft

15. $7\frac{1}{2}$ in. = _____ ft

Objective B To perform arithmetic operations with measurements of length

For Exercises 16 to 30, perform the arithmetic operation.

16. 100 in. =
___ ft ___ in.

17. 6400 ft =
___ mi ___ ft

18. 15 in. =
___ ft ___ in.

19. 6 ft 7 in.
+ 3 ft 4 in.

20. 9 ft 11 in.
+ 3 ft 16 in.

21. 5 ft 3 in.
− 2 ft 6 in.

22. 9 yd 1 ft
− 3 yd 2 ft

23. 2 ft 5 in.
× 2 ft 6 in.

24. $3\frac{2}{3}$ ft × 4

25. 2)5 ft 4 in.

26. $12\frac{1}{2}$ in. ÷ 3

27. $4\frac{2}{3}$ ft + $6\frac{1}{2}$ ft

28. 3 yd 2 ft
+ 6 yd 2 ft

29. 1 mi 4200 ft
+ 2 mi 3600 ft

30. 5 yd 1 ft
− 2 yd 2 ft

Objective C   **To solve application problems**

31. **Interior Decorating**   A kitchen counter is to be covered with tile that is 4 in. square. How many tiles can be placed along one row of a counter top that is 4 ft 8 in. long?

32. **Interior Decorating**   Thirty-two yards of material were used for making pleated draperies. How many feet of material were used?

33. **Measurement**   Find the missing dimension.

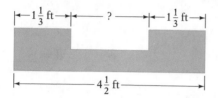

34. **Measurement**   Find the total length of the shaft.

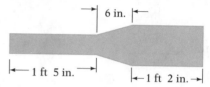

35. **Measurement**   What length of material is needed to drill two holes 3 in. in diameter and leave $\frac{1}{2}$ in. between the holes and on either side as shown in the diagram?

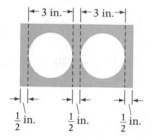

36. **Measurement**   Find the missing dimension in the figure.

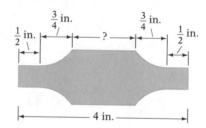

37. **Carpentry**   A board $6\frac{2}{3}$ ft long is cut into four equal pieces. How long is each piece?

38. **Carpentry**   How long must a board be if four pieces, each 3 ft 4 in. long, are to be cut from it?

39. **Interior Decorating**   A picture is 1 ft 9 in. high and 1 ft 6 in. wide. Find the length of framing needed to frame the picture.

40. **Interior Decorating**   You bought 32 ft of baseboard to install in the kitchen of your house. How many inches of baseboard did you purchase?

41. **Masonry**   Forty-five bricks, each 9 in. long, are laid end to end to make the base for a wall. Find the length of the wall in feet.

42. **Construction**   A roof is constructed with nine rafters, each 8 ft 4 in. long. Find the total number of feet of material needed to build the rafters.

APPLYING THE CONCEPTS

43. **Measurement**   There are approximately 200,000,000 adults living in the United States. Assume that the average adult is 19 in. wide from shoulder to shoulder. If all the adults in the United States are standing shoulder to shoulder, could they reach around Earth at the equator, a distance of approximately 25,000 mi?

44. How good are you at estimating lengths or distances? Estimate the length of a pencil, the width of your room, the length of a block, and the distance to the grocery store. Then measure these lengths and compare the results with your estimates.

8.2 Weight

Objective A

To convert measurements of weight in the U.S. Customary System

Point of Interest

The Romans used two different systems of weights. In both systems, the smallest unit was the *uncia*, abbreviated to "oz," from which the term *ounce* is derived. In one system, there were 16 ounces to 1 pound. In the second system, a pound, which was called the libra, equaled 12 unciae. The abbreviation "lb" for pound comes from the word *libra*.

The avoirdupois system of measurement and the troy system of measurement have their heritage in the two Roman systems.

Weight is a measure of how strongly Earth is pulling on an object. The unit of weight called the pound is defined as the weight of a standard solid kept at the Bureau of Standards in Washington, D.C. The U.S. Customary System units of weight are **ounce, pound,** and **ton.**

> **Equivalences Between Units of Weight in the U.S. Customary System**
>
> 16 ounces (oz) = 1 pound (lb)
>
> 2000 lb = 1 ton

These equivalences can be used to form conversion rates to change one unit of measurement to another. For example, because 16 oz = 1 lb, the conversion rates $\frac{16 \text{ oz}}{1 \text{ lb}}$ and $\frac{1 \text{ lb}}{16 \text{ oz}}$ are both equivalent to 1.

HOW TO Convert 62 oz to pounds.

$$62 \text{ oz} = 62 \text{ oz} \times \boxed{\frac{1 \text{ lb}}{16 \text{ oz}}}$$

$$= \frac{62 \text{ oz}}{1} \times \frac{1 \text{ lb}}{16 \text{ oz}}$$

$$= \frac{62 \text{ lb}}{16}$$

$$= 3\frac{7}{8} \text{ lb}$$

- **The conversion rate must contain lb (the unit desired in the answer) in the numerator and must contain oz (the original unit) in the denominator.**

Example 1 Convert $3\frac{1}{2}$ tons to pounds.

Solution

$$3\frac{1}{2} \text{ tons} = \frac{7}{2} \text{ tons} \times \frac{2000 \text{ lb}}{1 \text{ ton}}$$

$$= \frac{14{,}000 \text{ lb}}{2} = 7000 \text{ lb}$$

You Try It 1 Convert 3 lb to ounces.

Your solution

Example 2 Convert 42 oz to pounds.

Solution

$$42 \text{ oz} = 42 \text{ oz} \times \frac{1 \text{ lb}}{16 \text{ oz}}$$

$$= \frac{42 \text{ lb}}{16} = 2\frac{5}{8} \text{ lb}$$

You Try It 2 Convert 4200 lb to tons.

Your solution

Objective B   **To perform arithmetic operations with measurements of weight**

When performing arithmetic operations with measurements of weight, write the answer in simplest form. For example, 1 lb 22 oz should be written 2 lb 6 oz.

Example 3   Find the difference between 14 lb 5 oz and 8 lb 14 oz.

Solution

$$
\begin{array}{r}
\overset{13\ lb}{\cancel{14\ lb}}\ \overset{21\ oz}{\cancel{15\ oz}} \\
-\ 18\ lb\ 14\ oz \\
\hline
5\ lb\ 17\ oz
\end{array}
$$

• Borrow 1 lb (16 oz) from 14 lb and add it to 5 oz.

You Try It 3   Find the difference between 7 lb 1 oz and 3 lb 4 oz.

Your solution

Example 4   Divide: 7 lb 14 oz ÷ 3

Solution

$$
\begin{array}{r}
2\ lb = 10\ oz \\
3\overline{)\ 7\ lb = 14\ oz} \\
-6\ lb = 16\ oz \\
\hline
1\ lb = 16\ oz \\
30\ oz \\
-30\ oz \\
\hline
0\ oz
\end{array}
$$

You Try It 4   Multiply: 3 lb 6 oz × 4

Your solution

Objective C   **To solve application problems**

Example 5

Sirina Jasper purchased 4 lb 8 oz of oat bran and 2 lb 11 oz of wheat bran. She plans to blend the two brans and then repackage the mixture in 3-ounce packages for a diet supplement. How many 3-ounce packages can she make?

Strategy

To find the number of 3-ounce packages:

• Add the amount of oat bran (4 lb 8 oz) to the amount of wheat bran (2 lb 11 oz).
• Convert the sum to ounces.
• Divide the total ounces by the weight of each package (3 oz).

Solution

$$
\begin{array}{r}
4\ lb\ 18\ oz \\
+\ 2\ lb\ 11\ oz \\
\hline
6\ lb\ 19\ oz = 7\ lb\ 3\ oz = 115\ oz
\end{array}
$$

$$\frac{115\ oz}{3\ oz} \approx 38.3$$

She can make 38 packages.

You Try It 5

Find the weight in pounds of 12 bars of soap. Each bar weighs 7 oz.

Your strategy

Your solution

8.2 Exercises

Objective A   **To convert measurements of weight in the U.S. Customary System**

For Exercises 1 to 18, convert.

1. 64 oz = _____ lb

2. 36 oz = _____ lb

3. 8 lb = _____ oz

4. 7 lb = _____ oz

5. 3200 lb = _____ tons

6. 9000 lb = _____ tons

7. 6 tons = _____ lb

8. $1\frac{1}{4}$ tons = _____ lb

9. 66 oz = _____ lb

10. 90 oz = _____ lb

11. $1\frac{1}{2}$ lb = _____ oz

12. $2\frac{5}{8}$ lb = _____ oz

13. $1\frac{3}{10}$ tons = _____ lb

14. $\frac{4}{5}$ ton = _____ lb

15. 500 lb = _____ ton

16. 5000 lb = _____ tons

17. 180 oz = _____ lb

18. 12 oz = _____ lb

Objective B   **To perform arithmetic operations with measurements of weight**

For Exercises 19 to 33, perform the arithmetic operation.

19. 9000 lb = _____ tons _____ lb

20. 85 oz = _____ lb _____ oz

21. 40 oz = _____ lb _____ oz

22. 4 lb 17 oz
     + 3 lb 12 oz

23. 1 ton 1800 lb
     + 3 tons 1600 lb

24. 7 lb 5 oz
     − 3 lb 8 oz

25. 3 tons 500 lb
     − 1 tons 800 lb

26. 3 lb 6 oz
     × 3 lb 4 oz

27. $5\frac{1}{2}$ lb × 6

28. 2)$\overline{3 \text{ lb } 8 \text{ oz}}$

29. $4\frac{2}{3}$ lb × 3

30. 7 lb 7 oz
     + 6 lb 9 oz

31. $6\frac{1}{2}$ oz
     + $2\frac{1}{2}$ oz

32. $6\frac{3}{8}$ lb
     − $2\frac{5}{6}$ lb

33. 5 lb 12 oz ÷ 4

Objective C **To solve application problems**

34. Iron Works A machinist has 25 iron rods to mill. Each rod weighs 20 oz. Find the total weight of the rods in pounds.

35. Masonry A fireplace brick weighs $2\frac{1}{2}$ lb. What is the weight of a load of 800 bricks?

36. Weights A college bookstore received 1200 textbooks, each weighing 9 oz. Find the total weight of the 1200 textbooks in pounds.

37. Weights A 4- × 4-inch tile weighs 7 oz. Find the weight, in pounds, of a package of 144 tiles.

38. Ranching A farmer ordered 20 tons of feed for 100 cattle. After 15 days, the farmer has 5 tons of feed left. On average, how many pounds of food has each cow eaten per day?

39. Weights A case of soft drinks contains 24 cans, each weighing 6 oz. Find the weight, in pounds, of the case of soft drinks.

40. Child Development A baby weighed 7 lb 8 oz at birth. At 6 months of age, the baby weighed 15 lb 13 oz. Find the baby's increase in weight during the 6 months.

41. Packaging Shampoo weighing 5 lb 4 oz is divided equally and poured into four containers. How much shampoo is in each container?

42. Weights A steel rod weighing 16 lb 11 oz is cut into three pieces. Find the weight of each piece of steel rod.

43. Consumerism Find the cost of a ham roast that weighs 5 lb 10 oz if the price per pound is $4.80.

44. Markup A candy store buys candy weighing 12 lb for $14.40. The candy is repackaged and sold in 6-ounce packages for $1.15 each. Find the markup on the 12 lb of candy.

45. Shipping A manuscript weighing 2 lb 3 oz is mailed at the parcel post rate of $.25 per ounce. Find the cost of mailing the manuscript.

APPLYING THE CONCEPTS

46. Write a paragraph describing the growing need for precision in our measurements as civilization progressed. Include a discussion of the need for precision in the space industry.

47. Estimate the weight of a nickel, a textbook, a friend, and a car. Then find the actual weights and compare them with your estimates.

8.3 Capacity

Objective A   **To convert measurements of capacity in the U.S. Customary System**

Liquid substances are measured in units of **capacity.** The standard U.S. Customary units of capacity are the **fluid ounce, cup, pint, quart,** and **gallon.**

Point of Interest

The word *quart* has its root in the Medieval Latin word *quartus*, which means "fourth." Thus a quart is $\frac{1}{4}$ of a gallon.

The same Latin word is the source of such other English words as *quarter*, *quartile*, *quadrilateral*, and *quartet*.

Equivalences Between Units of Capacity in the U.S. Customary System

$$8 \text{ fluid ounces (fl oz)} = 1 \text{ cup (c)}$$
$$2 \text{ c} = 1 \text{ pint (pt)}$$
$$2 \text{ pt} = 1 \text{ quart (qt)}$$
$$4 \text{ qt} = 1 \text{ gallon (gal)}$$

These equivalences can be used to form conversion rates to change one unit of measurement to another. For example, because 8 fl oz = 1 c, the conversion rates $\frac{8 \text{ fl oz}}{1 \text{ c}}$ and $\frac{1 \text{ c}}{8 \text{ fl oz}}$ are both equivalent to 1.

HOW TO   Convert 36 fl oz to cups.

$$36 \text{ fl oz} = 36 \text{ fl oz} \times \boxed{\frac{1 \text{ c}}{8 \text{ fl oz}}}$$

$$= \frac{36 \text{ fl oz}}{1} \times \frac{1 \text{ c}}{8 \text{ fl oz}}$$

$$= \frac{36 \text{ c}}{8}$$

$$= 4\frac{1}{2} \text{ c}$$

- **The conversion rate must contain c in the numerator and fl oz in the denominator.**

HOW TO   Convert 3 qt to cups.

$$3 \text{ qt} = 3 \text{ qt} \times \boxed{\frac{2 \text{ pt}}{1 \text{ qt}}} \times \boxed{\frac{2 \text{ c}}{1 \text{ pt}}}$$

$$= \frac{3 \text{ qt}}{1} \times \frac{2 \text{ pt}}{1 \text{ qt}} \times \frac{2 \text{ c}}{1 \text{ pt}}$$

$$= \frac{12 \text{ c}}{1}$$

$$= 12 \text{ c}$$

- **The direct equivalence is not given above. Use two conversion rates. First convert quarts to pints, and then convert pints to cups. The unit in the denominator of the second conversion rate and the unit in the numerator of the first conversion rate must be the same in order to cancel.**

Example 1   Convert 42 c to quarts.

Solution $42 \text{ c} = 42 \text{ c} \times \dfrac{1 \text{ pt}}{2 \text{ c}} \times \dfrac{1 \text{ qt}}{2 \text{ pt}}$

$= \dfrac{42 \text{ qt}}{4} = 10\dfrac{1}{2} \text{ qt}$

You Try It 1   Convert 18 pt to gallons.

Your solution

Objective B   **To perform arithmetic operations with measurements of capacity**

When performing arithmetic operations with measurements of capacity, write the answer in simplest form. For example, 1 c 12 fl oz should be written as 2 c 4 fl oz.

Example 2   What is 4 gal 1 qt decreased by 2 gal 3 qt?

Solution

$$
\begin{array}{r}
\overset{3 \text{ gal}}{\cancel{4 \text{ gal}}} \overset{5 \text{ qt}}{\cancel{1 \text{ qt}}} \\
- 2 \text{ gal } 3 \text{ qt} \\
\hline
1 \text{ gal } 2 \text{ qt}
\end{array}
$$

• Borrow 1 gal (4 qt) from 4 gal and add to 1 qt.

You Try It 2   Find the quotient of 4 gal 2 qt and 3.

Your solution

Objective C   **To solve application problems**

Example 3

A can of apple juice contains 25 fl oz. Find the number of quarts of apple juice in a case of 24 cans.

Strategy

To find the number of quarts of apple juice in one case:

• Multiply the number of cans (24) by the number of fluid ounces per can (25) to find the total number of fluid ounces in the case.
• Convert the number of fluid ounces in the case to quarts.

Solution
24 × 25 fl oz = 600 fl oz

$$600 \text{ fl oz} = \frac{600 \cancel{\text{ fl oz}}}{1} \cdot \frac{1 \cancel{c}}{8 \cancel{\text{ fl oz}}} \cdot \frac{1 \cancel{\text{ pt}}}{2 \cancel{c}} \cdot \frac{1 \text{ qt}}{2 \cancel{\text{ pt}}}$$

$$= \frac{600 \text{ qt}}{32} = 18\frac{3}{4} \text{ qt}$$

One case of apple juice contains $18\frac{3}{4}$ qt.

You Try It 3

Five students are going backpacking in the desert. Each student requires 5 qt of water per day. How many gallons of water should they take for a 3-day trip?

Your strategy

Your solution

8.3 Exercises

Objective A   **To convert measurements of capacity in the U.S. Customary System**

For Exercises 1 to 18, convert.

1.   60 fl oz = _____ c

2.   48 fl oz = _____ c

3.   3 c = _____ fl oz

4. $2\frac{1}{2}$ c = _____ fl oz

5.   8 c = _____ pt

6.   5 c = _____ pt

7. $3\frac{1}{2}$ pt = _____ c

8.   12 pt = _____ qt

9.   22 qt = _____ gal

10.   10 qt = _____ gal

11. $2\frac{1}{4}$ gal = _____ qt

12.   7 gal = _____ qt

13. $7\frac{1}{2}$ pt = _____ qt

14. $3\frac{1}{2}$ qt = _____ pt

15.   20 fl oz = _____ pt

16. $1\frac{1}{2}$ pt = _____ fl oz

17.   17 c = _____ qt

18. $1\frac{1}{2}$ qt = _____ c

Objective B   **To perform arithmetic operations with measurements of capacity**

For Exercises 19 to 36, perform the arithmetic operation.

19.   14 qt = _____ gal _____ qt

20.   9 pt = _____ qt _____ pt

21.   5 pt = _____ qt _____ pt

22.   3 gal 2 qt
         + 4 gal 3 qt

23.   4 qt 1 pt
         + 2 qt 1 pt

24.   3 gal 1 qt
         − 1 gal 2 qt

25.   3 c 3 fl oz
         − 2 c 5 fl oz

26.   2 qt 1 pt
         × 2 qt 5 pt

27. $3\frac{1}{2}$ pt × 5

28.   5$\overline{)6\text{ gal 1 qt}}$

29. $3\frac{1}{2}$ gal ÷ 4

30.   5 c 3 fl oz
         + 3 c 6 fl oz

31.   3 gal 3 qt
         + 1 gal 2 qt

32.   4 c 6 fl oz
         − 2 c 7 fl oz

33.   3 gal 2 qt
         − 1 gal 2 qt

34. $1\dfrac{1}{2}$ pt $+ 2\dfrac{2}{3}$ pt

35. $4\dfrac{1}{2}$ gal $- 1\dfrac{3}{4}$ gal

36. $2\overline{)3 \text{ gal } 2 \text{ qt}}$

Objective C   **To solve application problems**

37. Catering   Sixty adults are expected to attend a book signing. Each adult will drink 2 c of coffee. How many gallons of coffee should be prepared?

38. Catering   The Bayside Playhouse serves punch during intermission. Assume that 200 people will each drink 1 c of punch. How many gallons of punch should be ordered?

39. Chemistry   A solution needed for a chemistry class required 72 fl oz of water, 16 fl oz of one solution, and 48 fl oz of another solution. Find the number of quarts of the final solution.

40. Food Service   A cafeteria sold 124 cartons of milk in 1 day. Each carton contained 1 c of milk. How many quarts of milk were sold that day?

41. Vehicle Maintenance   A farmer changed the oil in a tractor seven times during the year. Each oil change required 5 qt of oil. How many gallons of oil did the farmer use in the seven oil changes?

42. Capacity   There are 24 cans in a case of tomato juice. Each can contains 10 fl oz of tomato juice. Find the number of 1-cup servings in the case of tomato juice.

43. Consumerism   One brand of tomato juice costs $1.59 for 1 qt. Another brand costs $1.25 for 24 fl oz. Which is the more economical purchase?

44. Camping   Mandy carried 12 qt of water for 3 days of desert camping. Water weighs $8\dfrac{1}{3}$ lb per gallon. Find the weight of water that she carried.

45. Business   A department store bought hand lotion in 5-quart containers and then repackaged the lotion in 8-fluid-ounce bottles. The lotion and bottles cost $81.50, and each 8-fluid-ounce bottle was sold for $8.25. How much profit was made on each 5-quart package of lotion?

46. Business   Orlando bought oil in 50-gallon containers for changing the oil in his customers' cars. He paid $240 for the 50 gal of oil and charged customers $2.10 per quart. Find the profit Orlando made on one 50-gallon container of oil.

APPLYING THE CONCEPTS

47. Define the following units: grain, dram, furlong, and rod. Give an example where each would be used.

48. Assume that you wanted to invent a new measuring system. Discuss some of the features that would have to be incorporated into the system.

8.4 Time

Objective A   **To convert units of time**

The units in which time is generally measured are the **second, minute, hour, day,** and **week**.

> **Equivalences Between Units of Time**
>
> 60 seconds (s) = 1 minute (min)
> 60 min = 1 hour (h)
> 24 h = 1 day
> 7 days = 1 week

These equivalences can be used to form conversion rates to change one unit of time to another. For example, because 24 h = 1 day, the conversion rates $\frac{24\text{ h}}{1\text{ day}}$ and $\frac{1\text{ day}}{24\text{ h}}$ are both equivalent to 1. An example using each of these two rates is shown below.

HOW TO   Convert $5\frac{1}{2}$ days to hours.

$$5\frac{1}{2}\text{ days} = 5\frac{1}{2}\text{ days} \times \boxed{\frac{24\text{ h}}{1\text{ day}}}$$

$$= \frac{11\ \cancel{\text{days}}}{2} \times \frac{24\text{ h}}{1\ \cancel{\text{day}}}$$

$$= \frac{264\text{ h}}{2}$$

$$= 132\text{ h}$$

• The conversion rate must contain h (the unit desired in the answer) in the numerator and must contain day (the original unit) in the denominator.

HOW TO   Convert 156 h to days.

$$156\text{ h} = 156\text{ h} \times \boxed{\frac{1\text{ day}}{24\text{ h}}}$$

$$= \frac{156\ \cancel{\text{h}}}{1} \times \frac{1\text{ day}}{24\ \cancel{\text{h}}}$$

$$= \frac{156\text{ days}}{24}$$

$$= 6\frac{1}{2}\text{ days}$$

• The conversion rate must contain day (the unit desired in the answer) in the numerator and must contain h (the original unit) in the denominator.

Example 1   Convert 2880 min to days.

Solution

$$2880\text{ min} = 2880\ \cancel{\text{min}} \times \frac{1\ \cancel{\text{h}}}{60\ \cancel{\text{min}}} \times \frac{1\text{ day}}{24\ \cancel{\text{h}}}$$

$$= \frac{2880\text{ days}}{1440} = 2\text{ days}$$

You Try It 1   Convert 18,000 s to hours.

Your solution

8.4 Exercises

Objective A **To convert units of time**

For Exercises 1 to 24, convert.

1. 98 days = _____ weeks

2. 12 weeks = _____ days

3. $6\frac{1}{4}$ days = _____ h

4. 114 h = _____ days

5. 555 min = _____ h

6. $7\frac{3}{4}$ h = _____ min

7. $18\frac{1}{2}$ min = _____ s

8. 750 s = _____ min

9. 12,600 s = _____ h

10. 15,300 s = _____ h

11. $6\frac{1}{2}$ h = _____ s

12. $5\frac{3}{4}$ h = _____ s

13. 5040 min = _____ days

14. 6840 min = _____ days

15. $2\frac{1}{2}$ days = _____ min

16. $6\frac{1}{4}$ days = _____ min

17. 672 h = _____ weeks

18. 588 h = _____ weeks

19. 3 weeks = _____ h

20. $5\frac{1}{2}$ weeks = _____ h

21. 172,800 s = _____ days

22. 20,160 min = _____ weeks

23. 3 days = _____ s

24. 3 weeks = _____ min

APPLYING THE CONCEPTS

Another unit of time is the year. One year is equivalent to $365\frac{1}{4}$ days. However, our calendar does not include quarter days. Instead, we say that a year is 365 days, and every fourth year is a leap year of 366 days. If a year is divisible by 4, it is a leap year, unless it is a year at the beginning of a century not divisible by 400. 1600, 2000, 2004, 2008, and 2012 are leap years. 1700, 1800, and 1900 are not leap years. For Exercises 25 to 27, state whether the given year is a leap year.

25. 1984

26. 1994

27. 2144

For Exercises 28 to 33, convert. Use a 365-day year.

28. 1825 days = _____ years

29. 2555 days = _____ years

30. 4 years = _____ days

31. 6 years = _____ days

32. 2 years = _____ h

33. $3\frac{1}{2}$ years = _____ h

8.5   Energy and Power

Objective A   **To use units of energy in the U.S. Customary System**

Energy can be defined as the ability to do work. Energy is stored in coal, in gasoline, in water behind a dam, and in one's own body.

One **foot-pound** (ft · lb) of energy is the amount of energy necessary to lift 1 pound a distance of 1 foot.

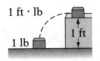

To lift 50 lb a distance of 5 ft requires 50 × 5 = 250 ft · lb of energy.

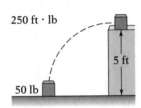

Consumer items that use energy, such as furnaces, stoves, and air conditioners, are rated in terms of the **British thermal unit** (Btu). For example, a furnace might have a rating of 35,000 Btu per hour, which means that it releases 35,000 Btu of energy in one hour (1 h).

Because 1 Btu = 778 ft · lb, the following conversion rate, equivalent to 1, can be written:

$$\frac{778 \text{ ft} \cdot \text{lb}}{1 \text{ Btu}} = 1$$

Example 1

Convert 250 Btu to foot-pounds.

Solution

$$250 \text{ Btu} = 250 \text{ B\!t\!u} \times \frac{778 \text{ ft} \cdot \text{lb}}{1 \text{ B\!t\!u}}$$

$$= 194,500 \text{ ft} \cdot \text{lb}$$

You Try It 1

Convert 4.5 Btu to foot-pounds.

Your solution

Example 2

Find the energy required for a 125-pound person to climb a mile-high mountain.

Solution

In climbing the mountain, the person is lifting 125 lb a distance of 5280 ft.

Energy = 125 lb × 5280 ft
     = 660,000 ft · lb

You Try It 2

Find the energy required for a motor to lift 800 lb a distance of 16 ft.

Your solution

Example 3

A furnace is rated at 80,000 Btu per hour. How many foot-pounds of energy are released in 1 h?

Solution

$$80{,}000 \text{ Btu} = 80{,}000 \text{ Btu} \times \frac{778 \text{ ft} \cdot \text{lb}}{1 \text{ Btu}}$$
$$= 62{,}240{,}000 \text{ ft} \cdot \text{lb}$$

You Try It 3

A furnace is rated at 56,000 Btu per hour. How many foot-pounds of energy are released in 1 h?

Your solution

Objective B | **To use units of power in the U.S. Customary System**

Power is the rate at which work is done or the rate at which energy is released.

Power is measured in **foot-pounds per second** $\left(\frac{\text{ft} \cdot \text{lb}}{\text{s}} \right)$. In each of the following examples, the amount of energy released is the same, but the time taken to release the energy is different; thus the power is different.

100 lb is lifted 10 ft in 10 s.

$$\text{Power} = \frac{10 \text{ ft} \times 100 \text{ lb}}{10 \text{ s}} = 100 \, \frac{\text{ft} \cdot \text{lb}}{\text{s}}$$

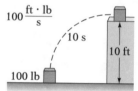

100 lb is lifted 10 ft in 5 s.

$$\text{Power} = \frac{10 \text{ ft} \times 100 \text{ lb}}{5 \text{ s}} = 200 \, \frac{\text{ft} \cdot \text{lb}}{\text{s}}$$

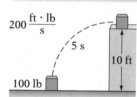

The U.S. Customary unit of power is the **horsepower**. A horse doing average work can pull 550 lb a distance of 1 ft in 1 s and can continue this work all day.

$$\textbf{1 horsepower (hp)} = \textbf{550} \, \frac{\textbf{ft} \cdot \textbf{lb}}{\textbf{s}}$$

Example 4

Find the power needed to raise 300 lb a distance of 30 ft in 15 s.

Solution
$$\text{Power} = \frac{30 \text{ ft} \times 300 \text{ lb}}{15 \text{ s}}$$
$$= 600 \, \frac{\text{ft} \cdot \text{lb}}{\text{s}}$$

You Try It 4

Find the power needed to raise 1200 lb a distance of 90 ft in 24 s.

Your solution

Example 5

A motor has a power of 2750 $\frac{\text{ft} \cdot \text{lb}}{\text{s}}$. Find the horsepower of the motor.

Solution $\quad \dfrac{2750}{550} = 5 \text{ hp}$

You Try It 5

A motor has a power of 3300 $\frac{\text{ft} \cdot \text{lb}}{\text{s}}$. Find the horsepower of the motor.

Your solution

8.5 Exercises

Objective A   To use units of energy in the U.S. Customary System

1. Convert 25 Btu to foot-pounds.

2. Convert 6000 Btu to foot-pounds.

3. Convert 25,000 Btu to foot-pounds.

4. Convert 40,000 Btu to foot-pounds.

5. Find the energy required to lift 150 lb a distance of 10 ft.

6. Find the energy required to lift 300 lb a distance of 16 ft.

7. Find the energy required to lift a 3300-pound car a distance of 9 ft.

8. Find the energy required to lift a 3680-pound elevator a distance of 325 ft.

9. Three tons are lifted 5 ft. Find the energy required in foot-pounds.

10. Seven tons are lifted 12 ft. Find the energy required in foot-pounds.

11. A construction worker carries 3-pound blocks up a 10-foot flight of stairs. How many foot-pounds of energy are required to carry 850 blocks up the stairs?

12. A crane lifts an 1800-pound steel beam to the roof of a building 36 ft high. Find the amount of energy the crane requires in lifting the beam.

13. A furnace is rated at 45,000 Btu per hour. How many foot-pounds of energy are released by the furnace in 1 h?

14. A furnace is rated at 22,500 Btu per hour. How many foot-pounds of energy does the furnace release in 1 h?

15. Find the amount of energy in foot-pounds given off when 1 lb of coal is burned. One pound of coal gives off 12,000 Btu of energy when burned.

16. Find the amount of energy in foot-pounds given off when 1 lb of gasoline is burned. One pound of gasoline gives off 21,000 Btu of energy when burned.

Objective B   **To use units of power in the U.S. Customary System**

17. Convert 1100 $\frac{\text{ft} \cdot \text{lb}}{\text{s}}$ to horsepower.

18. Convert 6050 $\frac{\text{ft} \cdot \text{lb}}{\text{s}}$ to horsepower.

19. Convert 4400 $\frac{\text{ft} \cdot \text{lb}}{\text{s}}$ to horsepower.

20. Convert 1650 $\frac{\text{ft} \cdot \text{lb}}{\text{s}}$ to horsepower.

21. Convert 9 hp to foot-pounds per second.

22. Convert 4 hp to foot-pounds per second.

23. Convert 7 hp to foot-pounds per second.

24. Convert 8 hp to foot-pounds per second.

25. Find the power in foot-pounds per second needed to raise 125 lb a distance of 12 ft in 3 s.

26. Find the power in foot-pounds per second needed to raise 500 lb a distance of 60 ft in 8 s.

27. Find the power in foot-pounds per second needed to raise 3000 lb a distance of 40 ft in 25 s.

28. Find the power in foot-pounds per second of an engine that can raise 12,000 lb to a height of 40 ft in 60 s.

29. Find the power in foot-pounds per second of an engine that can raise 180 lb to a height of 40 ft in 5 s.

30. Find the power in foot-pounds per second of an engine that can raise 1200 lb to a height of 18 ft in 30 s.

31. A motor has a power of 4950 $\frac{\text{ft} \cdot \text{lb}}{\text{s}}$. Find the horsepower of the motor.

32. A motor has a power of 16,500 $\frac{\text{ft} \cdot \text{lb}}{\text{s}}$. Find the horsepower of the motor.

33. A motor has a power of 6600 $\frac{\text{ft} \cdot \text{lb}}{\text{s}}$. Find the horsepower of the motor.

APPLYING THE CONCEPTS

34. Pick a source of energy and write an article about it. Include the source, possible pollution problems, and future prospects associated with this form of energy.

Focus on Problem Solving

Applying Solutions to Other Problems

Problem solving in the previous chapters concentrated on solving specific problems. After a problem is solved, however, there is an important question to be asked: "Does the solution to this problem apply to other types of problems?"

To illustrate this extension of problem solving, we will consider *triangular numbers,* which were studied by ancient Greek mathematicians. The numbers 1, 3, 6, 10, 15, and 21 are the first six triangular numbers. What is the next triangular number?

To answer this question, note in the diagram below that a triangle can be formed using the number of dots that correspond to a triangular number.

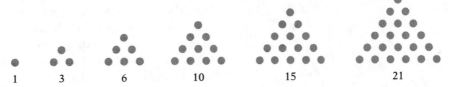

Observe that the number of dots in each row is one more than the number of dots in the row above. The total number of dots can be found by addition.

The pattern suggests that the next triangular number (the seventh one) is the sum of the first 7 natural numbers. The seventh triangular number is 28. The diagram at the right shows the seventh triangular number.

Using the pattern for triangular numbers, it is easy to determine that the tenth triangular number is

$$1 + 2 + 3 + 4 + 5 + 6 + 7 + 8 + 9 + 10 = 55$$

Now consider a situation that may seem to be totally unrelated to triangular numbers. Suppose you are in charge of scheduling softball games for a league. There are seven teams in the league, and each team must play every other team once. How many games must be scheduled?

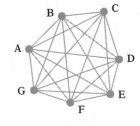

We label the teams A, B, C, D, E, F, and G. (See the figure at the left.) A line between two teams indicates that the two teams play each other. Beginning with A, there are 6 lines for the 6 teams that A must play. There are 6 teams that B must play, but the line between A and B has already been drawn, so there are only 5 remaining games to schedule for B. Now move on to C. The lines between C and A and between C and B have already been drawn, so there are only 4 additional lines to be drawn to represent the teams C will play. Moving on to D, we see that the lines between D and A, D and B, and D and C have already been drawn, so there are 3 more lines to be drawn to represent the teams D will play.

Note that each time we move from team to team, one fewer line needs to be drawn. When we reach F, there is only one line to be drawn, the one between F and G. The total number of lines drawn is $6 + 5 + 4 + 3 + 2 + 1 = 21$, the sixth triangular number. For a league with 7 teams, the number of games that must be scheduled so that each team plays every other team once is the sixth triangular number. If there were ten teams in the league, the number of games that must be scheduled would be the ninth triangular number, which is 45.

A college chess team wants to schedule a match so that each of its 15 members plays each other member of the team once. How many matches must be scheduled?

Projects and Group Activities

Nomographs

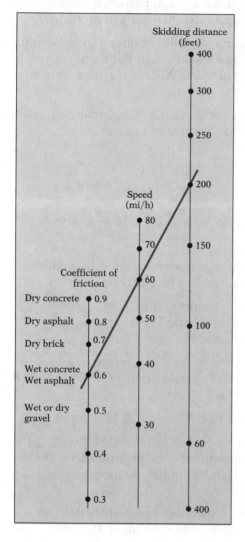

A chart is another tool that is used in problem solving. The chart at the left is a nomograph. A **nomograph** is a chart that represents numerical relationships among variables.

One of the details a traffic accident investigator checks when looking into a car accident is the length of the skid marks of the car. This length can help the investigator determine the speed of the car when the brakes were applied.

The nomograph at the left can be used to determine the speed of a car under given conditions. It shows the relationship among the speed of the car, the skidding distance, and the *coefficient of friction*.

The coefficient of friction is an experimentally obtained value that reflects how easy or hard it is to drag one object over another. For instance, it is easier to drag a box across ice than to drag it across a carpet. The coefficient of friction is smaller for the box and ice than it is for the box and carpet.

To use the nomograph at the left, an investigator would draw a line from the coefficient of friction to the skidding distance. The point at which the line crosses the speed line shows how fast the car was going when the brakes were applied. The line from 0.6 to 200 intersects the speed line at 60. This indicates that a car that skidded 200 ft on wet asphalt or wet concrete was traveling at 60 mi/h.

1. Use the nomograph to determine the speed of a car when the brakes were applied for a car traveling on gravel and for skid marks of 100 ft.

2. Use the nomograph to determine the speed of a car when the brakes were applied for a car traveling on dry concrete and for skid marks of 150 ft.

3. Suppose a car is traveling 80 mi/h when the brakes are applied. Find the difference in skidding distance if the car is traveling on wet concrete rather than dry concrete.

Averages

If two towns are 150 mi apart and you drive between the two towns in 3 h, then your

$$\text{Average speed} = \frac{\text{total distance}}{\text{total time}} = \frac{150 \text{ mi}}{3 \text{ h}} = 50 \text{ mi/h}$$

It is highly unlikely that your speed was *exactly* 50 mi/h the entire time of the trip. Sometimes you will have traveled faster than 50 mi/h, and other times you will have traveled slower than 50 mi/h. Dividing the total distance you traveled by the total time it took to go that distance is an example of calculating an average.

There are many other averages that may be calculated. For instance, the Environmental Protection Agency calculates an estimated miles per gallon (mpg) for new cars. Miles per gallon is an average calculated from the formula

$$\frac{\text{Miles traveled}}{\text{Gallons of gasoline consumed}}$$

For instance, the miles per gallon for a car that travels 308 mi on 11 gal of gas is $\frac{308 \text{ mi}}{11 \text{ gal}} = 28$ mpg.

A pilot would not use miles per gallon as a measure of fuel efficiency. Rather, pilots use gallons per hour. A plane that travels 5 h and uses 400 gal of fuel has an average that is calculated as

$$\frac{\text{Gallons of fuel}}{\text{Hours flown}} = \frac{400 \text{ gal}}{5 \text{ h}} = 80 \text{ gal/h}$$

Using the examples above, calculate the following averages.

1. Determine the average speed of a car that travels 355 mi in 6 h. Round to the nearest tenth.

2. Determine the miles per gallon of a car that can travel 405 mi on 12 gal of gasoline. Round to the nearest tenth.

3. If a plane flew 2000 mi in 5 h and used 1000 gal of fuel, determine the average number of gallons per hour that the plane used.

Another type of average is grade-point average (GPA). It is calculated by multiplying the units for each class by the grade point for that class, adding the results, and dividing by the total number of units taken. Here is an example using the grading scale A = 4, B = 3, C = 2, D = 1, and F = 0.

Class	Units	Grade
Math	4	B (= 3)
English	3	A (= 4)
French	5	C (= 2)
Biology	3	B (= 3)

$$\text{GPA} = \frac{4 \cdot 3 + 3 \cdot 4 + 5 \cdot 2 + 3 \cdot 3}{4 + 3 + 5 + 3} = \frac{43}{15} \approx 2.87$$

4. A grading scale that provides for plus or minus grades uses A = 4, A− = 3.7, B+ = 3.3, B = 3, B− = 2.7, C+ = 2.3, C = 2, C− = 1.7, D+ = 1.3, D = 1, D− = 0.7, and F = 0. Calculate the GPA of the student whose grades are given below.

Class	Units	Grade
Math	5	B +
English	3	C +
Spanish	5	A −
Physical science	3	B −

Chapter Summary

Key Words	Examples
A *measurement* includes a number and a unit.	9 inches, 6 feet, 3 yards, and 50 miles are measurements.
Equivalent measures are used to form *conversion rates* to change one unit in the U.S. Customary System of measurement to another. In the conversion rate chosen, the unit in the numerator is the same as the unit desired in the answer. The unit in the denominator is the same as the unit in the given measurement.	Because 12 in. = 1 ft, the conversion rate $\frac{12 \text{ in.}}{1 \text{ ft}}$ is used to convert feet to inches. The conversion rate $\frac{1 \text{ ft}}{12 \text{ in.}}$ is used to convert inches to feet.

Energy is the ability to do work. One *foot-pound* (ft · lb) of energy is the amount of energy necessary to lift 1 pound a distance of 1 foot. Consumer items that use energy are rated in *British thermal units* (Btu).

Find the energy required for a 110-pound person to climb a set of stairs 12 ft high.

Energy = 110 lb × 12 ft = 1320 ft · lb

Power is the rate at which work is done or energy is released.

Power is measured in *foot-pounds per second* $\left(\frac{\text{ft} \cdot \text{lb}}{\text{s}}\right)$ and *horsepower* (hp).

Find the power needed to raise 250 lb a distance of 20 ft in 10 s.

$$\text{Power} = \frac{20 \text{ ft} \times 250 \text{ lb}}{10 \text{ s}} = 500 \frac{\text{ft} \cdot \text{lb}}{\text{s}}$$

Essential Rules and Procedures

Examples

Equivalences Between Units of Length
The U.S. Customary units of length are inch (in.), foot (ft), yard (yd), and mile (mi).
12 in. = 1 ft
3 ft = 1 yd
36 in. = 1 yd
5280 ft = 1 mi

Convert 52 in. to ft.

$$52 \text{ in.} = 52 \text{ in.} \times \frac{1 \text{ ft}}{12 \text{ in.}}$$
$$= \frac{52 \text{ ft}}{12} = 4\frac{1}{3} \text{ ft}$$

Equivalences Between Units of Weight
Weight is a measure of how strongly Earth is pulling on an object. The U.S. Customary units of weight are ounce (oz), pound (lb), and ton.
16 oz = 1 lb
2000 lb = 1 ton

Convert 9 lb to ounces.

$$9 \text{ lb} = 9 \text{ lb} \times \frac{16 \text{ oz}}{1 \text{ lb}} = 144 \text{ oz}$$

Equivalences Between Units of Capacity
Liquid substances are measured in units of *capacity*. The U.S. Customary units of capacity are fluid ounce (fl oz), cup (c), pint (pt), quart (qt), and gallon (gal).
8 fl oz = 1 c
2 c = 1 pt
2 pt = 1 qt
4 qt = 1 gal

Convert 14 qt to gallons.

$$14 \text{ qt} = 14 \text{ qt} \times \frac{1 \text{ gal}}{4 \text{ qt}}$$
$$= \frac{14 \text{ gal}}{4} = 3\frac{1}{2} \text{ gal}$$

Equivalences Between Units of Time
Units of time are seconds (s), minutes (min), hours (h), days, and weeks.
60 s = 1 min
60 min = 1 h
24 h = 1 day
7 days = 1 week

Convert 8 days to hours.

$$8 \text{ days} = 8 \text{ days} \times \frac{24 \text{ h}}{1 \text{ day}} = 192 \text{ h}$$

Equivalences Between Units of Energy
1 Btu = 778 ft · lb

Convert 70 Btu to foot-pounds.

$$70 \text{ Btu} = 70 \text{ Btu} \times \frac{778 \text{ ft} \cdot \text{lb}}{1 \text{ Btu}}$$
$$= 54,460 \text{ ft} \cdot \text{lb}$$

Equivalences Between Units of Power
The U.S. Customary unit of power is the horsepower (hp).

$$1 \text{ hp} = 550 \frac{\text{ft} \cdot \text{lb}}{\text{s}}$$

Convert 5 hp to foot-pounds per second.

$$5 \times 550 = 2750 \frac{\text{ft} \cdot \text{lb}}{\text{s}}$$

Chapter Review Exercises

1. Convert 4 ft to inches.

2. What is 7 ft 6 in. divided by 3?

3. Find the energy needed to lift 200 lb a distance of 8 ft.

4. Convert $2\frac{1}{2}$ pt to fluid ounces.

5. Convert 14 ft to yards.

6. Convert 2400 lb to tons.

7. Find the quotient of 7 lb 5 oz and 3.

8. Convert $3\frac{3}{8}$ lb to ounces.

9. Add: 3 ft 9 in.
      + 5 ft 6 in.

10. Subtract: 3 tons 1500 lb
        − 1 tons 1500 lb

11. Add: 4 c 7 fl oz
       + 2 c 3 fl oz

12. Subtract: 5 yd 1 ft
        − 3 yd 2 ft

13. Convert 12 c to quarts.

14. Convert 375 min to hours.

15. Convert 2.5 hp to foot-pounds per second. $\left(1 \text{ hp} = 550 \,\frac{\text{ft} \cdot \text{lb}}{\text{s}}.\right)$

16. Multiply: 5 lb 8 oz
                      $\times$ 5 lb 8 oz

17. Convert 50 Btu to foot-pounds. (1 Btu = 778 ft · lb.)

18. Convert $3850 \,\frac{\text{ft} \cdot \text{lb}}{\text{s}}$ to horsepower. $\left(1 \text{ hp} = 550 \,\frac{\text{ft} \cdot \text{lb}}{\text{s}}.\right)$

19. **Carpentry**   A board 6 ft 11 in. long is cut from a board 10 ft 5 in. long. Find the length of the remaining piece of board.

20. **Shipping**   A book weighing 2 lb 3 oz is mailed at the parcel post rate of $.24 per ounce. Find the cost of mailing the book.

21. **Capacity**   A can of pineapple juice contains 18 fl oz. Find the number of quarts in a case of 24 cans.

22. **Food Service**   A cafeteria sold 256 cartons of milk in one school day. Each carton contains 1 c of milk. How many gallons of milk were sold that day?

23. **Energy**   A furnace is rated at 35,000 Btu per hour. How many foot-pounds of energy does the furnace release in 1 h? (1 Btu = 778 ft · lb)

24. **Power**   Find the power in foot-pounds per second of an engine that can raise 800 lb to a height of 15 ft in 25 s.

Chapter Test

1. Convert $2\frac{1}{2}$ ft to inches.

2. Subtract: 4 ft 2 in. $- 1$ ft 9 in. $\frac{2}{3}$

3. **Carpentry** A board $6\frac{2}{3}$ ft long is cut into five equal pieces. How long is each piece?

4. **Masonry** Seventy-two bricks, each 8 in. long, are laid end to end to make the base for a wall. Find the length of the wall in feet.

5. Convert $2\frac{7}{8}$ lb to ounces.

6. Convert: 40 oz $= $ ___ lb ___ oz

7. Find the sum of 9 lb 6 oz and 7 lb 11 oz.

8. Divide: 6 lb 12 oz $\div$ 4

9. **Weights** A college bookstore received 1000 workbooks, each weighing 12 oz. Find the total weight of the 1000 workbooks in pounds.

10. **Recycling** An elementary school class gathered 800 aluminum cans for recycling. Four aluminum cans weigh 3 oz. Find the amount the class received if the rate of pay was $.75 per pound for the aluminum cans. Round to the nearest cent.

11. Convert 13 qt to gallons.

12. Convert $3\frac{1}{2}$ gal to pints.

13. What is $1\frac{3}{4}$ gal times 7?

14. Add: 5 gal 2 qt + 2 gal 3 qt

15. Convert 756 h to weeks.

16. Convert $3\frac{1}{4}$ days to minutes.

17. Capacity A can of grapefruit juice contains 20 fl oz. Find the number of cups of grapefruit juice in a case of 24 cans.

18. Business Nick, a mechanic, bought oil in 40-gallon containers for changing the oil in customers' cars. He paid $200 for the 40 gal of oil and charged customers $2.15 per quart. Find the profit Nick made on one 40-gallon container of oil.

19. Energy Find the energy required to lift 250 lb a distance of 15 ft.

20. Energy A furnace is rated at 40,000 Btu per hour. How many foot-pounds of energy are released by the furnace in 1 h? (1 Btu = 778 ft · lb)

21. Power Find the power needed to lift 200 lb a distance of 20 ft in 25 s.

22. Power A motor has a power of 2200 $\frac{\text{ft} \cdot \text{lb}}{\text{s}}$. Find the motor's horsepower. $\left(1 \text{ hp} = 550 \frac{\text{ft} \cdot \text{lb}}{\text{s}}\right)$

chapter

9

The Metric System of Measurement

OBJECTIVES

Section 9.1
A To convert units of length in the metric system of measurement
B To solve application problems

Section 9.2
A To convert units of mass in the metric system of measurement
B To solve application problems

Section 9.3
A To convert units of capacity in the metric system measurement
B To solve application problems

Section 9.4
A To use units of energy in the metric system of measurement

We use electrical energy in countless ways each and every day. When you turn on a light, use a microwave, start up the air conditioner, or turn on the television, you are using electrical energy. The watt-hour is used for measuring the amount of electrical energy an appliance uses. For example, light bulbs usually use 60 watts, and microwaves can use 500 watts.

Need help? For online student resources, such as section quizzes, visit this textbook's website at **math.college.hmco.com/students.**

For Exercises 1 to 10, add, subtract, multiply, or divide.

1. $3.732 \times 10{,}000$

2. 65.9×10^4

3. $41.07 \div 1000$

4. $28{,}496 \div 10^3$

5. $6 - 0.875$

6. $5 + 0.96$

7. 3.25×0.04

8. $35 \times \dfrac{1.61}{1}$

9. $1.67 \times \dfrac{1}{3.34}$

10. $4\dfrac{1}{2} \times 150$

GO FIGURE • • •

Suppose you threw six darts and all six hit the target shown. Which of the following could be your score?

4, 15, 58, 28, 29, 31

9.1 Length

Objective A

To convert units of length in the metric system of measurement

In 1789, an attempt was made to standardize units of measurement internationally in order to simplify trade and commerce between nations. A commission in France developed a system of measurement known as the **metric system.**

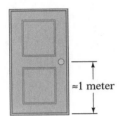

≈1 meter

The basic unit of length in the metric system is the **meter.** One meter is approximately the distance from a doorknob to the floor. All units of length in the metric system are derived from the meter. Prefixes to the basic unit denote the length of each unit. For example, the prefix "centi-" means one-hundredth, so 1 centimeter is 1 one-hundredth of a meter.

North Pole

Equator

Prefixes and Units of Length in the Metric System

kilo- = 1000	1 kilometer (km) = 1000 meters (m)
hecto- = 100	1 hectometer (hm) = 100 m
deca- = 10	1 decameter (dam) = 10 m
	1 meter (m) = 1 m
deci- = 0.1	1 decimeter (dm) = 0.1 m
centi- = 0.01	1 centimeter (cm) = 0.01 m
milli- = 0.001	1 millimeter (mm) = 0.001 m

Point of Interest

Originally the meter (spelled *metre* in some countries) was defined as $\frac{1}{10,000,000}$ of the distance from the equator to the North Pole. Modern scientists have redefined the meter as 1,650,763.73 wavelengths of the orange-red light given off by the element krypton.

Conversion between units of length in the metric system involves moving the decimal point to the right or to the left. Listing the units in order from largest to smallest will indicate how many places to move the decimal point and in which direction.

To convert 4200 cm to meters, write the units in order from largest to smallest.

km hm dam m dm cm mm

2 positions

4200 cm = 42.00 m

2 places

- **Converting cm to m requires moving 2 positions to the left.**

- **Move the decimal point the same number of places and in the same direction.**

A metric measurement that involves two units is customarily written in terms of one unit. Convert the smaller unit to the larger unit and then add.

To convert 8 km 32 m to kilometers, first convert 32 m to kilometers.

km hm dam m dm cm mm

32 m = 0.032 km

8 km 32 m = 8 km + 0.032 km
          = 8.032 km

- **Converting m to km requires moving 3 positions to the left.**

- **Move the decimal point the same number of places and in the same direction.**

- **Add the result to 8 km.**

Study Tip

The prefixes introduced here are used throughout the chapter. As you study the material in the remaining sections, use the table above for a reference or refer to the Chapter Summary at the end of this chapter.

Example 1 Convert 0.38 m to millimeters.

Solution 0.38 m = 380 mm

You Try It 1 Convert 3.07 m to centimeters.

Your solution

Example 2 Convert 4 m 62 cm to meters.

Solution 62 cm = 0.62 m

4 m 62 cm = 4 m + 0.62 m
= 4.62 m

You Try It 2 Convert 3 km 750 m to kilometers.

Your solution

Objective B   **To solve application problems**

TAKE NOTE

Although in this text we will always change units to the larger unit, it is possible to perform the calculation by changing to the smaller unit.

2 m − 85 cm
= 200 cm − 85 cm
= 115 cm

Note that
115 cm = 1.15 m.

In the application problems in this section, we perform arithmetic operations with the measurements of length in the metric system. It is important to remember that before measurements can be added or subtracted, they must be expressed in terms of the same unit. In this textbook, unless otherwise stated, the units should be changed to the larger unit before the arithmetic operation is performed.

To subtract 85 cm from 2 m, convert 85 cm to meters.

$$2 \text{ m} − 85 \text{ cm} = 2 \text{ m} − 0.85 \text{ m}$$
$$= 1.15 \text{ m}$$

Example 3

A piece measuring 142 cm is cut from a board 4.20 m long. Find the length of the remaining piece.

Strategy

To find the length of the remaining piece:

- Convert the length of the piece cut (142 cm) to meters.
- Subtract the length of the piece cut from the original length.

Solution

142 cm = 1.42 m

4.20 m − 142 cm = 4.20 m − 1.42 m
= 2.78 m

The length of the remaining piece is 2.78 m.

You Try It 3

A bookcase 175 cm long has four shelves. Find the cost of the shelves when the price of the lumber is $15.75 per meter.

Your strategy

Your solution

9.1 Exercises

Objective A   **To convert units of length in the metric system of measurement**

For Exercises 1 to 27, convert.

1. 42 cm = _____ mm

2. 62 cm = _____ mm

3. 81 mm = _____ cm

4. 68.2 mm = _____ cm

5. 6804 m = _____ km

6. 3750 m = _____ km

7. 2.109 km = _____ m

8. 32.5 km = _____ m

9. 432 cm = _____ m

10. 61.7 cm = _____ m

11. 0.88 m = _____ cm

12. 3.21 m = _____ cm

13. 7038 m = _____ km

14. 2589 m = _____ km

15. 3.5 km = _____ m

16. 9.75 km = _____ m

17. 260 cm = _____ m

18. 705 cm = _____ m

19. 1.685 m = _____ cm

20. 0.975 m = _____ cm

21. 14.8 cm = _____ mm

22. 6 m 42 cm = _____ m

23. 62 m 7 cm = _____ m

24. 42 cm 6 mm = _____ cm

25. 31 cm 9 mm = _____ cm

26. 62 km 482 m = _____ km

27. 8 km 75 m = _____ km

Objective B   **To solve application problems**

28. **Carpentry** How many shelves, each 140 cm long, can be cut from a board that is 4.20 m in length? Find the length of the board remaining after the shelves are cut.

29. Measurements Find the missing dimension, in centimeters, in the diagram at the right.

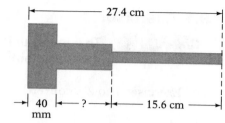

30. Sports A walk-a-thon had two checkpoints. One checkpoint was 1400 m from the starting point. The second checkpoint was 1200 m from the first checkpoint. The second checkpoint was 1800 m from the finish line. How long was the walk? Express the answer in kilometers.

31. Metal Works Twenty rivets are used to fasten two steel plates together. The plates are 3.4 m long, and the rivets are equally spaced, with a rivet at each end. Find the distance between the rivets. Round to the nearest tenth of a centimeter.

32. Measurements Find the total length, in centimeters, of the shaft in the diagram at the right.

33. Fencing You purchase a 50-meter roll of fencing, at a cost of $14.95 per meter, in order to build a dog run that is 340 cm wide and 1380 cm long. After you cut the four pieces of fencing from the roll, how much of the fencing is left on the roll?

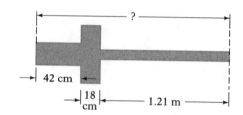

34. Highway Cleanup Carmine is a member of a group that has adopted 10 km of highway. During this week, Carmine cleaned up litter along the highway for 2500 m, 1500 m, 1200 m, 1300 m, and 1400 m. Find the average number of kilometers Carmine cleaned up on each of the 5 days this week.

35. Astronomy The distance between Earth and the sun is 150,000,000 km. Light travels 300,000,000 m in 1 s. How long does it take for light to reach Earth from the sun?

36. Earth Science The circumference of Earth is 40,000 km. How long would it take to travel the circumference of Earth at a speed of 85 km per hour? Round to the nearest tenth.

37. Physics Light travels 300,000 km in 1 s. How far does light travel in 1 day?

APPLYING THE CONCEPTS

38. Other prefixes in the metric system are becoming more commonly used as a result of technological advances. Find the meaning of the following prefixes: tera-, giga-, mega-, micro-, nano-, and pico.

39. Write a short history of the metric system.

9.2 Mass

To convert units of mass in the metric system of measurement

Mass and weight are closely related. Weight is a measure of how strongly Earth is pulling on an object. Therefore, an object's weight is less in space than on Earth's surface. However, the amount of material in the object, its **mass,** remains the same. On the surface of Earth, mass and weight can be used interchangeably.

1 gram = the
mass of water
in the box

The basic unit of mass in the metric system is the **gram.** If a box that is 1 cm long on each side is filled with water, then the mass of that water is 1 gram.

The gram is a very small unit of mass. A paper clip weighs about 1 gram. The kilogram (1000 grams) is a more useful unit of mass in consumer applications. This textbook weighs about 1 kilogram.

Point of Interest

An average snowflake weighs about $\frac{1}{300}$ g and contains approximately 100,000,000,000,000,000,000 water molecules. You may have heard the expression "No two snowflakes are the same." It was this large number of water molecules, and the number of their possible arrangements, that led to that statement.

The units of mass in the metric system have the same prefixes as the units of length.

> **Units of Mass in The Metric System**
>
> 1 kilogram (kg) = 1000 grams (g)
> 1 hectogram (hg) = 100 g
> 1 decagram (dag) = 10 g
> 1 gram (g) = 1 g
> 1 decigram (dg) = 0.1 g
> 1 centigram (cg) = 0.01 g
> 1 milligram (mg) = 0.001 g

Weight ≈ 1 gram

Conversion between units of mass in the metric system involves moving the decimal point to the right or to the left. Listing the units in order from largest to smallest will indicate how many places to move the decimal point and in which direction.

To convert 324 g to kilograms, first write the units in order from largest to smallest.

kg hg dag g dg cg mg
         3 positions

324 g = 0.324 kg
         3 places

• Converting g to kg requires moving 3 positions to the left.

• Move the decimal point the same number of places and in the same direction.

Example 1 Convert 4.23 g to milligrams.

Solution   4.23 g = 4230 mg

You Try It 1 Convert 42.3 mg to grams.

Your solution

Example 2   Convert 2 kg 564 g to kilograms.

Solution
$$564 \text{ g} = 0.564 \text{ kg}$$
$$2 \text{ kg } 564 \text{ g} = 2 \text{ kg} + 0.564 \text{ kg}$$
$$= 2.564 \text{ kg}$$

You Try It 2   Convert 3 g 54 mg to grams.

Your solution

Objective B   **To solve application problems**

TAKE NOTE

Although in this text we will always change units to the larger unit, it is possible to perform the calculation by changing to the smaller unit.

$$3 \text{ kg} - 750 \text{ g}$$
$$= 3000 \text{ g} - 750 \text{ g}$$
$$= 2250 \text{ g}$$

Note that
$$2250 \text{ g} = 2.250 \text{ kg}.$$

In the application problems in this section, we perform arithmetic operations with the measurements of mass in the metric system. Remember that before measurements can be added or subtracted, they must be expressed in terms of the same unit. In this textbook, unless otherwise stated, the units should be changed to the larger unit before the arithmetic operation is performed.

To subtract 750 g from 3 kg, convert 750 g to kilograms.

$$3 \text{ kg} - 750 \text{ g} = 3 \text{ kg} - 0.750 \text{ kg}$$
$$= 2.250 \text{ kg}$$

Example 3

Find the cost of three packages of ground meat weighing 540 g, 670 g, and 890 g if the price per kilogram is $9.89. Round to the nearest cent.

Strategy

To find the cost of the meat:

- Find the total weight of the three packages.
- Convert the total weight to kilograms.
- Multiply the weight by the cost per kilogram ($9.89).

Solution

$$540 \text{ g} + 670 \text{ g} + 890 \text{ g} = 2100 \text{ g}$$

$$2100 \text{ g} = 2.1 \text{ kg}$$

$$2.1 \times 9.89 = 20.769$$

The cost of the meat is $20.77.

You Try It 3

How many kilograms of fertilizer are required to fertilize 400 trees in an apple orchard if 300 g of fertilizer are used for each tree?

Your strategy

Your solution

9.2 Exercises

Objective A   To convert units of mass in the metric system of measurement

For Exercises 1 to 24, convert.

1. 420 g = _____ kg

2. 7421 g = _____ kg

3. 127 mg = _____ g

4. 43 mg = _____ g

5. 4.2 kg = _____ g

6. 0.027 kg = _____ g

7. 0.45 g = _____ mg

8. 325 g = _____ mg

9. 1856 g = _____ kg

10. 8900 g = _____ kg

11. 4057 mg = _____ g

12. 1970 mg = _____ g

13. 1.37 kg = _____ g

14. 5.1 kg = _____ g

15. 0.0456 g = _____ mg

16. 0.2 g = _____ mg

17. 18,000 g = _____ kg

18. 0.87 kg = _____ g

19. 3 kg 922 g = _____ kg

20. 1 kg 47 g = _____ kg

21. 7 g 891 mg = _____ g

22. 209 g 42 mg = _____ g

23. 4 kg 63 g = _____ kg

24. 18 g 5 mg = _____ g

Objective B   To solve application problems

25. **Consumerism** A 1.19-kilogram container of Quaker Oats contains 30 servings. Find the number of grams in one serving of the oatmeal. Round to the nearest whole number.

26. Nutrition A patient is advised to supplement her diet with 2 g of calcium per day. The calcium tablets she purchases contain 500 mg of calcium per tablet. How many tablets per day should the patient take?

27. Nutrition
   a. One egg contains 274 mg of cholesterol. How many grams of cholesterol are in a dozen eggs?
   b. One glass of milk contains 33 mg of cholesterol. How many grams of cholesterol are in four glasses of milk?

28. Gemology A carat is a unit of weight equal to 200 mg. Find the weight in grams of a 10-carat precious stone.

29. Consumerism The nutrition label for a corn bread mix is shown at the right.
   a. How many kilograms of mix are in the package?
   b. How many grams of sodium are contained in two servings of the corn bread?

Nutrition Facts		
Serving Size ⅙ pkg. (31g mix)		
Servings Per Container 6		
Amount Per Serving	**Mix**	**Prepared**
Calories	110	160
Calories from Fat	10	50
		% Daily Value*
Total Fat 1g	1%	9%
Saturated Fat 0g	0%	7%
Cholesterol 0mg	0%	12%
Sodium 210mg	9%	11%
Total Carbohydrate 24g	8%	8%
Sugars 6g		
Protein 2g		

30. Consumerism Find the cost of three packages of ground meat weighing 470 g, 680 g, and 590 g if the price per kilogram is $8.40.

31. Landscaping Eighty grams of grass seed are used for every 100 m² of lawn. How many kilograms of grass seed are needed to cover 2000 m²?

32. Airlines A commuter flight charges $9.95 for each kilogram or part of a kilogram over 15 kg of luggage weight. How much extra must be paid for three pieces of luggage weighing 6450 g, 5850 g, and 7500 g?

33. Business A health food store buys nuts in 10-kilogram containers and repackages the nuts for resale. The store packages the nuts in 200-gram bags, costing $.04 each, and sells them for $3.89 per bag. Find the profit on a 10-kilogram container of nuts costing $75.

34. Measurements A trailer is loaded with nine automobiles weighing 1405 kg each. Find the total weight of the automobiles.

35. Agriculture During 1 year the United States exported 37,141 million kg of wheat, 2680 million kg of rice, and 40,365 million kg of corn. What percent of the total of these grain exports was corn? Round to the nearest tenth of a percent.

APPLYING THE CONCEPTS

36. Define a metric ton. Convert the weights in Exercise 35 to metric tons.

37. Discuss the advantages and disadvantages of the U.S. Customary System and the metric system of measurement.

9.3 Capacity

Objective A   **To convert units of capacity in the metric system of measurement**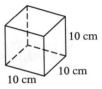

The basic unit of capacity in the metric system is the liter. One **liter** is defined as the capacity of a box that is 10 cm long on each side.

The units of capacity in the metric system have the same prefixes as the units of length.

1-liter bottle

1 cm
1 cm
1 cm
1 ml = 1 cm³

> **Units of Capacity in the Metric System**
>
> 1 kiloliter (kl) = 1000 L
> 1 hectoliter (hl) = 100 L
> 1 decaliter (dal) = 10 L
> 1 liter (L) = 1 L
> 1 deciliter (dl) = 0.1 L
> 1 centiliter (cl) = 0.01 L
> 1 milliliter (ml) = 0.001 L

10 cm
10 cm
10 cm

The milliliter is equal to 1 **cubic centimeter** (cm^3).

Conversion between units of capacity in the metric system involves moving the decimal point to the right or to the left. Listing the units in order from largest to smallest will indicate how many places to move the decimal point and in which direction.

To convert 824 ml to liters, first write the units in order from largest to smallest.

kl hl dal L dl cl ml
3 positions

824 ml = 0.824 L
3 places

- **Converting ml to L requires moving 3 positions to the left.**

- **Move the decimal point the same number of places and in the same direction.**

Example 1   Convert 4 L 32 ml to liters.

Solution   32 ml = 0.032 L

4 L 32 ml = 4 L + 0.032 L
          = 4.032 L

You Try It 1   Convert 2 kl 167 L to liters.

Your solution

Example 2 Convert 1.23 L to cubic centimeters.

Solution 1.23 L = 1230 ml = 1230 cm³

You Try It 2 Convert 325 cm³ to liters.

Your solution

Objective B **To solve application problems**

TAKE NOTE
Although in this text we will always change units to the larger unit, it is possible to perform the calculation by changing to the smaller unit.

2.5 kl + 875 L
= 2500 L + 875 L
= 3375 L
Note that
3375 L = 3.375 kl.

In the application problems in this section, we perform arithmetic operations with the measurements of capacity in the metric system. Remember that before measurements can be added or subtracted, they must be expressed in terms of the same unit. In this textbook, unless otherwise stated, the units should be changed to the larger unit before the arithmetic operation is performed.

To add 2.5 kl and 875 L, convert 875 L to kiloliters.

$$2.5 \text{ kl} + 875 \text{ L} = 2.5 \text{ kl} + 0.875 \text{ kl}$$
$$= 3.375 \text{ kl}$$

Example 3

A laboratory assistant is in charge of ordering acid for three chemistry classes of 30 students each. Each student requires 80 ml of acid. How many liters of acid should be ordered? (The assistant must order by the whole liter.)

Strategy
To find the number of liters to be ordered:
• Find the number of milliliters of acid needed by multiplying the number of classes (3) by the number of students per class (30) by the number of milliliters of acid required by each student (80).
• Convert milliliters to liters.
• Round up to the nearest whole number.

Solution
3(30)(80) = 7200 ml

7200 ml = 7.2 L

7.2 rounded up to the nearest whole number is 8.

The assistant should order 8 L of acid.

You Try It 3

For $299.50, a cosmetician buys 5 L of moisturizer and repackages it in 125-milliliter jars. Each jar costs the cosmetician $.85. Each jar of moisturizer is sold for $29.95. Find the profit on the 5 L of moisturizer.

Your strategy

Your solution

9.3 Exercises

Objective A   **To convert units of capacity in the metric system of measurement**

For Exercises 1 to 24, convert.

1. 4200 ml = _____ L

2. 7.5 ml = _____ L

3. 3.42 L = _____ ml

4. 0.037 L = _____ ml

5. 423 ml = _____ cm^3

6. 0.32 ml = _____ cm^3

7. 642 cm^3 = _____ ml

8. 0.083 cm^3 = _____ ml

9. 42 cm^3 = _____ L

10. 3075 cm^3 = _____ L

11. 0.435 L = _____ cm^3

12. 2.57 L = _____ cm^3

13. 4.62 kl = _____ L

14. 0.035 kl = _____ L

15. 1423 L = _____ kl

16. 897 L = _____ kl

17. 1.267 L = _____ cm^3

18. 4.105 L = _____ cm^3

19. 3 L 42 ml = _____ L

20. 1 L 127 ml = _____ L

21. 3 kl 4 L = _____ kl

22. 6 kl 32 L = _____ kl

23. 8 L 200 ml = _____ L

24. 9 kl 505 L = _____ kl

Objective B   **To solve application problems**

25. **Earth Science** The air in Earth's atmosphere is 78% nitrogen and 21% oxygen.
  a. Without calculating, determine whether the amount of oxygen in 50 L of air is more or less than 25 L.
  b. Find the amount of oxygen in 50 L of air.

26. **Consumerism** A can of tomato juice contains 1.36 L. How many 170-milliliter servings are in one can of tomato juice?

27. **Measurements** An athletic club uses 800 ml of chlorine each day for its swimming pool. How many liters of chlorine are used in a month of 30 days?

28. **Consumerism** The printed label from a container of milk is shown at the right. How many 230-milliliter servings are in the container? Round to the nearest whole number.

29. **Medicine** A flu vaccine is being given for the coming winter season. A medical corporation buys 12 L of flu vaccine. How many patients can be immunized if each person receives 3 cm³ of the vaccine?

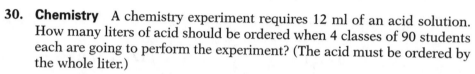

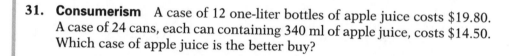

1 GAL (3.78 L)

30. **Chemistry** A chemistry experiment requires 12 ml of an acid solution. How many liters of acid should be ordered when 4 classes of 90 students each are going to perform the experiment? (The acid must be ordered by the whole liter.)

31. **Consumerism** A case of 12 one-liter bottles of apple juice costs $19.80. A case of 24 cans, each can containing 340 ml of apple juice, costs $14.50. Which case of apple juice is the better buy?

32. **Business** For $195, a pharmacist purchases 5 L of cough syrup and repackages it in 250-milliliter bottles. Each bottle costs the pharmacist $.55. Each bottle of cough syrup is sold for $23.89. Find the profit on the 5 L of cough syrup.

33. **Business** A service station operator bought 85 kl of gasoline for $23,750. The gasoline was sold for $.379 per liter. Find the profit on the 85 kl of gasoline.

34. **Business** A wholesale distributor purchased 32 kl of cooking oil for $44,480. The wholesaler repackaged the cooking oil in 1.25-liter bottles. The bottles cost $.21 each. Each bottle of cooking oil was sold for $2.97. Find the distributor's profit on the 32 kl of cooking oil.

APPLYING THE CONCEPTS

35. After a 280-milliliter serving is taken from a 3-liter bottle of water, how much water remains in the container? Write the answer in three different ways.

36. Write an essay describing problems in trade and manufacturing that arise between the United States and Europe because they use different systems of measurement.

9.4 Energy

Objective A   **To use units of energy in the metric system of measurement**

Two commonly used units of energy in the metric system are the calorie and the watt-hour.

Heat is generally measured in units called calories or in larger units called Calories (with a capital C). A **Calorie** is 1000 calories and should be called a kilocalorie, but it is common practice in nutritional references and food labeling to simply call it a Calorie. A Calorie is the amount of heat required to raise the temperature of 1 kg of water 1 degree Celsius. One Calorie is also the energy required to lift 1 kg a distance of 427 m.

HOW TO   Swimming uses 480 Calories per hour. How many Calories are used by swimming $\frac{1}{2}$ h each day for 30 days?

Strategy To find the number of Calories used:

- Find the number of hours spent swimming.
- Multiply the number of hours spent swimming by the Calories used per hour.

Solution $\frac{1}{2} \times 30 = 15$

$15(480) = 7200$

7200 Calories are used by swimming $\frac{1}{2}$ h each day for 30 days.

The **watt-hour** is used for measuring electrical energy. One watt-hour is the amount of energy required to lift 1 kg a distance of 370 m. A light bulb rated at 100 watts (W) will emit 100 watt-hours (Wh) of energy each hour. A **kilowatt-hour** is 1000 watt-hours.

1000 watt-hours (Wh) = 1 kilowatt-hour (kWh)

> **TAKE NOTE**
> Recall that the prefix kilo- means 1000.

HOW TO   A 150-watt bulb is on for 8 h. At 8¢ per kilowatt-hour, find the cost of the energy used.

Strategy To find the cost:

- Find the number of watt-hours used.
- Convert to kilowatt-hours.
- Multiply the number of kilowatt-hours used by the cost per kilowatt-hour.

Solution $150 \times 8 = 1200$

1200 Wh = 1.2 kWh

$1.2 \times 0.08 = 0.096$

The cost of the energy used is $.096.

> **Integrating Technology**
> To convert watt-hours to kilowatt-hours, divide by 1000. To use a calculator to determine the number of kilowatt-hours used in the problem at the right, enter the following:
>
> 150 ✕ 8 ÷ 1000 =
>
> The calculator display reads 1.2.

Example 1

Walking uses 180 Calories per hour. How many Calories will you burn off by walking $5\frac{1}{4}$ h during one week?

Strategy

To find the number of Calories, multiply the number of hours spent walking by the Calories used per hour.

Solution

$$5\frac{1}{4} \times 180 = \frac{21}{4} \times 180 = 945$$

You will burn off 945 Calories.

You Try It 1

Housework requires 240 Calories per hour. How many Calories are burned off by doing $4\frac{1}{2}$ h of housework?

Your strategy

Your solution

Example 2

A clothes iron is rated at 1200 W. If the iron is used for 1.5 h, how much energy, in kilowatt-hours, is used?

Strategy

To find the energy used:
• Find the number of watt-hours used.
• Convert watt-hours to kilowatt-hours.

Solution

$1200 \times 1.5 = 1800$

1800 Wh $= 1.8$ kWh

1.8 kWh of energy are used.

You Try It 2

Find the number of kilowatt-hours of energy used when a 150-watt light bulb burns for 200 h.

Your strategy

Your solution

Example 3

A TV set rated at 1800 W is on for an average of 3.5 h per day. At 7.2¢ per kilowatt-hour, find the cost of operating the set for 1 week.

Strategy

To find the cost:
• Multiply to find the total number of hours the set is used per week.
• Multiply the product by the number of watts to find the watt-hours.
• Convert watt-hours to kilowatt-hours.
• Multiply the number of kilowatt-hours by the cost per kilowatt-hour.

Solution

$3.5 \times 7 = 24.5$

$24.5 \times 1800 = 44{,}100$

$44{,}100$ Wh $= 44.1$ kWh

$44.1 \times 0.072 = 3.1752$

The cost is $3.1752.

You Try It 3

A microwave oven rated at 500 W is used an average of 20 min per day. At 8.7¢ per kilowatt-hour, find the cost of operating the oven for 30 days.

Your strategy

Your solution

9.4 Exercises

Objective A To use units of energy in the metric system of measurement

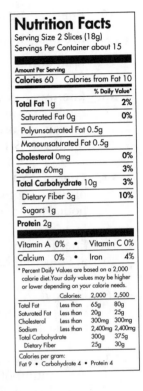

Nutrition Facts

Serving Size 2 Slices (18g)
Servings Per Container about 15

Amount Per Serving

Calories 60	Calories from Fat 10

	% Daily Value*
Total Fat 1g	2%
Saturated Fat 0g	0%
Polyunsaturated Fat 0.5g	
Monounsaturated Fat 0.5g	
Cholesterol 0mg	0%
Sodium 60mg	3%
Total Carbohydrate 10g	3%
Dietary Fiber 3g	10%
Sugars 1g	
Protein 2g	

Vitamin A 0%	•	Vitamin C 0%
Calcium 0%	•	Iron 4%

* Percent Daily Values are based on a 2,000 calorie diet. Your daily values may be higher or lower depending on your calorie needs.

	Calories:	2,000	2,500
Total Fat	Less than	65g	80g
Saturated Fat	Less than	20g	25g
Cholesterol	Less than	300mg	300mg
Sodium	Less than	2,400mg	2,400mg
Total Carbohydrate		300g	375g
Dietary Fiber		25g	30g

Calories per gram:
Fat 9 • Carbohydrate 4 • Protein 4

1. **Health** How many Calories can you eliminate from your diet by omitting 1 slice of bread per day for 30 days? One slice of bread contains 110 Calories.

2. **Health** How many Calories can you eliminate from your diet in 2 weeks by omitting 400 Calories per day?

3. **Nutrition** A nutrition label from a package of crisp bread is shown at the right.
   a. How many Calories are in $1\frac{1}{2}$ servings?
   b. How many Calories from fat are in 6 slices of the bread?

4. **Health** Moderately active people need 20 Calories per pound of body weight to maintain their weight. How many Calories should a 150-pound, moderately active person consume per day to maintain that weight?

5. **Health** People whose daily activity level would be described as light need 15 Calories per pound of body weight to maintain their weight. How many Calories should a 135-pound, lightly active person consume per day to maintain that weight?

6. **Health** For a healthful diet, it is recommended that 55% of the daily intake of Calories come from carbohydrates. Find the daily intake of Calories from carbohydrates that is appropriate if you want to limit your Calorie intake to 1600 Calories.

7. **Health** Playing singles tennis requires 450 Calories per hour. How many Calories do you burn in 30 days playing 45 min per day?

8. **Health** After playing golf for 3 h, Ruben had a banana split containing 550 Calories. Playing golf uses 320 Calories per hour.
   a. Without doing the calculations, did the banana split contain more or fewer Calories than Ruben burned off playing golf?
   b. Find the number of Calories Ruben gained or lost from these two activities.

9. **Health** Hiking requires approximately 315 Calories per hour. How many hours would you have to hike to burn off the Calories in a 375-Calorie sandwich, a 150-Calorie soda, and a 280-Calorie ice cream cone? Round to the nearest tenth.

10. **Health** Riding a bicycle requires 265 Calories per hour. How many hours would Shawna have to ride a bicycle to burn off the Calories in a 320-Calorie milkshake, a 310-Calorie cheeseburger, and a 150-Calorie apple? Round to the nearest tenth.

11. Energy An oven uses 500 W of energy. How many watt-hours of energy are used to cook a 5-kilogram roast for $2\frac{1}{2}$ h?

12. Energy A 21-inch color TV set is rated at 90 W. The TV is used an average of $3\frac{1}{2}$ h each day for a week. How many kilowatt-hours of energy are used during the week?

13. Energy A fax machine is rated at 9 W when the machine is in standby mode and at 36 W when in operation. How many kilowatt-hours of energy are used during a week in which the fax machine is in standby mode for 39 h and in operation for 6 h?

14. Energy A 120-watt CD player is on an average of 2 h a day. Find the cost of listening to the CD player for 2 weeks at a cost of 9.4¢ per kilowatt-hour. Round to the nearest cent.

15. Energy How much does it cost to run a 2200-watt air conditioner for 8 h at 9¢ per kilowatt-hour? Round to the nearest cent.

16. Energy A space heater is used for 3 h. The heater uses 1400 W per hour. Electricity costs 11.1¢ per kilowatt-hour. Find the cost of using the electric heater. Round to the nearest cent.

17. Energy A 60-watt Sylvania Long Life Soft White Bulb has a light output of 835 lumens and an average life of 1250 h. A 34-watt Sylvania Energy Saver Bulb has a light output of 400 lumens and an average life of 1500 h.
  a. Is the light output of the Energy Saver Bulb more or less than half that of the Long Life Soft White Bulb?
  b. If electricity costs 10.8¢ per kilowatt-hour, what is the difference in cost between using the Long Life Soft White Bulb for 150 h and using the Energy Saver Bulb for 150 h? Round to the nearest cent.

18. Energy A house is insulated to save energy. The house used 265 kWh of electrical energy per month before insulation and saves 45 kWh of energy per month after insulation. What percent decrease does this amount represent? Round to the nearest tenth of a percent.

19. Energy A welder uses 6.5 kWh of energy each hour. Find the cost of using the welder for 6 h a day for 30 days. The cost is 9.4¢ per kilowatt-hour.

APPLYING THE CONCEPTS

20. Write an essay on how to improve the energy efficiency of a home.

21. A maintenance intake of Calories allows a person to neither gain nor lose weight. Consult a book on nutrition in order to make a table of weights and the corresponding maintenance intake of Calories. Then, for each weight, add another column indicating the appropriate Calorie intake when an individual at that weight wants to lose 1 lb per week.

Focus on Problem Solving

Working Backward

Sometimes the solution to a problem can be found by *working backward*. This problem-solving technique can be used to find a winning strategy for a game called Nim.

There are many variations of this game. For our game, there are two players, Player A and Player B, who alternately place 1, 2, or 3 matchsticks in a pile. The object of the game is to place the 32nd matchstick in the pile. Is there a strategy that Player A can use to guarantee winning the game?

Working backward, if there are 29, 30, or 31 matchsticks in the pile when it is A's turn to play, A can win by placing 3 matchsticks (29 + 3 = 32), 2 matchsticks, (30 + 2 = 32), or 1 matchstick (31 + 1 = 32) on the pile. If there are to be 29, 30, or 31 matchsticks in the pile when it is A's turn, there must be 28 matchsticks in the pile when it is B's turn.

Working backward from 28, if there are to be 28 matches in the pile at B's turn, there must be 25, 26, or 27 at A's turn. Player A can then add 3 matchsticks, 2 matchsticks, or 1 matchstick to the pile to bring the number to 28. For there to be 25, 26, or 27 matchsticks in the pile at A's turn, there must be 24 matchsticks at B's turn.

Now working backward from 24, if there are to be 24 matches in the pile at B's turn, there must be 21, 22, or 23 at A's turn. Player A can then add 3 matchsticks, 2 matchsticks, or 1 matchstick to the pile to bring the number to 24. For there to be 21, 22, or 23 matchsticks in the pile at A's turn, there must be 20 matchsticks at B's turn.

So far, we have found that for Player A to win, there must be 28, 24, or 20 matchsticks in the pile when it is B's turn to play. Note that each time, the number is decreasing by 4. Continuing this pattern, Player A will win if there are 16, 12, 8, or 4 matchsticks in the pile when it is B's turn.

Player A can guarantee winning by making sure that the number of matchsticks in the pile is a multiple of 4. To ensure this, Player A allows Player B to go first and then adds exactly enough matchsticks to the pile to bring the total to a multiple of 4.

For example, suppose B places 3 matchsticks in the pile; then A places 1 matchstick (3 + 1 = 4). Now B places 2 matchsticks in the pile. The total is now 6 matchsticks. Player A then places 2 matchsticks in the pile to bring the total to 8, a multiple of 4. If play continues in this way, Player A will win.

Here are some variations of Nim. See whether you can develop a winning strategy for Player A.

1. Suppose the goal is to place the last matchstick in a pile of 30 matches.

2. Suppose the players make two piles of matchsticks, with the final number of matchsticks in each pile to be 20.

3. In this variation of Nim, there are 40 matchsticks in a pile. Each player alternately removes 1, 2, or 3 matches from the pile. The player who removes the last match wins.

Projects and Group Activities

Name That Metric Unit

What unit in the metric system would be used to measure each of the following? If you are working in a group, be sure that each member agrees on the unit to be used and understands why that unit is used before going on to the next item.

1. The distance from Los Angeles to New York

2. The weight of a truck

3. A person's waist

4. The amount of coffee in a mug

5. The weight of a thumbtack

6. The amount of water in a swimming pool

7. The distance a baseball player hits a baseball

8. A person's hat size

9. The amount of protein needed daily

10. A person's weight

11. The amount of maple syrup served with pancakes

12. The amount of water in a water cooler

13. The amount of medication in an aspirin

14. The distance to the grocery store

15. The width of a hair

16. A person's height

17. The weight of a lawn mower

18. The amount of water a family uses monthly

19. The contents of a bottle of salad dressing

20. The newspapers collected at a recycling center

Metric Measurements for Computers

Other prefixes in the metric system are becoming more commonly used as a result of technological advances in the computer industry. For example, the speed of a computer used to be measured in microseconds and then in nanoseconds, but now computer speeds are measured in picoseconds.

tera-	= 1,000,000,000,000
giga-	= 1,000,000,000
mega-	= 1,000,000
micro-	= 0.000001
nano-	= 0.000000001
pico-	= 0.000000000001

1. Complete the table.

Metric System Prefix	Symbol	Magnitude	Means Multiply the Basic Unit By:
tera-	T	10^{12}	1,000,000,000,000
giga-	G	___	1,000,000,000
mega-	M	10^6	___
kilo-	___	___	1,000
hecto-	h	___	100
deca-	da	10^1	___
deci-	d	$\dfrac{1}{10}$	___
centi-	___	$\dfrac{1}{10^2}$	___
milli-	___	___	0.001
micro-	μ	$\dfrac{1}{10^6}$	___
nano-	n	$\dfrac{1}{10^9}$	___
pico-	p	___	0.000000000001

2. How can the Magnitude column in the table above be used to determine how many places to move the decimal point when converting to the basic unit in the metric system?

A **bit** is the smallest unit of code that computers can read; it is a binary digit, either a 0 or a 1. A bit is abbreviated b. Usually bits are grouped into **bytes** of 8 bits. Each byte stands for a letter, number, or any other symbol we might use in communicating information. For example, the letter W can be represented 01010111. A byte is abbreviated B.

The amount of memory in a computer hard drive is measured in terabytes (TB), gigabytes (GB), and megabytes (MB). Often a gigabyte is referred to as a gig, and a megabyte is referred to as a meg. Using the definitions of the prefixes given above, a kilobyte is 1000 bytes, a megabyte is 1,000,000 bytes, and a gigabyte is 1,000,000,000 bytes. However, these are not exact equivalences. Bytes are actually computed in powers of 2. Therefore, kilobytes, megabytes, gigabytes, and terabytes are powers of 2. The exact equivalences are shown below.

> 1 byte = 2^3 bits
> 1 kilobyte = 2^{10} bytes = 1,024 bytes
> 1 megabyte = 2^{20} bytes = 1,048,576 bytes
> 1 gigabyte = 2^{30} bytes = 1,073,741,824 bytes
> 1 terabyte = 2^{40} bytes = 1,099,511,627,776 bytes

Apple iBook 900MHz 14" (M9009LL/A) Memory

SALE
Maximum Memory **640MB**

3. Find an advertisement for a computer system. What is the computer's storage capacity? Convert the capacity to bytes. Use the exact equivalences given above.

Chapter Summary

Key Words

The *metric system* of measurement is an internationally standardized system of measurement. It is based on the decimal system. The basic unit of length in the metric system is the *meter*.

The basic unit of *mass* is the *gram*.

The basic unit of capacity is the *liter*.

Heat is commonly measured in units called *Calories*.

The *watt-hour* is used in the metric system for measuring electrical energy.

In the metric system, prefixes to the basic unit denote the magnitude of each unit.

kilo- = 1000   *deci-* = 0.1
hecto- = 100   *centi-* = 0.01
deca- = 10   *milli-* = 0.001

Examples

1 km = 1000 m
1 kg = 1000 g
1 kl = 1000 L

1 m = 100 cm
1 m = 1000 mm
1 g = 1000 mg
1 L = 1000 ml

Essential Rules and Procedures

Converting between units in the metric system involves moving the decimal point to the right or to the left. Listing the units in order from largest to smallest will indicate how many places to move the decimal point and in which direction.

1. When converting from a larger unit to a smaller unit, move the decimal point to the *right*.
2. When converting from a smaller unit to a larger unit, move the decimal point to the *left*.

Approximate equivalences between units in the U.S. Customary and the metric systems of measurement are used to form conversion rates to change one unit of measurement to another.

Units of Length
1 in. = 2.54 cm
1 m ≈ 3.28 ft
1 m ≈ 1.09 yd
1 mi ≈ 1.61 km

Units of Weight
1 oz ≈ 28.35 g
1 lb ≈ 454 g
1 kg ≈ 2.2 lb

Units of Capacity
1 L ≈ 1.06 qt
1 gal ≈ 3.79 L

Examples

Convert 3.7 kg to grams.
$$3.7 \text{ kg} = 3700 \text{ g}$$

Convert 2387 m to kilometers.
$$2387 \text{ m} = 2.387 \text{ km}$$

Convert 9.5 L to milliliters.
$$9.5 \text{ L} = 9500 \text{ ml}$$

Convert 20 mi/h to kilometers per hour.
$$\frac{20 \text{ mi}}{\text{h}} \approx \frac{20 \text{ mi}}{\text{h}} \times \frac{1.61 \text{ km}}{1 \text{ mi}}$$
$$\approx \frac{32.2 \text{ km}}{1 \text{ h}}$$
$$\approx 32.2 \text{ km/h}$$

Convert 1000 m to yards.
$$1000 \text{ m} \approx 1000 \text{ m} \times \frac{1.09 \text{ yd}}{1 \text{ m}}$$
$$\approx 1090 \text{ yd}$$

Chapter Review Exercises

1. Convert 1.25 km to meters.

2. Convert 0.450 g to milligrams.

3. Convert 0.0056 L to milliliters.

4. Convert the 1000-meter run to yards. ($1\ m \approx 1.09\ yd$)

5. Convert 79 mm to centimeters.

6. Convert 5 m 34 cm to meters.

7. Convert 990 g to kilograms.

8. Convert 2550 ml to liters.

9. Convert 4870 m to kilometers.

10. Convert 0.37 cm to millimeters.

11. Convert 6 g 829 mg to grams.

12. Convert 1.2 L to cubic centimeters.

13. Convert 4.050 kg to grams.

14. Convert 8.7 m to centimeters.

15. Convert 192 ml to cubic centimeters.

16. Convert 356 mg to grams.

17. Convert 372 cm to meters.

18. Convert 8.3 kl to liters.

19. Convert 2 L 89 ml to liters.

20. Convert 5410 cm^3 to liters.

21. Convert 3792 L to kiloliters.

22. Convert 468 cm^3 to milliliters.

23. **Measurements** Three pieces of wire are cut from a 50-meter roll. The three pieces measure 240 cm, 560 cm, and 480 cm. How much wire is left on the roll after the three pieces are cut?

24. **Consumerism** Find the total cost of three packages of chicken weighing 790 g, 830 g, and 655 g if the cost is $5.59 per kilogram.

25. **Consumerism** Cheese costs $3.40 per pound. Find the cost per kilogram. (1 kg ≈ 2.2 lb)

26. **Measurements** One hundred twenty-five guests are expected to attend a reception. Assuming that each person drinks 400 ml of coffee, how many liters of coffee should be prepared?

27. **Nutrition** A large egg contains approximately 90 Calories. How many Calories can you eliminate from your diet in a 30-day month by eliminating one large egg per day from your usual breakfast?

28. **Energy** A TV uses 240 W of energy. The set is on an average of 5 h a day in a 30-day month. At a cost of 9.5¢ per kilowatt-hour, how much does it cost to run the set for 30 days?

29. **Measurements** A backpack weighs 1.90 kg. Find the weight in pounds. Round to the nearest hundredth. (1 kg ≈ 2.2 lb)

30. **Health** Cycling burns up approximately 400 Calories per hour. How many hours of cycling are necessary to lose 1 lb? (3500 Calories are equivalent to 1 lb.)

31. **Business** Six liters of liquid soap were bought for $11.40 per liter. The soap was repackaged in 150-milliliter plastic containers. The cost of each container was $.26. Each container of soap sold for $3.29 per bottle. Find the profit on the 6 L of liquid soap.

32. **Energy** A color TV is rated at 80 W. The TV is used an average of 2 h each day for a week. How many kilowatt-hours of energy are used during the week?

33. **Agriculture** How many kilograms of fertilizer are necessary to fertilize 500 trees in an orchard if 250 g of fertilizer is used for each tree?

Chapter Test

1. Convert 2.96 km to meters.

2. Convert 0.378 g to milligrams.

3. Convert 0.046 L to milliliters.

4. Convert 919 cm^3 to milliliters.

5. Convert 42.6 mm to centimeters.

6. Convert 7 m 96 cm to meters.

7. Convert 847 g to kilograms.

8. Convert 3920 ml to liters.

9. Convert 5885 m to kilometers.

10. Convert 1.5 cm to millimeters.

11. Convert 3 g 89 mg to grams.

12. Convert 1.6 L to cubic centimeters.

13. Convert 3.29 kg to grams.

14. Convert 4.2 m to centimeters.

15. Convert 96 ml to cubic centimeters.

16. Convert 1375 mg to grams.

17. Convert 402 cm to meters.

18. Convert 8.92 kl to liters.

19. **Health** Sedentary people need 15 Calories per pound of body weight to maintain their weight. How many Calories should a 140-pound, sedentary person consume per day to maintain that weight?

20. **Energy** A color television is rated at 100 W. The television is used an average of $4\frac{1}{2}$ h each day for a week. Find the number of kilowatt-hours of energy used during the week for operating the television.

21. Carpentry   A carpenter needs 30 rafters, each 380 cm long. Find the total length of the rafters in meters.

22. Measurements   A tile measuring 20×20 cm weighs 250 g. Find the weight, in kilograms, of a box of 144 tiles.

23. Medicine   The community health clinic is giving flu shots for the coming flu season. Each flu shot contains 2 cm^3 of vaccine. How many liters of vaccine are needed to inoculate 2600 people?

24. Measurements   Convert 35 mi/h to kilometers per hour. Round to the nearest tenth. (1 mi $\approx$ 1.61 km)

25. Metal Works   Twenty-five rivets are used to fasten two steel plates together. The plates are 4.20 m long, and the rivets are equally spaced, with a rivet at each end. Find the distance, in centimeters, between the rivets.

26. Agriculture   Two hundred grams of fertilizer are used for each tree in an orchard containing 1200 trees. At \$2.75 per kilogram of fertilizer, how much does it cost to fertilize the orchard?

27. Energy   An air conditioner rated at 1600 W is operated an average of 4 h per day. Electrical energy costs 8.5¢ per kilowatt-hour. How much does it cost to operate the air conditioner for 30 days?

28. Chemistry   A laboratory assistant is in charge of ordering acid for three chemistry classes of 40 students each. Each student requires 90 ml of acid. How many liters of acid should be ordered? (The assistant must order by the whole liter.)

29.   **Sports**   Three ski jumping events are held at the Olympic Games: the individual normal hill, the individual large hill, and the team large hill. The normal hill measures 90 m. The large hill measures 120 m. Convert the measure of the large hill to feet. Round to the nearest tenth. (1 m $\approx$ 3.28 ft)

30.   **Sports**   In the archery competition at the Olympic Games, the center ring, or bull's eye, of the target is approximately 4.8 in. in diameter. Convert 4.8 in. to centimeters. Round to the nearest tenth. (1 in. = 2.54 cm)

chapter

10 Statistics and Probability

Every 10 years, the U.S. Census Bureau collects data about the country's population. It then issues statistical reports that indicate changes and trends in the U.S. population. For example, according to the 2000 Census, there were approximately 105 men for every 100 women in the category of people under the age of 20. Statistics are found in many different sources, such as the radio, television, newspapers, and the Internet. Statistics can also be about anything, from the habits of mall shoppers like those in the photo above, to unusual biological data like these two statistics from www.geocities.com: (1) 70% of the dust in your home consists of shed human skin and hair. (2) Every human spent about one-half hour as a single cell.

Need help? For online student resources, such as section quizzes, visit this textbook's website at **math.college.hmco.com/students.**

1. **Mail** Bill-related mail accounted for 49 billion of the 102 billion pieces of first-class mail handled by the U.S. Postal Service during a recent year. (*Source:* US Postal Service) What percent of the pieces of first-class mail handled by the U.S. Postal Service was bill-related mail? Round to the nearest tenth of a percent.

2. **Education** The table at the right shows the estimated costs of funding an education at a public college.
   a. Between which two enrollment years is the increase in cost greatest?

   b. What is the increase between these two years?

Enrollment Year	Cost of Public College
2005	$70,206
2006	$74,418
2007	$78,883
2008	$83,616
2009	$88,633
2010	$93,951

   Source: The College Board's Annual Survey of Colleges

3. **Sports** During the 1924 Summer Olympics in Paris, France, the United States won 45 gold medals, 27 silver medals, and 27 bronze medals. (*Source: The Ultimate Book of Sports Lists*)
   a. Find the ratio of gold medals won by the United States to silver medals won by the United States during the 1924 Summer Olympics. Write the ratio as a fraction in simplest form.

   b. Find the ratio of silver medals won by the United States to bronze medals won by the United States during the 1924 Summer Olympics. Write the ratio using a colon.

4. **Television** The table below shows the number of television viewers, in millions, who watch pay-cable channels, such as HBO and Showtime, each night of the week. (*Source:* Neilsen Media Research analyzed by Initiative Media North America)

Mon	Tue	Wed	Thu	Fri	Sat	Sun
3.9	4.5	4.2	3.9	5.2	7.1	5.5

   a. Arrange the numbers in the table from least to greatest.

   b. Find the average number of viewers per night.

5. **The Military** Approximately 90,000 women serve in the U.S. military. Five percent of these women serve in the Marine Corps. (*Source:* U.S. Department of Defense)
   a. Approximately how many women are in the Marine Corps?

   b. What fractional amount of women in the military are in the Marine Corps?

GO FIGURE ● ● ●

I have 2 brothers and 1 sister. My father's parents have 10 grandchildren. My mother's parents have 11 grandchildren. If no divorces or remarriages occurred, how many first cousins do I have?

10.1 Pictographs and Circle Graphs

Objective A   **To read a pictograph**

Statistics is the branch of mathematics concerned with **data,** or numerical information. **Graphs** are displays that provide a pictorial representation of data. The advantage of graphs is that they present information in a way that is easily read. The disadvantage of graphs is that they can be misleading. (See "Projects and Group Activities" at the end of this chapter.)

A **pictograph** uses symbols to represent information. The pictograph in Figure 1 represents the net worth of America's richest billionaires. Each symbol represents 10 billion dollars.

Bill Gates

Net Worth (in tens of billions of dollars)

Bill Gates
Warren Buffet
Paul Allen
Larry Ellison
Jim C. Walton

Figure 1 Net worth of America's richest billionaires

Source: **www.Forbes.com**

From the pictograph, we can determine that Bill Gates has the greatest net worth. Warren Buffet's net worth is $10 billion more than Paul Allen's net worth.

HOW TO   The pictograph in Figure 2 represents the responses of 600 young Americans when asked what they would like to have with them on a desert island. "Books" was the response of what percent of the respondents?

Strategy
Use the basic percent equation. The base is 600 (the total number of responses), and the amount is 90 (the number responding "Books").

Solution

Percent × base = amount

$$n \times 600 = 90$$
$$n = 90 \div 600$$
$$n = 0.15$$

15% of the respondents wanted books on a desert island.

Music
Parents
Computer
Books
TV

= 30 responses

Figure 2 What 600 young Americans want on a desert island

Source: Time Magazine

The pictograph in Figure 3 shows the number of new cellular phones purchased in a particular city during a 4-month period.

The ratio of the number of cellular phones purchased in March to the number purchased in January is

$$\frac{3000}{4500} = \frac{2}{3}$$

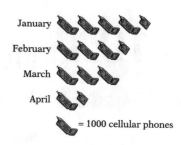

January

February

March

April

= 1000 cellular phones

Figure 3 Monthly cellular phone purchases

Example 1

Use Figure 3 to find the total number of cellular phones purchased during the 4-month period.

Strategy

To find the total number of cellular phones purchased in the 4-month period:

• Read the pictograph to determine the number of cellular phones purchased each month.
• Add the four numbers.

Solution

Purchases for January: 4500
Purchases for February: 3500
Purchases for March: 3000
Purchases for April: 1500

Total purchases for the 4-month period:

```
   4,500
   3,500
   3,000
+  1,500
  _____
  12,500
```

There were 12,500 cellular phones purchased in the 4-month period.

You Try It 1

According to Figure 3, the number of cellular phones purchased in March represents what percent of the total number of cellular phones purchased in that city during that 4-month period?

Your strategy

Your solution

Objective B   **To read a circle graph**

TAKE NOTE

One quadrillion is 1,000,000,000,000,000.

Point of Interest

Fossil fuels include coal, natural gas, and petroleum. Renewable energy includes hydroelectric power, solar energy, wood burning, and wind energy.

A **circle graph** represents data by the size of the sectors. A **sector of a circle** is one of the "pieces of the pie" into which a circle graph is divided.

The circle graph in Figure 4 shows the consumption of energy sources in the United States during a recent year. The complete circle graph represents the total amount of energy consumed, 96.6 quadrillion Btu. Each sector of the circle represents the consumption of energy from a different source.

To find the percent of the total energy consumed that originated from nuclear power, solve the basic percent equation for percent. The base is 96.6 quadrillion Btu, and the amount is 8.2 quadrillion Btu.

Percent × base = amount
$$n \times 96.6 = 8.2$$
$$n = 8.2 \div 96.6$$
$$n \approx 0.085$$

To the nearest tenth of a percent, 8.5% of the energy consumed originated from nuclear power.

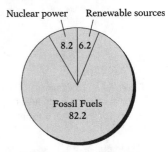

Figure 4 Annual energy consumption in quadrillion Btu in the United States
Source: The World Almanac and Book of Facts 2003

In a recent year, the top 25 companies in the United States spent a total of $17.8 billion for national advertising. The circle graph in Figure 5 shows what percents of the $17.8 billion went to the various advertising media. The complete circle represents 100% of all the money spent by these companies. Each sector of the graph represents the percent of the total spent for a particular medium.

HOW TO   According to Figure 5, how much money was spent for magazine advertising? Round to the nearest hundred million dollars.

Strategy
Use the basic percent equation. The base is $17.8 billion, and the percent is 16%.

Solution
Percent × base = amount
$$0.16 \times 17.8 = n$$
$$2.848 = n$$
2.848 billion = 2,848,000,000

To the nearest hundred million, the amount spent for magazine advertising was $2,800,000,000.

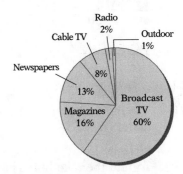

Figure 5 Distribution of advertising dollars for 25 companies
Source: Interep research

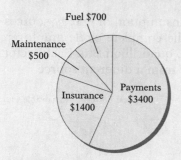

The circle graph in Figure 6 shows typical annual expenses of owning, operating, and financing a new car. Use this figure for Example 2 and You Try It 2.

Figure 6 Annual expenses of $6000 for owning, operating, and financing a car
Source: Based on data from IntelliChoice

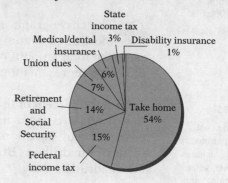

The circle graph in Figure 7 shows the distribution of an employee's gross monthly income. Use this figure for Example 3 and You Try It 3.

Figure 7 Distribution of gross monthly income of $2900

Example 2

Use Figure 6 to find the ratio of the annual insurance expense to the total annual cost of the car.

Strategy
To find the ratio:

- Locate the annual insurance expense in the circle graph.
- Write in simplest form the ratio of the annual insurance expense to the total annual cost of operating the car.

Solution
Annual insurance expense: $1400

$$\frac{1400}{6000} = \frac{7}{30}$$

The ratio is $\frac{7}{30}$.

You Try It 2

Use Figure 6 to find the ratio of the annual cost of fuel to the annual cost of maintenance.

Your strategy

Your solution

Example 3

Use Figure 7 to find the employee's take-home pay.

Strategy
To find the take-home pay:

- Locate the percent of the distribution that is take-home pay.
- Solve the basic percent equation for amount.

Solution
Take-home pay: 54%

Percent × base = amount
0.54   × 2900 = n
         1566 = n

The employee's take-home pay is $1566.

You Try It 3

Use Figure 7 to find the amount paid for medical/dental insurance.

Your strategy

Your solution

10.1 Exercises

Objective A   To read a pictograph

The Film Industry The pictograph in Figure 8 shows the approximate gross revenues in the United States from four Walt Disney animated movies. Use this graph for Exercises 1 to 3.

1. Find the total gross revenues from the four movies.

2. Find the ratio of the gross revenue of *Beauty and the Beast* to the gross revenue of *The Hunchback of Notre Dame*.

3. Find the percent of the total gross revenue that was earned by *The Lion King*.

Figure 8 Gross revenues of four Walt Disney animated movies
Source: **www.worldboxoffice.com**

Space Exploration The pictograph in Figure 9 is based on a survey of adults who were asked whether they agreed with each statement. Use this graph for Exercises 4 to 6.

4. Find the ratio of the number of people who agreed that space exploration impacts daily life to the number of people who agreed that space will be colonized in their lifetime.

5. How many more people agreed that humanity should explore planets than agreed that space exploration impacts daily life?

6. Is the number of people who said they would travel in space more than twice the number of people who agreed that space would be colonized in their lifetime?

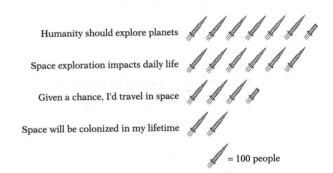

Figure 9 Number of adults who agree with the statement
Source: Opinion Research for Space Day Partners

Children's Behavior The pictograph in Figure 10 is based on a survey of children aged 7 through 12. The percent of children's responses to the survey are shown. Assume that 500 children were surveyed. Use this graph for Exercises 7 to 9.

7. Find the number of children who said they hid vegetables under a napkin.

8. What is the difference between the number of children who fed vegetables to the dog and the number who dropped them on the floor?

9. ✏ Were the responses given in the graph the only responses given by the children? Explain your answer.

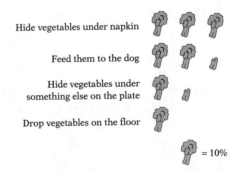

Figure 10 How children try to hide vegetables
Source: Strategic Consulting and Research for Del Monte

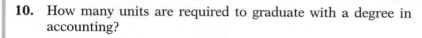

Education An accounting major recorded the number of units required in each discipline to graduate with a degree in accounting. The results are shown in the circle graph in Figure 11. Use this graph for Exercises 10 to 13.

10. How many units are required to graduate with a degree in accounting?

11. What is the ratio of the number of units in finance to the number of units in accounting?

12. What percent of the units required to graduate are taken in accounting? Round to the nearest tenth of a percent.

13. What percent of the units required to graduate are taken in mathematics? Round to the nearest tenth of a percent.

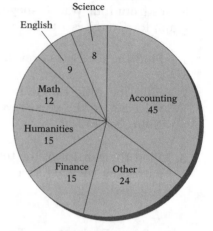

Figure 11 Number of units required to graduate with an accounting degree

Theaters The circle graph in Figure 12 shows the result of a survey in which people were asked, "What bothers you most about movie theaters?" Use this graph for Exercises 14 to 17.

14. **a.** What complaint was mentioned the most often?
    b. What complaint was mentioned the least often?

15. How many people were surveyed? 150

16. What is the ratio of the number of people responding "Dirty floors" to the number responding "High ticket prices"?

17. What percent of the respondents said that people talking bothered them most?

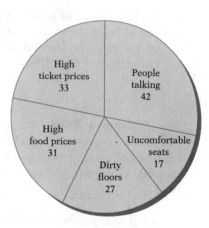

Figure 12 Distribution of responses in a survey

Video Games The circle graph in Figure 13 shows the breakdown of the approximately $3,100,000,000 that Americans spent on home video game equipment in one year. Use this graph for Exercises 18 to 21.

18. Find the amount of money spent on TV game machines.

19. Find the amount of money spent on portable game machines.

20. What fractional amount of the total money spent was spent on accessories?

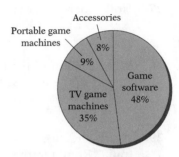

Figure 13 Percents of $3,100,000,000 spent annually on home video games

Source: The NPD Group, Toy Manufacturers of America

21. Is the amount spent for TV game machines more than three times the amount spent for portable game machines?

Demographics The circle graph in Figure 14 shows a breakdown, according to age, of the homeless in America. Use this graph for Exercises 22 to 25.

22. What age group represents the largest segment of the homeless population?

23. Is the number of homeless who are aged 25 to 34 more or less than twice the number who are under the age of 25?

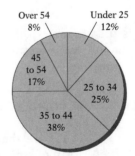

24. What percent of the homeless population is under the age of 35?

Figure 14 Ages of the homeless in America

Source: The Department of Housing and Urban Development

25. On average, how many of every 100,000 homeless people in America are over the age of 54?

Geography The circle graph in Figure 15 shows the land area of each of the seven continents in square miles. Use this graph for Exercises 26 to 29.

26. Find the total land area of the seven continents.

27. How much larger is North America than South America?

28. What percent of the total land area is the land area of Asia? Round to the nearest tenth of a percent.

29. What percent of the total land area is the land area of Australia? Round to the nearest tenth of a percent.

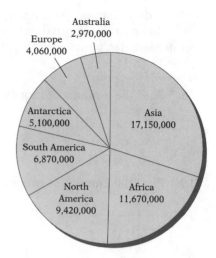

Figure 15 Land area of the seven continents (in square miles)

Cost of Living A typical household in the United States has an average after-tax income of $40,550. The circle graph in Figure 16 represents how this annual income is spent. (*Note:* It is because of rounding that the percents do not add up to 100%.) Use this graph for Exercises 30 to 33.

30. What amount is spent on food?

31. What amount is spent on health care?

32. How much more is spent on clothing than on entertainment?

33. Is the amount spent on housing more than twice the amount spent on transportation?

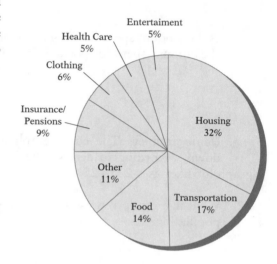

Figure 16 Average annual expenses in a U.S. household
Source: American Demographics

APPLYING THE CONCEPTS

34. a. What are the advantages of presenting data in the form of a pictograph?
    b. What are the disadvantages?

35. The circle graph at the right shows a couple's expenditures last month. Write two observations about this couple's expenses.

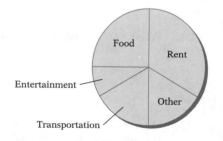

10.2 Bar Graphs and Broken-Line Graphs

Objective A To read a bar graph

A **bar graph** represents data by the height of the bars. The bar graph in Figure 17 shows temperature data recorded for Cincinnati, Ohio, for the months March through November. For each month, the height of the bar indicates the average daily high temperature during that month. The jagged line near the bottom of the graph indicates that the vertical scale is missing the numbers between 0 and 50.

The daily high temperature in September was 78°F. Because the bar for July is the tallest, the daily high temperature was highest in July.

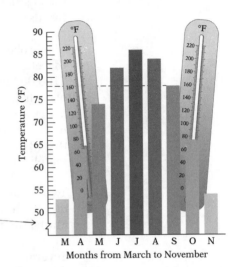

Figure 17 Daily high temperatures in Cincinnati, Ohio

Source: U.S. Weather Bureau

TAKE NOTE

The bar for athletic females is halfway between the marks for 50 and 60. Therefore, we estimate that the lung capacity is halfway between these two numbers, at 55.

A **double-bar graph** is used to display data for purposes of comparison. The double-bar graph in Figure 18 shows the lung capacity of inactive, versus that of athletic, 45-year-olds.

The lung capacity of an athletic female is 55 milliliters of oxygen per kilogram of body weight per minute.

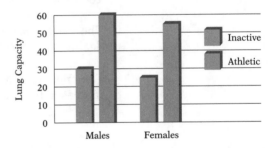

Figure 18 Lung capacity (in milliliters of oxygen per kilogram of body weight per minute)

Example 1

What is the ratio of the lung capacity of an inactive male to that of an athletic male?

Strategy
To write the ratio:

• Read the graph to find the lung capacity of an inactive male and of an athletic male.
• Write the ratio in simplest form.

Solution
Lung capacity of inactive male: 30
Lung capacity of athletic male: 60

$$\frac{30}{60} = \frac{1}{2}$$

The ratio is $\frac{1}{2}$.

You Try It 1

What is the ratio of the lung capacity of an inactive female to that of an athletic female?

Your strategy

Your solution

Objective B **To read a broken-line graph**

A **broken-line graph** represents data by the position of the lines. It is used to show trends.

The broken-line graph in Figure 19 shows the effect of inflation on the value of a $100,000 life insurance policy. The height of each dot indicates the value of the policy.

After 10 years, the purchasing power of the $100,000 has decreased to approximately $60,000.

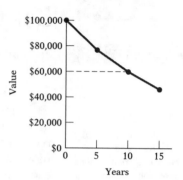

Figure 19 Effect of inflation on the value of a $100,000 life insurance policy

Two broken-line graphs are often shown in the same figure for comparison. Figure 20 shows the net incomes of two software companies, Math Associates and MatheMentors, before their merger.

Several things can be determined from the graph:

The net income for Math Associates in 2004 was $12 million.

The net income for MatheMentors declined from 2000 to 2001.

The net income for Math Associates increased for each year shown.

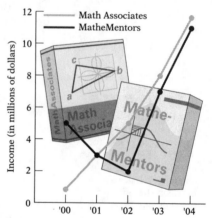

Figure 20 Net incomes of Math Associates and MatheMentors

Example 2

Use Figure 20 to approximate the difference between the net income of Math Associates and that of MatheMentors in 2002.

Strategy

To write the difference:

• Read the line graph to determine the net income of Math Associates and that of MatheMentors in 2002.
• Subtract to find the difference.

Solution

Net income for Math Associates: $5 million
Net income for MatheMentors: $2 million

$5 - 2 = 3$

The difference between the net incomes in 2002 was $3 million.

You Try It 2

Use Figure 20 to determine between which two years the net income of Math Associates increased the most.

Your strategy

Your solution

10.2 Exercises

Objective A   **To read a bar graph**

Automobile Production   The bar graph in Figure 21 shows the regions in which all the passenger cars were produced during a recent year. Use this graph for Exercises 1 to 3.

1. How many passenger cars were produced worldwide?

2. What is the difference between the number of passenger cars produced in Western Europe and the number produced in North America?

3. What percent of the passenger cars were produced in Asia? Round to the nearest percent.

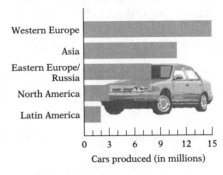

Figure 21 Number of passenger cars produced (in a recent year)
Source: Copyright © 2000 by the *Los Angeles Times*. Reprinted with permission.

Fuel Efficiency   The double-bar graph in Figure 22 shows the fuel efficiency of four vehicles, as rated by the Environmental Protection Agency. They are among the most fuel-efficient 2003 model-year cars for city and highway mileage. Use this graph for Exercises 4 to 6.

4. Is the fuel efficiency of the Toyota Prius greater on the highway or in city driving?

5. Approximately how many more miles per gallon does the Mini Cooper get while traveling on the highway than in the city?

6. Estimate the difference between the fuel efficiency of the Honda Insight in city driving and the fuel efficiency of the VW New Beetle in city driving.

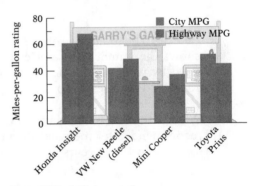

Figure 22 Fuel efficiency ratings
Source: Environmental Protection Agency

Compensation   The double-bar graph in Figure 23 shows maximum salaries for police officers in selected cities and the corresponding maximum salaries for officers in the suburbs of that city. Use this graph for Exercises 7 to 10.

7. Estimate the difference between the maximum salaries of police officers in the suburbs of New York City and in the city of New York.

8. Is there a city for which the maximum salary of a police officer in the city is greater than the salary in the suburbs?

9. For which city is the difference between the maximum salary in the suburbs and that in the city the greatest?

10. Of the cities shown on the graph, which city has the lowest maximum salary for police officers in the suburbs?

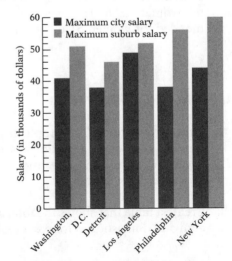

Figure 23 Maximum salaries of police officers in the city and the suburbs
Source: USA Today

Objective B   **To read a broken-line graph**

Meteorology The broken-line graph in Figure 24 shows the average monthly snowfall during ski season around Aspen, Colorado. Use this graph for Exercises 11 to 14.

11. What is the average snowfall during January?

12. During which month is the snowfall the greatest?

13. What is the total average snowfall during March and April?

14. Find the ratio of the average snowfall in November to the average snowfall in December.

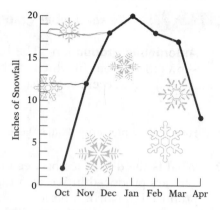

Figure 24 Average snowfall in Aspen, Colorado
Source: Weather America, by Alfred Garwood

Health The double-broken-line graph in Figure 25 shows the number of Calories per day that should be consumed by women and men in various age groups. Use this graph for Exercises 15 to 17.

15. What is the difference between the number of Calories recommended for men and the number recommended for women 19–22 years of age?

16. People of what age and gender have the lowest recommended number of Calories?

17. Find the ratio of the number of Calories recommended for women 15 to 18 years old to the number recommended for women 51 to 74 years old.

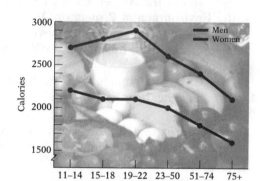

Figure 25 Recommended number of Calories per day for women and men
Source: Numbers, by Andrea Sutcliffe (HarperCollins)

APPLYING THE CONCEPTS

Drug Prevention The graph in Figure 26 shows the amount of money, in billions of dollars, spent by the U.S. government for drug prevention in the 1990s. Use this graph for Exercises 18 and 19.

18. Create a table that shows the total amount spent for foreign and domestic aid for each year from 1991 to 1999.

19. Create a table that shows the difference between the amount spent for foreign and for domestic aid in each year from 1991 to 1999.

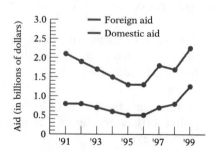

Figure 26 Aid provided by the U.S. government for drug prevention
Source: Reprinted by permission of the *San Diego Union-Tribune.*

10.3 Histograms and Frequency Polygons

Objective A   To read a histogram

A research group measured the fuel usage of 92 cars. The results are recorded in the histogram in Figure 27. A **histogram** is a special type of bar graph. The width of each bar corresponds to a range of numbers called a **class interval.** The height of each bar corresponds to the number of occurrences of data in each class interval and is called the **class frequency.**

Class Intervals (miles per gallon)	Class Frequencies (number of cars)
18–20	12
20–22	19
22–24	24
24–26	17
26–28	15
28–30	5

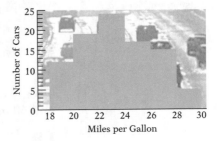

Figure 27

Twenty-four cars get between 22 and 24 miles per gallon.

A precision tool company has 85 employees. Their hourly wages are recorded in the histogram in Figure 28.

The ratio of the number of employees whose hourly wage is between $14 and $16 to the total number of employees is $\frac{17 \text{ employees}}{85 \text{ employees}} = \frac{1}{5}$.

Figure 28

Example 1

Use Figure 28 to find the number of employees whose hourly wage is between $16 and $20.

Strategy

To find the number of employees:

• Read the histogram to find the number of employees whose hourly wage is between $16 and $18 and the number whose hourly wage is between $18 and $20.
• Add the two numbers.

Solution

Number with wages between $16 and $18: 20
Number with wages between $18 and $20: 14

$20 + 14 = 34$

34 employees have an hourly wage between $16 and $20.

You Try It 1

Use Figure 28 to find the number of employees whose hourly wage is between $10 and $14.

Your strategy

Your solution

Objective B To read a frequency polygon

The speeds of 70 cars on a highway were measured by radar. The results are recorded in the frequency polygon in Figure 29. A **frequency polygon** is a graph that displays information in a manner similar to a histogram. A dot is placed above the center of each class interval at a height corresponding to that class's frequency. The dots are then connected to form a broken-line graph. The center of a class interval is called the **class midpoint.**

TAKE NOTE

The blue portion of the graph at the right is a histogram. The red portion of the graph is a frequency polygon.

Class Interval (miles per hour)	Class Midpoint	Class Frequency
30–40	35	7
40–50	45	13
50–60	55	25
60–70	65	21
70–80	75	4

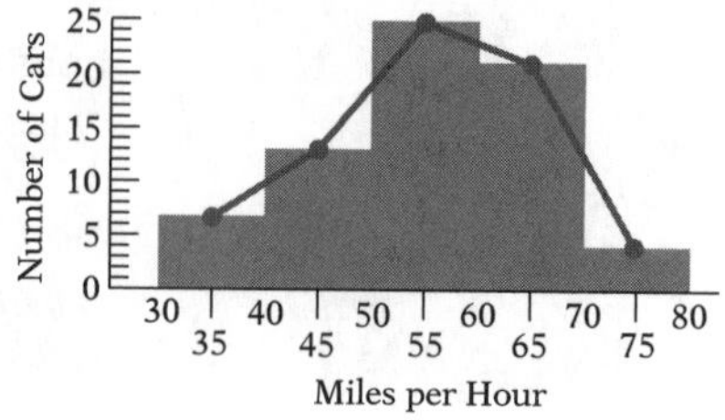

Figure 29

Twenty-five cars were traveling between 50 and 60 miles per hour.

The per capita incomes in a recent year for the 50 states are recorded in the frequency polygon in Figure 30.

The number of states with a per capita income between $24,000 and $28,000 is 14.

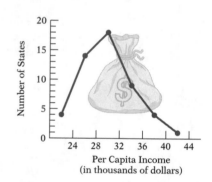

Figure 30

Source: Bureau of Economic Analysis

Example 2

According to Figure 30, what percent of the states have a per capita income between $24,000 and $28,000?

Strategy

To find the percent, solve the basic percent equation for percent. The base is 50. The amount is 14.

Solution

Percent × base = amount

n × 50 = 14

$n = 14 \div 50$

$n = 0.28$

28% of the states have a per capita income between $24,000 and $28,000.

You Try It 2

Use Figure 30 to find the ratio of the number of states with a per capita income between $28,000 and $32,000 to the number with a per capita income between $32,000 and $36,000.

Your strategy

Your solution

10.3 Exercises

Objective A   **To read a histogram**

Education   The annual tuition for undergraduate college students attending 4-year institutions varies depending on the college. The histogram in Figure 31 shows the tuition amounts for a representative sample of 120 students from various parts of the United States. Use this figure for Exercises 1 to 4.

1. How many students have a tuition that is between $3000 and $6000 per year?

2. What is the ratio of the number of students whose tuition is between $9000 per year and $12,000 per year to the total number of students represented?

3. How many students pay more than $12,000 annually for tuition?

4. What percent of the total number of students spend less than $6000 annually?

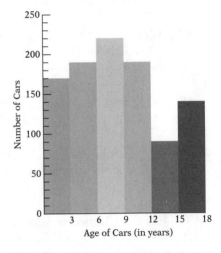

Figure 31
Source: Educational Testing Service

Automobiles   The histogram in Figure 32 is based on data from the American Automobile Manufacturers Association. It shows the ages of a sample of 1000 cars in a typical city in the United States. Use this figure for Exercises 5 to 8.

5. How many cars are between 6 and 12 years old?

6. Find the ratio of the number of cars between 12 and 15 years old to the total number of cars.

7. Find the number of cars more than 12 years old.

8. Find the percent of cars that are less than 9 years old.

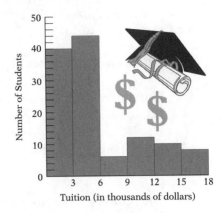

Figure 32
Source: American Automobile Manufacturers Association

Malls   According to a Maritz AmeriPoll, the average U.S. adult goes to a shopping mall about two times a month. The histogram in Figure 33 shows the average time 100 adults spend in the mall per trip. Use this figure for Exercises 9 to 12.

9. Find the number of adults who spend between 1 and 2 hours at the mall.

10. Find the number of adults who spend between 3 and 4 hours at the mall.

11. What percent of the adults spend less than 1 hour at the mall?

12. What percent of the adults spend 5 or more hours at the mall?

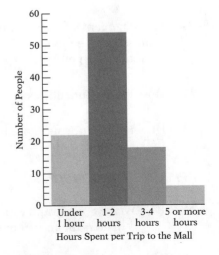

Figure 33
Source: Maritz AmeriPoll

Objective B **To read a frequency polygon**

Sports The frequency polygon in Figure 34 shows the distances thrown by the entrants in the University and College Discus Finals at the 2003 Drake Relays. Use this figure for Exercises 13 to 15.

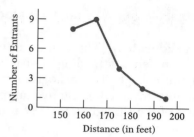
Figure 34

13. Determine the number of entrants in the discus finals.

14. Find the number of entrants with distances of more than 170 feet.

15. What percent of the entrants had distances between 160 feet and 170 feet?

The Lottery The frequency polygon in Figure 35 is based on data from a Gallup poll survey of 74 people who purchased lottery tickets. Use this figure for Exercises 16 to 19.

16. How many people purchased between 0 and 10 tickets?

17. What percent of the people purchased between 20 and 30 tickets each month? Round to the nearest tenth of a percent.

18. What percent of the people purchased more than 10 tickets each month? Round to the nearest tenth of a percent.

19. Is it possible to determine from the graph how many people purchased 15 lottery tickets? Explain.

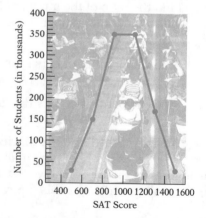
Figure 35

Education The frequency polygon in Figure 36 shows the distribution of scores of the approximately 1,080,000 students who took an SAT exam. Use this figure for Exercises 20 to 23.

20. How many students scored between 1200 and 1400 on the exam?

21. What percent of the number of students who took the exam scored between 800 and 1000? Round to the nearest tenth of a percent.

22. How many students scored below 1000?

23. How many students scored above 800?

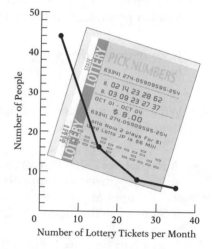
Figure 36
Source: Educational Testing Service

APPLYING THE CONCEPTS

24. Write a paragraph explaining the difference between a histogram and a bar graph.

25. In your own words, describe a frequency table.

10.4 Statistical Measures

Objective A   To find the mean, median, and mode of a distribution

The average score on the math portion of the SAT was 432. The EPA estimates that a 2005 Ford Focus averages 35 miles per gallon on the highway. The average rainfall for portions of Kauai is 350 inches per year. Each of these statements uses one number to describe an entire collection of numbers. Such a number is called an *average*.

In statistics there are various ways to calculate an average. Three of the most common—*mean, median,* and *mode*—are discussed here.

An automotive engineer tests the miles-per-gallon ratings of 15 cars and records the results as follows:

Miles-per-Gallon Ratings of 15 Cars

25	22	21	27	25	35	29	31	25	26	21	39	34	32	28

The **mean** of the data is the sum of the measurements divided by the number of measurements. The symbol for the mean is $\bar{x}$.

> **Formula for the Mean**
>
> $$\bar{x} = \frac{\text{sum of the data values}}{\text{number of data values}}$$

To find the mean for the data above, add the numbers and then divide by 15.

$$\bar{x} = \frac{25 + 22 + 21 + 27 + 25 + 35 + 29 + 31 + 25 + 26 + 21 + 39 + 34 + 32 + 28}{15}$$

$$= \frac{420}{15} = 28$$

The mean number of miles per gallon for the 15 cars tested was 28 miles per gallon.

The mean is one of the most frequently computed averages. It is the one that is commonly used to calculate a student's performance in a class.

Integrating Technology

When using a calculator to calculate the mean, use parentheses to group the sum in the numerator.

(78 + 82 + 91 + 87 + 93) ÷ 5 =

HOW TO   The test scores for a student taking American history were 78, 82, 91, 87, and 93. What was the mean score for this student?

Strategy
To find the mean, divide the sum of the test scores by 5, the number of scores.

Solution

$$\bar{x} = \frac{78 + 82 + 91 + 87 + 93}{5} = \frac{431}{5} = 86.2$$

The mean score for the history student was 86.2.

The **median** of the data is the number that separates the data into two equal parts when the numbers are arranged from smallest to largest (or from largest to smallest). There is an equal number of values above the median and below the median.

To find the median of a set of numbers, first arrange the numbers from smallest to largest. The median is the number in the middle.

The result of arranging the miles-per-gallon ratings given on the previous page from smallest to largest is shown below.

21 21 22 25 25 25 26 27 28 29 31 32 34 35 39

7 values below the median   Middle number **Median**   7 values above the median

The median is 27 miles per gallon.

If data contain an *even* number of values, the median is the mean of the two middle numbers.

HOW TO   The selling prices of the last six homes sold by a real estate agent were $175,000, $150,000, $250,000, $130,000, $245,000, and $190,000. Find the median selling price of these homes.

Strategy
To find the median, arrange the numbers from smallest to largest. Because there is an even number of values, the median is the mean of the two middle numbers.

Solution
130,000 150,000 175,000 190,000 245,000 250,000

Middle 2 numbers

$$\text{Median} = \frac{175,000 + 190,000}{2} = 182,500$$

The median selling price was $182,500.

The **mode** of a set of numbers is the value that occurs most frequently. If a set of numbers has no number occurring more than once, then the data have no mode.

Here again are the data for the gasoline mileage ratings of 15 cars.

Miles-per-Gallon Ratings of 15 Cars														
25	22	21	27	25	35	29	31	25	26	21	39	34	32	28

25 is the number that occurs most frequently.

The mode is 25 miles per gallon.

Note from the miles-per-gallon example that the mean, median, and mode may be different.

Example 1

Twenty students were asked the number of units in which they were enrolled. The responses were as follows:

| 15 | 12 | 13 | 15 | 17 | 18 | 13 | 20 | 9 | 16 |
| 14 | 10 | 15 | 12 | 17 | 16 | 6 | 14 | 15 | 12 |

Find the mean number of units taken by these students.

Strategy

To find the mean number of units:
- Find the sum of the 20 numbers.
- Divide the sum by 20.

Solution

15 + 12 + 13 + 15 + 17 + 18 + 13 + 20 + 9 +
    16 + 14 + 10 + 15 + 12 + 17 + 16 + 6 +
    14 + 15 + 12 = 279

$$\bar{x} = \frac{279}{20} = 13.95$$

The mean is 13.95 units.

Example 2

The starting hourly wages for an apprentice electrician for six different work locations are $10.90, $11.25, $10.10, $11.08, $11.56, and $10.55. Find the median starting hourly wage.

Strategy

To find the median starting hourly wage:
- Arrange the numbers from smallest to largest.
- Because there is an even number of values, the median is the mean of the two middle numbers.

Solution

10.10, 10.55, 10.90, 11.08, 11.25, 11.56

$$\text{Median} = \frac{10.90 + 11.08}{2} = 10.99$$

The median starting hourly wage is $10.99.

You Try It 1

The amounts spent by 12 customers at a McDonald's restaurant were as follows:

| 6.26 | 8.23 | 5.09 | 8.11 | 7.50 | 6.69 |
| 5.66 | 4.89 | 5.25 | 9.36 | 6.75 | 7.05 |

Find the mean amount spent by these customers. Round to the nearest cent.

Your strategy

Your solution

You Try It 2

The amounts of weight lost, in pounds, by 10 participants in a 6-month weight-reduction program were 22, 16, 31, 14, 27, 16, 29, 31, 40, and 10. Find the median weight loss for these participants.

Your strategy

Your solution

Objective B **To draw a box-and-whiskers plot**

Recall from the last objective that an average is one number that helps to describe all the numbers in a set of data. For example, we know from the following statement that Erie gets a lot of snow each winter.

The average annual snowfall in Erie, Pennsylvania, is 85 inches.

Now look at these two statements.

The average annual temperature in San Francisco, California, is 57°F.
The average annual temperature in St. Louis, Missouri, is 57°F.

The average annual temperature in both cities is the same. However, we do not expect the climate in St. Louis to be like San Francisco's climate. Although both cities have the same average annual temperature, their temperature ranges differ. In fact, the difference between the average monthly high temperatures in July and January in San Francisco is 14°F, whereas the difference between the average monthly high temperatures in July and January in St. Louis is 50°F.

Note that for this example, a single number (the average annual temperature) does not provide us with a very comprehensive picture of the climate of either of these two cities.

San Francisco

St. Louis

One method used to picture an entire set of data is a box-and-whiskers plot. To prepare a box-and-whiskers plot, we begin by separating a set of data into four parts, called quartiles. We will illustrate this by using the average monthly high temperatures for St. Louis, in degrees Fahrenheit. These are listed below from January through December.

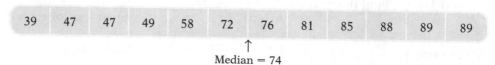

| 39 | 47 | 58 | 72 | 81 | 88 | 89 | 89 | 85 | 76 | 49 | 47 |

Source: The Weather Channel

First list the numbers in order from smallest to largest and determine the median.

| 39 | 47 | 47 | 49 | 58 | 72 | 76 | 81 | 85 | 88 | 89 | 89 |

↑
Median = 74

Now find the median of the data values below the median. The median of the data values below the median is called the **first quartile,** symbolized by Q_1. Also find the median of the data values above the median. The median of the data values above the median is called the **third quartile,** symbolized by Q_3.

|← 3 values →|* ← 3 values →|* ← 3 values →|* ← 3 values →|

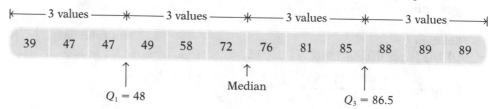

| 39 | 47 | 47 | 49 | 58 | 72 | 76 | 81 | 85 | 88 | 89 | 89 |

↑   ↑   ↑
$Q_1 = 48$ Median $Q_3 = 86.5$

The first quartile, Q_1, is the number that one-quarter of the data lie below. This means that 25% of the data lie below the first quartile. The third quartile, Q_3, is the number that one-quarter of the data lie above. This means that 25% of the data lie above the third quartile.

The **range** of a set of numbers is the difference between the largest number and the smallest number in the set. The range describes the spread of the data. For the data above,

$$\text{Range} = \text{largest value} - \text{smallest value} = 89 - 39 = 50$$

The **interquartile range** is the difference between the third quartile, Q_3, and the first quartile, Q_1. For the data above,

$$\text{Interquartile range} = Q_3 - Q_1 = 86.5 - 48 = 38.5$$

The interquartile range is the distance that spans the "middle" 50% of the data values. Because it excludes the bottom fourth of the data values and the top fourth of the data values, it excludes any extremes in the numbers in the set.

A **box-and-whiskers plot,** or **boxplot,** is a graph that shows five numbers: the smallest value, the first quartile, the median, the third quartile, and the greatest value. Here are these five values for the data on St. Louis temperatures.

The smallest number	39
The first quartile, Q_1	48
The median	74
The third quartile, Q_3	86.5
The largest number	89

Think of a number line that includes the five values listed above. With this in mind, mark off the five values. Draw a box that spans the distance from Q_1 to Q_3. Draw a vertical line the height of the box at the median.

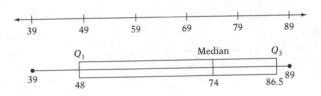

Listed below are the average monthly high temperatures for San Francisco.

57	60	61	64	68	71	71	73	74	73	60	59

Source: The Weather Channel

We can perform the same calculations on these data to determine the five values needed for the box-and-whiskers plot.

The smallest number	57
The first quartile, Q_1	60
The median	66
The third quartile, Q_3	72
The largest number	74

The box-and-whiskers plot is shown at the right with the same scale used for the data on the St. Louis temperatures.

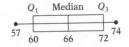

Note that by comparing the two boxplots, we can see that the range of temperatures in St. Louis is greater than the range of temperatures in San Francisco. For the St. Louis temperatures, there is a greater spread of the data below the median than above the median, whereas the spreads of the data above and below the median of the San Francisco boxplot are nearly equal.

HOW TO The numbers of avalanche deaths in the United States during each of nine consecutive winters were 8, 24, 29, 13, 28, 30, 22, 26, and 32. (*Source:* Colorado Avalanche Information Center) Draw a box-and-whiskers plot of the data and determine the interquartile range.

Strategy

To draw the box-and-whiskers plot, arrange the data from smallest to largest. Then find the median, Q_1, and Q_3. Use the smallest value, Q_1, the median, Q_3, and the largest value to draw the box-and-whiskers plot.

To find the interquartile range, find the difference between Q_3 and Q_1.

Solution

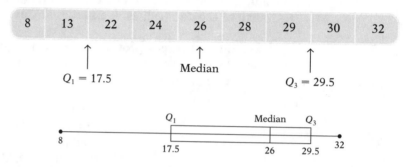

Interquartile range $= Q_3 - Q_1 = 29.5 - 17.5 = 12$

The interquartile range is 12 deaths.

TAKE NOTE

Note that the left whisker in this box-and-whiskers plot is quite long. This indicates a set of data in which the median is closer to the largest data value. If a boxplot has a long whisker on the right, the median is closer to the smallest data value. If the two whiskers are approximately the same length, then the smallest and largest values are about the same distance from the median. See Example 3.

Example 3

The average monthly snowfall, in inches, in Buffalo, New York, from October through April is 1, 12, 24, 25, 18, 12, and 3. (*Source:* The Weather Channel) Draw a box-and-whiskers plot of the data.

Strategy

To draw the box-and-whiskers plot:

- Arrange the data from smallest to largest.
- Find the median, Q_1, and Q_3.
- Use the smallest value, Q_1, the median, Q_3, and the largest value to draw the box-and-whiskers plot.

Solution

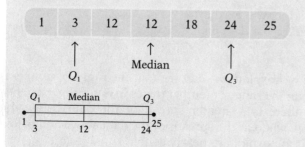

You Try It 3

The average monthly snowfall, in inches, in Denver, Colorado, from October through April is 4, 7, 7, 8, 8, 9, and 13. (*Source:* The Weather Channel)
a. Draw a box-and-whiskers plot of the data.
b. How does the spread of the data within the interquartile range compare with that in Example 3?

Your strategy

Your solution

10.4 Exercises

Objective A   **To find the mean, median, and mode of a distribution**

1. State whether the mean, median, or mode is being used.
   a. Half of the houses in the new development are priced under $125,000.
   b. The average bill for lunch at the college union is $7.95.
   c. The college bookstore sells more green college sweatshirts than any other color.
   d. In a recent year, there were as many people age 26 and younger in the world as there were people age 26 and older.
   e. The majority of full-time students carry a load of 12 credit hours per semester.
   f. The average annual return on this investment is 6.5%.

2. **Consumerism**   The number of big-screen televisions sold each month for one year was recorded by an electronics store. The results were 15, 12, 20, 20, 19, 17, 22, 24, 17, 20, 15, and 27. Calculate the mean, the median, and the mode of the number of televisions sold per month.

3. **The Airline Industry**   The number of seats occupied on a jet for 16 trans–Atlantic flights was recorded. The numbers were 309, 422, 389, 412, 401, 352, 367, 319, 410, 391, 330, 408, 399, 387, 411, and 398. Calculate the mean, the median, and the mode of the number of seats occupied per flight.

4. **Sports**   The times, in seconds, for a 100-meter dash at a college track meet were 10.45, 10.23, 10.57, 11.01, 10.26, 10.90, 10.74, 10.64, 10.52, and 10.78.
   a. Calculate the mean time for the 100-meter dash.
   b. Calculate the median time for the 100-meter dash.

5. **Consumerism**   A consumer research group purchased identical items in eight grocery stores. The costs for the purchased items were $45.89, $52.12, $41.43, $40.67, $48.73, $42.45, $47.81, and $45.82. Calculate the mean and the median costs of the purchased items.

6. **Computers**   One measure of a computer's hard-drive speed is called access time; this is measured in milliseconds (thousandths of a second). Find the mean and median for 11 hard drives whose access times were 5, 4.5, 4, 4.5, 5, 5.5, 6, 5.5, 3, 4.5, and 4.5. Round to the nearest tenth.

7. **Health Plans**   Eight health maintenance organizations (HMOs) presented group health insurance plans to a company. The monthly rates per employee were $423, $390, $405, $396, $426, $355, $404, and $430. Calculate the mean and the median monthly rates for these eight companies.

8. **Government**   The lengths of the terms, in years, of all the former Supreme Court chief justices are given in the table below. Find the mean and median length of term for the chief justices.

5	0	4	34	28	8	14	21
10	8	11	4	7	15	17	

9. **Life Expectancy** The life expectancies, in years, in ten selected Central and South American countries are given at the right.
   a. Find the mean life expectancy in this group of countries.
   b. Find the median life expectancy in this group of countries.

Country	Life Expectancy
Brazil	62
Chile	75
Costa Rica	78
Ecuador	70
Guatemala	64
Panama	75
Peru	66
Trinidad and Tobago	71
Uruguay	74
Venezuela	73

10. **Education** Your scores on six history tests were 78, 92, 95, 77, 94, and 88. If an "average score" of 90 receives an A for the course, which average, the mean or the median, would you prefer that the instructor use?

11. **Education** One student received scores of 85, 92, 86, and 89. A second student received scores of 90, 97, 91, and 94 (exactly 5 points more on each exam). Are the means of the two students the same? If not, what is the relationship between the means of the two students?

12. **Defense Spending** The table below shows the defense expenditures, in billions of dollars, by the federal government for 1965 through 1973, years during which the United States was actively involved in the Vietnam War.
   a. Calculate the mean annual defense expenditure. Round to the nearest tenth of a billion.
   b. Find the median annual defense expenditure.
   c. If the year 1965 were eliminated from the data, how would that affect the mean? The median?

Year	1965	1966	1967	1968	1969	1970	1971	1972	1973
Expenditures	$49.6	$56.8	$70.1	$80.5	$81.2	$80.3	$77.7	$78.3	$76.0

Source: Statistical Abstract of the United States

Objective B   **To draw a box-and-whiskers plot**

13. **a.** What percent of the data in a set of numbers lie above Q_3?
    b. What percent of the data in a set of numbers lie above Q_1?
    c. What percent of the data in a set of numbers lie below Q_3?
    d. What percent of the data in a set of numbers lie below Q_1?

14. **U.S. Presidents** The box-and-whiskers plot below shows the distribution of the ages of presidents of the United States at the time of their inauguration.
    a. What is the youngest age in the set of data?
    b. What is the oldest age?
    c. What is the first quartile?
    d. What is the third quartile?
    e. What is the median?
    f. Find the range.
    g. Find the interquartile range.

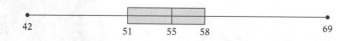

15. 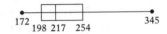 **Compensation**   The box-and-whiskers plot below shows the distribution of median incomes for 50 states and the District of Columbia. What is the lowest value in the set of data? The highest value? The first quartile? The third quartile? The median? Find the range and the interquartile range.

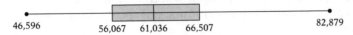

46,596   56,067   61,036   66,507   82,879

16. Education   An aptitude test was taken by 200 students at the Fairfield Middle School. The box-and-whiskers plot at the right shows the distribution of their scores.

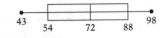

43   54   72   88   98

   a. How many students scored over 88?
   b. How many students scored below 72?
   c. How many scores are represented in each quartile?
   d. What percent of the students had scores of at least 54?

17. Health   The cholesterol levels for 80 adults were recorded and then displayed in the box-and-whiskers plot shown at the right.

172 198 217 254   345

   a. How many adults had a cholesterol level above 217?
   b. How many adults had a cholesterol level below 254?
   c. How many cholesterol levels are represented in each quartile?
   d. What percent of the adults had a cholesterol level of not more than 198?

18. Fuel Efficiency   The gasoline consumption of 19 cars was tested, and the results were recorded in the table below.
   a. Find the range, the first quartile, the third quartile, and the interquartile range.
   b. Draw a box-and-whiskers plot of the data.
   c. Is the data value 21 in the interquartile range?

Miles per Gallon for 19 Cars									
33	21	30	32	20	31	25	20	16	24
22	31	30	28	26	19	21	17	26	

19. 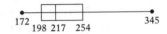 **Environment**   Carbon dioxide is among the gases that contribute to global warming. The world's biggest emitters of carbon dioxide are listed below. The figures are emissions in millions of metric tons per year.
   a. Find the range, the first quartile, the third quartile, and the interquartile range.
   b. Draw a box-and-whiskers plot of the data.
   c. What data value is responsible for the long "whisker" at the right?

Carbon Dioxide Emissions (in millions of metric tons per year)			
Canada	0.41	Japan	1.06
China	2.60	Russian Federation	2.10
Germany	0.87	Ukraine	0.61
India	0.76	United Kingdom	0.56
Italy	0.41	United States	4.80

Source: U.S. State Department

20. **Meteorology** The average monthly amounts of rainfall, in inches, from January through December for Seattle, Washington, and Houston, Texas, are listed below.
a. Is the difference between the means greater than 1 inch?
b. What is the difference between the medians?
c. Draw a box-and-whiskers plot of each set of data. Use the same scale.
d. Describe the difference between the distributions of the data for Seattle and Houston.

| Seattle | 6.0 | 4.2 | 3.6 | 2.4 | 1.6 | 1.4 | 0.7 | 1.3 | 2.0 | 3.4 | 5.6 | 6.3 |
| Houston | 3.2 | 3.3 | 2.7 | 4.2 | 4.7 | 4.1 | 3.3 | 3.7 | 4.9 | 3.7 | 3.4 | 3.7 |

Source: The Weather Channel

21. **Meteorology** The average monthly amounts of rainfall, in inches, from January through December for Orlando, Florida, and Portland, Oregon, are listed below.
a. Is the difference between the means greater than 1 inch?
b. What is the difference between the medians?
c. Draw a box-and-whiskers plot of each set of data. Use the same scale.
d. Describe the difference between the distributions of the data for Orlando and Portland.

| Orlando | 2.1 | 2.8 | 3.2 | 2.2 | 4.0 | 7.4 | 7.8 | 6.3 | 5.6 | 2.8 | 1.8 | 1.8 |
| Portland | 6.2 | 3.9 | 3.6 | 2.3 | 2.1 | 1.5 | 0.5 | 1.1 | 1.6 | 3.1 | 5.2 | 6.4 |

Source: The Weather Channel

APPLYING THE CONCEPTS

22. **a.** Explain how to determine the mean of a set of data.
b. Explain how to determine the median of a set of data.
c. Explain how to determine the mode of a set of data.

23. Write a set of data with five data values for which the mean, median, and mode are all 55.

24. A set of data has a mean of 16, a median of 15, and a mode of 14. Which of these numbers must be a value in the data? Explain your answer.

25. Explain each notation.
a. Q_1 **b.** Q_3 **c.** $\bar{x}$

26. What values are shown on a box-and-whiskers plot? Explain how each is displayed.

27. The box in a box-and-whiskers plot represents 50%, or one-half, of the data in a set. Why is the box in Example 3 in this section not one-half of the entire length of the box-and-whiskers plot?

28. Create a set of data containing 25 numbers that would correspond to the box-and-whiskers plot shown at the right.

10.5 Introduction to Probability

Objective A   **To calculate the probability of simple events**

A weather forecaster estimates that there is a 75% chance of rain. A state lottery director claims that there is a $\frac{1}{9}$ chance of winning a prize in a new game offered by the lottery. Each of these statements involves uncertainty to some extent. The degree of uncertainty is called **probability.** For the statements above, the probability of rain is 75%, and the probability of winning a prize in the new lottery game is $\frac{1}{9}$.

A probability is determined from an **experiment,** which is any activity that has an observable outcome. Examples of experiments include

Tossing a coin and observing whether it lands heads or tails

Interviewing voters to determine their preference for a political candidate

Drawing a card from a standard deck of 52 cards

All the possible outcomes of an experiment are called the **sample space** of the experiment. The outcomes are listed between braces. For example:

The number cube shown at the left is rolled once. Any of the numbers from 1 to 6 could show on the top of the cube. The sample space is

$$\{1, 2, 3, 4, 5, 6\}$$

A fair coin is tossed once. (A fair coin is one for which heads and tails have an equal chance of landing face up.) If H represents "heads up" and T represents "tails up," then the sample space is

$$\{H, T\}$$

An **event** is one or more outcomes of an experiment. For the experiment of rolling the six-sided cube described above, some possible events are

The number is even: $\{2, 4, 6\}$

The number is a multiple of 3: $\{3, 6\}$

The number is less than 10: $\{1, 2, 3, 4, 5, 6\}$

Note that in this case, the event is the entire sample space.

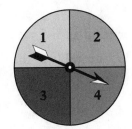

HOW TO   The spinner at the left is spun once. Assume that the spinner does not come to rest on a line.

a. What is the sample space?

The arrow could come to rest on any one of the four sectors.
The sample space is $\{1, 2, 3, 4\}$.

b. List the outcomes in the event that the spinner points to an odd number.

$\{1, 3\}$

In discussing experiments and events, it is convenient to refer to the **favorable outcomes** of an experiment. These are the outcomes of an experiment that satisfy the requirements of a particular event.

For instance, consider the experiment of rolling a fair die once. The sample space is

$$\{1, 2, 3, 4, 5, 6\}$$

and one possible event would be rolling a number that is divisible by 3. The outcomes of the experiment that are favorable to the event are 3 and 6:

$$\{3, 6\}$$

The outcomes of the experiment of tossing a fair coin are *equally likely*. Either one of the outcomes is just as likely as the other. If a fair coin is tossed once, the probability of a head is $\frac{1}{2}$, and the probability of a tail is $\frac{1}{2}$. Both events are equally likely. The theoretical probability formula, given below, applies to experiments for which the outcomes are equally likely.

Theoretical Probability Formula

The theoretical probability of an event is a fraction with the number of favorable outcomes of the experiment in the numerator and the total number of possible outcomes in the denominator.

$$\text{Probability of an event} = \frac{\text{number of favorable outcomes}}{\text{number of possible outcomes}}$$

A probability of an event is a number from 0 to 1 that tells us how likely it is that this outcome will happen.

A probability of 0 means that the event is impossible.
The probability of getting a heads when rolling the die shown at the left is 0.

A probability of 1 means that the event must happen.
The probability of getting either a heads or tails when tossing a coin is 1.

A probability of $\frac{1}{4}$ means that it is expected that the outcome will happen 1 in every 4 times the experiment is performed.

TAKE NOTE

The phrase **at random** means that each card has an equal chance of being drawn.

HOW TO Each of the letters of the word *TENNESSEE* is written on a card, and the cards are placed in a hat. If one card is drawn at random from the hat, what is the probability that the card has the letter *E* on it?

Count the possible outcomes of the experiment.

There are 9 letters in *TENNESSEE*.
There are 9 possible outcomes of the experiment.

Count the number of outcomes of the experiment that are favorable to the event that a card with the letter *E* on it is drawn.

There are 4 cards with an *E* on them.

Use the probability formula.

$$\text{Probability of the event} = \frac{\text{number of favorable outcomes}}{\text{number of possible outcomes}} = \frac{4}{9}$$

The probability of drawing an *E* is $\frac{4}{9}$.

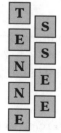

As shown above, calculating the probability of an event requires counting the number of possible outcomes of an experiment and the number of outcomes that are favorable to the event. One way to do this is to list the outcomes of the experiment in a systematic way. Using a table is often helpful.

When two dice are rolled, the sample space for the experiment can be recorded systematically as in the following table.

Point of Interest

Romans called a die that was marked on four faces a *talus*, which meant "anklebone." The anklebone was considered an ideal die because it is roughly a rectangular solid and it has no marrow, so loose anklebones from sheep were more likely than other bones to be lying around after the wolves had left their prey.

Possible Outcomes from Rolling Two Dice

HOW TO Two dice are rolled once. Calculate the probability that the sum of the numbers on the two dice is 7.

Use the table above to count the number of possible outcomes of the experiment.

There are 36 possible outcomes.

Count the number of outcomes of the experiment that are favorable to the event that a sum of 7 is rolled.

There are 6 favorable outcomes: (1, 6), (2, 5), (3, 4), (4, 3), (5, 2), and (6, 1).

Use the probability formula.

$$\text{Probability of the event} = \frac{\text{number of favorable outcomes}}{\text{number of possible outcomes}} = \frac{6}{36} = \frac{1}{6}$$

The probability of a sum of 7 is $\frac{1}{6}$.

The probabilities calculated above are theoretical probabilities. The calculation of a **theoretical probability** is based on theory—for example, that either side of a coin is equally likely to land face up or that each of the six sides of a fair die is equally likely to land face up. Not all probabilities arise from such assumptions.

An **empirical probability** is based on observations of certain events. For instance, a weather forecast of a 75% chance of rain is an empirical probability. From historical records kept by the weather bureau, when a similar weather pattern existed, rain occurred 75% of the time. It is theoretically impossible to predict the weather, and only observations of past weather patterns can be used to predict future weather conditions.

> **Empirical Probability Formula**
>
> The empirical probability of an event is a ratio of the number of observations of the event to the total number of observations.
>
> $$\text{Probability of an event} = \frac{\text{number of observations of the event}}{\text{total number of observations}}$$

For example, suppose the records of an insurance company show that of 2549 claims for theft filed by policy holders, 927 were claims for more than $5000. The empirical probability that the next claim for theft that this company receives will be a claim for more than $5000 is the ratio of the number of claims for over $5000 to the total number of claims.

$$\frac{927}{2549} \approx 0.36$$

The probability is approximately 0.36.

Example 1

There are three choices, a, b, or c, for each of the two questions on a multiple-choice quiz. If the instructor randomly chooses which questions will have an answer of a, b, or c, what is the probability that the two correct answers on this quiz will be the same letter?

Strategy

To find the probability:

- List the outcomes of the experiment in a systematic way.
- Count the number of possible outcomes of the experiment.
- Count the number of outcomes of the experiment that are favorable to the event that the two correct answers on the quiz will be the same letter.
- Use the probability formula.

Solution

Possible outcomes: (a, a) (b, a) (c, a)
                    (a, b) (b, b) (c, b)
                    (a, c) (b, c) (c, c)

There are 9 possible outcomes.

There are 3 favorable outcomes:
(a, a), (b, b), (c, c)

$$\text{Probability} = \frac{\text{number of favorable outcomes}}{\text{number of possible outcomes}}$$

$$= \frac{3}{9} = \frac{1}{3}$$

The probability that the two correct answers will be the same letter is $\frac{1}{3}$.

You Try It 1

A professor writes three true/false questions for a quiz. If the professor randomly chooses which questions will have a true answer and which will have a false answer, what is the probability that the test will have 2 true questions and 1 false question?

Your strategy

Your solution

10.5 Exercises

Objective A **To calculate the probability of simple events**

1. A coin is tossed four times. List all the possible outcomes of the experiment as a sample space.

2. Three cards—one red, one green, and one blue—are to be arranged in a stack. Using R for red, G for green, and B for blue, list all the different stacks that can be formed. (Some computer monitors are called RGB monitors for the colors red, green, and blue.)

Red Green Blue

3. A tetrahedral die is one with four triangular sides. The sides show the numbers from 1 to 4. Say two tetrahedral dice are rolled. List all the possible outcomes of the experiment as a sample space.

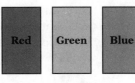

Tetrahedral die

4. A coin is tossed and then a die is rolled. List all the possible outcomes of the experiment as a sample space. [To get you started, (H, 1) is one of the possible outcomes.]

5. The spinner at the right is spun once. Assume that the spinner does not come to rest on a line.
   a. What is the sample space?
   b. List the outcomes in the event that the number is less than 4.

6. A coin is tossed four times.
   a. What is the probability that the outcomes of the tosses are exactly in the order HHTT? (See Exercise 1.)
   b. What is the probability that the outcomes of the tosses consist of two heads and two tails?
   c. What is the probability that the outcomes of the tosses consist of one head and three tails?

7. Two dice are rolled.
   a. What is the probability that the sum of the dots on the upward faces is 5?
   b. What is the probability that the sum of the dots on the upward faces is 15?
   c. What is the probability that the sum of the dots on the upward faces is less than 15?
   d. What is the probability that the sum of the dots on the upward faces is 2?

8. A dodecahedral die has 12 sides numbered from 1 to 12. The die is rolled once.
   a. What is the probability that the upward face shows an 11?
   b. What is the probability that the upward face shows a 5?

9. A dodecahedral die has 12 sides numbered from 1 to 12. The die is rolled once.
   a. What is the probability that the upward face shows a number divisible by 4?
   b. What is the probability that the upward face shows a number that is a multiple of 3?

Dodecahedral die

10. Two tetrahedral dice are rolled (see Exercise 3).
    a. What is the probability that the sum on the upward faces is 4?
    b. What is the probability that the sum on the upward faces is 6?

11. Two dice are rolled. Which has the greater probability, throwing a sum of 10 or throwing a sum of 5?

12. Two dice are rolled once. Calculate the probability that the two numbers on the dice are equal.

13. Each of the letters of the word *MISSISSIPPI* is written on a card, and the cards are placed in a hat. One card is drawn at random from the hat.
a. What is the probability that the card has the letter *I* on it?
b. Which is greater, the probability of choosing an *S* or that of choosing a *P*?

14. There are five choices—choices *a* through *e*—for each question on a multiple-choice test. What is the probability of choosing the correct answer for a certain question by just guessing?

15. Three blue marbles, four green marbles, and five red marbles are placed in a bag. One marble is chosen at random.
a. What is the probability that the marble chosen is green?
b. Which is greater, the probability of choosing a blue marble or that of choosing a red marble?

16. Which has the greater probability, drawing a jack, queen, or king from a deck of cards or drawing a spade?

17. In a history class, a set of exams earned the following grades: 4 A's, 8 B's, 22 C's, 10 D's, and 3 F's. If a single student's exam is chosen from this class, what is the probability that it received a B?

18. A survey of 95 people showed that 37 preferred (to using a credit card) a cash discount of 2% if an item was purchased using cash or a check. Judging on the basis of this survey, what is the empirical probability that a person prefers a cash discount? Write the answer as a decimal rounded to the nearest hundredth.

19. A survey of 725 people showed that 587 had a group health insurance plan where they worked. On the basis of this survey, what is the empirical probability that an employee has a group health insurance plan? Write the answer as a decimal rounded to the nearest hundredth.

20. A television cable company surveyed some of its customers and asked them to rate the cable service as excellent, satisfactory, average, unsatisfactory, or poor. The results are recorded in the table at the right. What is the probability that a customer who was surveyed rated the service as satisfactory or excellent?

Quality of Service	Number Who Voted
Excellent	98
Satisfactory	87
Average	129
Unsatisfactory	42
Poor	21

APPLYING THE CONCEPTS

21. If the spinner at the right is spun once, is each of the numbers 1 through 5 equally likely? Why or why not?

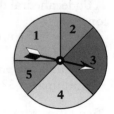

22. The probability of tossing a coin and having it land heads up is $\frac{1}{2}$.

Does this mean that if that coin is tossed 100 times, it will land heads up 50 times? Explain your answer.

23. Why can the probability of an event not be $\frac{5}{3}$?

Focus on Problem Solving

Inductive Reasoning   Suppose that, beginning in January, you save $25 each month. The total amount you have saved at the end of each month can be described by a list of numbers.

25	50	75	100	125	150	175	
Jan	Feb	Mar	Apr	May	June	July	. . .

The list of numbers that indicates your total savings is an *ordered* list of numbers called a **sequence.** Each of the numbers in a sequence is called a **term** of the sequence. The list is ordered because the position of a number in the list indicates the month in which that total amount has been saved. For example, the 7th term of the sequence (indicating July) is 175. This number means that a total of $175 has been saved by the end of the 7th month.

Now consider a person who has a different savings plan. The total amount saved by this person for the first seven months is given by the sequence

$$20, 35, 50, 65, 80, 95, 110, \ldots$$

The process you use to discover the next number in the above sequence is *inductive reasoning.* **Inductive reasoning** involves making generalizations from specific examples; in other words, we reach a conclusion by making observations about particular facts or cases. In the case of the above sequence, the person saved $15 per month after the first month.

Here is another example of inductive reasoning. Find the next two letters of the sequence A, B, E, F, I, J, ...

By trying different patterns, we can determine that a pattern for this sequence is

$$\underline{A, B}, C, D, \underline{E, F}, G, H, \underline{I, J}, \ldots$$

That is, write two letters, skip two letters, write two letters, skip two letters, and so on. The next two letters are M, N.

Use inductive reasoning to solve the following problems.

1. What is the next term of the sequence, ban, ben, bin, bon, . . . ?

2. 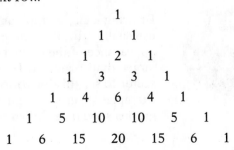 Using a calculator, determine the decimal representation of several proper fractions that have a denominator of 99. For instance, you may use $\frac{8}{99}$, $\frac{23}{99}$, and $\frac{75}{99}$. Now use inductive reasoning to explain the pattern, and use your reasoning to find the decimal representation of $\frac{53}{99}$ without a calculator.

3. Find the next number in the sequence 1, 1, 2, 3, 5, 8, 13, 21, ...

4. The decimal representation of a number begins 0.10100100010000100000 . . . . What are the next 10 digits in this number?

5. The first seven rows of a triangle of numbers called Pascal's triangle are given below. Find the next row.

```
                    1
                 1     1
              1     2     1
           1     3     3     1
        1     4     6     4     1
     1     5    10    10     5     1
  1     6    15    20    15     6     1
```

Projects and Group Activities

Deceptive Graphs   A graphical representation of data can sometimes be misleading. Consider the graphs shown below. A financial advisor with an investment firm claims that an investment with the firm grew as shown in the graph on the left, whereas an investment with a competitor grew as shown in the graph on the right. Apparently, one would have accumulated more money by choosing the investment on the left.

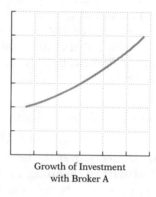

Growth of Investment
with Broker A

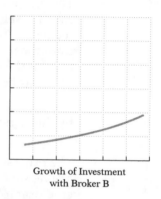

Growth of Investment
with Broker B

However, these graphs have a serious flaw. There are no labels on the horizontal and vertical axes. Therefore, it is impossible to tell which investment increased more or over what time interval. When labels are not placed on the axes of a graph, the data represented are meaningless. This is one way in which advertisers use a visual impact to distort the true meaning of data.

The graphs below are the same as those drawn above except that scales have been drawn along each axis. Now it is possible to tell how each investment performed. Note that both turned in exactly the same performance!

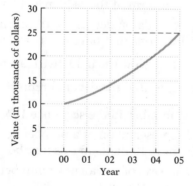

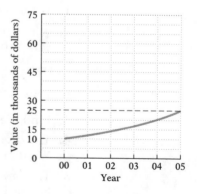

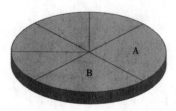

Drawing a circle graph as an oval is another way of distorting data. This is especially true if a three-dimensional representation is given. From the appearance of the circle graph at the left, one would think that region *B* is larger than region *A*. However, that isn't true. Measure the angle of each sector to see this for yourself. As you read newspapers and magazines, find examples of graphs that may distort the actual data. Discuss how these graphs should be drawn to be more accurate.

Collecting, Organizing, Displaying, and Analyzing Data

Before standardized units of measurement, measurements were made in terms of the human body. For example, the cubit was the distance from the end of the elbow to the tips of the fingers. The yard was the distance from the tip of the nose to the tip of the fingers on an outstretched arm.

For each student in the class, find the measure from the tip of the nose to the tip of the fingers on an outstretched arm. Round each measure to the nearest centimeter. Record all the measurements on the board.

1. From the data collected, determine each of the following.

   Mean _____

   Median _____

   Mode _____

   Range _____

   First quartile, Q_1 _____

   Third quartile, Q_3 _____

   Interquartile range _____

2. Prepare a box-and-whiskers plot of the data.

3. Write a description of the spread of the data.

4. Explain why we need standardized units of measurement.

Chapter Summary

Key Words

Statistics is the branch of mathematics concerned with *data*, or numerical information. A *graph* is a pictorial representation of data. A *pictograph* represents data by using a symbol that is characteristic of the data.

Examples

The pictograph shows the annual per capita turkey consumption in different counties.

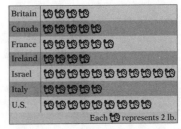

Per Capita Turkey Consumption
Source: National Turkey Federation

A *circle graph* represents data by the size of the sectors.

The circle graph shows the result of a survey of 300 people who were asked to name their favorite sport.

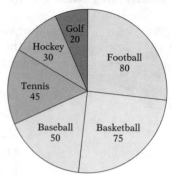

Distribution of Responses in a Survey

A *bar graph* represents data by the height of the bars.

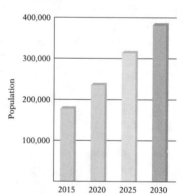 The bar graph shows the expected U.S. population aged 100 and over.

Expected U.S. Population Aged 100 and Over
Source: Census Bureau

A *broken-line graph* represents data by the position of the lines and shows trends or comparisons.

The line graph shows a recent graduate's cumulative debt in college loans at the end of each of the four years of college.

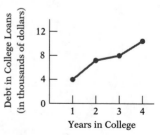

Cumulative Debt in College Loans

A *histogram* is a special kind of bar graph. In a histogram, the width of each bar corresponds to a range of numbers called a *class interval*. The height of each bar corresponds to the number of occurrences of data in each class interval and is called the *class frequency*.

An Internet service provider (ISP) surveyed 1000 of its subscribers to determine the time required for each subscriber to download a particular file. The results of the survey are shown in the histogram below.

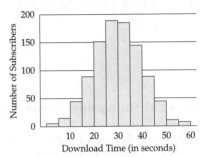

A *frequency polygon* is a graph that displays information in a manner similar to a histogram. A dot is placed above the center of each class interval at a height corresponding to that class's frequency. The dots are connected to form a broken-line graph. The center of a class interval is called the *class midpoint*.

Below is a frequency polygon for the data in the histogram above.

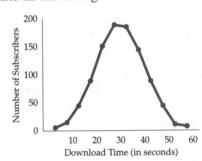

The *mean, median,* and *mode* are three types of averages used in statistics. The *mean* of the set of data is the sum of the data values divided by the number of values in the set. The *median* of a set of data is the number that separates the data into two equal parts when the data have been arranged from least to greatest (or greatest to least). There is an equal number of values above the median and below the median. The *mode* of a set of numbers is the value that occurs most frequently.

Consider the following set of data.

24, 28, 33, 45, 45

The median is 33.
The mode is 45.

A *box-and-whiskers plot*, or *boxplot*, is a graph that shows five numbers: the least value, the first quartile, the median, the third quartile, and the greatest value. The *first quartile*, Q_1, is the number below which one-fourth of the data lie. The *third quartile*, Q_3, is a number above which one-fourth of the data lie. The box is placed around the values between the first quartile and the third quartile. The *range* is the difference between the largest number and the smallest number in the set. The range describes the spread of the data. The *interquartile range* is the difference between Q_3 and Q_1.

The box-and-whiskers plot for a set of test scores is shown below.

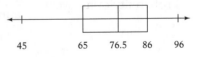

45   65   76.5   86   96

The range = $96 - 45 = 51$
$Q_1 = 65$
$Q_3 = 86$
The interquartile range
$$= Q_3 - Q_1 = 86 - 65 = 21$$

Probability is a number from 0 to 1 that tells us how likely it is that a certain outcome of an experiment will happen. An *experiment* is an activity with an observable outcome. All the possible outcomes of an experiment are called the *sample space* of the experiment. An *event* is one or more outcomes of an experiment. The *favorable outcomes* of an experiment are the outcomes that satisfy the requirements of a particular event.

Tossing a single die is an example of an experiment. The sample space for this experiment is the set of possible outcomes:

$$\{1, 2, 3, 4, 5, 6\}$$

The event that the number landing face up is an odd number is represented by

$$\{1, 3, 5\}$$

Essential Rules and Procedures

Examples

To Find the Mean of a Set of Data

Divide the sum of the numbers by the number of values in the set.

$$\overline{x} = \frac{\text{sum of the data values}}{\text{number of data values}}$$

Consider the following set of data.

$$24, 28, 33, 45, 45$$

$$\overline{x} = \frac{24 + 28 + 33 + 45 + 45}{5} = 35$$

To Find the Median

1. Arrange the numbers from least to greatest.
2. If there is an *odd* number of values in the set of data, the median is the middle number. If there is an *even* number of values in the set of data, the median is the mean of the two middle numbers.

Consider the following set of data.

$$24, 28, 33, 35, 45, 45$$

The median is $\dfrac{33 + 35}{2} = 34$.

To Find Q_1

Arrange the numbers from least to greatest and locate the median. Q_1 is the median of the lower half of the data.

Consider the following data.

8	10	12	14	16	19	22
	↑		↑			
	Q_1		Median			

To Find Q_3

Arrange the numbers from least to greatest and locate the median, Q_3 is the median of the upper half of the data.

Consider the following data.

8	10	12	14	16	19	22
			↑		↑	
			Median		Q_3	

Theoretical Probability Formula

$$\text{Probability of an event} = \frac{\text{number of favorable outcomes}}{\text{number of possible outcomes}}$$

A die is rolled. The probability of rolling a 2 or a 4 is $\frac{2}{6} = \frac{1}{3}$.

Empirical Probability Formula

$$\text{Probability of an event} = \frac{\text{number of observations of the event}}{\text{total number of observations}}$$

A thumbtack is tossed 100 times. It lands point up 15 times and lands on its side 85 times. From this experiment, the empirical probability of "point up" is $\frac{15}{100} = \frac{3}{20}$.

Chapter Review Exercises

Internal The circle graph in Figure 37 shows the approximate amount of money that government agencies spent on maintaining Internet websites for a 3-year period. Use this graph for Exercises 1 to 3.

1. Find the total amount of money that these agencies spent on maintaining websites.

2. What is the ratio of the amount spent by the Department of Commerce to the amount spent by the EPA?

3. What percent of the total money spent did NASA spend? Round to the nearest tenth of a percent.

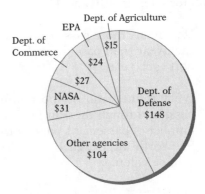

Figure 37 Millions of dollars that federal agencies spent on websites
Source: General Accounting Office

Demographics The double-line graph in Figure 38 shows the populations of California and Texas. Use this graph for Exercises 4 to 6.

4. In 1900, which state had the larger population?

5. In 2000, approximately how much greater was the population of California than the population of Texas?

6. During which 25-year period did the population of Texas increase the least?

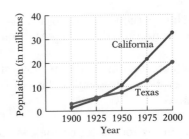

Figure 38 Populations of California and Texas

Sports The frequency polygon in Figure 39 shows the range of scores for the first 80 games of a season for the New York Knicks basketball team. Use this figure for Exercises 7 to 9.

7. Find the number of games in which fewer than 100 points were scored by the Knicks.

8. What is the ratio of the number of games in which 90 to 100 points were scored to the number of games in which 110 to 120 points were scored?

9. In what percent of the games were 110 points or more scored? Round to the nearest tenth of a percent.

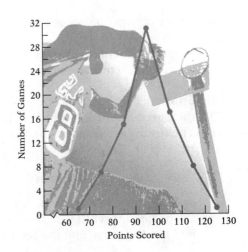

Figure 39
Source: Sports Illustrated website at
http://CNNSI.com

Airports The pictograph in Figure 40 shows the numbers of passengers annually passing through the five busiest airports in the United States. Use this graph for Exercises 10 and 11.

10. How many more passengers pass through O'Hare each year than pass through the Los Angeles airport each year?

11. What is the ratio of the number of passengers passing through the San Francisco airport to the number of passengers passing through the Dallas/Ft. Worth airport each year? Write your answer using a colon.

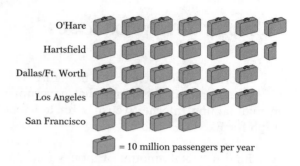

Figure 40 The busiest U.S. airports
Source: Airports Association Council International–North America; Air Transport Association of America

Sports The double-bar graph in Figure 41 shows the total days open and the days of full operation of ski resorts in different regions of the country. Use this graph for Exercises 12 to 14.

12. Find the difference between the total days open and the days of full operation for Midwest ski areas.

13. What percent of the total days open were the days of full operation for the Rocky Mountain ski areas?

14. Which region had the lowest number of days of full operation? How many days of full operation did this region have?

15. A coin is tossed four times. What is the probability that the outcomes of the tosses consist of one tail and three heads?

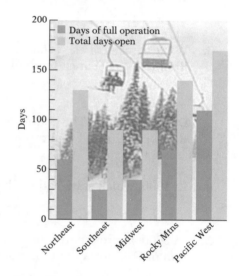

Figure 41
Source: Economic Analysis of United States Ski Areas

Health Based on a Gallup poll, the numbers of hours that the 46 people surveyed slept during a typical weekday night are shown in the histogram in Figure 42. Use this figure for Exercises 16 and 17.

16. How many people slept 8 hours or more?

17. What percent of the people surveyed slept 7 hours? Round to the nearest tenth of a percent.

18. **Sports** The heart rates of 24 women tennis players were measured after each of them had run one-quarter of a mile. The results are listed in the table below.

| 80 | 82 | 99 | 91 | 93 | 87 | 103 | 94 | 73 | 96 | 86 | 80 |
| 97 | 94 | 108 | 81 | 100 | 109 | 91 | 84 | 78 | 96 | 96 | 100 |

  a. Find the mean, median, and mode for the data. Round to the nearest tenth.

  b. Find the range and the interquartile range for the data.

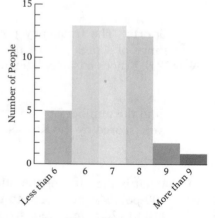

Hours of Sleep per Night

Figure 42

Chapter Test

Consumerism   Forty college students were surveyed to see how much money they spent each week on dining out in restaurants. The results are recorded in the frequency polygon shown in Figure 43. Use this figure for Exercises 1 to 3.

1. How many students spent between $15 and $25 per week?

2. Find the ratio of the number of students who spent between $10 and $15 to the number who spent between $15 and $20.

3. What percent of the students surveyed spent less than $15 per week?

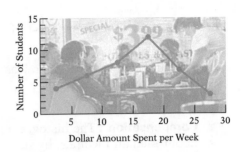

Figure 43

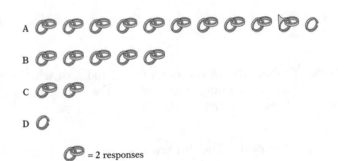

Marriage   The pictograph in Figure 44 is based on the results of a Gallup poll survey of married couples. Each individual was asked to give a letter grade to the marriage. Use this graph for Exercises 4 to 6.

4. Find the total number of people who were surveyed.

5. Find the ratio of the number of people who gave their marriage a B to the number who gave it a C.

6. What percent of the total number of people surveyed gave their marriage an A? Round to the nearest tenth of a percent.

= 2 responses

Figure 44 Survey of married couples rating their marriage

Amusement Rides   The bar graph in Figure 45 shows the number of fatalities that occurred in accidents on amusement rides in the 1990s in the United States. Use this graph for Exercises 7 to 9.

7. During which two consecutive years were the numbers of fatalities the same?

8. Find the total number of fatalities on amusement rides during 1991 through 1999.

9. How many more such fatalities occurred during the years 1995 through 1998 than occurred during the years 1991 through 1994?

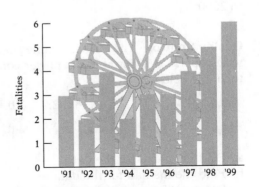

Figure 45 Number of fatalities in accidents on amusement rides

Source: USA Today, April 7, 2000

The Film Industry The circle graph in Figure 46 categorizes the 655 films released during a recent year by their ratings. Use this graph for Exercises 10 to 12.

10. How many more R-rated films were released than PG films?

11. How many times more PG-13 films were released than NC-17?

12. What percent of the films released were rated G? Round to the nearest tenth of a percent.

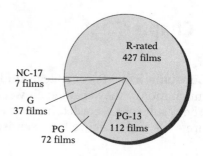

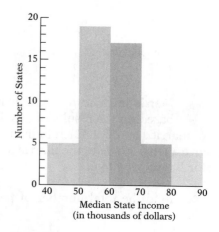

Figure 46 Ratings of films released
Source: MPA Worldwide Market Research

Compensation The histogram in Figure 47 gives information about median incomes, by state, in the United States. Use this figure for Exercises 13 to 15.

13. How many states have median incomes between $40,000 and $60,000?

14. What percent of the states have a median income that is between $50,000 and $70,000?

15. What percent of the states have a median income that is $70,000 or more?

16. **Probability** A box contains 50 balls, of which 15 are red. If 1 ball is randomly selected from the box, what is the probability of the ball's being red?

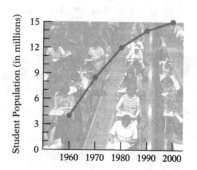

Figure 47
Source: U.S. Census Bureau

Education The broken-line graph in Figure 48 shows the number of students enrolled in colleges. Use this figure for Exercises 17 and 18.

17. During which decade did the student population increase the least?

18. Approximate the increase in the college enrollment from 1960 to 2000.

19. **Quality Control** The length of time (in days) that various batteries operated a portable CD player continuously are given in the table below.

| 2.9 | 2.4 | 3.1 | 2.5 | 2.6 | 2.0 | 3.0 | 2.3 | 2.4 | 2.7 |
| 2.0 | 2.4 | 2.6 | 2.7 | 2.1 | 2.9 | 2.8 | 2.4 | 2.0 | 2.8 |

a. Find the mean for the data.
b. Find the median for the data.
c. Draw a box-and-whiskers plot for the data.

Figure 48 Student enrollment in public and private colleges
Source: National Center for Educational Statistics

CHAPTER 10: *Additional Material From:*

MATHEMATICAL EXCURSIONS | SECOND EDITION

Aufmann • Lockwood • Nation • Clegg

| **Measures of Dispersion**

Table 12.3 *Test Scores*

Alan	Tara
55	80
80	76
97	77
80	83
68	84
100	80
Mean: 80	Mean: 80
Median: 80	Median: 80
Mode: 80	Mode: 80

The Range

In the preceding section we introduced the mean, the median, and the mode. Each of these statistics is a type of average that is designed to measure central tendencies of the data from which it was derived. Some characteristics of a set of data may not be evident from an examination of averages. For instance, consider the test scores for Alan and Tara, as shown in Table 12.3.

The mean, the median, and the mode of Alan's test scores and Tara's test scores are identical; however, an inspection of the test scores shows that Alan's scores are widely scattered, whereas all of Tara's scores are within a few units of the mean. This example shows that average values do not reflect the *spread* or *dispersion* of data. To measure the spread or dispersion of data, we must introduce statistical values known as the *range* and the *standard deviation*.

> **Range**
>
> The **range** of a set of data values is the difference between the largest data value and the smallest data value.

EXAMPLE 1 ■ Find a Range

Find the range of Alan's test scores in Table 12.3.

Solution
Alan's largest test score is 100 and his smallest test score is 55. The range of Alan's test scores is 100 − 55 = 45.

CHECK YOUR PROGRESS 1   Find the range of Tara's test scores in Table 12.3.

Solution   *See page B-9.*

Robert Wadlow

MathMatters   **A World Record Range**

The tallest man for whom there is irrefutable evidence was Robert Pershing Wadlow. On June 27, 1940, Wadlow was 8 feet 11.1 inches tall. The shortest man for whom there is reliable evidence is Gul Mohammad. On July 19, 1990, he was 22.5 inches tall. (*Source:* Guinness World Records 2001) The range of the heights of these men is 107.1 − 22.5 = 84.6 inches.

The Standard Deviation

The range of a set of data is easy to compute, but it can be deceiving. The range is a measure that depends only on the two most extreme values, and as such it is very sensitive. For instance, the table at the left shows the times for two sprinters in six

220-Yard Dash (times in seconds)

Race	Sprinter 1	Sprinter 2
1	23.8	24.1
2	24.0	24.2
3	24.1	24.1
4	24.4	24.2
5	23.9	24.1
6	24.5	25.8
Range	0.7	1.7

Deviations from the Mean

x	$x - \bar{x}$
2	$2 - 9 = -7$
6	$6 - 9 = -3$
11	$11 - 9 = 2$
12	$12 - 9 = 3$
14	$14 - 9 = 5$
Sum of the deviations 	0

✔ **TAKE NOTE**

You may question why a denominator of $n - 1$ is used instead of n when we compute a sample standard deviation. The reason is that a sample standard deviation is often used to estimate the population standard deviation, and it can be shown mathematically that the use of $n - 1$ tends to yield better estimates.

track meets. The range of times for the first sprinter is 0.7 second, and the range for the second sprinter is 1.7 seconds. If you consider only range values, then you might conclude that the first sprinter's times are more consistent than those of the second sprinter. However, a closer examination shows that if you exclude the time of 25.8 seconds by the second sprinter in the sixth race, then the second sprinter has a range of 0.1 second. On this basis one could argue that the second sprinter has a more consistent performance record.

The next measure of dispersion that we will consider is called the *standard deviation*. It is less sensitive to a change in an extreme value than is the range. The standard deviation of a set of numerical data makes use of the individual amount that each data value deviates from the mean. These deviations, represented by $(x - \bar{x})$, are positive when the data value x is greater than the mean $\bar{x}$, and are negative when x is less than the mean $\bar{x}$. The sum of all the deviations $(x - \bar{x})$ is 0 for all sets of data. For instance, consider the sample data 2, 6, 11, 12, 14. For these data, $\bar{x} = 9$. The individual deviation of each data value from the mean is shown in the table on the following page. Note that the sum of the deviations is 0.

Because the sum of all the deviations of the data values from the mean is *always* 0, we cannot use the sum of the deviations as a measure of dispersion for a set of data. What is needed is a procedure that can be applied to the deviations so that the sum of the numbers that are derived by adjusting the deviations is not always 0. The procedure that we will make use of *squares* each of the deviations $(x - \bar{x})$ to make each of them nonnegative. The sum of the squares of the deviations is then divided by a constant that depends on the number of data values. We then compute the square root of this result. The following definitions show that the formula for calculating the standard deviation of a population differs slightly from the formula used to calculate the standard deviation of a sample.

Standard Deviations for Samples and Populations

If $x_1, x_2, x_3, \ldots, x_n$ is a *population* of n numbers with a mean of μ, then the **standard deviation** of the population is $\sigma = \sqrt{\dfrac{\Sigma(x - \mu)^2}{n}}$ (1).

If $x_1, x_2, x_3, \ldots, x_n$ is a *sample* of n numbers with a mean of $\bar{x}$, then the **standard deviation** of the sample is $s = \sqrt{\dfrac{\Sigma(x - \bar{x})^2}{n - 1}}$ (2).

Most statistical applications involve a sample rather than a population, which is the complete set of data values. Sample standard deviations are designated by the lower-case letter s. In those cases in which we *do* work with a population, we designate the standard deviation of the population by σ, which is the lower-case Greek letter sigma. To calculate the standard deviation of n numbers, it is helpful to use the following procedure.

Procedure for Computing a Standard Deviation

1. Determine the mean of the n numbers.

2. For each number, calculate the deviation (difference) between the number and the mean of the numbers.

3. Calculate the square of each of the deviations and find the sum of these squared deviations.

4. If the data is a *population*, then divide the sum by n. If the data is a *sample*, then divide the sum by $n - 1$.

5. Find the square root of the quotient in Step 4.

EXAMPLE 2 ■ Find the Standard Deviation

The following numbers were obtained by sampling a population.

2, 4, 7, 12, 15

Find the standard deviation of the sample.

Solution

Step 1: The mean of the numbers is

$$\bar{x} = \frac{2 + 4 + 7 + 12 + 15}{5} = \frac{40}{5} = 8$$

Step 2: For each number, calculate the deviation between the number and the mean.

x	$x - \bar{x}$
2	$2 - 8 = -6$
4	$4 - 8 = -4$
7	$7 - 8 = -1$
12	$12 - 8 = 4$
15	$15 - 8 = 7$

✓ **TAKE NOTE**
Because the sum of the deviations is always 0, you can use this as a means to check your arithmetic. That is, if your deviations from the mean do not have a sum of 0, then you know you have made an error.

Step 3: Calculate the square of each of the deviations in Step 2, and find the sum of these squared deviations.

x	$x - \bar{x}$	$(x - \bar{x})^2$
2	$2 - 8 = -6$	$(-6)^2 = 36$
4	$4 - 8 = -4$	$(-4)^2 = 16$
7	$7 - 8 = -1$	$(-1)^2 = 1$
12	$12 - 8 = 4$	$4^2 = 16$
15	$15 - 8 = 7$	$7^2 = \underline{49}$
		118 ⟵ **The sum of the squared deviations**

Step 4: Because we have a sample of $n = 5$ values, divide the sum 118 by $n - 1$, which is 4.

$$\frac{118}{4} = 29.5$$

Step 5: The standard deviation of the sample is $s = \sqrt{29.5}$. To the nearest hundredth, the standard deviation is $s = 5.43$.

CHECK YOUR PROGRESS 2   A student has the following quiz scores: 5, 8, 16, 17, 18, 20. Find the standard deviation for this population of quiz scores.

Solution   *See page B-9.*

In the next example we use standard deviations to determine which company produces batteries that are most consistent with regard to their life expectancy.

EXAMPLE 3 ■ Use Standard Deviations

A consumers group has tested a sample of eight size D batteries from each of three companies. The results of the tests are shown in the following table. According to these tests, which company produces batteries for which the values representing hours of constant use have the least standard deviation?

Company	Hours of Constant Use per Battery
EverSoBright	6.2, 6.4, 7.1, 5.9, 8.3, 5.3, 7.5, 9.3
Dependable	6.8, 6.2, 7.2, 5.9, 7.0, 7.4, 7.3, 8.2
Beacon	6.1, 6.6, 7.3, 5.7, 7.1, 7.6, 7.1, 8.5

Solution
The mean for each sample of batteries is 7 hours.
The batteries from EverSoBright have a standard deviation of

$$s_1 = \sqrt{\frac{(6.2 - 7)^2 + (6.4 - 7)^2 + \cdots + (9.3 - 7)^2}{7}}$$

$$= \sqrt{\frac{12.34}{7}} \approx 1.328 \text{ hours}$$

The batteries from Dependable have a standard deviation of

$$s_2 = \sqrt{\frac{(6.8 - 7)^2 + (6.2 - 7)^2 + \cdots + (8.2 - 7)^2}{7}}$$

$$= \sqrt{\frac{3.62}{7}} \approx 0.719 \text{ hours}$$

The batteries from Beacon have a standard deviation of

$$s_3 = \sqrt{\frac{(6.1 - 7)^2 + (6.6 - 7)^2 + \cdots + (8.5 - 7)^2}{7}}$$

$$= \sqrt{\frac{5.38}{7}} \approx 0.877 \text{ hours}$$

The batteries from Dependable have the *least* standard deviation. According to these results, the Dependable company produces the most consistent batteries with regard to life expectancy under constant use.

CHECK YOUR PROGRESS 3   A consumer testing agency has tested the strengths of three brands of $\frac{1}{8}$-inch rope. The results of the tests are shown in the following table. According to the sample test results, which company produces $\frac{1}{8}$-inch rope for which the breaking point has the least standard deviation?

Company	Breaking Point of $\frac{1}{8}$-inch Rope, in Pounds
Trustworthy	122, 141, 151, 114, 108, 149, 125
Brand X	128, 127, 148, 164, 97, 109, 137
NeverSnap	112, 121, 138, 131, 134, 139, 135

Solution   *See page B-9.*

Many calculators have built-in features for calculating the mean and standard deviation of a set of numbers. The next example illustrates these features on a TI-83/84 graphing calculator.

EXAMPLE 4 ■ Use a Calculator to Find the Mean and Standard Deviation

Use a graphing calculator to find the mean and standard deviation of the times in the following table. Because the table contains all the winning times for this race (up to the year 2004), the data set is a population.

Olympic Women's 400-Meter Dash Results, in Seconds, 1964–2004

52.0	52.0	51.08	49.29	48.88	48.83	48.65	48.83	48.25	49.11	49.41

Solution
On a TI-83/84 calculator, press ⟨STAT⟩⟨ENTER⟩ and then enter the above times into list ⟨L1⟩. See the calculator display below. Press ⟨STAT⟩⟨▶⟩⟨ENTER⟩⟨ENTER⟩. The calculator displays the mean and standard deviations shown below. Because we are working with a population, we are interested in the population standard deviation. From the calculator screen, $\bar{x} \approx 49.666$ and $\sigma x \approx 1.296$ seconds.

✔ **TAKE NOTE**

Because the calculation of the population mean and the sample mean are the same, a graphing calculator uses the same symbol $\bar{x}$ for both. The symbols for the population standard deviation, σx, and the sample standard deviation, $s x$, are different.

TI-83/84 **Display of List 1**

L1	L2	L3	1
52	------	------	
52			
51.08			
49.29			
48.88			
48.83			
48.65			
L₁(1) = 52			

TI-83/84 **Display of** $\bar{x}$, s **and** σ

1-Var Stats
$\bar{x}$=49.66636364   ← **Mean**
Σx=546.33
Σx^2=27152.6879
Sx=1.358802949   ← **Sample standard deviation**
σx=1.295567778   ← **Population standard deviation**
↓n=11

CHECK YOUR PROGRESS 4   Use a calculator to find the mean and the population standard deviation of the race times in the following table.

Olympic Men's 400-Meter Dash Results, in Seconds, 1896–2004

54.2	49.4	49.2	53.2	50.0	48.2	49.6	47.6	47.8
46.2	46.5	46.2	45.9	46.7	44.9	45.1	43.8	44.66
44.26	44.60	44.27	43.87	43.50	43.49	43.84	44.00	

Solution   See page B-9.

The Variance

A statistic known as the *variance* is also used as a measure of dispersion. The **variance** for a given set of data is the square of the standard deviation of the data. The following chart shows the mathematical notations that are used to denote standard deviations and variances.

Notations for Standard Deviation and Variance

σ is the standard deviation of a population.

σ^2 is the variance of a population.

s is the standard deviation of a sample.

s^2 is the variance of a sample.

EXAMPLE 5 ■ Find the Variance

Find the variance for the sample given in Example 2.

Solution

In Example 2, we found $s = \sqrt{29.5}$. Variance is the square of the standard deviation. Thus the variance is $s^2 = \left(\sqrt{29.5}\right)^2 = 29.5$.

CHECK YOUR PROGRESS 5   Find the variance for the population given in Check Your Progress 2.

Solution   See page B-9.

QUESTION   *Can the variance of a data set be smaller than the standard deviation of the data set?*

Although the variance of a set of data is an important measure of dispersion, it has a disadvantage that is not shared by the standard deviation: the variance does not have the same unit of measure as the original data. For instance, if a set of data consists of times measured in hours, then the variance of the data will be measured in *square* hours. The standard deviation of this data set is the square root of the variance, and as such it is measured in hours, which is a more intuitive unit of measure.

ANSWER   *Yes. The variance is smaller than the standard deviation whenever the standard deviation is less than 1.*

Excursion

A Geometric View of Variance and Standard Deviation[1]

The following geometric explanation of the variance and standard deviation of a set of data is designed to provide you with a deeper understanding of these important concepts.

Consider the data $x_1, x_2, \ldots, x_n$, which are arranged in ascending order. The average, or mean, of these data is

$$\mu = \frac{\Sigma x_i}{n}$$

and the variance is

$$\sigma^2 = \frac{\Sigma(x_i - \mu)^2}{n}$$

In the last formula, each term $(x_i - \mu)^2$ can be pictured as the area of a square whose sides are of length $|x_i - \mu|$, the distance between the ith data value and the mean. We will refer to these squares as *tiles*, denoting by T_i the area of the tile associated with the data value x_i. Thus $\sigma^2 = \frac{\Sigma T_i}{n}$, which means that the variance may be thought of as the *area of the averaged-sized tile* and the standard deviation σ as the length of a side of this averaged-sized tile. By drawing the tiles associated with a data set, as shown below, you can visually estimate an averaged-size tile and thus you can roughly approximate the variance and standard deviation.

(continued)

✓ TAKE NOTE

Up to this point we have used $\mu = \frac{\Sigma x}{n}$ as the formula for the mean. However, many statistics texts use the formula $\mu = \frac{\Sigma x_i}{n}$ for the mean. Letting the subscript i vary from 1 to n helps us to remember that we are finding the sum of all the numbers $x_1, x_2, \ldots, x_n$.

---

1. Adapted with permission from "Chebyshev's Theorem: A Geometric Approach," *The College Mathematics Journal*, Vol. 26, No. 2, March 1995. Article by Pat Touhey, College Misericordia, Dallas, PA 18612.

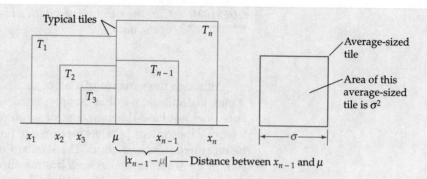

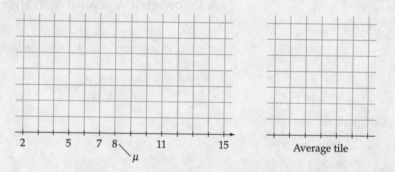

A typical data set, with its associated tiles and average-sized tile

These geometric representations of variance and standard deviation enable us to see visually how these values are used as measures of the dispersion of a set of data. If all of the data are bunched up near the mean, it is clear that the average-sized tile will be small and, consequently, so will its side length, which represents the standard deviation. But if even a small portion of the data lies far from the mean, the average-sized tile may be rather large, and thus its side length will also be large.

Excursion Exercises

1. This exercise makes use of the geometric procedure just explained to calculate the variance and standard deviation of the population 2, 5, 7, 11, 15. The following figure shows the given set of data labeled on a number line, along with its mean, which is 8.

a. Draw the tile associated with each of the five data values 2, 5, 7, 11, and 15.

b. Label each tile with its area.

c. Find the sum of the areas of all the tiles.

d. Find the average (mean) of the areas of all five tiles.

e. To the right of the above number line, draw a tile whose area is the average found in part d.

f. What is the variance of the data? What geometric figure represents the variance?

g. What is the standard deviation of the data? What geometric figure represents the standard deviation?

2. **a. to g.** Repeat all of the steps described in Excursion Exercise 1 for the data set

6, 8, 9, 11, 16

h. Which of the data sets in these two Excursion Exercises has the larger mean? Which data set has the larger standard deviation?

Exercise Set 12.2

1. **Meteorology** During a 12-hour period on December 24, 1924, the temperature in Fairfield, Montana dropped from a high of 63°F to a low of −21°F. What was the range of the temperatures during this period? (*Source: Time Almanac 2002, page 609*)

2. **Meteorology** During a two-hour period on January 12, 1911, the temperature in Rapid City, South Dakota dropped from a high of 49°F to a low of −13°F. What was the range of the temperatures during this period? (*Source: Time Almanac 2002, page 609*)

In Exercises 3–12, find the range, the standard deviation, and the variance for the given *samples*. Round noninteger results to the nearest tenth.

3. 1, 2, 5, 7, 8, 19, 22

4. 3, 4, 7, 11, 12, 12, 15, 16

5. 2.1, 3.0, 1.9, 1.5, 4.8

6. 5.2, 11.7, 19.1, 3.7, 8.2, 16.3

7. 48, 91, 87, 93, 59, 68, 92, 100, 81

8. 93, 67, 49, 55, 92, 87, 77, 66, 73, 96, 54

9. 4, 4, 4, 4, 4, 4, 4, 4, 4, 4, 4, 4, 4, 4, 4, 4, 4

10. 8, 6, 8, 6, 8, 6, 8, 6, 8, 6, 8, 6, 8

11. −8, −5, −12, −1, 4, 7, 11

12. −23, −17, −19, −5, −4, −11, −31

13. **Mountain Climbing** A mountain climber plans to buy some rope to use as a lifeline. Which of the following would be the better choice? Explain why you think your choice is the better choice.

 Rope A: Mean breaking strength: 500 pounds; standard deviation of 300 pounds

 Rope B: Mean breaking strength: 400 pounds; standard deviation of 40 pounds

14. **Lotteries** Which would you expect to be the larger: the standard deviation of five random numbers picked from 1 to 47 in the California Super Lotto, or the standard deviation of five random numbers picked from 1 to 51 in the multi-state PowerBall lottery?

15. **Heights of Students** Which would you expect to be the larger standard deviation: the standard deviation of the weights of 25 students in a first-grade class, or the standard deviation of the weights of 25 students in a college statistics course?

16. Evaluate the accuracy of the following statement: When the mean of a data set is large, the standard deviation will be large.

17. **Super Bowl** The following table lists the winning and losing scores for the Super Bowl games from 1972 through 2005.

Super Bowl Results, 1972–2005

33–14	16–6	26–21	20–16	27–17
16–7	21–17	27–17	55–10	35–21
23–7	32–14	38–9	20–19	31–24
16–13	27–10	38–16	37–24	34–19
24–3	35–31	46–10	52–17	23–16
14–7	31–19	39–20	30–13	34–7
20–17	48–21	32–29	24–21	

a. Find the mean and the *population* standard deviation of the winning scores. Round each result to the nearest tenth.

b. Find the mean and the *population* standard deviation of the losing scores. Round each result to the nearest tenth.

c. Which of the two data sets has the larger mean? Which of the two data sets has the larger standard deviation?

18. **Academy Awards** The following tables list the ages of female and male actors when they starred in their Oscar-winning Best Actor performances.

Ages of Best Female Actor Award Recipients, Academy Awards, 1971–2004

34	26	37	42	41	35	31	41	33	31	74	33
49	38	61	21	41	26	80	42	29	33	35	
45	49	39	34	26	25	33	35	35	28	30	

Ages of Best Male Actor Award Recipients, Academy Awards, 1971–2004

41	48	48	56	38	60	30	40	42	37	76	39
52	45	35	61	43	51	32	42	54	52	37	
38	31	45	60	46	40	36	47	29	43	37	

a. Find the mean and the *sample* standard deviation of the ages of the female recipients. Round each result to the nearest tenth.

b. Find the mean and the *sample* standard deviation of the ages of the male recipients. Round each result to the nearest tenth.

c. Which of the two data sets has the larger mean? Which of the two data sets has the larger standard deviation?

19. **Baseball** The following tables list the numbers of home runs hit by the leaders in the National and American Leagues from 1971 to 2004.

Home Run Leaders, 1971–2004

National League											
48	40	44	36	38	38	52	40	48	48	31	37
40	36	37	37	49	39	47	40	38	35	46	
43	40	47	49	70	65	50	73	49	47	48	

American League											
33	37	32	32	36	32	39	46	45	41	22	39
39	43	40	40	49	42	36	51	44	43	46	
40	50	52	56	56	48	47	52	57	47	43	

a. Find the mean and the *population* standard deviation of the number of home runs hit by the leaders in the National League. Round each result to the nearest tenth.

b. Find the mean and the *population* standard deviation of the number of home runs hit by the leaders in the American League. Round each result to the nearest tenth.

c. Which of the two data sets has the larger mean? Which of the two data sets has the larger standard deviation?

20. **Triathlon** The following table lists the winning times for the men's and women's Ironman Triathlon World Championships, held in Kailua-Kona, Hawaii.

Ironman Triathlon World Championships (Winning times rounded to the nearest minute)

Men	**(1980 – 2003)**		**Women**	**(1980 – 2003)**	
9:25	8:31	8:04	11:21	9:01	9:07
9:38	8:09	8:33	12:01	9:01	9:32
9:08	8:28	8:24	10:54	9:14	9:24
9:06	8:19	8:17	10:44	9:08	9:13
8:54	8:09	8:21	10:25	8:55	9:26
8:51	8:08	8:31	10:25	8:58	9:29
8:29	8:20	8:30	9:49	9:20	9:08
8:34	8:21	8:23	9:35	9:17	9:12

a. Find the mean and the *population* standard deviation of the winning times of the female athletes. *Note:* Convert each time to hours. For instance, a time of 12:55 (12 hours 55 minutes) is equal to $12 + \frac{55}{60} = 12.91\overline{6}$ hours. Round each result to the nearest tenth.

b. Find the mean and the *population* standard deviation of the winning times of the male athletes. Round each result to the nearest tenth.

c. Which of the two data sets has the larger mean? Which of the two data sets has the larger standard deviation?

21. Political Science The table on the following page lists the U.S. presidents and their ages at inauguration. President Cleveland has two entries because he served two nonconsecutive terms.

Washington	57	J. Adams	61
Jefferson	57	Madison	57
Monroe	58	J. Q. Adams	57
Jackson	61	Van Buren	54
W. H. Harrison	68	Tyler	51
Polk	49	Taylor	64
Fillmore	50	Pierce	48
Buchanan	65	Lincoln	52
A. Johnson	56	Grant	46
Hayes	54	Garfield	49
Arthur	50	Cleveland	47, 55
B. Harrison	55	McKinley	54
T. Roosevelt	42	Taft	51
Wilson	56	Harding	55
Coolidge	51	Hoover	54
F. D. Roosevelt	51	Truman	60
Eisenhower	62	Kennedy	43
L. B. Johnson	55	Nixon	56
Ford	61	Carter	52
Reagan	69	G. H. W. Bush	64
Clinton	46	G. W. Bush	54

Source: The World Almanac and Book of Facts, 2005

Find the mean and the *population* standard deviation of the ages. Round each result to the nearest tenth.

22. Political Science The following table lists the deceased U.S. presidents as of November 2004, and their ages at death.

Washington	67	J. Adams	90
Jefferson	83	Madison	85
Monroe	73	J. Q. Adams	80
Jackson	78	Van Buren	79
W. H. Harrison	68	Tyler	71
Polk	53	Taylor	65
Fillmore	74	Pierce	64
Buchanan	77	Lincoln	56
A. Johnson	66	Grant	63
Hayes	70	Garfield	49
Arthur	56	Cleveland	71
B. Harrison	67	McKinley	58
T. Roosevelt	60	Taft	72
Wilson	67	Harding	57
Coolidge	60	Hoover	90
F. D. Roosevelt	63	Truman	88
Eisenhower	78	Kennedy	46
L. B. Johnson	64	Nixon	81
Reagan	93		

Source: The World Almanac and Book of Facts, 2005

Find the mean and the *population* standard deviation of the ages. Round each result to the nearest tenth.

Extensions

CRITICAL THINKING

23. Pick five numbers and compute the *population* standard deviation of the numbers.

  a. Add a nonzero constant c to each of your original numbers and compute the standard deviation of this new population.

  b. Use the results of part a and inductive reasoning to state what happens to the standard deviation of a population when a nonzero constant c is added to each data item.

24. Pick six numbers and compute the *population* standard deviation of the numbers.

  a. Double each of your original numbers and compute the standard deviation of this new population.

  b. Use the results of part a and inductive reasoning to state what happens to the standard deviation of a population when each data item is multiplied by a positive constant k.

25. a. All of the numbers in a sample are the same number. What is the standard deviation of the sample?

  b. If the standard deviation of a sample is 0, must all of the numbers in the sample be the same number?

  c. If two samples both have the same standard deviation, are the samples necessarily identical?

26. Under what condition would the variance of a sample be equal to the standard deviation of the sample?

EXPLORATIONS

27. a. Use a calculator to compare the standard deviation of the population 1, 2, 3, 4, 5 and the value $\sqrt{\dfrac{5^2 - 1}{12}}$.

  b. Use a calculator to compare the standard deviation of the population 1, 2, 3, ..., 10 and the value $\sqrt{\dfrac{10^2 - 1}{12}}$.

  c. Use a calculator to compare the standard deviation of the population 1, 2, 3, ..., 15 and the value $\sqrt{\dfrac{15^2 - 1}{12}}$.

  d. Make a conjecture about the standard deviation of the population 1, 2, 3, ..., n and the value $\sqrt{\dfrac{n^2 - 1}{12}}$.

28. Find, without using a calculator, the standard deviation of the population

$$3001, 3002, 3003, 3004, \ldots, 3010$$

Hint: Use your answer to part b of Exercise 23 and your conjecture from part d of Exercise 27.

chapter

11

Linear Equations in Two Variables

This tennis player gets the energy for his workout from carbohydrates. Carbohydrates are the body's primary source of fuel for exercise. They can be released quickly and easily to fulfill the demands that exercise puts on the body. Since carbohydrates also fuel most of our muscular contractions, it is important to eat enough carbohydrates before any rigorous exercise.

OBJECTIVES

Section 11.1

A To graph points in a rectangular coordinate system

B To determine ordered-pair solutions of an equation in two variables

C To determine whether a set of ordered pairs is a function

D To evaluate a function written in functional notation

Section 11.2

A To graph an equation of the form $y = mx + b$

B To graph an equation of the form $Ax + By = C$

C To solve application problems

Section 11.3

A To find the x- and y-intercepts of a straight line

B To find the slope of a straight line

C To graph a line using the slope and the y-intercept

Need help? For online student resources, such as section quizzes, visit this textbook's website at **math.college.hmco.com/students.**

1. Simplify: $-\dfrac{5-(-7)}{4-8}$

2. Evaluate $\dfrac{a-b}{c-d}$ when $a=3$, $b=-2$, $c=-3$, and $d=2$.

3. Simplify: $-3(x-4)$

4. Solve: $3x+6=0$

5. Solve $4x+5y=20$ when $y=0$.

6. Solve $3x-7y=11$ when $x=-1$.

7. Divide: $\dfrac{12x-15}{-3}$

8. Solve: $\dfrac{2x+1}{3}=\dfrac{3x}{4}$

9. Solve $3x-5y=15$ for y.

10. Solve $y+3=-\dfrac{1}{2}(x+4)$ for y.

Points A, B, C, and D lie on the same line and in that order. The ratio of AB to AC is $\dfrac{1}{4}$ and the ratio of BC to CD is $\dfrac{1}{2}$. Find the ratio of AB to CD.

11.1 The Rectangular Coordinate System

Objective A   To graph points in a rectangular coordinate system

Before the 15th century, geometry and algebra were considered separate branches of mathematics. That all changed when René Descartes, a French mathematician who lived from 1596 to 1650, founded **analytic geometry.** In this geometry, a *coordinate system* is used to study relationships between variables.

A **rectangular coordinate system** is formed by two number lines, one horizontal and one vertical, that intersect at the zero point of each line. The point of intersection is called the **origin.** The two lines are called **coordinate axes,** or simply **axes.** The axes determine a **plane,** which can be thought of as a large, flat sheet of paper. The two axes divide the plane into four regions called **quadrants,** which are numbered counterclockwise from I to IV.

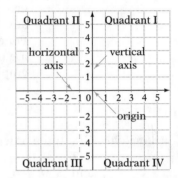

Each point in the plane can be identified by a pair of numbers called an **ordered pair.** The first number of the pair measures a horizontal distance and is called the **abscissa.** The second number of the pair measures a vertical distance and is called the **ordinate.** The **coordinates of a point** are the numbers in the ordered pair associated with the point. The abscissa is also called the **first coordinate** of the ordered pair, and the ordinate is also called the **second coordinate** of the ordered pair.

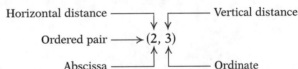

When drawing a rectangular coordinate system, we often label the horizontal axis x and the vertical axis y. In this case, the coordinate system is called an **xy-coordinate system.** The coordinates of the points are given by ordered pairs (x, y), where the abscissa is called the **x-coordinate** and the ordinate is called the **y-coordinate.**

To **graph or plot a point in the plane,** place a dot at the location given by the ordered pair. The **graph of an ordered pair** (x, y) is the dot drawn at the coordinates of the point in the plane. The points whose coordinates are $(3, 4)$ and $(-2.5, -3)$ are graphed in the figures below.

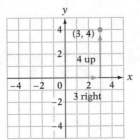 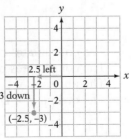

The points whose coordinates are (3, −1) and (−1, 3) are graphed at the right. Note that the graphed points are in different locations. *The order of the coordinates of an ordered pair is important.*

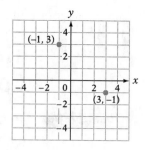

Each point in the plane is associated with an ordered pair, and each ordered pair is associated with a point in the plane. Although only the labels for integers are given on a coordinate grid, the graph of any ordered pair can be approximated. For example, the points whose coordinates are (−2.3, 4.1) and (π, 1) are shown on the graph at the right.

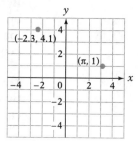

Example 1 Graph the ordered pairs (−2, −3), (3, −2), (0, −2), and (3, 0).

You Try It 1 Graph the ordered pairs (−4, 1), (3, −3), (0, 4), and (−3, 0).

Solution

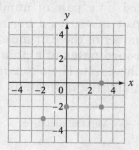

Your solution

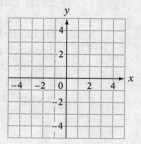

Example 2 Give the coordinates of the points labeled *A* and *B*. Give the abscissa of point *C* and the ordinate of point *D*.

You Try It 2 Give the coordinates of the points labeled *A* and *B*. Give the abscissa of point *D* and the ordinate of point *C*.

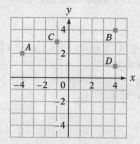

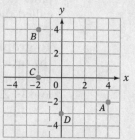

Solution The coordinates of *A* are (−4, 2).
The coordinates of *B* are (4, 4).
The abscissa of *C* is −1.
The ordinate of *D* is 1.

Your solution

Objective B

To determine ordered-pair solutions of an equation in two variables

An xy-coordinate system is used to study the relationship between two variables. Frequently this relationship is given by an equation. Examples of equations in two variables include

$$y = 2x - 3 \qquad 3x + 2y = 6 \qquad x^2 - y = 0$$

A **solution of an equation in two variables** is an ordered pair (x, y) whose coordinates make the equation a true statement.

HOW TO   Is $(-3, 7)$ a solution of $y = -2x + 1$?

$$y = -2x + 1$$

$$\begin{array}{c|c} 7 & -2(-3) + 1 \\ & 6 + 1 \end{array}$$ • Replace x by -3; replace y by 7.

$$7 = 7$$ • The results are equal.

$(-3, 7)$ is a solution of the equation $y = -2x + 1$.

Besides $(-3, 7)$, there are many other ordered-pair solutions of $y = -2x + 1$. For example, $(0, 1)$, $\left(-\frac{3}{2}, 4\right)$, and $(4, -7)$ are also solutions. In general, an equation in two variables has an infinite number of solutions. By choosing any value of x and substituting that value into the equation, we can calculate a corresponding value of y.

HOW TO   Find the ordered-pair solution of $y = \frac{2}{3}x - 3$ that corresponds to $x = 6$.

$$y = \frac{2}{3}x - 3$$

$$= \frac{2}{3}(6) - 3$$ • Replace x by 6.

$$= 4 - 3 = 1$$ • Simplify.

The ordered-pair solution is $(6, 1)$.

The solutions of an equation in two variables can be graphed in an xy-coordinate system.

HOW TO   Graph the ordered-pair solutions of $y = -2x + 1$ when $x = -2, -1, 0, 1,$ and 2.

Use the values of x to determine ordered-pair solutions of the equation. It is convenient to record these in a table.

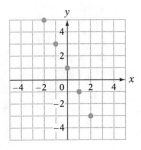

x	$y = -2x + 1$	y	(x, y)
-2	$-2(-2) + 1$	5	$(-2, 5)$
-1	$-2(-1) + 1$	3	$(-1, 3)$
0	$-2(0) + 1$	1	$(0, 1)$
1	$-2(1) + 1$	-1	$(1, -1)$
2	$-2(2) + 1$	-3	$(2, -3)$

Example 3

Is $(3, -2)$ a solution of $3x - 4y = 15$?

Solution

$$3x - 4y = 15$$

$$\begin{array}{c|c} 3(3) - 4(-2) & 15 \\ 9 + 8 & \\ & 17 \neq 15 \end{array}$$

• Replace x by 3 and y by -2.

No. $(3, -2)$ is not a solution of $3x - 4y = 15$.

You Try It 3

Is $(-2, 4)$ a solution of $x - 3y = -14$?

Your solution

Example 4

Graph the ordered-pair solutions of $2x - 3y = 6$ when $x = -3, 0, 3,$ and 6.

Solution

$$2x - 3y = 6$$ • Solve $2x - 3y = 6$ for y.

$$-3y = -2x + 6$$

$$y = \frac{2}{3}x - 2$$

Replace x in $y = \frac{2}{3}x - 2$ by $-3, 0, 3,$ and 6. For each value of x, determine the value of y.

You Try It 4

Graph the ordered-pair solutions of $x + 2y = 4$ when $x = -4, -2, 0,$ and 2.

Your solution

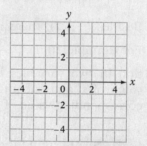

x	$y = \frac{2}{3}x = 2$	y	(x, y)
-3	$\frac{2}{3}(-3) - 2$	-4	$(-3, -4)$
0	$\frac{2}{3}(0) - 2$	-2	$(0, -2)$
3	$\frac{2}{3}(3) - 2$	0	$(3, 0)$
6	$\frac{2}{3}(6) - 2$	2	$(6, 2)$

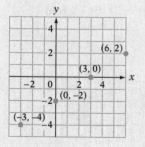

Objective C   To determine whether a set of ordered pairs is a function

Discovering a relationship between two variables is an important task in the application of mathematics. Here are some examples.

- Botanists study the relationship between the number of bushels of wheat yielded per acre and the amount of watering per acre.
- Environmental scientists study the relationship between the incidents of skin cancer and the amount of ozone in the atmosphere.
- Business analysts study the relationship between the price of a product and the number of products that are sold at that price.

Each of these relationships can be described by a set of ordered pairs.

> **Definition of a Relation**
>
> A **relation** is any set of ordered pairs.

The following table shows the number of hours that each of 9 students spent studying for a midterm exam and the grade that each of these 9 students received.

Hours	3	3.5	2.75	2	4	4.5	3	2.5	5
Grade	78	75	70	65	85	85	80	75	90

This information can be written as the relation

{(3, 78), (3.5, 75), (2.75, 70), (2, 65), (4, 85), (4.5, 85), (3, 80), (2.5, 75), (5, 90)}

where the first coordinate of the ordered pair is the hours spent studying and the second coordinate is the score on the midterm.

The **domain** of a relation is the set of first coordinates of the ordered pairs; the **range** is the set of second coordinates. For the relation above,

Domain = {2, 2.5, 2.75, 3, 3.5, 4, 4.5, 5}   Range = {65, 70, 75, 78, 80, 85, 90}

The **graph of a relation** is the graph of the ordered pairs that belong to the relation. The graph of the relation given above is shown at the right. The horizontal axis represents the hours spent studying (the domain); the vertical axis represents the test score (the range). The axes could be labeled H for hours studied and S for test score.

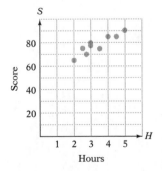

A *function* is a special type of relation in which no two ordered pairs have the same first coordinate.

> **Definition of a Function**
>
> A **function** is a relation in which no two ordered pairs have the same first coordinate.

The table at the right is the grading scale for a 100-point test. This table defines a relationship between the *score* on the test and a *letter grade*. Some of the ordered pairs of this function are (78, C), (97, A), (84, B), and (82, B).

Score	Grade
90–100	A
80–89	B
70–79	C
60–69	D
0–59	F

The grading-scale table defines a function, because no two ordered pairs can have the *same* first coordinate and *different* second coordinates. For instance, it is not possible to have the ordered pairs (72, C), and (72, B)—same first coordinate (test score) but different second coordinates (test grade). The domain of this function is {0, 1, 2,…, 99, 100}. The range is {A, B, C, D, F}.

The example of hours spent studying and test score given earlier is *not* a function, because (3, 78) and (3, 80) are ordered pairs of the relation that have the *same* first coordinate but *different* second coordinates.

Consider, again, the grading-scale example. Note that (84, B) and (82, B) are ordered pairs of the function. Ordered pairs of a function may have the same *second* coordinates but not the same first coordinates.

Although relations and functions can be given by tables, they are frequently given by an equation in two variables.

The equation $y = 2x$ expresses the relationship between a number, x, and twice the number, y. For instance, if $x = 3$, then $y = 6$, which is twice 3. To indicate exactly which ordered pairs are determined by the equation, the domain (values of x) is specified. If $x \in \{-2, -1, 0, 1, 2\}$, then the ordered pairs determined by the equation are {(−2, −4), (−1, −2), (0, 0), (1, 2), (2, 4)}. This relation is a function because no two ordered pairs have the same first coordinate.

The graph of the function $y = 2x$ with domain {−2, −1, 0, 1, 2} is shown at the right. The horizontal axis (domain) is labeled x; the vertical axis (range) is labeled y.

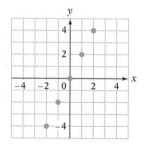

The domain {−2, −1, 0, 1, 2} was chosen arbitrarily. Other domains could have been selected. The type of application usually influences the choice of the domain.

For the equation $y = 2x$, we say that "y is a function of x" because the set of ordered pairs is a function.

Not all equations, however, define a function. For instance, the equation $|y| = x + 2$ does not define y as a function of x. The ordered pairs (2, 4) and (2, −4) both satisfy the equation. Thus there are two ordered pairs with the same first coordinate but different second coordinates.

Example 5

The number of tournaments and the total earnings of the top five Ladies Professional Golf Association (LPGA) players is given in the following table.

Player	Tournaments	Winnings
A. Sorenstam	16	$1,914,506
Se Ri Pak	25	$1,561,928
Grace Park	25	$1,374,702
Hee-Won Han	26	$1,101,060
Juli Inkster	20	$1,012,455

Write a relation where the first coordinate is the number of tournaments played and the second coordinate is the winnings per tournament rounded to the nearest dollar. Is the relation a function?

Solution

Find the winnings per tournament for each player by dividing the player's winnings by the number of tournaments played.

Sorenstam: $1,914,506 \div 16 \approx 119,657$
Pak: $1,561,928 \div 25 \approx 62,477$
Park: $1,374,702 \div 25 \approx 54,988$
Han: $1,101,060 \div 26 \approx 42,348$
Inkster: $1,012,455 \div 20 \approx 50,623$

The relation is {(16, 119,657), (25, 62,477), (25, 54,988), (26, 42,348), (20, 50,623)}. The relation is not a function. Two ordered pairs have the same first coordinate but different second coordinates.

You Try It 5

Six students decided to go on a diet and fitness program over the summer. Their weights (in pounds) at the beginning and end of the program are given in the table below.

Beginning	End
145	140
140	125
150	130
165	150
140	130
165	160

Write a relation wherein the first coordinate is the weight at the beginning of the summer and the second coordinate is the weight at the end of the summer. Is the relation a function?

Your solution

Example 6

Does $y = x^2 + 3$, where $x \in \{-2, -1, 1, 3\}$, define y as a function of x?

Solution

Determine the ordered pairs defined by the equation. Replace x in $y = x^2 + 3$ by the given values and solve for y.

{(−2, 7), (−1, 4), (1, 4), (3, 12)}

No two ordered pairs have the same first coordinate. Therefore, the relation is a function and the equation $y = x^2 + 3$ defines y as a function of x.

Note that (−1, 4) and (1, 4) are ordered pairs that belong to this function. Ordered pairs of a function may have the same *second* coordinate but not the same *first* coordinate.

You Try It 6

Does $y = \frac{1}{2}x + 1$, where $x \in \{-4, 0, 2\}$, define y as a function of x?

Your solution

Objective D   **To evaluate a function written in functional notation**

When an equation defines y as a function of x, **functional notation** is frequently used to emphasize that the relation is a function. In this case, it is common to replace y in the function's equation with the symbol $f(x)$, where

$$f(x) \text{ is read "} f \text{ of } x \text{" or "the value of } f \text{ at } x\text{."}$$

For instance, the equation $y = x^2 + 3$ from Example 6 defined y as a function of x. The equation can also be written in functional notation as

$$f(x) = x^2 + 3$$

where y has been replaced by $f(x)$.

The symbol $f(x)$ is called the **value of a function at x** because it is the result of evaluating a variable expression. For instance, $f(4)$ means to replace x by 4 and then simplify the resulting numerical expression.

$$f(x) = x^2 + 3$$
$$f(4) = 4^2 + 3 \qquad \text{• Replace } x \text{ by 4.}$$
$$= 16 + 3 = 19$$

This process is called **evaluating a function.**

> **HOW TO**   Given $f(x) = x^2 + x - 3$, find $f(-2)$.
>
> $$f(x) = x^2 + x - 3$$
> $$f(-2) = (-2)^2 + (-2) - 3 \qquad \text{• Replace } x \text{ by } -2.$$
> $$= 4 - 2 - 3 = -1$$
> $$f(-2) = -1$$

In this example, $f(-2)$ is the second coordinate of an ordered pair of the function; the first coordinate is -2. Therefore, an ordered pair of this function is $(-2, f(-2))$, or, because $f(-2) = -1$, $(-2, -1)$.

For the function given by $y = f(x) = x^2 + x - 3$, y is called the **dependent variable** because its value depends on the value of x. The **independent variable** is x.

Functions can be written using other letters or even combinations of letters. For instance, some calculators use $ABS(x)$ for the absolute-value function. Thus the equation $y = |x|$ would be written $ABS(x) = |x|$, where $ABS(x)$ replaces y.

Example 7

Given $G(t) = \dfrac{3t}{t + 4}$, find $G(1)$.

Solution

$$G(t) = \frac{3t}{t + 4}$$
$$G(1) = \frac{3(1)}{1 + 4} \qquad \text{• Replace } t \text{ by 1. Then simplify.}$$
$$G(1) = \frac{3}{5}$$

You Try It 7

Given $H(x) = \dfrac{x}{x - 4}$, find $H(8)$.

Your solution

11.1 Exercises

Objective A   To graph points in a rectangular coordinate system

1. Graph (−2, 1), (3, −5), (−2, 4), and (0, 3).

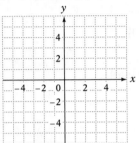

2. Graph (5, −1), (−3, −3), (−1, 0), and (1, −1).

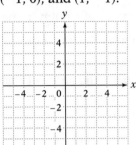

3. Graph (0, 0), (0, −5), (−3, 0), and (0, 2).

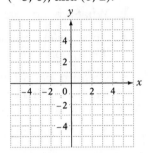

4. Graph (−4, 5), (−3, 1), (3, −4), and (5, 0).

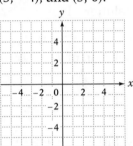

5. Graph (−1, 4), (−2, −3), (0, 2), and (4, 0).

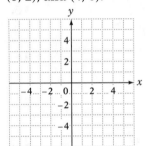

6. Graph (5, 2), (−4, −1), (0, 0), and (0, 3).

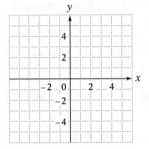

7. Find the coordinates of each of the points.

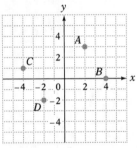

8. Find the coordinates of each of the points.

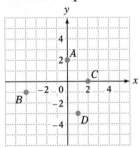

9. Find the coordinates of each of the points.

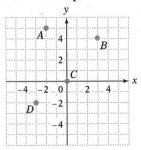

10. Find the coordinates of each of the points.

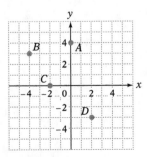

11. **a.** Name the abscissas of points A and C.
   b. Name the ordinates of points B and D.

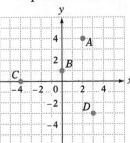

12. **a.** Name the abscissas of points A and C.
   b. Name the ordinates of points B and D.

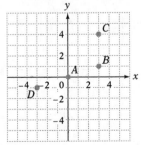

13. Suppose you are helping a student who is having trouble graphing ordered pairs. The work of the student is at the right. What can you say to this student to correct the error that is being made?

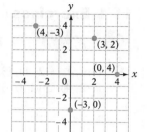

14. **a.** What are the signs of the coordinates of a point in the third quadrant?

b. What are the signs of the coordinates of a point in the fourth quadrant?

c. On an *xy*-coordinate system, what is the name of the axis for which all the *x*-coordinates are zero?

d. On an *xy*-coordinate system, what is the name of the axis for which all the *y*-coordinates are zero?

Objective B **To determine ordered-pair solutions of an equation in two variables**

15. Is (3, 4) a solution of $y = -x + 7$?

16. Is (2, −3) a solution of $y = x + 5$?

17. Is (−1, 2) a solution of $y = \frac{1}{2}x - 1$?

18. Is (1, −3) a solution of $y = -2x - 1$?

19. Is (4, 1) a solution of $2x - 5y = 4$?

20. Is (−5, 3) a solution of $3x - 2y = 9$?

21. Is (0, 4) a solution of $3x - 4y = -4$?

22. Is (−2, 0) a solution of $x + 2y = -1$?

For Exercises 23 to 28, graph the ordered-pair solutions of the equation for the given values of *x*.

23. $y = 2x; x = -2, -1, 0, 2$

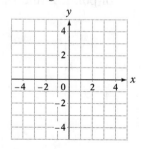

24. $y = -2x; x = -2, -1, 0, 2$

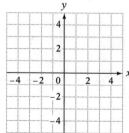

25. $y = \frac{2}{3}x + 1; x = -3, 0, 3$

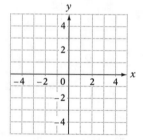

26. $y = -\frac{1}{3}x - 2; x = -3, 0, 3$

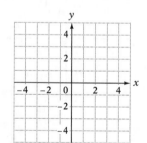

27. $2x + 3y = 6; x = -3, 0, 3$

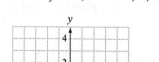

28. $x - 2y = 4; x = -2, 0, 2$

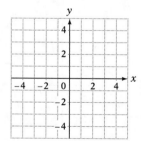

Objective C   **To determine whether a set of ordered pairs is a function**

29.   **Biology**   The table below shows the length, in centimeters, of the humerus (the long bone of the forelimb, from shoulder to elbow) and the total wingspan, in centimeters, of several pterosaurs, which are extinct flying reptiles of the order Pterosauria. Write a relation where the first coordinate is the length of the humerus and the second is the wingspan. Is the relation a function?

Humerus (in centimeters)	24	32	22	15	4.4	17	15	4.4
Wingspan (in centimeters)	600	750	430	300	68	370	310	55

30.   **Environmental Science**   The table below, based in part on data from the National Oceanic and Atmospheric Administration, shows the average annual concentration of atmospheric carbon dioxide (in parts per million) and the average sea surface temperature (in degrees Celsius) for eight consecutive years. Write a relation wherein the first coordinate is the carbon dioxide concentration and the second coordinate is the average sea surface temperature. Is the relation a function?

Carbon dioxide concentration (in parts per million)	352	353	354	355	356	358	360	361
Surface sea temperature (in degrees Celsius)	15.4	15.4	15.1	15.1	15.2	15.4	15.3	15.5

31.   **Sports**   The table at the right shows the number of home runs and the number of at-bats for the top five home runs leaders in the National League for the 2003 season. Write a relation where the first coordinate is the number of at-bats and the second coordinate is the number of home runs per at-bats rounded to the nearest thousand. Is the relation a function?

Player	At-bats	Home runs
Barry Bonds	390	45
Albert Pujois	591	43
Sammy Sosa	517	40
Gary Sheffield	576	39
Jeff Bagwell	605	39

32.   **Nielsen Ratings**   The ratings (each rating point is 1,055,000 households) and share (the percentage of television sets in use tuned to a specific program) for selected television shows for a week in November 2003 are shown in the table at the right. Write a relation where the first coordinate is the ratings and the second coordinate is the share. Is the relation a function?

Television Show	Rating	Share
CSI	18.1	27.0
E.R.	13.6	22.0
Friends	13.4	21.0
CSI: Miami	13.2	21.0
60 Minutes	11.3	18.0

33.   Does $y = -2x - 3$, where $x \in \{-2, -1, 0, 3\}$, define y as a function of x?

34.   Does $y = 2x + 3$, where $x \in \{-2, -1, 1, 4\}$, define y as a function of x?

35.   Does $|y| = x - 1$, where $x \in \{1, 2, 3, 4\}$, define y as a function of x?

36.   Does $|y| = x + 2$, where $x \in \{-2, -1, 0, 3\}$, define y as a function of x?

37.   Does $y = x^2$, where $x \in \{-2, -1, 0, 1, 2\}$, define y as a function of x?

38.   Does $y = x^2 - 1$, where $x \in \{-2, -1, 0, 1, 2\}$, define y as a function of x?

Objective D   To evaluate a function written in functional notation

39. Given $f(x) = 3x - 4$, find $f(4)$.

40. Given $f(x) = 5x + 1$, find $f(2)$.

41. Given $f(x) = x^2$, find $f(3)$.

42. Given $f(x) = x^2 - 1$, find $f(1)$.

43. Given $G(x) = x^2 + x$, find $G(-2)$.

44. Given $H(x) = x^2 - x$, find $H(-2)$.

45. Given $s(t) = \dfrac{3}{t - 1}$, find $s(-2)$.

46. Given $P(x) = \dfrac{4}{2x + 1}$, find $P(-2)$.

47. Given $h(x) = 3x^2 - 2x + 1$, find $h(3)$.

48. Given $Q(r) = 4r^2 - r - 3$, find $Q(2)$.

49. Given $f(x) = \dfrac{x}{x + 5}$, find $f(-3)$.

50. Given $v(t) = \dfrac{2t}{2t + 1}$, find $v(3)$.

51. Given $g(x) = x^3 - x^2 + 2x - 7$, find $g(0)$.

52. Given $F(z) = \dfrac{z}{z^2 + 1}$, find $F(0)$.

APPLYING THE CONCEPTS

53. ✏ Write a few sentences that describe the similarities and differences between relations and functions.

54. ✏ The graph of $y^2 = x$, where $x \in \{0, 1, 4, 9\}$, is shown at the right. Is this the graph of a function? Explain your answer.

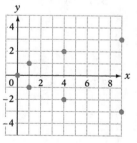

55. ✏ Is it possible to evaluate $f(x) = \dfrac{5}{x - 1}$ when $x = 1$? If so, what is $f(1)$? If not, explain why not.

11.2 Linear Equations in Two Variables

Objective A   **To graph an equation of the form $y = mx + b$**

The **graph of an equation in two variables** is a graph of the ordered-pair solutions of the equation.

Consider $y = 2x + 1$. Choosing $x = -2, -1, 0, 1$, and 2 and determining the corresponding values of y produces some of the ordered pairs of the equation. These are recorded in the table at the right. See the graph of the ordered pairs in Figure 1.

x	$y = 2x + 1$	y	(x, y)
-2	$2(-2) + 1$	-3	$(-2, -3)$
-1	$2(-1) + 1$	-1	$(-1, -1)$
0	$2(0) + 1$	1	$(0, 1)$
1	$2(1) + 1$	3	$(1, 3)$
2	$2(2) + 1$	5	$(2, 5)$

Choosing values of x that are not integers produces more ordered pairs to graph, such as $\left(-\frac{5}{2}, -4\right)$ and $\left(\frac{3}{2}, 4\right)$, as shown in Figure 2. Choosing still other values of x would result in more and more ordered pairs being graphed. The result would be so many dots that the graph would appear as the straight line shown in Figure 3, which is the graph of $y = 2x + 1$.

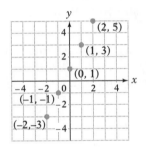

Figure 1

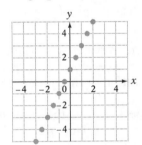

Figure 2

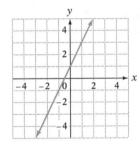

Figure 3

Equations in two variables have characteristic graphs. The equation $y = 2x + 1$ is an example of a *linear equation*, or *linear function*, because its graph is a straight line. It is also called a *first-degree equation* in two variables because the exponent on each variable is the first power.

> **Linear Equation in Two Variables**
>
> Any equation of the form $y = mx + b$, where m is the coefficient of x and b is a constant, is a **linear equation in two variables,** or a **first-degree equation in two variables** or a **linear function.** The graph of a linear equation in two variables is a straight line.

Examples of linear equations are shown at the right. These equations represent linear functions because there is only one possible y for each x. Note that for $y = 3 - 2x$, m is the coefficient of x and b is the constant.

$$y = 2x + 1 \qquad (m = 2, b = 1)$$
$$y = x - 4 \qquad (m = 1, b = -4)$$
$$y = -\frac{3}{4}x \qquad \left(m = -\frac{3}{4}, b = 0\right)$$
$$y = 3 - 2x \qquad (m = -2, b = 3)$$

The equation $y = x^2 + 4x + 3$ is not a linear equation in two variables because there is a term with a variable squared. The equation $y = \frac{3}{x - 4}$ is not a linear equation because a variable occurs in the denominator of a fraction.

To graph a linear equation, choose some values of x and then find the corresponding values of y. Because a straight line is determined by two points, it is sufficient to find only two ordered-pair solutions. However, it is recommended that at least three ordered-pair solutions be used to ensure accuracy.

HOW TO   Graph $y = -\frac{3}{2}x + 2$.

This is a linear equation with $m = -\frac{3}{2}$ and $b = 2$. Find at least three solutions. Because m is a fraction, choose values of x that will simplify the calculations. We have chosen -2, 0, and 4 for x. (Any values of x could have been selected.)

x	$y = -\frac{3}{2}x = 2$	y	(x, y)
-2	$-\frac{3}{2}(-2) + 2$	5	$(-2, 5)$
0	$-\frac{3}{2}(0) + 2$	2	$(0, 2)$
4	$-\frac{3}{2}(4) + 2$	-4	$(4, -4)$

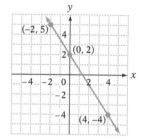

The graph of $y = -\frac{3}{2}x + 2$ is shown at the right.

Remember that a graph is a drawing of the ordered-pair solutions of the equation. Therefore, every point on the graph is a solution of the equation, and every solution of the equation is a point on the graph.

The graph at the right is the graph of $y = x + 2$. Note that $(-4, -2)$ and $(1, 3)$ are points on the graph and that these points are solutions of $y = x + 2$. The point whose coordinates are $(4, 1)$ is not a point on the graph and is not a solution of the equation.

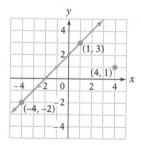

Example 1   Graph $y = 3x - 2$.

Solution

x	y
0	-2
-1	-5
2	4

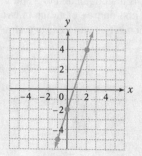

You Try It 1   Graph $y = 3x + 1$.

Your solution

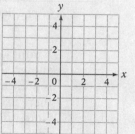

Example 2   Graph $y = 2x$.

Solution

x	y
0	0
2	4
−2	−4

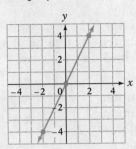

You Try It 2   Graph $y = -2x$.

Your solution

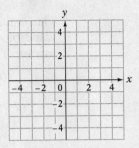

Example 3   Graph $y = \dfrac{1}{2}x - 1$.

Solution

x	y
0	−1
2	0
−2	−2

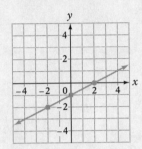

You Try It 3   Graph $y = \dfrac{1}{3}x - 3$.

Your solution

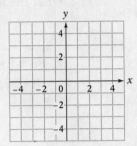

Objective B   **To graph an equation of the form $Ax + By = C$**

The equation $Ax + By = C$, where A and B are coefficients and C is a constant, is called the **standard form of a linear equation in two variables.** Examples are shown at the right.

$2x + 3y = 6$ $(A = 2, B = 3, C = 6)$
$x - 2y = -4$ $(A = 1, B = -2, C = -4)$
$2x + y = 0$ $(A = 2, B = 1, C = 0)$
$4x - 5y = 2$ $(A = 4, B = -5, C = 2)$

To graph an equation of the form $Ax + By = C$, first solve the equation for y. Then follow the same procedure used for graphing $y = mx + b$.

Study Tip

Remember that a How To example indicates a worked-out example. Using paper and pencil, work through the example. See *AIM for Success*.

HOW TO   Graph $3x + 4y = 12$.

$3x + 4y = 12$
$\quad\quad 4y = -3x + 12$

$\quad\quad\quad y = -\dfrac{3}{4}x + 3$

x	y
0	3
4	0
−4	6

- Solve for y.
- Subtract $3x$ from each side of the equation.

- Divide each side of the equation by 4.
- Find three ordered-pair solutions of the equation.

- Graph the ordered pairs and then draw a line through the points.

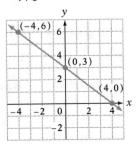

The graph of a linear equation with one of the variables missing is either a horizontal or a vertical line.

The equation $y = 2$ could be written $0 \cdot x + y = 2$. Because $0 \cdot x = 0$ for any value of x, the value of y is always 2 no matter what value of x is chosen. For instance, replace x by -4, by -1, by 0, and by 3. In each case, $y = 2$.

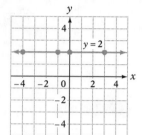

$$0x + y = 2$$
$$0(-4) + y = 2 \qquad (-4, 2) \text{ is a solution.}$$
$$0(-1) + y = 2 \qquad (-1, 2) \text{ is a solution.}$$
$$0(0) + y = 2 \qquad (0, 2) \text{ is a solution.}$$
$$0(3) + y = 2 \qquad (3, 2) \text{ is a solution.}$$

The solutions are plotted in the graph at the right, and a line is drawn through the plotted points. Note that the line is horizontal.

Graph of a Horizontal Line

The graph of $y = b$ is a horizontal line passing through $(0, b)$.

The equation $x = -2$ could be written $x + 0 \cdot y = -2$. Because $0 \cdot y = 0$ for any value of y, the value of x is always -2 no matter what value of y is chosen. For instance, replace y by -2, by 0, by 2, and by 3. In each case, $x = -2$.

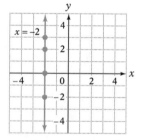

$$x + 0y = -2$$
$$x + 0(-2) = -2 \qquad (-2, -2) \text{ is a solution.}$$
$$x + 0(0) = -2 \qquad (-2, 0) \text{ is a solution.}$$
$$x + 0(2) = -2 \qquad (-2, 2) \text{ is a solution.}$$
$$x + 0(3) = -2 \qquad (-2, 3) \text{ is a solution.}$$

The solutions are plotted in the graph at the right, and a line is drawn through the plotted points. Note that the line is vertical.

Graph of a Vertical Line

The graph of $x = a$ is a vertical line passing through $(a, 0)$.

HOW TO   Graph $x = -3$ and $y = 1$ on the same coordinate grid.

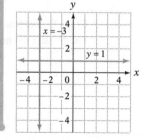

• The graph of $x = -3$ is a vertical line passing through $(-3, 0)$.

• The graph of $y = 1$ is a horizontal line passing through $(0, 1)$.

Example 4 Graph $2x - 5y = 10$.

Solution   Solve $2x - 5y = 10$ for y.

$2x - 5y = 10$

$\quad -5y = -2x + 10$

$\qquad y = \dfrac{2}{5}x - 2$

x	y
0	-2
5	0
-5	-4

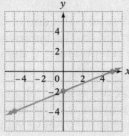

You Try It 4 Graph $5x - 2y = 10$.

Your solution

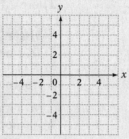

Example 5 Graph $x + 2y = 6$.

Solution   Solve $x + 2y = 6$ for y.

$x + 2y = 6$

$\quad 2y = -x + 6$

$\quad\ y = -\dfrac{1}{2}x + 3$

x	y
0	3
-2	4
4	1

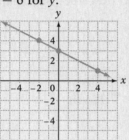

You Try It 5 Graph $x - 3y = 9$.

Your solution

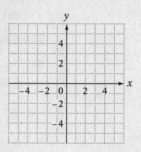

Example 6 Graph $y = -2$.

Solution

The graph of an equation of the form $y = b$ is a horizontal line passing through the point $(0, b)$.

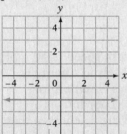

You Try It 6 Graph $y = 3$.

Your solution

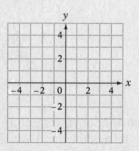

Example 7 Graph $x = 3$.

Solution

The graph of an equation of the form $x = a$ is a vertical line passing through the point $(a, 0)$.

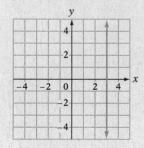

You Try It 7 Graph $x = -4$.

Your solution

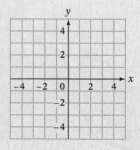

Objective C **To solve application problems**

There are a variety of applications of linear functions.

HOW TO Solve: The temperature of a cup of water that has been placed in a microwave oven to be heated can be approximated by the equation $T = 0.7s + 65$, where T is the temperature of the water s seconds after the microwave oven is turned on.

a. Graph this equation for $0 \le s \le 220$. (Note: In many applications, the domain of the variable is given so that the equation makes sense. For instance, it would not be sensible to have values of s that are less than 0. This would correspond to negative time. The choice of 220 is somewhat arbitrary and was chosen so that the water would not boil over.)

b. The point whose coordinates are (120, 149) is on the graph of this equation. Write a sentence that describes the meaning of this ordered pair.

Solution

a.

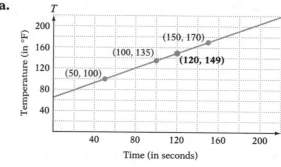

• Choosing $s = 50, 100$, and 150, you find the corresponding ordered pairs (50, 100), (100, 135), and (150, 170). Plot these points and draw a line through the points.

b. The point whose coordinates are (120, 149) means that 120 s (2 min) after the oven is turned on, the water temperature is 149°F.

Example 8

The number of kilobytes, K, of an MP3 file that remain to be downloaded t seconds after starting the download is given by $K = 935 - 5.5t$. Graph this equation for $0 \le t \le 170$. The point whose coordinates are (50, 660) are on this graph. Write a sentence that describes the meaning of this ordered pair.

Solution

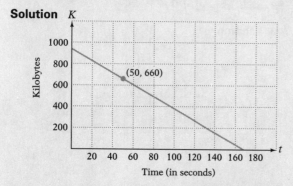

The ordered pair (50, 660) means that after 50 s, there are 660 K remaining to be downloaded.

You Try It 8

A car is traveling at a uniform speed of 40 mph. The distance, d, the car travels in t hours is given by $d = 40t$. Graph this equation for $0 \le t \le 5$. The point whose coordinates are (3, 120) is on the graph. Write a sentence that describes the meaning of this ordered pair.

Your solution

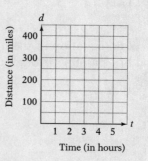

11.2 Exercises

Objective A   To graph an equation of the form $y = mx + b$

For Exercises 1 to 18, graph.

1. $y = 2x - 3$

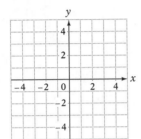

2. $y = -2x + 2$

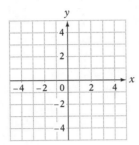

3. $y = \dfrac{1}{3}x$

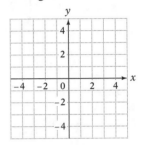

4. $y = -3x$

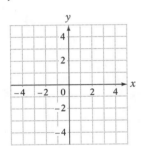

5. $y = \dfrac{2}{3}x - 1$

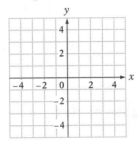

6. $y = \dfrac{3}{4}x + 2$

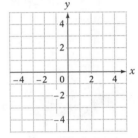

7. $y = -\dfrac{1}{4}x + 2$

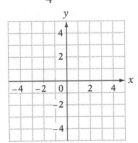

8. $y = -\dfrac{1}{3}x + 1$

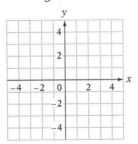

9. $y = -\dfrac{2}{5}x + 1$

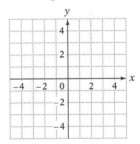

10. $y = -\dfrac{1}{2}x + 3$

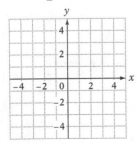

11. $y = 2x - 4$

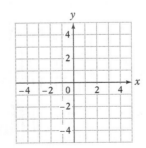

12. $y = 3x - 4$

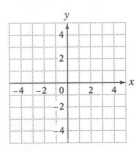

13. $y = x - 3$

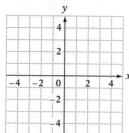

14. $y = x + 2$

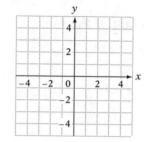

15. $y = -x + 2$

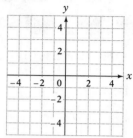

16. $y = -x - 1$

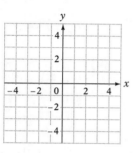

17. $y = -\dfrac{2}{3}x + 1$

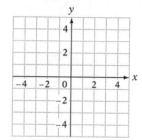

18. $y = 5x - 4$

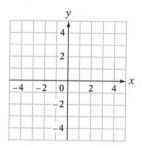

Objective B **To graph an equation of the form $Ax = By + C$**

For Exercises 19 to 36, graph.

19. $3x + y = 3$

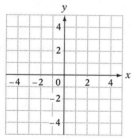

20. $2x + y = 4$

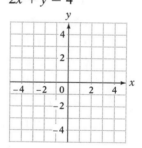

21. $2x + 3y = 6$

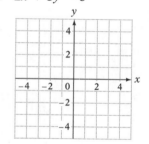

22. $3x + 2y = 4$

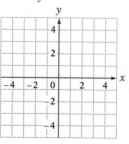

23. $x - 2y = 4$

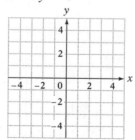

24. $x - 3y = 6$

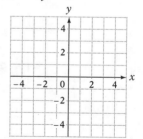

25. $2x - 3y = 6$

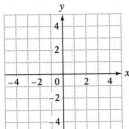

26. $3x - 2y = 8$

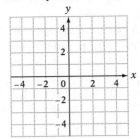

27. $2x + 5y = 10$

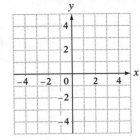

28. $3x + 4y = 12$

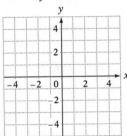

29. $x = 3$

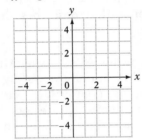

30. $y = -4$

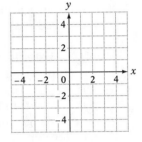

31. $x + 4y = 4$

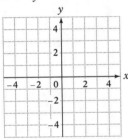

32. $4x - 3y = 12$

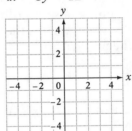

33. $y = 4$

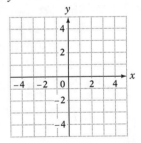

34. $x = -2$

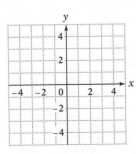

35. $\dfrac{x}{5} + \dfrac{y}{4} = 1$

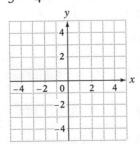

36. $\dfrac{x}{4} - \dfrac{y}{3} = 1$

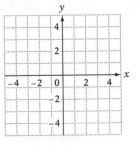

Objective C   **To solve application problems**

37. ✏️   **Emergency Response**   A rescue helicopter is rushing at a constant speed of 150 mph to reach several people stranded in the ocean 11 mi away after their boat sank. The rescuers can determine how far they are from the victims using the equation $D = 11 - 2.5t$, where D is the distance in miles and t is the time elapsed in minutes. Graph this equation for $0 \leq t \leq 4$. The point $(3, 3.5)$ is on the graph. Write a sentence that describes the meaning of this ordered pair.

38. ✏️   **Business**   A custom-illustrated sign or banner can be commissioned for a cost of $25 for the material and $10.50 per square foot for the artwork. The equation that represents this cost is given by $y = 10.50x + 25$, where y is the cost and x is the number of square feet in the sign. Graph this equation for $0 \leq x \leq 20$. The point $(15, 182.5)$ is on the graph. Write a sentence that describes the meaning of this ordered pair.

39. ✏️   **Veterinary Science**   According to some veterinarians, the age, x, of a dog can be translated to "human years" by using the equation $H = 4x + 16$, where H is the human equivalent age for the dog. Graph this equation for $2 \leq x \leq 21$. The point whose coordinates are $(6, 40)$ is on this graph. Write a sentence that explains the meaning of this ordered pair.

40. 🥧   **Business**   Judging on the basis of data from the Consumer Electronics Association, the projected number, N (in millions), of sales of high-definition televisions (HDTVs) can be approximated by $N = 3t + 4$, where $0 \leq t \leq 4$ and $t = 0$ corresponds to the year 2003. Graph this equation. The point whose coordinates are $(3, 13)$ is on this graph. Write a sentence that explains the meaning of this ordered pair in the context of the problem.

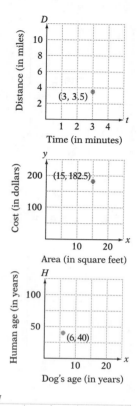

APPLYING THE CONCEPTS

41. ✏️   Graph $y = 2x - 2$, $y = 2x$, and $y = 2x + 3$. What observation can you make about the graphs?

42. ✏️   Graph $y = x + 3$, $y = 2x + 3$, and $y = -\frac{1}{2}x + 3$. What observation can you make about the graphs?

43. For the equation $y = 3x + 2$, when the value of x changes from 1 to 2, does the value of y increase or decrease? What is the change in y? Suppose that the value of x changes from 13 to 14. What is the change in y?

44. For the equation $y = -2x + 1$, when the value of x changes from 1 to 2, does the value of y increase or decrease? What is the change in y? Suppose the value of x changes from 13 to 14. What is the change in y?

45. **Telecommunications**   A long-distance telephone company offers a flat rate of $.99 for the first 15 minutes of a phone call and then $.15 for each additional minute. The graph of this situation is a combination of the graphs of two linear equations: $C = 0.99$ when $0 < t \leq 15$ and $C = 0.15(t - 15) + 0.99$ when $t > 15$. The graph is shown at the right.
a. What is the cost of a telephone call that lasts 5 minutes?
b. What is the cost of a telephone call that lasts 20 minutes?

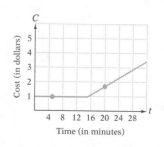

11.3 Intercepts and Slopes of Straight Lines

Objective A   To find the *x*- and *y*-intercepts of a straight line

The graph of the equation $2x + 3y = 6$ is shown at the right. The graph crosses the *x*-axis at the point (3, 0) and crosses the *y*-axis at the point (0, 2). The point at which a graph crosses the *x*-axis is called the **x-intercept.** At the *x*-intercept, the *y*-coordinate is 0. The point at which a graph crosses the *y*-axis is called the **y-intercept.** At the *y*-intercept, the *x*-coordinate is 0.

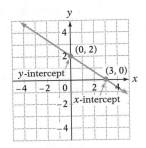

HOW TO   Find the *x*- and *y*-intercepts of the graph of the equation $2x - 3y = 12$.

> **TAKE NOTE**
> To find the *x*-intercept, let $y = 0$ and solve for *x*.
> To find the *y*-intercept, let $x = 0$ and solve for *y*.

To find the *x*-intercept, let $y = 0$. (Any point on the *x*-axis has *y*-coordinate 0.)

$$2x - 3y = 12$$
$$2x - 3(0) = 12$$
$$2x = 12$$
$$x = 6$$

The *x*-intercept is (6, 0).

To find the *y*-intercept, let $x = 0$. (Any point on the *y*-axis has *x*-coordinate 0.)

$$2x - 3y = 12$$
$$2(0) - 3y = 12$$
$$-3y = 12$$
$$y = -4$$

The *y*-intercept is (0, −4).

HOW TO   Find the *y*-intercept of $y = 3x + 4$.

$$y = 3x + 4 = 3(0) + 4 = 4 \qquad \bullet \text{ Let } x = 0.$$

The *y*-intercept is (0, 4).

For any equation of the form $y = mx + b$, the *y*-intercept is (0, *b*).

Some linear equations can be graphed by finding the *x*- and *y*-intercepts and then drawing a line through these two points.

Example 1   Find the *x*- and *y*-intercepts for $x - 2y = 4$. Graph the line.

Solution

To find the *x*-intercept, let $y = 0$ and solve for *x*.
$$x - 2y = 4$$
$$x - 2(0) = 4$$
$$x = 4 \qquad (4, 0)$$

To find the *y*-intercept, let $x = 0$ and solve for *y*.
$$x - 2y = 4$$
$$0 - 2y = 4$$
$$-2y = 4$$
$$y = -2 \qquad (0, -2)$$

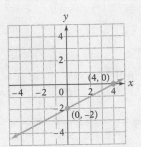

You Try It 1   Find the *x*- and *y*-intercepts for $y = 2x - 4$. Graph the line.

Your solution

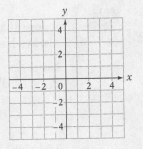

Objective B   **To find the slope of a straight line**

The graphs of $y = \frac{2}{3}x + 1$ and $y = 2x + 1$ are shown in Figure 1. Each graph crosses the y-axis at the point $(0, 1)$, but the graphs have different slants. The **slope** of a line is a measure of the slant of the line. The symbol for slope is m.

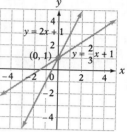

Figure 1

TAKE NOTE

The change in the y values can be thought of as the *rise* of the line, and the change in the x values can be thought of as the *run*. Then

$$\text{Slope} = m = \frac{\text{rise}}{\text{run}}$$

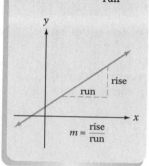

$$m = \frac{\text{rise}}{\text{run}}$$

The slope of a line containing two points is the ratio of the change in the y values of the two points to the change in the x values. The line containing the points $(-2, -3)$ and $(6, 1)$ is graphed in Figure 2. The change in the y values is the difference between the two ordinates.

$$\text{Change in } y = 1 - (-3) = 4$$

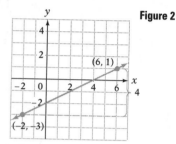

Figure 2

The change in the x values is the difference between the two abscissas (Figure 3).

$$\text{Change in } x = 6 - (-2) = 8$$

$$\text{Slope} = m = \frac{\text{change in } y}{\text{change in } x} = \frac{4}{8} = \frac{1}{2}$$

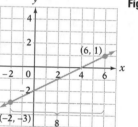

Figure 3

Slope Formula

If $P_1(x_1, y_1)$ and $P_2(x_2, y_2)$ are two points on a line and $x_1 \neq x_2$, then $m = \dfrac{y_2 - y_1}{x_2 - x_1}$ (Figure 4). If $x_1 = x_2$, the slope is undefined.

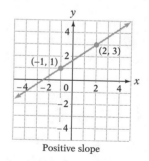

Figure 4

HOW TO Find the slope of the line containing the points $(-1, 1)$ and $(2, 3)$.

Let P_1 be $(-1, 1)$ and P_2 be $(2, 3)$. Then $x_1 = -1, y_1 = 1, x_2 = 2,$ and $y_2 = 3$.

$$m = \frac{y_2 - y_1}{x_2 - x_1} = \frac{3 - 1}{2 - (-1)} = \frac{2}{3}$$

The slope is $\frac{2}{3}$.

Positive slope

A line that slants upward to the right always has a **positive slope.**

TAKE NOTE

Positive slope means that the value of y increases as the value of x increases.

Note that you obtain the same results if the points are named oppositely. Let P_1 be $(2, 3)$ and P_2 be $(-1, 1)$. Then $x_1 = 2, y_1 = 3, x_2 = -1,$ and $y_2 = 1$.

$$m = \frac{y_2 - y_1}{x_2 - x_1} = \frac{1 - 3}{-1 - 2} = \frac{-2}{-3} = \frac{2}{3}$$

The slope is $\frac{2}{3}$. Therefore, it does not matter which point is named P_1 and which is named P_2; the slope remains the same.

> **TAKE NOTE**
> Negative slope means that the value of y decreases as x increases. Compare this to positive slope.

HOW TO Find the slope of the line containing the points $(-3, 4)$ and $(2, -2)$.

Let P_1 be $(-3, 4)$ and P_2 be $(2, -2)$.

$$m = \frac{y_2 - y_1}{x_2 - x_1} = \frac{-2 - 4}{2 - (-3)} = \frac{-6}{5} = -\frac{6}{5}$$

The slope is $-\frac{6}{5}$.

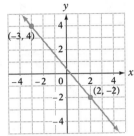
Negative slope

A line that slants downward to the right always has a **negative slope.**

HOW TO Find the slope of the line containing the points $(-1, 3)$ and $(4, 3)$.

Let P_1 be $(-1, 3)$ and P_2 be $(4, 3)$.

$$m = \frac{y_2 - y_1}{x_2 - x_1} = \frac{3 - 3}{4 - (-1)} = \frac{0}{5} = 0$$

The slope is 0.

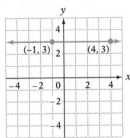
Zero slope

A horizontal line has **zero slope.**

HOW TO Find the slope of the line containing the points $(2, -2)$ and $(2, 4)$.

Let P_1 be $(2, -2)$ and P_2 be $(2, 4)$.

$$m = \frac{y_2 - y_1}{x_2 - x_1} = \frac{4 - (-2)}{2 - 2} = \frac{6}{0}$$ Division by zero is not defined.

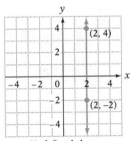
Undefined slope

A vertical line has undefined slope.

Two lines in the plane that never intersect are called parallel lines. The lines l_1 and l_2 in the figure at the right are parallel. Calculating the slope of each line, we have

Slope of l_1: $m_1 = \dfrac{y_2 - y_1}{x_2 - x_1} = \dfrac{5 - 1}{3 - (-3)} = \dfrac{4}{6} = \dfrac{2}{3}$

Slope of l_2: $m_2 = \dfrac{y_2 - y_1}{x_2 - x_1} = \dfrac{-1 - (-5)}{3 - (-3)} = \dfrac{4}{6} = \dfrac{2}{3}$

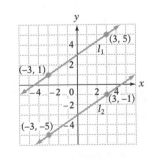

Note that these parallel lines have the same slope. This is always true.

> **TAKE NOTE**
> We must separate the description of parallel lines at the right because vertical lines in the plane are parallel but their slopes are undefined.

> **Parallel Lines**
> Two nonvertical lines in the plane are parallel if and only if they have the same slope. Vertical lines in the plane are parallel.

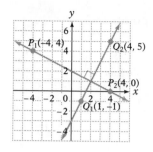

Two lines that intersect at a 90° angle (right angle) are perpendicular lines. The lines at the left are perpendicular.

> **Perpendicular Lines**
>
> Two nonvertical lines in the plane are perpendicular if and only if the product of their slopes is −1. A vertical and horizontal line are perpendicular.

The slope of the line between P_1 and P_2 is $m_1 = \dfrac{0 - 4}{4 - (-4)} = -\dfrac{4}{8} = -\dfrac{1}{2}$. The slope of the line between Q_1 and Q_2 is $m_2 = \dfrac{5 - (-1)}{4 - 1} = \dfrac{6}{3} = 2$. The product of the slopes is $\left(-\dfrac{1}{2}\right)2 = -1$. Because the product of the slopes is −1, the graphs are perpendicular.

There are many applications of the concept of slope. Here is a possibility.

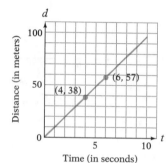

When Florence Griffith-Joyner set the world record for the 100-meter dash, her average rate of speed was approximately 9.5 meters per second. The graph at the right shows the distance she ran during her record-setting run. From the graph, note that after 4 s she had traveled 38 m and that after 6 s she had traveled 57 m. The slope of the line between these two points is

$$m = \frac{57 - 38}{6 - 4} = \frac{19}{2} = 9.5$$

Note that the slope of the line is the same as the rate she was running, 9.5 meters per second. The average speed of an object is related to slope.

Example 2

Find the slope of the line containing the points with coordinates $(-2, -3)$ and $(3, 4)$.

Solution

Let $P_1 = (-2, -3)$ and $P_2 = (3, 4)$.

$m = \dfrac{y_2 - y_1}{x_2 - x_1} = \dfrac{4 - (-3)}{3 - (-2)}$ • $y_2 = 4, y_1 = -3,$
$x_2 = 3, x_1 = -2$

$\quad = \dfrac{7}{5}$

The slope is $\dfrac{7}{5}$.

You Try It 2

Find the slope of the line containing the points with coordinates $(1, 4)$ and $(-3, 8)$.

Your solution

Example 3

Find the slope of the line containing the points with coordinates $(-1, 4)$ and $(-1, 0)$.

Solution

Let $P_1 = (-1, 4)$ and $P_2 = (-1, 0)$.

$m = \dfrac{y_2 - y_1}{x_2 - x_1} = \dfrac{0 - 4}{-1 - (-1)}$ • $y_2 = 0, y_1 = 4,$
$x_2 = -1, x_1 = -1$

$\quad = \dfrac{-4}{0}$

The slope is undefined.

You Try It 3

Find the slope of the line containing the points with coordinates $(-1, 2)$ and $(4, 2)$.

Your solution

Example 4

The graph below shows the height of a plane above an airport during its 30-minute descent from cruising altitude to landing. Find the slope of the line. Write a sentence that explains the meaning of the slope.

Solution

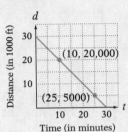

$$m = \frac{5000 - 20{,}000}{25 - 10} = \frac{-15{,}000}{15}$$

$$= -1000$$

A slope of -1000 means that the height of the plane is *decreasing* at the rate of 1000 ft/min.

You Try It 4

The graph below shows the approximate decline in the value of a used car over a 5-year period. Find the slope of the line. Write a sentence that states the meaning of the slope.

Your solution

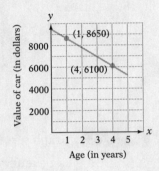

Objective C   **To graph a line using the slope and the *y*-intercept**

The graph of the equation $y = \frac{2}{3}x + 1$ is shown at the right. The points $(-3, -1)$ and $(3, 3)$ are on the graph. The slope of the line between the two points is

$$m = \frac{3 - (-1)}{3 - (-3)} = \frac{4}{6} = \frac{2}{3}$$

Observe that the slope of the line is the coefficient of x in the equation $y = \frac{2}{3}x + 1$. Also recall that the y-intercept is $(0, 1)$, where 1 is the constant term of the equation.

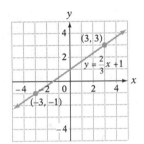

> *TAKE NOTE*
>
> Here are some equations in slope-intercept form.
>
> $y = 2x - 3$: Slope is 2; y-intercept is $(0, -3)$.
>
> $y = -x + 2$: Slope is -1 (recall that $-x = -1x$); y-intercept is $(0, 2)$.
>
> $y = \frac{x}{2}$: Because $\frac{x}{2} = \frac{1}{2}x$, slope is $\frac{1}{2}$; y-intercept is $(0, 0)$.

> **Slope-Intercept Form of a Linear Equation**
>
> An equation of the form $y = mx + b$ is called the **slope-intercept form** of a straight line. The slope of the line is m, the coefficient of x. The y-intercept is $(0, b)$, where b is the constant term of the equation.

If a linear equation is not in slope-intercept form, solve the equation for y.

HOW TO   Find the slope and y-intercept for the graph of $3x + 2y = 12$.

$$3x + 2y = 12$$
$$2y = -3x + 12$$
$$y = -\frac{3}{2}x + 6$$

• Write the equation in slope-intercept form by solving for y.

The slope is $-\frac{3}{2}$; the y-intercept is $(0, 6)$.

When an equation of a line is in slope-intercept form, the graph can be drawn using the slope and the y-intercept. First locate the y-intercept. Use the slope to find a second point on the line. Then draw a line through the two points.

HOW TO   Graph $y = 2x - 3$.

y-intercept $= (0, b) = (0, -3)$

$m = 2 = \dfrac{2}{1} = \dfrac{\text{change in } y}{\text{change in } x}$

Beginning at the y-intercept, move right 1 unit (change in x) and then up 2 units (change in y).

$(1, -1)$ is a second point on the graph.

Draw a line through the two points $(0, -3)$ and $(1, -1)$.

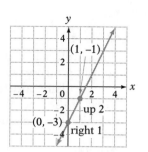

Example 5   Graph $y = -\dfrac{2}{3}x + 1$ by using the slope and y-intercept.

Solution y-intercept $= (0, b) = (0, 1)$

$m = -\dfrac{2}{3} = \dfrac{-2}{3} = \dfrac{\text{change in } y}{\text{change in } x}$

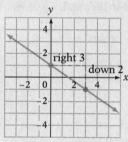

You Try It 5   Graph $y = -\dfrac{1}{4}x - 1$ by using the slope and y-intercept.

Your solution

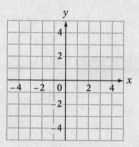

Example 6   Graph $2x - 3y = 6$ by using the slope and y-intercept.

Solution   Solve the equation for y.

$2x - 3y = 6$

$-3y = -2x + 6$

$y = \dfrac{2}{3}x - 2$

y-intercept $= (0, -2)$; $m = \dfrac{2}{3}$

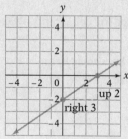

You Try It 6   Graph $x - 2y = 4$ by using the slope and y-intercept.

Your solution

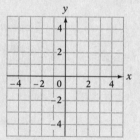

11.3 Exercises

Objective A   **To find the *x*- and *y*-intercepts of a straight line**

For Exercises 1 to 12, find the *x*- and *y*-intercepts.

1. $x - y = 3$ **2.** $3x + 4y = 12$ **3.** $y = 3x - 6$ **4.** $y = 2x + 10$

5. $x - 5y = 10$ **6.** $3x + 2y = 12$ **7.** $y = 3x + 12$ **8.** $y = 5x + 10$

9. $2x - 3y = 0$ **10.** $3x + 4y = 0$ **11.** $y = -\dfrac{1}{2}x + 3$ **12.** $y = \dfrac{2}{3}x - 4$

For Exercises 13 to 18, find the *x*- and *y*-intercepts and then graph.

13. $5x + 2y = 10$

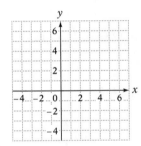

14. $x - 3y = 6$

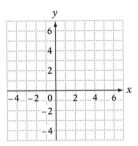

15. $y = \dfrac{3}{4}x - 3$

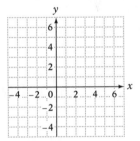

16. $y = \dfrac{2}{5}x - 2$

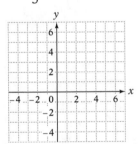

17. $5y - 3x = 15$

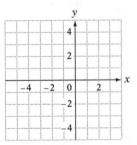

18. $9y - 4x = 18$

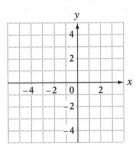

Objective B   **To find the slope of a straight line**

19.   Explain how to find the slope of a line given two points on the line.

20.   What is the difference between a line that has zero slope and one that has undefined slope?

For Exercises 21 to 32, find the slope of the line containing the given points.

21. $P_1(4, 2), P_2(3, 4)$ **22.** $P_1(2, 1), P_2(3, 4)$ **23.** $P_1(-1, 3), P_2(2, 4)$ **24.** $P_1(-2, 1), P_2(2, 2)$

25. $P_1(2, 4), P_2(4, -1)$ **26.** $P_1(1, 3), P_2(5, -3)$ **27.** $P_1(3, -4), P_2(3, 5)$ **28.** $P_1(-1, 2), P_2(-1, 3)$

29. $P_1(4, -2), P_2(3, -2)$ **30.** $P_1(5, 1), P_2(-2, 1)$ **31.** $P_1(0, -1), P_2(3, -2)$ **32.** $P_1(3, 0), P_2(2, -1)$

For Exercises 33 to 40, determine whether the line through P_1 and P_2 is parallel, perpendicular, or neither parallel nor perpendicular to the line through Q_1 and Q_2.

33. $P_1(-3, 4), P_2(2, -5); Q_1(3, 6), Q_2(-2, -3)$ **34.** $P_1(4, -5), P_2(6, -9); Q_1(5, -4), Q_2(1, 4)$

35. $P_1(0, 1), P_2(2, 4); Q_1(-4, -7), Q_2(2, 5)$ **36.** $P_1(5, 1), P_2(3, -2); Q_1(0, -2), Q_2(3, -4)$

37. $P_1(-2, 4), P_2(2, 4); Q_1(-3, 6), Q_2(4, 6)$ **38.** $P_1(1, -1), P_2(3, -2); Q_1(-4, 1), Q_2(2, -5)$

39. $P_1(7, -1), P_2(-4, 6); Q_1(3, 0), Q_2(-5, 3)$ **40.** $P_1(5, -2), P_2(-1, 3); Q_1(3, 4), Q_2(-2, -2)$

41. **Business** The graph at the right is based on data from *InfoSync World*. It shows the projected camera-phone sales worldwide through 2008. Find the slope of the line. Write a sentence that states the meaning of the slope in the context of this problem.

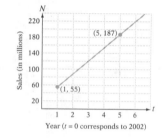

42. **Deep-Sea Diving** The pressure, in pounds per square inch, on a diver is shown in the graph at the right. Find the slope of the line. Write a sentence that explains the meaning of the slope.

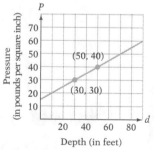

43. **Depreciation** The graph at the right, based on data from *Kelley Blue Book*, shows the decline in value of a 2002 Porsche Boxster as the number of miles the car is driven increases. Find the slope of the line. Write a sentence that states the meaning of the slope in the context of this problem.

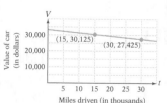

44. **Environmental Science**   The stratosphere extends from approximately 11 km to 50 km above Earth. The graph at the right shows how the temperature, in degrees Celsius, changes in the stratosphere. Explain the meaning of the horizontal line segment from A to B. Find the slope of the line from B to C and explain its meaning.

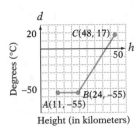

Objective C   **To graph a line using the slope and the *y*-intercept**

For Exercises 45 to 50, find the slope and *y*-intercept for the graph of the equation.

45. $2x - 3y = 6$

46. $4x + 3y = 12$

47. $2x + 5y = 10$

48. $2x + y = 0$

49. $x - 4y = 0$

50. $2x + 3y = 8$

For Exercises 51 to 65, graph by using the slope and *y*-intercept.

51. $y = 3x + 1$

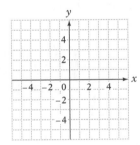

52. $y = -2x - 1$

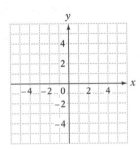

53. $y = \dfrac{2}{5}x - 2$

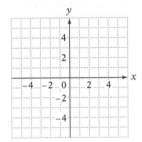

54. $y = \dfrac{3}{4}x + 1$

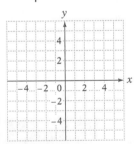

55. $2x + y = 3$

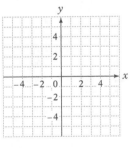

56. $3x - y = 1$

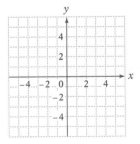

57. $x - 2y = 4$

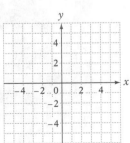

58. $x + 3y = 6$

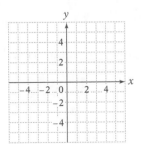

59. $y = \dfrac{2}{3}x$

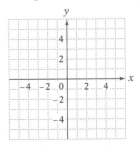

60. $y = \dfrac{1}{2}x$

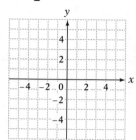

61. $y = -x + 1$

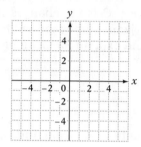

62. $y = -x - 3$

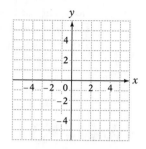

63. $3x - 4y = 12$

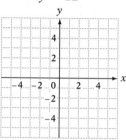

64. $5x - 2y = 10$

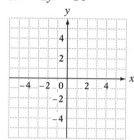

65. $y = -4x + 2$

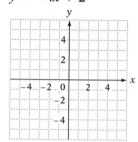

APPLYING THE CONCEPTS

66. Do all straight lines have a *y*-intercept? If not, give an example of one that does not.

67. If two lines have the same slope and the same *y*-intercept, must the graphs of the lines be the same? If not, give an example.

68. **a.** Graph: $\dfrac{x}{3} + \dfrac{y}{4} = 1$ **b.** Graph: $\dfrac{x}{2} - \dfrac{y}{3} = 1$ **c.** Graph: $-\dfrac{x}{4} + \dfrac{y}{2} = 1$

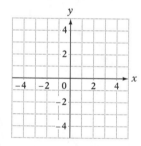
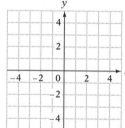
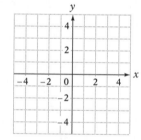

d. What observation can you make about the *x*- and *y*-intercepts of these graphs and the coefficients of *x* and *y*? Use this observation to draw the graph of $\dfrac{x}{4} - \dfrac{y}{3} = 1$.

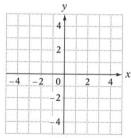

69. 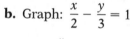 **Safety**   What does the highway sign at the right have to do with slope?

Focus on Problem Solving

Counterexamples Some of the exercises in this text ask you to determine whether a statement is true or false. For instance, the statement "Every real number has a reciprocal" is false because 0 is a real number and 0 does not have a reciprocal.

Finding an example, such as "0 has no reciprocal," to show that a statement is not always true is called finding a counterexample. A **counterexample** is an example that shows that a statement is not always true.

Here are some counterexamples to the statement "The square of a number is always larger than the number."

$$\left(\frac{1}{2}\right)^2 = \frac{1}{4} \quad \text{but} \quad \frac{1}{4} < \frac{1}{2} \qquad 1^2 = 1 \quad \text{but} \quad 1 = 1$$

For Exercises 1 to 9, answer true if the statement is always true. If there is an instance when the statement is false, give a counterexample.

1. The product of two integers is always a positive number.

2. The sum of two prime numbers is never a prime number.

3. For all real numbers, $|x + y| = |x| + |y|$.

4. If x and y are nonzero real numbers and $x > y$, then $x^2 > y^2$.

5. The quotient of any two nonzero real numbers is less than either one of the numbers.

6. The reciprocal of a positive number is always smaller than the number.

7. If $x < 0$, then $|x| = -x$.

8. For any two real numbers x and y, $x + y > x - y$.

9. The list of numbers 1, 11, 111, 1111, 11111, ... contains infinitely many composite numbers. (*Hint:* A number is divisible by 3 if the sum of the digits of the number is divisible by 3.)

Projects and Group Activities

Graphing Linear Equations with a Graphing Utility A computer or graphing calculator screen is divided into *pixels*. There are approximately 6000 to 790,000 pixels available on the screen (depending on the computer or calculator). The greater the number of pixels, the smoother a graph will appear. A portion of a screen is shown at the left. Each little rectangle represents one pixel.

The graphing utilities that are used by computers or calculators to graph an equation do basically what we have shown in the text: They choose values of x and, for each, calculate the corresponding value of y. The pixel corresponding to the ordered pair is then turned on. The graph is jagged because pixels are much larger than the dots we draw on paper.

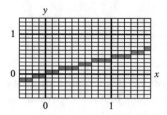

The graph of $y = 0.45x$ is shown at the left as the calculator drew it (jagged). The x- and y-axes have been chosen so that each pixel represents $\frac{1}{10}$ of a unit. Consider the region of the graph where $x = 1$, 1.1, and 1.2.

The corresponding values of y are 0.45, 0.495, and 0.54. Because the y-axis is in tenths, the numbers 0.45, 0.495, and 0.54 are rounded to the nearest tenth before plotting. Rounding 0.45, 0.495, and 0.54 to the nearest tenth results in 0.5 for each number. Thus the ordered pairs (1, 0.45), (1.1, 0.495), and (1.2, 0.54) are graphed as (1, 0.5), (1.1, 0.5), and (1.2, 0.5). These points appear as three illuminated horizontal pixels. However, if you use the TRACE feature of the calculator (see the Appendix), the actual y-coordinate for each value of x is displayed.

> **TAKE NOTE**
>
> Xmin and Xmax are the smallest and largest values of x that will be shown on the screen. Ymin and Ymax are the smallest and largest values of y that will be shown on the screen.

Here are the keystrokes for a TI-83 calculator to graph $y = \frac{2}{3}x + 1$. First the equation is entered. Then the domain (Xmin to Xmax) and the range (Ymin to Ymax) are entered. This is called the **viewing window.**

By changing the keystrokes 2 [X,T,θ,n] [÷] 3 [+] 1, you can graph different equations.

Integrating Technology

See the Keystroke Guide: [Y=] and WINDOW for assistance.

For Exercises 1 to 4, graph on a graphing calculator.

1. $y = 2x + 1$ **2.** $y = -\frac{1}{2}x - 2$ **3.** $3x + 2y = 6$ **4.** $4x + 3y = 75$

Graphs of Motion

A graph can be useful in analyzing the motion of a body. For example, consider an airplane in uniform motion traveling at 100 m/s. The table at the right shows the distance, in meters, traveled by the plane at the end of each of five one-second intervals.

Time (in seconds)	Distance (in meters)
0	0
1	100
2	200
3	300
4	400
5	500

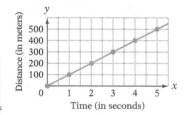

These data can be graphed on a rectangular coordinate system and a straight line drawn through the points plotted. The travel time is shown along the horizontal axis, and the distance traveled by the plane is shown along the vertical axis. (Note that the units along the two axes are not the same length.)

To write the equation for the line just graphed, use the coordinates of any two points on the line to find the slope. The y-intercept is (0, 0).

Let $(x_1, y_1) = (1, 100)$ and $(x_2, y_2) = (2, 200)$.

$$m = \frac{y_2 - y_1}{x_2 - x_1} = \frac{200 - 100}{2 - 1} = 100$$

$y = mx + b$
$y = 100x + 0$
$y = 100x$

Note that the slope of the line, 100, is equal to the speed, 100 m/s. *The slope of a distance-time graph represents the speed of the object.*

The distance-time graphs for two planes are shown at the left. One plane is traveling at 100 m/s, and the other is traveling at 200 m/s. The slope of the line representing the faster plane is greater than the slope of the line representing the slower plane.

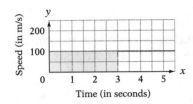

In the speed-time graph at the left, the time a plane has been flying at 100 m/s is shown along the horizontal axis, and its speed is shown along the vertical axis. Because the speed is constant, the graph is a horizontal line.

The area between the horizontal line graphed and the horizontal axis is equal to the distance traveled by the plane up to that time. For example, the area of the shaded region on the graph is

$$\text{Length} \cdot \text{width} = (3 \text{ s})(100 \text{ m/s}) = 300 \text{ m}$$

The distance traveled by the plane in 3 s is equal to 300 m.

1. A car in uniform motion is traveling at 20 m/s.
   a. Prepare a distance-time graph for the car for 0 s to 5 s.
   b. Find the slope of the line.
   c. Find the equation of the line.
   d. Prepare a speed-time graph for the car for 0 s to 5 s.
   e. Find the distance traveled by the car after 3 s.

2. One car in uniform motion is traveling at 10 m/s. A second car in uniform motion is traveling at 15 m/s.
   a. Prepare one distance-time graph for both cars for 0 s to 5 s.
   b. Find the slope of each line.
   c. Find the equation of each line graphed.
   d. Assuming that the cars started at the same point at 0 s, find the distance between the cars at the end of 5 s.

Chapter Summary

Key Words

Examples

A *rectangular coordinate system* is formed by two number lines, one horizontal and one vertical, that intersect at the zero point of each line. The number lines that make up a rectangular coordinate system are called the *coordinate axes*, or simply *axes*. The *origin* is the point of intersection of the two coordinate axes. Generally, the horizontal axis is labeled the *x*-axis and the vertical axis is labeled the *y*-axis. The coordinate system divides the plane into four regions called *quadrants*. The *coordinates of a point* in the plane are given by an *ordered pair* (x, y). The first number in the ordered pair is called the *abscissa* or *x-coordinate*. The second number in the ordered pair is the *ordinate* or *y-coordinate*. The *graph of an ordered pair* (x, y) is the dot drawn at the coordinates of the point in the plane.

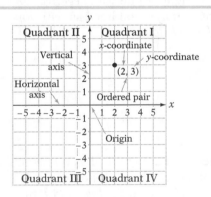

A *solution of an equation in two variables* is an ordered pair (x, y) that makes the equation a true statement.

The ordered pair $(-1, 1)$ is a solution of the equation $y = 2x + 3$ because when -1 is substituted for x and 1 is substituted for y, the result is a true equation.

A *relation* is any set of ordered pairs. The *domain* of a relation is the set of first coordinates of the ordered pairs. The *range* is the set of second coordinates of the ordered pairs.

For the relation $\{(-1, 2), (2, 4), (3, 5), (3, 7)\}$, the domain is $\{-1, 2, 3\}$; the range is $\{2, 4, 5, 7\}$.

A *function* is a relation in which no two ordered pairs have the same first coordinate.

The relation $\{(-2, -3), (0, 4), (1, 5)\}$ is a function. No two ordered pairs have the same first coordinate.

The *graph of an equation in two variables* is a graph of the ordered-pair solutions of the equation. An equation of the form $y = mx + b$ is a *linear equation in two variables*.

$y = 2x + 3$ is a linear equation in two variables. Its graph is shown at the right.

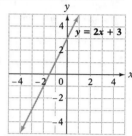

An equation written in the form $Ax + By = C$ is the *standard form of a linear equation in two variables*.

$2x + 7y = 10$ is an example of a linear equation in two variables written in standard form.

The point at which a graph crosses the x-axis is called the *x-intercept*. At the x-intercept, the y-coordinate is 0. The point at which a graph crosses the y-axis is called the *y-intercept*. At the y-intercept, the x-coordinate is 0.

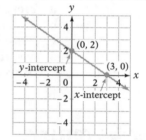

The *slope* of a line is a measure of the slant of the line. The symbol for slope is m. A line with *positive slope* slants upward to the right. A line with *negative slope* slants downward to the right. A horizontal line has *zero slope*. A vertical line has an *undefined slope*.

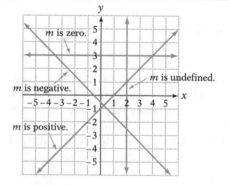

When data are graphed as points in a coordinate system, the graph is called a *scatter diagram*. A line drawn to approximate the data is called the *line of best fit*.

The graph shown at the right is the scatter diagram and line of best fit for the spring data on page 388.

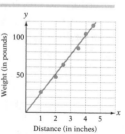

Essential Rules and Procedures

Examples

Functional Notation

The equation of a function is written in functional notation when y is replaced by the symbol $f(x)$, where $f(x)$ is read "f of x" or "the value of f at x." To evaluate a function at a given value of x, replace x by the given value and then simplify the resulting numerical expression to find the value of $f(x)$.

$y = x^2 + 2x - 1$ is written in functional notation as $f(x) = x^2 + 2x - 1$. To evaluate $f(x) = x^2 + 2x - 1$ at $x = -3$, find $f(-3)$.

$$f(-3) = (-3)^2 + 2(-3) - 1$$
$$= 9 - 6 - 1 = 2$$

Horizontal and Vertical Lines

The graph of $y = b$ is a horizontal line passing through $(0, b)$.
The graph of $x = a$ is a vertical line passing through $(a, 0)$.

The graph of $y = -2$ is a horizontal line passing through $(0, -2)$. The graph of $x = 3$ is a vertical line passing through $(3, 0)$.

To find the x-intercept, let $y = 0$ and solve for x.
To find the y-intercept, let $x = 0$ and solve for y.

To find the x-intercept of $4x - 5y = 20$, let $y = 0$ and solve for x. To find the y-intercept, let $x = 0$ and solve for y.

$$4x - 5y = 20 \qquad\qquad 4x - 5y = 20$$
$$4x - 5(0) = 20 \qquad\quad 4(0) - 5y = 20$$
$$4x = 20 \qquad\qquad\quad -5y = 20$$
$$x = 5 \qquad\qquad\qquad y = -4$$

The x-intercept is $(5, 0)$. The y-intercept is $(0, -4)$.

Slope Formula

If $P_1(x_1, y_1)$ and $P_2(x_2, y_2)$ are two points on a line and $x_1 \neq x_2$, then

$$m = \frac{y_2 - y_1}{x_2 - x_1}$$

To find the slope of the line between the points $(1, -2)$ and $(-3, -1)$, let $P_1 = (1, -2)$ and $P_2 = (-3, -1)$. Then

$$m = \frac{y_2 - y_1}{x_2 - x_1} = \frac{-1 - (-2)}{-3 - 1} = \frac{1}{-4} = -\frac{1}{4}.$$

Parallel Lines

Two nonvertical lines in the plane are parallel if and only if they have the same slope. Vertical lines in the plane are parallel.

The slope of the line through $P_1(3, -6)$ and $P_2(5, -10)$ is $m_1 = \frac{-10 - (-6)}{5 - 3} = -2.$

The slope of the line through $Q_1(4, -5)$ and $Q_2(0, 3)$ is $m_2 = \frac{3 - (-5)}{0 - 4} = -2.$

Because $m_1 = m_2$, the lines are parallel.

Perpendicular Lines

Two nonvertical lines in the plane are perpendicular if and only if the product of their slopes is -1. A vertical and horizontal line are perpendicular.

The slope of the line through $P_1(5, -3)$ and $P_2(2, -1)$ is $m_1 = \frac{-1 - (-3)}{2 - 5} = -\frac{2}{3}.$

The slope of the line through $Q_1(1, -4)$ and $Q_2(3, -1)$ is $m_2 = \frac{-1 - (-4)}{3 - 1} = \frac{3}{2}.$

Because $m_1 m_2 = \left(-\frac{2}{3}\right)\left(\frac{3}{2}\right) = -1$, the lines are perpendicular.

Slope-Intercept Form of a Linear Equation

An equation of the form $y = mx + b$ is called the slope-intercept form of a straight line. The slope of the line is m, the coefficient of x. The y-intercept is $(0, b)$, where b is the constant term of the equation.

For the line with equation $y = -3x + 2$, the slope is -3 and the y-intercept is $(0, 2)$.

Point-Slope Formula

If (x_1, y_1) is a point on a line with slope m, then

$$y - y_1 = m(x - x_1)$$

The equation of the line that passes through the point $(5, -3)$ and has slope -2 is:

$$y - y_1 = m(x - x_1)$$
$$y - (-3) = -2(x - 5)$$
$$y + 3 = -2x + 10$$
$$y = -2x + 7$$

Chapter Review Exercises

1. **a.** Graph the ordered pairs $(-2, 4)$ and $(3, -2)$.
 b. Name the abscissa of point A.
 c. Name the ordinate of point B.

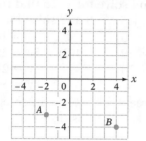

2. Graph the ordered-pair solutions of $y = -\frac{1}{2}x - 2$ when $x \in \{-4, -2, 0, 2\}$.

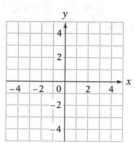

3. Determine the equation of the line that passes through the points $(-1, 3)$ and $(2, -5)$.

4. Determine the equation of the line that passes through the point $(6, 1)$ and has slope $-\frac{5}{2}$.

5. Graph $y = \frac{1}{4}x + 3$.

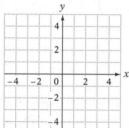

6. Graph $5x + 3y = 15$.

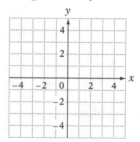

7. Is the line that passes through $(7, -5)$ and $(6, -1)$ parallel, perpendicular, or neither parallel nor perpendicular to the line that passes through $(4, 5)$ and $(2, -3)$?

8. Given $f(x) = x^2 - 2$, find $f(-1)$.

9. Determine the equation of the line that passes through the points $(-2, 5)$ and $(4, 1)$.

10. Does $y = -x + 3$, where $x \in \{-2, 0, 3, 5\}$, define y as a function of x?

11. Find the slope of the line containing the points $(9, 8)$ and $(-2, 1)$.

12. Find the x- and y-intercepts of $3x - 2y = 24$.

13. Find the slope of the line containing the points $(-2, -3)$ and $(4, -3)$.

14. Graph the line that has slope $\frac{1}{2}$ and y-intercept $(0, -1)$.

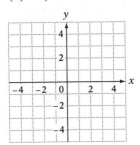

15. Graph $x = -3$.

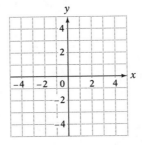

16. Graph the line that has slope $-\frac{2}{3}$ and y-intercept $(0, 2)$.

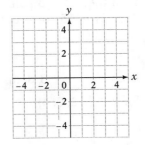

17. Graph $y = -2x - 1$.

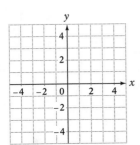

18. Graph the line that has slope 2 and y-intercept $(0, -4)$.

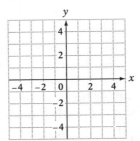

19. Graph $3x - 2y = -6$.

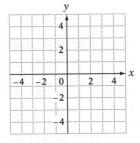

20. **Health** The height and weight of 8 seventh-grade students are shown in the following table. Write a relation where the first coordinate is height, in inches, and the second coordinate is weight, in pounds. Is the relation a function?

Height (in inches)	55	57	53	57	60	61	58	54
Weight (in pounds)	95	101	94	98	100	105	97	95

21. **Business** An online research service charges a monthly access fee of $75 plus $.45 per minute to use the service. An equation that represents the monthly cost to use this service is $C = 0.45x + 75$, where C is the monthly cost and x is the number of minutes of access used. Graph this equation for $0 \le x \le 100$. The point $(50, 97.5)$ is on the graph. Write a sentence that describes the meaning of this ordered pair.

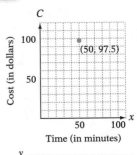

22. **Telecommunications** The data in the table below are estimates of the projected annual increase in average telephone bills for a family. The line of best fit is $y = 34x + 657$, where x is the year (with $x = 0$ corresponding to 1999) and y is the annual cost, in dollars, of telephone bills.

Year, x	0	1	2	3	4	5	6
Telephone bills, y (in dollars)	658	690	708	772	809	830	849

Graph the data and the line of best fit in the coordinate system at the right. Write a sentence that describes the meaning of the slope of the line of best fit.

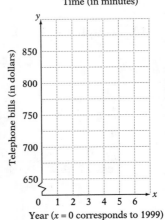

Chapter Test

1. Find the ordered-pair solution of $2x - 3y = 15$ corresponding to $x = 3$.

2. Graph the ordered-pair solutions of $y = -\dfrac{3}{2}x + 1$ for $x \in \{-2, 0, 4\}$.

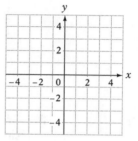

3. Does $y = \dfrac{1}{2}x - 3$ define y as a function of x for $x \in \{-2, 0, 4\}$?

4. Given $f(t) = t^2 + t$, find $f(2)$.

5. Given $f(x) = x^2 - 2x$, find $f(-1)$.

6. **Emergency Response** The distance a house is from a fire station and the amount of damage that the house sustained in a fire are given in the following table. Write a relation wherein the first coordinate of the ordered pair is the distance, in miles, from the fire station and the second coordinate is the amount of damage in thousands of dollars. Is the relation a function?

Distance (in miles)	3.5	4.0	5.2	5.0	4.0	6.3	5.4
Damage (in thousands of dollars)	25	30	45	38	42	12	34

7. Graph $y = 3x + 1$.

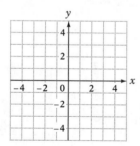

8. Graph $y = -\dfrac{3}{4}x + 3$.

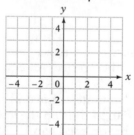

9. Graph $3x - 2y = 6$.

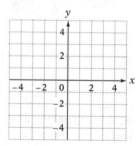

10. Graph $x + 3 = 0$.

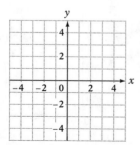

11. Graph the line that has slope $-\dfrac{2}{3}$ and y-intercept $(0, 4)$.

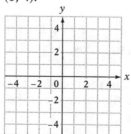

12. Graph the line that has slope 2 and y-intercept -2.

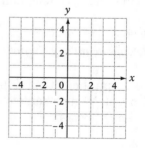

13. 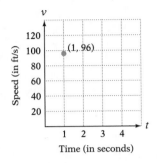 **Sports** The equation for the speed of a ball that is thrown straight up with an initial speed of 128 ft/s is $v = 128 - 32t$, where v is the speed of the ball after t seconds. Graph this equation for $0 \le t \le 4$. The point whose coordinates are (1, 96) is on the graph. Write a sentence that describes this ordered pair.

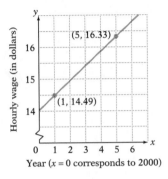

14. 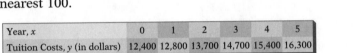 **Wages** The graph at the right shows the projected increase in the average hourly wage of a U.S. worker for the years 2000 through 2006 (with $x = 0$ corresponding to 2000). Find the slope of the line. Write a sentence that states the meaning of the slope.

15. 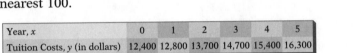 **Tuition** The data in the table below are the average annual tuition costs for 4-year private colleges in the United States. The line of best fit is $y = 809x + 12,195$, where x is the year (with $x = 0$ corresponding to 1995) and y is the annual tuition cost in dollars rounded to the nearest 100.

Year, x	0	1	2	3	4	5
Tuition Costs, y (in dollars)	12,400	12,800	13,700	14,700	15,400	16,300

Graph the data and the line of best fit in the coordinate system at the right. Write a sentence that describes the meaning of the slope of the line of best fit.

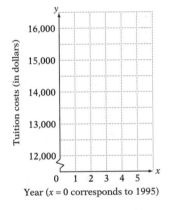

16. Find the x- and y-intercepts for $6x - 4y = 12$.

17. Find the x- and y-intercepts for $y = \frac{1}{2}x + 1$.

18. Find the slope of the line containing the points (2, −3) and (4, 1).

19. Is the line that passes through (2, 5) and (−1, 1) parallel, perpendicular, or neither parallel nor perpendicular to the line that passes through (−2, 3) and (4, 11)?

20. Find the slope of the line containing the points (−5, 2) and (−5, 7).

21. Find the slope of the line whose equation is $2x + 3y = 6$.

22. Find the equation of the line that contains the point (0, −1) and has slope 3.

23. Find the equation of the line that contains the point (−3, 1) and has slope $\frac{2}{3}$.

24. Find the equation of the line that passes through the points (5, −4) and (−3, 1).

25. Find the equation of the line that passes through the points (−2, 0) and (5, −2).

Quadratic Equations

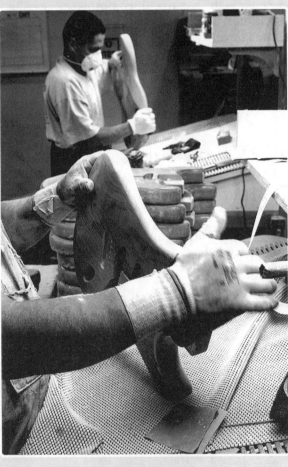

This photo shows employees at the Fender factory in Corona, California, in the process of making guitars. During this stage, the Fender Stratocaster bodies are hand-sanded. The objective of the Fender Musical Instruments Corporation, as with any business, is to earn a profit. Profit is the difference between a company's revenue (the total amount of money the company earns by selling its products or services) and its costs (the total amount of money the company spends in doing business).

OBJECTIVES

Section 12.1

A To graph a quadratic equation of the $y = ax^2 + bx + c$

12.1 Graphing Quadratic Equations in Two Variables

Objective A

Point of Interest

Mirrors in some telescopes are ground into the shape of a parabola. The mirror at the Palomar Mountain Observatory is 2 ft thick at the ends and weighs 14.75 tons. The mirror has been ground to a true paraboloid (the three-dimensional version of a parabola) to within 0.0000015 in. A possible equation of the mirror is $y = 2640x^2$.

T A K E   N O T E

One of the equations at the right was written as $y = 2x^2 + 3x - 2$ and the other using functional notation as $f(x) = -x^2 + 3x + 2$. Remember that y and $f(x)$ are different symbols for the same quantity.

Integrating Technology

One of the Projects and Group Activities at the end of this chapter shows how to graph a quadratic equation by using a graphing calculator. You may want to verify the graphs you draw in this section by drawing them on a graphing calculator.

To graph a quadratic equation of the form $y = ax^2 + bx + c$

An equation of the form $y = ax^2 + bx + c$, $a \neq 0$, is a **quadratic equation in two variables.** Examples of quadratic equations in two variables are shown at the right.

$$y = 3x^2 - x + 1$$
$$y = -x^2 - 3$$
$$y = 2x^2 - 5x$$

For these equations, y is a function of x, and we can write $f(x) = ax^2 + bx + c$. This equation represents a **quadratic function.**

HOW TO Evaluate $f(x) = 2x^2 - 3x + 4$ when $x = -2$.

$$f(x) = 2x^2 - 3x + 4$$
$$f(-2) = 2(-2)^2 - 3(-2) + 4 \qquad \bullet \text{ Replace } x \text{ by } -2.$$
$$= 2(4) + 6 + 4 = 18 \qquad \bullet \text{ Simplify.}$$

The value of the function when $x = -2$ is 18.

The graph of $y = ax^2 + bx + c$ or $f(x) = ax^2 + bx + c$ is a **parabola.** The graph is ∪-shaped and opens up when a is positive, and down when a is negative. The graphs of two parabolas are shown below.

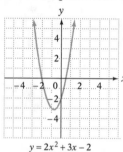

$y = 2x^2 + 3x - 2$
$a = 2$, a positive number
Parabola opens up.

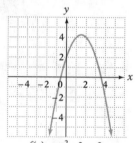

$f(x) = -x^2 + 3x + 2$
$a = -1$, a negative number
Parabola opens down.

HOW TO Graph $y = x^2 - 2x - 3$.

x	y
-2	5
-1	0
0	-3
1	-4
2	-3
3	0
4	5

• Find several solutions of the equation. Because the graph is not a straight line, several solutions must be found in order to determine the ∪-shape. Record the ordered pairs in a table.

• Graph the ordered-pair solutions on a rectangular coordinate system. Draw a parabola through the points.

For the graph of $y = x^2 - 2x - 3$, shown here again below, note that the graph crosses the x-axis at $(-1, 0)$ and $(3, 0)$. This is also confirmed from the table for the graph (see the preceding page). From the table, note that $y = 0$ when $x = -1$ and when $x = 3$. The x-intercepts of the graph are $(-1, 0)$ and $(3, 0)$.

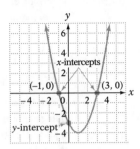

The y-intercept is the point at which the graph crosses the y-axis. At this point, $x = 0$. From the graph, we can see that the y-intercept is $(0, -3)$.

We can find the x-intercepts algebraically by letting $y = 0$ and solving for x.

$$y = x^2 - 2x - 3$$
$$0 = x^2 - 2x - 3$$ • Replace y by 0 and solve for x.
$$0 = (x + 1)(x - 3)$$ • This equation can be solved by factoring. However, it
$$x + 1 = 0 \qquad x - 3 = 0$$ will be necessary to use the quadratic formula to
$$\qquad x = -1 \qquad\quad x = 3$$ solve some quadratic equations.

The x-intercepts are $(-1, 0)$ and $(3, 0)$.

Integrating Technology

The first of the Projects and Group Activities at the end of this chapter shows how to use a graphing calculator to draw the graph of a parabola and how to find the x-intercepts.

We can find the y-intercept algebraically by letting $x = 0$ and solving for y.

$$y = x^2 - 2x - 3$$
$$y = 0^2 - 2(0) - 3$$ • Replace x by 0 and simplify.
$$\ = -3$$

The y-intercept is $(0, -3)$.

Graph of a Quadratic Equation in Two Variables

To graph a quadratic equation in two variables, find several solutions of the equation. Graph the ordered-pair solutions on a rectangular coordinate system. Draw a parabola through the points.

To find the x-intercepts of the graph of a quadratic equation in two variables, let $y = 0$ and solve for x.

To find the y-intercept, let $x = 0$ and solve for y.

Example 1 Graph $y = x^2 - 2x$.

Solution

x	y
-1	3
0	0
1	-1
2	0
3	3

- **Find several solutions of the equation.**

- **Graph the ordered-pair solutions. Draw a parabola through the points.**

You Try It 1 Graph $y = x^2 + 2$.

Your solution

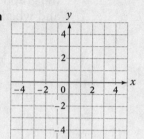

Example 2 Find the x- and y-intercepts of the graph of $y = x^2 - 2x - 5$.

Solution

To find the x-intercepts, let $y = 0$ and solve for x. This gives the equation $0 = x^2 - 2x - 5$, which is not factorable over the integers. Use the quadratic formula.

$$x = \frac{-b \pm \sqrt{b^2 - 4ac}}{2a}$$

$$= \frac{-(-2) \pm \sqrt{(-2)^2 - 4(1)(-5)}}{2(1)} \quad \bullet\ a = 1, b = -2, c = -5$$

$$= \frac{2 \pm \sqrt{24}}{2}$$

$$= \frac{2 \pm 2\sqrt{6}}{2}$$

$$= 1 \pm \sqrt{6}$$

The x-intercepts are $(1 - \sqrt{6}, 0)$ and $(1 + \sqrt{6}, 0)$.

To find the y-intercept, let $x = 0$ and solve for y.

$$y = x^2 - 2x - 5$$
$$= 0^2 - 2(0) - 5 \quad \bullet\ \textbf{Replace } x \textbf{ by 0.}$$
$$= -5$$

The y-intercept is $(0, -5)$.

You Try It 2 Find the x- and y-intercepts of the graph of $f(x) = x^2 - 6x + 9$.

Your solution

12.1 Exercises

Objective A **To graph a quadratic equation of the form $y = ax^2 + bx + c$**

For Exercises 1 to 4, determine whether the graph of the equation opens up or down.

1. $y = -\dfrac{1}{3}x^2$ **2.** $y = x^2 - 2x - 3$ **3.** $y = 2x^2 - 4$ **4.** $f(x) = 3 - 2x - x^2$

For Exercises 5 to 10, evaluate the function for the given value of x.

5. $f(x) = x^2 - 2x + 1; x = 3$ **6.** $f(x) = 2x^2 + x - 1; x = -2$

7. $f(x) = 4 - x^2; x = -3$ **8.** $f(x) = x^2 + 6x + 9; x = -3$

9. $f(x) = -x^2 + 5x - 6; x = -4$ **10.** $f(x) = -2x^2 + 2x - 1; x = -3$

For Exercises 11 to 25, graph.

11. $y = x^2$

12. $y = -x^2$

13. $y = -x^2 + 1$

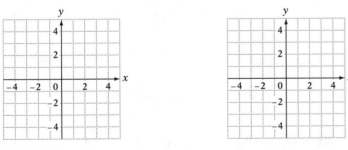

14. $y = x^2 - 1$

15. $y = 2x^2$

16. $y = \dfrac{1}{2}x^2$

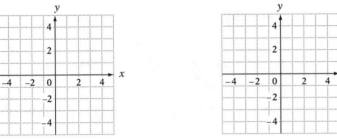
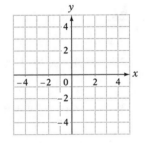

17. $y = -\dfrac{1}{2}x^2 + 1$

18. $y = 2x^2 - 1$

19. $y = x^2 - 4x$

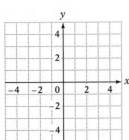
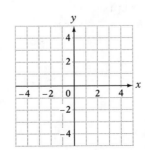
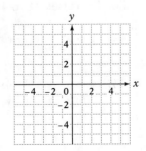

20. $y = x^2 + 4x$

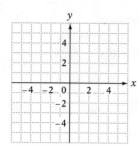

21. $y = x^2 - 2x + 3$

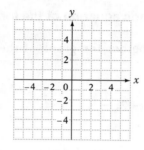

22. $y = x^2 - 4x + 2$

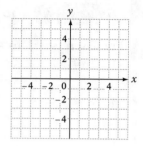

23. $y = -x^2 + 2x + 3$

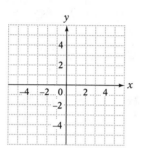

24. $y = -x^2 - 2x + 3$

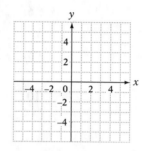

25. $y = -x^2 + 4x - 4$

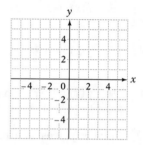

For Exercises 26 to 37, determine the *x*- and *y*-intercepts.

26. $y = x^2 - 5x + 6$

27. $y = x^2 + 5x - 6$

28. $f(x) = 9 - x^2$

29. $f(x) = x^2 + 12x + 36$

30. $y = x^2 + 2x - 6$

31. $f(x) = x^2 + 4x - 2$

32. $y = x^2 + 2x + 3$

33. $y = x^2 - x + 1$

34. $f(x) = 2x^2 - x - 3$

35. $f(x) = 2x^2 - 13x + 15$

36. $y = 4 - x - x^2$

37. $y = 2 - 3x - 3x^2$

APPLYING THE CONCEPTS

For Exercises 38 to 41, show that the equation is a quadratic equation in two variables by writing it in the form $y = ax^2 + bx + c$.

38. $y + 1 = (x - 4)^2$

39. $y - 2 = 3(x + 1)^2$

40. $y - 4 = 2(x - 3)^2$

41. $y + 3 = 3(x - 1)^2$

For Exercises 42 to 45, find the *x*-intercepts.

42. $y = x^3 - x^2 - 6x$

43. $y = x^3 - 4x^2 - 5x$

44. $y = x^3 + x^2 - 4x - 4$
Hint: Factor by grouping.

45. $y = x^3 + 3x^2 - x - 3$
Hint: Factor by grouping.

Focus on Problem Solving

Algebraic Manipulation and Graphing Techniques

Problem solving is often easier when we have both algebraic manipulation and graphing techniques at our disposal. Solving quadratic equations and graphing quadratic equations in two variables are used here to solve problems involving profit.

A company's revenue, R, is the total amount of money the company earned by selling its products. The cost, C, is the total amount of money the company spent to manufacture and sell its products. A company's profit, P, is the difference between the revenue and the cost: $P = R - C$. A company's revenue and cost may be represented by equations.

A company manufactures and sells woodstoves. The total monthly cost, in dollars, to produce n woodstoves is $C = 30n + 2000$. Write a variable expression for the company's monthly profit if the revenue, in dollars, obtained from selling all n woodstoves is $R = 150n - 0.4n^2$.

$$P = R - C$$
$$P = 150n - 0.4n^2 - (30n + 2000)$$
$$P = -0.4n^2 + 120n - 2000$$

• Replace R by $150n - 0.4n^2$ and C by $30n + 2000$. Then simplify.

How many woodstoves must the company manufacture and sell in order to make a profit of $6000 a month?

$$P = -0.4n^2 + 120n - 2000$$
$$6000 = -0.4n^2 + 120n - 2000$$
$$0 = -0.4n^2 + 120n - 8000$$

$$0 = n^2 - 300n + 20{,}000$$

$$0 = (n - 100)(n - 200)$$

$$n - 100 = 0 \qquad n - 200 = 0$$
$$n = 100 \qquad n = 200$$

• Substitute 6000 for P.
• Write the equation in standard form.
• Divide each side of the equation by -0.4.
• Factor.
• Solve for n.

The company will make a monthly profit of $6000 if either 100 or 200 woodstoves are manufactured and sold.

The graph of $P = -0.4n^2 + 120n - 2000$ is shown at the right. Note that when $P = 6000$, the values of n are 100 and 200.

Also note that the coordinates of the highest point on the graph are (150, 7000). This means that the company makes a *maximum* profit of $7000 per month when 150 woodstoves are manufactured and sold.

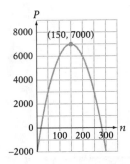

1. The total cost, in dollars, for a company to produce and sell n guitars per month is $C = 240n + 1200$. The company's revenue, in dollars, from selling all n guitars is $R = 400n - 2n^2$.

   a. How many guitars must the company produce and sell each month in order to make a monthly profit of $1200?

   b. Graph the profit equation. What is the maximum monthly profit that the company can make?

Projects and Group Activities

Graphical Solutions of Quadratic Equations

A real number x is called a **zero of a function** if the function evaluated at x is 0. That is, if $f(x) = 0$, then x is called a zero of the function. For instance, evaluating $f(x) = x^2 + x - 6$ when $x = -3$, we have

$$f(x) = x^2 + x - 6$$
$$f(-3) = (-3)^2 + (-3) - 6 \qquad \bullet \text{ Replace } x \text{ by } -3.$$
$$f(-3) = 9 - 3 - 6 = 0$$

For this function $f(-3) = 0$, so -3 is a zero of the function.

Verify that 2 is a zero of $f(x) = x^2 + x - 6$ by showing that $f(2) = 0$.

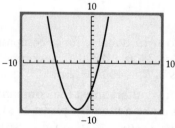

The graph of $f(x) = x^2 + x - 6$ is shown at the left. Note that the graph crosses the x-axis at -3 and 2, the two zeros of the function. The points $(-3, 0)$ and $(2, 0)$ are x-intercepts of the graph.

Or consider the equation $0 = x^2 + x - 6$, which is $f(x) = x^2 + x - 6$ with $f(x)$ replaced by 0. Solving $0 = x^2 + x - 6$, we have

$$0 = x^2 + x - 6$$
$$0 = (x + 3)(x - 2) \qquad \bullet \text{ Solve by factoring and using the}$$
$$x + 3 = 0 \qquad x - 2 = 0 \qquad \quad \text{Principle of Zero Products.}$$
$$x = -3 \qquad \qquad x = 2$$

Observe that the solutions of the equation are the zeros of the function. This important connection among the real zeros of a function, the x-intercepts of its graph, and the solutions of the equation is the basis for using a graphing calculator to solve an equation.

The following method of solving a quadratic equation by using a graphing calculator is based on a TI-83 or TI-83 Plus calculator. Other calculators will require a slightly different approach.

HOW TO Approximate the solutions of $x^2 + 4x = 6$ by using a graphing calculator.

Write the equation in standard form. $\qquad\qquad\qquad x^2 + 4x = 6$

1. Press ⬛Y= ⬛ and enter $x^2 + 4x - 6$ for Y1. $\qquad x^2 + 4x - 6 = 0$

2. Press ⬛GRAPH⬛. If the graph does not appear on the screen, press ⬛ZOOM⬛ 6.

3. Press ⬛2nd⬛ CALC 2. Note that the selection for 2 says **zero**. This will begin the calculation of the zeros of the function, which are the solutions of the equation.

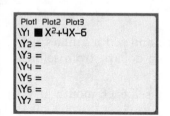

Step 1

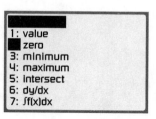

Step 2

Step 3

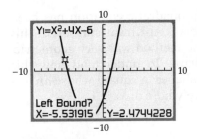

Step 4

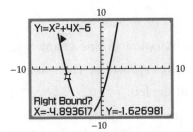

Step 5

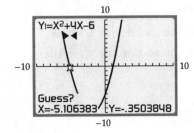

Step 6

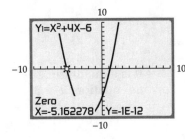

Step 7

4. At the bottom of the screen you will see **LeftBound?** This is asking you to move the blinking cursor so that it is to the *left* of the first *x*-intercept. Use the left arrow key to move the cursor to the left of the first *x*-intercept. The values of *x* and *y* that appear on your calculator may be different from the ones shown here. Just be sure that you are to the left of the *x*-intercept. When you are done, press [ENTER].

5. At the bottom of the screen you will see **RightBound?** This is asking you to move the blinking cursor so that it is to the *right* of the *x*-intercept. Use the right arrow key to move the cursor to the right of the *x*-intercept. The values of *x* and *y* that appear on your calculator may be different from the ones shown here. Just be sure that you are to the right of the *x*-intercept. When you are done, press [ENTER].

6. At the bottom of the screen you will see **Guess?** Press [ENTER].

7. The zero of the function is approximately -5.162278. Thus one solution of $x^2 + 4x = 6$ is -5.162278. Also note that the value of *y* is given as Y1 = ‾1E‾12. This is the way the calculator writes a number in scientific notation. We would normally write Y1 $= -1 \times 10^{-12}$. This number is very close to zero.

To find the other solution, we repeat Steps 3 through 7. The screens are shown below.

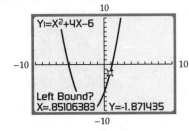

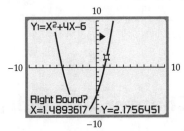

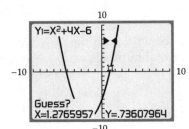

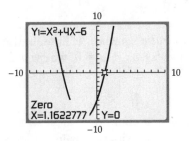

A second zero of the function is approximately 1.1622777. Thus the two solutions of $x^2 + 4x = 6$ are approximately -5.162278 and 1.1622777.

Use a graphing calculator to approximate the solutions of the following equations.

1. $x^2 + 3x - 4 = 0$ **2.** $x^2 - 4x - 5 = 0$

3. $x^2 + 3.4x = 4.15$ **4.** $2x^2 - \dfrac{5}{9}x = \dfrac{3}{8}$

5. $\pi x^2 - \sqrt{17}x - 2 = 0$ **6.** $\sqrt{2}x^2 + x - \sqrt{7} = 0$

Chapter Summary

Geometric Construction of Completing the Square

Completing the square as a method for solving a quadratic equation has been known for centuries. The Persian mathematician Al-Khwarismi used this method in a textbook written around 825 A.D. The method was very geometric. That is, Al-Khwarismi literally completed a square. To understand how this method works, consider the following geometric shapes: a square whose area is x^2, a rectangle whose area is x, and another square whose area is 1.

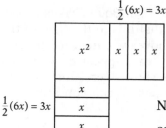

Now consider the expression $x^2 + 6x$. From our discussion in this chapter, to complete the square, we added $\left(\frac{1}{2} \cdot 6\right)^2 = 3^2 = 9$ to the expression. The geometric construction that Al-Khwarismi used is shown at the left.

Note that it is necessary to add 9 squares to the figure to "complete the square." One of the difficulties of using a geometric method such as this is that it cannot easily be extended to $x^2 - 6x$. There is no way to draw an area of $-6x$! That really did not bother Al-Khwarismi much. Negative numbers were not a significant part of mathematics until well into the 13th century.

1. Show how Al-Khwarismi would have completed the square for $x^2 + 4x$.
2. Show how Al-Khwarismi would have completed the square for $x^2 + 10x$.

9 squares were added

Chapter Summary

Key Words

Key Words	Examples
A *quadratic equation* is an equation that can be written in the form $ax^2 + bx + c = 0$, where a, b, and c are real numbers and $a \neq 0$.	$3x^2 - 5x - 3 = 0$ is a quadratic equation. For this equation, $a = 3$, $b = -5$, $c = -3$.
A quadratic equation is in *standard form* when the polynomial is in descending order and equal to zero.	$2x - 4 + 5x^2 = 0$ is not in standard form. The same equation in standard form is $5x^2 + 2x - 4 = 0$.
Adding to a binomial the constant term that makes it a perfect-square trinomial is called *completing the square*.	Adding to $x^2 - 8x$ the constant term 16 results in a perfect square trinomial: $x^2 - 8x + 16 = (x - 4)^2$.
An equation of the form $y = ax^2 + bx + c$, $a \neq 0$, is a *quadratic equation in two variables*.	$y = 2x^2 + 3x - 4$ is a quadratic equation in two variables.

The graph of an equation of the form $y = ax^2 + bx + c$, $a \neq 0$, is a *parabola*. The graph is U-shaped and opens up when $a > 0$ and opens down when $a < 0$.

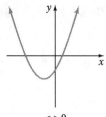

$a > 0$
Parabola opens up

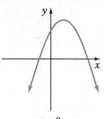

$a < 0$
Parabola opens down

Essential Rules and Procedures

Examples

Solving a Quadratic Equation by Factoring

Write the equation in standard form, factor the polynomial, apply the Principle of Zero Products, and solve for the variable.

$$x^2 - 3x = 10$$
$$x^2 - 3x - 10 = 0$$
$$(x + 2)(x - 5) = 0$$
$$x + 2 = 0 \qquad x - 5 = 0$$
$$x = -2 \qquad\qquad x = 5$$

Principle of Taking the Square Root of Each Side of an Equation

If $x^2 = a$, then $x = \pm\sqrt{a}$.

This principle is used to solve quadratic equations by taking square roots.

$$2x^2 - 36 = 0$$
$$2x^2 = 36$$
$$x^2 = 18$$
$$\sqrt{x^2} = \sqrt{18}$$
$$x = \pm\sqrt{18} = \pm 3\sqrt{2}$$

Solving a Quadratic Equation by Completing the Square

When the quadratic equation is in the form $x^2 + bx = c$, add to each side of the equation the term that completes the square on $x^2 + bx$. Factor the perfect-square trinomial, and write it as the square of a binomial. Take the square root of each side of the equation and solve for x.

$$x^2 + 6x = 5$$
$$x^2 + 6x + 9 = 5 + 9$$
$$(x + 3)^2 = 14$$
$$\sqrt{(x + 3)^2} = \sqrt{14}$$
$$x + 3 = \pm\sqrt{14}$$
$$x = -3 \pm \sqrt{14}$$

The Quadratic Formula

The solutions of $ax^2 + bx + c = 0$, $a \neq 0$, are

$$x = \frac{-b \pm \sqrt{b^2 - 4ac}}{2a}.$$

$$2x^2 + 3x - 6 = 0$$
$$x = \frac{-b \pm \sqrt{b^2 - 4ac}}{2a}$$
$$= \frac{-3 \pm \sqrt{(3)^2 - 4(2)(-6)}}{2(2)}$$
$$= \frac{-3 \pm \sqrt{9 + 48}}{4} = \frac{-3 \pm \sqrt{57}}{4}$$

Graph of a Quadratic Equation in Two Variables

To graph a quadratic equation in two variables, find several solutions of the equation. Graph the ordered-pair solutions on a rectangular coordinate system. Draw a parabola through the points.

To find the x-intercepts of the graph of a quadratic equation in two variables, let $y = 0$ and solve for x.

To find the y-intercept, let $x = 0$ and solve for y.

$$y = x^2 - x - 2$$

x	y
-2	4
-1	0
0	-2
1	-2
2	0
3	4

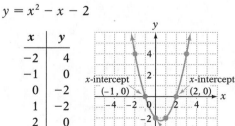

x-intercept
$(-1, 0)$

x-intercept
$(2, 0)$

y-intercept
$(0, -2)$

Chapter Review Exercises

1. Solve by factoring: $6x^2 + 13x - 28 = 0$

2. Solve by taking square roots: $49x^2 = 25$

3. Solve by completing the square: $x^2 + 2x - 24 = 0$

4. Solve by using the quadratic formula: $x^2 + 5x - 6 = 0$

5. Solve by completing the square: $2x^2 + 5x = 12$

6. Solve by factoring: $12x^2 + 10 = 29x$

7. Solve by taking square roots: $(x + 2)^2 - 24 = 0$

8. Solve by using the quadratic formula: $2x^2 + 3 = 5x$

9. Solve by factoring: $6x(x + 1) = x - 1$

10. Solve by taking square roots: $4y^2 + 9 = 0$

11. Solve by completing the square: $x^2 - 4x + 1 = 0$

12. Solve by using the quadratic formula: $x^2 - 3x - 5 = 0$

13. Solve by completing the square: $x^2 + 6x + 12 = 0$

14. Solve by factoring: $(x + 9)^2 = x + 11$

15. Solve by taking square roots: $\left(x - \dfrac{1}{2}\right)^2 = \dfrac{9}{4}$

16. Solve by completing the square: $4x^2 + 16x = 7$

17. Solve by using the quadratic formula:
$x^2 - 4x + 8 = 0$

18. Solve by using the quadratic formula:
$2x^2 + 5x + 2 = 0$

19. Graph $y = -3x^2$.

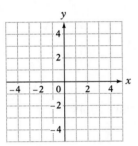

20. Graph $y = -\dfrac{1}{4}x^2$.

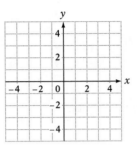

21. Graph $y = 2x^2 + 1$.

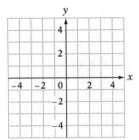

22. Graph $y = x^2 - 4x + 3$.

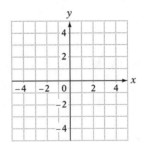

23. Graph $y = -x^2 + 4x - 5$.

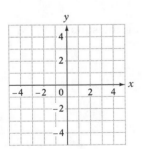

24. Find the x- and y-intercepts of the graph of
$y = x^2 - 2x - 15$.

25. **Travel** It took a hawk half an hour longer to fly 70 mi against the wind than to fly 40 mi with the wind. The rate of the wind was 5 mph. Find the rate of the hawk in calm air.

Chapter Test

1. Solve by factoring: $x^2 - 5x - 6 = 0$

2. Solve by factoring: $3x^2 + 7x = 20$

3. Solve by taking square roots:
$2(x - 5)^2 - 50 = 0$

4. Solve by taking square roots:
$3(x + 4)^2 - 60 = 0$

5. Solve by completing the square:
$x^2 + 4x - 16 = 0$

6. Solve by completing the square:
$x^2 + 3x = 8$

7. Solve by completing the square:
$2x^2 - 6x + 1 = 0$

8. Solve by completing the square:
$2x^2 + 8x = 3$

9. Solve by using the quadratic formula:
$x^2 + 4x + 2 = 0$

10. Solve by using the quadratic formula:
$x^2 - 3x = 6$

11. Solve by using the quadratic formula:
$2x^2 - 5x - 3 = 0$

12. Solve by using the quadratic formula:
$3x^2 - x = 1$

13. Graph $y = x^2 + 2x - 4$.

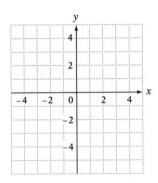

14. Find the x- and y-intercepts of the graph of $f(x) = x^2 + x - 12$.

15. Geometry The length of a rectangle is 2 ft less than twice the width. The area of the rectangle is 40 ft². Find the length and width of the rectangle.

16. Travel It took a motorboat 1 h longer to travel 60 mi against a current than it took the boat to travel 60 mi with the current. The rate of the current was 1 mph. Find the rate of the boat in calm water.

chapter 13

Exponential and Logarithmic Functions

OBJECTIVES

Section 13.1

A To evaluate an exponential function

B To graph an exponential function

This archaeopteryx skeleton is an exciting find for archaeologists. The archaeopteryx is thought to be from the Upper Jurassic period, and is considered by some scientists to be the most primitive of all birds. To determine exactly how old the bones are, archaeologists will use the carbon-dating method, which involves an exponential function. Instruments are used to detect the amount of carbon-14 left in an object. Since carbon-14 occurs naturally in living things and gradually decays after death, the amount of carbon-14 remaining can reveal the object's age.

Need help? For online student resources, such as section quizzes, visit this textbook's website at **math.college.hmco.com/students.**

13.1 Exponential Functions

Objective A   **To evaluate an exponential function**

The growth of a $500 savings account that earns 5% annual interest compounded daily is shown in the graph at the right. In approximately 14 years, the savings account contains approximately $1000, twice the initial amount. The growth of this savings account is an example of an exponential function.

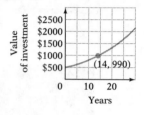

The pressure of the atmosphere at a certain height is shown in the graph at the right. This is another example of an exponential function. From the graph, we read that the air pressure is approximately 6.5 lb/in² at an altitude of 20,000 ft.

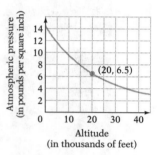

Definition of an Exponential Function

The **exponential function** with base b is defined by

$$f(x) = b^x$$

where $b > 0$, $b \neq 1$, and x is any real number.

In the definition of an exponential function, b, the base, is required to be positive. If the base were a negative number, the value of the function would be a complex number for some values of x. For instance, the value of $f(x) = (-4)^x$ when $x = \frac{1}{2}$ is $f\left(\frac{1}{2}\right) = (-4)^{1/2} = \sqrt{-4} = 2i$. To avoid complex number values of a function, the base of the exponential function is always a positive number.

Integrating Technology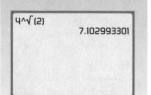

A graphing calculator can be used to evaluate an exponential expression for an irrational number.

```
4^√(2)
            7.102993301
```

HOW TO   Evaluate $f(x) = 2^x$ at $x = 3$ and $x = -2$.

$f(3) = 2^3 = 8$ • **Substitute 3 for x and simplify.**

$f(-2) = 2^{-2} = \dfrac{1}{2^2} = \dfrac{1}{4}$ • **Substitute −2 for x and simplify.**

To evaluate an exponential expression for an irrational number such as $\sqrt{2}$, we obtain an approximation to the value of the function by approximating the irrational number. For instance, the value of $f(x) = 4^x$ when $x = \sqrt{2}$ can be approximated by using an approximation of $\sqrt{2}$.

$$f(\sqrt{2}) = 4^{\sqrt{2}} \approx 4^{1.4142} \approx 7.1029$$

Because $f(x) = b^x$ ($b > 0$, $b \neq 1$) can be evaluated at both rational and irrational numbers, the domain of f is all real numbers. And because $b^x > 0$ for all values of x, the range of f is the positive real numbers.

A frequently used base in applications of exponential functions is an irrational number designated by e. **The number e is approximately 2.71828183.** It is an irrational number, so it has a nonterminating, nonrepeating decimal representation.

TAKE NOTE

The natural exponential function is an extremely important function. It is used extensively in applied problems in virtually all disciplines, from archaeology to zoology. Leonhard Euler (1707–1783) was the first to use the letter e as the base of the natural exponential function.

Natural Exponential Function

The function defined by $f(x) = e^x$ is called the **natural exponential function.**

The e^x key on a calculator can be used to evaluate the natural exponential function. The graph of $y = e^x$ is shown at the left.

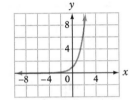

Example 1

Evaluate $f(x) = \left(\frac{1}{2}\right)^x$ at $x = 2$ and $x = -3$.

Solution

$f(x) = \left(\frac{1}{2}\right)^x$

$f(2) = \left(\frac{1}{2}\right)^2 = \frac{1}{4}$ • **$x = 2$**

$f(-3) = \left(\frac{1}{2}\right)^{-3} = 2^3 = 8$ • **$x = -3$**

You Try It 1

Evaluate $f(x) = \left(\frac{2}{3}\right)^x$ at $x = 3$ and $x = -2$.

Your solution

Example 2

Evaluate $f(x) = 2^{3x-1}$ at $x = 1$ and $x = -1$.

Solution

$f(x) = 2^{3x-1}$
$f(1) = 2^{3(1)-1} = 2^2 = 4$ • **$x = 1$**

$f(-1) = 2^{3(-1)-1} = 2^{-4} = \frac{1}{2^4} = \frac{1}{16}$ • **$x = -1$**

You Try It 2

Evaluate $f(x) = 2^{2x+1}$ at $x = 0$ and $x = -2$.

Your solution

Example 3

Evaluate $f(x) = e^{2x}$ at $x = 1$ and $x = -1$.
Round to the nearest ten-thousandth.

Solution

$f(x) = e^{2x}$
$f(1) = e^{2 \cdot 1} = e^2 \approx 7.3891$ • **$x = 1$**
$f(-1) = e^{2(-1)} = e^{-2} \approx 0.1353$ • **$x = -1$**

You Try It 3

Evaluate $f(x) = e^{2x-1}$ at $x = 2$ and $x = -2$.
Round to the nearest ten-thousandth.

Your solution

Objective B   **To graph an exponential function**

Integrating Technology
See the Keystroke Guide: *Graph* for instructions on using a graphing calculator to graph functions.

Some properties of an exponential function can be seen from its graph.

HOW TO   Graph $f(x) = 2^x$.

Think of this as the equation $y = 2^x$.

Choose values of x and find the corresponding values of y. The results can be recorded in a table.

Graph the ordered pairs on a rectangular coordinate system.

Connect the points with a smooth curve.

x	$f(x) = y$
-2	$2^{-2} = \frac{1}{4}$
-1	$2^{-1} = \frac{1}{2}$
0	$2^0 = 1$
1	$2^1 = 2$
2	$2^2 = 4$
3	$2^3 = 8$

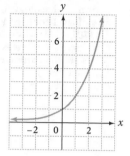

Note that any vertical line would intersect the graph at only one point. Therefore, by the vertical-line test, the graph of $f(x) = 2^x$ is the graph of a function. Also note that any horizontal line would intersect the graph at only one point. Therefore, the graph of $f(x) = 2^x$ is the graph of a one-to-one function.

HOW TO   Graph $f(x) = \left(\frac{1}{2}\right)^x$.

Think of this as the equation $y = \left(\frac{1}{2}\right)^x$.

Choose values of x and find the corresponding values of y.

Graph the ordered pairs on a rectangular coordinate system.

Connect the points with a smooth curve.

x	$f(x) = y$
-3	$\left(\frac{1}{2}\right)^{-3} = 8$
-2	$\left(\frac{1}{2}\right)^{-2} = 4$
-1	$\left(\frac{1}{2}\right)^{-1} = 2$
0	$\left(\frac{1}{2}\right)^{0} = 1$
1	$\left(\frac{1}{2}\right)^{1} = \frac{1}{2}$
2	$\left(\frac{1}{2}\right)^{2} = \frac{1}{4}$

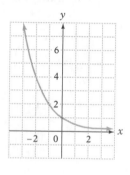

Applying the vertical-line and horizontal-line tests reveals that the graph of $f(x) = \left(\frac{1}{2}\right)^x$ is also the graph of a one-to-one function.

HOW TO   Graph $f(x) = 2^{-x}$.

Think of this as the equation $y = 2^{-x}$.

Choose values of x and find the corresponding values of y.

Graph the ordered pairs on a rectangular coordinate system.

Connect the points with a smooth curve.

x	y
-3	8
-2	4
-1	2
0	1
1	$\frac{1}{2}$
2	$\frac{1}{4}$

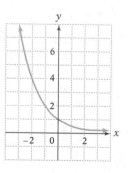

TAKE NOTE
Note that because $2^{-x} = (2^{-1})^x = \left(\frac{1}{2}\right)^x$, the graphs of $f(x) = 2^{-x}$ and $f(x) = \left(\frac{1}{2}\right)^x$ are the same.

Example 4 Graph: $f(x) = 3^{\frac{1}{2}x - 1}$

Solution

x	y
-2	$\frac{1}{9}$
0	$\frac{1}{3}$
2	1
4	3

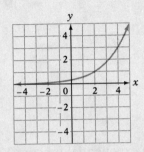

You Try It 4 Graph: $f(x) = 2^{-\frac{1}{2}x}$

Your solution

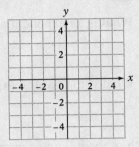

Example 5 Graph: $f(x) = 2^x - 1$

Solution

x	y
-2	$-\frac{3}{4}$
-1	$-\frac{1}{2}$
0	0
1	1
2	3
3	7

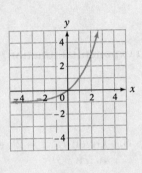

You Try It 5 Graph: $f(x) = 2^x + 1$

Your solution

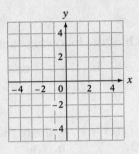

Example 6 Graph: $f(x) = \left(\frac{1}{3}\right)^x - 2$

Solution

x	y
-2	7
-1	1
0	-1
1	$-\frac{5}{3}$
2	$-\frac{17}{9}$

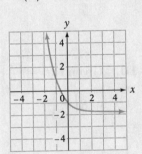

You Try It 6 Graph: $f(x) = 2^{-x} + 2$

Your solution

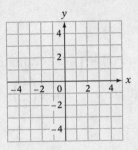

Example 7 Graph: $f(x) = 2^{-\frac{1}{2}x} - 1$

Solution

x	y
-6	7
-4	3
-2	1
0	0
2	$-\frac{1}{2}$
4	$-\frac{3}{4}$

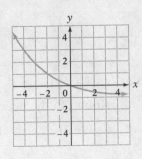

You Try It 7 Graph: $f(x) = \left(\frac{1}{2}\right)^{-\frac{1}{2}x} + 2$

Your solution

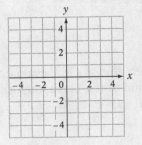

13.1 Exercises

Objective A   **To evaluate an exponential function**

1. What is an exponential function?

2. What is the natural exponential function?

3. Which of the following cannot be the base of an exponential function?

   a. 7   **b.** $\dfrac{1}{4}$ **c.** -5 **d.** 0.01

4. Which of the following cannot be the base of an exponential function?

   a. 0.9   **b.** 476   **c.** 8   **d.** $-\dfrac{1}{2}$

5. Given $f(x) = 3^x$, evaluate the following.
   a. $f(2)$ **b.** $f(0)$ **c.** $f(-2)$

6. Given $H(x) = 2^x$, evaluate the following.
   a. $H(-3)$ **b.** $H(0)$ **c.** $H(2)$

7. Given $g(x) = 2^{x+1}$, evaluate the following.
   a. $g(3)$ **b.** $g(1)$ **c.** $g(-3)$

8. Given $F(x) = 3^{x-2}$, evaluate the following.
   a. $F(-4)$ **b.** $F(-1)$ **c.** $F(0)$

9. Given $P(x) = \left(\dfrac{1}{2}\right)^{2x}$, evaluate the following.

   a. $P(0)$ **b.** $P\left(\dfrac{3}{2}\right)$ **c.** $P(-2)$

10. Given $R(t) = \left(\dfrac{1}{3}\right)^{3t}$, evaluate the following.

    a. $R\left(-\dfrac{1}{3}\right)$ **b.** $R(1)$ **c.** $R(-2)$

11. Given $G(x) = e^{x/2}$, evaluate the following. Round to the nearest ten-thousandth.

    a. $G(4)$ **b.** $G(-2)$ **c.** $G\left(\dfrac{1}{2}\right)$

12. Given $f(x) = e^{2x}$, evaluate the following. Round to the nearest ten-thousandth.

    a. $f(-2)$ **b.** $f\left(-\dfrac{2}{3}\right)$ **c.** $f(2)$

13. Given $H(r) = e^{-r+3}$, evaluate the following. Round to the nearest ten-thousandth.
    a. $H(-1)$ **b.** $H(3)$ **c.** $H(5)$

14. Given $P(t) = e^{-\frac{1}{2}t}$, evaluate the following. Round to the nearest ten-thousandth.

    a. $P(-3)$ **b.** $P(4)$ **c.** $P\left(\dfrac{1}{2}\right)$

15. Given $F(x) = 2^{x^2}$, evaluate the following.

    a. $F(2)$ **b.** $F(-2)$ **c.** $F\left(\dfrac{3}{4}\right)$

16. Given $Q(x) = 2^{-x^2}$, evaluate the following.

    a. $Q(3)$ **b.** $Q(-1)$ **c.** $Q(-2)$

17. Given $f(x) = e^{-x^2/2}$, evaluate the following. Round to the nearest ten-thousandth.

    a. $f(-2)$ **b.** $f(2)$ **c.** $f(-3)$

18. Given $f(x) = e^{-2x} + 1$, evaluate the following. Round to the nearest ten-thousandth.

    a. $f(-1)$ **b.** $f(3)$ **c.** $f(-2)$

Objective B   **To graph an exponential function**

Graph the functions in Exercises 19 to 30.

19. $f(x) = 3^x$

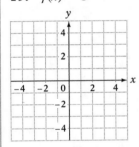

20. $f(x) = 3^{-x}$

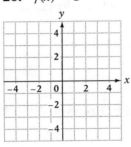

21. $f(x) = 2^{x+1}$

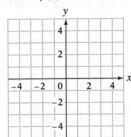

22. $f(x) = 2^{x-1}$

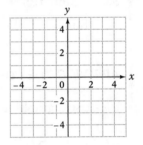

23. $f(x) = \left(\dfrac{1}{3}\right)^x$

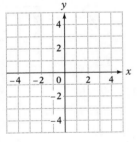

24. $f(x) = \left(\dfrac{2}{3}\right)^x$

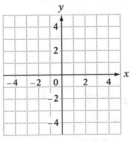

25. $f(x) = 2^{-x} + 1$

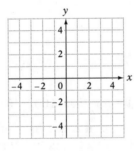

26. $f(x) = 2^x - 3$

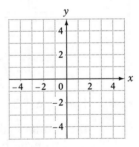

27. $f(x) = \left(\dfrac{1}{3}\right)^{-x}$

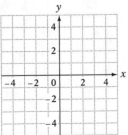

28. $f(x) = \left(\dfrac{3}{2}\right)^{-x}$

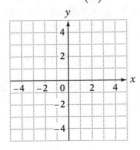

29. $f(x) = \left(\dfrac{1}{2}\right)^{-x} + 2$

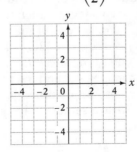

30. $f(x) = \left(\dfrac{1}{2}\right)^x - 1$

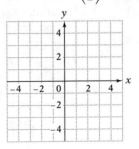

31. Which of the following functions have the same graph?

   a. $f(x) = 3^x$ **b.** $f(x) = \left(\dfrac{1}{3}\right)^x$ **c.** $f(x) = x^3$ **d.** $f(x) = 3^{-x}$

32. Which of the following functions have the same graph?

   a. $f(x) = x^4$ **b.** $f(x) = 4^{-x}$ **c.** $f(x) = 4^x$ **d.** $f(x) = \left(\dfrac{1}{4}\right)^x$

33. Graph $f(x) = 3^x$ and $f(x) = 3^{-x}$ and find the point of intersection of the two graphs.

34. Graph $f(x) = 2^{x+1}$ and $f(x) = 2^{-x+1}$ and find the point of intersection of the two graphs.

35. Graph $f(x) = \left(\dfrac{1}{3}\right)^x$. What are the x- and y-intercepts of the graph of the function?

36. Graph $f(x) = \left(\dfrac{1}{3}\right)^{-x}$. What are the x- and y-intercepts of the graph of the function?

APPLYING THE CONCEPTS

 Use a graphing calculator to graph the functions in Exercises 37 to 39.

37. $P(x) = \left(\sqrt{3}\right)^x$

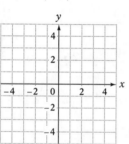

38. $Q(x) = \left(\sqrt{3}\right)^{-x}$

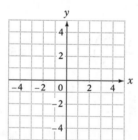

39. $f(x) = \pi^x$

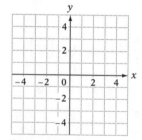

40. Evaluate $\left(1 + \dfrac{1}{n}\right)^n$ for $n = 100, 1000, 10{,}000,$ and $100{,}000$ and compare the results with the value of e, the base of the natural exponential function. On the basis of your evaluation, complete the following sentence: As n increases, $\left(1 + \dfrac{1}{n}\right)^n$ becomes closer to _____.

41. **Physics** If air resistance is ignored, the speed v, in feet per second, of an object t seconds after it has been dropped is given by $v = 32t$. However, if air resistance is considered, then the speed depends on the mass (and on other things). For a certain mass, the speed t seconds after it has been dropped is given by $v = 32(1 - e^{-t})$.

   a. Graph this equation. *Suggestion:* Use Xmin = 0, Xmax = 5.5, Ymin = 0, Ymax = 40, and Yscl = 5.

   b. The point whose approximate coordinates are (2, 27.7) is on this graph. Write a sentence that explains the meaning of these coordinates.

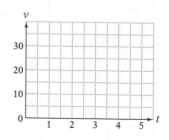

Appendix

Table of Geometric Formulas

Pythagorean Theorem

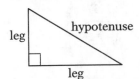

$\text{Hypotenuse} = \sqrt{(\text{leg})^2 + (\text{leg})^2}$

$\text{Leg} = \sqrt{(\text{hypotenuse})^2 - (\text{leg})^2}$

Perimeter and Area of a Triangle

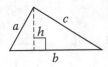

$P = a + b + c$

$A = \dfrac{1}{2}bh$

Perimeter and Area of a Rectangle

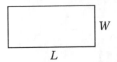

$P = 2L + 2W$

$A = LW$

Perimeter and Area of a Square

$P = 4s$

$A = s^2$

Circumference and Area of a Circle

$C = 2\pi r$ or $C = \pi d$

$A = \pi r^2$

Area of a Trapezoid

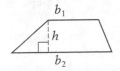

$A = \dfrac{1}{2}h(b_1 + b_2)$

Volume of a Rectangular Solid

$V = LWH$

Volume of a Cube

$V = s^3$

Volume of a Sphere

$V = \dfrac{4}{3}\pi r^3$

Volume of a Right Circular Cylinder

$V = \pi r^2 h$

Compound Interest Table

Compounded Annually

	4%	5%	6%	7%	8%	9%	10%
1 year	1.04000	1.05000	1.06000	1.07000	1.08000	1.09000	1.10000
5 years	1.21665	1.27628	1.33823	1.40255	1.46933	1.53862	1.61051
10 years	1.48024	1.62890	1.79085	1.96715	2.15893	2.36736	2.59374
15 years	1.80094	2.07893	2.39656	2.75903	3.17217	3.64248	4.17725
20 years	2.19112	2.65330	3.20714	3.86968	4.66095	5.60441	6.72750

Compounded Semiannually

	4%	5%	6%	7%	8%	9%	10%
1 year	1.04040	1.05062	1.06090	1.07123	1.08160	1.09203	1.10250
5 years	1.21899	1.28008	1.34392	1.41060	1.48024	1.55297	1.62890
10 years	1.48595	1.63862	1.80611	1.98979	2.19112	2.41171	2.65330
15 years	1.81136	2.09757	2.42726	2.80679	3.24340	3.74531	4.32194
20 years	2.20804	2.68506	3.26204	3.95926	4.80102	5.81634	7.03999

Compounded Quarterly

	4%	5%	6%	7%	8%	9%	10%
1 year	1.04060	1.05094	1.06136	1.07186	1.08243	1.09308	1.10381
5 years	1.22019	1.28204	1.34686	1.41478	1.48595	1.56051	1.63862
10 years	1.48886	1.64362	1.81402	2.00160	2.20804	2.43519	2.68506
15 years	1.81670	2.10718	2.44322	2.83182	3.28103	3.80013	4.39979
20 years	2.21672	2.70148	3.29066	4.00639	4.87544	5.93015	7.20957

Compounded Monthly

	4%	5%	6%	7%	8%	9%	10%
1 year	1.04074	1.051162	1.061678	1.072290	1.083000	1.093807	1.104713
5 years	1.220997	1.283359	1.348850	1.417625	1.489846	1.565681	1.645309
10 years	1.490833	1.647009	1.819397	2.009661	2.219640	2.451357	2.707041
15 years	1.820302	2.113704	2.454094	2.848947	3.306921	3.838043	4.453920
20 years	2.222582	2.712640	3.310204	4.038739	4.926803	6.009152	7.328074

Compounded Daily

	4%	5%	6%	7%	8%	9%	10%
1 year	1.04080	1.05127	1.06183	1.07250	1.08328	1.09416	1.10516
5 years	1.22139	1.28400	1.34983	1.41902	1.49176	1.56823	1.64861
10 years	1.49179	1.64866	1.82203	2.01362	2.22535	2.45933	2.71791
15 years	1.82206	2.11689	2.45942	2.85736	3.31968	3.85678	4.48077
20 years	2.22544	2.71810	3.31979	4.05466	4.95217	6.04830	7.38703

To use this table:
1. Locate the section that gives the desired compounding period.
2. Locate the interest rate in the top row of that section.
3. Locate the number of years in the left-hand column of that section.
4. Locate the number where the interest-rate column and the number-of-years row meet. This is the compound interest factor.

Example   An investment yields an annual interest rate of 10% compounded quarterly for 5 years.
The compounding period is "compounded quarterly."
The interest rate is 10%.
The number of years is 5.
The number where the row and column meet is 1.63862. This is the compound interest factor.

Compound Interest Table

Compounded Annually						
	11%	**12%**	**13%**	**14%**	**15%**	**16%**	**17%**
1 year	1.11000	1.12000	1.13000	1.14000	1.15000	1.16000	1.17000
5 years	1.68506	1.76234	1.84244	1.92542	2.01136	2.10034	2.19245
10 years	2.83942	3.10585	3.39457	3.70722	4.04556	4.41144	4.80683
15 years	4.78459	5.47357	6.25427	7.13794	8.13706	9.26552	10.53872
20 years	8.06239	9.64629	11.52309	13.74349	16.36654	19.46076	23.10560

Compounded Semiannually						
	11%	**12%**	**13%**	**14%**	**15%**	**16%**	**17%**
1 year	1.11303	1.12360	1.13423	1.14490	1.15563	1.16640	1.17723
5 years	1.70814	1.79085	1.87714	1.96715	2.06103	2.15893	2.26098
10 years	2.91776	3.20714	3.52365	3.86968	4.24785	4.66096	5.11205
15 years	4.98395	5.74349	6.61437	7.61226	8.75496	10.06266	11.55825
20 years	8.51331	10.28572	12.41607	14.97446	18.04424	21.72452	26.13302

Compounded Quarterly						
	11%	**12%**	**13%**	**14%**	**15%**	**16%**	**17%**
1 year	1.11462	1.12551	1.13648	1.14752	1.15865	1.16986	1.18115
5 years	1.72043	1.80611	1.89584	1.98979	2.08815	2.19112	2.29891
10 years	2.95987	3.26204	3.59420	3.95926	4.36038	4.80102	5.28497
15 years	5.09225	5.89160	6.81402	7.87809	9.10513	10.51963	12.14965
20 years	8.76085	10.64089	12.91828	15.67574	19.01290	23.04980	27.93091

Compounded Monthly						
	11%	**12%**	**13%**	**14%**	**15%**	**16%**	**17%**
1 year	1.115719	1.126825	1.138032	1.149342	1.160755	1.172271	1.183892
5 years	1.728916	1.816697	1.908857	2.005610	2.107181	2.213807	2.325733
10 years	2.989150	3.300387	3.643733	4.022471	4.440213	4.900941	5.409036
15 years	5.167988	5.995802	6.955364	8.067507	9.356334	10.849737	12.579975
20 years	8.935015	10.892554	13.276792	16.180270	19.715494	24.019222	29.257669

Compounded Daily						
	11%	**12%**	**13%**	**14%**	**15%**	**16%**	**17%**
1 year	1.11626	1.12747	1.13880	1.15024	1.16180	1.17347	1.18526
5 years	1.73311	1.82194	1.91532	2.01348	2.11667	2.22515	2.33918
10 years	3.00367	3.31946	3.66845	4.05411	4.48031	4.95130	5.47178
15 years	5.20569	6.04786	7.02625	8.16288	9.48335	11.01738	12.79950
20 years	9.02203	11.01883	13.45751	16.43582	20.07316	24.51534	29.94039

Monthly Payment Table

	4%	5%	6%	7%	8%	9%
1 year	0.0851499	0.0856075	0.0860664	0.0865267	0.0869884	0.0874515
2 years	0.0434249	0.0438714	0.0443206	0.0447726	0.0452273	0.0456847
3 years	0.0295240	0.0299709	0.0304219	0.0308771	0.0313364	0.0317997
4 years	0.0225791	0.0230293	0.0234850	0.0239462	0.0244129	0.0248850
5 years	0.0184165	0.0188712	0.0193328	0.0198012	0.0202764	0.0207584
15 years	0.0073969	0.0079079	0.0084386	0.0089883	0.0095565	0.0101427
20 years	0.0060598	0.0065996	0.0071643	0.0077530	0.0083644	0.0089973
25 years	0.0052784	0.0058459	0.0064430	0.0070678	0.0077182	0.0083920
30 years	0.0047742	0.0053682	0.0059955	0.0066530	0.0073376	0.0080462

	10%	11%	12%	13%
1 year	0.0879159	0.0883817	0.0888488	0.0893173
2 years	0.0461449	0.0466078	0.0470735	0.0475418
3 years	0.0322672	0.0327387	0.0332143	0.0336940
4 years	0.0253626	0.0258455	0.0263338	0.0268275
5 years	0.0212470	0.0217424	0.0222445	0.0227531
15 years	0.0107461	0.0113660	0.0120017	0.0126524
20 years	0.0096502	0.0103219	0.0110109	0.0117158
25 years	0.0090870	0.0098011	0.0105322	0.0112784
30 years	0.0087757	0.0095232	0.0102861	0.0110620

To use this table:
1. Locate the desired interest rate in the top row.
2. Locate the number of years in the left-hand column.
3. Locate the number where the interest-rate column and the number-of-years row meet. This is the monthly payment factor.

Example   A home has a 30-year mortgage at an annual interest rate of 12%.
The interest rate is 12%.
The number of years is 30.
The number where the row and column meet is 0.0102861. This is the monthly payment factor.

Table of Measurements

Prefixes in the Metric System of Measurement

kilo-	1000	deci-	0.1
hecto-	100	centi-	0.01
deca-	10	milli-	0.001

Measurement Abbreviations
U.S. Customary System

Length

in.	inches
ft	feet
yd	yards
mi	miles

Capacity

oz	fluid ounces
c	cups
qt	quarts
gal	gallons

Weight

| oz | ounces |
| lb | pounds |

Area

in^2	square inches
ft^2	square feet
yd^2	square yards
mi^2	square miles

Rate

| ft/s | feet per second |
| mi/h | miles per hour |

Time

h	hours
min	minutes
s	seconds

Metric System

Length

mm	millimeters
cm	centimeters
m	meters
km	kilometers

Capacity

ml	milliliters
cl	centiliters
L	liters
kl	kiloliters

Weight/Mass

mg	milligrams
cg	centigrams
g	grams
kg	kilograms

Area

cm^2	square centimeters
m^2	square meters
km^2	square kilometers

Rate

m/s	meters per second
km/s	kilometers per second
km/h	kilometers per hour

Time

h	hours
min	minutes
s	seconds

Table of Properties

Properties of Real Numbers

Commutative Property of Addition

If a and b are real numbers, then $a + b = b + a$.

Commutative Property of Multiplication

If a and b are real numbers, then $a \cdot b = b \cdot a$.

Associative Property of Addition

If a, b, and c are real numbers, then
$(a + b) + c = a + (b + c)$.

Associative Property of Multiplication

If a, b, and c are real numbers, then
$(a \cdot b) \cdot c = a \cdot (b \cdot c)$.

Addition Property of Zero

If a is a real number, then $a + 0 = 0 + a = a$.

Multiplication Property of Zero

If a is a real number, then $a \cdot 0 = 0 \cdot a = 0$.

Multiplication Property of One

If a is a real number, then $a \cdot 1 = 1 \cdot a = a$.

Inverse Property of Addition

If a is a real number, then $a + (-a) = (-a) + a = 0$.

Inverse Property of Multiplication

If a is a real number and $a \neq 0$, then
$a \cdot \dfrac{1}{a} = \dfrac{1}{a} \cdot a = 1$.

Distributive Property

If a, b, and c are real numbers, then
$a(b + c) = ab + ac$.

Properties of Zero and One in Division

Any number divided by 1 is the number.
Division by zero is not allowed.

Any number other than zero divided by itself is 1.
Zero divided by a number other than zero is zero.

Appendix A

Keystroke Guide for the TI-83 and TI-83 Plus

Basic Operations

Numerical calculations are performed on the **home screen.** You can always return to the home screen by pressing 〔2nd〕 QUIT. Pressing 〔CLEAR〕 erases the home screen.

To evaluate the expression $-2(3 + 5) - 8 \div 4$, use the following keystrokes.

〔(-)〕 2 〔(〕 3 〔+〕 5 〔)〕 〔−〕 8 〔÷〕 4 〔ENTER〕

−2(3+5)−8/4
-18

Note: There is a difference between the key to enter a negative number, 〔(-)〕, and the key for subtraction, 〔−〕. You cannot use these keys interchangeably.

The 〔2nd〕 key is used to access the commands in gold writing above a key. For instance, to evaluate the $\sqrt{49}$, press 〔2nd〕 √ 49 〔)〕 〔ENTER〕.

√(49)
7

The 〔ALPHA〕 key is used to place a letter on the screen. One reason to do this is to store a value of a variable. The following keystrokes give A the value of 5.

5 〔STO▸〕 〔ALPHA〕 A 〔ENTER〕

5→A
5

This value is now available in calculations. For instance, we can find the value of $3a^2$ by using the following keystrokes: 3 〔ALPHA〕 A 〔x²〕. To display the value of the variable on the screen, press 〔2nd〕 RCL 〔ALPHA〕 A.

3A²
75

Note: When you use the 〔ALPHA〕 key, only capital letters are available on the TI-83 calculator.

Complex Numbers

To perform operations on complex numbers, first press 〔MODE〕 and then use the arrow keys to select a+bi. Then press 〔ENTER〕 〔2nd〕 QUIT.

Addition of complex numbers To add $(3 + 4i) + (2 - 7i)$, use the keystrokes

〔(〕 3 〔+〕 4 〔2nd〕 i 〔)〕 〔+〕

〔(〕 2 〔−〕 7 〔2nd〕 i 〔)〕 〔ENTER〕.

(3+4i)+(2−7i)
5−3i

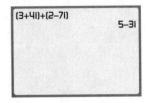

Division of complex numbers. To divide $\frac{26 + 2i}{2 + 4i}$, use the keystrokes 〔(〕 26 〔+〕 2 〔2nd〕 i 〔)〕 〔÷〕 〔(〕 2 〔+〕 4 〔2nd〕 i 〔)〕 〔ENTER〕.

(26+2i)/(2+4i)
3−5i

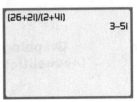

Note: Operations for subtraction and multiplication are similar.

TAKE NOTE

The descriptions in the margins (for example, Basic Operations and Complex Numbers) are the same as those used in the text and are arranged alphabetically.

Additional operations on complex numbers can be found by selecting CPX under the [MATH] key.

To find the absolute value of $2 - 5i$, press [MATH] (scroll to CPX) (scroll to abs) [ENTER] (2 [−] 5 [2nd] i [)] [ENTER].

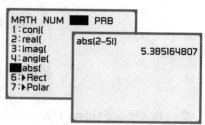

Evaluating Functions

There are various methods of evaluating a function but all methods require that the expression be entered as one of the ten functions Y1 to Y0. To evaluate $f(x) = \frac{x^2}{x - 1}$ when $x = -3$, enter the expression into, for instance, Y1, and then press [VARS] ▸ 11 ([(-)] 3 [)] [ENTER].

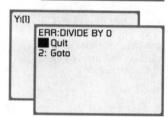

> **TAKE NOTE**
> Use the down arrow key to scroll past Y7 to see Y8, Y9, and Y0.

Note: If you try to evaluate a function at a number that is not in the domain of the function, you will get an error message. For instance, 1 is not in the domain of $f(x) = \frac{x^2}{x - 1}$. If we try to evaluate the function at 1, the error screen at the right appears.

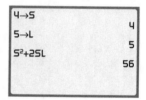

Evaluating Variable Expressions

To evaluate a variable expression, first store the values of each variable. Then enter the variable expression. For instance, to evaluate $s^2 + 2sl$ when $s = 4$ and $l = 5$, use the following keystrokes.

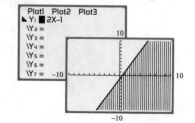

4 [STO▸] [ALPHA] S [ENTER] 5 [STO▸] [ALPHA] L [ENTER] [ALPHA] S
 [x²] [+] 2 [ALPHA] S [ALPHA] L [ENTER]

Graph

To graph a function, use the [Y=] key to enter the expression for the function, select a suitable viewing window, and then press [GRAPH]. For instance, to graph $f(x) = 0.1x^3 - 2x - 1$ in the standard viewing window, use the following keystrokes.

[Y=] 0.1 [X,T,θ,n] [^] 3 [−] 2 [X,T,θ,n] [−] 1 [ZOOM] (scroll to 6) [ENTER]

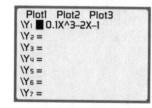 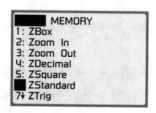 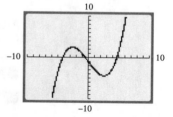

Note: For the keystrokes above, you do not have to scroll to 6. Alternatively, use [ZOOM] 6. This will select the standard viewing window and automatically start the graph. Use the [WINDOW] key to create a custom window for a graph.

Graphing Inequalities

To illustrate this feature, we will graph $y \le 2x - 1$. Enter $2x - 1$ into Y1. Because $y \le 2x - 1$, we want to shade below the graph. Move the cursor to the left of Y1 and press [ENTER] three times. Press [GRAPH].

Note: To shade above the graph, move the cursor to the left of Y_1 and press **ENTER** two times. An inequality with the symbol $\le$ or $\ge$ should be graphed with a solid line, and an inequality with the symbol $<$ or $>$ should be graphed with a dashed line. However, the graph of a linear inequality on a graphing calculator does not distinguish between a solid line and a dashed line.

To graph the solution set of a system of inequalities, solve each inequality for y and graph each inequality. The solution set is the intersection of the two inequalities. The solution set of $\begin{array}{l} 3x + 2y > 10 \\ 4x - 3y \le 5 \end{array}$ is shown at the right.

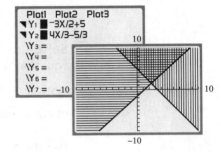

Intersect   The INTERSECT feature is used to solve a system of equations. To illustrate this feature, we will use the system of equations $\begin{array}{l} 2x - 3y = 13 \\ 3x + 4y = -6 \end{array}$.

Note: Some equations can be solved by this method. See the section "Solve an equation" below. Also, this method is used to find a number in the domain of a function for a given number in the range. See the section "Find a domain element."

Solve each of the equations in the system of equations for y. In this case, we have $y = \frac{2}{3}x - \frac{13}{3}$ and $y = -\frac{3}{4}x - \frac{3}{2}$.

Use the Y-editor to enter $\frac{2}{3}x - \frac{13}{3}$ into Y_1 and $-\frac{3}{4}x - \frac{3}{2}$ into Y_2. Graph the two functions in the standard viewing window. (If the window does not show the point of intersection of the two graphs, adjust the window until you can see the point of intersection.)

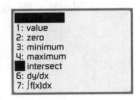

Press **2nd** CALC (scroll to 5, intersect) **ENTER**.

Alternatively, you can just press **2nd** CALC 5.

First curve? is shown at the bottom of the screen and identifies one of the two graphs on the screen. Press **ENTER**.

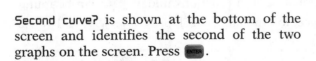

Second curve? is shown at the bottom of the screen and identifies the second of the two graphs on the screen. Press **ENTER**.

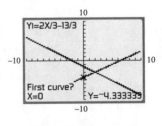

Guess? shown at the bottom of the screen asks you to use the left or right arrow key to move the cursor to the *approximate* location of the point of intersection. (If there are two or more points of intersection, it does not matter which one you choose first.) Press **ENTER**.

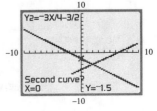

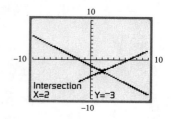

The solution of the system of equations is $(2, -3)$.

Solve an equation To illustrate the steps involved, we will solve the equation $2x + 4 = -3x - 1$. The idea is to write the equation as the system of equations $\begin{array}{l} y = 2x + 4 \\ y = -3x - 1 \end{array}$ and then use the steps for solving a system of equations.

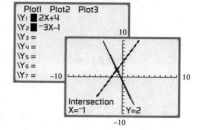

Use the Y-editor to enter the left and right sides of the equation into Y_1 and Y_2. Graph the two functions and then follow the steps for Intersect.

The solution is -1, the x-coordinate of the point of intersection.

Find a domain element For this example, we will find a number in the domain of $f(x) = -\frac{2}{3}x + 2$ that corresponds to 4 in the range of the function. This is like solving the system of equations $y = -\frac{2}{3}x + 2$ and $y = 4$.

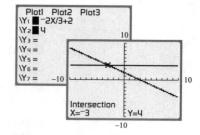

Use the Y= editor to enter the expression for the function in Y_1 and the desired output, 4, in Y_2. Graph the two functions and then follow the steps for Intersect.

The point of intersection is $(-3, 4)$. The number -3 in the domain of f produces an output of 4 in the range of f.

Math Pressing ⬛MATH gives you access to many built-in functions. The following keystrokes will convert 0.125 to a fraction: .125 ⬛MATH 1 ⬛ENTER .

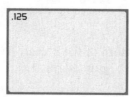
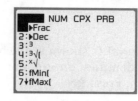

Additional built-in functions under ⬛MATH can be found by pressing ⬛MATH ▶. For instance, to evaluate $-|-25|$, press ⊙(-) ⬛MATH ▶ 1 ⊙(-) 25 ⬛) ⬛ENTER .

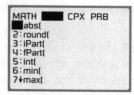
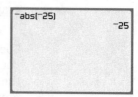

See your owner's manual for assistance with other functions under the ⬛MATH key.

Min and Max The local minimum and the local maximum values of a function are calculated by accessing the CALC menu. For this demonstration, we will find the minimum value and the maximum value of $f(x) = 0.2x^3 + 0.3x^2 - 3.6x + 2$.

Enter the function into Y₁. Press 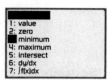 CALC (scroll to 3 for minimum of the function) ■.

Alternatively, you can just press ■ CALC 3.

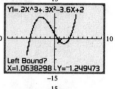

Left Bound? shown at the bottom of the screen asks you to use the left or right arrow key to move the cursor to the *left* of the minimum. Press ■.

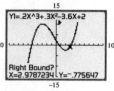

Right Bound? shown at the bottom of the screen asks you to use the left or right arrow key to move the cursor to the *right* of the minimum. Press ■.

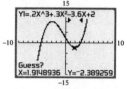

Guess? shown at the bottom of the screen asks you to use the left or right arrow key to move the cursor to the *approximate* location of the minimum. Press ■.

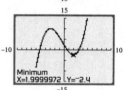

The minimum value of the function is the *y*-coordinate. For this example, the minimum value of the function is −2.4.

The *x*-coordinate for the minimum is 2. However, because of rounding errors in the calculation, it is shown as a number close to 2.

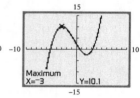

To find the maximum value of the function, follow the same steps as above except select maximum under the CALC menu. The screens for this calculation are shown below.

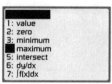 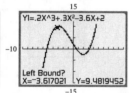 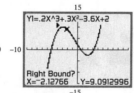 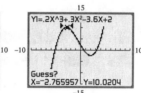

The maximum value of the function is 10.1.

Radical Expressions To evaluate a square-root expression, press ■ √.

For instance, to evaluate $0.15\sqrt{p^2 + 4p + 10}$ when $p = 100,000$, first store 100,000 in P. Then press 0.15 ■ √ ALPHA P ■ ■ 4 ALPHA P ■ 10 ■ ■.

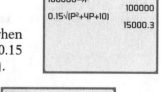

To evaluate a radical expression other than a square root, access $\sqrt[x]{}$ by pressing ■. For instance, to evaluate $\sqrt[4]{67}$, press 4 (the index of the radical) ■ (scroll to 5) ■ 67 ■.

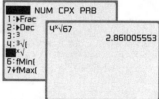

Scientific Notation

To enter a number in scientific notation, use 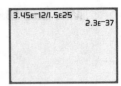 EE. For instance, to find $\frac{3.45 \times 10^{-12}}{1.5 \times 10^{25}}$, press 3.45 2nd EE (-) 12 ÷ 1.5 2nd EE 25 ENTER. The answer is 2.3×10^{-37}.

Sequences and Series

The terms of a sequence and the sum of a series can be calculated by using the 2nd LIST feature.

Store a sequence A sequence is stored in one of the lists L_1 through L_6. For instance, to store the sequence 1, 3, 5, 7, 9 in L_1, use the following keystrokes.

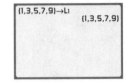

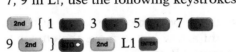

Display the terms of a sequence The terms of a sequence are displayed by using the function seq(expression, variable, begin, end, increment). For instance, to display the 3rd through 8th terms of the sequence given by $a_n = n^2 + 6$, enter the following keystrokes.

2nd LIST ● (scroll to 5)

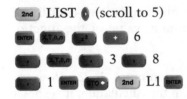

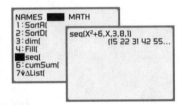

The keystrokes STO 2nd L1 ENTER store the terms of the sequence in L_1. This is not necessary but is sometimes helpful if additional work will be done with that sequence.

Find a sequence of partial sums To find a sequence of partial sums, use the cumSum(function. For instance, to find the sequence of partial sums for 2, 4, 6, 8, 10, use the following keystrokes.

2nd LIST ● (scroll to 6)

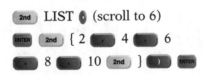

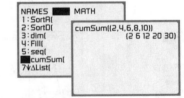

If a sequence is stored as a list in L_1, then the sequence of partial sums can be calculated by pressing 2nd LIST ● (scroll to 6 [or press 6]) ENTER 2nd L1) ENTER.

Find the sum of a series The sum of a series is calculated using sum<list, start, end>. For instance, to find $\sum_{n=3}^{6} (n^2 + 2)$, enter the following keystrokes.

2nd LIST ● ● (scroll to 5)

ENTER 2nd LIST ● (scroll to 5 [or press 5])

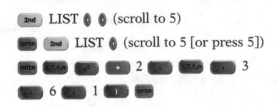

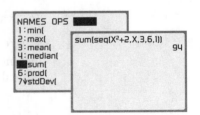

Table
There are three steps in creating an input/output table for a function. First use the ⬛ editor to input the function. The second step is setting up the table, and the third step is displaying the table.

To set up the table, press **2nd** TBLSET. TblStart is the first value of the independent variable in the input/output table. △Tbl is the difference between successive values. Setting this to 1 means that, for this table, the input values are $-2, -1, 0, 1, 2\ldots$. If $\triangle$Tbl $= 0.5$, then the input values are $-2, -1.5, -1, -0.5, 0, 0.5, \ldots$

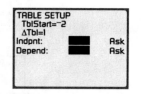

Indpnt is the independent variable. When this is set to Auto, values of the independent variable are automatically entered into the table. Depend is the dependent variable. When this is set to Auto, values of the dependent variable are automatically entered into the table.

To display the table, press **2nd** TABLE. An input/output table for $f(x) = x^2 - 1$ is shown at the right.

Once the table is on the screen, the up and down arrow keys can be used to display more values in the table. For the table at the right, we used the up arrow key to move to $x = -7$.

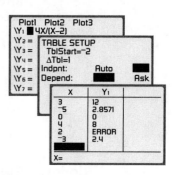

An input/output table for any given input can be created by selecting Ask for the independent variable. The table at the right shows an input/output table for $f(x) = \dfrac{4x}{x-2}$ for selected values of x. Note the word ERROR when 2 was entered. This occurred because f is not defined when $x = 2$.

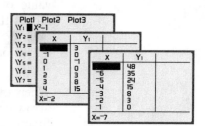

> Note: Using the table feature in Ask mode is the same as evaluating a function for given values of the independent variable. For instance, from the table at the right, we have $f(4) = 8$.

Test
The TEST feature has many uses, one of which is to graph the solution set of a linear inequality in one variable. To illustrate this feature, we will graph the solution set of $x - 1 < 4$. Press **Y=** ⬛ ⬛ 1 **2nd** TEST (scroll to 5) **ENTER** 4 **GRAPH** .

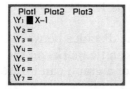

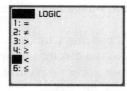

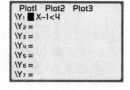

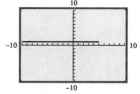

Trace
Once a graph is drawn, pressing **TRACE** will place a cursor on the screen, and the coordinates of the point below the cursor are shown at the bottom of the screen. Use the left and right arrow keys to move the cursor along the graph. For the graph at the right, we have $f(4.8) = 3.4592$, where $f(x) = 0.1x^3 - 2x + 2$ is shown at the top left of the screen.

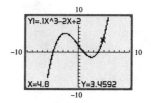

In TRACE mode, you can evaluate a function at any value of the independent variable that is within Xmin and Xmax. To do this, first graph the function. Now press (the value of x) ⬛. For the graph at the left below, we used $x = -3.5$. If a value of x is chosen outside the window, an error message is displayed.

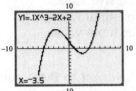 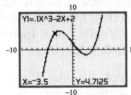 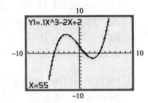 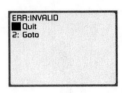

In the example above where we entered -3.5 for x, the value of the function was calculated as 4.7125. This means that $f(-3.5) = 4.7125$. The keystrokes ⬛ QUIT ⬛ ⬥ 11 ⬛ 1 ⬛ will convert the decimal value to a fraction.

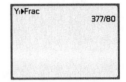

When the TRACE feature is used with two or more graphs, the up and down arrow keys are used to move between the graphs. The graphs below are for the functions $f(x) = 0.1x^3 - 2x + 2$ and $g(x) = 2x - 3$. By using the up and down arrows, we can place the cursor on either graph. The right and left arrows are used to move along the graph.

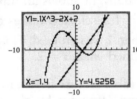 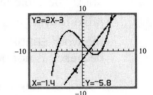

Window The viewing window for a graph is controlled by pressing ⬛. Xmin and Xmax are the minimum value and maximum value, respectively, of the independent variable shown on the graph. Xscl is the distance between tic marks on the x-axis. Ymin and Ymax are the minimum value and maximum value, respectively, of the dependent variable shown on the graph. Yscl is the distance between tic marks on the y-axis. Leave Xres as 1.

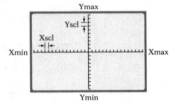

Note: In the standard viewing window, the distance between tic marks on the x-axis is different from the distance between tic marks on the y-axis. This will distort a graph. A more accurate picture of a graph can be created by using a square viewing window. See ZOOM.

⬛ Y= The ⬛ Y= editor is used to enter the expression for a function. There are ten possible functions, labeled Y_1 to Y_0, that can be active at any one time. For instance, to enter $f(x) = x^2 + 3x - 2$ as Y_1, use the following keystrokes.

⬛ Y= ⬛ ⬛ ⬛ + 3 ⬛ ⬛ − 2

Note: If an expression is already entered for Y_1, place the cursor anywhere on that expression and press 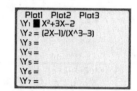.

To enter $s = \frac{2v - 1}{v^3 - 3}$ into Y_2, place the cursor to the right of the equals sign for Y_2. Then press (2 █ ▄ 1 █ ÷ (▄ ▄ 3 █ 3).

Note: When we enter an equation, the independent variable, v in the expression above, is entered using ▄. The dependent variable, s in the expression above, is one of Y_1 to Y_0. Also note the use of parentheses to ensure the correct order of operations.

Observe the black rectangle that covers the equals sign for the two examples we have shown. This rectangle means that the function is "active." If we were to press ▄, then the graph of both functions would appear. You can make a function inactive by using the arrow keys to move the cursor over the equals sign of that function and then pressing ▄. This will remove the black rectangle. We have done that for Y_2, as shown at the right. Now if ▄ is pressed, only Y_1 will be graphed.

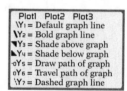

It is also possible to control the appearance of the graph by moving the cursor on the ▄ screen to the left of any Y. With the cursor in this position, pressing ▄ will change the appearance of the graph. The options are shown at the right.

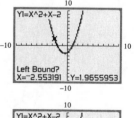

Zero The ZERO feature of a graphing calculator is used for various calculations: to find the x-intercepts of a function, to solve some equations, and to find the zero of a function.

x-intercepts To illustrate the procedure for finding x-intercepts, we will use $f(x) = x^2 + x - 2$.

First, use the Y-editor to enter the expression for the function and then graph the function in the standard viewing window. (It may be necessary to adjust this window so that the intercepts are visible.) Once the graph is displayed, use the keystrokes below to find the x-intercepts of the graph of the function.

Press ▄ CALC (scroll to 2 for zero of the function) ▄.

Alternatively, you can just press ▄ CALC 2.

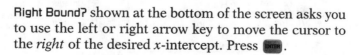

Left Bound? shown at the bottom of the screen asks you to use the left or right arrow key to move the cursor to the *left* of the desired x-intercept. Press ▄.

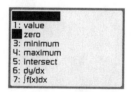

Right Bound? shown at the bottom of the screen asks you to use the left or right arrow key to move the cursor to the *right* of the desired x-intercept. Press ▄.

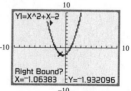

Guess? shown at the bottom of the screen asks you to use the left or right arrow key to move the cursor to the *approximate* location of the desired *x*-intercept. Press ▇.

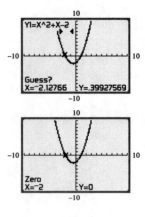

The *x*-coordinate of an *x*-intercept is −2. Therefore, an *x*-intercept is (−2, 0).

To find the other *x*-intercept, follow the same steps as above. The screens for this calculation are shown below.

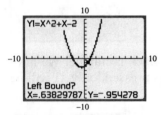 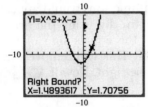 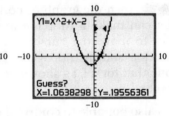 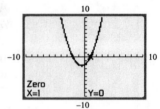

A second *x*-intercept is (1, 0).

Solve an equation   To use the ZERO feature to solve an equation, first rewrite the equation with all terms on one side. For instance, one way to solve the equation $x^3 - x + 1 = -2x + 3$ is first to rewrite it as $x^3 + x - 2 = 0$. Enter $x^3 + x - 2$ into Y₁ and then follow the steps for finding *x*-intercepts.

Find the real zeros of a function   To find the real zeros of a function, follow the steps for finding *x*-intercepts.

Zoom   Pressing ▇▇▇ allows you to select some preset viewing windows. This key also gives you access to ZBox, Zoom In, and Zoom Out. These functions enable you to redraw a selected portion of a graph in a new window. Some windows used frequently in this text are shown below.

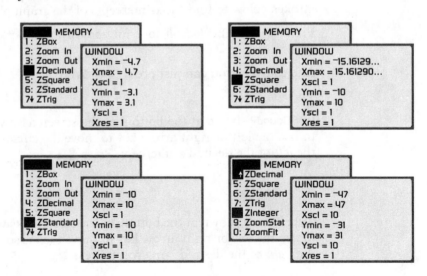

Appendix B

Proofs and Tables

Proofs of Logarithmic Properties

In each of the following proofs of logarithmic properties, it is assumed that the Properties of Exponents are true for all real number exponents.

The Logarithm Property of the Product of Two Numbers

For any positive real numbers x, y, and b, $b \neq 1$, $\log_b xy = \log_b x + \log_b y$.

Proof: Let $\log_b x = m$ and $\log_b y = n$.

Write each equation in its equivalent exponential form.	$x = b^m \qquad y = b^n$
Use substitution and the Properties of Exponents.	$xy = b^m b^n$
	$xy = b^{m+n}$
Write the equation in its equivalent logarithmic form.	$\log_b xy = m + n$
Substitute $\log_b x$ for m and $\log_b y$ for n.	$\log_b xy = \log_b x + \log_b y$

The Logarithm Property of the Quotient of Two Numbers

For any positive real numbers x, y, and b, $b \neq 1$, $\log_b \dfrac{x}{y} = \log_b x - \log_b y$.

Proof: Let $\log_b x = m$ and $\log_b y = n$.

Write each equation in its equivalent exponential form.	$x = b^m \qquad y = b^n$
Use substitution and the Properties of Exponents.	$\dfrac{x}{y} = \dfrac{b^m}{b^n}$
	$\dfrac{x}{y} = b^{m-n}$
Write the equation in its equivalent logarithmic form.	$\log_b \dfrac{x}{y} = m - n$
Substitute $\log_b x$ for m and $\log_b y$ for n.	$\log_b \dfrac{x}{y} = \log_b x - \log_b y$

The Logarithm Property of the Power of a Number

For any real numbers x, r, and b, $b \neq 1$, $\log_b x^r = r \log_b x$.

Proof: Let $\log_b x = m$.

Write the equation in its equivalent exponential form.	$x = b^m$
Raise both sides to the r power.	$x^r = (b^m)^r$
	$x^r = b^{mr}$
Write the equation in its equivalent logarithmic form.	$\log_b x^r = mr$
Substitute $\log_b x$ for m.	$\log_b x^r = r \log_b x$

Proof of the Formula for the Sum of *n* Terms of a Geometric Series

Theorem: The sum of the first n terms of a geometric sequence whose nth term is ar^{n-1} is given by $S_n = \dfrac{a(1 - r^n)}{1 - r}$.

Proof: Let S_n represent the sum of n terms of the sequence.	$S_n = a + ar + ar^2 + \cdots + ar^{n-2} + ar^{n-1}$
Multiply each side of the equation by r.	$rS_n = ar + ar^2 + ar^3 + \cdots + ar^{n-1} + ar^n$
Subtract the two equations.	$S_n - rS_n = a - ar^n$
Assuming $r \neq 1$, solve for S_n.	$(1 - r)S_n = a(1 - r^n)$
	$S_n = \dfrac{a(1 - r^n)}{1 - r}$

Proof of the Formula for the Sum of *n* Terms of an Arithmetic Series

Each term of the arithmetic sequence shown at the right was found by adding 3 to the previous term.

2, 5, 8,...,17, 20

Each term of the reverse arithmetic sequence can be found by subtracting 3 from the previous term.

20, 17, 14,...,5, 2

This idea is used in the following proof.

Theorem: The sum of the first n terms of an arithmetic sequence for which a_1 is the first term, n is the number of terms, a_n is the last term, and d is the common difference is given by $S_n = \dfrac{n}{2}(a_1 + a_n)$.

Proof: Let S_n represent the sum of the sequence.

$S_n = a_1 + (a_1 + d) + (a_1 + 2d) + \cdots + a_n$

Write the terms of the sum of the sequence in reverse order. The sum will be the same.

$S_n = a_n + (a_n - d) + (a_n - 2d) + \cdots + a_1$

Add the two equations.

$2S_n = (a_1 + a_n) + (a_1 + a_n) + (a_1 + a_n) + \cdots + (a_1 + a_n)$

Simplify the right side of the equation by using the fact that there are n terms in the sequence.

$2S_n = n(a_1 + a_n)$

Solve for S_n.

$S_n = \dfrac{n}{2}(a_1 + a_n)$

Table of Symbols

$+$	add	$<$	is less than
$-$	subtract	$\leq$	is less than or equal to
$\cdot, \times, (a)(b)$	multiply	$>$	is greater than
$\dfrac{a}{b}, \div$	divide	$\geq$	is greater than or equal to
		(a, b)	an ordered pair whose first component is a and whose second component is b
$(\,)$	parentheses, a grouping symbol		
$[\,]$	brackets, a grouping symbol	$\circ$	degree (for angles)
π	pi, a number approximately equal to $\dfrac{22}{7}$ or 3.14	$\sqrt{a}$	the principal square root of a
		$\varnothing, \{\,\}$	the empty set
$-a$	the opposite, or additive inverse, of a	$|a|$	the absolute value of a
		$\cup$	union of two sets
$\dfrac{1}{a}$	the reciprocal, or multiplicative inverse, of a	$\cap$	intersection of two sets
		$\in$	is an element of (for sets)
$=$	is equal to	$\notin$	is not an element of (for sets)
$\approx$	is approximately equal to		
$\neq$	is not equal to		

Table of Measurement Abbreviations

U.S. Customary System

Length		**Capacity**		**Weight**		**Area**	
in.	inches	oz	fluid ounces	oz	ounces	in²	square inches
ft	feet	c	cups	lb	pounds	ft²	square feet
yd	yards	qt	quarts				
mi	miles	gal	gallons				

Metric System

Length		**Capacity**		**Weight/Mass**		**Area**	
mm	millimeter (0.001 m)	ml	milliliter (0.001 L)	mg	milligram (0.001 g)	cm²	square centimeters
cm	centimeter (0.01 m)	cl	centiliter (0.01 L)	cg	centigram (0.01 g)	m²	square meters
dm	decimeter (0.1 m)	dl	deciliter (0.1 L)	dg	decigram (0.1 g)		
m	meter	L	liter	g	gram		
dam	decameter (10 m)	dal	decaliter (10 L)	dag	decagram (10 g)		
hm	hectometer (100 m)	hl	hectoliter (100 L)	hg	hectogram (100 g)		
km	kilometer (1000 m)	kl	kiloliter (1000 L)	kg	kilogram (1000 g)		

Time

h	hours	min	minutes	s	seconds

Table of Properties

Properties of Real Numbers

The Associative Property of Addition
If a, b, and c are real numbers, then
$(a + b) + c = a + (b + c)$.

The Associative Property of Multiplication
If a, b, and c are real numbers, then
$(a \cdot b) \cdot c = a \cdot (b \cdot c)$.

The Commutative Property of Addition
If a and b are real numbers, then
$a + b = b + a$.

The Commutative Property of Multiplication
If a and b are real numbers, then
$a \cdot b = b \cdot a$.

The Addition Property of Zero
If a is a real number, then
$a + 0 = 0 + a = a$.

The Multiplication Property of One
If a is a real number, then
$a \cdot 1 = 1 \cdot a = a$.

The Multiplication Property of Zero
If a is a real number, then
$a \cdot 0 = 0 \cdot a = 0$.

The Inverse Property of Multiplication
If a is a real number and $a \neq 0$, then
$a \cdot \dfrac{1}{a} = \dfrac{1}{a} \cdot a = 1$.

The Inverse Property of Addition
If a is a real number, then
$a + (-a) = (-a) + a = 0$.

Distributive Property
If a, b, and c are real numbers, then
$a(b + c) = ab + ac$.

Properties of Equations

Addition Property of Equations
If $a = b$, then $a + c = b + c$.

Multiplication Property of Equations
If $a = b$ and $c \neq 0$, then $a \cdot c = b \cdot c$.

Properties of Inequalities

Addition Property of Inequalities
If $a > b$, then $a + c > b + c$.
If $a < b$, then $a + c < b + c$.

Multiplication Property of Inequalities
If $a > b$ and $c > 0$, then $ac > bc$.
If $a < b$ and $c > 0$, then $ac < bc$.
If $a > b$ and $c < 0$, then $ac < bc$.
If $a < b$ and $c < 0$, then $ac > bc$.

Properties of Exponents

If m and n are integers, then $x^m \cdot x^n = x^{m+n}$.
If m and n are integers, then $(x^m)^n = x^{mn}$.

If $x \neq 0$, then $x^0 = 1$.

If m and n are integers and $x \neq 0$, then $\dfrac{x^m}{x^n} = x^{m-n}$.

If m, n, and p are integers, then $(x^m \cdot y^n)^p = x^{mp}y^{np}$.
If n is a positive integer and $x \neq 0$, then

$x^{-n} = \dfrac{1}{x^n}$ and $\dfrac{1}{x^{-n}} = x^n$.

If m, n, and p are integers and $y \neq 0$, then $\left(\dfrac{x^m}{y^n}\right)^p = \dfrac{x^{mp}}{y^{np}}$.

Principle of Zero Products

If $a \cdot b = 0$, then $a = 0$ or $b = 0$.

Properties of Radical Expressions

If a and b are positive real numbers, then $\sqrt{ab} = \sqrt{a}\sqrt{b}$.

If a and b are positive real numbers, then $\sqrt{\dfrac{a}{b}} = \dfrac{\sqrt{a}}{\sqrt{b}}$.

Property of Squaring Both Sides of an Equation

If a and b are real numbers and $a = b$, then $a^2 = b^2$.

Properties of Logarithms

If x, y, and b are positive real numbers and $b \neq 1$, then
$\log_b(xy) = \log_b x + \log_b y$.
If x, y, and b are positive real numbers and $b \neq 1$, then
$\log_b \dfrac{x}{y} = \log_b x - \log_b y$.

If x and b are positive real numbers, $b \neq 1$, and r is
any real number, then $\log_b x^r = r \log_b x$.
If x and b are positive real numbers and $b \neq 1$, then
$\log_b b^x = x$.

Table of Algebraic and Geometric Formulas

Slope of a line

$$m = \frac{y_2 - y_1}{x_2 - x_1}, x_1 \neq x_2$$

Slope-intercept form of a straight line

$$y = mx + b$$

Point-slope formula for a line

$$y - y_1 = m(x - x_1)$$

Quadratic Formula

$$x = \frac{-b \pm \sqrt{b^2 - 4ac}}{2a}$$

$$\text{discriminant} = b^2 - 4ac$$

Perimeter and Area of a Triangle, and Sum of the Measures of the Angles

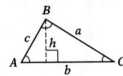

$$P = a + b + c$$

$$A = \frac{1}{2}bh$$

$$A + B + C = 180°$$

Pythagorean Theorem

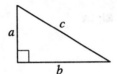

$$a^2 + b^2 = c^2$$

Perimeter and Area of a Rectangle

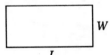

$$P = 2L + 2W$$

$$A = LW$$

Perimeter and Area of a Square

$$P = 4s$$

$$A = s^2$$

Area of a Trapezoid

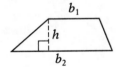

$$A = \frac{1}{2}h(b_1 + b_2)$$

Circumference and Area of a Circle

$$C = 2\pi r \quad \text{or} \quad C = \pi d$$

$$A = \pi r^2$$

Volume and Surface Area of a Rectangular Solid

$$V = LWH$$

$$SA = 2LW + 2LH + 2WH$$

Volume of a Cube

$$V = s^3$$

Table of Algebraic and Geometric Formulas

Volume and Surface Area of a Right Circular Cylinder

$$V = \pi r^2 h$$
$$SA = 2\pi r^2 + 2\pi rh$$

Volume and Surface Area of a Sphere

$$V = \frac{4}{3}\pi r^3$$

$$SA = 4\pi r^2$$

Volume and Surface Area of a Right Circular Cone

$$V = \frac{1}{3}\pi r^2 h$$

$$SA = \pi r^2 + \pi rl$$

Solutions to Chapter 1 "You Try It"

SECTION 1.1

You Try It 1 -232 ft

You Try It 2

$$\xleftarrow{\;\blacklozenge\;|\;\;|\;\;|\;\;|\;\;|\;\;|\;\;|\;\;|\;\;|\;}\rightarrow$$
$$\quad -4\;-3\;-2\;-1\;\;0\;\;1\;\;2\;\;3\;\;4$$

You Try It 3 $-12 < -8$ • **-12 is to the left of -8 on the number line.**

You Try It 4 $|-7| = 7; \;|21| = 21$

You Try It 5 $|2| = 2; \;|-9| = 9$

You Try It 6 $-|-12| = -12$

SECTION 1.2

You Try It 1 $-154 + (-37) = -191$ • **The signs of the addends are the same.**

You Try It 2 $-5 + (-2) + 9 + (-3)$
$$= -7 + 9 + (-3)$$
$$= 2 + (-3)$$
$$= -1$$

You Try It 3 $-8 - 14$
$$= -8 + (-14) \quad \text{• Rewrite "$-$" as "$+$";}$$
$$= -22 \qquad\qquad\text{the opposite of 14 is -1}$$

You Try It 4 $3 - (-15)$
$$= 3 + 15 \quad \text{• Rewrite "$-$" as "$+$";}$$
$$= 18 \qquad\text{the opposite of -15 is 15.}$$

You Try It 5 $4 - (-3) - 12 - (-7) - 20$
$$= 4 + 3 + (-12) + 7 + (-20)$$
$$= 7 + (-12) + 7 + (-20)$$
$$= -5 + 7 + (-20)$$
$$= 2 + (-20)$$
$$= -18$$

You Try It 6

Strategy   To find the temperature, add the increase (12°C) to the previous temperature (-10°C).

Solution $-10 + 12 = 2$

After an increase of 12°C, the temperature is 2°C.

SECTION 1.3

You Try It 1 $(-3)(-5) = 15$ • **The signs are the same. The product is positive.**

You Try It 2   The signs are different. The product is negative.

$$-38 \cdot 51 = -1938$$

You Try It 3 $-7(-8)(9)(-2) = 56(9)(-2)$
$$= 504(-2)$$
$$= -1008$$

You Try It 4 $(-135) \div (-9) = 15$

You Try It 5 $84 \div (-6) = -14$ • **The signs are the same. The quotient is positive**

You Try It 6 $-72 \div 4 = -18$ • **The signs are different. The quotient is negative.**

You Try It 7   Division by zero is undefined.
$-39 \div 0$ is undefined.

You Try It 8

Strategy   To find the melting point of argon, multiply the melting point of mercury (-38°C) by 5.

Solution $5(-38) = -190$

The melting point of argon is -190°C.

You Try It 9

Strategy   To find the average daily low temperature:
• Add the seven temperature readings.
• Divide by 7.

Solution
$-6 + (-7) + 1 + 0 + (-5) + (-10) + (-1)$
$$= -13 + 1 + 0 + (-5) + (-10) + (-1)$$
$$= -12 + 0 + (-5) + (-10) + (-1)$$
$$= -12 + (-5) + (-10) + (-1)$$
$$= -17 + (-10) + (-1)$$
$$= -27 + (-1)$$
$$= -28$$

$-28 \div 7 = -4$

The average daily low temperature was -4°F.

SECTION 1.4

You Try It 1   The LCM of 9 and 12 is 36.

$$\frac{5}{9} - \frac{11}{12} = \frac{20}{36} - \frac{33}{36} = \frac{20}{36} + \frac{-33}{36}$$

$$= \frac{20 + (-33)}{36} = \frac{-13}{36}$$

$$= -\frac{13}{36}$$

You Try It 2   The LCM of 8, 6, and 3 is 24.

$$-\frac{7}{8} - \frac{5}{6} + \frac{2}{3}$$

$$= -\frac{21}{24} - \frac{20}{24} + \frac{16}{24}$$

$$= \frac{-21}{24} + \frac{-20}{24} + \frac{16}{24}$$

$$= \frac{-21 + (-20) + 16}{24} = \frac{-25}{24}$$

$$= -\frac{25}{24} = -1\frac{1}{24}$$

You Try It 3 $16.127 - 67.91 = 16.127 + (-67.91)$

$$\begin{array}{r} 67.910 \\ -16.127 \\ \hline 51.783 \end{array}$$

$16.127 - 67.91 = -51.783$

You Try It 4 $2.7 + (-9.44) + 6.2$
$= -6.74 + 6.2$
$= -0.54$

You Try It 5   The product is positive.

$$\left(-\frac{2}{3}\right)\left(-\frac{9}{10}\right) = \frac{2 \cdot 9}{3 \cdot 10}$$

$$= \frac{3}{5}$$

You Try It 6   The quotient is negative.

$$-\frac{5}{8} \div \frac{5}{40} = -\left(\frac{5}{8} \div \frac{5}{40}\right)$$

$$= -\left(\frac{5}{8} \times \frac{40}{5}\right)$$

$$= -\left(\frac{5 \cdot 40}{8 \cdot 5}\right)$$

$$= -5$$

You Try It 7   The product is negative.

$$\begin{array}{r} 5.44 \\ \times\ 3.8 \\ \hline 4352 \\ 16322 \\ \hline 20.672 \end{array}$$

$-5.44 \times 3.8 = -20.672$

You Try It 8 $3.44 \times (-1.7) \times 0.6$
$= (-5.848) \times 0.6$
$= -3.5088$

You Try It 9

$$\begin{array}{r} 0.231 \\ 1.7\overline{)0.3.940} \\ -3.440 \\ \hline 540 \\ -510 \\ \hline 30 \\ -17 \\ \hline 13 \end{array}$$

$-0.394 \div 1.7 \approx -0.23$

You Try It 10

Strategy   To find how many degrees the temperature fell, subtract the lower temperature ($-13.33°C$) from the higher temperature ($12.78°C$).

Solution $12.78 - (-13.33) = 12.78 + 13.33$
$= 26.11$

The temperature fell $26.11°C$ in the 15-min period.

SECTION 1.5

You Try It 1   The number is less than 1. Move the decimal point 7 places to the right. The exponent on 10 is -7.

$$0.000000961 = 9.61 \times 10^{-7}$$

You Try It 2   The exponent on 10 is positive. Move the decimal point 6 places to the right.

$$7.329 \times 10^6 = 7,329,000$$

You Try It 3 $9 - 9 \div (-3)$
$= 9 - (-3)$ • **Do the division.**
$= 9 + 3$ • **Rewrite as addition. Add**
$= 12$

You Try It 4 $8 \div 4 \cdot 4 - (-2)^2$
$= 8 \div 4 \cdot 4 - 4$ • **Exponents**
$= 2 \cdot 4 - 4$ • **Division**
$= 8 - 4$ • **Multiplication**
$= 8 + (-4)$ • **Subtraction**
$= 4$

You Try It 5 $8 - (-15) \div (2 - 7)$
$= 8 - (-15) \div (-5)$
$= 8 - 3$
$= 8 + (-3)$
$= 5$

You Try It 6 $(-2)^2 \times (3 - 7)^2 - (-16) \div (-4)$
$= (-2)^2 \times (-4)^2 - (-16) \div (-4)$
$= 4 \times 16 - (-16) \div (-4)$
$= 64 - (-16) \div (-4)$
$= 64 - 4$
$= 64 + (-4)$
$= 60$

You Try It 7 $7 \div \left(\dfrac{1}{7} - \dfrac{3}{14} \right) - 9$

$= 7 \div \left(-\dfrac{1}{14} \right) - 9$

$= 7(-14) - 9$
$= -98 - 9$
$= -98 + (-9)$
$= -107$

Solutions to Chapter 2 "You Try It"

SECTION 2.1

You Try It 1 $6a - 5b$

$$6(-3) - 5(4) = -18 - 20$$
$$= -18 + (-20)$$
$$= -38$$

You Try It 2 $-3s^2 - 12 \div t$

$$-3(-2)^2 - 12 \div 4 = -3(4) - 12 \div 4$$
$$= -12 - 12 \div 4$$
$$= -12 - 3$$
$$= -12 + (-3)$$
$$= -15$$

You Try It 3 $-\dfrac{2}{3}m + \dfrac{3}{4}n^3$

$$-\frac{2}{3}(6) + \frac{3}{4}(2)^3 = -\frac{2}{3}(6) + \frac{3}{4}(8)$$
$$= -4 + 6$$
$$= 2$$

You Try It 4 $-3yz - z^2 + y^2$

$$-3\left(-\frac{2}{3}\right)\left(\frac{1}{3}\right) - \left(\frac{1}{3}\right)^2 + \left(-\frac{2}{3}\right)^2$$
$$= -3\left(-\frac{2}{3}\right)\left(\frac{1}{3}\right) - \frac{1}{9} + \frac{4}{9}$$
$$= \frac{2}{3} - \frac{1}{9} + \frac{4}{9} = \frac{6}{9} - \frac{1}{9} + \frac{4}{9} = \frac{9}{9}$$
$$= 1$$

You Try It 5 $5a^2 - 6b^2 + 7a^2 - 9b^2$
$$= 5a^2 + (-6)b^2 + 7a^2 + (-9)b^2$$
$$= 5a^2 + 7a^2 + (-6)b^2 + (-9)b^2$$
$$= 12a^2 + (-15)b^2$$
$$= 12a^2 - 15b^2$$

You Try It 6 $-6x + 7 + 9x - 10$
$$= (-6)x + 7 + 9x + (-10)$$
$$= (-6)x + 9x + 7 + (-10)$$
$$= 3x + (-3)$$
$$= 3x - 3$$

You Try It 7 $\dfrac{3}{8}w + \dfrac{1}{2} - \dfrac{1}{4}w - \dfrac{2}{3}$

$$= \frac{3}{8}w + \frac{1}{2} + \left(-\frac{1}{4}\right)w + \left(-\frac{2}{3}\right)$$
$$= \frac{3}{8}w + \left(-\frac{1}{4}\right)w + \frac{1}{2} + \left(-\frac{2}{3}\right)$$
$$= \frac{3}{8}w + \left(-\frac{2}{8}\right)w + \frac{3}{6} + \left(-\frac{4}{6}\right)$$
$$= \frac{1}{8}w + \left(-\frac{1}{6}\right)$$
$$= \frac{1}{8}w - \frac{1}{6}$$

You Try It 8 $5(a - 2) = 5a - 5(2)$
$$= 5a - 10$$

You Try It 9 $8s - 2(3s - 5)$
$$= 8s - 2(3s) - (-2)(5)$$
$$= 8s - 6s + 10$$
$$= 2s + 10$$

You Try It 10 $4(x - 3) - 2(x + 1)$
$$= 4x - 4(3) - 2x - 2(1)$$
$$= 4x - 12 - 2x - 2$$
$$= 4x - 2x - 12 - 2$$
$$= 2x - 14$$

SECTION 2.2

You Try It 1

$$\dfrac{x(x + 3) = 4x + 6}{}$$

$$(-2)(-2 + 3) \overset{?}{=} 4(-2) + 6$$
$$(-2)(1) \overset{?}{=} (-8) + 6$$
$$-2 = -2$$

Yes, -2 is a solution.

You Try It 2

$$\dfrac{x^2 - x = 3x + 7}{}$$

$$(-3)^2 - (-3) \overset{?}{=} 3(-3) + 7$$
$$9 + 3 \overset{?}{=} -9 + 7$$
$$12 \neq -2$$

No, -3 is not a solution.

You Try It 3

$$-2 + y = -5$$
$$-2 + 2 + y = -5 + 2 \qquad \bullet \textbf{ Add 2 to}$$
$$0 + y = -3 \qquad\qquad \textbf{each side.}$$
$$y = -3$$

The solution is -3.

You Try It 4

$$7 = y + 8$$
$$7 - 8 = y + 8 - 8$$
$$-1 = y + 0$$
$$-1 = y$$

• Subtract 8 from each side.

The solution is -1.

You Try It 5

$$\frac{1}{5} = z + \frac{4}{5}$$
$$\frac{1}{5} - \frac{4}{5} = z + \frac{4}{5} - \frac{4}{5}$$
$$-\frac{3}{5} = z + 0$$
$$-\frac{3}{5} = z$$

• Subtract $\frac{4}{5}$ from each side.

The solution is $-\frac{3}{5}$.

You Try It 6

$$4z = -20$$
$$\frac{4z}{4} = \frac{-20}{4}$$
$$1z = -5$$
$$z = -5$$

• Divide each side by 4.

The solution is -5.

You Try It 7

$$8 = \frac{2}{5}n$$
$$\left(\frac{5}{2}\right)(8) = \left(\frac{5}{2}\right)\frac{2}{5}n$$
$$20 = 1n$$
$$20 = n$$

• Multiply each side by $\frac{5}{2}$.

The solution is 20.

You Try It 8

$$\frac{2}{3}t - \frac{1}{3}t = -2$$
$$\frac{1}{3}t = -2$$
$$\left(\frac{3}{1}\right)\frac{1}{3}t = \left(\frac{3}{1}\right)(-2)$$
$$1t = -6$$
$$t = -6$$

• Combine like terms.
• Multiply each side by 3.

The solution is -6.

You Try It 9

Strategy   To find the regular price, replace the variables S and D in the formula by the given values and solve for R.

Solution

$$S = R - D$$
$$44 = R - 16$$
$$44 + 16 = R - 16 + 16$$
$$60 = R$$

The regular price is $60.

You Try It 10

Strategy   To find the monthly payment, replace the variables A and N in the formula by the given values and solve for M.

Solution

$$A = MN$$
$$6840 = M \cdot 24$$
$$6840 = 24M$$
$$\frac{6840}{24} = \frac{24M}{24}$$
$$285 = M$$

The monthly payment is $285.

SECTION 2.3

You Try It 1

$$5x + 8 = 6$$
$$5x + 8 - 8 = 6 - 8$$
$$5x = -2$$
$$\frac{5x}{5} = \frac{-2}{5}$$
$$x = -\frac{2}{5}$$

• Subtract 8 from each side.
• Divide each side by 5.

The solution is $-\frac{2}{5}$.

You Try It 2

$$7 - x = 3$$
$$7 - 7 - x = 3 - 7$$
$$-x = -4$$
$$(-1)(-x) = (-1)(-4)$$
$$x = 4$$

• Subtract 7 from each side.
• Multiply each side by -1.

The solution is 4.

You Try It 3

Strategy To find the Celsius temperature, replace the variable F in the formula by the given value and solve for C.

Solution
$$F = 1.8C + 32$$
$$-22 = 1.8C + 32 \quad \bullet \text{ Substitute } -22 \text{ for } F.$$
$$-22 - 32 = 1.8C + 32 - 32 \quad \bullet \text{ Subtract 32 from each side.}$$
$$-54 = 1.8C \quad \bullet \text{ Combine like terms.}$$
$$\frac{-54}{1.8} = \frac{1.8C}{1.8} \quad \bullet \text{ Divide each side by 1.8.}$$
$$-30 = C$$

The temperature is $-30°C$.

You Try It 4

Strategy To find the cost per unit, replace the variables T, N, and F in the formula by the given values and solve for U.

Solution
$$T = U \cdot N + F$$
$$4500 = U \cdot 250 + 1500$$
$$4500 = 250U + 1500$$
$$4500 - 1500 = 250U + 1500 - 1500$$
$$3000 = 250U$$
$$\frac{3000}{250} = \frac{250U}{250}$$
$$12 = U$$

The cost per unit is $12.

SECTION 2.4

You Try It 1 $\quad \frac{1}{5}x - 2 = \frac{2}{5}x + 4$

$$\frac{1}{5}x - \frac{2}{5}x - 2 = \frac{2}{5}x - \frac{2}{5}x + 4 \quad \bullet \text{ Subtract}$$
$$-\frac{1}{5}x - 2 = 4 \qquad \qquad \qquad \frac{2}{5}x \text{ from}$$
$$\text{each side.}$$
$$-\frac{1}{5}x - 2 + 2 = 4 + 2 \quad \bullet \text{ Add 2 to each side.}$$
$$-\frac{1}{5}x = 6$$
$$(-5)\left(-\frac{1}{5}x\right) = (-5)6 \quad \bullet \text{ Multiply each side by } -5.$$
$$x = -30$$

The solution is -30.

You Try It 2 $\quad 4(x - 1) - x = 5$
$$4x - 4 - x = 5$$
$$3x - 4 = 5$$
$$3x - 4 + 4 = 5 + 4$$
$$3x = 9$$
$$\frac{3x}{3} = \frac{9}{3}$$
$$x = 3$$

The solution is 3.

You Try It 3
$$2x - 7(3x + 1) = 5(5 - 3x)$$
$$2x - 21x - 7 = 25 - 15x \quad \bullet \text{ Distributive Property}$$
$$-19x - 7 = 25 - 15x \quad \bullet \text{ Combine like terms.}$$
$$-19x + 15x - 7 = 25 - 15x + 15x \quad \bullet \text{ Add } 15x \text{ to both sides.}$$
$$-4x - 7 = 25 \quad \bullet \text{ Combine like terms.}$$
$$-4x - 7 + 7 = 25 + 7 \quad \bullet \text{ Add 7 to both sides.}$$
$$-4x = 32 \quad \bullet \text{ Combine like terms.}$$
$$\frac{-4x}{-4} = \frac{32}{-4} \quad \bullet \text{ Divide each side by } -4.$$
$$x = -8$$

The solution is -8.

SECTION 2.5

You Try It 1 $\quad 8 - 2t$

You Try It 2 $\quad \dfrac{5}{7x}$

You Try It 3 The product of a number and one-half of the number

The unknown number: x

One-half the number: $\frac{1}{2}x$

$$(x)\left(\frac{1}{2}x\right)$$

SECTION 2.6

You Try It 1   The unknown number: x

A number increased by four	equals	twelve

$$x + 4 = 12$$
$$x + 4 - 4 = 12 - 4$$
$$x = 8$$

The number is 8.

You Try It 2   The unknown number: x

The product of two and a number	is	ten

$$2x = 10$$
$$\frac{2x}{2} = \frac{10}{2}$$
$$x = 5$$

The number is 5.

You Try It 3   The unknown number: x

The sum of three times a number and six	equals	four

$$3x + 6 = 4$$
$$3x + 6 - 6 = 4 - 6$$
$$3x = -2$$
$$\frac{3x}{3} = \frac{-2}{3}$$
$$x = -\frac{2}{3}$$

The number is $-\frac{2}{3}$.

You Try It 4   The unknown number: x

Three more than one-half of a number	is	nine

$$\frac{1}{2}x + 3 = 9$$
$$\frac{1}{2}x + 3 - 3 = 9 - 3$$
$$\frac{1}{2}x = 6$$
$$2 \cdot \frac{1}{2}x = 2 \cdot 6$$
$$x = 12$$

The number is 12.

You Try It 5

Strategy   To find the regular price, write and solve an equation using R to represent the regular price of the slacks.

Solution

$38.95	is	$11 less than the regular price

$$38.95 = R - 11$$
$$38.95 + 11 = R - 11 + 11$$
$$49.95 = R$$

The regular price of the slacks is $49.95.

You Try It 6

Strategy   To find the rpm of the engine when it is in third gear, write and solve an equation using R to represent the rpm of the engine in third gear.

Solution

2500	is	two-thirds of the rpm of the engine in third gear

$$2500 = \frac{2}{3}R$$
$$\frac{3}{2}(2500) = \left(\frac{3}{2}\right)\frac{2}{3}R$$
$$3750 = R$$

The rpm of the engine when in third gear is 3750 rpm.

You Try It 7

Strategy   To find the number of hours of labor, write and solve an equation using H to represent the number of hours of labor required.

Solution

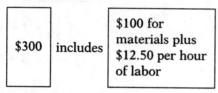

$$300 = 100 + 12.50H$$
$$300 - 100 = 100 - 100 + 12.50H$$
$$200 = 12.50H$$
$$\frac{200}{12.50} = \frac{12.50H}{12.50}$$
$$16 = H$$

16 h of labor are required.

You Try It 8

Strategy   To find the total sales, write and solve an equation using S to represent the total sales.

Solution

2500 is the sum of $800 and an 8% commission on total sales

$$2500 = 800 + 0.08S$$
$$2500 - 800 = 800 - 800 + 0.08S$$
$$1700 = 0.08S$$
$$\frac{1700}{0.08} = \frac{0.08S}{0.08}$$
$$21{,}250 = S$$

Natalie's total sales for the month were $21,250.

Solutions to Chapter 3 "You Try It"

SECTION 3.1

You Try It 1

$$x + 2 < -2$$
$$x + 2 - 2 < -2 - 2 \quad \bullet \text{ Subtract 2.}$$
$$x < -4$$

You Try It 2

$$5x + 3 > 4x + 5$$
$$5x - 4x + 3 > 4x - 4x + 5 \quad \bullet \text{ Subtract 4.}$$
$$x + 3 > 5$$
$$x + 3 - 3 > 5 - 3 \quad \bullet \text{ Subtract 3.}$$
$$x > 2$$

You Try It 3

$$-3x > -9$$
$$\frac{-3x}{-3} < \frac{-9}{-3} \quad \bullet \text{ Divide by } -3.$$
$$x < 3$$

You Try It 4

$$-\frac{3}{4}x \geq 18$$
$$-\frac{4}{3}\left(-\frac{3}{4}x\right) \leq -\frac{4}{3}(18) \quad \bullet \text{ Multiply by } -\frac{4}{3}.$$
$$x \leq -24$$

You Try It 5

Strategy   To find the selling prices, write and solve an inequality using p to represent the possible selling prices.

Solution $0.70p > 314$
$$p > 448.571 \quad \bullet \text{ Divide by 0.70.}$$

The dealer will make a profit with any selling price greater than or equal to $448.58.

SECTION 3.2

You Try It 1

$$5 - 4x > 9 - 8x$$
$$5 - 4x + 8x > 9 - 8x + 8x \quad \bullet \text{ Add 8x.}$$
$$5 + 4x > 9$$
$$5 - 5 + 4x > 9 - 5 \quad \bullet \text{ Subtract 5.}$$
$$4x > 4$$
$$\frac{4x}{4} > \frac{4}{4} \quad \bullet \text{ Divide by 4.}$$
$$x > 1$$

You Try It 2

$$8 - 4(3x + 5) \leq 6(x - 8)$$
$$8 - 12x - 20 \leq 6x - 48 \quad \bullet \text{ Distributive Property}$$
$$-12 - 12x \leq 6x - 48$$
$$-12 - 12x - 6x \leq 6x - 6x - 48 \quad \bullet \text{ Subtract 6x.}$$
$$-12 - 18x \leq -48$$
$$-12 + 12 - 18x \leq -48 + 12 \quad \bullet \text{ Add 12.}$$
$$-18x \leq -36$$
$$\frac{-18x}{-18} \geq \frac{-36}{-18} \quad \bullet \text{ Divide by } -18.$$
$$x \geq 2$$

You Try It 3

Strategy   To find the maximum number of miles:
- Write an expression for the cost of each car, using x to represent the number of miles driven during the week.
- Write and solve an inequality.

Solution

Cost of a Company A car	is less than	cost of a Company B car

$$8(7) + 0.10x < 10(7) + 0.08x$$
$$56 + 0.10x < 70 + 0.08x$$
$$56 + 0.10x - 0.08x < 70 + 0.08x - 0.08x \quad \bullet \text{ Subtract 0.08x.}$$
$$56 + 0.02x < 70$$
$$56 - 56 + 0.02x < 70 - 56 \quad \bullet \text{ Subtract 56.}$$
$$0.02x < 14$$
$$\frac{0.02x}{0.02} < \frac{14}{0.02} \quad \bullet \text{ Divide by 0.02.}$$
$$x < 700$$

The maximum number of miles is 699 mi.

SECTION 3.3

You Try It 1

$$x - 3y < 2$$
$$x - x - 3y < -x + 2$$
$$-3y < -x + 2 \qquad \bullet \text{ Subtract } x.$$
$$\frac{-3y}{-3} > \frac{-x + 2}{-3} \qquad \bullet \text{ Divide by } -3.$$
$$y > \frac{1}{3}x - \frac{2}{3}$$

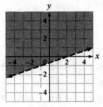

You Try It 2

$$2x - 4y \le 8$$
$$2x - 2x - 4y \le -2x + 8 \qquad \bullet \text{ Subtract } 2x.$$
$$-4y \le -2x + 8$$
$$\frac{-4y}{-4} \ge \frac{-2x + 8}{-4} \qquad \bullet \text{ Divide by } -4.$$
$$y \ge \frac{1}{2}x - 2$$

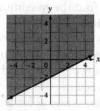

You Try It 3 $\quad x < 3$

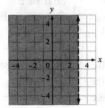

Solutions to Chapter 4 "You Try It"

SECTION 4.1

You Try It 1

$$\frac{20 \text{ pounds}}{24 \text{ pounds}} = \frac{20}{24} = \frac{5}{6}$$

20 pounds : 24 pounds = 20 : 24 = 5 : 6

20 pounds to 24 pounds = 20 to 24
$$= 5 \text{ to } 6$$

You Try It 2

$$\frac{64 \text{ miles}}{8 \text{ miles}} = \frac{64}{8} = \frac{8}{1}$$

64 miles : 8 miles = 64 : 8 = 8 : 1

64 miles to 8 miles = 64 to 8 = 8 to 1

You Try It 3

Strategy To find the ratio, write the ratio of board feet of cedar (12,000) to board feet of ash (18,000) in simplest form.

Solution $\dfrac{12,000}{18,000} = \dfrac{2}{3}$

The ratio is $\dfrac{2}{3}$.

You Try It 4

Strategy To find the ratio, write the ratio of the amount spent on radio advertising (45,000) to the amount spent on radio and television advertising (45,000 + 60,000) in simplest form.

Solution $\dfrac{\$45,000}{\$45,000 + \$60,000} = \dfrac{45,000}{105,000} = \dfrac{3}{7}$

The ratio is $\dfrac{3}{7}$.

SECTION 4.2

You Try It 1

$$\frac{15 \text{ pounds}}{12 \text{ trees}} = \frac{5 \text{ pounds}}{4 \text{ trees}}$$

You Try It 2

$$\frac{260 \text{ miles}}{8 \text{ hours}}$$

$$\begin{array}{r} 32.5 \\ 8)\overline{260.0} \end{array}$$

32.5 miles/hour

You Try It 3

Strategy To find Erik's profit per ounce:
- Find the total profit by subtracting the cost (\$1625) from the selling price (\$1720).
- Divide the total profit by the number of ounces (5).

Solution $1720 - 1625 = 95$

$95 \div 5 = 19$

The profit was \$19/ounce.

SECTION 4.3

You Try It 1

$$\frac{6}{10} \bowtie \frac{9}{15} \begin{array}{l} \rightarrow 10 \times 9 = 90 \\ \rightarrow 6 \times 15 = 90 \end{array}$$

The cross products are equal. The proportion is true.

You Try It 2

$$\frac{32}{6} \bowtie \frac{90}{8} \begin{array}{l} \rightarrow 6 \times 90 = 540 \\ \rightarrow 32 \times 8 = 256 \end{array}$$

The cross products are not equal. The proportion is not true.

You Try It 3

$$\frac{n}{14} = \frac{3}{7}$$

- **Find the cross products. Then solve for *n*.**

$n \times 7 = 14 \times 3$

$n \times 7 = 42$

$n = 42 \div 7$

$n = 6$

Check: $\dfrac{6}{14} \bowtie \dfrac{3}{7} \begin{array}{l} \rightarrow 14 \times 3 = 42 \\ \rightarrow 16 \times 7 = 42 \end{array}$

You Try It 4
$$\frac{5}{7} = \frac{n}{20}$$

• Find the cross products. Then solve for n.

$$5 \times 20 = 7 \times n$$
$$100 = 7 \times n$$
$$100 \div 7 = n$$
$$14.3 \approx n$$

You Try It 5
$$\frac{15}{20} = \frac{12}{n}$$

• Find the cross products. Then solve for n.

$$15 \times n = 20 \times 12$$
$$15 \times n = 240$$
$$n = 240 \div 15$$
$$n = 16$$

Check: $\dfrac{15}{20} \bowtie \dfrac{12}{16}$ → $20 \times 12 = 240$
→ $15 \times 16 = 240$

You Try It 6
$$\frac{12}{n} = \frac{7}{4}$$

$$12 \times 4 = n \times 7$$
$$48 = n \times 7$$
$$48 \div 7 = n$$
$$6.86 \approx n$$

You Try It 7
$$\frac{n}{12} = \frac{4}{1}$$

$$n \times 1 = 12 \times 4$$
$$n \times 1 = 48$$
$$n = 48 \div 1$$
$$n = 48$$

Check: $\dfrac{48}{12} \bowtie \dfrac{4}{1}$ → $12 \times 4 = 48$
→ $48 \times 1 = 48$

You Try It 8

Strategy To find the number of tablespoons of fertilizer needed, write and solve a proportion using n to represent the number of tablespoons of fertilizer.

Solution
$$\frac{3 \text{ tablespoons}}{4 \text{ gallons}} = \frac{n \text{ tablespoons}}{10 \text{ gallons}}$$

• The unit "tablespoons" is in the numerator. The unit "gallons" is in the denominator.

$$3 \times 10 = 4 \times n$$
$$30 = 4 \times n$$
$$30 \div 4 = n$$
$$7.5 = n$$

For 10 gallons of water, 7.5 tablespoons of fertilizer are required.

You Try It 9

Strategy To find the number of jars that can be packed in 15 boxes, write and solve a proportion using n to represent the number of jars.

Solution
$$\frac{24 \text{ jars}}{6 \text{ boxes}} = \frac{n \text{ jars}}{15 \text{ boxes}}$$

$$24 \times 15 = 6 \times n$$
$$360 = 6 \times n$$
$$360 \div 6 = n$$
$$60 = n$$

60 jars can be packed in 15 boxes.

Solutions to Chapter 5 "You Try It"

SECTION 5.1

You Try It 1   a. $125\% = 125 \times \dfrac{1}{100} = \dfrac{125}{100} = 1\dfrac{1}{4}$

b. $125\% = 125 \times 0.01 = 1.25$

You Try It 2 $33\dfrac{1}{3}\% = 33\dfrac{1}{3} \times \dfrac{1}{100}$

$= \dfrac{100}{3} \times \dfrac{1}{100}$

$= \dfrac{100}{300} = \dfrac{1}{3}$

You Try It 3 $0.25\% = 0.25 \times 0.01 = 0.0025$

You Try It 4 $0.048 = 0.048 \times 100\% = 4.8\%$

You Try It 5 $3.67 = 3.67 \times 100\% = 367\%$

You Try It 6 $0.62\dfrac{1}{2} = 0.62\dfrac{1}{2} \times 100\%$

$= 62\dfrac{1}{2}\%$

You Try It 7 $\dfrac{5}{6} = \dfrac{5}{6} \times 100\% = \dfrac{500}{6}\% = 83\dfrac{1}{3}\%$

You Try It 8 $1\dfrac{4}{9} = \dfrac{13}{9} = \dfrac{13}{9} \times 100\%$

$= \dfrac{1300}{9}\% \approx 144.4\%$

SECTION 5.2

You Try It 1   Percent $\times$ base = amount
$0.063 \times 150 = n$
$9.45 = n$

You Try It 2   Percent $\times$ base = amount
$\dfrac{1}{6} \times 66 = n$ • $16\dfrac{2}{3}\% = \dfrac{1}{6}$
$11 = n$

You Try It 3

Strategy   To determine the amount that came from corporations, write and solve the basic percent equation using n to represent the amount. The percent is 4%. The base is $212 billion.

Solution   Percent $\times$ base = amount
$4\% \times 212 = n$
$0.04 \times 212 = n$
$8.48 = n$

Corporations gave $8.48 billion to charities.

You Try It 4

Strategy   To find the new hourly wage:
• Find the amount of the raise. Write and solve the basic percent equation using n to represent the amount of the raise (amount). The percent is 8%. The base is $33.50.
• Add the amount of the raise to the old wage (33.50).

Solution $\begin{aligned} 8\% \times 33.50 &= n \\ 0.08 \times 33.50 &= n \\ 2.68 &= n \end{aligned}$ $\begin{aligned} 33.50 \\ +12.68 \\ \hline 36.18 \end{aligned}$

The new hourly wage is $36.18.

SECTION 5.3

You Try It 1   Percent $\times$ base = amount
$n \times 32 = 16$
$n = 16 \div 32$
$n = 0.50$
$n = 50\%$

You Try It 2   Percent $\times$ base = amount
$n \times 15 = 48$
$n = 48 \div 15$
$n = 3.2$
$n = 320\%$

You Try It 3   Percent $\times$ base = amount
$n \times 45 = 30$
$n = 30 \div 45$
$n = \dfrac{2}{3} = 66\dfrac{2}{3}\%$

You Try It 4

Strategy   To find what percent of the income the income tax is, write and solve the basic percent equation using n to represent the percent. The base is $33,500 and the amount is $5025.

Solution
$$n \times 33{,}500 = 5025$$
$$n = 5025 \div 33{,}500$$
$$n = 0.15 = 15\%$$

The income tax is 15% of the income.

You Try It 5

Strategy To find the percent who were women:
- Subtract to find the number of enlisted personnel who were women (518,921 − 512,370).
- Write and solve the basic percent equation using n to represent the percent. The base is 518,921, and the amount is the number of enlisted personnel who were women.

Solution $518{,}921 - 512{,}370 = 6551$

$$n \times 518{,}921 = 6551$$
$$n = 6551 \div 518{,}921$$
$$n \approx 0.013$$

In 1950, 1.3% of the enlisted personnel in the U.S. Army were women.

SECTION 5.4

You Try It 1 Percent × base = amount
$$0.86 \times n = 215$$
$$n = 215 \div 0.86$$
$$n = 250$$

You Try It 2 Percent × base = amount
$$0.025 \times n = 15$$
$$n = 15 \div 0.025$$
$$n = 600$$

You Try It 3 Percent × base = amount
$$\frac{1}{6} \times n = 5 \qquad \bullet\ 16\tfrac{2}{3}\% = \frac{1}{6}$$
$$n = 5 \div \frac{1}{6}$$
$$n = 30$$

You Try It 4

Strategy To find the original value of the car, write and solve the basic percent equation using n to represent the original value (base). The percent is 42% and the amount is $10,458.

Solution
$$42\% \times n = 10{,}458$$
$$0.42 \times n = 10{,}458$$
$$n = 10{,}458 \div 0.42$$
$$n = 24{,}900$$

The original value of the car was $24,900.

You Try It 5

Strategy To find the difference between the original price and the sale price:
- Find the original price. Write and solve the basic percent equation using n to represent the original price (base). The percent is 80% and the amount is $89.60.
- Subtract the sale price (89.60) from the original price.

Solution
$$80\% \times n = 89.60$$
$$0.80 \times n = 89.60$$
$$n = 89.60 \div 0.80$$
$$n = 112.00 \quad \text{(original price)}$$

$$112.00 - 89.60 = 22.40$$

The difference between the original price and the sale price is $22.40.

SECTION 5.5

You Try It 1
$$\frac{26}{100} = \frac{22}{n}$$
$$26 \times n = 100 \times 22$$
$$26 \times n = 2200$$
$$n = 2200 \div 26$$
$$n \approx 84.62$$

You Try It 2
$$\frac{16}{100} = \frac{n}{132}$$
$$16 \times 132 = 100 \times n$$
$$2112 = 100 \times n$$
$$2112 \div 100 = n$$
$$21.12 = n$$

You Try It 3

Strategy To find the number of days it snowed, write and solve a proportion using n to represent the number of days it snowed (amount). The percent is 64% and the base is 150.

Solution
$$\frac{64}{100} = \frac{n}{150}$$
$$64 \times 150 = 100 \times n$$
$$9600 = 100 \times n$$
$$9600 \div 100 = n$$
$$96 = n$$

It snowed 96 days.

You Try It 4

Strategy To find the percent of pens that were not defective:
- Subtract to find the number of pens that were not defective $(200 - 5)$.
- Write and solve a proportion using n to represent the percent of pens that were not defective. The base is 200, and the amount is the number of pens not defective.

Solution $200 - 5 = 195$ (number of pens not defective)

$$\frac{n}{100} = \frac{195}{200}$$
$$n \times 200 = 100 \times 195$$
$$n \times 200 = 19,500$$
$$n = 19,500 \div 200$$
$$n = 97.5$$

97.5% of the pens were not defective.

Solutions to Chapter 6 "You Try It"

SECTION 6.1

You Try It 1

Strategy   To find the unit cost, divide the total cost by the number of units.

Solution   **a.** $7.67 \div 8 = 0.95875$
$.959 per battery
b. $2.29 \div 15 \approx 0.153$
$.153 per ounce

You Try It 2

Strategy   To find the more economical purchase, compare the unit costs.

Solution $5.70 \div 6 = 0.95$
$3.96 \div 4 = 0.99$
$.95 < $.99

The more economical purchase is 6 cans for $5.70.

You Try It 3

Strategy   To find the total cost, multiply the unit cost (9.96) by the number of units (7).

Solution
$$\boxed{\text{Unit cost}} \times \boxed{\text{number of units}} = \boxed{\text{total cost}}$$
$$9.96 \quad \times \quad 7 \quad = \quad 69.72$$
The total cost is $69.72.

SECTION 6.2

You Try It 1

Strategy   To find the percent increase:
• Find the amount of the increase.
• Solve the basic percent equation for *percent*.

Solution
$$\boxed{\text{New value}} - \boxed{\text{original value}} = \boxed{\text{amount of increase}}$$
$$1.83 \quad - \quad 1.46 \quad = \quad 0.37$$
Percent × base = amount
$$n \quad \times 1.46 = \quad 0.37$$
$$n = 0.37 \div 1.46$$
$$n \approx 0.25 = 25\%$$

The percent increase was 25%.

You Try It 2

Strategy   To find the new hourly wage:
• Solve the basic percent equation for *amount*.
• Add the amount of the increase to the original wage.

Solution   Percent × base = amount
$$0.14 \quad \times 12.50 = \quad n$$
$$1.75 = n$$
$$12.50 + 1.75 = 14.25$$
The new hourly wage is $14.25.

You Try It 3

Strategy   To find the markup, solve the basic percent equation for *amount*.

Solution   Percent × base = amount
$$\boxed{\text{Markup rate}} \times \boxed{\text{cost}} = \boxed{\text{markup}}$$
$$0.20 \quad \times \quad 8 \quad = \quad n$$
$$1.60 = n$$
The markup is $1.60.

You Try It 4

Strategy   To find the selling price:
• Find the markup by solving the basic percent equation for *amount*.
• Add the markup to the cost.

Solution   Percent × base = amount
$$\boxed{\text{Markup rate}} \times \boxed{\text{cost}} = \boxed{\text{markup}}$$
$$0.55 \quad \times \quad 72 \quad = \quad n$$
$$39.60 = n$$

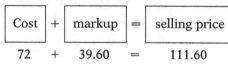
$$\boxed{\text{Cost}} + \boxed{\text{markup}} = \boxed{\text{selling price}}$$
$$72 \quad + \quad 39.60 \quad = \quad 111.60$$
The selling price is $111.60.

You Try It 5

Strategy   To find the percent decrease:
• Find the amount of the decrease.
• Solve the basic percent equation for *percent*.

Solution
$$\boxed{\text{Original value}} - \boxed{\text{new value}} = \boxed{\text{amount of decrease}}$$
$$261{,}000 \quad - \quad 215{,}000 = \quad 46{,}000$$

Percent × base = amount
$$n \times 261{,}000 = 46{,}000$$
$$n = 46{,}000 \div 261{,}000$$
$$n \approx 0.176$$

The percent decrease is 17.6%.

You Try It 6

Strategy To find the visibility:
- Find the amount of decrease by solving the basic percent equation for *amount*.
- Subtract the amount of decrease from the original visibility.

Solution Percent × base = amount
$$0.40 \times 5 = n$$
$$2 = n$$
$$5 - 2 = 3$$

The visibility was 3 miles.

You Try It 7

Strategy To find the discount rate:
- Find the discount.
- Solve the basic percent equation for *percent*.

Solution

Regular price	−	sale price	=	discount
12.50	−	10.99	=	1.51

Percent	×	base	=	amount
Discount rate	×	regular price	=	discount
n	×	12.50	=	1.51

$$n = 1.51 \div 12.50$$
$$n = 0.1208$$

The discount rate is 12.1%.

You Try It 8

Strategy To find the sale price:
- Find the discount by solving the basic percent equation for *amount*.
- Subtract to find the sale price.

Solution

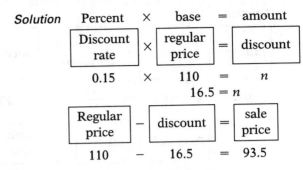

Percent	×	base	=	amount
Discount rate	×	regular price	=	discount
0.15	×	110	=	n
			16.5	= n

Regular price	−	discount	=	sale price
110	−	16.5	=	93.5

The sale price is $93.50.

SECTION 6.3

You Try It 1

Strategy To find the simple interest due, multiply the principal (15,000) times the annual interest rate (8% = 0.08) times the time, in years $\left(18 \text{ months} = \frac{18}{12} \text{ years} = 1.5 \text{ years}\right)$.

Solution

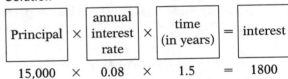

Principal	×	annual interest rate	×	time (in years)	=	interest
15,000	×	0.08	×	1.5	=	1800

The interest due is $1800.

You Try It 2

Strategy To find the maturity value:
- Use the simple interest formula to find the simple interest due.
- Find the maturity value by adding the principal and the interest.

Solution

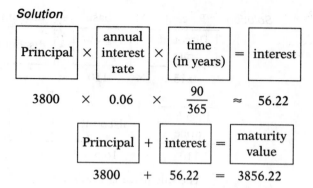

3800 × 0.06 × $\frac{90}{365}$ ≈ 56.22

Principal	+	interest	=	maturity value
3800	+	56.22	=	3856.22

The maturity value is $3856.22.

You Try It 3

Strategy To find the monthly payment:
- Find the maturity value by adding the principal and the interest.
- Divide the maturity value by the length of the loan in months (12).

Solution Principal + interest = maturity value
    1900   +   152   =   2052

Maturity value ÷ length of the loan = payment
    2052   ÷   12   =   171

The monthly payment is $171.

You Try It 4

Strategy To find the finance charge, multiply the principal, or unpaid balance (1250), times the monthly interest rate (1.6%) times the number of months (1).

Solution

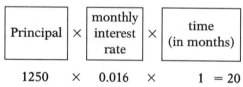

1250 × 0.016 × 1 = 20

The simple interest due is $20.

You Try It 5

Strategy To find the interest earned:
- Find the new principal by multiplying the original principal (1000) by the factor found in the Compound Interest Table (3.29066).
- Subtract the original principal from the new principal.

Solution 1000 × 3.29066 = 3290.66

The new principal is $3290.66.

3290.66 − 1000 = 2290.66

The interest earned is $2290.66.

SECTION 6.4

You Try It 1

Strategy To find the worker's earnings:
- Find the worker's overtime wage by multiplying the hourly wage by 2.
- Multiply the number of overtime hours worked by the overtime wage.

Solution 18.50 × 2 = 37

The hourly wage for overtime is $37.

37 × 8 = 296

The construction worker earns $296.

You Try It 2

Strategy To find the salary per month, divide the annual salary by the number of months in a year (12).

Solution 48,228 ÷ 12 = 4019

The contractor's monthly salary is $4019.

You Try It 3

Strategy   To find the total earnings:
- Find the sales over $50,000.
- Multiply the commission rate by sales over $50,000.
- Add the commission to the annual salary.

Solution $175,000 - 50,000 = 125,000$

Sales over $50,000 totaled $125,000.

$125,000 \times 0.095 = 11,875$

Earnings from commissions totaled $11,875.

$27,000 + 11,875 = 38,875$

The insurance agent earned $38,875.

SECTION 6.5

You Try It 1

Strategy   To find the current balance:
- Subtract the amount of the check from the old balance.
- Add the amount of each deposit.

Solution

$$\begin{array}{r} 302.46 \\ -\ 320.59 \end{array} \text{check}$$

$$\begin{array}{r} 281.87 \\ 176.86 \quad \text{first deposit} \\ +\ 194.73 \quad \text{second deposit} \\ \hline 553.46 \end{array}$$

The current checking account balance is $553.46.

You Try It 2

Current checkbook balance:	623.41
Check: 237	+ 678.73
	702.14
Interest:	+ 702.11
	704.25
Deposit:	− 523.84
	180.41

Closing bank balance from bank statement: $180.41

Checkbook balance: $180.41

The bank statement and the checkbook balance.

Solutions to Chapter 7 "You Try It"

SECTION 7.1

You Try It 1
$$QT = QR + RS + ST$$
$$62 = 24 + RS + 17$$
$$62 = 41 + RS$$
$$62 - 41 = 41 - 41 + RS$$
$$21 = RS$$

You Try It 2 Let x represent the supplement of a $32°$ angle. The sum of supplementary angles is $180°$.
$$x + 32° = 180°$$
$$x + 32° - 32° = 180° - 32°$$
$$x = 148°$$

$148°$ is the supplement of $32°$.

You Try It 3
$$\angle a + 68° = 118°$$
$$\angle a + 68° - 68° = 118° - 68°$$
$$\angle a = 50°$$

You Try It 4 In a right triangle, one angle measures $90°$ and the two acute angles are complementary.
$$\angle A + \angle B = 90°$$
$$\angle A + 7° = 90°$$
$$\angle A + 7° - 7° = 90° - 7°$$
$$\angle A = 83°$$

The other angles measure $90°$ and $83°$.

You Try It 5 The sum of the three angles of a triangle is $180°$.
$$\angle A + \angle B + \angle C = 180°$$
$$\angle A + 62° + 45° = 180°$$
$$\angle A + 107° = 180°$$
$$\angle A + 107° - 107° = 180° - 107°$$
$$\angle A = 73°$$

The measure of the other angle is $73°$.

You Try It 6
$$r = \frac{1}{2}d$$
$$r = \frac{1}{2}(8 \text{ in.}) = 4 \text{ in.}$$

The radius is 4 in.

You Try It 7 Angles a and b are supplementary angles.
$$\angle a + \angle b = 180°$$
$$125° + \angle b = 180°$$
$$125° - 125° + \angle b = 180° - 125°$$
$$\angle b = 55°$$

You Try It 8 $\angle c$ and $\angle a$ are corresponding angles. Corresponding angles are equal.
$$\angle c = \angle a = 120°$$

$\angle b$ and $\angle c$ are supplementary angles.
$$\angle b + \angle c = 180°$$
$$\angle b + 120° = 180°$$
$$\angle b + 120° - 120° = 180° - 120°$$
$$\angle b = 60°$$

SECTION 7.2

You Try It 1
$$P = 2L + 2W$$
$$= 2(2 \text{ m}) + 2(0.85 \text{ m})$$
$$= 4 \text{ m} + 1.7 \text{ m}$$
$$= 5.7 \text{ m}$$

The perimeter of the rectangle is 5.7 m.

You Try It 2
$$P = a + b + c$$
$$= 12 \text{ cm} + 15 \text{ cm} + 18 \text{ cm}$$
$$= 45 \text{ cm}$$

The perimeter of the triangle is 45 cm.

You Try It 3
$$C = \pi d$$
$$\approx 3.14 \cdot 6 \text{ in.}$$
$$= 18.84 \text{ in.}$$

The circumference is approximately 18.84 in.

You Try It 4 $$\text{Perimeter of composite figure} = \text{two lengths of a rectangle} + \text{the circumference of a circle}$$

$$P = 2L + \pi d$$
$$\approx 2(8 \text{ in.}) + 3.14(3 \text{ in.})$$
$$= 16 \text{ in.} + 9.42 \text{ in.}$$
$$= 25.42 \text{ in.}$$

The perimeter is approximately 25.42 in.

You Try It 5

Strategy To find the perimeter, use the formula for the perimeter of a rectangle.

Solution $$P = 2L + 2W$$
$$= 2(11 \text{ in.}) + 2\left(8\frac{1}{2} \text{ in.}\right)$$
$$= 22 \text{ in.} + 17 \text{ in.}$$
$$= 39 \text{ in.}$$

The perimeter of the computer paper is 39 in.

You Try It 6

Strategy To find the cost:
• Find the perimeter of the workbench.
• Multiply the perimeter by the per meter cost of the stripping.

Solution $$P = 2L + 2W$$
$$= 2(3 \text{ m}) + 2(0.74 \text{ m})$$
$$= 6 \text{ m} + 1.48 \text{ m}$$
$$= 7.48 \text{ m}$$

$$\$2.76 \times 7.48 = \$20.6448$$

The cost is $20.64.

SECTION 7.3

You Try It 1 $$A = \frac{1}{2}bh = \frac{1}{2}(24 \text{ in.})(14 \text{ in.}) = 168 \text{ in}^2$$

The area is 168 in².

You Try It 2

$$A = \text{area of rectangle} - \text{area of triangle}$$
$$A = LW - \frac{1}{2}bh$$
$$= (10 \text{ in.} \times 6 \text{ in.}) - \left(\frac{1}{2} \times 6 \text{ in.} \times 4 \text{ in.}\right)$$
$$= 60 \text{ in}^2 - 12 \text{ in}^2$$
$$= 48 \text{ in}^2$$

The area is 48 in².

You Try It 3

Strategy To find the area of the room:
• Find the area in square feet.
• Convert to square yards.

Solution $$A = LW$$
$$= 12 \text{ ft} \cdot 9 \text{ ft}$$
$$= 108 \text{ ft}^2$$

$$108 \text{ ft}^2 \times \frac{1 \text{ yd}^2}{9 \text{ ft}^2} = \frac{108}{9} \text{ yd}^2$$
$$= 12 \text{ yd}^2$$

The area of the room is 12 yd².

SECTION 7.4

You Try It 1 $$V = LWH$$
$$= (8 \text{ cm})(3.5 \text{ cm})(4 \text{ cm})$$
$$= 112 \text{ cm}^3$$

The volume is 112 cm³.

You Try It 2 $$V = s^3$$
$$= (5 \text{ cm})^3$$
$$= 125 \text{ cm}^3$$

The volume is 125 cm³.

You Try It 3 $$r = \frac{1}{2}d = \frac{1}{2}(14 \text{ in.}) = 7 \text{ in.}$$

$$V = \pi r^2 h$$
$$\approx \frac{22}{7}(7 \text{ in.})^2(15 \text{ in.})$$
$$= 2310 \text{ in}^3$$

The volume is approximately 2310 in³.

You Try It 4 $$V = \frac{4}{3}\pi r^3$$
$$\approx \frac{4}{3}(3.14)(3 \text{ m})^3$$
$$= 113.04 \text{ m}^3$$

The volume is approximately 113.04 m³.

You Try It 5
$$V = \text{volume of rectangular solid} + \text{volume of cylinder}$$

$$V = LWH + \pi r^2 h$$
$$\approx (1.5 \text{ m})(0.4 \text{ m})(0.4 \text{ m}) + 3.14(0.8 \text{ m})^2(0.2 \text{ m})$$
$$= 0.24 \text{ m}^3 + 0.40192 \text{ m}^3$$
$$= 0.64192 \text{ m}^3$$

The volume is approximately 0.64192 m³.

You Try It 6

V = volume of rectangular solid

$\quad + \dfrac{1}{2}$ the volume of cylinder

$V = LWH + \dfrac{1}{2}\pi r^2 h$

$\quad \approx (24 \text{ in.})(6 \text{ in.})(4 \text{ in.}) + \dfrac{1}{2}(3.14)(3 \text{ in.})^2(24 \text{ in.})$

$\quad = 576 \text{ in}^3 + 339.12 \text{ in}^3$

$\quad = 915.12 \text{ in}^3$

The volume is approximately 915.12 in³.

You Try It 7

Strategy To find the volume of the freezer, use the formula for the volume of a rectangular solid.

Solution $V = LWH$
$\quad = (7 \text{ ft})(2.5 \text{ ft})(3 \text{ ft})$
$\quad = 52.5 \text{ ft}^3$

The volume of the freezer is 52.5 ft³.

You Try It 8

Strategy
To find the volume of the channel iron, subtract the volume of the cut-out rectangular solid from the large rectangular solid.

Solution

$V = LWH - LWH$
$\quad = (10 \text{ ft})(0.5 \text{ ft})(0.8 \text{ ft}) - (10 \text{ ft})(0.3 \text{ ft})(0.2 \text{ ft})$
$\quad = 4 \text{ ft}^3 - 0.6 \text{ ft}^3$
$\quad = 3.4 \text{ ft}^3$

The volume of the channel iron is 3.4 ft³.

SECTION 7.5

You Try It 1 **a.** $\sqrt{16} = 4$
$\qquad \sqrt{169} = 13$

b. $\sqrt{32} \approx 5.657$
$\quad \sqrt{162} \approx 12.728$

You Try It 2 Hypotenuse $= \sqrt{(\text{leg})^2 + (\text{leg})^2}$
$\qquad\qquad = \sqrt{8^2 + 11^2}$
$\qquad\qquad = \sqrt{64 + 121}$
$\qquad\qquad = \sqrt{185}$
$\qquad\qquad \approx 13.601$

The hypotenuse is approximately 13.601 in.

You Try It 3 Leg $= \sqrt{(\text{hypotenuse})^2 - (\text{leg})^2}$
$\qquad\quad = \sqrt{12^2 - 5^2}$
$\qquad\quad = \sqrt{144 - 25}$
$\qquad\quad = \sqrt{119}$
$\qquad\quad \approx 10.909$

The length of the leg is approximately 10.909 ft.

You Try It 4

Strategy To find the distance between the holes, use the Pythagorean Theorem. The hypotenuse is the distance between the holes. The length of each leg is given (3 cm and 8 cm).

Solution Hypotenuse $= \sqrt{(\text{leg})^2 + (\text{leg})^2}$
$\qquad\qquad = \sqrt{3^2 + 8^2}$
$\qquad\qquad = \sqrt{9 + 64}$
$\qquad\qquad = \sqrt{73}$
$\qquad\qquad \approx 8.544$

The distance is approximately 8.544 cm.

Solutions to Chapter 8 "You Try It"

SECTION 8.1

You Try It 1 $14 \text{ ft} = 14 \cancel{\text{ft}} \times \dfrac{1 \text{ yd}}{3 \cancel{\text{ft}}} = \dfrac{14 \text{ yd}}{3} = 4\dfrac{2}{3} \text{ yd}$

You Try It 2 $9240 \text{ ft} = 9240 \cancel{\text{ft}} \times \dfrac{1 \text{ mi}}{5280 \cancel{\text{ft}}}$

$= \dfrac{9240 \text{ mi}}{5280} = 1\dfrac{3}{4} \text{ mi}$

You Try It 3

$$12\overline{)\begin{array}{r} 3 \text{ ft } 6 \text{ in.} \\ -42 \\ \hline \end{array}}$$
$$\begin{array}{r} -36 \\ \hline 6 \end{array}$$

• **12 in. = 1 ft**

42 in. = 3 ft 6 in.

You Try It 4

$$3\overline{)\begin{array}{r} 4 \text{ yd } 2 \text{ ft} \\ -14 \\ \hline \end{array}}$$
$$\begin{array}{r} -12 \\ \hline 2 \end{array}$$

• **3 ft = 1 yd**

14 ft = 4 yd 2 ft

You Try It 5

$$\begin{array}{r} 3 \text{ ft } 15 \text{ in.} \\ + 4 \text{ ft } 19 \text{ in.} \\ \hline 7 \text{ ft } 14 \text{ in.} \end{array}$$

• **14 in. = 1 ft 2 in.**

7 ft 14 in. = 8 ft 2 in.

You Try It 6

$$\begin{array}{r} {}^{3 \text{ ft}}{}^{14 \text{ in.}} \\ \cancel{4 \text{ ft } 2 \text{ in.}} \\ - 1 \text{ ft } 8 \text{ in.} \\ \hline 2 \text{ ft } 6 \text{ in.} \end{array}$$

• **Borrow 1 ft (12 in.) from 4 ft and add it to 2 in.**

You Try It 7

$$\begin{array}{r} 4 \text{ yd } 1 \text{ ft} \\ \times \ 4 \text{ yd } 8 \text{ ft} \\ \hline 32 \text{ yd } 8 \text{ ft} \end{array}$$

• **8 ft = 2 yd 2 ft**

32 yd 8 ft = 34 yd 2 ft

You Try It 8

$$2\overline{)\begin{array}{r} 3 \text{ yd} = 2 \text{ ft} \\ -7 \text{ yd} = 1 \text{ ft} \\ \hline \end{array}}$$
$$\begin{array}{r} -6 \text{ yd} = 3 \text{ ft} \\ \hline 1 \text{ yd} = 3 \text{ ft} \\ 4 \text{ ft} \\ -4 \text{ ft} \\ \hline 0 \end{array}$$

You Try It 9 $6\dfrac{1}{4} \text{ ft} = 6\dfrac{3}{12} \text{ ft} = 5\dfrac{15}{12} \text{ ft}$

$$\begin{array}{r} -3\dfrac{2}{3} \text{ ft} = 3\dfrac{8}{12} \text{ ft} = 3\dfrac{8}{12} \text{ ft} \\ \hline 2\dfrac{7}{12} \text{ ft} \end{array}$$

You Try It 10

Strategy   To find the width of the storage room:
• Multiply the number of tiles (8) by the width of each tile (9 in.).
• Divide the result by the number of inches in 1 foot (12) to find the width in feet.

Solution   9 in. × 8 = 72 in.

$72 \div 12 = 6$

The width is 6 ft.

You Try It 11

Strategy   To find the length of each piece, divide the total length (9 ft 8 in.) by the number of pieces (4).

Solution

$$4\overline{)\begin{array}{r} 2 \text{ ft} = 15 \text{ in.} \\ -9 \text{ ft} = 18 \text{ in.} \\ \hline \end{array}}$$
$$\begin{array}{r} -8 \text{ ft} = 12 \text{ in.} \\ \hline 1 \text{ ft} = 12 \text{ in.} \\ 20 \text{ in.} \\ -20 \text{ in.} \\ \hline 0 \text{ in.} \end{array}$$

Each piece is 2 ft 5 in. long.

SECTION 8.2

You Try It 1 $3 \text{ lb} = 3 \cancel{\text{lb}} \times \dfrac{16 \text{ oz}}{1 \cancel{\text{lb}}} = 48 \text{ oz}$

You Try It 2 $4200 \text{ lb} = 4200 \cancel{\text{lb}} \times \dfrac{1 \text{ ton}}{2000 \cancel{\text{lb}}}$

$= \dfrac{4200 \text{ tons}}{2000} = 2\dfrac{1}{10} \text{ tons}$

You Try It 3

$$\begin{array}{r} {}^{6 \text{ lb}}{}^{17 \text{ oz}} \\ \cancel{7 \text{ lb } 11 \text{ oz}} \\ - 3 \text{ lb } 14 \text{ oz} \\ \hline 3 \text{ lb } 13 \text{ oz} \end{array}$$

• **Borrow 1 lb (16 oz) from 7 lb and add it to 1 oz.**

You Try It 4

$$\begin{array}{r} 3 \text{ lb } 6 \text{ oz} \\ \times \ 3 \text{ lb } 4 \text{ oz} \\ \hline 12 \text{ lb } 24 \text{ oz} = 13 \text{ lb } 8 \text{ oz} \end{array}$$

You Try It 5

Strategy   To find the weight of 12 bars of soap:
- Multiply the number of bars (12) by the weight of each bar (7 oz).
- Convert the number of ounces to pounds.

Solution

$$\begin{array}{r} 12 \text{ oz} \\ \times\ 17 \text{ oz} \\ \hline 84 \text{ oz} \end{array} \qquad 84 \cancel{\text{oz}} \times \frac{1 \text{ lb}}{16 \cancel{\text{oz}}} = 5\frac{1}{4} \text{ lb}$$

The 12 bars of soap weigh $5\frac{1}{4}$ lb.

SECTION 8.3

You Try It 1

$$18 \text{ pt} = 18 \cancel{\text{pt}} \times \frac{1 \cancel{\text{qt}}}{2 \cancel{\text{pt}}} \times \frac{1 \text{ gal}}{4 \cancel{\text{qt}}}$$
$$= \frac{18 \text{ gal}}{8} = 2\frac{1}{4} \text{ gal}$$

You Try It 2

$$\begin{array}{r} 1 \text{ gal} = 2 \text{ qt} \\ 3\overline{)-4 \text{ gal} = 2 \text{ qt}} \\ \underline{-3 \text{ gal} = 4 \text{ qt}} \\ 1 \text{ gal} = \underline{4 \text{ qt}} \\ 6 \text{ qt} \\ \underline{-6 \text{ qt}} \\ 0 \text{ qt} \end{array}$$

You Try It 3

Strategy   To find the number of gallons of water needed:
- Find the number of quarts required by multiplying the number of quarts one student needs per day (5) by the number of students (5) by the number of days (3).
- Convert the number of quarts to gallons.

Solution $5 \times 5 \times 3 = 75$ qt

$$75 \cancel{\text{qt}} \cdot \frac{1 \text{ gal}}{4 \cancel{\text{qt}}} = \frac{75 \text{ gal}}{4} = 18\frac{3}{4} \text{ gal}$$

The students should take $18\frac{3}{4}$ gal of water.

SECTION 8.4

You Try It 1

$$18{,}000 \text{ s} = 18{,}000 \cancel{\text{s}} \times \frac{1 \cancel{\text{min}}}{60 \cancel{\text{s}}} \times \frac{1 \text{ h}}{60 \cancel{\text{min}}}$$
$$= \frac{18{,}000 \text{ h}}{3600} = 5 \text{ h}$$

SECTION 8.5

You Try It 1

$$4.5 \text{ Btu} = 4.5 \cancel{\text{Btu}} \times \frac{778 \text{ ft} \cdot \text{lb}}{1 \cancel{\text{Btu}}}$$
$$= 3501 \text{ ft} \cdot \text{lb}$$

You Try It 2

$$\text{Energy} = 800 \text{ lb} \times 16 \text{ ft} = 12{,}800 \text{ ft} \cdot \text{lb}$$

You Try It 3

$$56{,}000 \text{ Btu} =$$
$$56{,}000 \cancel{\text{Btu}} \times \frac{778 \text{ ft} \cdot \text{lb}}{1 \cancel{\text{Btu}}} =$$
$$43{,}568{,}000 \text{ ft} \cdot \text{lb}$$

You Try It 4

$$\text{Power} = \frac{90 \text{ ft} \times 1200 \text{ lb}}{24 \text{ s}}$$
$$= 4500 \frac{\text{ft} \cdot \text{lb}}{\text{s}}$$

You Try It 5

$$\frac{3300}{550} = 6 \text{ hp}$$

Solutions to Chapter 9 "You Try It"

SECTION 9.1

You Try It 1   3.07 m = 307 cm

You Try It 2   750 m = 0.750 km

3 km 750 m = 3 km + 0.750 km
                    = 3.750 km

You Try It 3

Strategy   To find the cost of the shelves:
- Multiply the length of the bookcase (175 cm) by the number of shelves (4).
- Convert centimeters to meters.
- Multiply the number of meters by the cost per meter ($15.75).

Solution   175 cm
              $\times$ 114
                700 cm

700 cm = 7 m

                15.75
            $\times$ $15.77
              110.25

The cost of the shelves is $110.25.

SECTION 9.2

You Try It 1   42.3 mg = 0.0423 g

You Try It 2   54 mg = 0.054 g

3 g 54 mg = 3 g + 0.054 g
                 = 3.054 g

You Try It 3

Strategy   To find how much fertilizer is required:
- Convert 300 g to kilograms.
- Multiply the number of kilograms by the number of trees (400).

Solution   300 g = 0.3 kg

               400 kg
           $\times$ 40.3 kg
             120.0 kg

To fertilize the trees, 120 kg of fertilizer are required.

SECTION 9.3

You Try It 1   2 kl = 2000 L

2 kl 167 L = 2000 L + 167 L
                   = 2167 L

You Try It 2   325 cm^3 = 325 ml = 0.325 L

You Try It 3

Strategy   To find the profit:
- Convert 5 L to milliliters.
- Find the number of jars by dividing the number of milliliters by the number of milliliters in each jar (125).
- Multiply the number of jars by the cost per jar ($.85).
- Find the total cost by adding the cost of the jars to the cost for the moisturizer ($299.50).
- Find the income by multiplying the number of jars by the selling price per jar ($29.95).
- Subtract the total cost from the income.

Solution   5 L = 5000 ml

5000 $\div$ 125 = 40   This is the number of jars.

              0.85
        $\times$ 40
             34.00   This is the cost of the jars.

          299.50
        +   34.00
          333.50   This is the total cost.

           29.95
        $\times$ 40
         1198.00   This is the income from sales.

         1198.00
        − $333.50
          864.50

The profit on the 5 L of moisturizer is $864.50.

SECTION 9.4

You Try It 1

Strategy   To find the number of Calories burned off, multiply the number of hours spent doing housework $\left(4\frac{1}{2}\right)$ by the Calories used per hour (240).

Solution $4\frac{1}{2} \times 240 = \frac{9}{2} \times 240 = 1080$

Doing $4\frac{1}{2}$ h of housework burns off 1080 Calories.

You Try It 2

Strategy   To find the number of kilowatt-hours used:
- Find the number of watt-hours used.
- Convert watt-hours to kilowatt-hours.

Solution $150 \times 200 = 30,000$
30,000 Wh = 30 kWh

30 kWh of energy are used.

You Try It 3

Strategy   To find the cost:
- Convert 20 min to hours.
- Multiply to find the total number of hours the oven is used.
- Multiply the number of hours used by the number of watts to find the watt-hours.
- Convert watt-hours to kilowatt-hours.
- Multiply the number of kilowatt-hours by the cost per kilowatt-hour.

Solution $20 \text{ min} = 20 \text{ min} \times \dfrac{1 \text{ h}}{60 \text{ min}}$

$\qquad\qquad = \dfrac{20}{60} \text{ h} = \dfrac{1}{3} \text{ h}$

$\dfrac{1}{3} \text{ h} \times 30 = 10 \text{ h}$

$10 \text{ h} \times 500 \text{ W} = 5000 \text{ Wh}$

$5000 \text{ Wh} = 5 \text{ kWh}$

$5 \times 8.7¢ = 43.5¢$

Solutions to Chapter 10 "You Try It"

SECTION 10.1

You Try It 1

Strategy   To find what percent of the total number of cellular phones purchased the number purchased in March represents:
- Read the pictograph to determine the number of cellular phones purchased for each month.
- Find the total cellular phone purchases for the 4-month period.
- Solve the basic percent equation for percent (n). Amount = 3000; the base is the total sales for the 4-month period.

Solution   4,500
3,500
3,000
$\underline{11,500}$
12,500

$$\text{Percent} \times \text{base} = \text{amount}$$
$$n \times 12{,}500 = 3000$$
$$n = 3000 \div 12{,}500$$
$$n = 0.24$$

The number of cellular phones purchased in March represents 24% of the total number of cellular phones purchased.

You Try It 2

Strategy   To find the ratio of the annual cost of fuel to the annual cost of maintenance:
- Locate the annual fuel cost and the annual maintenance cost in the circle graph.
- Write the ratio of the annual fuel cost to the annual maintenance cost in simplest form.

Solution   Annual fuel cost: $700
Annual maintenance cost: $500
$$\frac{700}{500} = \frac{7}{5}$$

The ratio is $\frac{7}{5}$.

You Try It 3

Strategy   To find the amount paid for medical/dental insurance:
- Locate the percent of the distribution that is medical/dental insurance.
- Solve the basic percent equation for amount.

Solution   The percent of the distribution that is medical/dental insurance: 6%

$$\text{Percent} \times \text{base} = \text{amount}$$
$$0.06 \times 2900 = n$$
$$174 = n$$

The amount paid for medical/dental insurance is $174.

SECTION 10.2

You Try It 1

Strategy   To write the ratio:
- Read the graph to find the lung capacity of an inactive female and of an athletic female.
- Write the ratio in simplest form.

Solution   Lung capacity of an inactive female: 25
Lung capacity of an athletic female: 55

$$\frac{25}{55} = \frac{5}{11}$$

The ratio is $\frac{5}{11}$.

You Try It 2

Strategy To determine between which two years the net income of Math Associates increased the most:
- Read the line graph to determine the net income of Math Associates for each of the years shown.
- Subtract to find the difference between each two years.
- Find the greatest difference.

Solution 2000: $1 million
2001: $3 million
2002: $5 million
2003: $8 million
2004: $12 million

Between 2000 and 2001: $3 - 1 = 2$
Between 2001 and 2002: $5 - 3 = 2$
Between 2002 and 2003: $8 - 5 = 3$
Between 2003 and 2004: $12 - 8 = 4$

$4 > 3 > 2$

The net income of Math Associates increased the most between 2003 and 2004.

SECTION 10.3

You Try It 1

Strategy To find the number of employees:
- Read the histogram to find the number of employees whose hourly wage is between $10 and $12 and the number whose hourly wage is between $12 and $14.
- Add the two numbers.

Solution Number whose wage is between $10 and $12: 7
Number whose wage is between $12 and $14: 15

$7 + 15 = 22$

22 employees earn between $10 and $14.

You Try It 2

Strategy To write the ratio:
- Read the graph to find the number of states with a per capita income between $28,000 and $32,000 and the number with a per capita income between $32,000 and $36,000.
- Write the ratio in simplest form.

Solution Number of states with a per capita income between $28,000 and $32,000: 18
Number of states with a per capita income between $32,000 and $36,000: 9

$$\frac{18}{9} = \frac{2}{1}$$

The ratio is $\frac{2}{1}$.

SECTION 10.4

You Try It 1

Strategy To find the mean amount spent by the 12 customers:
- Find the sum of the numbers.
- Divide the sum by the number of customers (12).

Solution $6.26 + 8.23 + 5.09 + 8.11 + 7.50 + 6.69 + 5.66 + 4.89 + 5.25 + 9.36 + 6.75 + 7.05 = 80.84$

$$\bar{x} = \frac{80.84}{12} \approx 6.74$$

The mean amount spent by the 12 customers was $6.74.

You Try It 2

Strategy To find the median weight loss:
- Arrange the weight losses from smallest to largest.
- Because there is an even number of values, the median is the mean of the middle two numbers.

Solution   10, 14, 16, 16, 22, 27, 29, 31, 31, 40

$$\text{Median} = \frac{22 + 27}{2} = \frac{49}{2} = 24.5$$

The median weight loss was 24.5 pounds.

You Try It 3

Strategy   To draw the box-and-whiskers plot:
- Find the median, Q_1, and Q_3.
- Use the smallest value, Q_1, the median, Q_3, and the largest value to draw the box-and-whiskers plot.

Solution

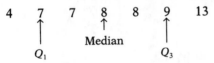

a.

Median

Q_1 | Q_3

4   7 8 9   13

b. Answers about the spread of the data will vary. For example, in You Try It 3, the values in the interquartile range are all very close to the median. They are not so close to the median in Example 3. The whiskers are long with respect to the box in You Try It 3, whereas they are short with respect to the box in Example 3. This shows that the data values outside the interquartile range are closer together in Example 3 than in You Try It 3.

SECTION 10.5

You Try It 1

Strategy   To find the probability:
- List the outcomes of the experiment in a systematic way. We will use a table.
- Use the table to count the number of possible outcomes of the experiment.
- Count the number of outcomes of the experiment that are favorable to the event of 2 true questions and 1 false question.
- Use the probability formula.

Solution

Question 1	Question 2	Question 3
T	T	T
T	T	F
T	F	T
T	F	F
F	T	T
F	T	F
F	F	T
F	F	F

There are 8 possible outcomes:

$S = \{\text{TTT, TTF, TFT, TFF, FTT, FTF, FFT, FFF}\}$

There are 3 outcomes favorable to the event:

$\{\text{TTF, TFT, FTT}\}$

Probability of an event

$$= \frac{\text{number of favorable outcomes}}{\text{number of possible outcomes}} = \frac{3}{8}$$

The probability of 2 true questions and 1 false question is $\frac{3}{8}$.

Solutions to Chapter 11 "You Try It"

SECTION 11.1

SECTION 11.2

You Try It 1

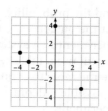

You Try It 2 $A(4, -2), B(-2, 4)$.
The abscissa of D is 0.
The ordinate of C is 0.

You Try It 3

$$x - 3y = -14$$
$$-2 - 3(4) \overset{?}{=} -14$$
$$-2 - 12 \overset{?}{=} -14$$
$$-14 = -14$$

Yes, $(-2, 4)$ is a solution of
$x - 3y = -14$.

You Try It 4 $x + 2y = 4$
$$2y = -x + 4$$
$$y = -\frac{1}{2}x + 2$$

You Try It 5

$\{(145, 140), (140, 125), (150, 130), (165, 150), (140, 130), (165, 160)\}$

No, the relation is not a function. The two ordered
pairs $(140, 125)$ and $(140, 130)$ have the same first
coordinate but different second coordinates.

You Try It 6   Determine the ordered pairs defined
by the equation. Replace x in
$y = \frac{1}{2}x + 1$ by the given values and
solve for y. $\{(-4, -1), (0, 1), (2, 2)\}$
Yes, y is a function of x.

You Try It 7 $H(x) = \dfrac{x}{x - 4}$

$H(8) = \dfrac{8}{8 - 4}$ • Replace x by 8.

$H(8) = \dfrac{8}{4} = 2$

You Try It 1

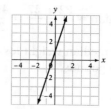

You Try It 2

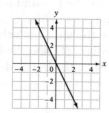

You Try It 3

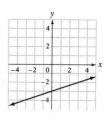

You Try It 4 $5x - 2y = 10$ • **Solve for y.**
$$-2y = -5x + 10$$
$$y = \frac{5}{2}x - 5$$

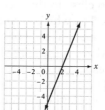

You Try It 5 $x - 3y = 9$ • **Solve for y.**
$$-3y = -x + 9$$
$$y = \frac{1}{3}x - 3$$

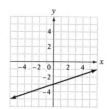

You Try It 6

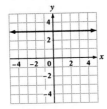

You Try It 7

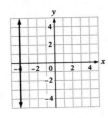

You Try It 8

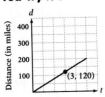

The ordered pair $(3, 120)$ means that in 3 h the car will travel 120 mi.

SECTION 11.3

You Try It 1

x-intercept: y-intercept:

$$y = 2x - 4 \qquad (0, b)$$
$$0 = 2x - 4 \qquad b = -4$$
$$-2x = -4 \qquad (0, -4)$$
$$x = 2$$
$$(2, 0)$$

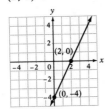

You Try It 2

Let $P_1 = (1, 4)$ and $P_2 = (-3, 8)$.

$$m = \frac{y_2 - y_1}{x_2 - x_1} = \frac{8 - 4}{-3 - 1} = \frac{4}{-4} = -1$$

The slope is -1.

You Try It 3

Let $P_1 = (-1, 2)$ and $P_2 = (4, 2)$.

$$m = \frac{y_2 - y_1}{x_2 - x_1} = \frac{2 - 2}{4 - (-1)} = \frac{0}{5} = 0$$

The slope is 0.

You Try It 4

$$m = \frac{8650 - 6100}{1 - 4} = \frac{2550}{-3}$$
$$m = -850$$

A slope of -850 means that the value of the car is decreasing at a rate of $850 per year.

You Try It 5

y-intercept $= (0, b) = (0, -1)$

$$m = -\frac{1}{4}$$

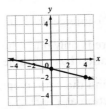

You Try It 6

Solve the equation for y.

$$x - 2y = 4$$
$$-2y = -x + 4$$
$$y = \frac{1}{2}x - 2$$

y-intercept $= (0, b) = (0, -2)$

$$m = \frac{1}{2}$$

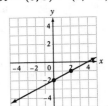

Solutions to Chapter 12 "You Try It"

SECTION 12.1

You Try It 1 $y = x^2 + 2$

x	y
-2	6
-1	3
0	2
1	3
2	6

You Try It 2   To find the x-intercept, let $f(x) = 0$
and solve for x.

$$f(x) = x^2 - 6x + 9$$
$$0 = x^2 - 6x + 9$$
$$0 = (x - 3)(x - 3) \quad \text{• Factor.}$$
$$x - 3 = 0 \qquad x - 3 = 0 \quad \text{• Principle of}$$
$$x = 3 \qquad\qquad x = 3 \qquad \text{Zero Products}$$

The x-intercept: $(3, 0)$.

There is only one x-intercept. The
equation has a double root.

To find the y-intercept, evaluate the
function at $x = 0$.

$$f(x) = x^2 - 6x + 9$$
$$f(0) = 0^2 - 6(0) + 9 = 9$$

The y-intercept: $(0, 9)$.

Solutions to Chapter 13 "You Try It"

You Try It 1

$$f(x) = \left(\frac{2}{3}\right)^x$$

$$f(3) = \left(\frac{2}{3}\right)^3 = \frac{8}{27} \qquad \bullet \; x = 3$$

$$f(-2) = \left(\frac{2}{3}\right)^{-2} = \left(\frac{3}{2}\right)^2 = \frac{9}{4} \qquad \bullet \; x = -2$$

You Try It 2

$$f(x) = 2^{2x+1}$$

$$f(0) = 2^{2(0)+1} = 2^1 = 2 \qquad \bullet \; x = 0$$

$$f(-2) = 2^{2(-2)+1} = 2^{-3} = \frac{1}{2^3} = \frac{1}{8} \qquad \bullet \; x = -2$$

You Try It 3

$$f(x) = e^{2x-1}$$

$$f(2) = e^{2\cdot 2 - 1} = e^3 \approx 20.0855 \qquad \bullet \; x = 2$$

$$f(-2) = e^{2(-2)-1} = e^{-5} \approx 0.0067 \qquad \bullet \; x = -2$$

You Try It 4

x	y
-4	4
-2	2
0	1
2	$\frac{1}{2}$
4	$\frac{1}{4}$

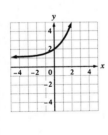

You Try It 5

x	y
-2	$\frac{5}{4}$
-1	$\frac{3}{2}$
0	2
1	3
2	5

You Try It 6

x	y
-2	6
-1	4
0	3
1	$\frac{5}{2}$
2	$\frac{9}{4}$

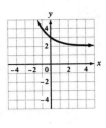

You Try It 7

x	y
-4	$\frac{9}{4}$
-2	$\frac{5}{2}$
0	3
2	4
4	6

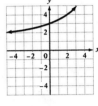
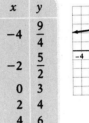

Answers to Chapter 1 Odd-Numbered Exercises

PREP TEST

1. $54 > 45$ **2.** 4   **3.** 15,847   **4.** 3779   **5.** 26,432   **6.** 6

7. $1\frac{4}{15}$ **8.** $\frac{7}{16}$ **9.** 11.058   **10.** 3.781   **11.** $\frac{2}{5}$ **12.** $\frac{5}{9}$

13. 9.4   **14.** 0.4   **15.** 31

SECTION 1.1

1. -120 ft   **3.** $+2$ dollars   **5.**   **7.**

9. 1   **11.** -1 **13.** 3   **15. a.** A is -4.   **b.** C is -2.   **17. a.** A is -7.   **b.** D is -4.   **19.** $-2 > -5$

21. $-16 < 1$ **23.** $3 > -7$ **25.** $-11 < -8$ **27.** $35 > 28$ **29.** $-42 < 27$ **31.** $21 > -34$ **33.** $-27 > -39$

35. $-87 < 63$ **37.** $86 > -79$ **39.** $-62 > -84$ **41.** $-131 < 101$ **43.** $-7, -2, 0, 3$ **45.** $-5, -3, 1, 4$

47. $-4, 0, 5, 9$ **49.** $-10, -7, -5, 4, 12$ **51.** $-11, -7, -2, 5, 10$ **53.** -16 **55.** 3   **57.** -45 **59.** 59

61. 88   **63.** 4   **65.** 9   **67.** 11   **69.** 12   **71.** 2   **73.** 6   **75.** 5   **77.** 1   **79.** -5 **81.** 16   **83.** 12

85. -29 **87.** -14 **89.** 15   **91.** -33 **93.** 32   **95.** -42 **97.** 61   **99.** -52 **101.** $|-12| > |8|$

103. $|6| < |13|$ **105.** $|-1| < |-17|$ **107.** $|17| = |-17|$ **109.** $-9, -|6|, -4, |-7|$ **111.** $-9, -|-7|, |4|, 5$

113. $-|10|, -|-8|, -3, |5|$ **115. a.** 8 and -2 are 5 units from 3.   **b.** 2 and -4 are 3 units from -1.   **117.** -12 min and counting is closer to blastoff.   **119.** The loss was greater during the first quarter.   **121.** $11, -11$

SECTION 1.2

1. $-14, -364$ **3.** -2 **5.** 20   **7.** -11 **9.** -9 **11.** -3 **13.** 1   **15.** -5 **17.** -30 **19.** 9   **21.** 1

23. -10 **25.** -28 **27.** -41 **29.** -392 **31.** -20 **33.** -23 **35.** -2 **37.** -6 **39.** -6

41. Negative six minus positive four   **43.** Positive six minus negative four   **45.** $9 + 5$ **47.** $1 + (-8)$ **49.** 8

51. -7 **53.** -9 **55.** 36   **57.** -3 **59.** 18   **61.** -9 **63.** 11   **65.** 0   **67.** 11   **69.** 2   **71.** -138

73. 86   **75.** -337 **77.** 4   **79.** -12 **81.** -12 **83.** 3   **85.** The temperature is $-1°$C.   **87.** Nick's score was -15 points after his opponent shot the moon.   **89.** The change in the price of the stock is -9 dollars.   **91.** The temperature is 115°F.   **93.** The difference in elevation is 7046 m.   **95.** The difference is 82°C.   **97.** The difference in temperature is 13°C.   **99.**

-3	2	1
4	0	-4
-1	-2	3

SECTION 1.3

1. Subtraction   **3.** Multiplication   **5.** 42   **7.** -24 **9.** 6   **11.** 18   **13.** -20 **15.** -16 **17.** 25   **19.** 0

21. -72 **23.** -102 **25.** 140   **27.** -228 **29.** -320 **31.** -156 **33.** -70 **35.** 162   **37.** 120

39. 36   **41.** 192   **43.** -108 **45.** -2100 **47.** 20   **49.** -48 **51.** 140   **53.** $3(-12) = -36$

55. $-5(11) = -55$ **57.** -2 **59.** 8   **61.** 0   **63.** -9 **65.** -9 **67.** 9   **69.** -24 **71.** -12 **73.** 31

75. 17   **77.** 15   **79.** -13 **81.** -18 **83.** 19   **85.** 13   **87.** -19 **89.** 17   **91.** 26   **93.** 23   **95.** 25

97. -34 **99.** 11   **101.** -13 **103.** 13   **105.** 12   **107.** -14 **109.** -14 **111.** -6 **113.** -4

115. The average high temperature was $-4°$F.   **117.** The average score was -2.   **119.** The wind chill factor is $-45°$F.

121. a. 25   **b.** -17 **123. a.** True   **b.** True

SECTION 1.4

1. $-\dfrac{5}{24}$ **3.** $-\dfrac{19}{24}$ **5.** $\dfrac{5}{26}$ **7.** $\dfrac{7}{24}$ **9.** $-\dfrac{19}{60}$ **11.** $-1\dfrac{3}{8}$ **13.** $\dfrac{3}{4}$ **15.** $-\dfrac{47}{48}$ **17.** $\dfrac{3}{8}$ **19.** $-\dfrac{7}{60}$ **21.** $\dfrac{13}{24}$

23. -3.4 **25.** -8.89 **27.** -8.0 **29.** -0.68 **31.** -181.51 **33.** 2.7 **35.** -20.7 **37.** -37.19

39. -34.99 **41.** 6.778 **43.** -8.4 **45.** $\dfrac{1}{21}$ **47.** $\dfrac{2}{9}$ **49.** $-\dfrac{2}{9}$ **51.** $-\dfrac{45}{328}$ **53.** $\dfrac{2}{3}$ **55.** $\dfrac{15}{64}$ **57.** $-\dfrac{3}{7}$

59. $-1\dfrac{1}{9}$ **61.** $\dfrac{5}{6}$ **63.** $-2\dfrac{2}{7}$ **65.** $-13\dfrac{1}{2}$ **67.** 31.15 **69.** -112.97 **71.** 0.0363 **73.** 97 **75.** 2.2

77. -4.14 **79.** -3.8 **81.** -22.70 **83.** 0.07 **85.** 0.55 **87.** The temperature fell 32.22°C in 27 min.

89. The difference between the boiling point and the melting point of oxygen is 35.438°C.   **91. a.** The closing price was

$19.39.   **b.** The closing price was $72.46.   **93.** Answers will vary. $-\dfrac{17}{24}$ is one example.

SECTION 1.5

1. 2.37×10^{6} **3.** 4.5×10^{-4} **5.** 3.09×10^{5} **7.** 6.01×10^{-7} **9.** 5.7×10^{10} **11.** 1.7×10^{-8} **13.** $710{,}000$

15. 0.000043 **17.** $671{,}000{,}000$ **19.** 0.00000713 **21.** $5{,}000{,}000{,}000{,}000$ **23.** 0.00801 **25.** 1.6×10^{10} mi

27. $\$3.1 \times 10^{12}$ **29.** 3.7×10^{-6} m   **31.** 4 **33.** 0 **35.** 12 **37.** -6 **39.** -5 **41.** 2 **43.** -3 **45.** 1

47. 2 **49.** -3 **51.** 14 **53.** -4 **55.** 33 **57.** -13 **59.** -12 **61.** 17 **63.** 0 **65.** 30 **67.** 94

69. -8 **71.** 39 **73.** 22 **75.** 0.21 **77.** -0.96 **79.** -0.29 **81.** -1.76 **83.** 2.1 **85.** $\dfrac{3}{16}$ **87.** $\dfrac{7}{16}$

89. $-\dfrac{5}{16}$ **91.** $-\dfrac{5}{8}$ **93. a.** $3.45 \times 10^{-14} > 3.45 \times 10^{-15}$ **b.** $5.23 \times 10^{18} > 5.23 \times 10^{17}$

c. $3.12 \times 10^{12} > 3.12 \times 10^{11}$ **95. a.** 100 **b.** -100 **c.** 225 **d.** -225 **99. a.** 1.99×10^{30} kg

b. 1.67×10^{-27} kg

Chapter Review

1. -22 **2.** 1 **3.** $-\dfrac{5}{24}$ **4.** 0.21 **5.** $\dfrac{8}{25}$ **6.** -1.28

7. 10 **8.** $-\dfrac{7}{18}$ **9.** 4 **10.** $0 > -3$ **11.** -6 **12.** 6

13. $\dfrac{17}{24}$ **14.** $-\dfrac{1}{4}$ **15.** $1\dfrac{5}{8}$ **16.** 24 **17.** -26 **18.** 2

19. 3.97×10^{-5} **20.** -0.08 **21.** $\dfrac{1}{36}$ **22.** $\dfrac{3}{40}$ **23.** -0.042

24. $\dfrac{1}{3}$ **25.** 5 **26.** $-2 > -40$ **27.** -26 **28.** 1.33

29. $-\dfrac{1}{4}$ **30.** -7.4 **31.** $\dfrac{15}{32}$ **32.** $240{,}000$ **33.** $-4°$

34. The student's score was 98.   **35.** The difference between the boiling and melting points is 395.45°C.

Chapter Test

1. 3 **2.** -2 **3.** $\dfrac{1}{15}$ **4.** -0.0608 **5.** $-8 > -10$

6. -1.88 **7.** -26 **8.** 90 **9.** -4.014 **10.** -9 **11.** -7

12. $\dfrac{7}{24}$ **13.** 8.76×10^{10} **14.** -48 **15.** 0 **16.** 10

17. $-\dfrac{4}{5}$ **18.** $0 > -4$ **19.** -14 **20.** -4 **21.** $\dfrac{3}{10}$

22. 0.00000009601 **23.** 3.4 **24.** $\dfrac{1}{12}$ **25.** $\dfrac{1}{12}$ **26.** 3.213

27. The temperature is 7°C.   **28.** The melting point of oxygen is −213°C.   **29.** The temperature
fell 46.62°C.   **30.** The average low temperature was −2°F.

Answers to Chapter 2 Odd-Numbered Exercises

PREP TEST

1. -7 **2.** -20 **3.** 0 **4.** 1 **5.** 1 **6.** $\dfrac{1}{15}$

7. $\dfrac{19}{24}$ **8.** 4 **9.** -21

SECTION 2.1

1. -33 **3.** -12 **5.** -4 **7.** -3 **9.** -22 **11.** -40 **13.** -1 **15.** 14 **17.** 32 **19.** 6 **21.** 7

23. 49 **25.** -24 **27.** 63 **29.** 9 **31.** 4 **33.** $-\dfrac{2}{3}$ **35.** 0 **37.** $-3\dfrac{1}{4}$ **39.** 8.5023

41. -18.950658 **43.** $2x^2, 3x, \underline{-4}$ **45.** $3a^2, -4a, \underline{8}$ **47.** $\underline{3x^2}, \underline{-4x}$ **49.** $\underline{1y^2}, 6a$ **51.** $16z$ **53.** $9m$ **55.** $12at$

57. $3yt$ **59.** Unlike terms   **61.** $-2t^2$ **63.** $13c - 5$ **65.** $-2t$ **67.** $3y^2 - 2$ **69.** $14w - 8u$

71. $-23xy + 10$ **73.** $-11v^2$ **75.** $-8ab - 3a$ **77.** $4y^2 - y$ **79.** $-3a - 2b^2$ **81.** $7x^2 - 8x$ **83.** $-3s + 6t$

85. $-3m + 10n$ **87.** $5ab + 4ac$ **89.** $\dfrac{2}{3}a^2 + \dfrac{3}{5}b^2$ **91.** $6.994x$ **93.** $1.56m - 3.77n$ **95.** $5x + 20$ **97.** $4y - 12$

99. $-2a - 8$ **101.** $15x + 30$ **103.** $15c - 25$ **105.** $-3y + 18$ **107.** $7x + 14$ **109.** $4y - 8$ **111.** $5x + 24$

113. $y - 6$ **115.** $6n - 3$ **117.** $6y + 20$ **119.** $10x + 4$ **121.** $-6t - 6$ **123.** $z - 2$ **125.** $y + 6$

127. $9t + 15$ **129.** $5t + 24$ **131. a.** | 1 | 1 | 1 | x | x | **b.** | x | x | x | x | 1 | 1 | 1 | 1 | 1 | 1 |

c. | x | x | x | 1 | 1 | **d.** | x | x | 1 | 1 | 1 | 1 | **e.** | x | x | x | 1 | 1 | 1 | **f.** $3x + 3$

133. Answers will vary.

SECTION 2.2

1. Yes   **3.** No   **5.** Yes   **7.** Yes   **9.** Yes   **11.** Yes   **13.** Yes   **15.** Yes   **17.** No   **19.** No   **21.** Yes

23. -2 **25.** 14 **27.** 2 **29.** -4 **31.** -5 **33.** 0 **35.** 2 **37.** -3 **39.** 10 **41.** -5 **43.** -12

45. -7 **47.** $\dfrac{2}{3}$ **49.** -1 **51.** $\dfrac{1}{3}$ **53.** $-\dfrac{1}{8}$ **55.** $-\dfrac{3}{4}$ **57.** $-1\dfrac{1}{12}$ **59.** 6 **61.** -9 **63.** -5 **65.** 14

67. 8 **69.** -3 **71.** 20 **73.** -21 **75.** -15 **77.** 16 **79.** -42 **81.** 15 **83.** $-38\dfrac{2}{5}$ **85.** $9\dfrac{3}{5}$

87. $-10\dfrac{4}{5}$ **89.** $1\dfrac{17}{18}$ **91.** $-2\dfrac{2}{3}$ **93.** 3 **95.** The original investment was \$23,610.   **97.** The value of the fund increased by \$1190.   **99.** 18.5 gal of gasoline was used.   **101.** The car gets 34.2 mi/gal.   **103.** The markup on each stuffed animal is \$16.30.   **105.** The compact disc costs \$14.50.   **109.** Answers will vary. For example, $x + 5 = 1$.

SECTION 2.3

1. 3 **3.** 5 **5.** -1 **7.** -4 **9.** 1 **11.** 3 **13.** -2 **15.** -3 **17.** -2 **19.** -1 **21.** 3 **23.** -1

25. 7 **27.** 2 **29.** 2 **31.** 0 **33.** 2 **35.** 0 **37.** $\dfrac{2}{3}$ **39.** $2\dfrac{5}{6}$ **41.** $-2\dfrac{1}{2}$ **43.** $1\dfrac{1}{2}$ **45.** 2 **47.** -2

49. $2\dfrac{1}{3}$ **51.** $-1\dfrac{1}{2}$ **53.** 10 **55.** 5 **57.** 36 **59.** -6 **61.** -9 **63.** $-4\dfrac{4}{5}$ **65.** $-8\dfrac{3}{4}$ **67.** 36 **69.** $1\dfrac{1}{3}$

71. 2 **73.** 4 **75.** 9 **77.** 4 **79.** -3.125 **81.** 1 **83.** -3 **85.** -9 **87.** 4.95 **89.** -0.0862069

91. The temperature is $-40°$C.   **93.** The time is 14.5 s.   **95.** 2500 units were made.   **97.** The clerk's monthly income is \$1800.   **99.** The total sales were \$32,000.   **101.** Miguel's commission rate was 4.5%.

SECTION 2.4

1. $\frac{1}{2}$ **3.** -1 **5.** -4 **7.** -1 **9.** -4 **11.** 3 **13.** -1 **15.** 2 **17.** 3 **19.** 0 **21.** -2 **23.** -1

25. $-\frac{2}{3}$ **27.** -4 **29.** $\frac{1}{3}$ **31.** $-\frac{3}{4}$ **33.** $\frac{1}{4}$ **35.** 0 **37.** $-1\frac{3}{4}$ **39.** 1 **41.** -1 **43.** -5 **45.** $\frac{5}{12}$

47. $-\frac{4}{7}$ **49.** $2\frac{1}{3}$ **51.** 21 **53.** 21 **55.** 2 **57.** -1 **59.** -4 **61.** $-\frac{6}{7}$ **63.** 5 **65.** 3 **67.** 0

69. -1 **71.** 2 **73.** $1\frac{9}{10}$ **75.** 13 **77.** $2\frac{1}{2}$ **79.** 2 **81.** 0 **83.** $3\frac{1}{5}$ **85.** 4 **87.** $-6\frac{1}{2}$ **89.** $-\frac{3}{4}$

91. $-\frac{2}{3}$ **93.** -3 **95.** $-1\frac{1}{4}$ **97.** $2\frac{5}{8}$ **99.** 1.9936196 **101.** 13.383119 **103.** 48

SECTION 2.5

1. $y - 9$ **3.** $z + 3$ **5.** $\frac{2}{3}n + n$ **7.** $\frac{m}{m - 3}$ **9.** $9(x + 4)$ **11.** $n - (-5)n$ **13.** $c\left(\frac{1}{4}c\right)$ **15.** $m^2 + 2m^2$

17. $2(t + 6)$ **19.** $\frac{x}{9 + x}$ **21.** $3(b + 6)$ **23.** x^2 **25.** $\frac{x}{20}$ **27.** $4x$ **29.** $\frac{3}{4}x$ **31.** $4 + x$ **33.** $5x - x$

35. $x(x + 2)$ **37.** $7(x + 8)$ **39.** $x^2 + 3x$ **41.** $(x + 3) + \frac{1}{2}x$ **43.** $\frac{3x}{x}$ **45. a.** Answers will vary. For example,

the sum of twice x and 3. **b.** Answers will vary. For example, twice the sum of x and 3. **49.** carbon: $\frac{1}{2}x$; oxygen: $\frac{1}{2}x$

SECTION 2.6

1. $x + 7 = 12; 5$ **3.** $3x = 18; 6$ **5.** $x + 5 = 3; -2$ **7.** $6x = 14; 2\frac{1}{3}$ **9.** $\frac{5}{6}x = 15; 18$ **11.** $3x + 4 = 8; 1\frac{1}{3}$

13. $\frac{1}{4}x - 7 = 9; 64$ **15.** $\frac{x}{9} = 14; 126$ **17.** $\frac{x}{4} - 6 = -2; 16$ **19.** $7 - 2x = 13; -3$ **21.** $9 - \frac{x}{2} = 5; 8$

23. $\frac{3}{5}x + 8 = 2; -10$ **25.** $\frac{x}{4.186} - 7.92 = 12.529; 85.599514$ **27.** The price at Target is $76.75. **29.** The value of
the SUV last year was $20,000. **31.** The length of the Brooklyn Bridge is 486 m. **33.** The family's monthly income is
$5440. **35.** The monthly output a year ago was 5000 computers. **37.** The recommended daily allowance of sodium
is 2.5 g. **39.** It took 3 h to install the water softener. **41.** About 11,065 plants and animals are known to be at risk of
extinction in the world. **43.** The percent is 3.3%. **45.** The original water flow rate was 5 gal/min. **47.** The total
sales for the month were $42,540. **49.** The world carbon dioxide emissions in 1990 were 5.83 billion metric tons.

Chapter Review

1. $-2a + 2b$ **2.** Yes **3.** -4 **4.** 7 **5.** 13 **6.** -9

7. -18 **8.** $-3x + 4$ **9.** 5 **10.** -5 **11.** No **12.** 6

13. 5 **14.** 10 **15.** $-4bc$ **16.** $-2\frac{1}{2}$ **17.** $1\frac{1}{4}$ **18.** $\frac{71}{30}x^2$

19. $-\frac{1}{3}$ **20.** $10\frac{4}{5}$ **21.** The car averaged 23 mi/gal. **22.** The temperature

is 37.8°C. **23.** $n + \frac{n}{5}$ **24.** $(n + 5) + \frac{1}{3}n$ **25.** The number is 2. **26.** The

number is 10. **27.** The regular price of the CD player is $380. **28.** Last year's crop was 25,300
bushels.

Chapter Test

1. 95 **2.** 26 **3.** $-11x - 4y$ **4.** $3\frac{1}{5}$ **5.** -2 **6.** -38

7. No **8.** $-14ab + 9$ **9.** $-2\frac{4}{5}$ **10.** $8y - 7$ **11.** 0

12. $-\frac{1}{2}$ **13.** $-5\frac{5}{6}$ **14.** -16 **15.** -3 **16.** 11 **17.** The monthly payment is \$137.50. **18.** 4000 clocks were made during the month. **19.** The time required is 11.5 s. **20.** $x + \frac{1}{3}x$ **21.** $5(x + 3)$ **22.** $2x - 3 = 7; 5$

23. The number is $-3\frac{1}{2}$. **24.** Santos's total sales for the month were \$40,000. **25.** The mechanic worked for 3 h.

Answers to Chapter 3 Odd-Numbered Exercises

SECTION 3.1

1. $x < 2$　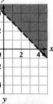　**3.** $x > 3$

5. $n \geq 3$　**7.** $x \leq -4$　**9.** $x < 1$　**11.** $x \leq -3$

13. $y \geq -9$　**15.** $x < 12$　**17.** $x \geq 5$　**19.** $x < -11$　**21.** $x \leq 10$　**23.** $x \geq -6$　**25.** $x > 2$　**27.** $d < -\dfrac{1}{6}$

29. $x \geq -\dfrac{31}{24}$　**31.** $x < \dfrac{5}{8}$　**33.** $x < \dfrac{5}{4}$　**35.** $x > \dfrac{5}{24}$　**37.** $x < -3.8$　**39.** $x \leq -1.2$　**41.** $x < 5.6$

43.　$x < 4$　**45.**　$y \geq 3$

47.　$x \leq 1$　**49.**　$x < -1$

51.　$b < -4$　**53.** $y \leq 0$　**55.** $x > \dfrac{2}{7}$　**57.** $x \leq -\dfrac{5}{2}$　**59.** $x < 16$　**61.** $x \geq 16$

63. $x \geq -14$　**65.** $x \leq 21$　**67.** $x > 0$　**69.** $x \leq -\dfrac{12}{7}$　**71.** $x > \dfrac{2}{3}$　**73.** $x \leq \dfrac{2}{3}$　**75.** $x \leq 2.3$　**77.** $x < -3.2$

79. $x \leq 5$　**81.** The team must win 11 or more games to be eligible for the tournament.　**83.** The service organization must collect more than 440 lb on the fourth drive to collect the bonus.　**85.** The person needs 50 or more milligrams of additional vitamin C to satisfy the recommended daily allowance.　**87.** No, the student cannot earn an A grade.
89. $\{c \mid c > 0\}$　**91.** $\{c \mid c > \in \text{ real numbers}\}$　**93.** $\{c \mid c > 0\}$

SECTION 3.2

1. $x < 4$　**3.** $x < -4$　**5.** $x \geq 1$　**7.** $x < 5$　**9.** $x < 0$　**11.** $x < 20$　**13.** $y \leq \dfrac{5}{2}$　**15.** $x < \dfrac{25}{11}$　**17.** $n \leq \dfrac{11}{18}$

19. $x \geq 6$　**21.** In one month the agent expects to make sales totaling \$20,000 or less.　**23.** A person must use more than 60 min to exceed \$10.　**25.** The amount of artificial flavors that can be added is less than or equal to 8 oz.
27. The distance to the ski resort must be greater than 38 mi.　**29.** $\{1, 2\}$　**31.** $\{3, 4, 5\}$　**33.** $\{x \mid x \in \text{ real numbers}\}$

SECTION 3.3

1. 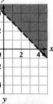　**3.**　**5.**　**7.**

9. 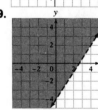　**11.** 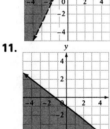　**13.** 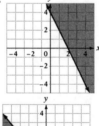　**15.**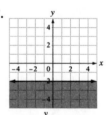

17. 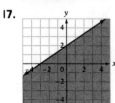　**19.** 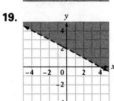　**21.** 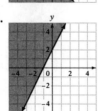　**23.** $x \leq 3$

Chapter Review

1. $x > 18$ [9.2A]   **2.** $A \cap B = \varnothing$ [9.1A]   **3.** $\{x \mid x > -8, x \in \text{odd integers}\}$

4. $A \cup B = \{2, 4, 6, 8, 10\}$ **5.** $A = \{1, 3, 5, 7\}$ **6.** $x \geq 4$

7. 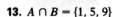   **8.** $x \geq -4$ **9.**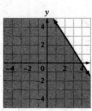

10. 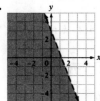   **11.** $\{x \mid x > 3, x \in \text{real numbers}\}$ **12.** $x > 2$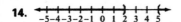

13. $A \cap B = \{1, 5, 9\}$ **14.** 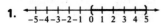   **15.**

16. $x \geq -3$ **17.** $x > -18$ **18.** $x < \dfrac{1}{2}$ **19.** $x < -\dfrac{8}{9}$

20. 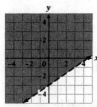   **21.** $x \geq 4$ **22.** For florist B to be more economical, there must be 5 or more residents in the nursing home.

23. The minimum length is 24 ft.   **24.** 32 is the smallest integer that satisfies the inequality.

25. 72 is the lowest score that the student can receive and still attain a minimum of 480 points.

Chapter Test

1. 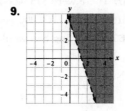   **2.** $\{x \mid x < 50, x \in \text{positive integers}\}$ **3.** $A = \{4, 6, 8\}$

4. $x \leq -3$ **5.** $x > \dfrac{1}{8}$ **6.**   **7.** $x < -1$

8. $\{x \mid x > -23, x \in \text{real numbers}\}$ **9.**   **10.**

11. $A \cap B = \{12\}$ **12.** $x < -3$ **13.** $x \geq -\dfrac{40}{3}$

14. $x < -\dfrac{22}{7}$ **15.** $x \geq 3$ **16.** $x \geq -4$ **17.** The child must grow 5 in. or more.   **18.** The width must be less than or equal to 11 ft.   **19.** The diameter must be between 0.0389 in. and 0.0395 in.   **20.** The total value of the stock processed by the broker was less than or equal to $75,000.

Answers to Chapter 4 Odd-Numbered Exercises

PREP TEST

1. $\frac{4}{5}$ **2.** $\frac{1}{2}$ **3.** 24.8   **4.** 4×33 **5.** 4

SECTION 4.1

1. $\frac{1}{5}$ 1:5   1 to 5   **3.** $\frac{2}{1}$ 2:1   2 to 1   **5.** $\frac{3}{8}$ 3:8   3 to 8   **7.** $\frac{37}{24}$ 37:24   37 to 24   **9.** $\frac{1}{1}$ 1:1   1 to 1

11. $\frac{7}{10}$ 7:10   7 to 10   **13.** $\frac{1}{2}$ 1:2   1 to 2   **15.** $\frac{2}{1}$ 2:1   2 to 1   **17.** $\frac{3}{4}$ 3:4   3 to 4   **19.** $\frac{5}{3}$ 5:3   5 to 3

21. $\frac{2}{3}$ 2:3   2 to 3   **23.** $\frac{2}{1}$ 2:1   2 to 1   **25.** The ratio is $\frac{1}{3}$.   **27.** The ratio is $\frac{3}{8}$.   **29.** The ratio is $\frac{2}{77}$.

31. The ratio is $\frac{1}{12}$.   **33. a.** The amount of increase is $20,000.   **b.** The ratio is $\frac{2}{9}$.   **35.** The ratio is $\frac{11}{31}$.

37. No, the ratio $= \frac{830}{1389} \approx 0.5976$ is greater than $\frac{2}{5}$ (0.4).

SECTION 4.2

1. $\frac{3\text{ pounds}}{4\text{ people}}$ **3.** $\frac{\$20}{3\text{ boards}}$ **5.** $\frac{20\text{ miles}}{1\text{ gallon}}$ **7.** $\frac{5\text{ children}}{2\text{ families}}$ **9.** $\frac{8\text{ gallons}}{1\text{ hour}}$ **11.** 2.5 feet/second   **13.** $975/week

15. 110 trees/acre   **17.** $18.84/hour   **19.** 52.4 miles/hour   **21.** 28 miles/gallon   **23.** $1.65/pound   **25.** The gas mileage was 28.4 miles/gallon.   **27.** The rocket uses 213,600 gallons/minute.   **29. a.** 175 pounds of beef was packaged.   **b.** The beef cost $2.09/pound.   **31. a.** The camera goes through film at the rate of 336 feet/minute. **b.** The camera uses the film at a rate of 89 seconds/roll.   **33. a.** The price of the computer hardware would be 109,236 euros.   **b.** The cost of the car would be 3,978,000 yen.

SECTION 4.3

1. True   **3.** Not true   **5.** Not true   **7.** True   **9.** True   **11.** Not true   **13.** True   **15.** True   **17.** True
19. Not true   **21.** True   **23.** Not true   **25.** 3   **27.** 6   **29.** 9   **31.** 5.67   **33.** 4   **35.** 4.38   **37.** 88
39. 3.33   **41.** 26.25   **43.** 96   **45.** 9.78   **47.** 3.43   **49.** 1.34   **51.** 50.4   **53.** A 0.5-ounce serving contains 50 calories.   **55.** Ron used 70 pounds of fertilizer.   **57.** There were 375 wooden bats produced.
59. The distance is 16 miles.   **61.** 1.25 ounces are required.   **63.** 160,000 people would vote.   **65.** The monthly payment is $176.75.   **67.** You will own 400 shares.   **69.** A bowling ball would weigh 2.67 pounds on the moon.
71. The dividend would be $1071.

Chapter Review

1. True **2.** $\frac{2}{5}$ 2:5 2 to 5 **3.** 62.5 miles/hour **4.** True **5.** 68

6. $7.50/hour **7.** $1.75/pound **8.** $\frac{2}{7}$ 2:7 2 to 7 **9.** 36 **10.** 19.44

11. $\frac{2}{5}$ 2:5 2 to 5 **12.** Not true **13.** $\frac{\$15}{4\text{ hours}}$ **14.** 27.2 miles/gallon

15. $\frac{1}{1}$ 1:1 1 to 1 **16.** True **17.** 65.45 **18.** $\frac{100\text{ miles}}{3\text{ hours}}$ **19.** The ratio

is $\frac{2}{5}$. **20.** The property tax is $6400. **21.** The ratio is $\frac{2}{1}$. **22.** The cost per phone

is $37.50. **23.** 1344 blocks would be needed. **24.** The ratio is $\frac{5}{2}$. **25.** The turkey costs

$.93/pound. **26.** The average was 56.8 miles/hour. **27.** The cost is $493.50. **28.** The cost

is $44.75/share. **29.** 22.5 pounds of fertilizer will be used. **30.** The ratio is $\frac{1}{2}$.

Chapter Test

1. $3836.40/month **2.** $\frac{1}{6}$ 1:6 1 to 6 **3.** $\frac{9\text{ supports}}{4\text{ feet}}$ **4.** Not true

5. $\frac{3}{2}$ 3:2 3 to 2 **6.** 144 **7.** 30.5 miles/gallon **8.** $\frac{1}{3}$ 1:3 1 to 3

9. True **10.** 40.5 **11.** $\frac{\$27}{4\text{ boards}}$ **12.** $\frac{3}{5}$ 3:5 3 to 5 **13.** The dividend is

$625. **14.** The ratio is $\frac{43}{56}$. **15.** The plane's speed is 538 miles/hour. **16.** The college

student's body contains 132 pounds of water. **17.** The cost of the lumber is $1.73/foot. **18.** The amount

of medication required is 0.875 ounce. **19.** The ratio is $\frac{4}{5}$. **20.** 36 defective hard drives are expected

to be found in the production of 1200 hard drives.

Answers to Chapter 5 Odd-Numbered Exercises

PREP TEST

1. $\frac{19}{100}$　　**2.** 0.23　　**3.** 47　　**4.** 2850　　**5.** 4000　　**6.** 32

7. 62.5　　**8.** $66\frac{2}{3}$　　**9.** 1.75

SECTION 5.1

1. $\frac{1}{4}$, 0.25　　**3.** $1\frac{3}{10}$, 1.30　　**5.** 1, 1.00　　**7.** $\frac{73}{100}$, 0.73　　**9.** $3\frac{83}{100}$, 3.83　　**11.** $\frac{7}{10}$, 0.70　　**13.** $\frac{22}{25}$, 0.88

15. $\frac{8}{25}$, 0.32　　**17.** $\frac{2}{3}$　　**19.** $\frac{5}{6}$　　**21.** $\frac{1}{9}$　　**23.** $3\frac{5}{11}$　　**25.** $\frac{3}{70}$　　**27.** $\frac{1}{15}$　　**29.** 0.065　　**31.** 0.123　　**33.** 0.0055

35. 0.0825　　**37.** 0.0505　　**39.** 0.02　　**41.** 0.804　　**43.** 0.049　　**45.** 73%　　**47.** 1%　　**49.** 294%　　**51.** 0.6%

53. 310.6%　　**55.** 70%　　**57.** 37%　　**59.** 40%　　**61.** 12.5%　　**63.** 150%　　**65.** 166.7%　　**67.** 87.5%　　**69.** 48%

71. $33\frac{1}{3}$%　　**73.** $166\frac{2}{3}$%　　**75.** $87\frac{1}{2}$%　　**77.** 6% of those surveyed named something other than corn on the cob, cole

slaw, corn bread, or fries.　　**79.** This represents $\frac{1}{2}$ off the regular price.　　**81. a.** False　　**b.** For example,

200% × 4 = 2 × 4 = 8

SECTION 5.2

1. 8　　**3.** 10.8　　**5.** 0.075　　**7.** 80　　**9.** 51.895　　**11.** 7.5　　**13.** 13　　**15.** 3.75　　**17.** 20　　**19.** 210

21. 5% of 95　　**23.** 79% of 16　　**25.** 72% of 40　　**27.** 25,805.0324　　**29.** About 13.2 million people aged 18 to 24 do

not have health insurance.　　**31.** 12,151 more faculty members described their political views as liberal than described

their views as far left.　　**33. a.** The sales tax is $1770.　　**b.** The total cost of the car is $31,270.　　**35.** 6232 respondents

did not answer yes to the question.　　**37.** Employees spend 48.2 hours with family and friends.　　**39.** There are

approximately 3.4 hours difference between the actual and preferred amounts of time the employees spent on self.

SECTION 5.3

1. 32%　　**3.** $16\frac{2}{3}$%　　**5.** 200%　　**7.** 37.5%　　**9.** 18%　　**11.** 0.25%　　**13.** 20%　　**15.** 400%　　**17.** 2.5%

19. 37.5%　　**21.** 0.25%　　**23.** 2.4%　　**25.** 9.6%　　**27.** 70% of couples disagree about financial matters.

29. Approximately 25.4% of the vegetables were wasted.　　**31.** The typical American household spends 6% of the total

amount spent on energy utilities on lighting.　　**33.** 27% of the food produced in the United States is wasted.

35. Approximately 27.4% of the total expenses is spent for food.　　**37.** 91.8% of the total is spent on all categories except

training.

SECTION 5.4

1. 75　　**3.** 50　　**5.** 100　　**7.** 85　　**9.** 1200　　**11.** 19.2　　**13.** 7.5　　**15.** 32　　**17.** 200　　**19.** 80　　**21.** 9

23. 504　　**25.** 108　　**27.** There were 15.8 million travelers who allowed their children to miss school to go along on

a trip.　　**29.** 3364 people responded to the survey.　　**31. a.** 3000 boards were tested.　　**b.** 2976 boards tested were not

defective.　　**33.** 200,935,308 people in the United States were age 20 and older in 2000.　　**35.** The recommended daily

allowance of copper for an adult is 2 milligrams.

SECTION 5.5

1. 65　　**3.** 25%　　**5.** 75　　**7.** 12.5%　　**9.** 400　　**11.** 19.5　　**13.** 14.8%　　**15.** 62.62　　**17.** 5　　**19.** 45

21. 15　　**23.** The total amount collected was $24,500.　　**25.** The world's total land area is 58,750,000 square miles.

27. 22,577 hotels in the United States are located along highways.　　**29.** 14,000,000 ounces of gold were mined in the

United States that year.　　**31.** 46.8% of the deaths were due to traffic accidents.　　**33.** The 108th House of

Representatives had the larger percent of Republicans.

Chapter Review

1. 60　　　　**2.** 20%　　　　**3.** 175%　　　　**4.** 75　　　　**5.** $\frac{3}{25}$　　　　**6.** 19.36

7. 150%　　　　**8.** 504　　　　**9.** 0.42　　　　**10.** 5.4　　　　**11.** 157.5　　　　**12.** 0.076

13. 77.5　　　　**14.** $\frac{1}{6}$　　　　**15.** 160%　　　　**16.** 75　　　　**17.** 38%　　　　**18.** 10.9

19. 7.3%　　　　**20.** 613.3%　　　　**21.** The student answered 85% of the questions correctly.

22. The company spent $4500 for newspaper advertising.　　　　**23.** 31.7% of the cost is for electricity.

24. The total cost of the video camera is $1041.25.　　　　**25.** Approximately 78.6% of the women wore sunscreen often.　　　　**26.** The world's population in 2000 was approximately 6,100,000,000 people.　　　　**27.** The cost of the computer 4 years ago was $3000.　　　　**28.** The dollar value of all the online transactions made that year was $52 billion.

Chapter Test

1. 0.973　　　　**2.** $\frac{5}{6}$　　　　**3.** 30%　　　　**4.** 163%　　　　**5.** 150%　　　　**6.** $66\frac{2}{3}\%$

7. 50.05　　　　**8.** 61.36　　　　**9.** 76% of 13　　　　**10.** 212% of 12　　　　**11.** The amount spent for for advertising is $4500.　　　　**12.** 1170 pounds of vegetables were not spoiled.　　　　**13.** 14.7% of the daily recommended amount of potassium is provided.　　　　**14.** 9.1% of the daily recommended number of calories is provided.　　　　**15.** 16% of the permanent employees are hired.　　　　**16.** The student answered approximately 91.3% of the questions correctly.　　　　**17.** 80　　　　**18.** 28.3　　　　**19.** 32,000 PDAs were tested.

20. The increase was 60% of the original price.　　　　**21.** 143.0　　　　**22.** 1000%　　　　**23.** The dollar increase is $1.74.　　　　**24.** The population now is 220% of what it was 10 years ago.　　　　**25.** The value of the car is $12,500.

Answers to Chapter 6 Odd-Numbered Exercises

PREP TEST

1. 0.75 **2.** 52.05 **3.** 504.51 **4.** 9750 **5.** 45 **6.** 1417.24
7. 3.33 **8.** 0.605 **9.** $0.379 < 0.397$

SECTION 6.1

1. The unit cost is $.055 per ounce. **3.** The unit cost is $.374 per ounce. **5.** The unit cost is $.080 per tablet.
7. The unit price is $6.975 per clamp. **9.** The unit cost is $.199 per ounce. **11.** The unit cost is $.119 per screw.
13. The Sutter Home pasta sauce is the more economical purchase. **15.** 20 ounces is the more economical purchase.
17. 400 tablets is the more economical purchase. **19.** Land O' Lakes cheddar cheese is the more economical purchase.
21. Maxwell House coffee is the more economical purchase. **23.** Friskies Chef's Blend is the more economical purchase.
25. The total cost is $13.77. **27.** The total cost is $1.84. **29.** The total cost is $6.37. **31.** The total cost is $2.71.
33. The total cost is $5.96.

SECTION 6.2

1. The percent increase is 19.6%. **3.** The percent increase is 117.6%. **5.** The percent increase is 457.1%.
7. The population 8 years later was 157,861 people. **9.** The average age of American mothers giving birth in 2000 was
24.9 years. **11.** The markup is $35.70. **13.** The markup rate is 30%. **15. a.** The markup is $77.76. **b.** The
selling price is $239.76. **17. a.** The markup is $1.10. **b.** The selling price is $3.10. **19.** The selling price is $74.
21. The amount represents a decrease of 40%. **23.** There is a decrease of 540 employees. **25. a.** The amount of
decrease is 13 minutes. **b.** The amount represents a decrease of 25%. **27. a.** The amount of decrease is $.60.
b. The new dividend is $1.00. **29.** The amount represents a decrease of 6.6%. **31.** The discount rate is $33\frac{1}{3}\%$.
33. The discount is $68. **35.** The discount rate is 30%. **37. a.** The discount is $.25 per pound. **b.** The sale price
is $1.00 per pound. **39. a.** The amount of the discount is $4. **b.** The discount rate is 20%. **41.** Yes

SECTION 6.3

1. a. $10,000 **b.** $850 **c.** 4.25% **d.** 2 years **3.** The simple interest owed is $960. **5.** The simple interest
due is $3375. **7.** The simple interest due is $1320. **9.** The simple interest due is $92.47. **11.** The simple interest
due is $84.76. **13.** The maturity value is $5120. **15.** The maturity value is $164,250. **17.** The total amount due
on the loan is $12,875. **19.** The maturity value is $14,543.70. **21.** The monthly payment is $6187.50.
23. a. The interest charged is $1080. **b.** The monthly payment is $545. **25.** The monthly payment is $1332.50.
27. The finance charge is $1.48. **29.** The finance charge is $185.53. **31.** The difference in finance charges is $10.07.
33. The value of the investment after 1 year is $780.60. **35.** The value of the investment after 15 years is $7281.78.
37. a. The value of the investment in 5 years will be $111,446.25. **b.** The amount of interest earned will be $36,446.25.
39. The amount of interest earned is $5799.48. **41.** The interest owed is $16.

SECTION 6.4

1. Lewis earns $380. **3.** The real estate agent's commission is $3930. **5.** The stockbroker's commission is $84.
7. The teacher's monthly salary is $3244. **9.** The overtime wage is $51.60/hour. **11.** The golf pro's commission was
$112.50. **13.** The typist earns $618.75. **15.** Maxine's hourly wage is $85. **17. a.** Mark's hourly wage on Saturday
is $23.85. **b.** Mark earns $190.80. **19. a.** The nurse's increase in hourly pay is $2.15. **b.** The nurse's hourly pay
is $23.65. **21.** Nicole's earnings were $475. **23.** The starting salary for a chemical engineer increased $922 over that
of the previous year. **25.** The starting salary for a political science major decreased $4115 from that of the previous year.

SECTION 6.5

1. Your current checking account balance is $486.32.   **3.** The real estate firm's current checking account balance is $1222.47.   **5.** The nutritionist's current balance is $825.27.   **7.** The current checking account balance is $3000.82.   **9.** Yes, there is enough money in the carpenter's account to purchase the refrigerator.   **11.** Yes, there is enough money in the account to make the two purchases.   **13.** The bank statement and checkbook balance.   **15.** The bank statement and checkbook balance.   **17.** added   **19.** subtract

Chapter Review

1. The unit cost is $.195 per ounce or 19.5¢ per ounce.   **2.** The cost is $.164 or 16.4¢ per mile.   **3.** The percent increase is 30.4%.   **4.** The markup is $72.   **5.** The simple interest due is $3000.   **6.** The value of the investment after 10 years is $45,550.75.   **7.** The percent increase is 15%.   **8.** The total monthly payment for the mortgage and property tax is $578.53.   **9.** The monthly payment is $518.02.   **10.** The value of the investment will be $53,593.   **11.** The down payment is $18,750.   **12.** The total cost of the sales tax and license fee is $1471.25.   **13.** The selling price is $2079.   **14.** The interest paid is $97.33.   **15.** The commission was $3240.   **16.** The sale price is $141.   **17.** The current checkbook balance is $943.68.   **18.** The maturity value is $31,200.   **19.** The origination fee is $1875.   **20.** The more economical purchase is 33 ounces for $6.99.   **21.** The monthly mortgage payment is $934.08.   **22.** The total income was $655.20.   **23.** The donut shop's checkbook balance is $8866.58.   **24.** The monthly payment is $14,093.75.   **25.** The finance charge is $7.20.

Chapter Test

1. The cost per foot is $6.92.   **2.** The more economical purchase is 3 pounds for $7.49.   **3.** The total cost is $14.53.   **4.** The percent increase in the cost of the exercise bicycle is 20%.   **5.** The selling price of the compact disc player is $301.   **6.** The percent decrease is 7.7%.   **7.** The percent decrease is 20%.   **8.** The sale price of the corner hutch is $209.30.   **9.** The discount rate is 40%.   **10.** The simple interest due is $2000.   **11.** The maturity value is $26,725.   **12.** The finance charge is $4.50.   **13.** The amount of interest earned in 10 years will be $24,420.60.   **14.** The loan origination fee is $3350.   **15.** The monthly mortgage payment is $1713.44.   **16.** The amount financed is $19,000.   **17.** The monthly truck payment is $482.68.   **18.** Shaney earns $1071.   **19.** The current checkbook balance is $6612.25.   **20.** The bank statement and the checkbook balance.

Answers to Chapter 7 Odd-Numbered Exercises

PREP TEST

1. 43 **2.** 51 **3.** 56 **4.** 56.52 **5.** 113.04 **6.** 14.4

SECTION 7.1

1. 0°; 90° **3.** 180° **5.** 30 **7.** 21 **9.** 14 **11.** 59° **13.** 108° **15.** 77° **17.** 53° **19.** 77° **21.** 118°
23. 133° **25.** 86° **27.** 180° **29.** Rectangle or square **31.** Cube **33.** Parallelogram, rectangle, or square
35. Cylinder **37.** 102° **39.** 90° and 45° **41.** 14° **43.** 90° and 65° **45.** 8 in. **47.** $4\frac{2}{3}$ ft **49.** 7 cm
51. 2 ft 4 in. **53.** $\angle a = 106°$, $\angle b = 74°$ **55.** $\angle a = 112°$, $\angle b = 68°$ **57.** $\angle a = 38°$, $\angle b = 142°$
59. $\angle a = 58°$, $\angle b = 58°$ **61.** $\angle a = 152°$, $\angle b = 152°$ **63.** $\angle a = 130°$, $\angle b = 50°$ **65. a.** 1° **b.** 90°

SECTION 7.2

1. 56 in. **3.** 20 ft **5.** 92 cm **7.** 47.1 cm **9.** 9 ft 10 in. **11.** 50.24 cm **13.** 240 m **15.** 157 cm
17. 121 cm **19.** 50.56 m **21.** 3.57 ft **23.** 139.3 m **25.** The amount of fencing needed is 60 ft. **27.** The
amount of binding needed is 24 ft. **29.** The total cost of the fence is $24,422.50. **31.** The bicycle travels 31.4 ft.
33. a. The perimeter of the rink is larger than the perimeter of the rectangle. The perimeter of the rink is more than 70 m.
b. The perimeter of the rink is 81.4 m. **35.** Approximately 20.71 ft of weather stripping are installed. **37.** The
circumference of Earth is approximately 39,915.68 km. **39.** 22 units **41.** $14\frac{1}{4}$ cm

SECTION 7.3

1. 144 ft² **3.** 81 in² **5.** 50.24 ft² **7.** 20 in² **9.** 2.13 cm² **11.** 16 ft² **13.** 817 in² **15.** 154 in²
17. 26 cm² **19.** 2220 cm² **21.** 150.72 in² **23.** 8.851323 ft² **25.** The area of the playing field is 7500 yd².
27. The area watered by the irrigation system is approximately 7850 ft². **29.** You should buy 2 qt. **31.** The area of
the driveway is 1250 ft². **33.** The cost to wallpaper the two walls is $114. **35.** $17.25 should be budgeted for grass
seed. **37.** The total area of the park is 125.1492 mi². **39. a.** The amount of the increase is about 113.04 in².
b. The amount of the increase is about 235.5 cm². **41. a.** If the length and width are doubled, the area is increased
4 times. **b.** If the radius is doubled, the area is quadrupled. **c.** If the diameter is doubled, the area is quadrupled.
43. a. Sometimes true **b.** Sometimes true **c.** Always true

SECTION 7.4

1. 144 cm³ **3.** 512 in³ **5.** 2143.57 in³ **7.** 150.72 cm³ **9.** 6.4 m³ **11.** 5572.45 mm³ **13.** 3391.2 ft³
15. $42\frac{7}{8}$ ft³ **17.** 82.26 in³ **19.** 1.6688 m³ **21.** 69.08 in³ **23.** The volume of the water in the tank is 40.5 m³.
25. The volume is approximately 17,148.59 ft³. **27.** The amount of oil is approximately 75.36 m³. **29.** The volume of
the auditorium is approximately 809,516.25 ft³. **31.** The volume of the bushing is approximately 212.64 in³. **33.** The
tank will hold 3.7 gal. **35.** The cost is approximately $6526.41. **37. a.** 4 times larger **b.** 8 times larger
c. 8 times larger

SECTION 7.5

1. 2.646 **3.** 6.481 **5.** 12.845 **7.** 13.748 **9.** 5 in. **11.** 8.602 cm **13.** 11.180 ft **15.** 4.472 cm
17. 12.728 yd **19.** 10.392 ft **21.** 21.213 cm **23.** 8.944 m **25.** 7.879 yd **27.** The ramp is 9.66 ft long.
29. The distance is 21.6 mi. **31.** The length of the diagonal is 12.1 mi. **33.** The ladder is 7.4 m high on the building.
35. The perimeter is 27.7 in. **37.** The distance is 250 ft. **39.** The distance is 4.243 in. **41. a.** Always true
b. Always true **45.** 8 m

Chapter Review

1. 0.75 m **2.** 31.4 cm **3.** 26 ft **4.** 3 **5.** 200 ft³

6. 26 cm **7.** 75° **8.** 3.873 **9.** 16 cm **10.** 63.585 cm²

11. a. 45° **b.** 135° **12.** 55 m² **13.** 240 in³ **14.** 57.12 in²

15. 267.9 ft³ **16.** 64.8 m² **17.** 47.7 in. **18. a.** 80° **b.** 100°

19. The ladder will reach 15 ft up the building. **20.** The other angles of the triangle are 90° and 58°.

21. The bicycle travels approximately 73.3 ft in 10 revolutions. **22.** The area of the room is 28 yd².

23. The volume of the silo is approximately 1144.53 ft³. **24.** The area is 11 m².

25. The distance from the starting point is 29 mi.

Chapter Test

1. 169.56 m³ **2.** 6.8 m **3.** 1406.72 cm³ **4.** 10 m **5.** 58°

6. $3\frac{1}{7}$ m² **7.** 150° **8.** 15.85 ft **9.** 13.748 **10.** 9.747 ft

11. 10.125 ft² **12.** $\angle a = 45°$; $\angle b = 135°$ **13.** $1\frac{1}{5}$ ft **14.** 90° and 50°

15. The width of the canal is 25 ft. **16.** The amount of extra pizza is 113.04 in². **17.** It will cost $1113.69 to carpet the area. **18.** The area is 103.82 ft². **19.** The length of the rafter is 15 ft.

20. The volume of the interior of the toolbox is 780 in³.

Answers to Chapter 8 Odd-Numbered Exercises

PREP TEST

1. 702   **2.** 58   **3.** 4   **4.** 10   **5.** 25   **6.** 46   **7.** 238
8. 1.5

SECTION 8.1

1. 72 in.   **3.** $2\frac{1}{2}$ ft   **5.** 39 ft   **7.** $5\frac{1}{3}$ yd   **9.** 84 in.   **11.** $3\frac{1}{3}$ yd   **13.** 10,560 ft   **15.** $\frac{5}{8}$ ft   **17.** 1 mi 1120 ft

19. 9 ft 11 in.   **21.** 2 ft 9 in.   **23.** 14 ft 6 in.   **25.** 2 ft 8 in.   **27.** $11\frac{1}{6}$ ft   **29.** 4 mi 2520 ft   **31.** 14 tiles can

be placed along one row.   **33.** The missing dimension is $1\frac{5}{6}$ ft.   **35.** The length of material needed is $7\frac{1}{2}$ in.

37. The length of each piece is $1\frac{2}{3}$ ft.   **39.** The length of framing needed is 6 ft 6 in.   **41.** The total length of the wall

is $33\frac{3}{4}$ ft.   **43.** Yes.

SECTION 8.2

1. 4 lb   **3.** 128 oz   **5.** $1\frac{3}{5}$ tons   **7.** 12,000 lb   **9.** $4\frac{1}{8}$ lb   **11.** 24 oz   **13.** 2600 lb   **15.** $\frac{1}{4}$ ton

17. $11\frac{1}{4}$ lb   **19.** 4 tons 1000 lb   **21.** 2 lb 8 oz   **23.** 5 tons 400 lb   **25.** 1 ton 1700 lb   **27.** 33 lb

29. 14 lb   **31.** 9 oz   **33.** 1 lb 7 oz   **35.** The load of bricks weighs 2000 lb.   **37.** The package of tiles weighs 63 lb.
39. The weight of the case of soft drinks is 9 lb.   **41.** Each container holds 1 lb 5 oz of shampoo.   **43.** The ham roast
costs $27.   **45.** The cost of mailing the manuscript is $8.75.   **47.** Answers will vary.

SECTION 8.3

1. $7\frac{1}{2}$ c   **3.** 24 fl oz   **5.** 4 pt   **7.** 7 c   **9.** $5\frac{1}{2}$ gal   **11.** 9 qt   **13.** $3\frac{3}{4}$ qt   **15.** $1\frac{1}{4}$ pt   **17.** $4\frac{1}{4}$ qt

19. 3 gal 2 qt   **21.** 2 qt 1 pt   **23.** 7 qt   **25.** 6 fl oz   **27.** $17\frac{1}{2}$ pt   **29.** $\frac{7}{8}$ gal   **31.** 5 gal 1 qt

33. 1 gal 2 qt   **35.** $2\frac{3}{4}$ gal   **37.** $7\frac{1}{2}$ gal of coffee should be prepared.   **39.** There are $4\frac{1}{4}$ qt of final solution.

41. The farmer used $8\frac{3}{4}$ gal of oil.   **43.** The more economical purchase is $1.59 for 1 qt.   **45.** The profit made was

$83.50.   **47.** 1 grain = 0.002286 oz; 1 dram = 0.0625 oz; 1 furlong = $\frac{1}{8}$ mi; 1 rod = 16.5 ft

SECTION 8.4

1. 14 weeks   **3.** 150 h   **5.** $9\frac{1}{4}$ h   **7.** 1110 s   **9.** $3\frac{1}{2}$ h   **11.** 23,400 s   **13.** $3\frac{1}{2}$ days   **15.** 3600 min

17. 4 weeks   **19.** 504 h   **21.** 2 days   **23.** 259,200 s   **25.** Yes   **27.** Yes   **29.** 7 years   **31.** 2190 days
33. 30,660 h

SECTION 8.5

1. 19,450 ft · lb   **3.** 19,450,000 ft · lb   **5.** 1500 ft · lb   **7.** 29,700 ft · lb   **9.** 30,000 ft · lb   **11.** 25,500 ft · lb

13. 35,010,000 ft · lb   **15.** 9,336,000 ft · lb   **17.** 2 hp   **19.** 8 hp   **21.** 4950 $\frac{\text{ft} \cdot \text{lb}}{\text{s}}$ **23.** 3850 $\frac{\text{ft} \cdot \text{lb}}{\text{s}}$

25. 500 $\frac{\text{ft} \cdot \text{lb}}{\text{s}}$ **27.** 4800 $\frac{\text{ft} \cdot \text{lb}}{\text{s}}$ **29.** 1440 $\frac{\text{ft} \cdot \text{lb}}{\text{s}}$ **31.** 9 hp   **33.** 12 hp

Chapter Review

1. 48 in. **2.** 2 ft 6 in. **3.** 1600 ft · lb **4.** 40 fl oz **5.** $4\frac{2}{3}$ yd

6. $1\frac{1}{5}$ tons **7.** 2 lb 7 oz **8.** 54 oz **9.** 9 ft 3 in. **10.** 1 ton 1000 lb

11. 7 c 2 fl oz **12.** 1 yd 2 ft **13.** 3 qt **14.** $6\frac{1}{4}$ h **15.** $1375\frac{\text{ft} \cdot \text{lb}}{\text{s}}$

16. 44 lb **17.** 38,900 ft · lb **18.** 7 hp **19.** The length of the remaining piece is 3 ft 6 in.

20. The cost of mailing the book is $8.40. **21.** There are $13\frac{1}{2}$ qt in a case.

22. 16 gal of milk were sold that day. **23.** 27,230,000 ft · lb **24.** $480\frac{\text{ft} \cdot \text{lb}}{\text{s}}$

Chapter Test

1. 30 in. **2.** 2 ft 5 in. **3.** $1\frac{1}{3}$ ft **4.** The wall is 48 ft long. **5.** 46 oz

6. 2 lb 8 oz **7.** 17 lb 1 oz **8.** 1 lb 11oz **9.** The total weight of the workbooks is 750 lb.

10. The amount the class received for recycling was $28.13. **11.** $3\frac{1}{4}$ gal **12.** 28 pt

13. $12\frac{1}{4}$ gal **14.** 8 gal 1 qt **15.** $4\frac{1}{2}$ weeks **16.** 4680 min **17.** There are 60 c in a case. **18.** Nick's profit is $144. **19.** 3750 ft · lb **20.** 31,120,000 ft · lb

21. $160\frac{\text{ft} \cdot \text{lb}}{\text{s}}$ **22.** 4 hp

Answers to Chapter 9 Odd-Numbered Exercises

PREP TEST

1. 37,320   **2.** 659,000   **3.** 0.04107   **4.** 28.496   **5.** 5.125
6. 5.96   **7.** 0.13   **8.** 56.35   **9.** 0.5   **10.** 675

SECTION 9.1

1. 420 mm   **3.** 8.1 cm   **5.** 6.804 km   **7.** 2109 m   **9.** 4.32 m   **11.** 88 cm   **13.** 7.038 km   **15.** 3500 m
17. 2.60 m   **19.** 168.5 cm   **21.** 148 mm   **23.** 62.07 m   **25.** 31.9 cm   **27.** 8.075 km   **29.** The missing dimension is 7.8 cm.   **31.** The distance between the rivets is 17.9 cm.   **33.** The amount of fencing left on the roll is 15.6 m.   **35.** It takes 500 s for light to travel from the sun to Earth.   **37.** Light travels 25,920,000,000 km in 1 day.

SECTION 9.2

1. 0.420 kg   **3.** 0.127 g   **5.** 4200 g   **7.** 450 mg   **9.** 1.856 kg   **11.** 4.057 g   **13.** 1370 g   **15.** 45.6 mg
17. 18.000 kg   **19.** 3.922 kg   **21.** 7.891 g   **23.** 4.063 kg   **25.** There are 40 g in 1 serving.   **27. a.** There are 3.288 g of cholesterol in 12 eggs.   **b.** There are 0.132 g of cholesterol in four glasses of milk.   **29. a.** There is 0.186 kg of mix in the package.   **b.** There is 0.42 g of sodium in two servings.   **31.** The amount of seed needed is 1.6 kg.
33. The profit from repackaging the nuts is $117.50.   **35.** Corn was 50.3% of the total exports.

SECTION 9.3

1. 4.2 L   **3.** 3420 ml   **5.** 423 cm^3 **7.** 642 ml   **9.** 0.042 L   **11.** 435 cm^3 **13.** 4620 L   **15.** 1.423 kl
17. 1267 cm^3 **19.** 3.042 L   **21.** 3.004 kl   **23.** 8.200 L   **25. a.** There is less than 25 L of oxygen in 50 L of air.
b. There are 10.5 L of oxygen in 50 L of air.   **27.** 24 L of chlorine were used in a month.   **29.** 4000 patients can be immunized.   **31.** The 12 one-liter bottles are the better buy.   **33.** The profit on the gasoline was $8465.   **35.** 2.72 L; 2720 ml; 2L 720 ml

SECTION 9.4

1. 3300 Calories can be omitted from your diet.   **3. a.** There are 90 Calories in $1\frac{1}{2}$ servings.   **b.** There are 30 fat Calories in 6 slices of bread.   **5.** 2025 Calories would be needed.   **7.** You burn 10,125 Calories.   **9.** You would have to hike for 2.6 h.   **11.** 1250 Wh are used.   **13.** The fax machine used 0.567 kWh.   **15.** The cost of running an air conditioner is $1.58.   **17. a.** 400 lumens is less than half the output of Soft White bulb.   **b.** The energy saver bulb costs $.42 less to operate.   **19.** The cost of using the welder is $109.98.   **21.** Answers will vary.

Chapter Review

1. 1250 m   **2.** 450 mg   **3.** 5.6 ml   **4.** 1090 yd   **5.** 7.9 cm
6. 5.34 m   **7.** 0.990 kg   **8.** 2.550 L   **9.** 4.870 km   **10.** 3.7 mm
11. 6.829 g   **12.** 1200 cm^3 **13.** 4050 g   **14.** 870 cm   **15.** 192 cm^3
16. 0.356 g   **17.** 3.72 m   **18.** 8300 L   **19.** 2.089 L   **20.** 5.410 L
21. 3.792 kl   **22.** 468 ml   **23.** There are 37.2 m of wire left on the roll.   **24.** The total cost of the chicken is $12.72.   **25.** $7.48/kg   **26.** The amount of coffee that should be prepared is 50 L.
27. You can eliminate 2700 Calories.   **28.** The cost of running the TV set is $3.42.
29. 4.18 lb   **30.** 8.75 h of cycling are needed.   **31.** The profit was $52.80.
32. The color TV used 1.120 kWh of electricity.   **33.** The amount of fertilizer used was 125 kg.

Chapter Test

1. 2960 m   **2.** 378 mg   **3.** 46 ml   **4.** 919 ml   **5.** 4.26 cm

6. 7.96 m   **7.** 0.847 kg   **8.** 3.920 L   **9.** 5.885 km   **10.** 15 mm

11. 3.089 g   **12.** 1600 cm³   **13.** 3290 g   **14.** 420 cm   **15.** 96 cm³

16. 1.375 g   **17.** 4.02 m   **18.** 8920 L   **19.** A 140-pound sedentary person should consume 2100 Calories per day to maintain that weight.   **20.** 3.15 kWh of energy is used during the week for operating the television.   **21.** The total length of the rafters is 114 m.   **22.** The weight of the box is 36 kg.

23. The amount of vaccine needed is 5.2 L.   **24.** 56.4 km/h   **25.** The distance between the rivets is 17.5 cm.   **26.** The cost to fertilize the trees is $660.   **27.** The total cost is $16.32.   **28.** The assistant should order 11 L of acid.   **29.** The measure of the large hill is 393.6 ft.

30. 4.8 in. is approximately 12.2 cm.

Answers to Chapter 10 Odd-Numbered Exercises

PREP TEST

1. 48.0% was bill-related mail.　　**2. a.** The greatest cost increase is between 2009 and 2010.　　**b.** Between those years, there was an increase of $5318.　　**3. a.** The ratio is $\frac{5}{3}$.　　**b.** The ratio is $1:1$.

4. a. 3.9, 3.9, 4.2, 4.5, 5.2, 5.5, 7.1　**b.** The average is 4.9 million viewers per night.

5. a. 4500 women are in the Marine Corps.　　　　**b.** $\frac{1}{20}$ of the women in the military are in the Marine Corps.

SECTION 10.1

1. The gross revenue is $750 million.　　**3.** The percent is 40%.　　**5.** 50 more people agreed that humanity should explore space than agreed that space exploration impacts daily life.　　**7.** 150 children said they hid their vegetables under a napkin.　　**11.** The ratio is $\frac{1}{3}$.　　**13.** The percent is 9.4%.　　**15.** The number of people surveyed is 150 people.

17. The percent is 28%.　　**19.** Americans spent $279,000,000 on portable game machines.　　**21.** Yes.

23. The number of homeless aged 25 to 34 is more than twice the number of homeless under the age of 25.

25. Out of every 100,000 homeless people, there are 8000 people over age 54.　　**27.** North America is 2,550,000 square miles larger than South America.　　**29.** Australia is 5.2% of the total land area.　　**31.** $2027.50 is spent on health care.

33. No, the amount spent on housing is not more than twice the amount spent on transporation.

SECTION 10.2

1. 39 million passenger cars were produced worldwide.　　**3.** The percent is 28%.　　**5.** The Mini Cooper gets approximately 10 more miles per gallon while traveling on the highway.　　**7.** The maximum salary of police officers in the suburbs is $16,000 higher than the maximum salary of police officers in the city.　　**9.** The greatest difference in salaries is in Philadelphia.　　**11.** The average snowfall during January is 20 inches.　　**13.** The snowfall during March and April was 25 inches.　　**15.** The difference is 800 Calories.　　**17.** The ratio is $\frac{7}{6}$.

19.

Year	Difference Between the Amount Spent for Foreign and for Domestic Aid (in billions of dollars)
1991	$1.3
1992	$1.1
1993	$1.0
1994	$0.9
1995	$0.8
1996	$0.8
1997	$1.1
1998	$0.9
1999	$1.0

SECTION 10.3

1. 44 students have a tuition that is between $3000 and $6000.　　**3.** 18 students paid more than $12,000.　　**5.** There are 410 cars between 6 and 12 years old.　　**7.** 230 cars are more than 12 years old.　　**9.** 54 adults spend between 1 and 2 hours at the mall.　　**11.** The percent is 22%.　　**13.** There were 24 entrants in the discus finals.　　**15.** 37.5% of the entrants had distances between 160 feet and 170 feet.　　**17.** The percent is 10.8%.　　**21.** The percent is 32.4%.

23. 900,000 students scored above 800.

SECTION 10.4

1. a. Median   **b.** Mean   **c.** Mode   **d.** Median   **e.** Mode   **f.** Mean   **3.** The mean number of seats filled is 381.5625 seats. The median number of seats filled is 394.5 seats. Since each number occurs only once, there is no mode. **5.** The mean cost is $45.615. The median cost is $45.855.   **7.** The mean monthly rate is $403.625. The median monthly rate is $404.50.   **9.** The mean life expectancy is 70.8 years. The median life expectancy is 72 years.   **13. a.** 25% **b.** 75%   **c.** 75%   **d.** 25%   **15.** Lowest is $46,596. Highest is $82,879. Q_1 = $56,067. Q_3 = $66,507. Median = $61,036. Range = $36,283. Interquartile range = $10,440.   **17. a.** There were 40 adults who had cholesterol levels above 217.   **b.** There were 60 adults who had cholesterol levels below 254.   **c.** There are 20 cholesterol levels in each quartile.   **d.** 25% of the adults had cholesterol levels not more than 198.   **19. a.** Range = 4.39 million metric tons. Q_1 = 0.56 million metric tons. Q_3 = 2.10 million metric tons. Interquartile range = 1.54 million metric tons

b. 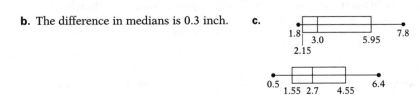   **c.** 4.80   **21. a.** No, the difference in the means is not greater than 1 inch.

b. The difference in medians is 0.3 inch.   **c.**

23. Answers will vary. For example, 55, 55, 55, 55, 55, or 50, 55, 55, 55, 60

SECTION 10.5

1. {(HHHH), (HHHT), (HHTT), (HHTH), (HTTT), (HTHH), (HTTH), (HTHT), (TTTT), (TTTH), (TTHH), (THHH), (TTHT), (THHT), (THTT), (THTH)}   **3.** {(1, 1), (1, 2), (1, 3), (1, 4), (2, 1), (2, 2), (2, 3), (2, 4), (3, 1), (3, 2), (3, 3), (3, 4), (4, 1), (4, 2), (4, 3), (4, 4)}   **5. a.** {1, 2, 3, 4, 5, 6, 7, 8}   **b.** {1, 2, 3}   **7. a.** The probability that the sum is 5 is $\frac{1}{9}$.

b. The probability that the sum is 15 is 0.   **c.** The probablity that the sum is less than 15 is 1.   **d.** The probability that the sum is 2 is $\frac{1}{36}$.   **9. a.** The probability that the number is divisible by 4 is $\frac{1}{4}$.   **b.** The probability that the number is a multiple of 3 is $\frac{1}{3}$.   **11.** The probability of throwing a sum of 5 is greater.   **13. a.** The probability is $\frac{4}{11}$ that the letter I is drawn.   **b.** The probability of choosing an S is greater.   **15. a.** The probability is $\frac{1}{3}$ that the marble chosen is green.   **b.** The probability of choosing a red marble is greater.   **17.** The probability is $\frac{8}{47}$ that the paper has a B grade.   **19.** The probability is 0.81 that an employee has a group health insurance plan.

Chapter Review

1. The agencies spent $349 million on maintaining websites.   **2.** The ratio is $\frac{9}{8}$.   **3.** 8.9% of the total amount of money was spent by NASA.   **4.** Texas had the larger population.   **5.** The population of California is 12.5 million people more than the population of Texas.   **6.** The Texas population increased the least from 1925 to 1950.   **7.** There were 54 games in which the Knicks scored fewer than 100 points.

8. The ratio is $\frac{31}{8}$.   **9.** The percent is 11.3%.   **10.** From the pictograph, O'Hare airport has 10 million more passengers than Los Angeles airport.   **11.** The ratio is 2:3.   **12.** The difference was 50 days.   **13.** The percent is 50%.   **14. a.** The Southeast had the lowest number of days of full operation.   **b.** This region had 30 days of full operation.   **15.** The probability of one tail and three heads is $\frac{1}{4}$.   **16.** There were 15 people who slept 8 or more hours.   **17.** The percent is 28.3%.

18. a. The mean heart rate is 91.6 heartbeats per minute. The median heart rate is 93.5 heartbeats per minute. The mode is 96 heartbeats per minute.   **b.** The range is 36 heartbeats per minute. The interquartile range is 15 heartbeats per minute.

Chapter Test

1. 19 students spent between $15 and $25 each week.   **2.** The ratio is $\frac{2}{3}$.   **3.** The percent is 45%.   **4.** There were 36 people that were surveyed for the Gallup poll.   **5.** The ratio is $\frac{5}{2}$.

6. The percent is 58.3%.   **7.** During 1995 and 1996, the number of fatalities was the same.   **8.** There were 32 fatal accidents from 1991 to 1999.   **9.** There were 4 more fatalities from 1995 to 1998.   **10.** There were 355 more films rated R.   **11.** There were 16 times more films rated PG-13.   **12.** The percent of films rated G was 5.6%.   **13.** There are 24 states that have a median income between $40,000 and $60,000.   **14.** The percent is 72%.   **15.** The percent is 18%.   **16.** The probability is $\frac{3}{10}$ that the ball chosen is red.   **17.** The student enrollment increased the least during the 1990s.   **18.** The increase in the enrollment was 11 million students.   **19. a.** The mean time is 2.53 days.   **b.** The median time is 2.55 days.   **c.**

2.0   2.35 2.55 2.8   3.1

Answers to Chapter 11 Odd-Numbered Exercises

PREP TEST

1. 3   **2.** −1   **3.** −3x + 12   **4.** −2   **5.** x = 5   **6.** y = −2

7. −4x + 5   **8.** 4   **9.** $y = \frac{3}{5}x - 3$ **10.** $y = -\frac{1}{2}x - 5$

SECTION 11.1

1.   **3.** 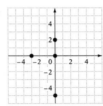   **5.** 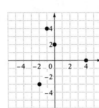   **7.** A(2, 3), B(4, 0), C(−4, 1), D(−2, −2)

9. A(−2, 5), B(3, 4), C(0, 0), D(−3, −2)   **11. a.** 2, −4   **b.** 1, −3   **15.** Yes   **17.** No   **19.** No   **21.** No

23. 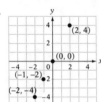   **25.** 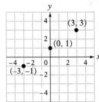   **27.**

29. {(24, 600), (32, 750), (22, 430), (15, 300), (4.4, 68), (17, 370), (15, 310), (4.4, 55)}; No

31. {(390, 0.115), (591, 0.073), (517, 0.077), (576, 0.068), (605, 0.064)}; Yes   **33.** Yes   **35.** No   **37.** Yes   **39.** 8

41. 9   **43.** 2   **45.** −1   **47.** 22   **49.** $-\frac{3}{2}$ **51.** −7

SECTION 11.2

1. 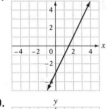   **3.** 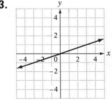   **5.** 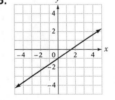   **7.**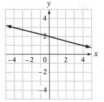

9. 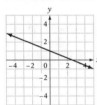   **11.** 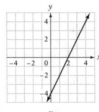   **13.** 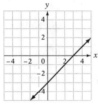   **15.**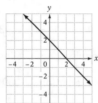

7. 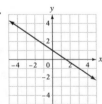   **19.** 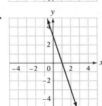   **21.** 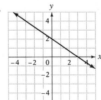   **23.**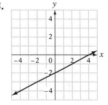

SECTION 11.2

25. 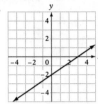 **27.** 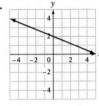 **29.** 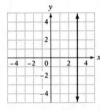 **31.**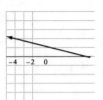

33. 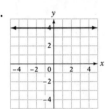 **35.**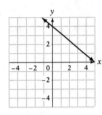

37. After flying for 3 min, the helicopter is 3.5 mi away from the victims.

39. A dog 6 years is equivalent in age to a human 40 years old.

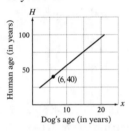

43. Increases; 3; 3   **45. a.** The cost is $.99.   **b.** The cost is $1.74.

SECTION 11.3

1. $(3, 0), (0, -3)$ **3.** $(2, 0), (0, -6)$ **5.** $(10, 0), (0, -2)$ **7.** $(-4, 0), (0, 12)$ **9.** $(0, 0), (0, 0)$ **11.** $(6, 0), (0, 3)$

13. 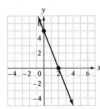   **15.**    **17.** 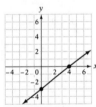   **21.** -2 **23.** $\dfrac{1}{3}$ **25.** $-\dfrac{5}{2}$

27. Undefined   **29.** 0   **31.** $-\dfrac{1}{3}$ **33.** Neither   **35.** Neither   **37.** Parallel   **39.** Neither   **41.** $m = 33$. The worldwide sales of camera-phones are increasing by 33 million units per year.   **43.** $m = -180$. The value of the car is decreasing $180 for each additional 1000 miles the car is driven.   **45.** $m = \dfrac{2}{3}$; $(0, -2)$ **47.** $m = -\dfrac{2}{5}$; $(0, 2)$

SECTION 11.3

49. $m = \dfrac{1}{4}$; $(0, 0)$ **51.** 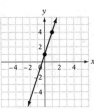   **53.** 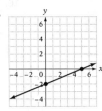   **55.**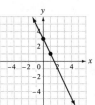

57. 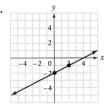   **59.** 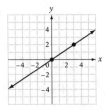   **61.**   **63.**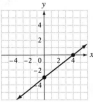

65. 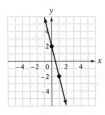   **67.** Yes

Chapter Review

1. a. 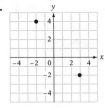   **2.** 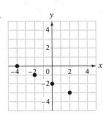   **3.** $y = -\dfrac{8}{3}x + \dfrac{1}{3}$ **4.** $y = -\dfrac{5}{2}x + 16$

b. -2

c. -4

5. 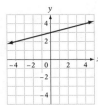   **6.** 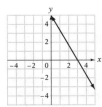   **7.** Neither   **8.** -1

9. $y = -\dfrac{2}{3}x + \dfrac{11}{3}$ **10.** Yes   **11.** $\dfrac{7}{11}$ **12.** $(8, 0), (0, -12)$ **13.** 0

Chapter Review

14.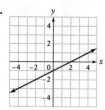

15.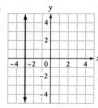

16.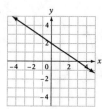

17.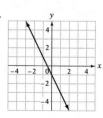

18.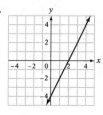

19.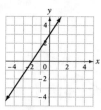

20. {(55, 95), (57, 101), (53, 94), (57, 98), (60, 100), (61, 105), (58, 97), (54, 95)}; No

21. The cost of 50 min of access time for one month is $97.50.

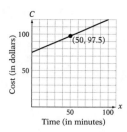

22. The average annual telephone bill for a family is increasing by $34 per year.

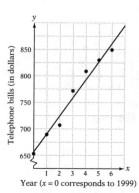

Chapter Test

1. $(3, -3)$

2.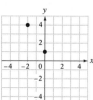

3. Yes

4. 6

5. 3

6. {(3.5, 25), (4.0, 30), (5.2, 45), (5.0, 38), (4.0, 42), (6.3, 12), (5.4, 34)}; No

7.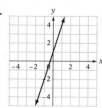

Chapter Test

8.

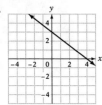

9.

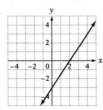

10.

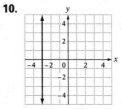

11.

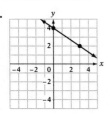

12.

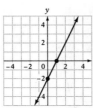

13. After 1 s, the speed of the ball is 96 ft/s.

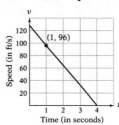

14. $m = 0.46$. The average hourly wage is increasing by \$.46 per year.

15.

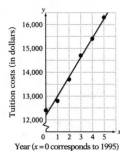

The average annual tuition for a private 4-year college is increasing \$809 per year.

16. $(2, 0), (0, -3)$

17. $(-2, 0), (0, 1)$

18. 2

19. Parallel

20. Undefined

21. $-\dfrac{2}{3}$

22. $y = 3x - 1$

23. $y = \dfrac{2}{3}x + 3$

24. $y = -\dfrac{5}{8}x - \dfrac{7}{8}$

25. $y = -\dfrac{2}{7}x - \dfrac{4}{7}$

Answers to Chapter 12 Odd-Numbered Exercises

SECTION 12.1

1. Down   **3.** Up   **5.** 4   **7.** -5 **9.** -42 **11.** 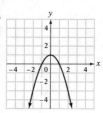   **13.**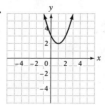

15. 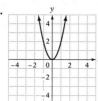   **17.** 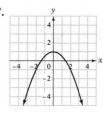   **19.** 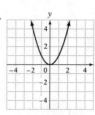   **21.**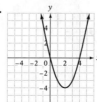

23. 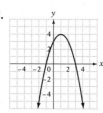   **25.** 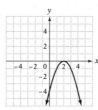   **27.** $(-6, 0), (1, 0); (0, -6)$ **29.** $(-6, 0); (0, 36)$

31. $(-2 - \sqrt{6}, 0), (-2 + \sqrt{6}, 0); (0, -2)$ **33.** No x-intercepts; $(0, 1)$ **35.** $\left(\dfrac{3}{2}, 0\right), (5, 0); (0, 15)$

37. $\left(\dfrac{-3 - \sqrt{33}}{6}, 0\right), \left(\dfrac{-3 + \sqrt{33}}{6}, 0\right); (0, 2)$ **39.** $y = 3x^2 + 6x + 5$ **41.** $y = 3x^2 - 6x$ **43.** $(-1, 0), (0, 0), (5, 0)$

45. $(-3, 0), (-1, 0), (1, 0)$

Chapter Review

1. $-\dfrac{7}{2}, \dfrac{4}{3}$ **2.** $-\dfrac{5}{7}, \dfrac{5}{7}$ **3.** $-6, 4$ **4.** $-6, 1$ **5.** $-4, \dfrac{3}{2}$

6. $\dfrac{5}{12}, 2$ **7.** $-2 - 2\sqrt{6}, -2 + 2\sqrt{6}$ **8.** $1, \dfrac{3}{2}$ **9.** $-\dfrac{1}{2}, -\dfrac{1}{3}$

10. No real number solution   **11.** $2 - \sqrt{3}, 2 + \sqrt{3}$ **12.** $\dfrac{3 - \sqrt{29}}{2}, \dfrac{3 + \sqrt{29}}{2}$

13. No real number solution   **14.** $-10, -7$ **15.** $-1, 2$

16. $\dfrac{-4 - \sqrt{23}}{2}, \dfrac{-4 + \sqrt{23}}{2}$ **17.** No real number solution   **18.** $-2, -\dfrac{1}{2}$

19. 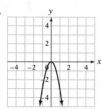   **20.** 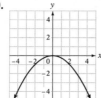   **21.**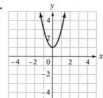

Chapter Review

22.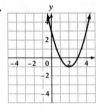

23.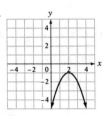

24. $(-3, 0), (5, 0); (0, -15)$ 　　　　 **25.** The rate of the hawk in calm air is 75 mph.

Chapter Test

1. $-1, 6$ 　　　　 **2.** $-4, \dfrac{5}{3}$ 　　　　 **3.** $0, 10$ 　　　　 **4.** $-4 - 2\sqrt{5}, -4 + 2\sqrt{5}$

5. $-2 - 2\sqrt{5}, -2 + 2\sqrt{5}$ 　　 **6.** $\dfrac{-3 - \sqrt{41}}{2}, \dfrac{-3 + \sqrt{41}}{2}$ 　　 **7.** $\dfrac{3 - \sqrt{7}}{2}, \dfrac{3 + \sqrt{7}}{2}$

8. $\dfrac{-4 - \sqrt{22}}{2}, \dfrac{-4 + \sqrt{22}}{2}$ 　　 **9.** $-2 - \sqrt{2}, -2 + \sqrt{2}$ 　　 **10.** $\dfrac{3 - \sqrt{33}}{2}, \dfrac{3 + \sqrt{33}}{2}$

11. $-\dfrac{1}{2}, 3$ 　　　　 **12.** $\dfrac{1 - \sqrt{13}}{6}, \dfrac{1 + \sqrt{13}}{6}$ 　　　　 **13.**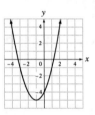

14. $(-4, 0), (3, 0); (0, -12)$ 　　　　 **15.** The width is 5 ft. The length is 8 ft.

16. The rate of the boat in calm water is 11 mph.

Answers to Chapter 13 Odd-Numbered Exercises

SECTION 13.1

3. c **5. a.** 9 **b.** 1 **c.** $\frac{1}{9}$ **7. a.** 16 **b.** 4 **c.** $\frac{1}{4}$ **9. a.** 1 **b.** $\frac{1}{8}$ **c.** 16 **11. a.** 7.3891

b. 0.3679 **c.** 1.2840 **13. a.** 54.5982 **b.** 1 **c.** 0.1353 **15. a.** 16 **b.** 16 **c.** 1.4768

17. a. 0.1353 **b.** 0.1353 **c.** 0.0111 **19.** 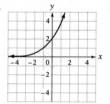 **21.**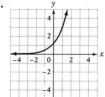

23. 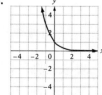 **25.** 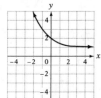 **27.** 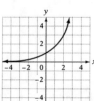 **29.**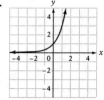

31. **b** and **d** **33.** (0, 1) **35.** No x-intercept; (0, 1) **37.** 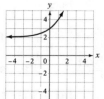 **39.**

41. a.   **b.** The point (2, 27.7) means that after 2 s, the object is falling at a speed of 27.7 ft/s.

SOLUTIONS TO CHECK YOUR PROGRESS PROBLEMS, SECTIONS 10.3, 10.4 AND 10.5, ADDITIONAL MATERIAL TO CHAPTER 6

SECTION 10.3

CHECK YOUR PROGRESS 1

Date	Payments or Purchases	Balance Each Day	Number of Days Until Balance Changes	Unpaid Balance Times Number of Days
July 1–6		$1024	6	$6144
July 7–14	$315	$1339	8	$10,712
July 15–21	−$400	$939	7	$6573
July 22–31	$410	$1349	10	$13,490
Total				$36,919

$$\text{Average daily balance} = \frac{\text{sum of the total amounts owed each day of the month}}{\text{number of days in the billing period}}$$
$$= \frac{36,919}{31} \approx \$1190.94$$

$I = Prt$
$I = 1190.94(0.012)(1)$
$I \approx 14.29$

The finance charge on the August 1 bill is $14.29.

CHECK YOUR PROGRESS 2

a. Down payment = Percent down × purchase price
           = 0.20 × 750 = 150

Amount financed = purchase price − down payment
           = 750 − 150 = 600

Interest owed = finance rate × amount financed
           = 0.08 × 600 = 48

The finance charge is $48.

b. $\text{APR} \approx \dfrac{2Nr}{N+1}$

$\approx \dfrac{2(12)(0.08)}{12+1} \approx \dfrac{1.92}{13} \approx 0.148$

The annual percentage rate is approximately 14.8%.

CHECK YOUR PROGRESS 3

Sales tax amount = sales tax rate × purchase price
$$= 0.0425 \times 1499 \approx 63.71$$

Amount financed = purchase price + sales tax amount
$$= 1499 + 63.71 = 1562.71$$

$$i = \frac{\text{annual interest rate}}{\text{number of payments per year}} = \frac{0.084}{12} = 0.007$$
$$n = 3(12) = 36$$

$$PMT = A\left(\frac{i}{1 - (1 + i)^{-n}}\right)$$

$$PMT = 1562.71\left(\frac{0.007}{1 - (1 + 0.007)^{-36}}\right)$$

$$PMT \approx 49.26$$

The monthly payment is $49.26.

CHECK YOUR PROGRESS 4

a. Sales tax = 0.0525(26,788) = 1406.37

b. Loan amount
$$= \text{purchase price} + \text{sales tax} + \text{license fee} - \text{down payment}$$
$$= 26,788 + 1406.37 + 145 - 2500$$
$$= 25,839.37$$

c. $i = \dfrac{APR}{12} = \dfrac{0.081}{12} = 0.00675; n = 12 \times 5 = 60$

$$PMT = A\left(\frac{i}{1 - (1 + i)^{-n}}\right)$$

$$PMT = 25,839.37\left(\frac{0.00675}{1 - (1 + 0.00675)^{-60}}\right)$$

$$PMT \approx 525.17$$

The monthly payment is $525.17.

CHECK YOUR PROGRESS 5

$$i = \frac{APR}{12} = \frac{0.084}{12} = 0.007$$

$$A = PMT\left(\frac{1 - (1 + i)^{-n}}{i}\right)$$

$$A = 592.57\left(\frac{1 - (1 + 0.007)^{-24}}{0.007}\right)$$

$$A \approx 13,049.34$$

The loan payoff is $13,049.34.

CHECK YOUR PROGRESS 6

Residual value = 0.40(33,395) = 13,358

$$\text{Money factor} = \frac{\text{annual interest rate as a percent}}{2400} = \frac{8}{2400}$$
$$\approx 0.00333333$$

Average monthly finance charge
$$= (\text{net capitalized cost} + \text{residual value}) \times \text{money factor}$$
$$= (31,900 + 13,358) \times 0.00333333$$
$$\approx 150.86$$

Average monthly depreciation
$$= \frac{\text{net capitalized cost} - \text{residual value}}{\text{term of the lease in months}}$$
$$= \frac{31,900 - 13,358}{60}$$
$$\approx 309.03$$

Monthly lease payment
$$= \text{average monthly finance charge} + \text{average monthly depreciation}$$
$$= 150.86 + 309.03$$
$$= 459.89$$

The monthly lease payment is $459.89.

SECTION 10.4

CHECK YOUR PROGRESS 1

($.72 per share) × (550 shares) = $396

The shareholder receives $396 in dividends.

CHECK YOUR PROGRESS 2

$$I = Prt$$

$0.82 = 51.25r(1)$ • **Let I = annual dividend and P = the stock price. The time is 1 year.**

$0.82 = 51.25r$

$0.016 = r$ • **Divide each side of the equation by 51.25.**

The dividend yield is 1.6%.

CHECK YOUR PROGRESS 3

a. From Table 10.2, the 52-week low is $29.43, and the 52-week high is $38.89.

Profit = selling price − purchase price

= 300($38.89) − 300($29.43)

= $11,667 − $8829 = $2838

The profit on the sale of the stock was $2838.

b. Commission = 2.1%(selling price)

= 0.021($11,667) ≈ $245.01

The broker's commission was $245.01.

CHECK YOUR PROGRESS 4

Use the simple interest formula to find the annual interest payments. Substitute the following values into the formula: $P = 15,000$, $r = 3.5\% = 0.035$, and $t = 1$.

$I = Prt$

$I = 15,000(0.035)(1)$

$I = 525$

Multiply the annual interest payments by the term of the bond.

$525(4) = 2100$

The total of the interest payments paid to the bondholder is $2100.

CHECK YOUR PROGRESS 5

a. $A - L = (750 \text{ million} + 0.75 \text{ million}$

$+ 1.5 \text{ million}) - 1.5 \text{ million}$

$= 750.75 \text{ million}, N = 20 \text{ million}$

$\text{NAV} = \dfrac{A - L}{N} = \dfrac{750.75 \text{ million}}{20 \text{ million}} = 37.5375$

The NAV of the fund is $37.5375.

b. $\dfrac{10,000}{37.5375} \approx 266$ • **Divide the amount invested by the cost per share of the fund. Round down to the nearest whole number.**

You will purchase 266 shares of the mutual fund.

CHECK YOUR PROGRESS 1

Down payment = 25% of 410,000 = 0.25(410,000)

= 102,500

Mortgage = selling price − down payment

= 410,000 − 102,500

= 307,500

Points = 1.75% of 307,500 = 0.0175(307,500)

= 5381.25

Total = 102,500 + 375 + 5381.25 = 108,256.25

The total of the down payment and the closing costs is $108,256.25.

CHECK YOUR PROGRESS 2

a. $i = \dfrac{0.07}{12} \approx 0.00583333$

$n = 25(12) = 300$

$PMT = A\left(\dfrac{i}{1 - (1 + i)^{-n}}\right)$

$PMT \approx 223,000\left(\dfrac{0.00583333}{1 - (1 + 0.00583333)^{-300}}\right)$

$PMT \approx 1576.12$

The monthly payment is $1576.12.

b. Total = 1576.12(300) = 472,836

The total of the payments over the life of the loan is $472,836.

c. Interest = 472,836 − 223,000 = 249,836

The amount of interest paid over the life of the loan is $249,836.

CHECK YOUR PROGRESS 3

Down payment = 0.25(295,000) = 73,750

Mortgage = 295,000 − 73,750 = 221,250

$i = \dfrac{0.0675}{12} = 0.005625$

$n = 30(12) = 360$

$PMT = A\left(\dfrac{i}{1 - (1 + i)^{-n}}\right)$

$PMT = 221,250\left(\dfrac{0.005625}{1 - (1 + 0.005625)^{-360}}\right)$

$PMT \approx 1435.02$

The monthly payment is $1435.02.

$I = Prt$

$= 221,250(0.0675)\left(\dfrac{1}{12}\right)$

≈ 1244.53

The interest paid on the first payment is $1244.53.

Principal = 1435.02 − 1244.53 = 190.49

The principal paid on the first payment is $190.49.

CHECK YOUR PROGRESS 4

$$i = \frac{0.069}{12} = 0.00575$$

$$n = 25(12) - 4(12) = 300 - 48 = 252$$

$$A = PMT\left(\frac{1 - (1 + i)^{-n}}{i}\right)$$

$$A = 846.82\left(\frac{1 - (1 + 0.00575)^{-252}}{0.00575}\right)$$

$$A \approx 112{,}548.79$$

The mortgage payoff is $112,548.79.

CHECK YOUR PROGRESS 5

Monthly property tax = 2332.80 ÷ 12 = 194.40
Monthly fire insurance = 450 ÷ 12 = 37.50
Total monthly payment = 1492.89 + 194.40 + 37.50 = 1724.79

The total monthly payment for mortgage, property tax, and fire insurance is $1724.79.

ANSWERS TO ALL EXERCISES, SECTIONS 10.3, 10.4 AND 10.5, ADDITIONAL MATERIAL TO CHAPTER 6

EXCURSION EXERCISES, SECTION 10.3

1. $23,617   **2.** $456.58   **3.** $29,894.80   **4.** $18,869.80   **5.** $22,000   **6.** $280.08
7. $19,304.80   **8.** Buying the car   **9.** Answers will vary.

EXERCISE SET 10.3

1. $1.48   **2.** $6.85   **3.** $152.32   **4.** $254.34   **5.** $335.87   **6.** $955.20   **7.** $15.34
8. $6.81   **9.** $5.00   **10.** $5.65   **11.** $26.93   **12.** $20.37   **13.** 13.5%   **14.** 13.7%
15. 19.2%   **16.** 12.9%   **17.** $34.59   **18.** $56.03   **19. a.** $696.05   **b.** $174.01   **c.** $88.46
20. a. $40,736.25   **b.** $8147.25   **c.** $987.00   **21. a.** $68,569.73   **b.** $13,713.95   **c.** $641.17
22. a. $2680.82   **b.** $402.12   **c.** $103.23   **23.** $874.88   **24.** $826.28   **25.** $571.31
26. $636.32   **27. a.** $621.19   **b.** $4372.12   **28. a.** $432.37   **b.** $4517.20   **29.** $13,575.25
30. $9990.66   **31.** $3472.57   **32.** $9900.81   **33. a.** $22,740   **b.** $101.90   **c.** $161.25
d. $263.15   **34. a.** $31,165   **b.** $166.83   **c.** $244.42   **d.** $411.25   **35. a.** $21,100   **b.** 0.003375
c. $121.84   **d.** $169.44   **e.** $291.28   **36. a.** $160,000   **b.** 0.0035   **c.** $857.50   **d.** $1250
e. $2107.50   **37.** The monthly payment for the loan is *PMT*. The interest rate per period, *i*, is the annual interest rate divided by 12. The term of the loan, *n*, is the number of years of the loan times 12. Substitute these values into the Payment Formula for an APR Loan and solve for *A*, the selling price of the car. The selling price of the car is $9775.72.   **38. a.** $2704.15
b. $20,938.15   **c.** $515.10   **39. a.** $168.48   **b.** $2669   **c.** $11,391.04   **40. a.** $15.24
b. $20.62   **c.** $5.38   **d.** $5.38   **e.** In part c, the credit card company is charging interest on the additional $299 of unpaid balance. In part d, the interest is earned on the $299 invested.   **41. a.** $336.04   **b.** $339.29   **c.** $1.40
d. $22.63   **42. a.** 92 months   **b.** $1200.66   **c.** Answers will vary.

EXCURSION EXERCISES, SECTION 10.4

1. $29,663.13   **2.** $19,850.36   **3.** $59,924.80   **4.** $39,819.64

EXERCISE SET 10.4

1. $382.50   **2.** $870.00   **3.** $535.50   **4.** $364.00   **5.** 2.51%   **6.** 1.25%   **7.** 1.83%
8. 0.8%   **9. a.** $8.73   **b.** $67.50   **c.** 3,750,600 shares   **d.** Decrease   **e.** $22.59   **10. a.** $19.44
b. $1500   **c.** 5,711,500 shares   **d.** Decrease   **e.** $43.30   **11.** 50 shares   **12.** 212 shares
13. a. Profit of $290   **b.** $78.66   **14. a.** Profit of $2028   **b.** $328.70   **15. a.** Profit of $9096
b. $472.33   **16. a.** Profit of $6504   **b.** $1327.59   **17.** $252   **18.** $562.50   **19.** $840   **20.** $2832
21. $22.50   **22.** $16.50   **23.** 714 shares   **24.** 250 shares   **25.** 240 shares   **26.** 500 shares
27. The no-load fund's value ($2800.57) is $2.05 greater than the load fund's value ($2798.52).   **28.** Answers will vary.
29. Answers will vary.

EXCURSION EXERCISES, SECTION 10.5

1. $1801.39   **2.** $4275   **3.** $289,275   **4.** 6.36%   **5.** Option 1: $682.18; Option 2: $665.30
6. Option 1: $1500; Option 2: $2000   **7.** Option 1: $17,872.32; Option 2: $17,967.20   **8.** Option 1: $26,058.48;
Option 2: $25,950.80   **9.** Option 1 is more cost effective if you stay in the home for 2 years or less. Option 2 is more cost effective
if you stay in the home for 3 years or more. Explanations will vary.

EXERCISE SET 10.5

1. $64,500; $193,500   **2.** $32,500; $292,500   **3.** $5625   **4.** $4675   **5.** $99,539   **6.** $56,801
7. $34,289.38   **8.** $34,841   **9.** $974.37   **10.** $1548.57   **11.** $2155.28   **12.** $1300.87
13. a. $1088.95   **b.** $392,022   **c.** $240,022   **14. a.** $1569.02   **b.** $470,706   **c.** $271,706
15. $174,606   **16.** $664,141.60   **17.** Interest: $1407.38; principal: $495.89   **18.** Interest: $1297.13; principal: $37.49
19. Interest: $1347.68; principal: $123.62   **20.** Interest: $986.59; principal: $110.44   **21.** $112,025.49
22. $126,874.00   **23.** $61,039.75   **24.** $96,924.63   **25.** $1071.10   **26.** $1903.71   **27.** $2022.50
28. $1827.28   **29. a.** $330.57   **b.** $140,972.40   **30. a.** $804.08   **b.** $325,058.40   **31. a.** $390.62
b. $178,273.20   **32. a.** $343.07   **b.** $188,254.80   **33.** $125,000   **34.** $120,000   **35.** $212,065
36. 260th payment   **37.** No   **38.** Yes. If the interest rate is lower, it will take fewer months.   **39.** You pay less total
interest on a 15-year mortgage loan.   **40. a.** $65,641.88   **b.** $138,596.60   **c.** $28,881.52   **d.** 44%
41. a. $29,805; yes   **b.** $862.56   **c.** $1145.60   **d.** $3333.78   **e.** 25.6%   **f.** Answers will vary.

CHAPTER 10 REVIEW EXERCISES

11. a. $11,318.23   **b.** $3318.23 [Sec. 10.2]
12. $19,225.50 [Sec. 10.2]   **13.** 1.1% [Sec. 10.4]   **14.** $9000 [Sec. 10.4]   **15.** $2.31 [Sec. 10.2]
16. $43,650.68 [Sec. 10.2]   **17.** 6.06% [Sec. 10.2]   **18.** 5.4% compounded semiannually [Sec. 10.2]
19. $431.16 [Sec. 10.3]   **20.** $6.12 [Sec. 10.3]   **21. a.** $259.38   **b.** 12.9% [Sec. 10.3]
22. a. $36.03   **b.** 12.9% [Sec. 10.3]   **23.** $45.41 [Sec. 10.3]   **24. a.** $10,092.69   **b.** $2018.54
c. $253.01 [Sec. 10.3]   **25.** $704.85 [Sec. 10.3]   **26. a.** $540.02   **b.** $12,196.80 [Sec. 10.3]
27. a. $29,450   **b.** $181.80   **c.** $224.17   **d.** $436.42 [Sec. 10.3]   **28. a.** Profit of $5325
b. $256.10 [Sec. 10.4]   **29.** 200 shares [Sec. 10.4]   **30.** $99,041 [Sec. 10.5]
31. a. $1659.11   **b.** $597,279.60   **c.** $341,479.60 [Sec. 10.5]   **32. a.** $1396.69
b. $150,665.74 [Sec. 10.5]   **33.** $2658.53 [Sec. 10.5]

CHAPTER 10 TEST

1. $108.28 [Sec. 10.1]   **2.** $202.50 [Sec. 10.1]   **3.** $8408.89 [Sec. 10.1]   **4.** 9% [Sec. 10.1]
5. $7340.87 [Sec. 10.2]   **6.** $312.03 [Sec. 10.2]   **7. a.** $15,331.03   **b.** $4831.03 [Sec. 10.2]
8. $21,949.06 [Sec. 10.2]   **9.** 1.2% [Sec. 10.4]   **10.** $1900 [Sec. 10.4]   **11.** $612,184.08 [Sec. 10.2]
12. 6.40% [Sec. 10.2]   **13.** 4.6% compounded semiannually [Sec. 10.2]   **14.** $7.79 [Sec. 10.3]   **15. a.** $48.56
b. 16.6% [Sec. 10.3]   **16.** $60.61 [Sec. 10.3]   **17. a.** loss of $4896   **b.** $226.16 [Sec. 10.4]
18. 208 shares [Sec. 10.4]   **19. a.** $6985.94   **b.** $1397.19   **c.** $174.62 [Sec. 10.3]
20. $60,083.50 [Sec. 10.5]   **21. a.** $1530.69   **b.** $221,546.46 [Sec. 10.5]   **22.** $2595.97 [Sec. 10.5]

SOLUTIONS TO CHECK YOUR PROGRESS PROBLEMS, SECTION 8.5, ADDITIONAL MATERIAL TO CHAPTER 7

SECTION 8.5

CHECK YOUR PROGRESS 1

Use the Pythagorean Theorem to find the length of the hypotenuse.

$$a^2 + b^2 = c^2$$
$$3^2 + 4^2 = c^2$$
$$9 + 16 = c^2$$
$$25 = c^2$$
$$\sqrt{25} = \sqrt{c^2}$$
$$5 = c$$

$$\sin \theta = \frac{\text{opp}}{\text{hyp}} = \frac{3}{5},$$

$$\cos \theta = \frac{\text{adj}}{\text{hyp}} = \frac{4}{5},$$

$$\tan \theta = \frac{\text{opp}}{\text{adj}} = \frac{3}{4}$$

CHECK YOUR PROGRESS 2

$$\tan 37.1° = 0.7563$$

CHECK YOUR PROGRESS 3

We are given the measure of $\angle B$ and the hypotenuse. We want to find the length of side a. The cosine function involves the side adjacent and the hypotenuse.

$$\cos B = \frac{\text{adj}}{\text{hyp}}$$

$$\cos 48° = \frac{a}{12}$$

$$12(\cos 48°) = a$$

$$8.03 \approx a$$

The length of side a is approximately 8.03 ft.

CHECK YOUR PROGRESS 4

$$\tan^{-1}(0.3165) \approx 17.6°$$

CHECK YOUR PROGRESS 5

$$\theta \approx \tan^{-1}(0.5681)$$
$$\theta \approx 29.6°$$

CHECK YOUR PROGRESS 6

We want to find the measure of $\angle A$, and we are given the length of the side opposite $\angle A$ and the hypotenuse. The sine function involves the side opposite an angle and the hypotenuse.

$$\sin A = \frac{\text{opp}}{\text{hyp}}$$

$$\sin A = \frac{7}{11}$$

$$A = \sin^{-1} \frac{7}{11}$$

$$A \approx 39.5°$$

The measure of $\angle A$ is approximately 39.5°.

CHECK YOUR PROGRESS 7

Let d be the distance from the base of the lighthouse to the boat.

$$\tan 25° = \frac{20}{d}$$

$$d(\tan 25°) = 20$$

$$d = \frac{20}{\tan 25°}$$

$$d \approx 42.9$$

The boat is approximately 42.9 m from the base of the lighthouse.

ANSWERS TO ALL EXERCISES, SECTION 8.5, ADDITIONAL MATERIAL TO CHAPTER 7

EXCURSION EXERCISES, SECTION 8.5

Drawings should be similar to that shown in the text. Approximate values will vary. As produced by a calculator, $\sin 35° = 0.5736$, $\cos 35° = 0.8192$, and $\tan 35° = 0.7002$.

EXERCISE SET 8.5

1. a. $\dfrac{a}{c}$ **b.** $\dfrac{b}{c}$ **c.** $\dfrac{b}{c}$ **d.** $\dfrac{a}{c}$ **e.** $\dfrac{a}{b}$ **f.** $\dfrac{b}{a}$ **2.** $y = \sin^{-1}(x)$ means that y is the angle whose sine is x. $y = \cos^{-1}(x)$ means that y is the angle whose cosine is x. $y = \tan^{-1}(x)$ means that y is the angle whose tangent is x.

3. $\sin\theta = \dfrac{5}{13}$, $\cos\theta = \dfrac{12}{13}$, $\tan\theta = \dfrac{5}{12}$ **4.** $\sin\theta = \dfrac{15}{17}$, $\cos\theta = \dfrac{8}{17}$, $\tan\theta = \dfrac{15}{8}$ **5.** $\sin\theta = \dfrac{24}{25}$, $\cos\theta = \dfrac{7}{25}$, $\tan\theta = \dfrac{24}{7}$

6. $\sin\theta = \dfrac{20}{29}$, $\cos\theta = \dfrac{21}{29}$, $\tan\theta = \dfrac{20}{21}$ **7.** $\sin\theta = \dfrac{8}{\sqrt{113}}$, $\cos\theta = \dfrac{7}{\sqrt{113}}$, $\tan\theta = \dfrac{8}{7}$

8. $\sin\theta = \dfrac{3}{\sqrt{10}}$, $\cos\theta = \dfrac{1}{\sqrt{10}}$, $\tan\theta = 3$ **9.** $\sin\theta = \dfrac{1}{2}$, $\cos\theta = \dfrac{\sqrt{3}}{2}$, $\tan\theta = \dfrac{1}{\sqrt{3}}$

10. $\sin\theta = \dfrac{3}{4}$, $\cos\theta = \dfrac{\sqrt{7}}{4}$, $\tan\theta = \dfrac{3}{\sqrt{7}}$ **11.** 0.6820 **12.** 0.8829 **13.** 1.4281 **14.** 0.9816

15. 0.9971 **16.** 0.9278 **17.** 1.9970 **18.** 0.1357 **19.** 0.8878 **20.** 0.2924 **21.** 0.8453
22. 0.8156 **23.** 0.8508 **24.** 0.7028 **25.** 0.6833 **26.** 0.7660 **27.** 38.6° **28.** 17.9°
29. 41.1° **30.** 26.6° **31.** 21.3° **32.** 47.3° **33.** 38.0° **34.** 52.9° **35.** 72.5° **36.** 57.8°
37. 0.6° **38.** 13.7° **39.** 66.1° **40.** 61.6° **41.** 29.5° **42.** 12.7° **43.** 841.79 ft
44. 86.95 ft **45.** 13.6° **46.** 247.07 ft **47.** 29.14 ft **48.** 360.78 ft **49.** 52.92 ft **50.** 1801.25 ft
51. 13.59 ft **52.** 55.1° **53.** 1056.63 ft **54.** 19.4° **55.** 29.58 yd **56.** 1467.84 ft

57. No. Explanations will vary. **58.** Yes. Explanations will vary. **59.** $\dfrac{\sqrt{5}}{3}$ **60.** $\dfrac{5}{\sqrt{41}}$ **61.** $\dfrac{\sqrt{7}}{3}$

62. $\dfrac{\sqrt{5}}{\sqrt{11}}$ **63.** $\sqrt{1 - a^2}$ **64.** $\dfrac{a}{\sqrt{a^2 + 1}}$ **65.** 4 radians

66. $\dfrac{1}{2}$ radian **67.** $\dfrac{2}{3}$ radian **68.** 1.2 radians **69.** $\left(\dfrac{180}{\pi}\right)^{\circ}$ **70.** larger than **71.** $\dfrac{\pi}{4}$ radian;

0.7854 radian **72.** π radians; 3.1416 radians **73.** $\dfrac{7\pi}{4}$ radians; 5.4978 radians **74.** $\dfrac{\pi}{2}$ radians; 1.5708 radians

75. $\dfrac{7\pi}{6}$ radians; 3.6652 radians **76.** $\dfrac{\pi}{10}$ radian; 0.3142 radian **77.** 60° **78.** 330° **79.** 240°

80. $\left(\dfrac{216}{\pi}\right)^{\circ}$; 68.7549° **81.** $\left(\dfrac{540}{\pi}\right)^{\circ}$; 171.8873° **82.** $\left(\dfrac{432}{\pi}\right)^{\circ}$; 137.5099°

CHAPTER 8 REVIEW EXERCISES

25. 9.75 ft [Sec. 8.3]

26. $\sin \theta = \dfrac{5\sqrt{89}}{89}$, $\cos \theta = \dfrac{8\sqrt{89}}{89}$, $\tan \theta = \dfrac{5}{8}$ [Sec. 8.5]　　**27.** $\sin \theta = \dfrac{\sqrt{3}}{2}$, $\cos \theta = \dfrac{1}{2}$, $\tan \theta = \sqrt{3}$ [Sec. 8.5]

28. 25.7° [Sec. 8.5]　　**29.** 29.2° [Sec. 8.5]　　**30.** 53.8° [Sec. 8.5]　　**31.** 1.9° [Sec. 8.5]　　**32.** 100.1 ft [Sec. 8.5]

CHAPTER 8 TEST

1. 169.65 m^3 [Sec. 8.4]　　**2.** 6.8 m [Sec. 8.2]　　**3.** a 58° angle [Sec. 8.1]　　**4.** 3.14 m^2 [Sec. 8.2]

5. 150° [Sec. 8.1]　　**6.** $m\angle a = 45°$; $m\angle b = 135°$ [Sec. 8.1]　　**7.** 5.0625 ft^2 [Sec. 8.2]　　**8.** 448π cm^3 [Sec. 8.4]

9. $1\dfrac{1}{5}$ ft [Sec. 8.3]　　**10.** 90° and 50° [Sec. 8.1]　　**11.** 125° [Sec. 8.1]　　**12.** 32 m^2 [Sec. 8.2]

13. 25 ft [Sec. 8.3]　　**14.** 113.10 in^2 [Sec. 8.2]　　**15.** The triangles are congruent by the SAS theorem. [Sec. 8.3]

16. 7.55 cm [Sec. 8.3]　　**17.** $\sin \theta = \dfrac{4}{5}$, $\cos \theta = \dfrac{3}{5}$, $\tan \theta = \dfrac{4}{3}$ [Sec. 8.5]　　**18.** 127 ft [Sec. 8.5]

19. 103.87 ft^2 [Sec. 8.2]　　**20.** 780 in^3 [Sec. 8.4]　　**21. a.** Through a given point not on a given line, exactly one line can be drawn parallel to the given line.　　**b.** Through a given point not on a given line, there exist no lines parallel to the given line. [Sec. 8.6]　　**22. a.** 1　　**b.** 3 [Sec. 8.6]　　**23.** A great circle of a sphere is a circle on the surface of the sphere whose center is at the center of the sphere. [Sec. 8.6]　　**24.** 80π ft$^2 \approx 251.3$ ft^2 [Sec. 8.6]

25. $d_E(P, Q) = \sqrt{82} \approx 9.1$ blocks, $d_C(P, Q) = 10$ blocks [Sec. 8.6]　　**26.** 16 [Sec. 8.6]

27.

Stage 2　　[Sec. 8.7]

28.

Stage 2　　[Sec. 8.7]

29. Replacement ratio: 2; scale ratio: 2; similarity dimension: 1 [Sec. 8.7]

30. Replacement ratio: 3; scale ratio: 2; similarity dimension: $\dfrac{\log 3}{\log 2} \approx 1.585$ [Sec. 8.7]

SOLUTIONS TO CHECK YOUR PROGRESS PROBLEMS, SECTION 12.2
ADDITIONAL MATERIAL TO CHAPTER 10

SECTION 12.2

CHECK YOUR PROGRESS 1

Tara's largest test score is 84 and her smallest test score is 76. The range of Tara's test scores is $84 - 76 = 8$.

CHECK YOUR PROGRESS 2

$$\mu = \frac{5 + 8 + 16 + 17 + 18 + 20}{6} = \frac{84}{6} = 14$$

x	$x - \mu$	$(x - \mu)^2$
5	$5 - 14 = -9$	$(-9)^2 = 81$
8	$8 - 14 = -6$	$(-6)^2 = 36$
16	$16 - 14 = 2$	$2^2 = 4$
17	$17 - 14 = 3$	$3^2 = 9$
18	$18 - 14 = 4$	$4^2 = 16$
20	$20 - 14 = 6$	$6^2 = 36$
		Sum: 182

$$\sigma = \sqrt{\frac{\Sigma(x - \mu)^2}{n}} = \sqrt{\frac{182}{6}} \approx \sqrt{30.33} \approx 5.51$$

The standard deviation for this population is approximately 5.51.

CHECK YOUR PROGRESS 3

The rope from Trustworthy has a breaking point standard deviation of

$$s_1 = \sqrt{\frac{(122 - 130)^2 + (141 - 130)^2 + \cdots + (125 - 130)^2}{6}}$$

$$= \sqrt{\frac{1752}{6}} \approx 17.1 \text{ pounds}$$

The rope from Brand X has a breaking point standard deviation of

$$s_2 = \sqrt{\frac{(128 - 130)^2 + (127 - 130)^2 + \cdots + (137 - 130)^2}{6}}$$

$$= \sqrt{\frac{3072}{6}} \approx 22.6 \text{ pounds}$$

The rope from NeverSnap has a breaking point standard deviation of

$$s_3 = \sqrt{\frac{(112 - 130)^2 + (121 - 130)^2 + \cdots + (135 - 130)^2}{6}}$$

$$= \sqrt{\frac{592}{6}} \approx 9.9 \text{ pounds}$$

The rope from NeverSnap has the lowest breaking point standard deviation.

CHECK YOUR PROGRESS 4

The mean is approximately 46.577.

The population standard deviation is approximately 2.876.

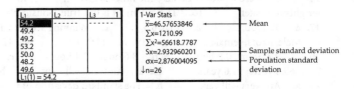

CHECK YOUR PROGRESS 5

In Check Your Progress 2 we found $\sigma \approx \sqrt{30.33}$. Variance is the square of the standard deviation. Thus the variance is $\sigma^2 \approx \left(\sqrt{30.33}\right)^2 = 30.33$.

ANSWERS TO ALL EXERCISES, SECTION 12.2, ADDITIONAL MATERIAL TO CHAPTER 10

EXCURSION EXERCISES, SECTION 12.2

1. a. and b.

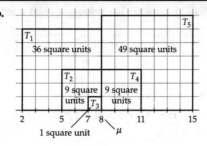 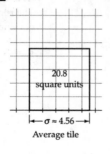

1 square unit

Average tile

c. 104 square units
d. 20.8 square units
e. See the figure at the left.
f. The variance is 20.8. It is the area of the average tile shown at the left.
g. The standard deviation is $\sqrt{20.8} \approx 4.56$. It is the width of the average tile.

2. a. and b.

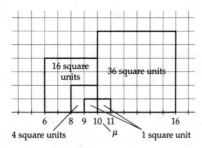 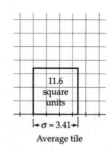

4 square units   1 square unit

Average tile

c. 58 square units
d. 11.6 square units
e. See the figure at the left.
f. The variance is 11.6. It is the area of the average tile shown at the left.
g. The standard deviation is $\sqrt{11.6} \approx 3.41$. It is the width of the average tile.
h. The data set in Excursion Exercise 2 has the larger mean, but the data set in Excursion Exercise 1 has the larger standard deviation.

EXERCISE SET 12.2

1. 84°F   **2.** 62°F   **3.** 21; 8.2; 67.1   **4.** 13; 4.8; 23.4   **5.** 3.3; 1.3; 1.7   **6.** 15.4; 6.1; 37.7
7. 52; 17.7; 311.6   **8.** 47; 16.9; 284.5   **9.** 0; 0; 0   **10.** 2; 1.0; 1.1   **11.** 23; 8.3; 69.6   **12.** 27; 9.8; 95.6
13. Opinions will vary. However, many climbers would consider rope B to be safer because of its small standard deviation.
14. The Powerball lottery because the range is greater.   **15.** The students in the college statistic course because the range of weights is greater.   **16.** The statement is not true. Consider, for example, the data sets 98, 99, 100, 101, 102 and 2, 4, 6, 8, 10.
17. a. 30.1; 10.1   **b.** 15.6; 6.5   **c.** Winning scores; winning scores   **18. a.** 38; 12.7   **b.** 44.4; 10.2
c. Male actors; female actors   **19. a.** 44.9; 9.3   **b.** 42.8; 7.7   **c.** National League; National League
20. a. 9.7 hours; 0.8 hour   **b.** 8.6 hours; 0.4 hour   **c.** Women; women   **21.** 54.8 years; 6.2 years
22. 69.8 years; 11.6 years   **23. a.** Answers will vary.   **b.** The population standard deviation remains the same.
24. a. Answers will vary.   **b.** The standard deviation of the new data is *k* times the standard deviation of the original data.
25. a. 0   **b.** Yes   **c.** No   **26.** If the variance is 0 or 1   **27. a.** Identical   **b.** Identical
c. Identical   **d.** They will be identical.   **28.** The standard deviation is the same as in Exercise 27b—about 2.87.

Glossary

abscissa The first number of an ordered pair; it measures a horizontal distance and is also called the first coordinate of an ordered pair.

absolute value equation An equation containing the absolute-value symbol.

absolute value function A function containing an absolute value symbol.

absolute value of a number The distance between zero and the number on the number line.

acute angle An angle whose measure is between 0 and 90.

acute triangle A triangle that has three acute angles.

addend In addition, one of the numbers added.

addition The process of finding the total of two numbers.

addition method An algebraic method of finding an exact solution of a system of linear equations.

Addition Property of Zero Zero added to a number does not change the number.

additive inverse of a polynomial The polynomial with the sign of every term changed.

additive inverses Numbers that are the same distance from zero on the number line but lie on different sides of zero; also called opposites.

adjacent angles Two angles that share a common side.

alternate exterior angles Two nonadjacent angles that are on opposite sides of the transversal and outside the parallel lines.

alternate interior angles Two nonadjacent angles that are on opposite sides of the transversal and between the parallel lines.

analytic geometry Geometry in which a coordinate system is used to study relationships between variables.

angle An angle is formed when two rays start at the same point; it is measured in degrees.

approximation An estimated value obtained by rounding an exact value.

area A measure of the amount of surface in a region.

arithmetic mean of values Average determined by calculating the sum of the values and then dividing that result by the number of values.

arithmetic progression A sequence in which the difference between any two consecutive terms is constant; also called an arithmetic sequence.

arithmetic sequence A sequence in which the difference between any two consecutive terms is constant; also called an arithmetic progression.

arithmetic series The indicated sum of the terms of an arithmetic sequence.

Associative Property of Addition Numbers to be added can be grouped (with parentheses, for example) in any order; the sum will be the same.

Associative Property of Multiplication Numbers to be multiplied can be grouped (with parentheses, for example) in any order; the product will be the same.

asymptotes The two straight lines that a hyperbola "approaches."

average The sum of all the numbers divided by the number of those numbers.

average value The sum of all values divided by the number of those values; also known as the mean value.

axes The two number lines that form a rectangular coordinate system; also called coordinate axes.

axes of symmetry of a hyperbola The line that passes through the vertices of the hyperbola.

axis of symmetry of a parabola A line of symmetry that passes through the vertex of the parabola and is parallel to the y-axis for an equation of the form $y = ax^2 + bx + c$ or parallel to the x-axis for an equation of the form $x = ay^2 + by + c$.

balancing a checkbook Determining whether the checking account balance is accurate.

bank statement A document showing all the transactions in a bank account during the month.

bar graph A graph that represents data by the height of the bars.

base In an exponential expression, the number that is taken as a factor as many times as indicated by the exponent.

base of a triangle The side that the triangle rests on.

basic percent equation Percent times base equals amount.

binomial A polynomial of two terms.

binomial factor A factor that has two terms.

borrowing In subtraction, taking a unit from the next larger place value in the minuend and adding it to the number in the given place value in order to make that number larger than the number to be subtracted from it.

box-and-whiskers plot A graph that shows the smallest value in a set of numbers, the first quartile, the median, the third quartile, and the greatest value.

British thermal unit A unit of energy. 1 British thermal unit = 778 foot-pounds.

broken-line graph A graph that represents data by the position of the lines and shows trends and comparisons.

Calorie A unit of energy in the metric system.

capacity A measure of liquid substances.

carrying In addition, transferring a number to another column.

center of a circle The point from which all points on the circle are equidistant.

center of a circle The central point that is equidistant from all the points that make up a circle.

center of a sphere The point from which all points on the surface of the sphere are equidistant.

center of an ellipse The intersection of the two axes of symmetry of the ellipse.

centi- The metric system prefix that means one-hundredth.

check A printed form that, when filled out and signed, instructs a bank to pay a specified sum of money to the person named on it.

checking account A bank account that enables you to withdraw money or make payments to other people, using checks.

circle A plane figure in which all points are the same distance from point O, which is called the center of the circle.

circle graph A graph that represents data by the size of the sectors.

circumference The distance around a circle.

class frequency The number of occurrences of data in a class interval on a histogram; represented by the height of each bar.

class interval Range of numbers represented by the width of a bar on a histogram.

class midpoint The center of a class interval in a frequency polygon.

clearing denominators Removing denominators from an equation that contains fractions by multiplying each side of the equation by the LCM of the denominators.

closed interval In interval notation, an interval that contains its endpoints.

coefficient The number part of a variable term.

cofactor of an element of a matrix $(-1)^{i+j}$ times the minor of that element, where i is the row number of the element and j is its column number.

combined variation A variation in which two or more types of variation occur at the same time.

combining like terms Using the Distributive Property to add the coefficients of like variable terms; adding like terms of a variable expression.

commission That part of the pay earned by a salesperson that is calculated as a percent of the salesperson's sales.

common difference of an arithmetic sequence The difference between any two consecutive terms in an arithmetic sequence.

common factor A number that is a factor of two or more numbers is a common factor of those numbers.

common logarithms Logarithms to the base 10.

common monomial factor A monomial factor that is a factor of the terms in a polynomial.

common multiple A number that is a multiple of two or more numbers is a common multiple of those numbers.

common ratio of a sequence In a geometric sequence, each successive term of the sequence is the same nonzero constant multiple of the preceding term. This common multiple is called the common ratio of the sequence.

Commutative Property of Addition Two numbers can be added in either order; the sum will be the same.

Commutative Property of Multiplication Two numbers can be multiplied in either order; the product will be the same.

complementary angles Two angles whose sum is 90.

completing the square Adding to a binomial the constant term that makes it a perfect-square trinomial.

complex fraction A fraction whose numerator or denominator contains one or more fractions.

complex number A number of the form $a + bi$, where a and b are real numbers and $i = \sqrt{-1}$.

composite geometric figure A figure made from two or more geometric figures.

composite geometric solid A solid made from two or more geometric solids.

composite number A number that has whole-number factors besides 1 and itself. For instance, 18 is a composite number.

composition of two functions The operation on two functions f and g denoted by $f \circ g$. The value of the composition of f and g is given by $(f \circ g)(x) = f[g(x)]$.

compound inequality Two inequalities joined with a connective word such as *and* or *or*.

compound interest Interest computed not only on the original principal but also on interest already earned.

compound interest formula $A = P(1 + i)$ where P is the original value of an investment, i is the interest rate per compounding period, n is the total number of compounding periods, and A is the value of the investment after n periods.

conditional equation An equation that is true if the variable it contains is replaced by the proper value. $x + 2 = 5$ is a conditional equation.

congruent objects Objects that have the same shape and the same size.

congruent triangles Triangles that have the same shape and the same size.

conic section A curve that can be constructed from the intersection of a plane and a right circular cone. The four conic sections are the parabola, hyperbola, ellipse, and circle.

conjugates Binomial expressions that differ only in the sign of a term. The expressions and are conjugates.

consecutive even integers Even integers that follow one another in order.

consecutive integers Integers that follow one another in order.

consecutive odd integers Odd integers that follow one another in order.

constant function A function given by $f(x) = b$, where b is a constant. Its graph is a horizontal line passing through $(0, b)$.

constant of proportionality k in a variation equation; also called the constant of variation.

constant of variation k in a variation equation; also called the constant of proportionality.

constant term A term that has no variables.

contradiction An equation in which any replacement for the variable will result in a false equation. is a contradiction.

conversion rate A relationship used to change one unit of measurement to another.

coordinate axes The two number lines that form a rectangular coordinate system; also called axes.

coordinates of a point The numbers in the ordered pair that is associated with the point.

corresponding angles Two angles that are on the same side of the transversal and are both acute angles or are both obtuse angles.

cost The price that a business pays for a product.

cross product In a proportion, the product of the numerator on the left side of the proportion times the denominator on the right, and the product of the denominator on the left side of the proportion times the numerator on the right.

cube A rectangular solid in which all six faces are squares.

cube root of a perfect cube One of the three equal factors of the perfect cube.

cubic centimeter A unit of capacity equal to 1 milliliter.

cubic function A third-degree polynomial function.

cup A U.S. Customary measure of capacity. 2 cups 1 pint.

cylinder A geometric solid in which the bases are circles and are perpendicular to the height.

data Numerical information.

day A unit of time. 24 hours 1 day.

decimal A number written in decimal notation.

decimal notation Notation in which a number consists of a whole-number part, a decimal point, and a decimal part.

decimal part In decimal notation, that part of the number that appears to the right of the decimal point.

decimal point In decimal notation, the point that separates the whole-number part from the decimal part.

degree Unit used to measure angles; one complete revolution is 360 .

degree of a monomial The sum of the exponents of the variables.

degree of a polynomial The greatest of the degrees of any of its terms.

degree of a polynomial in one variable The largest exponent that appears on the variable.

denominator The part of a fraction that appears below the fraction bar.

dependent system A system of equations that has an infinite number of solutions.

dependent system of equations A system of equations whose graphs coincide.

dependent variable A variable whose value depends on that of another variable known as the independent variable.

deposit slip A form for depositing money in a checking account.

descending order The terms of a polynomial in one variable are arranged in descending order when the exponents of the variable decrease from left to right. The polynomial $9x^5$ $2x^4$ $7x^3$ x^2 $8x$ 1 is in descending order.

determinant A number associated with a square matrix.

diameter Line segment across a circle that passes through the circle's center.

diameter of a circle A line segment with endpoints on the circle and going through the center.

diameter of a sphere A line segment with endpoints on the sphere and going through the center.

difference In subtraction, the result of subtracting two numbers.

difference of two perfect squares A polynomial in the form of a^2 b^2.

difference of two perfect cubes A polynomial in the form a^3 b^3.

direct variation A special function that can be expressed as the equation y kx, where k is a constant called the constant of variation or the constant of proportionality.

discount The difference between the regular price and the sale price.

discount rate The percent of a product's regular price that is represented by the discount.

discriminant For an equation of the form ax^2 bx c 0, the quantity b^2 $4ac$ is called the discriminant.

dividend In division, the number into which the divisor is divided to yield the quotient.

division The process of finding the quotient of two numbers.

divisor In division, the number that is divided into the dividend to yield the quotient.

domain The set of the first coordinates of all the ordered pairs of a function.

double-bar graph A graph used to display data for purposes of comparison.

double function A function that pairs a number with twice that number.

double root When a quadratic equation has two solutions that are the same number, the solution is called a double root of the equation.

down payment The percent of a home's purchase price that the bank, when issuing a mortgage, requires the borrower to provide.

element of a matrix A number in a matrix.

elements of a set The objects in the set.

ellipse An oval shape that is one of the conic sections.

empirical probability The ratio of the number of observations of an event to the total number of observations.

empty set The set that contains no elements.

endpoints of an interval In interval notation, the values that mark the interval's beginning and end, whether or not either or both of those values are included in the interval.

energy The ability to do work.

equation A statement of the equality of two mathematical expressions.

equation in two variables An equation in which two different variables appear.

equilateral triangle A triangle that has three sides of equal length; the three angles are also of equal measure.

equivalent equations Equations that have the same solution.

equivalent fractions Equal fractions with different denominators.

evaluating a function Determining $f(x)$ for a given value of x.

evaluating a variable expression Replacing the variable or variables with numbers and then simplifying the resulting numerical expression.

even integer An integer that is divisible by 2.

event One or more outcomes of an experiment.

expanded form The number 46,208 can be written in expanded form as 40,000 6000 200 0 8.

expanding by cofactors A technique for finding the value of a 3 3 or larger determinant.

expansion of the binomial $(a \quad b)^n$ To write the expression as the sum of its terms.

experiment Any activity that has an observable outcome.

exponent In exponential notation, the raised number that indicates how many times the number to which it is attached is taken as a factor.

exponential decay equation Any equation that can be written in the form $A \quad A_0 b^{kt}$ where A is the size at time t, A_0 is the initial size, b is between 0 and 1, and k is a positive real number.

exponential equation An equation in which a variable occurs in the exponent.

exponential form The expression 2^6 is in exponential form. Compare *factored form*

exponential function The exponential function with base b is defined by $f(x) \quad b^x$, where b is a positive real number not equal to 1.

exponential growth equation Any equation that can be written in the form $A \quad A_0 b^{kt}$, where A is the size at time t, is the initial size, b is greater than 1, and k is a positive real number.

exponential notation The expression of a number to some power, indicated by an exponent.

exterior angle of a triangle Angle adjacent to an interior angle of a triangle.

extraneous solution When each side of an equation is raised to an even power, the resulting equation may have a solution that is not a solution of the original equation. Such a solution is called an extraneous solution.

factor One number is a factor of another when it can be divided into that other number with a remainder of zero.

factor a polynomial Writing the polynomial as a product of other polynomials.

factor a quadratic trinomial Expressing the trinomial as the product of two binomials.

factor a trinomial of the form $x^2 \quad bx \quad c$ To express the trinomial as the product of two binomials.

factor by grouping Process of grouping and factoring terms in a polynomial in such a way that a common binomial factor is found.

factor completely Refers to writing a polynomial as a product of factors that are nonfactorable over the integers.

factored form The multiplication is in factored form. Compare exponential form.

factors In multiplication, the numbers that are multiplied.

factors of a number The whole-number factors of a number divide that number evenly.

favorable outcomes The outcomes of an experiment that satisfy the requirements of a particular event.

finance charges Interest charges on purchases made with a credit card.

finite sequence A sequence that contains a finite number of terms.

finite set A set for which all the elements can be listed.

first coordinate of an ordered pair The first number of the ordered pair; it measures a horizontal distance and is also called the abscissa.

first-degree equation in one variable An equation in which all variables have an exponent of 1 and all variable terms include one and the same variable.

first-degree equation in two variables An equation of the form $y \quad mx \quad b$, where m is the coefficient and b is a constant; also called a linear equation in two variables or a linear function.

first quartile In a set of numbers, the number below which one-quarter of the data lie.

fixed-rate mortgage A mortgage in which the monthly payment remains the same for the life of the loan.

fluid ounce A U.S. Customary measure of capacity. 8 fluid ounces 1 cup.

FOIL A method of finding the product of two binomials. The letters stand for First, Outer, Inner, and Last.

foot A U.S. Customary unit of length. 3 feet 1 yard.

foot-pound A U.S. Customary unit of energy. One foot-pound is the amount of energy required to lift 1 pound a distance of 1 foot.

foot-pounds per second A U.S. Customary unit of power.

formula An equation that expresses a relationship among variables.

fraction The notation used to represent the number of equal parts of a whole.

fraction bar The bar that separates the numerator of a fraction from the denominator.

frequency polygon A graph that displays information similarly to a histogram. A dot is placed above the center of each class interval at a height corresponding to that class's frequency.

function A relation in which no two ordered pairs that have the same first coordinate have different second coordinates.

functional notation Notation used for those equations that define functions. The letter f is commonly used to name a function.

gallon A U.S. Customary measure of capacity. 1 gallon 4 quarts.

general term of a sequence In the sequence $a_1, a_2, a_3, ..., a_n, ...$ the general term of the sequence is a_n.

geometric progression A sequence in which each successive term of the sequence is the same nonzero constant multiple of the preceding term; also called a geometric sequence.

geometric sequence A sequence in which each successive term of the sequence is the same nonzero constant multiple of the preceding term; also called a geometric progression.

geometric series The indicated sum of the terms of a geometric sequence.

geometric solid A figure in space.

gram The basic unit of mass in the metric system.

graph A display that provides a pictorial representation of data.

graph a point in the plane To place a dot at the location given by the ordered pair; also called plotting a point in the plane.

graph of a function A graph of the ordered pairs that belong to the function.

graph of a quadratic inequality in two variables A region of the plane that is bounded by one of the conic sections.

graph of a real number A heavy dot placed directly above the number on the number line.

graph of a relation The graph of the ordered pairs that belong to the relation.

graph of a whole number A heavy dot placed directly above that number on the number line.

graph of an equation in two variables A graph of the ordered-pair solutions of the equation.

graph of an integer A heavy dot directly above that number on the number line.

graph of an ordered pair The dot drawn at the coordinates of the point in the plane.

graph of x a A vertical line passing through the point.

graph of y b A horizontal line passing through the point.

graphing a point in the plane Placing a dot at the location given by the ordered pair; also called plotting a point in the plane.

graphing, or plotting, an ordered pair Placing a dot, on a rectangular coordinate system, at the location given by the ordered pair.

greater than A number that appears to the right of a given number on the number line is greater than the given number.

greater than or equal to The symbol means "is greater than or equal to."

greatest common factor (GCF) The largest common factor of two or more numbers.

greatest common factor (GCF) of two or more monomicals The product of the GCF of the coefficients and the common variable factors.

grouping symbols Parentheses ( ), brackets [ ], braces { }, the absolute value symbol, and the fraction bar.

half-open interval In set-builder notation, an interval that contains one of its endpoints.

half-plane The solution set of a linear inequality in two variables.

height of a parallelogram The distance between parallel sides.

height of a triangle A line segment perpendicular to the base from the opposite vertex.

histogram A bar graph in which the width of each bar corresponds to a range of numbers called a class interval.

horizontal-line test A graph of a function represents the graph of a one-to-one function if any horizontal line intersects the graph at no more than one point.

horsepower The U.S. Customary unit of power. 1 horsepower 550 foot-pounds per second.

hourly wage Pay calculated on the basis of a certain amount for each hour worked.

hyperbola A conic section formed by the intersection of a cone and a plane perpendicular to the base of the cone.

hypotenuse The side opposite the right angle in a right triangle.

identity An equation in which any replacement for the variable will result in a true equation. x 2 x 2 is an identity.

improper fraction A fraction greater than or equal to 1.

imaginary number A number of the form ai, where a is a real number and $i = \sqrt{-1}$.

imaginary part of a complex number For the complex number $a + bi$, b is the imaginary part.

inch A U.S. Customary unit of length. 12 inches = 1 foot.

inconsistent system of equations A system of equations that has no solution.

independent system of equations A system of equations whose graphs intersect at only one point.

independent variable A variable whose value determines that of another variable known as the dependent variable.

index In the expression $\sqrt[n]{a}$, n is the index of the radical.

index of a summation The variable used in summation notation.

inequality An expression that contains the symbol $\ne$, $>$, $<$, $\ge$ (is greater than or equal to), or $\le$ (is less than or equal to).

infinite geometric series The indicated sum of the terms of an infinite geometric sequence.

infinite sequence A sequence that contains an infinite number of terms.

infinite set A set in which the list of elements continues without end.

input In a function, the value of the independent variable.

input/output table A table that shows the results of evaluating a function for various values of the independent variable.

integers The numbers . . . , -3, -2, -1, 0, 1, 2, 3, ...

interest Money paid for the privilege of using someone else's money.

interest rate The percent used to determine the amount of interest.

interior angle of a triangle Angle within the region enclosed by a triangle.

interquartile range The difference between the third quartile and the first quartile.

intersecting lines Lines that cross at a point in the plane.

intersection of sets A and B The set that contains the elements that are common to both A and B.

intersection of two sets The set that contains all elements that are common to both of the sets.

interval notation A type of set notation in which the property that distinguishes the elements of the set is their location within a specified interval.

inverse of a function The set of ordered pairs formed by reversing the coordinates of each ordered pair of the function.

inverse variation A function that can be expressed as the equation $y = \dfrac{k}{x}$, where k is a constant.

inverting a fraction Interchanging the numerator and denominator.

irrational number The decimal representation of an irrational number never terminates or repeats and can only be approximated.

isosceles triangle A triangle that has two sides of equal length; the angles opposite the equal sides are of equal measure.

joint variation A variation in which a variable varies directly as the product of two or more variables. A joint variation can be expressed as the equation $z = kxy$, where k is a constant.

kilo- The metric system prefix that means one thousand.

kilowatt-hour A unit of electrical energy in the metric system equal to 1000-watt hours.

leading coefficient In a polynomial, the coefficient of the variable with the largest exponent.

least common denominator (LCD) The least common multiple of denominators.

least common multiple (LCM) The smallest common multiple of two or more numbers.

least common multiple (LCM) of two or more polynomials The simplest polynomial of least degree that contains the factors of each polynomial.

leg In a right triangle, one of the two sides that are not opposite the 90° angle.

legs of a right triangle The two shortest sides of a right triangle.

length A measure of distance.

less than A number that appears to the left of a given number on the number line is less than the given number.

less than or equal to The symbol $\le$ means "is less than or equal to".

license fees Fees charged for authorization to operate a vehicle.

like terms Terms of a variable expression that have the same variable part. Having no variable part, constant terms are like terms.

line A line extends indefinitely in two directions in a plane; it has no width.

line of best fit A line drawn to approximate data that are graphed as points in a coordinate system.

line segment Part of a line; it has two endpoints.

linear equation in three variables An equation of the form $Ax + By + Cz = D$, where A, B, and C are coefficients of the variables and D is a constant.

linear equation in two variables An equation of the form $y = mx + b$ or $Ax + By = C$.

linear function A function that can be expressed in the form $f(x) = mx + b$. Its graph is a straight line.

linear inequality in two variables An inequality of the form $y = mx + b$ or $Ax + By = C$. (The symbol $=$ could be replaced by $>$, $<$, or $\ge$, $\le$.)

linear model A first-degree equation that is used to describe a relationship between quantities.

liter The basic unit of capacity in the metric system.

literal equation An equation that contains more than one variable.

loan origination fee   The fee a bank charges for processing mortgage papers.

logarithm   For b greater than zero and not equal to 1, the statement $y = \log_b x$ (the logarithm of x to the base b) is equivalent to $x = b^y$.

lower limit   In a tolerance, the lowest acceptable value.

main fraction bar   The fraction bar that is placed between the numerator and denominator of a complex fraction.

mantissa   The decimal part of a common logarithm.

markdown   The amount by which a retailer reduces the regular price of a product for a promotional sale.

markup   The difference between selling price and cost.

markup rate   The percent of a product's cost that is represented by the markup.

mass   The amount of material in an object. On the surface of Earth, mass is the same as weight.

matrix   A rectangular array of numbers.

maturity value of a loan   The principal of a loan plus the interest owed on it.

maximum value of a function   The greatest value that the function can take on.

mean   The sum of all values divided by the number of those values; also known as the average value.

measurement   A measurement has both a number and a unit. Examples include 7 feet, 4 ounces, and 0.5 gallon.

median   The value that separates a list of values in such a way that there is the same number of values below the median as above it.

meter   The basic unit of length in the metric system.

metric system   A system of measurement based on the decimal system.

midpoint of a line segment   The point on a line segment that is equidistant from its endpoints.

mile   A U.S. Customary unit of length. 5280 feet = 1 mile.

milli-   The metric system prefix that means one-thousandth.

minimum value of a function   The least value that the function can take on.

minor of an element   The minor of an element in a 3×3 determinant is the 2×2 determinant obtained by eliminating the row and column that contain that element.

minuend   In subtraction, the number from which another number (the subtrahend) is subtracted.

minute   A unit of time. 60 minutes = 1 hour.

mixed number   A number greater than 1 that has a whole-number part and a fractional part.

mode   In a set of numbers, the value that occurs most frequently.

monomial   A number, a variable, or a product of a number and variables; a polynomial of one term.

monthly mortgage payment   One of 12 payments due each year to the lender of money to buy real estate.

mortgage   The amount borrowed to buy real estate.

moving average   The arithmetic mean of the changes in the value of a stock for a given number of days.

multiples of a number   The products of that number and the numbers 1, 2, 3, ...

multiplication   The process of finding the product of two numbers.

Multiplication Property of One   The product of a number and one is the number.

Multiplication Property of Zero   The product of a number and zero is zero.

multiplicative inverse   The multiplicative inverse of a nonzero real number a is $\frac{1}{a}$; also called the reciprocal.

n factorial   The product of the first n natural numbers; n factorial is written $n!$.

natural exponential function   The function defined by $f(x) = e^x$, where $e \approx 2.71828$.

natural logarithm   When e (the base of the natural exponential function) is used as the base of a logarithm, the logarithm is referred to as the natural logarithm and is abbreviated ln x.

natural numbers   The numbers 1, 2, 3, 4, 5, . . . ; also called the positive integers.

negative integers   The numbers . . . , -5, -4, -3, -2, -1.

negative numbers   Numbers less than zero.

negative reciprocal   The negative reciprocal of a nonzero real number a is $-1/a$.

negative slope   The slope of a line that slants downward to the right.

nonfactorable over the integers   A polynomial is nonfactorable over the integers if it does not factor using only integers.

nonlinear system of equations   A system of equations in which one or more of the equations are not linear equations.

nth root of a   A number b such that $b^n = a$. The nth root of a can be written $a^{1/n}$ or $\sqrt[n]{a}$.

null set   The set that contains no elements.

number line   A line on which a number can be graphed.

numerator   The part of a fraction that appears above the fraction bar.

numerical coefficient   The number part of a variable term. When the numerical coefficient is 1 or -1, the 1 is usually not written.

obtuse angle   An angle whose measure is between $90°$ and $180°$.

obtuse triangle   A triangle that has one obtuse angle.

odd integer   An integer that is not divisible by 2.

one-to-one function   In a one-to-one function, given any y, there is only one x that can be paired with the given y.

open interval   In set-builder notation, an interval that does not contain its endpoints.

opposite of a polynomial The polynomial created when the sign of each term of the original polynomial is changed.

opposite numbers Two numbers that are the same distance from zero on the number line, but on opposite sides, also called additive inverses.

opposites Numbers that are the same distance from zero on the number line, but on opposite sides; also called additive inverses.

order m **n** A matrix of m rows and n columns is of order m n.

Order of Operations Agreement A set of rules that tells us in what order to perform the operations that occur in a numerical expression.

ordered pair A pair of numbers expressed in the form (a, b) and used to locate a point in the plane determined by a rectangular coordinate system.

ordered triple Three numbers expressed in the form (x, y, z) and used to locate a point in the xyz-coordinate system.

ordinate The second number of an ordered pair; it measures a vertical distance and is also called the second coordinate of an ordered pair.

origin The point of intersection of the two number lines that form a rectangular coordinate system.

ounce A U.S. Customary unit of weight. 16 ounces 1 pound.

output The result of evaluating a function.

parabola The graph of a quadratic function is called a parabola.

parallel lines Lines that never meet; the distance between them is always the same.

parallelogram A quadrilateral that has opposite sides equal and parallel.

Pascal's Triangle A pattern for the coefficients of the terms of the expansion of the binomial $(a \quad b)^n$ that can be formed by writing the coefficients in a triangular array known as Pascal's Triangle.

percent Parts per hundred.

percent decrease A decrease of a quantity, expressed as a percent of its original value.

percent increase An increase of a quantity, expressed as a percent of its original value.

percent mixture problem A problem that involves combining two solutions or alloys that have different concentrations of the same substance.

perfect cube The product of the same three factors.

perfect square The product of a whole number and itself.

perfect-square trinomial The square of a binomial.

perimeter The distance around a plane figure.

period In a number written in standard form, each group of digits separated from other digits by a comma or commas.

perpendicular lines Intersecting lines that form right angles. The slopes of perpendicular lines are negative reciprocals of each other.

pictograph A graph that uses symbols to represent information.

pint A U.S. Customary measure of capacity. 2 pints 1 quart.

place value The position of each digit in a number written in standard form determines that digit's place value.

place-value chart A chart that indicates the place value of every digit in a number.

plane The infinitely extending, two-dimensional space in which a rectangular coordinate system lies; may be pictured as a large, flat piece of paper.

plane figures Figures that lie totally in a plane.

plotting a point in the plane Placing a dot at the location given by the ordered pair; also called graphing a point in the plane.

point-slope formula The equation , where m is the slope of a line and is a point on the line.

points A term banks use to mean percent of a mortgage; used to express the loan origination fee.

polygon A closed figure determined by three or more line segments that lie in a plane.

polynomial A variable expression in which the terms are monomials.

polynomial function An expression whose terms are monomials.

positive integers The numbers 1, 2, 3, 4, 5, . . . ; also called the natural numbers.

positive slope The slope of a line that slants upward to the right.

positive numbers Numbers greater than zero.

pound A U.S. Customary unit of weight. 1 pound 16 ounces.

power The rate at which work is done or energy is released. In an exponential expression, the number of times (indicated by the exponent) that the factor, or base, occurs in the multiplication.

prime factorization The expression of a number as the product of its prime factors.

prime number A number whose only whole-number factors are 1 and itself. For instance, 13 is a prime number.

prime polynomial A polynomial that is nonfactorable over the integers.

principal The amount of money originally deposited or borrowed.

principal square root The positive square root of a number.

Principle of Zero Products If the product of two factors is zero, then at least one of the factors must be zero.

probability A number from 0 to 1 that tells us how likely it is that a certain outcome of an experiment will happen.

product In multiplication, the result of multiplying two numbers.

product of the sum and difference of two terms A polynomial that can be expressed in the form $(a \ b)(a \ b)$.

proper fraction A fraction less than 1.

property tax A tax based on the value of real estate.

proportion An expression of the equality of two ratios or rates.

Pythagorean Theorem The square of the hypotenuse of a right triangle is equal to the sum of the squares of the two legs.

quadrant One of the four regions into which a rectangular coordinate system divides the plane.

quadratic equation An equation of the form $ax^2 \ bx \ c \ 0$, where a and b are coefficients, c is a constant, and $a \neq 0$; also called a second-degree equation.

quadratic equation in standard form A quadratic equation written in descending order and set equal to zero.

quadratic equation in two variables An equation of the form $y \ ax^2 \ bx \ c$, where a is not equal to zero.

quadratic formula A general formula, derived by applying the method of completing the square to the standard form of a quadratic equation, used to solve quadratic equations.

quadratic function A function that can be expressed by the equation $f(x) \ ax^2 \ bx \ c$, where a is not equal to zero.

quadratic inequality An inequality that can be written in the form $ax^2 \ bx \ c \ 0$ or $ax^2 \ bx \ c \ 0$, where a is not equal to zero. The symbols and can also be used.

quadratic in form A trinomial is quadratic in form if it can be written as $au^2 \ bu \ c$

quadratic trinomial A trinomial of the form $ax^2 \ bx \ c$ where a and b are nonzero coefficients and c is a nonzero constant.

quadrilateral A four-sided closed figure.

quart A U.S. Customary measure of capacity. 4 quarts 1 gallon.

quotient In division, the result of dividing the divisor into the dividend.

radical In a radical expression, the symbol $\sqrt{}$.

radical equation An equation that contains a variable expression in a radicand.

radical function A function containing a radical.

radical sign The symbol $\sqrt{}$, which is used to indicate the positive, or principal, square root of a number.

radicand The expression under a radical sign.

radius of a circle A line segment going from the center to a point on the circle.

radius of a sphere A line segment going from the center to a point on the sphere.

range In a set of numbers, the difference between the largest and smallest values.

rate A comparison of two quantities that have different units.

rate of work That part of a task that is completed in one unit of time.

ratio A comparison of two quantities that have the same units.

rational expression A fraction in which the numerator or denominator is a polynomial.

rational function A function that is written in terms of a rational expression.

rational number A number that can be written as the ratio of two integers, where the denominator is not zero.

rationalizing the denominator The procedure used to remove a radical from the denominator of a fraction.

ray A ray starts at a point and extends indefinitely in one direction.

real numbers The rational numbers and the irrational numbers taken together.

real part of a complex number For the complex number $a \ bi$, a is the real part.

reciprocal The reciprocal of a nonzero real number a is $\frac{1}{a}$; also called the multiplicative inverse.

reciprocal of a fraction The fraction with the numerator and denominator interchanged.

reciprocal of a rational expression The rational expression with the numerator and denominator interchanged.

rectangle A parallelogram that has four right angles.

rectangular coordinate system A coordinate system formed by two number lines, one horizontal and one vertical, that intersect at the zero point of each line.

rectangular solid A solid in which all six faces are rectangles.

regular polygon A polygon in which each side has the same length and each angle has the same measure.

relation A set of ordered pairs.

remainder In division, the quantity left over when it is not possible to separate objects or numbers into a whole number of equal groups.

Remainder Theorem If the polynoimal is divided by x a, the remainder is $P(a)$.

repeating decimal A decimal formed when dividing the numerator of its fractional counterpart by the denominator results in a decimal part wherein one or more digits repeat infinitely.

right angle A 90 angle.

right triangle A triangle that contains one right angle.

root(s) of an equation The replacement value(s) of the variable that will make the equation true; also called the solution(s) of the equation.

roster method A method of designating a set by enclosing a list of its elements in braces.

rounding Giving an approximate value of an exact number.

salary Pay based on a weekly, biweekly, monthly, or annual time schedule.

sale price The reduced price.

sales tax A tax levied by a state or municipality on purchases.

sample space All the possible outcomes of an experiment.

scalene triangle A triangle that has no sides of equal length; no two of its angles are of equal measure.

scatter diagram A graph of ordered-pair data.

scientific notation Notation in which a number is expressed as a product of two factors, one a number between 1 and 10 and the other a power of 10.

second A unit of time. 60 seconds 1 minute.

second coordinate of an ordered pair The second number of the ordered pair; it measures a vertical distance and is also called the ordinate.

second-degree equation An equation of the form ax^2 bx c 0, where a and b are coefficients, c is aconstant, and $a \neq 0$; also called a quadratic equation.

sector of a circle One of the "pieces of the pie" in a circle graph.

selling price The price for which a business sells a product to a customer.

service charge A sum of money charged by a bank for handling a transaction.

sequence An ordered list of numbers.

series The indicated sum of the terms of a sequence

set A collection of objects.

set-builder notation A method of designating a set that makes use of a variable and a certain property that only elements of that set possess.

sides of a polygon The line segments that form the polygon.

sigma notation Notation used to represent a series in a compact form; also called summation notation.

similar objects Objects that have the same shape but not necessarily the same size.

similar triangles Triangles that have the same shape but not necessarily the same size.

simple interest Interest computed on the original principal.

simplest form of a fraction A fraction is in simplest form when there are no common factors in the numerator and denominator.

simplest form of a rate A rate is in simplest form when the numbers that make up the rate have no common factor.

simplest form of a ratio A ratio is in simplest form when the two numbers do not have a common factor.

simplest form of a rational expression A rational expression is in simplest form when the numerator and denominator have no common factors.

simplifying a variable expression Combining like terms by adding their numerical coefficients.

slope A measure of the slant, or tilt, of a line. The symbol for slope is m.

slope-intercept form The slope-intercept form of an equation of a straight line is y mx b.

slope-intercept form of a straight line The equation y mx b, where m is the slope of the line and $(0, b)$ is the y-intercept.

solids Objects in space.

solution of a system of equations in three variables An ordered triple that is a solution of each equation of the system.

solution of a system of equations in two variables An ordered pair that is a solution of each equation of the system.

solution of an equation A number that, when substituted for the variable, results in a true equation.

solution of an equation in three variables An ordered triple (x, y, z) whose coordinates make the equation a true statement.

solution of an equation in two variables An ordered pair whose coordinates make the equation a true statement.

solution set of a system of inequalities The intersection of the solution sets of the individual inequalities.

solution set of an inequality A set of numbers, each element of which, when substituted for the variable, results in a true inequality.

solution(s) of an equation The replacement value(s) of the variable that will make the equation true; also called the root(s) of the equation.

solving an equation Finding a solution of the equation.

sphere A solid in which all points are the same distance from point O, which is called the center of the sphere.

square A rectangle that has four equal sides.

square function A function that pairs a number with its square.

square matrix A matrix that has the same number of rows as columns.

square of a binomial A polynomial that can be expressed in the form $(a$ $b)^2$.

square root A square root of a number is one of two identical factors of that number.

square root of a perfect square One of the two equal factors of the perfect square.

standard form A whole number is in standard form when it is written using the digits 0, 1, 2, . . . , 9. An example is 46,208.

standard form of a linear equation in two variables An equation of the form Ax By C, where A and B are coefficients and C is a constant.

standard form of a quadratic equation A quadratic equation is in standard form when the polynomial is in descending order and equal to zero.

statistics The branch of mathematics concerned with data, or numerical information.

straight angle A 180° angle.

substitution method An algebraic method of finding an exact solution of a system of linear equations.

subtraction The process of finding the difference between two numbers.

subtrahend In subtraction, the number that is subtracted from another number (the minuend).

sum In addition, the total of the numbers added.

summation notation Notation used to represent a series in a compact form; also called sigma notation.

sum of two perfect cubes A polynomial that can be written in the form $a^3 + b^3$.

sum of two perfect squares A binomial in the form $a^2 + b^2$, which is nonfactorable over the integers.

supplementary angles Two angles whose sum is 180°.

synthetic division A shorter method of dividing a polynomial by a binomial of the form $x - a$. This method uses only the coefficients of the variable terms.

system of equations Two or more equations considered together.

system of inequalities Two or more inequalities considered together.

term of a sequence A number in a sequence.

terminating decimal A decimal that has a finite number of digits after the decimal point, which means that it comes to an end and does not go on forever.

terms of a variable expression The addends of the expression.

theoretical probability A fraction with the number of favorable outcomes of an experiment in the numerator and the total number of possible outcomes of the experiment in the denominator.

third quartile In a set of numbers, the number above which one-quarter of the data lie.

tolerance of a component The amount by which it is acceptable for the component to vary from a given measurement.

ton A U.S. Customary unit of weight. 1 ton = 2000 pounds.

total cost The unit cost multiplied by the number of units purchased.

transversal A line intersecting two other lines at two different points.

triangle A three-sided closed figure.

trinomial A polynomial of three terms.

true proportion A proportion in which the fractions are equal.

undefined slope The slope of a vertical line is undefined.

uniform motion The motion of an object whose speed and direction do not change.

uniform motion problem A problem that involves the motion of an object whose speed and direction do not change.

union of two sets The set that contains all elements that belong to either of the sets.

unit cost The cost of one item.

unit rate A rate in which the number in the denominator is 1.

upper limit In a tolerance, the greatest acceptable value.

value mixture problem A problem that involves combining two ingredients that have different prices into a single blend.

value of a function The value of the dependent variable for a given value of the independent variable.

value of a function at x The result of evaluating a variable expression, represented by the symbol $f(x)$.

value of a variable The number assigned to the variable.

variable A letter used to stand for a quantity that is unknown or that can change.

variable expression An expression that contains one or more variables.

variable part In a variable term, the variable or variables and their exponents.

variable part of a variable term The variables, taken together, that occur in a variable term.

variable term A term composed of a numerical coefficient and a variable part. When the numerical coefficient is 1 or -1, the 1 is usually not written.

vertex The common endpoint of two rays that form an angle.

vertex of a parabola The point on the parabola with the smallest y-coordinate or the largest y-coordinate.

vertical angles Two angles that are on opposite sides of the intersection of two lines.

vertical-line test A graph defines a function if any vertical line intersects the graph at no more than one point.

volume A measure of the amount of space inside a closed surface.

watt-hour A unit of electrical energy in the metric system.

week A unit of time. 7 days = 1 week.

weight A measure of how strongly Earth is pulling on an object.

whole numbers The whole numbers are 0, 1, 2, 3, ...

whole-number part In decimal notation, that part of the number that appears to the left of the decimal point.

x-coordinate The abscissa in an xy-coordinate system.

x-intercept The point at which a graph crosses the x-axis.

xy-coordinate system A rectangular coordinate system in which the horizontal axis is labeled x and the vertical axis is labeled y.

xyz-coordinate system A three-dimensional coordinate system formed when a third coordinate axis (the z-axis) is located perpendicular to the xy-plane.

y-coordinate The ordinate in an xy-coordinate system.

y-intercept The point at which a graph crosses the y-axis.

yard A U.S. Customary unit of length. 36 inches = 1 yard.

Index

Photo Credits

Chapter 1: p. 1: Peter Johnson/CORBIS; p. 8: Tannen Maury/The Image Works; p. 16: DPA/The Image Works; p. 24: AP/Wide World Photos; p. 42: CORBIS

Chapter 2: p. 51: E. Dygas/TAXI/Getty Images; p. 71: Olson Scott/CORBIS SYGMA; p. 72: James Leynse/CORBIS SABA; p. 74:The Granger Collection; p. 78: Sandor Szabo/EPA/Landov; p. 96: Kaku Kurita/Time Life Pictures/Getty Images; p. 97: AP/Wide World Photos; p. 104: Ralf-Finn Hestoft/CORBIS; p. 106: Peter Beck/CORBIS

Chapter 3: p. 107, Michael Newman/PhotoEdit, Inc.; p. 115, Vic Bider/PhotoEdit, Inc.; p. 116, Spencer Grant/PhotoEdit, Inc.; p. 119, Spencer Grant/PhotoEdit, Inc.; p. 120, Dallas & John Heaton/CORBIS; p. 130, PictureArts/CORBIS

Chapter 4: p. 133: Joel Simon/STONE/Getty Images; p. 136: Charles O'Rear/CORBIS; p. 138: Mike Powell/Allsport Concepts/Getty Images; p. 140: John Madere/CORBIS; p. 141: AP/Wide World Photos; p. 142: Warner Brothers Television/Getty Images; p. 149: Michael Newman/PhotoEdit, Inc.; p. 150: Digital Image © 1996 CORBIS, Original Image Courtesy of NASA/CORBIS; p. 151: Reproduced by Permission of The State Hermitage Museum, St. Petersburg, Russia/CORBIS; p. 152: Dallas & John Heaton/CORBIS

Chapter 5: p. 159: David Sacks/The Image Bank/Getty Images; p. 164: David Chasey/Photodisc/Getty Images; p. 167: Galen Rowell/CORBIS; p. 168: Joe McBride/STONE/Getty Images; p. 172: Ulrike Welsch/Photoedit, Inc.; p. 175: Ariel Skelley/CORBIS; p. 176: Chuck Savage/CORBIS; p. 182: Ariel Skelley/CORBIS; p. 186: CORBIS

Chapter 6: p. 189: CORBIS; p. 190: Ainaco/CORBIS; p. 192: Myrleen Ferguson Cate/Photoedit, Inc.; p. 196: David Madison/STONE/Getty Images; p. 203: Todd A. Gipstein/CORBIS; p. 204: David Bartruff/CORBIS; p. 211: Richard Cummins/CORBIS; p. 213: Knut Platon/STONE/Getty Images; p. 217: Jeff Greenberg/PhotoEdit, Inc.

Chapter 6 Additional Material from Mathematical Excursions, Second Edition - Sections 10.3, 10.4, 10.5: p. 6-A: Tom Grill/CORBIS; p. 6-S: Topham/The Image Works, Inc.

Chapter 7: p. 237: Kevin Flemming/CORBIS; p. 251: CORBIS; p. 267: CORBIS; p. 277: Kevin R. Morris/CORBIS

Chapter 8: p. 295: CORBIS; p. 306: Tony Freeman/PhotoEdit, Inc.; p. 310: Michael Newman/PhotoEdit, Inc.; p. 315: CORBIS; p. 323: Tony Freeman/ PhotoEdit, Inc.

Chapter 9: p. 325: Robert W. Ginn/PhotoEdit, Inc.; p. 333: Michael Newman/PhotoEdit, Inc.; p. 334: Robert Essel NYC/CORBIS; p. 335: Rachel Epstein/ PhotoEdit, Inc.; p. 339: CORBIS; p. 341: Cleve Bryant/PhotoEdit. Inc.; p. 342: Dick Reed/CORBIS; p. 348: Randy M. Ury/CORBIS; p. 350: S. Carmona/CORBIS

Chapter 10: p. 351: Frederic J. Brown/AFP/Getty Images; p. 352: Roy Morsch/CORBIS; p. 353: Ethan Miller/CORBIS; p. 372 (top): CORBIS, (bottom): CORBIS; p. 375: Jason Reed/Reuters NewMedia, Inc./CORBIS; p. 376: Bettmann/CORBIS; p. 383: Tony Freeman/PhotoEdit, Inc.

Chapter 10 Additional Material from Mathematical Excursions, Second Edition - Section 12.2: p: 10-A: Bettmann/CORBIS; p 10-I: AP/World Wide Photos; p. 10-K: Francis Miller/Getty Images

Chapter 11: p. 395: AP/Wide World Photos; p. 401: Craig Tuttle/CORBIS; p. 428: Tony Freeman/PhotoEdit, Inc.

Chapter 12: p. 438: AP/Wide World Photos; p. 451: David Ponton/Getty Images; p. 453: Grafton Marshall Smith/CORBIS

Chapter 13: p. 454: Rudi Von Briel/PhotoEdit, Inc.